BEHIND THE BRICKS

ARTS IN ACTION

SERIES EDITOR:
Jennifer Pettit, Dean, Faculty of Arts, Mount Royal University

Co-published with Mount Royal University
ISSN 2371-6134 (Print)   ISSN 2371-6142 (Online)

This series focuses on illuminating, promoting, or demonstrating the fundamental significance of the Arts, Humanities, and Social Sciences to public well-being and contemporary society—culturally, spiritually, socially, politically, and economically—with the aim of raising awareness of the essential skills, perspectives, and critical understandings of societal issues these disciplines cultivate.

No. 1   *Understanding Atrocities: Remembering, Representing, and Teaching Genocide*
Edited by Scott W. Murray

No. 2   *Orange Chinook: Politics in the New Alberta*
Edited by Duane Bratt, Keith Brownsey, Richard Sutherland, and David Taras

No. 3   *Signs of Water: Community Perspectives on Water, Responsibility, and Hope*
Edited by Robert Boschman and Sonya L. Jakubec

No. 4   *Blue Storm: The Rise and Fall of Jason Kenney*
Edited by Duane Bratt, Richard Sutherland, and David Taras

No. 5   *Behind the Bricks: The Life and Times of the Mohawk Institute, Canada's Longest-Running Residential School*
Edited by Richard W. Hill, Sr., Alison Norman, Thomas Peace, and Jennifer Pettit

UNIVERSITY OF CALGARY
Press

BEHIND the BRICKS

The Life and Times of the Mohawk Institute, Canada's Longest-Running Residential School

EDITED BY
**Richard W. Hill, Sr.,
Alison Norman,
Thomas Peace,
and Jennifer Pettit**

Arts in Action Series
ISSN 2371-6134 (Print) ISSN 2371-6142 (Online)

© 2025 Richard W. Hill, Sr., Alison Norman, Thomas Peace, and Jennifer Pettit

University of Calgary Press
2500 University Drive NW
Calgary, Alberta
Canada T2N 1N4
press.ucalgary.ca

All rights reserved.

This book is available in an Open Access digital format published under a CC-BY-NCND 4.0 Creative Commons license. The publisher should be contacted for any commercial use which falls outside the terms of that license.

LIBRARY AND ARCHIVES CANADA CATALOGUING IN PUBLICATION

Title: Behind the bricks : the life and times of the Mohawk Institute, Canada's longest-running residential school / edited by Richard W. Hill, Sr., Alison Norman, Thomas Peace, and Jennifer Pettit.
Names: Hill, Richard W., Sr., editor | Norman, Alison (Historian), editor. | Peace, Thomas, 1980- editor. | Pettit, Jennifer, editor.
Series: Arts in action ; no. 5.
Description: Series statement: Arts in action, 2371-6134 ; no. 5 | Includes bibliographical references and index.
Identifiers: Canadiana (print) 20250223643 | Canadiana (ebook) 20250223740 | ISBN 9781773856513 (hardcover) | ISBN 9781773856520 (softcover) | ISBN 9781773856537 (Open Access PDF) | ISBN 9781773856544 (PDF) | ISBN 9781773856551 (EPUB)
Subjects: LCSH: Mohawk Institute (Brantford, Ont.)—History. | CSH: First Nations—Ontario—Brantford—Residential schools—History. | CSH: First Nations—Education—Ontario—Brantford—History. | CSH: First Nations students—Ontario—Brantford—History.
Classification: LCC E96.6.M64 B44 2025 | DDC 371.829/97071347—dc23

The University of Calgary Press acknowledges the support of the Government of Alberta through the Alberta Media Fund for our publications. We acknowledge the financial support of the Government of Canada. We acknowledge the financial support of the Canada Council for the Arts for our publishing program.

This book has been published with the support of Huron University, and with the support of Mount Royal University.

The manufacturer's authorized representative in the EU for product safety is Mare Nostrum Group B.V., Mauritskade 21D, 1091 GC Amsterdam, The Netherlands. Email: gpsr@mare-nostrum.co.uk

Copy editing by Ryan Perks
Cover design by Barrett Reid-Maroney Type Design Studio using images courtesy of Mary Baxter/TV Ontario. Students and staff in front of the Mohawk Institute," ca. 1934. Image courtesy of Richard Hill.
Cover production, page design, and typesetting by Melina Cusano

Because of that long driveway with those beautiful trees and orchards on either side . . . outwardly it looked like an attractive place. But behind the walls . . . there's things we left there. Our DNA is in there; it's not just benign walls.

    Former Mohawk Institute student Doug George, 2018

DEDICATION: THE MUSH HOLE RUBRIC

David Monture

Dedicated to the survivors of the Mohawk Institute

Having been administered
a psychological caning
and made to feel among
"The Other,"
in our own homeland.
Citations not quite in order
Not fitting into the paint
by number
linear boxes
Regurgitating the same old
same old

This is how you will
surely lose marks
boy . . .

Such are the metrics
of compliance
and obedience

Contents

Dedication: The Mush Hole Rubric ... vii
    David Monture

List of Figures ... xii
List of Tables ... xv
List of Abbreviations ... xvi
Preface ... xvii
    Richard W. Hill, Sr.

Introduction ... 1
    Jennifer Pettit

The Russ Moses Residential School Memoir ... 11
    John Moses and Russ Moses

Part 1. Historical Overview and Context of the Mohawk Institute ... 23

1. "To Shake Off the Rude Habits of Savage Life": The Foundations of the Mohawk Institute to the Early 1900s ... 25
    Jennifer Pettit

2. "The Difficulties of Making an Indian into a White Man, Were Not Thoroughly Appreciated": The Mohawk Institute, 1904 to the Present ... 59
    Jennifer Pettit

Part 2. Teachers, Curriculum, and Tools of Control ... 105

3. The Indian Normal School: The Role of the Mohawk Institute in the Training of Indigenous Teachers in the Late Nineteenth Century ... 107
    Alison Norman

4. Teaching Control and Service: The Use of Military Training at the Mohawk Institute ... 133
    Evan Habkirk

5. "New Weapons": Race, Indigeneity, and Intelligence 153
Testing at the Mohawk Institute, 1920–1949
Alexandra Giancarlo

Part 3. The Building, the Grounds, and Commemoration 169

6. A "Model" School: An Architectural History of the 171
Mohawk Institute
Magdalena Miłosz

7. The Stewardship, Preservation, and Commemoration of 225
the Mohawk Institute
Cody Groat

Part 4. Survival and Resistance 241

8. Ten Years of Student Resistance at the Mohawk Institute, 243
1903–1913
Diana Castillo

9. ęhǫwadihsadǫ ne:ʔhniʔ gadigyenǫ:gyeʔs ganahaǫgwęʔ 253
ęyagǫnhehgǫhǫ:k / They Buried Them, but They the Seeds
Floated Around What Will Sustain Them
Teri Lyn Morrow, Bonnie Freeman, and Sandra Juutilainen

Part 5. The New England Company and the Mohawk Institute 273

10. A Model to Follow? The Sussex Vale Indian School 275
Thomas Peace

11. Robert Ashton, the New England Company, and the 295
Mohawk Institute, 1872–1910
William Acres

| 12. | The Lands of the Mohawk Institute: Robert Ashton and the Demise of the New England Company's "Station," 1891–1922
William Acres | 323 |

Part 6. Student Experiences and Voices — 349

13.	Life at the Mohawk Institute During the 1860s *Thomas Peace and the 2018 Huron University College Students in HIS 3201E*	351
14.	Collecting the Evidence: Restoration and Archaeology at the Mohawk Institute *Sarah Clarke, Paul Racher, and Tara Froman*	375
15.	Collective Trauma and the Role of Religion in the Mohawk Institute Experience *Wendy Fletcher*	393
16.	Concluding Voices: Survivor Stories of Life Behind the Bricks *Richard W. Hill, Sr.*	415

Closing Poems — 449
  Jimmie Edgar
  Bud Whiteye

Appendix 1. History of Six Nations Education by Keith Jamieson — 453
Appendix 2. Mohawk Institute Students Who Became Teachers — 479
Suggested Reading — 485
Acknowledgements — 493
Contributors — 495
Index — 499

List of Figures

Figure 0.1.	Staff and students of the Mohawk Institute (possibly the 1920s)	xvii
Figure 0.2.	Russ and Thelma Moses, Mush Hole, October 1943	10
Figure 0.3.	Russ Moses in RCAF uniform, 1965	13
Figure 0.4.	Russ Moses's hand-drawn map (1999), "Mohawk Institute, 1942–1946 by # 12 Boy"	14
Figure 0.5.	New England Company medallion	23
Figure 1.1.	A nineteenth-century photo of the Mohawk Chapel and possibly the original Mohawk Institute	24
Figure 2.1.	Girls playing on a swing set in the girls' playground	59
Figure 2.2.	Mohawk Institute boys on the way to the Six Nations Fair, 1934	77
Figure 2.3.	Mohawk Institute trip to Christian Island, 1960s	80
Figure 2.4.	Summer camp at Christian Island, 1960s	81
Figure 2.5.	An image from May 1966 in *The Toronto Star*	85
Figure 0.6.	Mohawk Institute students	106
Figure 3.1.	Albert Anthony	113
Figure 3.2.	The Reverend Isaac Bearfoot, Christ Church	115
Figure 3.3.	"Teacher and Pupils in No. 3 School"	118
Figure 3.4.	"No. 3 School, with Pupils and Teachers, the Rev. Mr. and Mrs. Caswell and Others."	119
Figure 3.5.	"Miss F. K. Maracle, 1905, Toronto"	120
Figure 3.6.	Margaret Maracle's certificate from 1882	122
Figure 3.7.	Bishop Appleyard, the Reverend Canon Zimmerman, David Wilson, and Susan Hardie in the Mohawk Chapel	125
Figure 4.1.	The Mohawk Institute Cadet Corps, displayed at the Central Canada Exhibition, 1896	133
Figure 4.2.	Cadets at the Mohawk Institute, possibly 1890s	135
Figure 4.3.	A. Nelles Ashton and Mohawk Institute cadets with the Brantford Gala Day Trophy, 1896	138
Figure 4.4.	A. Nelles Ashton and Mohawk Institute cadets in front of the Mohawk Institute, 1909	140

Figure 4.5.	A. Nelles Ashton and Mohawk Institute cadets on the front steps of the Mohawk Institute, 1909	141
Figure 5.1.	Calum Miller, from Six Nations, in 1936. Photograph taken by D. F. Kidd.	152
Figure 5.2.	A page from C. A. F. Clark's report on the Mohawk Institute in 1948, with photos	159
Figure 0.7.	Undated photo, Mohawk Institute grounds	170
Figure 6.1.	The Mohawk Village School, 1780s.	175
Figure 6.2.	Map of Brantford showing "Site of the Old Institution Buildings" near the Mohawk Chapel. "Institution Buildings" indicates the location of the Mohawk Institute beginning in 1858.	178
Figure 6.3.	The Mohawk Institute, 1884	180
Figure 6.4.	Edward Lamson Henry, *Johnson Hall (Sir William Johnson Presenting Medals to the Indian Chiefs of the Six Nations at Johnstown, NY, 1772)*, 1903, oil on canvas	181
Figure 6.5.	The Mohawk Institute and its landscape, 1884	182
Figure 6.6.	Floor plan of the Mohawk Institute, 1879	186
Figure 6.7.	Boys' dormitory, possibly Mohawk Institute, before 1904	187
Figure 6.8.	The Mohawk Institute, following the 1886 addition	188
Figure 6.9.	The Mohawk Institute, following 1893–4 addition	190
Figure 6.10.	Mohawk Institute, 1917	194
Figure 6.11.	Students and staff in front of the Mohawk Institute, ca. 1934	195
Figure 6.12.	Elevations of proposed addition to the Mohawk Institute, 1922. R. Guerney Orr, architect.	199
Figure 6.13.	Plan of alterations and additions to the Mohawk Institute basement, 1922. R. Guerney Orr, architect	200
Figure 6.14.	Girls in the sewing room, Mohawk Institute, ca. 1943	203
Figure 6.15.	Mohawk Institute fields looking northwest, with the school and farm buildings in the background, 1917	205
Figure 6.16.	Detail of site plan showing the main building of the Mohawk Institute ("residential school"), classroom block built of army huts ("school building"), and other outbuildings, 1948	209

Figure 6.17.	Children in the army-hut classroom at the Mohawk Institute, 1948	210
Figure 6.18	Photograph of the Mohawk Institute kitchen, including Institute personnel, taken 21 January 1961	213
Figure 7.1.	Plaque unveiling at the Mohawk Institute, 17 June 1972	229
Figure 7.2.	Current plaque in front of the Woodland Cultural Centre	230
Figure 0.8.	Mohawk Chapel confirmation, 1918	242
Figure 9.1.	*Katsian[:ionte Hanging Flower*, Jake Thomas print	260
Figure 9.2.	Christine Skye, Six Nations Mohawk	261
Figure 0.9.	Boys farming at Mohawk Institute, 1943	274
Figure 11.1.	"Mohawk Institution, Regulations Relating to Pupils," 1872	301
Figure 11.2.	Mohawk Institute staff, with Robert and Alice Ashton standing in the centre, Isaac Bearfoot on the left next to Jennie Fisher, and likely Mr. Thomas, the notorious boys' master, on the right	306
Figure 12.1.	Glebe Farm Reserve no. 40B	325
Figure 0.10.	Elwood Burnham, Mohawk Institute, 1934	350
Figure 13.1.	A page in the register, April 1868	354
Figure 14.1.	(A) chipping "detritus"; (B) Woodland period pottery and projectile point; (C) silver earring; (D) cadet uniform button	378
Figure 14.2.	(E) enamelled pitchers; (F) enamelled cups; (G) slate tablet with "Leah" inscribed into it	380
Figure 14.3.	(H) "Government of Canada 1917" pencil; (I) child's pyjama shirt; (J) pencil sketches on paper; (K) sewing machine used at the Mohawk Institute	381
Figure 14.4.	(L) watch clock key; (M) labour ledger; (N) cigarette package; (O) comic strip	385
Figure 14.5.	(P) canned chicken; (Q) canned apples; (R) "2 Jan. 1951, Know Your Words"; (S) "Elvis the Pel, 1957" brick	387
Figure 15.1.	*Trauma* by R. G. Miller, depicting the artist as a young boy at the Mohawk Institute	394
Figure 15.2.	Photo of clergy in front of the Mohawk Chapel, ca. 1925	402

Figure 16.1.	Doug George	418
Figure 16.2.	Drawing of Emmert General, 1934, by Richard Hill	421
Figure 16.3.	Geronimo Henry at age fifteen at the Mohawk Institute	423
Figure 16.4.	Blanche Hill-Easton	426
Figure 16.5.	Pat Hill	427
Figure 16.6.	Raymond Hill	430
Figure 16.7.	John Elliot	431
Figure 16.8.	Bud Whiteye	435
Figure 16.9.	"Help me" brick	436
Figure 16.10.	Dawn and Roberta Hill in their first foster home after leaving the Mohawk Institute	438
Figure 16.11.	Roberta Hill in 1972	438
Figure 16.12.	Roberta Hill more recently	438
Figure 16.13.	Newspaper photograph of Roberta Hill and Rev. Zimmerman	440
Figure 16.14.	Ramona Kiyoshk, of Walpole Island, at the Mohawk Institute in July 1959	441
Figure 16.15.	Geraldine Maness with Violet Riley	444
Figure 16.16.	Geraldine Robertson	445

List of Tables

| Table 11.1. | Mohawk Institute daily schedule, January 1873 | 315 |
| Table 13.1. | Mohawk Institute curriculum, ca. 1869 | 359 |

List of Abbreviations

AFN	Assembly of First Nations
BCI	Brantford Collegiate Institute
BHS	Brant Historical Society
CTA	Calls to Action (TRC)
DIA	Department of Indian Affairs
HSMBC	Historic Sites and Monuments Board of Canada
IAB	Indian Affairs Branch (Department of Citizenship and Immigration)
INAC	Indian and Northern Affairs Canada
IODE	Imperial Order Daughters of the Empire
IRSSA	Indian Residential Schools Settlement Agreement
MI	Mohawk Institute
MSCC	Missionary Society of the Church of England in Canada
NCTR	National Centre for Truth and Reconciliation
NEC	New England Company
OHT	Ontario Heritage Trust
RCAF	Royal Canadian Air Force
RCAP	Royal Commission on Aboriginal Peoples
RCMP	Royal Canadian Mounted Police
SNC	Six Nations Council
SPG	Society for the Propagation of the Gospel
TRC	Truth and Reconciliation Commission of Canada
WCC	Woodland Cultural Centre

Preface

Richard W. Hill, Sr.

Figure 0.1. Staff and students of the Mohawk Institute (possibly the 1920s)
Source: Richard Hill Collection

The brick-covered building that still stands in Brantford, Ontario, housed the third version of the Mohawk Institute. It is a place of traumatic memory for many of the survivors. Behind the bricks of this former residential school rest many personal stories about life in the school, most of which are not to be found in the written record. There are also many stories from the nearly two-hundred-year history of the Mohawk Institute, including the years that it operated as a school, and its subsequent years when it had

xvii

an ongoing impact on the people who went there. We cannot share all the stories of this place. That would take several books. Of those we do share, we hope that you will continue to learn from them.

The story of the Mohawk Institute includes the writings of school officials, government agents, and church authorities. It is found in government policy and dusty records of the New England Company, as well as within the records of the Haudenosaunee Confederacy Council of Chiefs. The story is found in newspaper articles, handwritten notes, academic research, and dinner table conversations around the Six Nations community. It is also found in the informal documentation of some of the teachers and principals. In addition, there are those stories that, up until quite recently, have remained locked up in the hearts and minds of the survivors. Some were too ashamed to tell their stories. Some tried to forget. Some even pretended that they had no stories to tell. Some never survived to tell their stories. However, some have been brave enough to share their stories so that, for once, we can get a real glimpse behind the bricks of the Mohawk Institute.

One survivor, Doug George, from Akwesasne said, "We left our DNA in that building." Their stories became the DNA of school, a twisted matrix of facts, reports, memories, rumours, and fears. For some people that DNA also reflects good times, some great opportunities, and many personal successes. Some memories are found in what students stuffed behind the walls or under the floorboards. Some were scratched into the red bricks on the back side of the building. Some children did so as inmates of the school; others left their names when they returned to this place of memory, many years after they walked out the front door.

These red bricks have become our version of the Wailing Wall. People have stood before the bricks in honour of the victims of the school, shedding tears and praying for the souls of classmates or family members. Reading the names or initials etched on the bricks was a way of reclaiming a connection to the students. The officers of the school stripped them of their names and gave them numbers instead. They took away their clothing and forced them to wear handmade uniforms. They took away their hair. They tried to remake their minds, to transform their identities and beliefs. The brick wall continues to stand, offering a way for students to speak back to those in power and to leave evidence of their existence.

One young girl turned to the red bricks as a plea for help. She was being repeatedly molested by the officers of the Institute. Every time she was alone after swimming in the pool, she scratched the word "HELP" in the bricks. At first, her message was quite faint. Each time she did it, the word became bolder and bolder. Her one word was also a prayer that, somehow, something or someone would intervene to stop those who were hurting her. She survived her experiences at the school and returned to tell her story. She was not unscathed, and once we hear the story of the Mohawk Institute, we, too, will become marked by the power of this place.

As we were writing this book, the news came of the suspected graves of 215 students that were uncovered at the Kamloops Indian Residential School. It caused a national pause that forced Canadians to realize that, yes, it was real children who experienced this trauma. Yes, religious people reacted in a very cold and secular manner. Some children died, but their spirits have reached us from beyond the unmarked grave. Another voice to get our attention.

My ancestors say that we cannot carry the burden of grief into our future lives. We had ceremony by which that burden was lifted from our minds. We had to have someone step forward to remove the tears from our eyes to restore our vision so we can see hope more clearly. We had to have someone clear our ears so that we could restore our hearing so that the voices of the past would not be lost. Someone had to offer us a refreshing drink to wash away the dust of trauma that clogs our throats and stifles our speech. We need all of this to recover our humanity.

The purpose of this book is to better comprehend the reality of this place. Facing the people who operated the school and facing the students who once lived behind the bricks is our way of wiping away our collective tears so we can see the truth of what actually happened. The words and the historical photographs will help to clear our ears from the historical dust that have interfered with our understanding. The refreshing part is more difficult. As we search for hope, listen carefully to what the survivors have had to say, read carefully what the scholars have written, and then make up your own mind about the legacy of the Mohawk Institute, Canada's oldest and longest-running Indian Residential School. What does this place tell us about ourselves? How does this book help us better understand why reconciliation is necessary? It is something we just can't get over that easily. For reconciliation to happen, we first need to hear the truth of the Mohawk Institute. This is our effort to share truth as we have come to know it.

Introduction

Jennifer Pettit

Operating from the 1830s to 1970, the Mohawk Institute, Canada's first and longest-running residential school, and a model for the residential school system, still stands today as part of the Woodland Cultural Centre (WCC) in what is now known as Brantford, Ontario. The Mohawk Institute had, and continues to have, a significant impact on the students who attended and their families and communities. Yet, though it existed as a residential school for almost a century and a half, most people know little about what went on "behind the bricks" of the Institute. This is no accident. As determined by the Truth and Reconciliation Commission (TRC), Canada has historically downplayed or told outright mistruths about its settler-colonial past, at the heart of which was the residential school system that removed over 130,000 students from their homes and communities.

Like the TRC, the authors contributing to this collection believe this needs to change. Assembled and guided by Tuscarora historian Richard (Rick) W. Hill, Sr., *Behind the Bricks* brings together experts in a wide variety of areas to tell a more complete history of the school than has hitherto been published. The most unique feature of this book is that it brings together non-Indigenous writers and Haudenosaunee scholars from Six Nations who have been working on various aspects of the Mohawk Institute's history for decades. In doing so, it seeks to bring these separate studies into conversation with each other and make these bodies of work more accessible. The scope of the book is broad, covering an array of topics, such as the architecture and archaeology of the Institute, student experiences at the school, religion, food, etc. In *Behind the Bricks*, you will read not only about the school but about the students, the teachers, and the changing historical context in which the Mohawk Institute and other residential schools operated. While

Behind the Bricks can of course be read in its entirety, individual chapters also stand on their own.

Behind the Bricks begins with a memoir, introduced by John Moses, a member of the Delaware and Upper Mohawk bands from the Six Nations of the Grand River Territory, and written by his father, Russ Moses, who attended the Mohawk Institute in the 1940s. Russ's father attended the school in the 1910s, and his father before him in the 1880s, so John is the first of his family who was not a student at the Mohawk Institute. Despite this, the school continues to have a significant impact on him and his family and community. The memoir concludes with Russ's reminder that "This is not my story, but yours," calling attention to the fact that the truth of residential schools is something that should be known to all Canadians.

Following Moses's memoir, part 1, "Historical Overview and Context of the Mohawk Institute," begins with two overview chapters by historian Jennifer Pettit, who started writing about the Mohawk Institute in her 1993 master's thesis at the University of Western Ontario. The first of these chapters, "'To Shake Off the Rude Habits of Savage Life': The Foundations of the Mohawk Institute to the Early 1900s," traces the beginnings of the Mohawk Institute in present-day Brantford, Ontario, from its inception in the 1830s through to the early years of the twentieth century, when the second Mohawk Institute building was burned to the ground by students, and government aspirations for residential schools began to move from assimilation to a policy of segregation. The goals of church and state authorities and administrators over time, as well as the goals of community members, are analyzed in this introductory chapter, as are community and student responses to the school until the turn of the century. The second background chapter, "'The Difficulties of Making an Indian into a White Man, Were Not Thoroughly Appreciated': The Mohawk Institute, 1904 to the Present," continues by following and analyzing the history of the school from the opening of the third and final school building in 1904 to the closure of the Mohawk Institute in 1970. The school's legacy, the government's apology and settlement for student survivors, and the TRC's findings are also addressed. The chapter concludes that the school failed all three parties involved—church, government, and community.

Part 2, "Teachers, Curriculum, and Tools of Control," consists of three chapters. The first, by historian Alison Norman, entitled "The Indian Normal School: The Role of the Mohawk Institute in the Training of Indigenous Teachers in the Late Nineteenth Century," describes teacher training as a priority for principals Abraham Nelles and Robert Ashton. The

Mohawk Institute worked to educate high-performing students to continue their education and become teachers within the Institute, and later in day schools at Grand River and beyond. From little-known instructors to prominent teachers like Isaac Bearfoot, these students had a significant impact on their communities as educators. Norman stresses, however, that their success came despite their residential school experience, not because of it.

The next chapter, "Teaching Control and Service: The Use of Military Training at the Mohawk Institute," by Evan Habkirk, examines the use of military training at the Mohawk Institute. Habkirk concludes that this training was used as a tool to control Indigenous students while demonstrating to the non-Indigenous public that the school was "civilizing" students and having a positive effect on the children. In reality, military training served only to hide the negative experiences of students.

In the final chapter in part 2, "'New Weapons': Race, Indigeneity, and Intelligence Testing at the Mohawk Institute, 1920–1949," Alexandra Giancarlo assesses how intelligence testing affected the quality of education provided to Indigenous students and the curriculum of the Mohawk Institute and residential schools more broadly. Giancarlo explains how school authority figures used the "science" of intelligence to justify and legitimize a policy of segregation of Indigenous students and lower-quality "special" curricula well below the standards for non-Indigenous students in this period.

Part 3, "The Building, the Grounds, and Commemoration," begins with a chapter by Magdalena Miłosz entitled "A 'Model' School: An Architectural History of the Mohawk Institute." Miłosz analyzes the architectural history of the Mohawk Institute, studying who imagined, built, and maintained the school's buildings. She describes the important role that school architecture played not only in the experiences of students but also in advancing the broader goals of settler-colonial authorities.

The final chapter in part 3, "The Stewardship, Preservation, and Commemoration of the Mohawk Institute," by Cody Groat, examines how the Mohawk Institute has been remembered and memorialized. In 1972, the Institute was the first residential school to be recognized by the Province of Ontario through a heritage designation, and in 2013, the WCC, built on the site of the former residential school, launched the "Save the Evidence" campaign with the goal of supporting the restoration of the former Mohawk Institute school building. Despite being the longest-running residential school in Canada, and one of the few such schools still standing, the Mohawk Institute has not been designated a national historic site.

Part 4, "Survival and Resistance," provides examples of how students responded to the school. In "Ten Years of Student Resistance at the Mohawk Institute, 1903–1913," Diana Castillo examines student opposition during an important decade in the school's history. In addition to the destruction of the school by students via a fire, this decade also saw the prosecution of principal A. Nelles Ashton, who was tried and found guilty of harming students Ruth and Hazel Miller, who ran away from the Mohawk Institute and were severely punished by Ashton upon their return. These incidents helped bring about a move to more government control and oversight of the school.

In the next chapter, "ęhowadihsadǫ ne:ʔhniʔ gadigyenǫ:gye'ʔs ganahaǫgwęʔ ęyagǫnhehgǫhǫ:k / They Buried Them, but They the Seeds Floated Around What Will Sustain Them," Haudenosaunee community members and scholars Teri Lyn Morrow, Bonnie Freeman, and Sandra Juutilainen explore student experiences and perceptions of gardens, farming, and food, and how this has affected their lives and families after attending the Mohawk Institute. They stress the importance of food sovereignty and access and community-led programs to the understanding of and advancement of reconciliation.

Part 5 of *Behind the Bricks* consists of three chapters that examine the impact of the New England Company on the Mohawk Institute. This part of the book begins with a chapter by Thomas Peace entitled "A Model to Follow? The Sussex Vale Indian School." Built in 1787 in Sussex Vale, New Brunswick, by the New England Company, the same missionary society that would go on to build the Mohawk Institute, this school helps us to understand how and why the Mohawk Institute was created. Designed as a residential facility intended for the removal of children from their communities and families, and anchored in indentured servitude and facing several allegations of sexual assault, Sussex Vale ended in failure in 1826. As a result, the New England Company looked west to the Grand River, where they founded the Mohawk Institute in the 1830s in partnership with some of the Six Nations community (including the Six Nations' Council), though other community members rejected the school from the start. In this chapter, Peace traces the New England Company's aspirations for its school at Grand River and the impact of Sussex Vale on both the Mohawk Institute and the residential school system that grew from it.

In the next chapter, "Robert Ashton, the New England Company, and the Mohawk Institute, 1872–1910," historian William Acres examines Robert Ashton, superintendent of the Mohawk Institute for almost forty years. This chapter analyzes a school authority figure, a topic often ignored in residential school histories. Acres traces Ashton's vision for the Institute, his dealings with the New England Company, and the many troubles during his tenure, including the burning down of the Institute by disgruntled students.

Acres also authored the final chapter in part 5, entitled "The Lands of the Mohawk Institute: Robert Ashton and the Demise of the New England Company's 'Station,' 1891–1922." This chapter examines the land and properties of the New England Company at their Grand River Station. Conflicts over these lands were exacerbated by Ashton's choice to manage the Mohawk Institute more as a "Victorian agricultural reformatory" than a school. This approach, combined with a lack of consultation with the Six Nations community, resulted in a school that was a far cry from what the Six Nations had hoped for when the Institute was envisioned.

Part 6, "Student Experiences and Voices," begins with another chapter by Thomas Peace entitled "Life at the Mohawk Institute During the 1860s." This chapter was created as part of the Documenting the Early Residential Schools project, in which Peace and his students at Huron University College, in partnership with the WCC and others, transcribed the Mohawk Institute's only surviving attendance records from the 1800s. In the absence of survivor testimony, it is difficult to understand student experiences of the residential school system. This is especially the case for students who attended the school during the nineteenth century. This chapter details how the Mohawk Institute register covering 1860–73 provides a window into the life of over four hundred children who attended the school during this period, and touches on such topics as attendance, sickness, death, student activities, academics, runaways, and visitor observations. Peace concludes that there was no singular student experience at the Mohawk Institute during these years.

Drawing on materials recovered from the building during recent renovations and artifacts from an archaeological assessment, the next chapter, "Collecting the Evidence: Restoration and Archaeology at the Mohawk Institute," written by Sarah Clarke, Paul Racher, and Tara Froman, examines the archaeology of the Mohawk Institute, exploring the lived experiences of the students at the school through objects. Water damage at the Institute in 2017 necessitated an extensive renovation of the school, and no archaeological assessment had been completed before this time. The archaeological study completed as part of the renovation has already uncovered over thirty-five thousand artifacts, ranging from the pre-colonial Indigenous occupation of this land, through the residential school era, to the present. While ongoing, the archaeological assessment has much to tell us about student life at the Mohawk Institute.

The next chapter in part 6, "Collective Trauma and the Role of Religion in the Mohawk Institute Experience," by Wendy Fletcher, assesses the role that religion played in the socialization and harm of children at the Mohawk Institute. As this chapter demonstrates, notwithstanding the de facto lack of a signatory religious partner at the Mohawk Institute between 1922 and 1970, religion held a complex and multi-faceted place in the narrative of the Mohawk Institute, from the perspective of both those who wielded power and those who were harmed. Fletcher uses collective trauma theory as a vehicle to understand the experience of the survivors of the Mohawk Institute and concludes that religion was the framework for the collective traumatization of students through the destruction of their culture through a "civilization" process managed in a Christian context.

In the final chapter, "Concluding Voices: Survivor Stories of Life Behind the Bricks," Six Nations historian Richard (Rick) W. Hill, Sr. shares excerpts from a variety of interviews with former students. These are gathered from several sources, including Elizabeth Graham's book *The Mush Hole: Life at Two Residential Schools*, as well as interviews with former Mohawk Institute students conducted by the WCC. These oral history testimonies reveal shared themes such as hunger, loneliness, and abuse, and provide us with an insider's view of daily life at the school. Standing on their own with little interpretation, these interviews serve as a testament to the strength and resilience of those who survived their time at the Mohawk Institute, something they never should have had to face as children.

***

It is important to note that many of the authors of *Behind the Bricks* are non-Indigenous settler scholars who have benefited (and continue to benefit) from Canada's colonial past. We have attempted to grapple with this and approach our work in a manner that is respectful and produces a much more truthful assessment of the Mohawk Institute. In this journey, our work has been led and guided by Richard (Rick) W. Hill, Sr., a member of the Six Nations community, and co-editor of *Behind the Bricks*. Together, we formed the Mohawk Institute Research Group with the aim of sharing research related to the Mohawk Institute (both previously conducted and new) and making this information available to the public. We hope we have written a book that benefits, rather than takes from or harms, the Six

Nations community and that challenges past histories that justify settler colonialism.

Research methodology varies from chapter to chapter, but primary source analysis (including government and church documents, artifacts, and oral testimony) forms the basis of the research for the book. While many of these sources were produced by church and state authorities with their own biases and a goal of using residential schools to eradicate Indigenous culture and legitimize non-Indigenous rule, we have read these sources critically and juxtaposed them with oral testimony and non-written sources such as artwork created by survivors of the Mohawk Institute, as well as archaeological findings.

Photographs from various years of the Mohawk Institute's history have also been utilized and are found throughout *Behind the Bricks*. Some of these photographs are informal and taken by amateurs, while others were created by official church or state photographers. John Berger and Jean Mohr have written that "a photograph is a meeting place where the interests of the photographer, the photographed, the viewer and those who are using the photographs are often contradictory."[1] This is the case for the photographs included in *Behind the Bricks*. Some of these images were used as propaganda to convince church and state administrators and the public that the school's "civilization" program was succeeding and thus may not provide a "true" view of what went on behind the bricks of the Mohawk Institute. However, even these posed photographs sometimes tell us more than the photographer intended as they are another means of assessing administrators' goals for the school. In choosing which photos to include and which to leave out, we have attempted to be cognizant of the potential value of including photographs and drawings for our readers, while being mindful not to re-victimize former students.

Indeed, one of our goals for *Behind the Bricks* is for readers of this book not just to observe from a distance, but to take what they have learned and make concrete actions toward truth and reconciliation. Paulette Regan has written that we must be aware of "appropriating survivors' pain in voyeuristic ways that enable non-Indigenous people to feel good about feeling bad, but engender no critical awareness of themselves as colonial beneficiaries who bear a responsibility to address the inequities and injustices from which they have profited."[2] For too long, many histories of Canada have ignored or downplayed how non-Indigenous people have benefited from the residential school system and schools such as the Mohawk Institute.

Behind the Bricks thus aims to fill a gap in residential school literature. Despite the school's importance to Canada's history and the global history of colonial schooling, no comparable text is available. *Behind the Bricks* rests on a wide foundation of books about the residential school system, including works such as J. R. Miller's *Shingwauk's Vision: A History of Native Residential Schools* (1996); Agnes Grant's *No End of Grief: Native Residential Schools in Canada* (1996); John Milloy's *A National Crime: The Canadian Government and the Residential School System* (1999); and the many works produced more recently as part of the Truth and Reconciliation Commission, such as *A Knock on the Door: The Essential History of Residential Schools from the Truth and Reconciliation Commission of Canada* (2016) and the TRC's extensive six-volume final report, which provides a detailed historical overview of the residential school system in Canada.[3] More narrowly, many articles and books have focused on specific aspects of residential school history, such as health and sport. Many memoirs have also been written by former students. While there are case studies of individual schools such as Williams Lake, relatively little has been written about the Mohawk Institute specifically.

The two works that have to date provided the most complete examination of the Mohawk Institute are Jennifer Pettit's 1993 master's thesis, "From Longhouse to Schoolhouse: The Mohawk Institute, 1934–1970," and Elizabeth Graham's *The Mush Hole: Life at Two Residential Schools* (1997). Graham's book includes not only a brief narrative history of the Mohawk Institute and the Mount Elgin school but also an extensive collection of documents from government and church authorities, as well as the transcripts of interviews with sixty former students at the schools. *Behind the Bricks* builds on these works and is notable for the broad number of topics covered and for its focus on the early, middle, and later years of the residential school system, unlike many studies that tend to favour the more recent period. *Behind the Bricks* is also unique in that it is an edited collection with both Indigenous and non-Indigenous contributors rather than a single-author book, which is the case for many works that focus on the residential school system in Canada.

Behind the Bricks concludes with several appendices and a list of suggested readings for those who wish to continue to research and explore the history of the Mohawk Institute. Also included is a reproduction of Haudenosaunee scholar Keith Jamieson's important 1987 essay "History of Six Nations Education." This source was one of the first published by the WCC and sold to visitors, and it includes community knowledge, primary source research, and a section on Haudenosaunee history from Tom Hill, the director of the WCC at the time. As it is out of print, we have reproduced it here for the benefit of those wishing to learn more. None of our research on the Mohawk Institute would have been possible without the work of the Woodland Cultural Centre over the decades; and for that reason, among others, all proceeds from the sale of this book will go to the WCC.

We hope that *Behind the Bricks* contributes to the "truth" aspect of truth and reconciliation and inspires readers to continue their journey of learning about not only the Mohawk Institute and the residential school system more broadly but also the history of settler colonialism and its continued influence in Canada today. Without this truth, there can be no reconciliation.

NOTES

1. John Berger and Jean Mohr, *Another Way of Telling* (Pantheon, 1982), 7, quoted in Molly Fraust, "Visual Propaganda at the Carlisle Indian School," in *Visualizing a Mission: Artifacts and Imagery of the Carlisle Indian School, 1879 to 1918*, ed. Molly Fraust, Stephanie Latini, Kathleen McWeeney, Kathryn M. Moyer, Laura Turner, and Antonia Valdes-Dapena (Trout Gallery, 2004), 19.
2. Paulette Regan, *Unsettling the Settler Within: Indian Residential Schools, Truth Telling, and Reconciliation in Canada* (UBC Press, 2010), 47.
3. Detailed publication information about these sources can be found in the "Suggested Reading" section of *Behind the Bricks*.

Figure 0.2. Russ and Thelma Moses, Mush Hole, October 1943
Source: John Moses

The Russ Moses Residential School Memoir

John Moses and Russ Moses

The Russ Moses residential school memoir does not exist in a vacuum, and it requires appropriate words of introduction and context which I, as Russ's son, am pleased to provide herewith. My family members and I are Six Nations band members (Delaware and Upper Mohawk bands) living and working in Ottawa. My late father, Russ Moses (8 August 1932–22 May 2013), whose memoir is reproduced here, was a residential school survivor and Korean War veteran. He chose to relocate our family to Ottawa in 1965 upon leaving the military that year to pursue civilian employment with the federal government. My mother, Helen Monture Moses (aged ninety at the time of this writing), who followed her own mother, Edith Anderson Monture, into nursing, was one of the founding members of the National Native Nurses Association of Canada back in the 1970s.

On moving to Ottawa in the 1960s, our family—myself, my older brother Jim, and parents Russ and Helen—joined the bare handful of Indigenous families here in Ottawa comprising the city's urban Indigenous population at that time. There are now many thousands of Indigenous people in Ottawa from all over Canada, coming here for school, to work with the federal government, to join national Indigenous political organizations, or to work in the private sector. When we moved here, there were far fewer Indigenous families in the city, even counting those from the two nearest reserve communities at Kitigan Zibi (Maniwaki, Quebec) and Pikwakanagan (Golden Lake, Ontario).

Our 1965 arrival in Ottawa included moves to rental housing on Bayswater Avenue and Baseline Road, before my folks bought a place in a new subdivision called Briargreen in Nepean, in Ottawa's West End, in

1969. We moved into our new home in June of that year, and later that summer my folks hosted a large housewarming party that included friends and family from Six Nations, Tyendinaga, and from here in Ottawa. The housewarming party lasted two or three days, with tents and trailers in the front and backyards (the new neighbours were aghast), and included traditional blessings, food and drink, and singing and dancing to music on the record player.

During the 1970s and '80s and beyond, as we made twice-yearly trips back to Six Nations and spent many summers there, and as we hosted visiting Six Nations relatives and friends in Ottawa, we witnessed the flourishing of Ottawa's urban Indigenous community from the small beginnings I describe above. Our reality as a nuclear family of Status Indians who were registered band members living and working in Ottawa's urban and suburban environments unfolded always with the knowledge of our Six Nations identity. In respect to my father's family, this included the legacy of the residential schools.

The residential school experience thus looms large in the history of my family, just as it does for so many other Indigenous families across the country. While my mother's family, the Montures, were for the most part raised at home in traditional Six Nations family settings, things were rather different on my father's side. My late father, Russ Moses, was raised, along with his brother and sister, at the Mohawk Institute Indian Residential School in Brantford, Ontario, in the 1940s; their father/my grandfather, Ted Moses, was there in the 1910s, and my great-grandfather Nelson Moses was raised there even earlier, in the 1880s. So that makes me the first generation after three that was not sent there, for which I am of course grateful. The Mohawk Institute closed its doors as a residential school in 1970. My own elementary and secondary schooling was completed in Ottawa, in the public system, in the 1970s, when there was no public awareness regarding urban Indigenous issues, and any Indigenous curriculum content was confined to grade 8 history, as I recall, and was at any rate badly skewed by today's standards.

The following memoir was written by my father, Russ, upon his leaving the Canadian military in 1965 and starting new work that year as a civilian public servant, with what was then the Indian Affairs Branch (IAB) of the Department of Citizenship and Immigration. He was one of a handful of new Indigenous hires in the IAB, part of an innovation to bring more Indigenous public servants into the federal government. His hiring in August 1965 coincided with the planning of an annual symposium of residential school principals and administrators set for January 1966. It was

Figure 0.3. Russ Moses in RCAF uniform, 1965
Source: John Moses

decided to approach a number of new Indigenous hires whom IAB knew to be former residential school students to add their views to the gathering. Written from the vantage point of December 1965, when he was thirty-three years old, happily married, and the father of two young boys, the memoir recounts Russ's childhood experiences at the Mohawk Institute, which he attended from 1942 until 1947. Each residential school was a unique subculture in its own right: Different schools met different perceived needs in different regions of the country during different decades, and different conditions existed.

When my great-grandfather Nelson Moses was at the Mohawk in the 1880s, it was run as a mission school where young men and women from the Six Nations community were sent to be trained as Indigenous Anglican clergy and teachers. When my grandfather Ted Moses was there in the 1910s it was essentially a military-themed boarding school during the era of global militarization that would culminate with the outbreak of the Great War. It degenerated throughout the 1920s and '30s and the era of the Great Depression. My father and his siblings had the misfortune of being sent there during the 1940s, at the height of the Second World War, by which time any pretense toward education or training had been abandoned. Instead, the Indigenous children were there to provide the forced agricultural labour necessary to keep the large farm operation going, as a contribution to the civilian food-production effort on the Canadian home

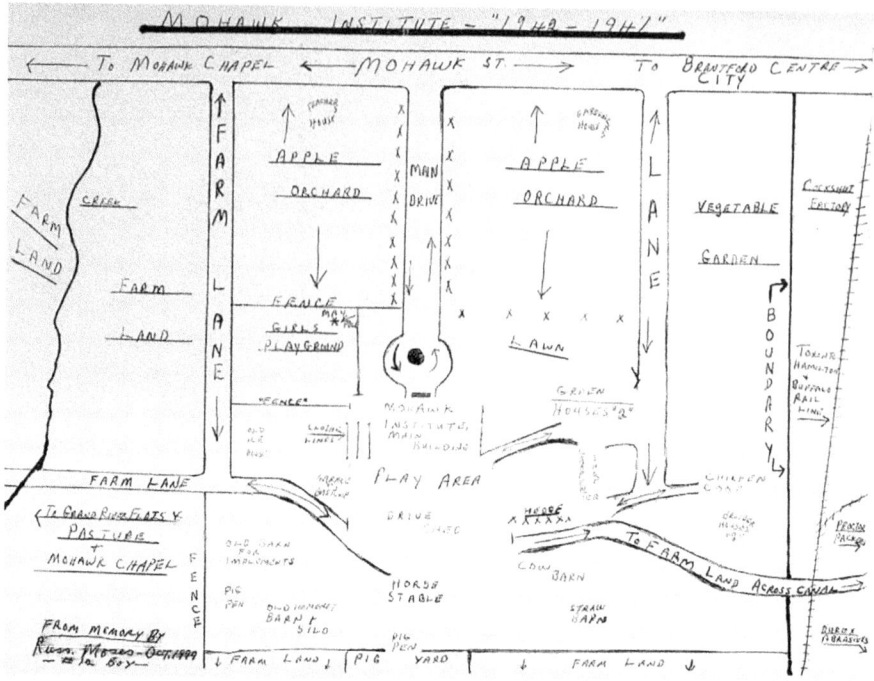

Figure 0.4. Russ Moses's hand-drawn map (1999), "Mohawk Institute, 1942–1946 by # 12 Boy."
Source: John Moses

front during wartime. Others were sent to provide forced labour in various factories in Brantford, with the city's major farm machinery companies by then likewise having been converted to meet wartime industrial production needs. As Russ's accompanying hand-drawn map illustrates, the Mohawk Institute itself sat on 350 acres of prime southern Ontario farmland with different varieties of crops, livestock, and orchards under cultivation. Sadly, the child inmates derived no benefit from their labours, and, as you will read, were reduced to begging on the streets of Brantford to help sustain themselves.

This unique first-person account is an important primary source document for an Indigenous auto-ethnography of the residential school experience in Canada wherein we assert, as Indigenous peoples, a leadership role in providing our own unfiltered testimonies and accounts, without representation or validation or mediation by others; and, since the memoir was produced in 1965 at the specific request of government officials, it obviously predates our current era of retrospection concerning the schools, as the Canadian state manoeuvres to contain its various liabilities. Thus, Russ's memoir is not a mere *representation* or *interpretation* of an Indigenous experience by some second- or third-hand narrator—it remains an actual first-hand, first-person Indigenous account that continues to speak truth to power despite the passage of many decades.

Recently there has been speculation concerning the extent to which the government (up to the most senior levels, including the minister of citizenship and immigration's office itself) knew about, or understood, residential school conditions at the time my father wrote his memoir. While Russ's memoir, even at the time of its first submission, could have been, and possibly was, dismissed as being of historical interest only to the extent that he was writing in 1965 and describing events that had occurred some twenty years previously, any recent statements by former government officials that they were unaware of these conditions is incorrect. The photograph of Russ and his sister (my aunt Thelma Davis) that accompanies the memoir is one of the few possessions that my father retained from childhood. The other photograph is of Russ upon his release from the Royal Canadian Air Force in 1965, the same year in which he wrote his memoir. The condition of their clothing in the first photograph speaks for itself. The second photo of Russ in uniform speaks to the twin legacies of residential school attendance and later military service shared by many Indigenous families. The first picture, according to Russ's note on the back, was taken in October 1943, during the course of one of the once-monthly, fifteen-minutes-only visiting sessions for brothers and sisters. I call this photograph *Proof of Life*. It was taken and kept on file by Mohawk Institute staff, to be provided to the Ontario Provincial Police and RCMP for identification purposes should the children attempt to run away home. Another photo was sent to family members on-reserve, as proof of the children's well-being at the school.

Notwithstanding the tragic circumstances of child abuse and neglect described in his memoir, as Russ's son it is important for me to convey to readers that Russ refused to be defined by his residential school experience. While Russ never hid his residential school experience, neither did he dwell upon it, and this imparts an important lesson for survivors of intergenerational trauma today. Beyond his upbringing, my father was a decorated naval veteran of the Korean War, an air force veteran of the Cold War, and an accomplished public servant whose many achievements included being deputy commissioner general of the groundbreaking Indians of Canada Pavilion at Montreal's Expo 67, a watershed in Indigenous self-representation before national and global audiences. Most importantly, Russ was a loving husband, father, grandfather, father-in-law, and uncle, with a tremendous sense of humour and irony, and an appreciation of the absurd, which I think is what helped him deal with so many things in life. As you read the memoir, I would ask you to reflect on the following questions:

- In what ways was the childhood and educational experience described here different from your own experiences, or what you might know about your own parents' or grandparents' experiences?

- What were some of the specific techniques used to sever bonds between siblings, and between children and their families, and to disrupt the cross-generational transmission of Indigenous cultures, heritage, and languages?

- Finally, how might some of the conditions described here account for the social pathologies experienced in some Indigenous families and communities today?

I will conclude with Russ's own admonition: "This is not my story, but yours."

INDIAN AFFAIRS BRANCH
DEPARTMENT OF CITIZENSHIP AND IMMIGRATION

DIRECTION DES AFFAIRES INDIENNES
MINISTÈRE DE LA CITOYENNETÉ ET DE L'IMMIGRATION

Ottawa 2, December 10, 1965.

OUR FILE NO. 1/25-20-1 (E.24)
Notre dossier nº

Mr. Russ Moses,
Information Section,
Room 425,
Bourque Building,
Ottawa, Ontario.

Dear Mr. Moses:

During the week beginning with January 10, 1966, the Residential School Principals from all regions will be meeting at Elliot Lake, Ontario, to discuss various aspects of residential schools.

In order to bring as many view points as possible to these deliberations, a selected number of Indians have been invited to submit their views and you are one of the persons who has been selected.

We would be most grateful to you if you would put your thoughts regarding residential schools down on paper and send this to me by the end of December. Please feel free to express your views candidly. We want to benefit both from your experience and your insights and frankness will be appreciated.

All the best to you and yours during the Yuletide Season and I will very much appreciate hearing from you at your earliest convenience.

Yours sincerely,

L. Jampolsky,
Chief Superintendent of
Vocational Training and
Special Services.

MOHAWK INSTITUTE – 1942-47   28/12/65

    First, a bit of what it was like in the "good old days".

    In August 1942, shortly before my 9th birthday a series of unfortunate family circumstances made it necessary that I along with my 7 year old sister and an older brother, be placed in the Mohawk Institute at Brantford, Ontario.

    Our home life prior to going to the "Mohawk" was considerably better than many of the other Indian children who were to be my friends in the following five years. At the "mushole" (this was the name applied to the school by the Indians for many years) I found to my surprise that one of the main tasks for a new arrival was to engage in physical combat with a series of opponents, this was done by the students, so that you knew exactly where you stood in the social structure that existed.

    The food at the Institute was disgraceful. The normal diet was as follows:

<u>Breakfast</u> – two slices of bread with either jam or honey as the dressing, oatmeal with worms or corn meal porridge which was <u>minimal</u> in quantity and appalling in quality. The beverage consisted of skim milk and when one stops to consider that we were milking from twenty to thirty head of pure bred Aolstein cattle, it seems odd that we did not <u>ever</u> receive whole milk and in my five years at the Institute we <u>never</u> received butter once.

This is very strange, for on entering the Institute our ration books for sugar and butter were turned in to the management – we never received sugar other than Christmas morning when we had a yearly feast of one shreaded wheat with a sprinkling of brown sugar.

<u>Lunch</u> – At the Institute this consisted of water as the beverage, if you were a senior boy or girl you received (Grade V or above) one and half slices of <u>dry</u> bread and the main course consisted of "rotten soup" (local terminology) (i.e. scraps of beef, vegetables some in a state of decay.) Desert would be restricted to nothing on some days and a type of tapioca pudding (fish eyes) or a crudely prepared custard, the taste of which I can taste to this day. Children under Grade V level received <u>one</u> slice of dry bread – incidentally we were not weight watchers.

Supper — This consisted of two slices of bread and jam, fried potatoes, <u>NO MEAT</u>, a bun baked by the girls (common terminology - "horse buns") and every other night a piece of cake or possibly an apple in the summer months.

The manner in which the food was prepared did not encourage overeating. The diet remained constant, hunger was never absent. I would say here that 90% of the children were suffering from diet deficiency and this was evident by the number of boils, warts and general malaise that existed within the school population.

I have seen Indian children eating from the swill barrel, picking out soggy bits of food that was intended for the pigs.

At the "mushole" we had several hundred laying hens (white leghorn). We received a yearly ration of <u>one</u> egg a piece - this was on Easter Sunday morning, the Easter Bunny apparently influenced this.

The whole milk was separated in the barn and the cream was then sold to a local dairy firm, "The Mohawk Creamery", which I believe is still in business. All eggs were sold as well as the chickens at the end of their laying life - we never had chicken - except on several occasions when we stole one or two and roasted them on a well concealed fire in the bush - half raw chicken is not too bad eating!

The policy of the Mohawk Institute was that both girls and boys would attend school for half days and work the other half. This was Monday to Friday inclusive. No school on Saturday but generally we worked,

The normal work method was that the children under Grade V level worked in the market garden in which every type of vegetable was grown and in the main sold - the only vegetables which were stored for our use were potatoes, beans, turnips of the animal fodder variety. The work was supervised by white people who were employed by the Institute and beatings were administered at the slightest pretext. We were not treated as human beings - we were the Indian who had to become shining examples of Anglican Christianity.

I have seen Indian children having their faces rubbed in human excrement, this was done by a gentleman who has now gone to his just reward.

The normal punishment for bed wetters (usually one of the smaller boys) was to have his face rubbed in his own urine.

- 3 -

The senior boys worked on the farm - and I mean worked, we were underfed, ill clad and out in all types of weather - there is certainly something to be said for Indian stamina. At harvest times, such as potatoe harvest, corn harvest for cattle fodder - we older boys would at times not attend school until well on into fall as we were needed to help with the harvest.

We arose at 6:00 a.m. each morning and went to the barn to do "chores". This included milking the cattle, feeding and then using curry comb and brush to keep them in good mental and physical condition.

After our usual sumptuous breakfast we returned to the barn to do "second chores" 8:00 to 9:00 a.m. - this included cleaning the stables, watering the young stock and getting hay down out of mow, as well as carrying ensilage from the silo to the main barn.

We also had some forty to eighty pigs depending on time of year - we never received pork or bacon of any kind except at Christmas when a single slice of pork along with mashed potatoes and gravy made up our Christmas dinner. A few rock candies along with an orange and Christmas pudding which was referred to as "dog shit" made up our Christmas celebrations. The I.O.D.E. sent us books as gifts.

Religion was pumped into us at a fast rate, chapel every evening, church on Sundays (twice). For some years after leaving the Institute, I was under the impression that my tribal affiliation was "Anglican" rather than Delaware.

Our formal education was sadly neglected, when a child is tired, hungry, lice infested and treated as a sub-human, how in heavens name do you expect to make a decent citizen out of him or her, when the formal school curriculum is the most disregarded aspect of his whole background. I speak of lice, this was an accepted part of "being Indian" at the Mohawk - heads were shaved in late spring. We had no tooth brushes, no underwear was issued in the summer, no socks in the summer. Our clothing was a disgrace to this country. Our so called "Sunday clothes" were cut down first world war army uniforms. Cold showers were provided summer and winter in which we were herded en masse by some of the bigger boys and if you did not keep under the shower you would be struck with a brass studded belt.

The soap for perfuming our ablutions was the green liquid variety which would just about take the hide off you.

Bullying by larger boys was terrible, younger boys were "slaves" to these fellows and were required to act as such - there were also cases of homosexual contact, but this is not strange when you consider that the boys were not even allowed to talk to the girls - even their own sisters, except for 15 minutes once a month when you met each other in the "visiting room" and you then spoke in hushed tones.

Any mail coming to any student or mail being sent was opened and read before ever getting to the addressee or to the Indian child - money was removed and held in "trust" for the child.

It was our practise at the "Mohawk" to go begging at various homes throughout Brantford. There were certain homes that we knew that the people were good to us, we would rap on the door and our question was: "Anything extra", whereupon if we were lucky, we would be rewarded with scraps from the household - survival of the fittest.

Many children tried to run away from the Institute and nearly all were caught and brought back to face the music - we had a form of running the gauntlet in which the offender had to go through the line, that is on his hand and knees, through widespread legs of all the boys and he would be struck with anything that was at hand - all this done under the fatherly supervision of the boys' master. I have seen boys after going through a line of fifty to seventy boys lay crying in the most abject human misery and pain with not a soul to care - <u>the dignity of man</u>!!

As I sit writing this paper, things that have been dormant in my mind for years come to the fore - we will sing Hymn No. 128!!

This situation divides the shame amongst the Churches, the Indian Affairs Branch and the Canadian public.

I could write on and on - and some day I will tell of how things used to be - sadness, pain and misery were my legacy as an Indian.

The staff at the Mohawk lived very well, separate dining room where they were waited on by our Indian girls - the food I am told, was excellent.

When I was asked to do this paper I had some misgivings, for if I were to be honest, I must tell of things as they were and really this is not my story, but yours.

- 5 -

There were and are some decent honourable people employed by the residential schools, but they were not sufficient in number to change things.

SUGGESTED IMPROVEMENTS FOR RESIDENTIAL SCHOOLS

1. Religion should <u>not</u> be the basic curriculum, therefore, it is my feeling that non-denominational residential schools should be established. (dreamer)
2. More people of Indian ancestry should be encouraged to work in residential schools as they have a much better understanding of the Indian "personality" and would also be more apt to be trusted and respected by the students.
3. Indian residential schools should be integrated – the residential school should be a "home" rather than an Institute.
4. Salaries paid to the staff members should be on a par with industrie – otherwise you tend to attract only social misfits and religious zealots.
5. The Indian students should have a certain amount of work (physical) to do – overwork is no good and no work is even worse. I believe that a limited amount of work gives responsibility to the individual and helps him or her to develop a well-balanced personality.
6. Parents of Indian children should be made to contribute to the financial upkeep of their children – I realize that this would be difficult, but it at least bears looking into.
7. Each child should be given individual attention – get to know him or her – encourage leadership, this could be accomplished by giving awards for certain achievements.
8. Last, but most important, solicit ideas from the students, we adults do not know all the answers.

SUMMATION – The years that an Indian child spends in an Indian residential school has a very great deal to do with his or her future outlook on life and in my own case it showed me that Indian are "different", simply because you made us different and so gentlemen I say to you, take pains in molding, not the Indian of to-morrow, but the Canadian citizen of to-morrow. <u>FOR</u> "As ye sow, so shall ye reap".

28/12/65

Russell Moses,
Former Pupil – Mohawk Institute, 1942-47.

PART 1
Historical Overview and Context of the Mohawk Institute

Figure 0.5. New England Company medallion.
Source: Woodland Cultural Centre

Figure 1.1. A nineteenth-century photo of the Mohawk Chapel, right, and possibly the original Mohawk Institute on the left.

Source: Richard Hill; photograph of an original photograph at the Mohawk Chapel

1

"To Shake Off the Rude Habits of Savage Life":[1] The Foundations of the Mohawk Institute to the Early 1900s

Jennifer Pettit

Senator Murray Sinclair, chief commissioner of the Truth and Reconciliation Commission of Canada (TRC), cautioned us that reconciliation is going to be a slow process given the significant and long-standing impact of the Indian Residential School system on Indigenous peoples. Before his passing, Sinclair explained that "we may not achieve reconciliation in my lifetime, or within the lifetime of my children."[2] According to Sinclair, the path to truth is equally challenging: "The road we travel is equal in importance to the destination we seek. There are no shortcuts. When it comes to truth and reconciliation we are forced to go the distance."[3] Where better to begin our journey toward the "truth" than a study of the Mohawk Institute in Brantford, Ontario, Canada's first and longest-running residential school and one that served as a foundation and "model" for the entire residential school system.[4]

Long before the TRC, Carl Urion suggested that "if we could understand the motivation for the establishment of residential, industrial and boarding schools for Indians in Canada and the United States . . . we would understand Indian-White relations in North America."[5] To that end, this chapter traces the beginnings of the Mohawk Institute, the first of what we would now call residential schools in Canada, from its inception in the 1830s through to the early years of the twentieth century, when students set fire to what was then the second set of Mohawk Institute school buildings.

It argues that church and state administrators and the Six Nations of the Grand River had very different visions for the Mohawk Institute. Based on the largely negative experiences that took place behind the bricks of the school, government and church officials should have abandoned their assimilationist agenda of "Christianizing and civilizing" Indigenous peoples instead of replicating schools like the Mohawk Institute across the rest of what would become Canada.

The story of the Mohawk Institute begins in the late 1700s with three groups—the British government, the New England Company, and the Six Nations. The school's subsequent history, stretching from 1904 to the present, is told in chapter 2. Together, these two chapters provide context for subsequent chapters in *Behind the Bricks*.

The Six Nations and the British in the 1700s

The Six Nations are Haudenosaunee, "people of the longhouse," who originally belonged to a confederacy of five nations—Cayuga, Mohawk, Oneida, Onondaga, and Seneca. When the Tuscarora joined the confederacy in the early 1700s, it became known as the Six Nations. Originally inhabiting lands in what is now New York and guided by the Great Law of Peace, each nation had their own languages and governing council of chiefs and clan mothers, and a political structure in which men and women held significant positions. The Six Nations also had their own education systems in which "children learned in unstructured and non-coercive ways, through participation, and studying their environment, and from instruction provided by older members of their communities."[6]

After the British settled in what would become the Thirteen Colonies, the Six Nations began to form ties with the new settlers. These relationships brought about treaties, the conversion by some Haudenosaunee to Christianity, the formation of schools, and trade and military partnerships. Throughout the eighteenth century the British saw the Six Nations as valuable economic partners in the fur trade.[7] Equally important, if not more so, the British also saw Indigenous nations as military allies, to the extent that the first British Indian Department for Canada was created in 1755 as a branch of the military portfolio to ensure a strong partnership with Indigenous peoples like the Six Nations during such conflicts as the American Revolution.[8] When the British lost the Revolutionary War to the American colonists in 1783, thousands of those who had fought alongside the British, including members of the Six Nations, fled to what would become Canada. Mohawk leader Joseph Brant (Thayendanegea) and others encouraged the Crown to provide the Six Nations with land as compensation for land lost during the American Revolution. To facilitate this, Frederick Haldimand, the governor of Quebec, signed the 1784 Haldimand Treaty with the Mississauga, establishing a large territory for the Haudenosaunee on both sides of the Grand River (six miles on each side, amounting to 674,910 acres); this territory would eventually become the location of the Six Nations Reserve and the future Mohawk Institute in Brantford. While the Haudenosaunee saw themselves as sovereign nations, the British began to view them as subjects under their control. By 1847 the Six Nations would occupy only "4.8 percent of the original Haldimand Tract."[9]

New Government Policy: To Christianize and Civilize

Not long after the Haldimand Treaty of 1784, military and commercial alliances with the Six Nations began to wane. Following the War of 1812 (1812–15), there was little need for Indigenous support in battle, as the threat of future North American wars had decreased; subsequently, Indigenous peoples' "warrior image had been replaced by that of an expensive social nuisance."[10] In addition, a substantial influx of settlers into Canada during the late 1700s and early 1800s exacerbated what was now the "problem" of what to do with Indigenous peoples who were no longer seen as valuable military partners, who were living on valuable farmland, and who were thus in the way of desirable non-Indigenous settlers during a time of significant population growth.[11] All of these changes meant it was becoming more and more difficult for Indigenous peoples in Canada to pursue their traditional ways of life. They became more and more reliant on what was known as the present system, which consisted of payments and gifts from the government. With the decline of the fur trade, Indigenous groups such as the Haudenosaunee were also no longer seen as important economic and commercial partners. Instead, they had become an exorbitant expense. With costs increasing and returns dwindling, the British sought out a new, more economical direction for their relationship with Indigenous peoples in Canada, one that would enable them to solve what they were now calling "the Indian Problem."[12]

British officials opted to undertake several inquiries in an attempt to find a solution. In 1828, Major General H. C. Darling, military secretary to the Governor General, led the first exploration of this situation in Canada. Darling felt the British government should "encourage the disposition now shown generally amongst the resident Indians of this province, to shake off the rude habits of savage life, and to embrace Christianity and civilization."[13] Darling's report would form the basis of a new "civilization" program. Darling's solution to eliminating these land and financial pressures and solving the "Indian problem" was to create a reserve system (in 1830) and make Indigenous peoples self-supporting sedentary Christian farmers who would be "educated" in schools and who would integrate into settler society (albeit as lower-class manual labourers). Government officials explained that

> experience has shown that Indians can no longer lead a wild and roving life, in the midst of a numerous and rapidly increasing white population. Their hunting grounds are broken up by settlements; the game is exhausted; their resources as hunters and trappers are cut off; want and disease spread rapidly among them, and gradually reduce their numbers. To escape these consequences, no choice is left, but to remove beyond the pale of civilization, or to settle and cultivate the land for a livelihood. . . . The settled and partially civilized Indians, when left to themselves, become exposed to a new class of evils. They hold large blocks of lands, generally of the most valuable description, which they can neither occupy nor protect against the encroachments of white squatters, with whom, in the vain attempt to guard their lands, they are brought into a state of constant hostility and collision. As they are exempt from any obligation to make or maintain roads through their lands, these reserves are serious obstacles to the settlement and improvement of the surrounding country, and their possessors become objects of jealousy and dislike to their neighbours.[14]

The "civilization" plan was not without recent precedent. In 1808 Major John Norton, who was adopted by Joseph Brant, Pine Tree Chief of Six Nations, proposed a "civilization programme comprising agricultural settlement, religious conversion, individual Indian land titles, and incentives to encourage local Indian enterprises."[15]

There were also other suggestions about how to solve the "Indian problem." For instance, Sir Francis Bond Head, the lieutenant-governor of Upper Canada from 1836 to 1838, felt a civilization policy was bound to fail and that all Indigenous peoples should be moved to Manitoulin Island, where they would eventually disappear. Here, they would be able to live away from the influence of settler society until they perished.[16] This obviously inhumane approach was not acceptable to church groups, such as the New England Company, who would become the government's partners. Lord Glenelg told Bond Head to stop his efforts and follow Darling's plan.[17] A "civilization" program was henceforth adopted.[18]

The "civilization" program was founded on three principles: "Indian protection, based on the Royal Proclamation; improvement of Indian living conditions; and Indian assimilation into the dominant society. The new policy had three systemic cornerstones: a system of land cession treaties, which we see in Upper Canada, which is now Ontario, and western Canada; a system of Indian reserves and supervisory Indian agents; and a system of schools to educate Indians, first at day and industrial schools, and later at residential schools."[19]

Like Darling, Sir James Kempt, an army officer and colonial official who became administrator of the Government in Canada, wrote in 1829 that nothing would civilize "the Indians" but "the education of a portion of their children." He went on to say, "I am aware that it has been the practice to look upon the Indians as useful only for war, but my object is, as far as it may be practicable, to alter this system, and to induce the Indians to adopt the habits of civilized life."[20] Civil authorities knew Indigenous peoples would have to learn to survive in the burgeoning industrial and agrarian society of the Canadas without government support. To sustain themselves, government and church officials believed that Indigenous peoples, especially children, needed to be taught Christianity and British culture, as well as work skills to keep in step with the social, economic, and technological changes taking place in the Canadas. Ideally, a "civilized" Indigenous person would support one of the Christian churches, would read and write English or French, and would dress and live in a manner similar to that of British people who were now living in Canada. Administrators hoped Indigenous groups such as the Haudenosaunee would begin to work toward this model of "civilized" personhood at an early age, when it supposedly would be easier for them to change their "savage" ways. Giving up speaking Indigenous languages was essential to this process, as was abandoning all Indigenous religious beliefs and practices, habits, customs, celebrations, and traditional dress and vocations. The laws, norms, and gender roles of Canadians would also have to be adopted. In virtually all aspects, Indigenous peoples were to become like the non-Indigenous settlers occupying their lands. Schools would teach Indigenous children to accept a subservient position in society and to acquiesce to upper-class authority.

The various church societies shared in many of these state aims. Schooling thus became the "joint enterprise of throne and altar."[21] The churches, like the government, sought Indigenous land, saw the schools as an employment opportunity for their followers, and often also held the same prejudiced ideas about Indigenous people. Yet, other issues also motivated church involvement in the industrial school system. The prime motivation for church members was the spreading of the word of God to "heathen" Indigenous peoples since the "Great Commission" in the Bible decreed that followers should bring the word of God to the world.[22] The motivations of missionary groups derived from what E. Brian Titley has called "misguided humanitarianism," since missionaries assumed that Indigenous groups were destined to be destroyed unless they embraced the values and cultures of the supposedly more advanced white society.[23] The state believed in the power of religion to speed up the civilization process, and perhaps more importantly, felt church involvement would save money.

Settler Colonialism

British North Americans' ideas about their cultural superiority shaped these civilization plans. Non-Indigenous settlers believed that agriculturalists were superior to those who lived by other means such as hunting. Moreover, drawing on the Bible and papal law known as the Doctrine of Discovery, non-Indigenous settlers believed that, since they had "subdued" the land, they possessed a greater right to it than did Indigenous peoples. Settlers also assumed that, as a result of their supposed "supremacy," Indigenous peoples would want to adopt Euro-Canadian language and ways of life. The British did not believe they needed to consult Indigenous people at length regarding their opinions or ideas about assimilation and assumed that they would want to convert. Many in the dominant settler society simply believed the disappearance of Indigenous peoples to be inevitable.

This replacing of Indigenous society by an "invasive settler society" has come to be known as "settler colonialism," which has been defined by Barker as "a distinct method of colonising involving the creation and consumption of a whole array of spaces by settler collectives that claim and transform places through the exercise of their sovereign capacity."[24] Settler colonialism continues to exist today in Canada, as non-Indigenous settlers are still living on appropriated land and many treaty promises remain unfulfilled.[25] All of this is built on the notion of *terra nullius*—the idea that Indigenous lands were unused. Barker and Lowman explain that settler colonialism differs from other forms of colonialism for three reasons: colonizers intend to stay; the "invasion is a structure, not an event," that results in "the assertion of state sovereignty and juridical control over their [Indigenous peoples'] lands"; and finally, the goal of settler colonialism is to "eliminate challenges posed to settler autonomy by indigenous peoples' claims to land by eliminating indigenous peoples themselves and asserting false narratives and structures of settler belonging."[26] Thomas Peace's recent book, *The Slow Rush of Colonization*, argues strongly that schools, both day schools and colonial colleges, played a critical role in the development during the late eighteenth and early nineteenth centuries of settler-colonial hegemony in the places that eventually became Canada.[27]

While church and state administrators throughout the history of the Mohawk Institute referred to having an agenda with the goals of "civilization" and assimilation, in reality, the goals are better described as management and elimination. Assimilation actually meant conformation as manual labourers and acceptance of upper-class white authority, and the destruction of traditional ways of knowing and life, with "British rhetoric calling for 'assimilation' of Aboriginal people into British North American Society . . . tempered by a long-standing colonialist view that Aboriginal peoples not only had an inferior culture to their own, but that this alleged inferiority demonstrated that Aboriginal peoples were simply not as intelligent or as capable as people of European origin."[28] The TRC has used the term "cultural genocide" to describe the real plans of church and state:

> For over a century, the central goals of Canada's Aboriginal policy were to eliminate Aboriginal governments; ignore Aboriginal rights; terminate the Treaties; and, through a process of assimilation, cause Aboriginal peoples to cease to exist as distinct legal, social, cultural, religious, and racial entities in Canada. The establishment and operation of residential schools were a central element of this policy, which can best be described as "cultural genocide. . . . *Physical genocide* is the mass killing of the members of a targeted group. . . . *Cultural genocide* is the destruction of those structures and practices that allow the group to continue as a group. States that engage in cultural genocide set out to destroy the political and social institutions of the targeted group. Land is seized, and populations are forcibly transferred and their movement is restricted. Languages are banned. Spiritual leaders are persecuted, spiritual practices are forbidden, and objects of spiritual value are confiscated and

destroyed. And, most significantly to the issue at hand, families are disrupted to prevent the transmission of cultural values and identity from one generation to the next.[29]

This is exactly what transpired at the Mohawk Institute over the course of its history.

Early Day Schools and the Arrival of the New England Company at Six Nations

When the Six Nations relocated to what would become Canada in the late 1700s, Governor Haldimand had promised them that they would thrive on the banks of the Grand River. In addition to a sawmill, a grist mill, and a church (the Mohawk Chapel), Haldimand committed to building a school and paying twenty-five pounds a year for a schoolteacher. This was in keeping with the wishes of Pine Tree Chief and Mohawk leader Joseph Brant, who wanted Haudenosaunee children to acquire a Western-based education and be taught about the Christian faith. As a result, in 1786, with the help of funding from the Crown, the Anglican Church opened the first day school in the Mohawk Village; children attended the school during the day and returned home at night. Teachers at the school used items such as prayer books and school primers in the Mohawk language.[30] The goal of leaders like Brant was the construction of more day schools. To that end, John Brant, the son of Joseph, visited England in 1822. While there, he approached the New England Company (NEC), an Anglican missionary group, to request a school and resident missionary for his community. The Company agreed to provide two hundred pounds for the school.[31] Brant "was instrumental in focusing the attention of the New England Company on the Six Nations."[32]

In keeping with its new plans for "civilizing" groups like the Six Nations, the British government supported the building of the day schools, endorsing the Church of England as the religious organization "most closely tuned to its official views."[33] The "Company for the Propagation of the Gospel in New England and the Parts Adjacent in America," or the "New England Company," as it would come to be known, was set up by an ordinance on 27 July 1649 and received a charter on 7 February 1662 from Charles II. The NEC was originally a Puritan missionary organization but later became an exclusively Anglican society.[34] The Company's missionaries assumed that the Indigenous groups such as the Six Nations would welcome their efforts; the seal of the NEC pictured an Indigenous person with the motto "Come Over and Help Us." The Company's 1662 charter explained that "we are resolved not only to seeke the outward welfare and prosperity of those colonies, by putting an industrious people into a way of trade and commerce, that they may be imployed and improved for their owne and the common benefitt of these our kingdoms; but more especially to endeavour the good and salvation of the most glorious gospel of Christ amongst them."[35] An extract from the 1874 correspondence of the NEC stressed the importance of their "civilization" focus, in keeping with government policy goals: "the first duty of the New England Company for more than 200 years has been, and still is, to civilize heathen natives in British North America. Their second duty is to christianize [sic] them."[36]

The Company's early efforts concentrated on the American colonies. After the American Revolution, however, the NEC moved to Sussex Vale, New Brunswick.[37] In 1786, missionaries decided to place Indigenous children in the homes of English-speaking settlers so that they could be "instructed in the principles of the Christian religion, reading, writing and also some trade or business."[38] The settlers, though, used the children "only as a means of financial gain, cheap labor, and sexual indulgence."[39] In 1822, the Reverend Oliver Arnold claimed that the children "appeared to be scattered all over the country,"[40] and by 1826 the Reverend John West asserted that "little or no good has accrued to the Natives from the Establishment at Sussex Vale. . . . Not an Individual is found to have settled upon Land on leaving his apprenticeship."[41] The plan had "utterly failed."[42]

The Company speculated that perhaps a more "advanced" Indigenous community such as the Six Nations would accomplish more than had the Mi'kmaq and Wolastoqey of Sussex Vale. The Six Nations were largely sedentary and they had an established system of government.[43] In addition, some of the Six Nations had already received religious instruction before they moved to Grand River and thus were Protestants and had been members of the Church of England for many years.[44] The Six Nations had also already encountered schooling while in the American colonies and had been exposed to reading and writing.[45] Joseph Brant, for example, had attended "Moor's School in Connecticut."[46] As a result, at Brant's urging, the NEC decided to move to Upper Canada to minister to the Six Nations. Eager to expand, the Company continued to fund and build more day schools in the 1830s in the communities of the Oneida, the Tuscarora, and the Cayuga. By 1900 there would be twelve day schools at Grand River.[47]

The NEC also established mission stations (as they were known) on the banks of the Grand River, near Lake Erie; on the shores of the Bay of Quinte, northeast of Lake Ontario; and on the banks of the Garden River, near Sault

Ste. Marie.[48] Writing in 1826, the Reverend John West said one of the day schools created by Thomas Davis, a Mohawk chief, proved to be a huge success. He went on to say he spoke with an Indigenous farmer who "expressed a warm Interest in the Education of the children of his Tribe," and said that "these Schools present[ed] every encouraging Prospect of further usefulness under the continued Patronage and Support of the Company."[49] West saw the Grand River station, home to over two thousand people (the Mohawks being the most numerous of the groups), as having great potential: "I beg leave respectfully to mention the importance should the Company have funds at their Disposal of having a Missionary resident at the Mohawk village. . . . I know not so promising a field of Missionary Labor or where the Labors of a liberal Enlightened Devoted Missionary would be found so efficient in benefitting a highly interesting, yet . . . neglected a portion of our fellow Men."[50]

The NEC chose the Reverend W. Hough as the first resident missionary at Grand River. He was there only a few months, however, before the Reverend Robert Lugger took over the role of resident missionary.[51] Lugger had some educational experience, having organized the National Negro School in Barbados in 1818, where he focused on the joining of education and evangelism. The NEC's 1829 annual report described Lugger as "a gentleman whose moral and religious character and earnest desire to be engaged as a missionary, well qualified him to carry into effect the objects of the Company."[52]

Opening of the Mohawk Institute

In 1828, the Reverend Abraham Nelles was appointed assistant missionary to Lugger and was tasked with overseeing the educational aspect of the Grand River mission. Lugger wanted to expand beyond the day schools, so the Company opted to open a Mechanics' Institute near the Mohawk Chapel that consisted of a mechanics' shop and four rooms, two for teaching girls to spin and weave, and two for instructing Indigenous boys in tailoring and carpentering.[53] This building had originally been occupied by Nelles as his home.[54] At first, the Institute operated as a day school for boys only, but by 1834 it opened "residential quarters" for ten boys and four girls from the Six Nations. Canada's first residential school was now in operation. Government officials would come to support the Institute since they viewed removing students from their parents in a positive light as it meant less community influence. It also guaranteed a higher rate of attendance than at day schools:

> The Day Schools are very inefficient for the purposes of education. In most cases there are no means of securing a regular attendance of the children at School. The abodes of the Indians are very scattered; the poverty and improvidence of the Indians in many instances so great that they are unable to provide suitable food and clothing to enable their children to attend regularly; the weather is often inclement, the roads bad, and parental restraint extremely lax. The only plan, therefore, to secure a systematical education, is to establish a Boarding School among them. The children should be removed to it at an early period from the injurious influence of their homes, and carefully and thoroughly reared in industrious and religious habits. By connecting a Farm with a School, the children might be usefully employed, and contribute much to defray the expenses of it.[55]

At schools like the Mechanics' Institute, children would be able to learn trades in addition to traditional academic subjects. Officials believed that training the young students in trades, farming, and household duties would be more useful by far than "book knowledge" on its own and would be the ideal means to fashion "Christianized and civilized" people.

Prior to the creation of the Mechanics' Institute, there were some models and attempts at boarding-type schooling, though not necessarily akin to what we today would consider a residential school. As early as the 1610s, French Récollets tried to school Innu children in their seminaries. Once they were replaced by the Jesuits, these efforts continued, always being somewhat short-lived. Female religious, such as the Augustinians and Ursulines, also boarded young girls. Though many of these children quickly left these schools, their legacy persisted into the eighteenth century.[56] Developments were similar in the Thirteen Colonies, with the early histories of Harvard, William & Mary, and Dartmouth all following similar trajectories.

The concept of the residential school originated in the eighteenth century in what was to become the United States. John Sergeant, a clergyman, first suggested the notion of an industrial school in 1743. Sergeant died, however, before his plan of establishing a school took shape.[57] The first industrial school in the United States would not open until 1804, when a Presbyterian missionary founded a school for Cherokee children, called a "manual labour residential school," that was to give equal time to work and study.[58] These schools were modelled upon "homes for vagrants, orphans and incorrigible children in Britain," thus "an institution ostensibly designed to reform those with a predilection for crime . . . [was] chosen as the premier form of schooling for Indian children."⁵⁹ These spaces were "designed for disciplining the bodies of those perceived to be unproductive, shiftless, or sinful."⁶⁰ Driving the creation of schools for children "was the belief that Indigenous adults were too stubborn in their traditions for effective assimilation, making children the best targets for a more rapid transformation of Indigenous communities away from their cultural past toward a more Europeanized future."⁶¹

Indigenous peoples, however, envisioned a different system of education than did the government and Indigenous missionaries. They wanted a school system that would teach their children to cope with the changing circumstances that imperilled their traditional ways. Most wanted to retain their separate status and the reserve system, and sought only the parts of the "civilizing" program that they felt would help them in some manner. They perceived the schools as more of a partnership between Indigenous peoples and church and state, and many believed that Indigenous communities would one day control their own education programs.⁶² As historian Douglas Leighton has explained, Indigenous groups such as the Six Nations were "active participants in the Indian-church relationship."⁶³ Indigenous missionaries such as Mississauga Reverend Peter Jones (Kahkewaquonaby) sought financial and moral support for schools. In an 1831 letter to Viscount Goderich, the colonial secretary, Jones wrote, "I want to speak a few words about the Indian schools in Upper Canada. I hope you will help all the schools which good White people have established for the Indians. . . . We have great regard for our teachers."⁶⁴ A number of Indigenous peoples felt schools would teach their children the skills needed to be self-reliant. Euro-Canadians appeared to be prospering, so Indigenous peoples sought to learn the same skills, which apparently made them successful. In addition, administrators could help establish contacts between Euro-Canadians seeking employees and Indigenous peoples seeking work. Schools would also instruct children in the English language and arithmetic, which would facilitate business transactions and would ensure that non-Indigenous peoples did not deceive Indigenous peoples in business dealings. Chief Shawahnahness of St. Clair, for instance, claimed in 1833 that his people "agreed to have their children instructed that they might understand the weights and measures used by the white people, and that they may be able to write and keep accounts that the white men may not cheat them."⁶⁵ Finally, some Indigenous peoples believed that conversion to Christianity would end social problems such as alcoholism, which now plagued some of their communities.⁶⁶ That said, their ability to respond and either support or resist the assimilationist plans of church and state varied over time.

While some community leaders initially backed the idea of schools, some Indigenous peoples responded rather apprehensively to the new Mechanics' Institute at Six Nations. Just as English-speaking Canada lived in two universes, Protestant and Catholic, the Six Nations community contained Catholic, Protestant and Longhouse adherents, followers of traditional spiritual belief.⁶⁷ Longhouse people were generally not supportive of schools, and a clear religious divide existed between Longhouse chiefs and Mohawk Anglican chiefs. In addition, the new Institute differed from the traditional education a child usually received. Indigenous children originally learned only the skills and knowledge that directly related to "the economic, social and cultural bases of their culture," and they learned through observation rather than through formal instruction.⁶⁸ Instead of being taught school concepts such as failure, Indigenous children traditionally were taught to be collaborators and to "act for others"—this was very different from what the school was teaching. The Anglican chiefs of the Six Nations, however, were hopeful about the new school. They backed the new Mechanics' Institute and asked that two hundred acres of their land be set aside for the Mohawk Chapel and the Institute.⁶⁹

Significant immigration in the 1820s meant more and more pressure on Indigenous lands. When the Reverend Robert Lugger arrived at Grand River, the Indigenous population was 2,233, and of the 355,000 acres remaining of the original tract government officials had allotted to Six Nations, less than 7,000 acres were under cultivation by Indigenous farmers.⁷⁰ In 1830, 800 acres of Six Nations land was alienated for the establishment of the village of Brantford.⁷¹ In 1841, under protest, the Six Nations saw the Crown reduce their remaining lands of 220,000 acres to a mere 20,000-acre reserve plus the land under cultivation. After further reductions, the reserve would eventually total about 44,900 acres.⁷² The NEC argued against the land reduction, and afterward the Mohawk Institute grounds were the only lands still considered Six Nations land in addition to the condensed reserve. By 1847, a sufficient number of non-Indigenous settlers arrived to justify the village of Brantford's incorporation into a town.⁷³ Farmers composed the majority of these settlers. By 1851, Brant County became the most productive farming community in Ontario. More than 50 per cent of local farmland was improved by this time in Brant County, the "greatest extent of 'farm progress'" in all of Ontario to that date. Net farm output for the county averaged over $350, yet net farm output for Six Nations farms during this period was less than $100.[74]

Early Years of the Mohawk Institute

In 1831, the Reverend Abraham Nelles took over school affairs, though he would not be made resident missionary for the New England Company for six more years. Nelles was born in Ontario, and his father and grandfather had been involved in the Indian Department in New York. He studied Iroquoian dialects as a student missionary. As he could speak Mohawk, he could communicate with the community in the Grand River.[75] Throughout its history the school would go by various names, though "Mohawk Institute" would be the most commonly used term. The NEC stated its goals for the school as follows: "the instruction of a number of the youth of both sexes in the arts, habits, and customs of civilized life, who may hereafter act as instruments in the hands of the Company, for the complete civilization of the Indians generally."[76] The NEC reported that the Six Nations welcomed the school, and that "it is the wish of the most civilized amongst them that their offspring would receive the benefit of instruction."[77] Shortly thereafter, farming became the most important subject in which the children received instruction, but trades still remained an integral part of the curriculum. In 1836, in a report to the Company's directors, Nelles made clear that that school was flourishing: "The progress of the children at the Institution he describes as very gratifying. They have been visited by many persons of respectability, some clergymen, who all expressed satisfaction and delight." By 1837, there were eighteen children at the "Institution," three of whom were day scholars.[78] In 1838, Nelles reported on the addition of six girls to the school, who "seemed to be contented, and promised to profit by the instructions given them, as much as the boys."[79]

When the government recommended in 1835 that the Haudenosaunee should move to the south side of the Grand River, the need for more residential places in the school increased; at the same time, NEC costs rapidly escalated from £750 to £4,000 per annum.[80] Conditions at the school continued to be favourable throughout the 1830s, and at the end of 1838 enough equipment and buildings existed to accommodate thirty boys and ten girls. The school was considered a "model institute." Besides being instructed in farming, the "older boys were trained as wagon-makers, blacksmiths and carpenters," while the girls learned "housekeeping and the arts of needlework, spinning and knitting."[81] In 1838 the Institute hired shoemaking and wheelwrighting teachers. Nelles recommended an increase in the number of children at the Institute as "he regard[ed it] . . . as the most useful part of the Company's establishment."[82] In the 1840s, graduates of the Institute began settling on small farms near the school, and in 1842 the NEC gave a grant of ten pounds to provide graduates with tools and materials. Nelles wrote in 1844 that he was worried, however, as most graduates returned to the reserve after completing their education and reverted back to their older practices.[83]

In these early years of the Mohawk Institute, government officials monitored the school and the general condition of Indigenous peoples. In 1842, Sir Charles Bagot, the governor general, was tasked with studying the Indian Department and Indigenous peoples in general. The Bagot Commission claimed that policy for Indigenous peoples lacked direction and argued that the approach that the Mohawk Institute was taking—removing children from their parents and sending them to school to learn farming and trades—was the desirable path forward. Rather than spending money on treaty payments, the commission's report said that the government should fund manual labour schools.[84] Shortly after, at the 1846 General Council at the Narrows of Lake Simcoe (present-day Orillia, Ontario), a number of the chiefs who gathered agreed that industrial schools for Indigenous children seemed to be the way of the future. To place Indigenous peoples "on the same ground as the white man,"[85] chiefs promised to support the erection of schools by giving one-quarter of their annuities for the next twenty-five years.[86] A government report in the year that the council took place indicated that over fifty children were on a waiting list for the Mohawk Institute.[87] In these early years, the Mohawk Institute drew its student body from Six Nations, with many Christian chiefs and families in the community eagerly sending their own children to the school.[88]

The popularity of the Mohawk Institute in particular stemmed in part from Nelles's ability to recognize what the Christian Six Nations desired; indeed, he is remembered as being "well-liked by both the students and the Six Nations community."[89] Nelles permitted the students to speak Indigenous languages at all times, "except while lessons were being conducted."[90] Nelles was also concerned about how the Six Nations were reacting to the Institute. For example, in 1847, when Egerton Ryerson, then superintendent of education in Canada West, recommended that more time should be spent on manual labour,[91] Nelles refused to make changes and retained the Mohawk Institute's system of one half day of instruction and one half day of labour as he knew that people from Six Nations would resist having students spend more time on work.

A Model Institute

In his 1847 *Report by Dr. Ryerson on Industrial Schools*, Ryerson made clear that he believed that schools such as the Mohawk Institute were intended to "give a plain English education adopted to the working farmer and mechanic."[92] Ryerson had visited an agricultural school for the poor in Hofwyl, Switzerland, that inspired much of his thinking. He believed there should be schools for Indigenous peoples that were intended to produce labourers, not professionals. Ryerson praised the Mohawk Institute and recommended that "a general education should be provided for the Indian youths ... similar to the New England Company's Establishment." He also recommended that such schools be the joint enterprise of church and state, and again emphasized that during most of the school year the "time occupied in labour should be from 8 to 12 hours a day ... and instruction from 2 to 4 hours ... [and] in the autumn, it may, perhaps, be well to omit instruction altogether."[93] He further suggested that schools such as the Mohawk Institute should be called "industrial schools" rather than "manual labour schools." Ryerson insisted that students must reside together at these schools and that the schools had to be connected to the churches: "the North American Indian cannot be civilized or preserved in a state of civilization (including habits of industry and sobriety) except in connection with, if not by the influence of, not only religious instruction and sentiment but of religious feelings."[94] Ryerson suggested that the day-to-day management of the schools be left with the churches, while the government would provide financial support. At this point, however, the NEC continued to financially support the Mohawk Institute.

Interest in schools and the "civilization" program remained strong and the Mohawk Institute became "a model of sorts" for other institutions.[95] In 1847, the chief superintendent of Indian Affairs was equally positive about the Mohawk Institute:

> I am of the opinion that a general Education should be provided for the Indian youths, both male and female, on a uniform system, *something similar to the New England Company's Establishment* [i.e., the Mohawk Institute; emphasis added]. The children should reside at the Establishment, and be placed under the constant supervision of a competent and attached Tutor, who should pay to their habits the same attention as to their minds. The course of Education should consist of reading, writing, and arithmetic, and religious instruction under

the superintendence of the Minister of the church to which they belong; they should also be in-structed in such mechanical arts as they display an aptitude to acquire, and in the theory and practice of husbandry; the more talented should be encouraged, by a more liberal education, to enter into Holy Orders, and become the resident Ministers among their Tribe. The girls, besides a similar elementary Education, should be instructed in such useful acquirements as are possessed by white people of the inferior class. The proceeds of their labours, as well as of the boys, in the mechanical arts, might be profitably disposed of in the neighbouring towns and surrounding country. This constant employment of their intellectual and bodily faculties, will alone reserve the Indians from extinction, and elevate their condition.[96]

After the opening of the Mohawk Institute, the first of these new schools was the Alnwick or Alderville Industrial School built in 1848 by Methodists. Shortly after, in 1851, Methodists opened the Mount Elgin Industrial School on the reserve belonging to the Chippewas of the Thames.[97] Unlike the situation with the NEC, which was still covering the costs for the Mohawk Institute, this time the government entered a financial partnership with the Methodist missionaries. The church was to be placed "in charge of the Industrial schools and responsible for providing books, supplies, and teachers' salaries. The missionaries also supplied farm stock and farm equipment for the attached model farms. For its part, the Indian Department agreed to maintain the school buildings and provide an annual per capita subsidy to defer food, clothing, and general education expenses."[98] Despite the government's faith in the "civilization" plan, both the Alderville and the Mount Elgin schools experienced troubles such as mismanagement and a lack of funding and student interest. In 1858 a government investigation recommended that both schools be closed.[99] The Methodists ignored this recommendation, but in 1859 the Alnwick school merged with the Mount Elgin school.[100] By 1862 administrators were forced to close the Mount Elgin school for a time to assess the various difficulties it was experiencing, though it would reopen and remain in operation until 1946.[101] Mary Jane McCallum's study of the Mount Elgin Industrial School provides us with a detailed look at the impact of a lack of funding on students, who were forced to work instead of going to school to offset the costs of running the schools.[102] School officials spent as little as they were able on food and care for the students, which meant that "poor nutrition, overexertion, stress, and unsafe conditions made students at Mount Elgin especially vulnerable to getting ill, and when they did, principals often delayed seeking medical advice and intervention to save money."[103]

The 1850s and '60s: Challenges and Possible Arson

While students at the Mohawk Institute faced similar conditions, by 1853 there were forty adults, "practically all graduates" of the Institute, who were following trades and farming and living near the school. By that time, the New England Company decided that since "the Mohawk Institute was meeting with so much more success than the day schools, that especial attention should be devoted to its activities."[104] Still, the day schools continued to serve an important role in the community, and Six Nations was home to more day schools than any other Indigenous nation in Ontario. In 1857, the government chose to pass the *Act to Encourage the Gradual Civilization of the Indian Tribes in the Province, and to Amend the Laws Respecting Indians*. In addition to new powers for the Indian Department such as control of reserve lands, the act focused on enfranchisement (terminating Indian status). At this time, Richard T. Pennefather, the civil secretary, wrote a report that recommended that the government's focus should be on education and that Canada should take over the control of Indian affairs in Canada from the British; this happened in 1860. To facilitate the success of the schools, a new system of agents was created to supervise the industrial schools, as they had come to be known.

Despite these government studies, in 1858 the Mohawk Institute burned to the ground, either by accident or, as some assumed, by arson. Undeterred, the NEC ignored these concerns and decided to rebuild the Institute after the fire. The new yellow-brick school opened in 1862. Much bigger than the first school, the new multi-storey building could hold approximately sixty students, though additions not long after meant it could hold ninety students—forty-five boys and forty-five girls.[105] The new school was built on a ten-acre parcel of land a few hundred yards from the Mohawk Chapel that had been purchased by the NEC from individual members of Six Nations.[106] Unlike many other residential schools, the school was just over a mile away from the nearest city (Brantford), and only seven miles from the Grand River Reserve, today commonly referred to as Six Nations of the Grand River Territory.

Conditions at the Institute appear to have improved in the 1860s. The Prince of Wales visited the Mohawk Institute in 1860 and H. J. Lister, sent by the NEC in 1868 to report on the school, described it as "very well managed."[107] By the middle of the 1860s the Mohawk Institute was the only technical education institution that had achieved its intended results.[108] During this period, Isaac Barefoot, an Onondaga member from Six Nations and a graduate of the Mohawk Institute, became the first Indigenous person appointed as a teacher at the school. He had trained to be a teacher at Egerton Ryerson's Toronto Normal School and eventually became a priest at Huron College in London, Ontario.[109] Several other graduates from the Institute excelled during this period as well. Three boys were sent to the Grammar School in Brantford, and three girls and two boys were sent to Hellmuth College in London, Ontario.[110] This development of Indigenous teachers and clergy was not outside the professed goals of church and state policies for Indigenous peoples. Such activities enhanced the influence of the Institute among its target population without changing the general goal of training the masses for labouring jobs. The NEC hired several more Indigenous teachers to work at the schools, and by the 1880s seven of the eight teachers at the day schools were Haudenosaunee.[111]

For a variety of reasons, the main one financial, the NEC made the decision in 1864 to pull back from trades instruction at the Mohawk Institute and concentrate mainly on farming. To facilitate this, the Company purchased what was known as the Babcock Lot, roughly thirty-three acres located between the Institute and the town of Brantford. The hope was that instructing the students on this land would lead to more students deciding to farm after they graduated from the school.

A few years later, the 1867 *British North America Act* not only officially made Canada a country but also transferred authority over Indigenous peoples to the federal government under section 91(24). The portfolio of Indian Affairs now fell under the guidance of the secretary of the state, who became the superintendent general of Indian Affairs. Administrators opted to retain much of the earlier colonial legislation, including the plan to use schools to "civilize" Indigenous peoples.

Shortly after, in 1869, the Canadian government passed the *Enfranchisement Act*. The act stated that the governor-in-council could remove from band council membership lists those who he felt were unqualified or unfit to hold office, and even minor bylaws were to be approved by the superintendent general of Indian Affairs. The goal was for Indigenous groups to give up traditional forms of government in favour of a top-down, centralized form of government.[112] While elected councils were supposed to be required under this legislation, the Six Nations kept their hereditary council until 1924, the last Indigenous community in Canada to do so.

The 1870s: Changes at the Institute and the Expansion of the School System

In 1870, an addition was added to the Mohawk Institute's main building, and a few years later additional spaces for staff were also built, as was a new principal's residence. These additions were financed by the NEC.[113] In 1872, when the Reverend Abraham Nelles retired as the Institute's principal, the Company named the Reverend Robert Ashton as his replacement. Ashton was English and had worked as a schoolmaster in England prior to moving to Brantford in 1872 after being hired by the NEC to manage the Mohawk Institute. Rather than finding a school in great shape, as Nelles had claimed, Ashton claimed to discover errors in Nelles's bookkeeping. He also reported other problems at the school such as a lack of proper bathing facilities for the children, and that numerous land claims problems existed. The NEC responded with surprise and wrote to Ashton that "it is quite amazing to the Committee that such a state of affairs as you describe should have been permitted by your predecessor."[114]

Ashton's discovery of Nelles's shortcomings can be interpreted in a number of ways. Ashton may simply have been promoting himself by discrediting his predecessor, a common enough tactic among rival professionals, but Ashton's insistence on more meticulous bookkeeping and management of the school is also reflective of a growing paternalism in government and Institute policy. This paternalism stemmed from population growth and economic development of the larger non-Indigenous society. Non-Indigenous people began filling the majority of the farm-labouring positions that Indigenous peoples had earlier held, and the growth of racism meant most graduates were not able to find off-reserve wage employment. The rise in paternalistic social control meant an increasing separation of Indigenous and non-Indigenous objectives for the Institute. There were fewer and fewer reasons for the Six Nations community to send their children to the school, especially since the number of day schools was increasing.

This situation was compounded by Ashton's management approach, which was far stricter and more paternalistic than Nelles's. He chose to remodel the Institute after British reformatory schools.[115] Ashton believed the children at the Institute were lazy and poorly disciplined and thus needed to be reformed, and students describe his appointment as the beginning of a "reign of terror."[116] At first, the NEC approved of Ashton's methods, writing to tell him in 1873 that "the Committee approves of your proceedings generally."[117] Ashton was keen to make the school more aesthetically pleasing and took on projects such as creating a lawn and planting trees and shrubs in front of the Institute; seeing this, the public and others would be less concerned about what went on behind the bricks of the Mohawk Institute. Ashton also enacted new measures to "prevent communication between the boys and girls in the Institution," and required parents to provide a doctor's note before a student could be removed from the school due to illness.[118] In addition, Ashton sent out a letter to the parents of all of the students informing them of the school's attendance policies."[119] Ashton decreed that only English, and no Indigenous languages, be spoken at the Mohawk Institute, and he used student monitors to enforce this rule. All of these actions were indicative of a growing control that the Six Nations increasingly resisted.

In keeping with the rise of paternalistic sentiments, the Reverend Robert Ashton's letters to the NEC seldom mentioned specific children and instead focused on school policies and the school buildings. For example, Ashton obtained a new laundry, bathroom, and bathhouse for the Institute.[120] Ashton also proudly informed the Company that the male students undertook all of the ploughing and seeding on the farm.[121] Government officials encouraged Ashton to have parents sign forms promising they would not interfere with their children for five years, but Ashton claimed such actions would be difficult since many parents already complained about the quality of education received by their children.[122]

The Six Nations resisted the growing paternalistic social control of the Anglican Church and state officials, and as a result, the Haudenosaunee Confederacy Council of Chiefs tried to take over control of the schools on the reserve. The Council failed in this attempt, but the NEC agreed in 1878 to the creation of a school board composed of the Indian superintendent, three Six Nations representatives who would be elected by the Council, and three officers of the NEC.[123] The Company said that this arrangement was to eventually lead to Six Nations taking over control of the day schools on the reserve.[124] The creation of such a board was rather unique and a significant step for the NEC, which was accustomed to having sole control over school matters, and well into the twentieth century (the school board existed until 1933) the board was the only one of its kind in all of Canada.[125] The Six Nations agreed to provide an annual grant of £1,500 for schools.[126] They said that it would be "a step in the wrong direction" for the NEC to give up its management of the Mohawk Institute.[127]

At this time, the Canadian government established the Indian Affairs Branch as part of the Department of the Interior (in 1873), and in 1876 the government passed the infamous *Indian Act*. This document consolidated previous legislation and would have an impact on virtually every aspect of the lives of Indigenous peoples in Canada.[128] In 1879, Nicholas Flood Davin, a Regina newspaper editor and the member of Parliament for Assiniboia West, was sent by the federal government to study the American system of industrial schools. Davin delivered his findings in his *Report on Industrial Schools for Indians and Half-Breeds* (1879). Based primarily on his research in the United States, Davin recommended building institutions similar to the Mohawk Institute in Western Canada despite disappointing results at most of the schools in Eastern Canada.[129] Davin did not sympathize with the challenges facing Indigenous peoples, and he professed, of the average Indigenous person, that "little can be done with him. He can be taught to do a little at farming, and at stock-raising, and to dress in a more civilized manner, but that is all."[130] Under this new plan, only the Qu'Appelle and Battleford schools in Saskatchewan and the High River or Dunbow school in Alberta were to be constructed. Shortly after, however, a number of industrial institutions appeared, and the 1890s witnessed the "heyday" of this type of school. At its peak, the industrial school system numbered in the twenties. Schools in Ontario, such as the Mohawk Institute, "served as models for [this] later development in western and northern Canada."[131] Given the negative reactions by this time to the schools in Ontario, administrators should have seriously reconsidered their decision to expand the system across the country. Had they done so, a great deal of harm could have been prevented.

The End of the Nineteenth Century and Changes to the Mohawk Institute

This apparent confidence in the industrial school system must be closely examined. The Mohawk Institute cannot be deemed a "success" as a major shift took place whereby the administrators began to focus on enrolling orphans and destitute children who formed the majority of students by the 1890s. The school principal became their legal guardian, and more rigid disciplinary systems were put in place. As time passed, Six Nations students attended the Institute only long enough to acquire the skills they needed to farm, or until they were able to find someone willing to adopt them. Some families, at their own expense, sent their children to Caledonia or Brantford to be educated. Many parents felt the administrators at the school overworked their children. Destitution became the prime motive for sending children to the Institute, and more and more children came from bands other than the Six Nations. By 1878, of the ninety students at the Institute, half came "from Indian Bands outside of the Six Nations."[132]

An agricultural depression in England forced the NEC in 1882 to reduce its grant to the school from £1,500 to £1,000.[133] In response, in 1885, the Indian Department gave its first grants to the Institute to protect it from the threat of closure, but management of the school was largely left under the auspices of the NEC. That year, J. Kelly, who was sent by the government to inspect the Mohawk Institute, claimed that the school possessed ample academic supplies such as globes, a chemical cabinet, two hundred books, and various periodicals. Kelly felt "the whole farm . . . present[ed] a park-like appearance and [was] very attractive."[134] Likewise, in 1885 visiting Superintendent and Commissioner J. T. Gilkison offered a very positive description of the school: "the extensive grounds in front of the Institute are much improved and beautified, rendering the place pleasing, attractive, and a most comfortable home for its fortunate inmates."[135] Clearly, he did not look too deeply into what was transpiring behind the bricks of the school, assuming instead that if the outside of the school looked wonderful, the inner workings must be equally positive.

Despite the federal government's faith in industrial schools, Principal Ashton was becoming increasingly frustrated with resistance to his efforts at the school and recommended that if students left the Institute, they should not be permitted to attend another school. Ashton said most students left "before the completion of their second year" and before they "derived much lasting advantage from the course of training provided." He thus sought "regulations as would permit pupils being admitted under a written agreement to remain [for] specified periods."[136] While demand for admission to the Mohawk Institute remained high, "far exceeding the accommodation that the building is capable of affording," it was still not completely meeting expectations.[137] Hayter Reed, the deputy superintendent general, visited the Mohawk Institute in 1889. He objected to the amount of time the children spent in classrooms and said they should spend even more time engaged in labour, "unless it be intended to train children to earn their bread by brainwork rather than by manual labour." Reed also disliked that some of the children spent summer vacation time at home on the reserve.[138]

By 1891, a larger government grant (now sixty dollars per student) meant that Indian Affairs would henceforth pay "the major portion of current expenses and . . . shared the responsibility for the conduct of the school."[139] The grant covered the majority of costs and the NEC agreed to make up the difference and maintain the property. Once again, trades instruction was reduced even further. The NEC in 1893 used the newly acquired funds to add a new wing to the school, which allowed it to increase the number of students at the school to 120.[140] The majority of these new students, however, were destitute or orphans who Ashton feared would lower the standards of the Institute even further. He emphasized that "the general standard of attainments is and will be lowered for a time owing to the admission of orphans and neglected children, who are generally quite ignorant on admission."[141] Ashton explained that at this time there were two "classes" of children—the children whose parents sent them to the Institute so that they would have access to higher education, and the orphaned and destitute children who began to attend in higher numbers.[142]

In an effort to gain control of the students, Principal Ashton decided to give "good conduct badges" to deserving pupils once a month.[143] The badges consisted of a small star and were to be worn on the left breast. A first badge entitled the student to one month with no corporal punishment and meant they could go out without a monitor. Two badges entitled a boy to go out on half-holidays and a girl to go on a walk to Brantford once a fortnight. Three badges earned a reward of two cents per week, four paid three cents per week, and so on, up to five cents per week. Once two "bad" reports were received in one month, a badge would have to be forfeited. Each additional bad report would mean the loss of another badge. Crimes such as "theft, absconding, direct insubordination or gross breach of discipline" meant the loss of all badges. A student who received more than four offences in one month would be put on a "black list."[144] Boys on this list were forced to wear a black strap over their left shoulder and girls had to wear a black apron.[145]

Discipline at the school was strict and was enforced by monitors. For example, children were locked in their dormitories at night and a "punishment room" existed, which was six feet by ten feet and "only lighted by a barred fanlight over the door." Ashton felt that this form of discipline had "a most salutary effect" and that "examples [had] to be made and punishment resorted to." Unruly students were also forced to participate in "Sentry Go," which consisted of a "solitary march around a well beaten square" during playtime.[146] It was said that Principal Ashton could "train an Indian child 'to work whether he likes work or no.'"[147] Besides the punishment room,

Ashton had students dig pits behind the school to serve as cells for those who misbehaved, and he resorted to the use of solitary confinement with bread and water as the only source of nourishment.[148]

In many ways the school mimicked a military-type establishment. In fact, the students were actually arranged into military squads.[149] Regimentation carried over into all aspects of life at the Institute. Bells were rung to inform children what activities they should be engaging in, and when the bell rang for supper, for example, all the students washed and then fell into "their proper places and march[ed] to the dining room," where they sat in "squads." Even the clothing of the children was intended to look like military uniforms: "[The boys] wear a neat dark grey uniform, blouse and trousers, with a black strip and glengarry cap, and with polished boots and neatly brushed hair they looked very smart and carried themselves like veterans."[150] Each student's clothing was marked with the number they had received when they arrived at the Institute.[151] Even the bathing towels were stamped with each student's number. Baths at the school were really quite degrading for the boys since once a week they were all gathered in a large basin and sprayed down. Sleeping arrangements were also very regimented and crowded. Forty-one girls slept in a room sixty by thirty-five feet and fifty-three boys slept in a room fifty by thirty-five feet.[152]

Disillusionment with Industrial Schools Like the Mohawk Institute

In 1894, to ensure children attended schools such as the Mohawk Institute, the federal government passed the first legislation regarding school attendance. Residential school attendance was voluntary unless an Indian agent or justice of the peace believed a child was not being properly cared for or re-educated. In these cases, children could be committed to schools such as the Mohawk Institute. According to the new regulations, truant students could be arrested and their parents fined (maximum two dollars) or imprisoned for ten days. Force could be used if necessary to keep children in custody, and the government was to appoint truant officers who were given the right to search homes for missing students.[153] Hayter Reed, deputy superintendent general of Indian Affairs, explained that, "in the past, no small amount of difficulty has been experienced in getting Indian parents to consent to leave their children in these institutions for terms sufficiently long to enable them to receive permanent benefit."[154] Less than half of Indigenous children attended schools of any sort in 1900.[155] Ashton explained that most of the applications to the Mohawk Institute now came from female students, which he saw as somewhat positive since previously parents "would not readily allow their girls away from home."[156] Church and state administrators encouraged female students to attend the Institute since they believed that Indigenous women would have a greater influence than Indigenous men on future generations of children:

> A boy leaves the school, returns to the Reserve, marries an Indian girl who has not had similar advantages and the result is he reverts to the Indian language, habits and customs and his children are Indians pure and simple. While a girl who has been thoroughly trained returns to her people, takes pride in her cooking and house-hold duties, and when she marries and has a family, her children are taught to speak English and are brought up to follow her habits of civilization. The man may be the breadwinner but the woman is the civilizer.[157]

By the beginning of the 1900s, continued immigration brought with it increasingly racist sentiments about Indigenous peoples. These immigrants, rather than graduates of residential schools, filled manual labour positions. By this time, the population of Indigenous peoples had dwindled to just 1.5 per cent of the population of Canada.[158] Schools such as the Mohawk Institute were proving to be expensive, there was discontent from both parents and students, and religious groups such as the NEC were becoming less and less keen to finance the schools. Parents were also increasingly disillusioned with the "education" their children received. To help finance the Institute, farming and gardening operations had to be expanded during the late 1890s, with the result that academic subjects faded farther into the background. In 1899 Ashton reported that "farming and gardening form the principal occupation of the boys."[159]

By this time, the high cost of running industrial schools was becoming increasingly obvious. In 1896, for example, the average yearly cost of a student's attendance at an industrial school like the Mohawk Institute was $132.18, while the average cost at boarding schools, where trades were not the focus, was just $81.27.[160] Anxious to reduce these costs, Clifford Sifton, the superintendent general of Indian Affairs, asked school inspector Martin Benson to launch a larger investigation to determine the value of industrial schools such as the Mohawk Institute. Benson's inquiry revealed that few officials had ever visited the schools or seriously considered the work being done there. He cited other issues such as poor-quality teaching and lack of farmland and said that departmental funds were being squandered: "I consider it a waste of time and money to force a trade on a boy who is not likely to make a success of the opportunities afforded to him. . . . What opening is there for printers, shoemakers, tailors and several other trades that are now taught at a loss of time, wages and materials at some of the schools?"[161] Frank Oliver, a member of Parliament and future superintendent general of Indian Affairs, went on to say that the graduates of schools like the Mohawk Institute were potentially an economic threat: "The position is this—that we are educating these Indians to compete industrially with our people, which seems to me to be a very undesirable use of public money, or else we are not able to educate them to compete, in which case our money is thrown away."[162]

In 1898, due to a lack of funds, the NEC was forced to terminate its grant to the Six Nations day schools. The Company, however, decided to retain the Mohawk Institute. To compensate for the lack of funding, the Institute forced children to spend more time on farm and garden work rather than learning trades or going to class.[163] The Six Nations believed they were doing a better job of running day schools than were the government and churches, and thus sought control of all the schools, especially since they were largely financing them. The Indian Department refused this request.[164]

"Utterly Destroyed" by Fire

On 19 April 1903, student discontent with the situation at the Institute culminated in the school's destruction by fire. The following day's edition of *The Toronto World* newspaper described the incident in the following terms: "The fire originated in the dormitory on the third storey shortly after 10 o'clock, where the 130 students in attendance were asleep. There was much confusion when the alarm was sounded, but fortunately the building was cleared before anyone was injured. The flames spread with great speed, and by midnight every department in the building had been utterly destroyed."[165] Principal Robert Ashton reported that "the institute, laundry and dairy were totally destroyed by fire on April 19 last; the farm buildings were burnt down on May 7, and the boys' play-house where the lads were temporarily housed was destroyed on June 21, the boys being accountable for the three fires."[166]

The question was whether to rebuild. The Mohawk Institute had now been burned to the ground twice—once in 1858 (possibly through arson) and again in 1903 (confirmed arson). A clearer message could not be sent—the school was not what the Six Nations wanted or imagined. Rather than a school to empower the Six Nations, the Institute now housed mainly orphans and destitute children. Likewise, what church and state administrators thought would be an inexpensive solution to the "Indian problem" instead became a costly enterprise that was failing to meet their shared goal of assimilating the Six Nations. By the time of the fire, the school had been running for seventy years. During that period, church and state administrators and the Six Nations had very different visions for the Mohawk Institute. Based on students' largely negative experiences at such schools, government and church officials should have abandoned their assimilationist agenda of "Christianizing and civilizing" Indigenous peoples. Instead, they ramped up construction of institutions such as the Mohawk Institute across the rest of Canada. It seemed that church and state administrators were either unwilling to formulate another plan. Their faith in the Mohawk Institute remained steadfast as well. Virtually everything was lost in the fire, and since insurance was not sufficient to cover the costs of rebuilding, the Indian Department provided a grant to finance reconstruction. As chapter 2 details, the Institute would rise from the flames once again.

NOTES

I would like to thank the Social Sciences and Humanities Research Council for providing financial support for this research, and George Emery, professor emeritus at Western University, for supervising my 1993 master's thesis on the Mohawk Institute, which sparked my interest in the history of residential schools. Since that time, as a result of the bravery of former students sharing their stories, and reports such as that from the Truth and Reconciliation Commission, our knowledge of the "truth" of the residential school system has been greatly expanded. As a settler scholar, I am thankful for those who have challenged long-held views of Canadian history that have told only the history of those who have benefited from settler colonialism. It is my hope that works such as this one contribute to our collective knowledge and move us toward reconciliation.

1   The title of this chapter comes from H. C. Darling's report from 1828, in which he recommended the creation of a system of education for Indigenous peoples in Canada so that they would "shake off the rude habits of savage life." See British Parliamentary Papers, "H. C. Darling Report upon the Indian Department," in *Irish University Press Series of British Parliamentary Papers*, vol. 3, *Anthropology: Aborigines* (Irish University Press, 1968), 24 July 1828.

2   Senator Murray Sinclair in Dave Rideout, "Chancellor Murray Sinclair Shares Thoughts on National ay for Truth and Reconciliation," *Queen's Gazette*, 29 September 2021, https://www.queensu.ca/gazette/stories/chancellor-murray-sinclair-shares-thoughts-ahead-national-day-truth-and-reconciliation.

3   Senator Murray Sinclair, "Keeping Reconciliation at the Forefront," *Queen's Gazette*, 12 September 2019, https://www.queensu.ca/gazette/stories/keeping-reconciliation-forefront.

4   Residential schools have been described in various ways over time, though most today use the term "residential school." It was not until the 1920s that the term "residential schools" was utilized. This chapter uses the terms "mechanics' institute," "manual labour school," "industrial school," and "residential school" interchangeably, though, as I demonstrate, historically there were some differences between these types of schools. Boarding schools were seen as separate from industrial schools until 1923.

5   C. Urion, "Introduction: The Experience of Indian Residential Schooling," *Canadian Journal of Native Education* 18 (Suppl. 1991): i.

6   Alison Norman, "The History of Education at Six Nations of the Grand River, 1828–1939," in *Ontario Since Confederation: A Reader*, 2nd ed., ed. Lori Chambers, Edgar-Andre Montigny, James Onusko, and Dimitry Anastakis (University of Toronto Press, 2024), 90.

7   See important foundational works on the fur trade such as Arthur J. Ray, *Indians in the Fur Trade: Their Role as Trappers, Hunters, and Middlemen in the Lands Southwest of Hudson Bay, 1660–1870* (University of Toronto Press, 1998); Jennifer S. H. Brown, *Strangers in Blood: Fur Trade Company Families in Indian Country* (University of British Columbia Press, 1980); and Daniel Francis and Toby Morantz, *Partners in Furs: A History of the Fur Trade in Eastern James Bay, 1600–1870* (McGill-Queen's University Press, 1983).

8   See Communications Branch, Indian and Northern Affairs Canada, *Indian Affairs and Northern Development 1755–1986* (Indian Affairs and Northern Development, 1986), for a detailed list of the managers responsible for Indigenous affairs in Canada.

9   See Rick Monture, *We Share Our Matters: Two Centuries of Writing and Resistance at Six Nations of the Grand River* (University of Manitoba Press, 2024); Michelle Filice, "Haldimand Proclamation," *Canadian Encyclopedia*, last modified 10 November 2020, https://www.thecanadianencyclopedia.ca/en/article/haldimand-proclamation .

10   John Leslie, *Commissions of Inquiry into Indian Affairs in the Canadas, 1828–1858* (Treaties and Historical Research Centre Research Branch, Corporate Policy, Indian Affairs and Northern Development Canada, 1985), 1.

11   During the period 1815 to 1851, the population of Upper Canada increased from 95,000 to over 950,000. Truth and Reconciliation Commission, *Final Report of the Truth and Reconciliation Commission of Canada*, vol. 1, *Canada's Residential Schools: The History, Part 2, 1939 to 2000* (McGill-Queen's University Press, 2015), 56.

12   See Noel Dyck, *What Is the Indian "Problem": Tutelage and Resistance in Canadian Indian Administration* (Institute of Social and Economic Research, Memorial University of Newfoundland, 1991).

13   See British Parliamentary Papers, "H. C. Darling Report," 29.

14   See Canada, "Report on the Affairs of the Indians of Canada," *Journals of the Legislative Assembly of the Province of Canada*, appendix T, sec. III, pt. I, 24 June 1847, 1.

15   John Leslie, *Commissions of Inquiry*, 2.

16   See Theodore Binnema and Kevin Hutchings, "The Emigrant and the Noble Savage: Sir Francis Bond Head's Romantic Approach to Aboriginal Policy in Upper Canada, 1836–1838," *Journal of Canadian Studies / Revue d d'études canadiennes* 39, no. 1 (Winter 2005): 115–38. Binnema and Hutchings argue that Bond used "Romantic notions that exalted primitivism and the 'noble savage' to justify this plan," and while it seemed like this may have been a benevolent approach, removing Indigenous people from their land was also his goal (see pp. 115 and 134).

17   See British Parliamentary Papers, "Instructions Addressed to the Governors of Upper and Lower Canada from Lord Glenelg," in *Irish University Press Series of British Parliamentary Papers*, 3:21 April 1836.

18   For a discussion of Canada's early policies toward Indigenous peoples, see John L. Tobias, "Protection, Civilization, Assimilation: An Outline History of Canada's Indian Policy," in *Sweet Promises: A Reader on Indian-White Relations in Canada*, ed. J. R. Miller (University of Toronto Press, 1991), 127–44.

19   Canada, 37th Parl., 1st Sess., Standing Committee on Aboriginal Affairs, Northern Development and Natural Resources, meeting 43, presentation by John Leslie, research consultant, 12 March 2002.

20   British Parliamentary Papers, "Despatch from Sir James Kempt to Sir George Murray," in *Irish University Press Series of British Parliamentary Papers*, 3:15 December 1829.

21   J. R. Miller, "The Irony of Residential Schooling," *Canadian Journal of Native Education* 14, no. 2 (1987): 5.

22   Quoted in Eugene Stock, *The History of the Church Missionary Society: Its Environment, Its Men and Its Work* (Church Missionary Society, 1899), 1:2–3.

23   E. Brian Titley, "Indian Industrial Schools in Western Canada," in *Schools in the West: Essays in Canadian Education*, ed. Nancy Sheehan, Donald Wilson, and David Jones (Detselig Enterprises, 1986), 133.

24   Adam J. Barker, "Locating Settler Colonialism," *Journal of Colonialism and Colonial History* 13, no. 3 (Winter 2012), https://dx.doi.org/10.1353/cch.2012.0035. For a basic overview of settler colonialism, see Adam Barker and Emma Battell Lowman, "Settler Colonialism," *Global Social Theory*, accessed 1 July 2024, https://globalsocialtheory.org/concepts/settler-colonialism/ .

25   See Linda Tuhiwai Smith, K. Wayne Yang, and Eve Tuck, eds., *Indigenous and Decolonizing Studies in Education: Mapping the Long View* (Routledge, 2019).

26   Barker and Lowman, "Settler Colonialism."

27 Thomas Peace, *The Slow Rush of Colonization: Spaces of Power in the Maritime Peninsula, 1680–1790* (UBC Press, 2023), chap. 10.

28 Truth and Reconciliation Commission, *Final Report of the Truth and Reconciliation Commission of Canada*, vol. 1, *Canada's Residential Schools: The History, Part 1, Origins to 1939* (McGill-Queen's University Press, 2015), 63.

29 Truth and Reconciliation Commission of Canada, *Final Report*, vol. 1, pt. 1:3.

30 Norman, "The History of Education at Six Nations of the Grand River," 92.

31 Norman, 92.

32 Duncan C. Scott, deputy superintendent general of Indian affairs, 18 December 1930, *Annual Report of the Department of Indian Affairs for the Year Ended March 31 1930* (F. A. Ackland, 1931), 15.

33 James Douglas Leighton, "The Development of Federal Indian Policy in Canada, 1840–1890," (PhD diss., University of Western Ontario, 1975), 53. See also the charter for the New England Company, 7 February 1662, File 7825-1B, Vol. 200, Record Group 10 [hereafter RG 10], Library and Archives Canada [hereafter LAC].

34 John Webster Grant, *Moon of Wintertime: Missionaries and the Indians of Canada in Encounter Since 1534* (University of Toronto Press, 1984), 72.

35 Charter for the New England Company, 7 February 1662, File 7825-1B, Vol. 2007, RG 10, LAC.

36 Correspondence, 1874, File 7928-1, B 3, Manuscript Group 17 [hereafter MG 17], New England Company Records [hereafter NEC], LAC.

37 See chapter 10 by Thomas Peace for more information about the New England Company and Sussex Vale.

38 Report by Robert Ashton, 12 March 1882, File 7825-1B, Vol. 2007, RG 10, LAC.

39 J. W. Chalmers, *Education Behind the Buckskin Curtain: A History of Indian Education in Canada* (University of Alberta, 1972), 42. See also Judith Fingard, "The New England Company and the New Brunswick Indians, 1786–1826: A Comment on the Colonial Perversion of British Benevolence," *Acadiensis* 1 (Spring 1972): 29–42.

40 Report by Reverend Oliver Arnold, 25 September 1822, File 7928-1, B3, MG 17, NEC, LAC.

41 Report by Reverend John West, 20 September 1826, File 7930, B3, MG 17, NEC, LAC.

42 Report by Lieutenant Governor Howard Douglas, 13 December 1824, File 7930, B3, MG 17, NEC, LAC.

43 The history of the Grand River Haudenosaunee is explored in more detail in Susan M. Hill, *The Clay We Are Made Of: Haudenosaunee Land Tenure on the Grand River* (University of Manitoba Press, 2017).

44 Charles M. Johnston, "To the Mohawk Station: The Making of a New England Company Missionary—the Rev. Robert Lugger," in *Extending the Rafters: Interdisciplinary Approaches to Iroquoian Studies*, ed. Michael K. Foster, Jack Campisi, and Marianee Mithun (State University of New York Press, 1984), 69.

45 Woodland Indian Cultural Educational Centre, *School Days* (Woodland Indian Cultural Educational Centre, 1984), 29.

46 Margaret Connell Szasz, *Indian Education in the American Colonies, 1607–1783* (University of New Mexico Press, 1988), 240.

47 Norman, "The History of Education at Six Nations of the Grand River," 92.

48 Finding aid of the New England Company Manuscripts, B3, MG 17, Reference Room, LAC.

49 John West, 20 September 1826, File 7970, B3, MG 17, NEC, LAC.

50 Report by Reverend John West, 20 September 1826, File 7970, B3, MG 17, NEC, LAC.

51 New England Company Sub-Committee, September 1877, File 7825-1B, Vol. 2007, RG 10, LAC.

52 New England Company, *Annual Report, 1839*, in John L. Duncan, "Church of England Missions Among the Indians in the Diocese of Huron to 1850" (master's thesis, University of Western Ontario, 1936), 12.

53 Agreement of New England Company with R. Ashton, 1872, File 7966, B3, MG 17, NEC, LAC.

54 *Report by a Committee of the Corporation Commonly Called the New England Company, of Their Proceedings, for the Civilization and Conversion of Indians, Blacks, and Pagans, in the British Colonies in American, and the West Indies, Since the Last Report in 1832* (J. Master, 1840), 6.

55 See Canada, "Report on the Affairs of the Indians of Canada" (pp. 3–4 of the document).

56 Thomas Peace, "Borderlands, Primary Sources, and the Longue Durée: Contextualizing Colonial Schooling at Odanak, Lorette, and Kahnawake, 1600–1850," *Historical Studies in Education / Revue d'histoire De l'éducation* 29, no. 1 (2017), https://doi.org/10.32316/hse/rhe.v29i1.4498.

57 See Robert F. Berkhofer, "Model Zions for the American Indian," *American Quarterly* 15, no. 2, pt. 1 (Summer 1963): 176–90.

58 Joan Scott-Brown, "The Short Life of St. Dunstan's Calgary Industrial School, 1896–1907," *Canadian Journal of Native Education* 14, no. 1 (1987): 41.
59 Titley, "Indian Industrial Schools in Western Canada," 133.
60 Andrew Woolford, *This Benevolent Experiment: Indigenous Boarding Schools, Genocide, and Redress in Canada and the United States* (University of Manitoba Press, 2015), 51.
61 Woolford, 63.
62 See *Minutes of the General Council of Indian Chiefs and Principal Men, Held at Orillia, Lake Simcoe Narrows, on Thursday the 30th, and Friday the 31st July, 1846 on the Proposed Removal of the Smaller Communities and the Establishment of Manual Labour Schools* (Canada Gazette Office, 1846).
63 Douglas Leighton, "The Ethnohistory of Missions in Southwestern Ontario," *Journal of the Canadian Church Historical Society* 26 (October 1984): 56.
64 British Parliamentary Papers, "Peter Jones to Viscount Goderich," in *Irish University Press Series of British Parliamentary Papers*, 3:26 July 1831.
65 Chief Shawahnahness in Elizabeth Graham, *Medicine Man to Missionary: Missionaries as Agents of Change Among the Indians of Southern Ontario, 1784–1867* (Peter Martin, 1975), 73.
66 For further discussion regarding why Indigenous communities chose to convert and support schools, see Donald B. Smith, *Sacred Feathers: The Reverend Peter Jones (Kahkewaquonaby) and the Mississauga Indians* (University of Toronto Press, 1987), 73.
67 For a further discussion of this split in the community, refer to Sally Weaver, "The Iroquois: The Consolidation of the Grand River Reserve in the Mid-Nineteenth Century, 1847–1875," and Weaver, "The Iroquois: The Grand River Reserve in the Late Nineteenth and Early Twentieth Centuries, 1875–1945," in *Aboriginal Ontario: Historical Perspectives on the First Nations*, ed. Edward S. Rogers and Donald B. Smith (Dundurn Press, 1994), 182–257.
68 Abate Wori Abate, "Iroquois Control of Iroquois Education: A Case Study of the Iroquois of the Grand River Valley in Ontario, Canada" (PhD diss., University of Toronto, 1984), 8.
69 See 1844 Council Minutes, pp. 286–300, Vol. 144, RG10, LAC.
70 Johnson, "To the Mohawk Station," 74.
71 Grand River Branch, United Empire Loyalists, *Loyalist Families of the Grand River Branch* (Pro Familia Publishing, 1991), 33.
72 Sally M. Weaver, "Six Nations of the Grand River, Ontario," in *Reserve Communities: A Six Nations History Unit*, ed. Woodland Indian Cultural Education Centre (Woodland Indian Cultural Educational Centre, 1987), 41–2.
73 H. R. Page & Co., *Illustrated Historical Atlas of Brant County, Ontario* (Mika Silk Screening, 1972), xiv.
74 See Marvin McInnis, "Ontario Agriculture at Mid-Century," in *Canadian Papers in Rural History*, ed. Donald H. Akenson (Langdale Press, 1992), 56.
75 See Douglas Leighton, "Abraham Nelles," in *Dictionary of Canadian Biography*, vol. 11, *1881–1890* (University of Toronto Press, 1982), 639–40.
76 *Report by a Committee of the Corporation Commonly Called the New England Company, of Their Proceedings*, 147.
77 *Report by a Committee of the Corporation Commonly Called the New England Company of Their Proceedings*, 147.
78 *Report by a Committee of the Corporation Commonly Called the New England Company, of Their Proceedings*, 24–6.
79 *Report by a Committee of the Corporation Commonly Called the New England Company, of Their Proceedings*, 91.
80 Scott, *Annual Report*, 16.
81 Scott, 16.
82 *Report by a Committee of the Corporation Commonly Called the New England Company, of Their Proceedings*, 105.
83 Abraham Nelles in Duncan, "Church of England Missions," 31.
84 The report was published in two parts in "Report on the Affairs of the Indians of Canada," *Journals of the Legislative Assembly of the Province of Canada*, 1844–5, appendix EEE, and 1847, appendix T.
85 See Henry Baldwin in *Minutes of the General Council of Indian Chiefs and Principal Men, Held at Orillia, Lake Simcoe Narrows*.

86 Most of the chiefs present at the Orillia meeting supported the donation, but some felt that one-quarter of annuity money was too generous a gift. See "Report of the Special Commissioners Appointed on the 8th of September, 1856, to Investigate Indian Affairs in Canada," *Journals of the Legislative Assembly of the Province of Canada*, vol. 16, appendix 21, 1858, n.p.

87 *Report on the Affairs on Indians in Canada*, 1844, in *The Valley of the Six Nations: A Collection of Documents on the Indian Lands of the Grand River*, ed. Charles M. Johnston (Champlain Society, 1964), 268.

88 Norman, "The History of Education at Six Nations of the Grand River," 97.

89 "A History of the Mohawk Institute," *Wadrihawa, Quarterly Newsletter of the Woodland Cultural Centre* 17–18, nos. 4 and 1 (June 2003): 4.

90 "A History of the Mohawk Institute," 4.

91 Egerton Ryerson to George Vardon, assistant superintendent general of Indian affairs, 26 May 1847, HR 6503. C73R4 Ex. 1, 3, Archives Deschâtelets [hereafter AD].

92 E. Ryerson to George Vardon, assistant superintendent general, *Report by Dr. Ryerson on Industrial Schools*, 26 May 1847, p. 73, File 202,239, Vol. 2952, RG 10, LAC. See also Egerton Ryerson, *Statistics Respecting Indian Schools with Dr. Ryerson's Report of 1847 Attached* (Government Printing Bureau, 1898). For a discussion of the debate over Ryerson's role in the creation of the residential school system, see Donald B. Smith, "Egerton Ryerson and the Mississauga, 1826 to 1856, an Appeal for Further Study," *Ontario History* 113, no. 2 (2021): 222–43.

93 E. Ryerson to George Vardon, assistant superintendent general, *Report by Dr. Ryerson on Industrial Schools*, 26 May 1847, p. 75, File 202,239, Vol. 2952, RG 10, LAC.

94 E. Ryerson to George Vardon, assistant superintendent general, *Report by Dr. Ryerson on Industrial Schools*, 26 May 1847, p. 73, File 202,239, Vol. 2952, RG 10, LAC.

95 Leighton, "The Development of Federal Indian Policy in Canada, 1840–1890," 237.

96 See Canada, "Report on the Affairs of the Indians of Canada" (p. 3 of the document).

97 See Mary Jane Logan McCallum, *Nii Ndahlohke: Boys' and Girls' Work at Mount Elgin Industrial School, 1890–1915* (Friesen Press, 2022).

98 Leslie, *Commissions of Inquiry*, 105–6.

99 See "Report of the Special Commissioners," *Journals of the Legislative Assembly*, n.p.

100 Memo by M. Benson to J. D. McLean, 15 July 1897, p. 3, File 160-1, Pt. 1, Vol. 6039, RG 10, LAC. In the memo, Benson claims that in 1855 Lord Bury (then superintendent general) suggested the amalgamation of the Alderville and the Mount Elgin institutes.

101 D. C. Scott notes, February 1898, File 468-1 Pt. 1, Vol. 6205, RG 10, LAC. The Mount Elgin school would reopen in 1867 and remain in operation until the 1940s.

102 McCallum, *Nii Ndahlohke*, 13.

103 McCallum, 55.

104 Scott, *Annual Report*, 16.

105 Agreement of the New England Company with R. Ashton, 1872, File 7966, B3, MG 17, NEC, LAC. See also the illustrations before the appendices.

106 Scott, *Annual Report*, 16.

107 J. H. Lister, 1868, in *Brantford Expositor*, 4 October 1955.

108 Leighton, "The Development of Federal Indian Policy in Canada, 1840–1890," 243. See also Keith Jamieson and Michelle A. Hamilton, *Dr. Oronhyatekha: Security, Justice, and Equality* (Dundurn, 2016).

109 Chapter 3 by Alison Norman explores in more detail the training of Indigenous teachers and their role at the Mohawk Institute.

110 Scott, *Annual Report*, 17.

111 Norman, "The History of Education at Six Nations of the Grand River," 93.

112 See Tobias, "Protection, Civilization, Assimilation," 45–6.

113 Scott, *Annual Report*, 17.

114 New England Company to Reverend Robert Ashton, 23 November 1872, File 7928-1, B3, MG 17, NEC, LAC.

115 See chapter 11 for an in-depth study of Ashton's time as principal of the Mohawk Institute.

116 "A History of the Mohawk Institute," 4.

117 New England Company Committee to Ashton, 13 February 1873, File 7928-1, B3, MG 17, NEC, LAC.

118 New England Company Committee, 16 May 1873, File 7928-1, B3, MG 17, NEC, LAC.
119 Robert Ashton, 31 July 1873, File 7928-1, B3, MG 17, NEC, LAC.
120 Robert Ashton, 26 May 1874, File 7928-1, B3, MG 17, NEC, LAC.
121 New England Company Committee, 30 July 1876, File 7928-2, B3, MG 17, NEC, LAC.
122 See File 7928-1 to -5, B3, MG 17, NEC, LAC.
123 Constitution of the School Board of the Six Nations Indians, 29 July 1878, File 7825-1B, Vol. 2007, RG 10, LAC.
124 New England Company Sub-Committee, September 1877, File 7825-1B, Vol. 2007, RG 10, LAC. This takeover never did transpire, and the Six Nations never had true control over the Council as they held only three seats.
125 Scott, *Annual Report*, 17.
126 This grant was to be voted on annually by the Six Nations. See Report of the Privy Council, 18 November 1878, File 7825-1B, Vol. 2007, RG 10, LAC.
127 School Board of Six Nations Indians, 29 July 1878, File 7825-1B, Vol. 2007, RG 10, LAC.
128 See Tobias, "Protection, Civilization, Assimilation," 44–5.
129 See Nicholas Flood Davin, *Report on Industrial Schools for Indians and Half-Breeds* ([publisher not identified], 1879).
130 See Davin, 2.
131 Agnes Grant, *No End of Grief: Indian Residential Schools in Canada* (Pemmican Publications, 1996), 60.
132 R. Ashton to Hayter Reed, 28 November 1894, File 154,845, Pt. 1, Vol. 2771, RG 10, LAC, and Superintendent Gilkison to Department of Indian Affairs, 29 August 1878, File 7825-1B, Vol. 2007, RG 10, LAC.
133 New England Company Committee Report, 14 May 1882, file 7928-3, B3, MG 17, NEC, LAC.
134 J. Kelly, 14 July 1885, Vol. 5991, RG 10, LAC.
135 J. T. Gilkison, Visiting Superintendent and Commissioner to Superintendent-General of Indian Affairs, 27 August 1885, *Annual Report of the Department of Indian Affairs for the Year Ended 31 December 1885* (MacLean, Rogers & Co., 1886), 2.
136 R. Ashton to Superintendent General of Indian Affairs, 25 August 1885, *Annual Report of the Department of Indian Affairs for the Year Ended 31 December 1885*, 17.
137 Superintendent General of Indian Affairs Report, 1 January 1889, *Annual Report of the Department of Indian Affairs for the Year Ended 31 December 1888* (A. Senecal, 1889), xv. Many of these children, however, were orphans or destitute.
138 Hayter Reed in Jacqueline Kennedy, "Qu'Appelle Industrial School: White 'Rites' for the Indians of the Old North-West" (master's thesis, Carleton University, 1970), 91.
139 Scott, *Annual Report*, 18.
140 R. Ashton to Superintendent of Indian Affairs, 14 September 1893, *Annual Report of the Department of Indian Affairs for the Year Ended 30 June 1893* (S. E. Dawson, 1894), 22.
141 R. Ashton, *Annual Report of the Department of Indian Affairs for the Year Ended 30 June 1893*, 22.
142 See R. Ashton to Hayter Reed, 28 November 1894, File 154,845, Pt.1, Vol. 2771, RG 10, LAC.
143 R. Ashton to Superintendent of Indian Affairs, *Annual Report of the Department of Indian Affairs for the Year Ended 31 December 1888*, 123.
144 Martin Benson, *Report on the Mohawk Institute and Six Nations Boarding Schools*, 30 August 1895, File 7825-1A, Vol. 2006, RG 10, LAC.
145 Benson, *Report*.
146 Benson, *Report*.
147 Benson, *Report*.
148 "A History of the Mohawk Institute," 5.
149 See chapter 4 for a detailed study of the use of military training at the Mohawk Institute.
150 Benson, *Report*.
151 The exact time students began to be assigned numbers is not clear. The deputy superintendent general of Indian affairs recommended it in a letter to Ashton in 1894. See Deputy Superintendent General to R. Ashton, File 154,845, Pt. 1, Vol. 2771, RG 10, LAC.
152 Benson, *Report*.

153 Regulations Relating to the Education of Indian Children, 1894, File 150-40A, Pt. 1, Vol. 6032, RG 10, LAC.

154 Hayter Reed, Report of the Deputy Superintendent General of Indian Affairs, 31 December 1894, *Annual Report of the Department of Indian Affairs for the Year Ended 30 June 1894* (S. E. Dawson, 1895), xxi-xxii.

155 In 1900, of twenty thousand Indigenous people aged six to fifteen years, 3,285 were enrolled in thirty-nine boarding and twenty-two industrial schools and 6,349 attended 226 day schools. See Barman et al., *Indian Education in Canada*, 1:8.

156 R. Ashton to Superintendent of Indian Affairs, *Annual Report of the Department of Indian Affairs for the Year Ended 30 June 1894*, 22.

157 Benson, *Report*.

158 Barman et al., *Indian Education in Canada*, 1:8. This statistic is from 1911.

159 R. Ashton to Superintendent General of Indian Affairs, 25 August 1899, *Annual Report of the Department of Indian Affairs for the Year Ended 30 June 1899* (S. E. Dawson, 1900), 291.

160 *Annual Report of the Department of Indian Affairs for the Year Ended 30 June 1896* (S. E. Dawson, 1897), 291.

161 M. Benson to J. D. Mclean, 15 July 1897, File 160-1, Pt. 1, Vol 6039, RG 10, LAC.

162 *Hansard*, 14 June 1897, 4076.

163 See R. Ashton, *Annual Report of the Department of Indian Affairs for the Year Ended 20 June 1899*, 291, and File 7825-1B, Vol. 2007, RG 10, LAC.

164 Keith Jamieson, *History of Six Nations Education* (Woodland Indian Cultural Education Centre, 1987), 16. This is reproduced in appendix 1 of this volume.

165 "Brantford's Big Blaze: Some Narrow Escapes," *Toronto World*, 20 April 1903.

166 R. Ashton to Superintendent General of Indian Affairs, 12 August 1903, *Annual Report of the Department of Indian Affairs for the Year Ended June 30 1903* (S. E. Dawson, 1904), 326.

2

"The Difficulties of Making an Indian into a White Man, Were Not Thoroughly Appreciated": The Mohawk Institute, 1904 to the Present

Jennifer Pettit

Figure 2.1. Girls playing on a swing set in the girls' playground
Source: The General Synod Archives, Anglican Church of Canada

Given that the Mohawk Institute had been burned to the ground twice, once by possible arson and another by confirmed arson, it was clear that the "difficulties of making an Indian into a white man, were not thoroughly appreciated."[1] As Superintendent General of Indian Affairs Frank Oliver told the House of Commons in 1909, when it came to the church and state's plan to assimilate Indigenous peoples such as the Six Nations, "there have been grave difficulties . . . that were not expected."[2] By 1904, when the Mohawk Institute met its second fiery demise, it was obvious that the school was not meeting the initial visions of anyone, and was, in fact, bringing great harm to Indigenous students who attended. Yet, incredulously, the school would remain open for decades more. By 1970, when the Mohawk Institute finally closed, it would be even more evident that the Institute had ultimately failed all three parties involved—the Six Nations, the New England Company (the Anglican religious group who founded and managed the school), and the Canadian government. The Anglican Church apologized in 1993, but it would take until 2008 for the federal government to apologize for its role in the residential school system. Canada is still grappling with the legacy left by schools such as the Mohawk Institute and much work remains to be done before we have either truth or reconciliation.[3]

New Directions for Government Policy

By the beginning of the twentieth century, the system of schooling for Indigenous peoples had evolved into three types of distinct schools: day schools on reserves where students returned home each evening; boarding schools where students lived at the school and received basic training, often related to farming and domestic duties; and industrial schools such as the Mohawk Institute where children lived at the school but received more intensive training in trades than they did at the boarding schools. By 1900, there were 226 day schools, 39 boarding schools, and 22 industrial schools in operation in Canada—a far cry from the 1830s, when the Mohawk Institute was the only residential school in existence.[4] The professed goal of church and state by the turn of the twentieth century was still "assimilation" into white, lower-class society. The question in the minds of church and government administrators, however, was whether the existing schools were working and whether assimilation should remain the goal of education policy.

The arrival of the twentieth century brought even greater pressure on Indigenous land; in the first twelve years of the 1900s alone, the population of Canada increased by almost 35 per cent.[5] Many of these settlers came to Ontario, the home of the Mohawk Institute. Government officials began to seriously question the expanding system of industrial and boarding schools, which had grown at an astonishing rate. Scandals also plagued a number of the schools, and increasingly the government felt that boarding schools might suffice since Indigenous peoples were not utilizing the trade skills they learned at the industrial schools due to immigrants filling many of the manual labour positions, especially in more populated areas. Besides, by the turn of the century, training at many of the boarding schools rivalled that received at industrial schools. David Laird, Indian commissioner, claimed in 1904 that "the training of the children in perhaps half of these schools may be said to be almost equal to that given in industrial schools."[6] Government expenditures for the schooling portfolio in Indian Affairs had also greatly increased, especially at the more expensive industrial schools such as the Mohawk Institute. Most importantly, though, the industrial school system had failed to "civilize" Indigenous peoples such as the Six Nations.[7] After attending, most students simply returned to the reserves. The 1906 Department of Indian Affairs annual report explained that industrial schools such as the Mohawk Institute would "turn out boys better equipped to live and work among other communities but [would] not apparently tend to produce amalgamation of races."[8]

Government administrators decided that a change in policy was once again necessary, as circumstances in Canada had shifted due to increasing school costs, immigration, and rising racist sentiments. In addition, assumptions made in the early to mid-1800s, when the Mohawk Institute had been founded, about Indigenous peoples eagerly embracing church and state visions for schools had not proven to be true. Both Indigenous parents and students had pushed back against conditions in schools, particularly when principals such as the Reverend Robert Ashton at the Mohawk Institute created a harsh and abusive environment for students.[9] It is not surprising that students chose to burn down the Mohawk Institute in 1903. Most Indigenous parents and students sought only the employment skills the schools could provide—"a means to an end"—rather than the cultural destruction the schools attempted to bring about. Frank Pedley, deputy superintendent general of Indian Affairs, explained that it "need not be expected that beyond the rare exceptions occasionally met with, they will manifest any desire for higher education."[10]

As a result of all of these challenges, by 1910 church and state administrators officially abandoned attempts to completely assimilate Indigenous peoples into Euro-Canadian society and instead fashioned a school system that taught groups such as the Six Nations to accept isolation on significantly smaller reserves away from land coveted by Euro-Canadians. Frank Oliver said they needed a new plan whose "results will tend rather to improving the conditions of the Indian as an Indian, than making the Indian into a white man."[11] Deputy Superintendent General Frank Pedley stressed "an effort [should now be] made to adapt the training to the requirements of the future pupils' environments, and to avoid the danger of such treatment as might create a distaste, for conditions from which there might be no means of escape."[12] In simple terms, government officials believed that Indigenous people only needed to be educated to a level sufficient to survive life on the reserves and nothing more. No longer were Indigenous peoples to be assimilated into lower-class society; now, they would exist segregated on reserves.

The main proponent of this new scheme was Duncan Campbell Scott, who became the superintendent of Indian education in 1909. In an about-face from previous policy, the Canadian government claimed that "it was never the policy, nor the end and aim of the endeavour to transform an Indian into a white man." Instead, the new goal was "to fit the Indian for civilized life in his own environment."[13] These policy changes affected the next half century of school policy. Research consultant David Hoffman has written that after the policy changes in 1910,

> the Department began to bring the churches' administration of the residential schools into the framework that was to last essentially unchanged for five decades. In return for increased appropriations, the government placed greater demands upon the management of the boarding schools; soon, the upkeep of the buildings, pupils' diets and classroom administration were to conform to standards established by the Department. Agreements were established between churches and the government specifying enrolment limits for each residence. The Department expected this to result in "greater efficiency."[14]

Even with a new policy, schools such as the Mohawk Institute could not be completely abandoned by church and state officials since schooling was the main method they had for "managing" and converting Indigenous peoples. The superintendent of Indian education professed that "Without education and with neglect the Indians would produce an undesirable and often a dangerous element in society. Not only are our schools every day removing intelligent Indian children from evil surroundings, but they are very often ministering to a class which would be outcasts without such aid."[15] Federal politician Clifford Sifton shared similar sentiments: "I have no hesitation in saying (we may as well be frank) that the Indian cannot go out from a school, making his own way and compete with the white man."[16]

Most of the churches were also not ready to abandon the school system as school officials remained committed to the religious conversion of the students throughout the life of the Institute. They agreed with the government's plan of focusing on day and boarding schools, as these cost far less to operate. As a result, boarding schools flourished while many industrial schools languished or closed altogether. Government spending on boarding schools increased to $521,076.44 in 1915, up from $241,756.53 in 1913. During the same period, funding for industrial schools fell from $316,836.66 in 1913 to $290,644.62 in 1915.[17] The Mohawk Institute, however, continued to function and grow. By the turn of the century "there were 125 children living at the Mohawk Institute (including some from other First Nations), and 520 children attending the nine local day schools. In 1920, there were 134 students living at the Mohawk Institute and 546 attending the eleven local day schools."[18]

The Mohawk Institute Rises from the Flames

After the fire in 1903, the NEC decided to rebuild the school. The newly rebuilt Mohawk Institute opened in October of 1904. It was an impressive, large brick building that is still standing today. Principal Robert Ashton described the school in the following way:

> The new building occupied in October last is in the form of the letter H, built of red brick, with cut stone basement, roofed with shingles, laid on asbestos paper. The main building is 79 x 42 feet, and has two wings 60 x 36½ feet each. The building is two stories high with basement and attic. *The Main Building.*—In the basement are the stores, including insulated cold store, officers' dining-rooms, boiler-room, girls' clothing-rooms and lavatory. On the first floor are the offices, sewing-room, and female officers' rooms. The second floor contains the superintendent's residence and two sick-rooms. *North Wing.*—In the basement is the kitchen and dining halls; on the first floor, class-room, master's room and farm men's rooms; on the second floor is the boy's dormitory. *South Wing.*—The basement comprises the girls' play-room, boot-room and flushwater-closets; on the first

floor is the class and assembly room, and on the second floor is the girls' dormitory. Each dormitory has an iron fire-escape and door opening into the main building. Boys' play-house, 74 x 20 feet, two and a half stories; laundry, 30 x 20.3 feet, two Stories; dairy, 18 x 13 feet; barn and cow-stable, 97 x 35 feet; silo (cement), 30 x 16 feet; hog-pens, 72 x 30 feet and 60 x 13.4 feet; horse and cattle stables, 82.8 x 22.5 feet, with room for sixteen horses and sixteen cattle. Other buildings are: carpenter's shop, implement-house, drive-house, wagon-shed, poultry-house, two greenhouses and an ice-house.[19]

School administrators like Ashton felt confident that the new Mohawk Institute would continue to be of use, claiming that the Six Nations possessed sufficient skills to permit them to subsist on the reserve with little interference.[20] W. F. Webster, for instance, sent by the NEC to report on the Six Nations in 1908, agreed, claiming that on the reserve "the farming was ... nearly as good as that of adjoining portions of Ontario farmed by White men."[21] To support the plan of turning students into farmers, Institute administrators reduced trades instruction almost completely and concentrated their efforts on teaching the children farm skills.

Complaints in this era about the lack of government concern for industrial schools were common. In 1904, for instance, the Presbyterian Committee to Investigate Schools claimed that the Department of Indian Affairs did not value the industrial schools or care about the happenings of the students.[22] In 1907, Peter H. Bryce, a medical inspector for the department, released his damning *Report on the Indian Schools of Manitoba and the North West Territories*. Bryce described the conditions in the schools as appalling, which he blamed on a lack of funding. He cited several issues with schools such as staff ineffectiveness and parental concerns and said the death rates of children in the schools was shocking—24 per cent of all pupils who attended school were known to be dead, and at File Hills, a boarding school in Saskatchewan, 69 per cent had died. Bryce claimed that boarding schools were preferable and that the government needed to undertake proper financial management and control of the schools.[23]

While Bryce did not examine the Mohawk Institute, there is no doubt that at least some of his findings can be applied to the school. As Kathleen McKenzie and Sean Carleton have demonstrated, Bryce's report was made public through numerous newspaper articles, yet very little was changed in response to the report.[24] A year after its release, in 1908, the government passed guidelines to further enhance compulsory attendance.[25] In 1920 the *Indian Act* made attendance at residential schools compulsory for status children between the ages of seven and fifteen.

Both the NEC and the Indian Department seemed pleased with how Ashton was managing the school, despite the dissatisfaction shown at Six Nations. The NEC, for instance, wrote about their "great satisfaction" with the school, and the Indian Department claimed that the school functioned "in a highly satisfactory manner."[26] Principal Ashton boasted that the girls trained at the Mohawk Institute were "in great demand" and that the boys were pursuing several vocations including that of printer, typewriter, and timekeeper, in addition to finding work in factories and as farmhands.[27] This conflicts with an investigation by Samuel H. Blake, an executive on the board of the Missionary Society of the Church of England in Canada, whose general investigation of the residential school system found that no trades were being taught at the majority of industrial schools, and that those that did offer trades instruction were limiting such training to just a few students.[28]

The Six Nations community was divided in their support for Ashton and the Institute. While some continued to show their support, others were not impressed with either Ashton or the Institute and claimed that "a widespread interest in the matters of education" was taking place on the reserve.[29] Discontent with the qualifications of teachers who graduated from the Mohawk Institute heightened during this period. According to one complaint, reported in *The Globe and Mail*, one school led by teachers who had graduated from the Mohawk Institute had "failed for twenty years to produce a pupil to pass the entrance examinations to the high schools."[30] Teachers did not have to be certified, and Indigenous teachers were paid less than teachers in non-Indigenous schools.[31] Increasingly, places in the Mohawk Institute were being filled by children deemed by the department to be orphans and destitute, and the school roster included only a small portion of the Six Nations community; there were only seventy children at the Institute in 1906, for instance, out of one thousand children of school age on the Six Nations reserve.[32] Parents who disliked sending their children away from home were angered that the high school accepted graduates of the Mohawk Institute before graduates of the day schools.[33] Rumours of harsh punishments at the school also caused discontent. The NEC wrote to Principal Ashton and requested that a "Punishment Book" be kept of any harsh punishments because of allegations that a "Davis" boy had been hurt at the Institute. The Company stressed that only a "birch rod" should be used to discipline the students.³⁴ To ensure their concerns about the school system would be heard, in 1906 the "Indian Rights Association" came to the Hamilton conference to air their grievances. In addition to many complaints about the reserve schools, the delegation said that children who wanted to go to the Mohawk Institute were being denied admission "because they were not orphans."³⁵ In 1911, shortly after the announcement of the new government policy to educate Indigenous peoples for life on the reserves, the Reverend Robert Ashton decided to retire (likely at the urging of the NEC); he stayed on as chaplain. His son, Alfred Nelles Ashton, assumed the role of principal.

The Tumultuous Years of Alfred Nelles Ashton

When Alfred Nelles Ashton was appointed principal (the first headmaster who was not an Anglican reverend), it was not due to his skills, but because he was the son of Robert Ashton, who had served as principal for four decades. His arrival corresponded with an increase in government funding; the Canadian government increased its per capita grant to $100 for 120 students.³⁶ The NEC thus agreed to take on the financial management of all the Mohawk Institute buildings. This increased funding should have led to better conditions "behind the bricks" of the school, but that would not be the case. Alfred Nelles Ashton's time as principal would be marred by scandal and discontent.

When Alfred Nelles Ashton took over the Mohawk Institute, he set about making physical improvements at the school such as new student desks and an improved lavatory. Ashton indicated that the Mohawk Institute now had "a staff of 12, including 3 farm-hands and a gardener." Academically, the Institute now followed the curriculum set by the Indian Department. He described the boys' work in the following manner: "Farming, gardening and the care of green-houses form the principal occupation of the boys, and include the management of a dairy of over 35 cows, and the raising of pigs, also the cultivation of plants and flowers for market." The girls' work was as follows: "The girls are trained for domestic work, including sewing, dress-making, cooking, backing, laundrying and butter-making. They make all their own clothes, also those of the boys."³⁷

As shown in Evan Habkirk's chapter in this volume, in 1912, Ashton proudly reported that the school's Cadet Corps had won first place in the central Ontario competition, and that new beds and laundry equipment had been ordered for the school. A new greenhouse and poultry house had also been constructed and improvements to the building's appearance such as renovations to the girls' dressing room and painting of the barns and outbuildings were carried out. Recreational activities expanded to include fishing and shooting at a miniature rifle range.[38]

During Alfred's tenure as principal, however, complaints were often raised by parents. Alfred was an alcoholic and concerns about his leadership began to mount. Parents said their children were "being so poorly fed and suffering such indignities at the hands of the officers of this Institute that many of the children [were] compelled to run away from the School." Others wrote the department to say "that the children are being punished from time to time in a shameful manner for trifling offences and that they are treated from time to time as though they were criminals. For instances [sic], boys are whipped until they are cut, girls have their hair cut off close to the scalp, for punishment, and parents are not allowed to see their children if they (the children) happen to be under punishment at the time."[39]

Fearing that schools like the Mohawk Institute might open their doors to a wider pool of prospective students due to complaints, the government reiterated in 1912 that such schools were not intended for children of mixed ancestry. According to Duncan Campbell Scott, "A Half-breed, being legally 'a person' within the meaning of the Act, that is not an Indian, he is an ordinary citizen of the country and the problem of his education belongs to the Provinces not to the Dominion."[40] In 1913, however, he said that if a child of mixed ancestry was living on a reserve then they could be admitted to a school at the federal government's cost: "it was conceded that all children, even those of mixed blood, whether legitimate or not who live upon a reserve and whose parents on either side live as Indians, even if not annuitants, should be eligible for admission to the schools."[41]

What stood out most about Alfred Nelles Ashton's tenure as principal was a court case, addressed in Diana Castillo's chapter, which involved female students—Ruth and Hazel Miller—who had absconded from the Institute. As a punishment they had their hair cut off and Ruth was locked in a small cell for three days without access to proper food. Ruth was whipped thirteen times as well. Her sister was also locked in a small room. Duncan Campbell Scott investigated the school but found no wrongdoing and said the case was unwarranted.[42] Ruth's father sued the school and the Ashtons; the jury awarded him $400 in damages.[43]

In the spring of 1914, as the dust was settling from the court case, Alfred's sister, Alice Boyce, expressed serious concerns about her brother's worsening alcoholism and his "physical unfitness" for the position of principal of the Mohawk Institute. As a result, the NEC requested that Alfred take a holiday to the United States and that Alice take over temporary management of the school at a salary of $800 per year. She would be the only woman to ever serve as principal. The Company planned to send out a deputation to Canada in the fall to further investigate, but the outbreak of the First World War halted this plan. Alfred Nelles Ashton publicly admitted his faults and pledged to do better, but Alice said she could not work under him if he were to return as principal, not even in the role of overseeing the female students. In 1914, Alfred enlisted in the Canadian Expeditionary Force. Alice was replaced in mid-1915 when the NEC sent Reverand Cyril M. Turnell to take over the management of the school. Ashton served with the 38th Regiment and was wounded in service. He did not return to the Mohawk Institute, instead becoming a fruit farmer in Grimsby. Having been replaced, Alice opted to care for her parents.[44]

Changes in the Approach to School Management

The Reverend Cyril M. Turnell served as principal for the duration of the First World War. He was an Englishman who came to Canada for this purpose, after having worked at several schools in the United Kingdom. His tenure was shaped by the events of the First World War. In recognition of the increased cost of the war, in 1918 the Department of Indian Affairs approved a temporary increase of ten dollars in the per capita grants given to schools.[45] That year, the department elaborated on the direction of its policy for the graduates of schools such as the Mohawk Institute. The goal, where possible, was to educate Indigenous students alongside non-Indigenous pupils, rather than build separate secondary or post-secondary institutions. The deputy superintendent general explained that "it is not the policy of the Department to establish schools for the higher education of Indian children. On the contrary our present policy is to make use in so far as possible of the educational institutions in the province [of Ontario]." Despite the policy, few graduates of the Institute pursued higher education.[46]

By 1918, enrolment grew to 140 students and Turnell attempted to make several improvements.[47] That year, the Mohawk Institute held "short courses in agriculture" for the Six Nations community on topics relating to the planting and growing of crops and vegetables, as well as raising dairy and beef cattle, horses and hogs. These lectures were "accompanied by practical work with the stock."[48] Principal Turnell attempted to relax some of the heavy disciplinary measures initiated by Alfred Nelles Ashton and to improve the diet of the students. There was said to be a "glimmer of hope" when he became principal.[49] Turnell attempted to keep communication lines open with Six Nations and he allowed children to go home during the holidays. There were said to be no truancies while he was principal.[50]

Turnell had grand plans for the school, such as further increasing enrolment. The NEC, however, felt Turnell was taking a softer approach to the school than they desired; they also claimed he was mismanaging the school and that he took too many vacations. He was thus fired. Duncan Campbell Scott made the case that Turnell should not be blamed for the issues facing the school and said he would like him to be reinstated. In the end, Turnell resigned and in 1918 moved to Jamaica, at which point Alice Boyce was reinstated as principal.

Alice Boyce said she was glad to return to the school as it would enable her to care for her elderly parents after she lost a large sum of money in an unsuccessful railroad investment. She had come to Canada with her father, Robert Ashton, as a child. She had grown up at the school and thus was very familiar with it. She trained as a nurse prior to becoming principal.[51] Boyce seemed to care more about the children than had her father or her brother, though she, too, was said to be a strong disciplinarian. This coincided with a growing lack of interest in Indigenous schooling. Many Indigenous peoples did not respond to the school as positively as they had when the Institute opened eighty years earlier because, increasingly, they felt the school had little to offer them other than serving a welfare function for impoverished or orphaned children or providing a home for children with disciplinary issues. School records in this era, for instance, describe children in the following ways: "orphan"; "illegitimate"; "deaf mother who was living with a man who was not the father of the child"; "parents dead"; "mother dead, father 'abnormal'"; "admitted on warrant, was 'uncontrollable' at home"; and "mother sick in hospital, father deserted." Since many of the children who attended were disadvantaged in some way, and thus had little prior exposure to schooling, the level of academic difficulty at the school had to be lowered to accommodate these students.[52]

Government officials did not seem to be particularly concerned with the quality of management at the school in the 1920s, likely because the government was concentrating on postwar recovery. When Edward, the Prince of Wales, visited the Mohawk Institute in 1919, Boyce allowed the children to sing hymns in Indigenous languages in his honour. While in Brantford, the Prince of Wales also unveiled a bronze tablet that listed eighty-eight members of Six Nations who had lost their lives fighting in the First World War.[53] That year, the Indian Department stressed that schools such as the Mohawk Institute "compare[d] favourably with white schools similarly situated with respect to the work in the classroom, and in accommodation and equipment provided."[54] Upon graduation, each male student was provided with "a grant of cattle, horses, implements and building material."[55]

The NEC, however, still found it difficult to fund the school during this era. They sold off part of the Manual Labour Farm and the Babcock Lot to help make ends meet. As a result, in 1918, the Department of Indian Affairs took on the responsibility for the majority of expenses at the school. The per capita grant went from $120 to $220 per year (though this would be reduced to $180 and then $160 by 1922). Indian Affairs also signed a lease for the Institute for twenty-one years and, in 1922, enlarged the main building.[56]

Boyce concentrated on trying to improve conditions for the children in the face of financial difficulty. To better the health of the children, she sent them to a dentist and oculist (her interest in health likely sprang from her background as a nurse). Boyce also worked to raise funds to send female students to business school. She succeeded in getting groups to issue invitations to the students for town events and the children entered contests at the local fairs to display their knowledge of carpentry, sewing, and agriculture. In addition, the cadets from the school marched in parades and local merchants sponsored a Sports Day.[57] The children were also rewarded with rides in the school truck, and on important occasions such as Christmas they received special treats like plum pudding, figs, and candies. Some parents asked the school to keep their children during the holidays since they could not afford to buy presents or transport them back home, and they assumed the children would be treated well.[58] Boyce reported that the children had access to many forms of recreation and that they attended the circus when it came to town. She claimed that while the children at the Mount Elgin residential school were dirty and only changed their clothing once a week, the uniforms of the students at the Mohawk Institute were clean and very attractive—the boys wearing marine uniforms with black and red stripes and the girls "dresses of aeroplane linen trimmed with blue and . . . black hats."[59] Much of this clothing, as well as other goods, had been donated by the Canadian military, and the older girls worked to sew uniforms for the children at the school. While the "Good Conduct Badges" had to be discontinued due to a lack of funds, pupils who were well-behaved were given fifteen cents per month; these funds were placed in a fund controlled by a committee of pupils who spent it on activities that benefited the students. Money was deducted from this fund when clothing was ruined or if school property was destroyed or lost.[60] Several letters of appreciation from students during this period can be found in Record Group 10 at Library and

Archives Canada. Emily Pheasant, for example, wrote in 1921 that she was "very glad to get home again . . . but . . . would sooner go back to school."[61]

Despite these positive aspects, the Institute was not without troubles. Children during this period still continued to run away and commit other offences. Boyce claimed that many were leaving to meet boyfriends or girlfriends, citing one student who ran away to spend the night with a suitor at the Brantford Hotel. Others ran away to go home and help with work on the reserve. When the public discovered that one student had contracted a sexually transmitted infection while in the care of the Institute, an investigation was launched. It was discovered that she had contracted the disease during a sexual assault.[62] Boyce's response to rule breakers was swift and harsh—she has since been described as being "over-vigilant in meting out discipline."[63] Duncan Campbell Scott, however, said that the general public did not comprehend the difficulties of running the school and disciplining the children, and claimed that Boyce was doing an excellent job of dealing with issues.[64]

Financial challenges meant increased manual labour, especially for the male students, though Boyce claimed that "in no single instance [did] any boy [have] to neglect his lessons or miss school in order that so much should be done."[65] To help offset costs, Boyce requested that her pay be reduced from $1,000 to $600 per year so that she could hire a "playground mistress" and "farmerette" to help teach the girls at the school.

The other industrial schools in Ontario seemed to experience more difficulties than did the Mohawk Institute from the 1880s to the early decades of the twentieth century. The Mount Elgin school expanded under little scrutiny, such that by 1906 conditions there had degenerated to the point where they were no longer acceptable.[66] Indigenous resistance, financial difficulties, and poor conditions also plagued the Wikwemikong and Shingwauk schools.[67] Unlike these institutions, the Mohawk Institute continued to maintain what government officials saw as fair conditions and reasonable attendance rates.[68]

The Indian Department was pleased with the efforts of Boyce and the Mohawk Institute. In 1922, when the courts decided that the Institute's farm belonged to the Six Nations, the department agreed to pay them $500 per year in rent so that the Institute could continue to use the land for farming purposes.[69] The Indian Department and the NEC made an agreement at this time that the department would rent the Mohawk Institute from the Company for one dollar per year for twenty-one years. In return, the Company stipulated that the principal be an Anglican minister and offered to provide a yearly grant of £1,000.[70] In 1922, the Schultz Brothers Company added an addition to the rear of the school at a cost of $35,180.[71] This was the first addition to the Mohawk Institute that had not been financed by the NEC. At the end of 1922, soon after the addition was completed, Alice Boyce married Sydney Rogers and, in keeping with what was "proper" for a married woman, resigned, at which point he took over as principal of the school. The department seemed keen on his appointment, saying that Rogers possessed "considerable administrative ability" and that they expected "a career of much usefulness in his case." This would not turn out to be the result.[72]

Declining Conditions Under Principal Sydney Rogers

Sydney Rogers was not a well-educated man, but he had previously been a book clerk and served in the First World War. Rogers came to the Institute in 1919 as the boys' master and married Alice at the end of 1922.[73] Since Boyce was retained as "lady principal" for the Institute, few changes initially occurred in terms of the school's daily functioning. The Mohawk Institute remained a "model" for industrial and residential schools in this period, and Russell Ferrier, the superintendent of Indian education, claimed that "no residential school in Canada ... [was] subjected to the same continuous stream of visitors as the Mohawk."[74] However, the Institute's finances continued to be an issue. Since most industrial schools were only receiving $120 per capita, in 1922 the government reduced its yearly grant to the Mohawk Institute to $160 per pupil. In addition to this amount, the Institute received about $50 per student from the NEC grant.[75]

The department continued to favour boarding schools during this period, and by 1923 the distinction between boarding and industrial schools had disappeared completely. The two categories thus merged to form the new classification of "residential school," and the focus on training students in the trades decreased even further.[76] "Residential school" is the term used most often today to refer to the church- and state-run school system created for Indigenous students. This name change fit with the policy of educating Indigenous students for life on the reserve rather than integration into non-Indigenous society—trades were far less important on the reserves than were farming activities.

The quality of instruction was not the main concern of Principal Rogers. A typical day at the school paralleled a regular day spent on a farm: The children rose at 6:00 a.m. and tended to the animals or made breakfast. Officially, work or school began at 8:15 a.m. and went until lunch at

12:15 p.m. Work or school continued from 1:30 to 4:00 p.m., supper was served at 5:45 p.m., and at 8:00 or 9:00 p.m. the children retired.[77] A school inspector in 1923 declared that "no provision for systemic instruction in the principles, either of household science, manual training or agriculture," existed at the Mohawk Institute.[78] It was clear that basic manual labour rather than academic schooling received the most attention, which is not surprising given church and government goals for the schools, and since the agricultural activities helped finance the Institute. Rogers's reports seldom mentioned classroom activities, and instead were filled with references to farming, gardening, and domestic activities. Rogers reported, for instance, that he had to discontinue classroom activities completely during harvest time.[79]

In 1923 the Institute became the focus of several newspaper articles. The Haudenosaunee Confederacy Council of Chiefs (the hereditary council) asked Evelyn Johnson, the sister of the poet Pauline Johnson, to raise public awareness about conditions in the school. Johnson vehemently criticized the Mohawk Institute in *The Toronto Sunday World*. She claimed the Institute was "a home for many orphaned boys and girls as well as other children," and that she spoke to a missionary on the reserve who said that "they had met no one . . . who likes the Mohawk Institution." Johnson said that the education the children received was inferior, that they ran away because they were hungry, and that they were being improperly disciplined.[80] The department, however, promptly dismissed her concerns, maintaining that the article contained "not one single word of truth."[81]

An official report commissioned by the department on the Six Nations that same year delved further into issues on the reserve with the hopes of finding evidence to replace the hereditary chiefs with an elected council. The report said that waiting lists continued at the Mohawk Institute and that a "large number of the Indians, both men and women, are keenly alive to the benefit of education."[82] The report also observed, however, that the Six Nations wanted to attend schools for white children: "the Indians . . . were unanimously of the opinion that it was very much to the advantage of their children to attend the white schools, and there to mingle with the white children. As one Indian put it, 'We do not wish to be a people apart, we want our children to grow up good Canadians like the rest.'"[83] The report said there was still a role for the Mohawk Institute, but again as more of a welfare provider than a school:

> The Mohawk Institute, situate [sic] in Brantford, already referred to, performs a function quite apart from the general educational system. As I have stated, it provides vocational and academic training for orphans, for deserted children, and for the children of the very poor. This function is necessary, and must not be interfered with. At the present time its accommodation is nearly all taken up by children of this class.[84]

In a supplement to the main report focusing specifically on the Mohawk Institute, Andrews interviewed staff who said the food, discipline, and conditions at the school were reasonable to very good.[85] Notably, he spoke to no current students in the school, who, as Rick Hill's conclusion in this book demonstrates, likely would have painted a different picture.[86]

As Principal Rogers took on more of a leadership role, conditions at the Mohawk Institute deteriorated. Fighting often occurred among the children; Rogers said a "Jesse James Gang" appeared among the girls and that fighting was common among the boys.[87] Health conditions were also far from ideal. Records show that Rogers ordered six pounds of vermin powder and one gallon of bed bug poison for the school.[88] Most students at the school in the 1920s, however, were fairly well-behaved, likely because many did not have a home and because they knew how few positions there were at the school.[89] Likewise, Rogers claimed that parents ensured the prompt return of their children after the holidays, and that when students ran away, few people on the reserve provided shelter for them.[90] After two girls ran away in 1929, Rogers claimed they were "the first in years to abscond."[91] The boys, though, were clearly less obedient. Two of them, armed with clubs, had "openly defied the Principal," and Rogers had to have a system of alarms installed to keep the boys from sneaking into the girls' dormitory at night.[92]

Rogers was a strong advocate of what he thought to be appropriate discipline. When graduates of the Institute failed to do well at the local collegiate school in Brantford, Rogers blamed their failure on the lack of discipline at the schools.[93] In her testimony to the 1923 investigation into the Mohawk Institute by Colonel Andrew Thompson, Alice tried to justify the discipline meted out by her husband, claiming that he used only a regulation school strap, and only struck students on the hands.[94] In her testimony to the investigation, Mohawk Institute teacher Susan Hardie claimed the following: "In answer to the question, 'What is the discipline imposed?,' Miss Hardie replied, 'It is not severe,' and to the question, 'Is whipping used?,' she said, 'Yes, and I have to do it for all the girls. I do not have to whip more than once a month on an average.'"[95] Hardie, a Mohawk woman from Six Nations, was a graduate of the Mohawk Institute who began teaching there in 1887. She would remain a teacher at the Institute for decades, retiring in 1936 at the age of seventy.[96] Though she was proud of her work, many former students do not remember her fondly.[97]

There were other issues plaguing the Institute in this era as well, many of them to do with finances and Rogers's generally poor administrative skills. In addition to asking for more hours of religious instruction,[98] the NEC asked the department to purchase the parts of the Institute still owned by the Company for £9,000; the department claimed that it could not afford this.[99] The entire time Rogers acted as principal, the department had been troubled by his poor accounting abilities, inadequate reporting, and his inability to make enough profit from the farm to help pay for the costs of running the school. Rogers was also criticized for making "unauthorized expenditures" and not paying bills on time.[100]

Rogers purchased a farm adjoining the Mohawk Institute, which he planned on turning into a riding school. The Indian Department discovered, however, that Rogers was using school labour and machinery on his personal farm. Soon after, the police arrested Rogers for drunk driving. As a result of these incidents, the department, without consulting the NEC, fired Rogers on 28 May 1929. This "precipitated a small crisis": Who would be the new principal, and how would they be chosen and appointed? The department assumed that its lease with the NEC stated that the new principal would have to be an Anglican clergyman, but this was mistaken (the lease did not dictate such terms). Regardless, the department consulted with the bishop of Huron, who nominated the Reverend Horace W. Snell as Rogers's replacement.[101]

Challenging Decades: The 1930s and '40s

Few government policy changes happened during the tenure of Principal Horace Snell. By 1923, when boarding and industrial schools were merged to form the new category of "residential" school, almost half of the industrial schools in Canada had closed, making the Mohawk Institute of particular note since it had been open almost one hundred years by this point. It is obvious that the schools had not lived up to policy-makers' expectations by this time. What officials thought would be a quick, easy, and inexpensive way of dealing with the "Indian problem" was in fact a costly failure. Instead of abandoning the failing system, however, some schools such as the Mohawk Institute remained open for another half century in another form—that of the residential school.

During this period schools would deteriorate even further. In 1936 the federal government made the Indian Department into a branch of the Department of Mines and Resources, but otherwise, as historian John L. Tobias writes, Indigenous affairs were left "in a state of flux" with the government making only "ad hoc decisions." Tobias believes this lack of a clear policy was possibly the "result of the realization that all previous policies had failed to attain the goal established for Canada's Indian administration."[102] Likewise, in a study prepared for the 1996 Royal Commission on Aboriginal Peoples, David Hoffman notes that there were very few changes to education policy between 1923 and 1950, the period roughly coinciding with Snell's time as principal of the Mohawk Institute. Hoffman found that the department rarely even made statements during this era about its objectives for residential schools.[103]

Since Principal Snell was brought up on a farm, NEC and government administrators were hopeful that he would be a competent principal. He had been born in Canada and raised in Oxford County, Ontario. He was ordained as an Anglican minister and served in several parishes in the southern part of the province. Overall, Snell made relatively few changes to how the Mohawk Institute was managed, though he did seem to want to make some improvements, such as buying the children toothbrushes (which he ended up purchasing with his own money). As principal, Snell generally waited to deal with problems as they arose, rather than making proactive changes, and he seems to have taken little initiative in school matters. The reports for the school from the 1930s are concerned primarily with the Institute's physical appearance, and such safety items as fire extinguishers and alarms.[104]

Snell, however, proved to be less concerned with the financial conditions of the school, and more than once the department warned him to watch his spending and to follow their orders.[105] The Mohawk Institute required a substantial amount of money to function—the costs of running the school exceeded the expense of operating all of the day schools on the reserve, even though many more students were enrolled in those schools. In 1929, for example, it cost $22,266 to run the day schools and $23,870 to run the Mohawk Institute.[106]

The safety of the school, the quality of teaching, and the conduct of the children also came under scrutiny during Snell's time as principal. In 1936, one student died when a maypole at the school came loose and crushed her,

Figure 2.2. Mohawk Institute boys on the way to the Six Nations Fair, 1934
Source: Kenneth Kidd Collection, Trent University Archives

causing internal injuries.[107] Children were still spending half of their day, at least, in work rather than in the classroom.[108] Peter Smith, who attended the Mohawk Institute in this period, said the following about his time at the schools: "We worked on the farm, we were hungry all the time. We had a team of horses—you had to clean all the stock, all the stables—you had to work all the time. We got up at 6 in the morning and we worked until 6 at night."[109] Snell told the Indian Department that he could not find suitable teachers for the vocational training that was supposed to be taking place.[110] Academic standards also decreased since more and more children were considered orphans or juvenile delinquents. The Indian agent at Walpole Island, for example, suggested that two boys who were caught breaking into houses should be sent to the Mohawk Institute.[111] The presence of such children suggested that the school had become more of a detention centre than an academic institution. Some citizens in Brantford complained that boys from the Institute stole money from milk bottles and pestered people to hire them to do odd jobs.[112] The department warned Snell that they had heard reports that the boys were visiting "the garbage dump early in the mornings, between seven and eight, to collect and eat scrap candies and biscuits."[113]

Despite all this, Principal Snell did not see the school as functioning poorly. He wrote that children were pleased with their time at the school and that they were "taking their places creditably in all walks of life"; some were "leading farmers on the Reserve, others [were] in business or industry, while many [were] making good wives in well-kept homes."[114] He claimed that "truancy [had] almost entirely ceased" and that "corporeal punishment [was used] only on very rare occasions."[115] These claims conflict with students' accounts. One student, for instance, complained that one Mr. Logan, who worked at the school, took him into the henhouse and hit him "with a belt" until he was "covered with bruises."[116] Snell responded to the complaint by saying he felt that the boy deserved such punishment.[117]

With the expiration of the government's lease with the NEC, coupled with the outbreak of war, faith in the residential school system was starting to wane. Robert A. Hoey, the superintendent of welfare and training, wrote in 1941 that the policy of the government was to promote day schools over residential schools: "The tendency on the part of the Government in recent years has been to multiply Indian day schools rather than residential schools. You may be interested to learn that a great deal of criticism has been directed against residential schools since I entered the Department about 5 years ago. There seems to be a growing feeling that with the exception of the remote northern regions our Indians have outgrown the necessity for such institutions."[118] At this time the Canadian government was grossly underfunding residential schools; in 1941, for instance, in the United States the "per capita grant for a boarding school with fewer than 200 pupils was $335. The 1941 per capita grant for the Canadian schools, most of which had fewer than 200 pupils, was only $170."[119]

In 1943, the NEC decided to end its grants to the Mohawk Institute. The Company agreed to care for the Mohawk Chapel and keep a clergyman at the Institute.[120] When the Second World War ended, a new lease was finally agreed between both parties. As had previously been the case, the NEC asked the Canadian government to purchase the Mohawk Institute. In the end, however, a new twenty-one-year lease was negotiated in 1946, after which management of the school remained in the hands of the Company.[121]

The Indian Department claimed that Snell had "never been a good administrator at any time."[122] As a result, a committee, including representatives from Six Nations, was formed to seek out a new principal. Joseph C. Hill, a teacher from Six Nations with excellent credentials, was suggested. Hill possessed certificates in areas such as manual training and religious instruction, and he had owned a grocery store and taught at day schools. He seemed perfect for the position, but the bishop of Huron felt that appointing an Indigenous person to the position would not be desirable.[123] In August

1945, he sent the Reverend W. J. Zimmerman to serve as principal. While it is impossible to know what might have happened under Hill at the school, it is likely that it would have been a much better experience for children than what occurred under Zimmerman.

The Dark Days Under the Reverend W. John Zimmerman

John Zimmerman was born in New Hamburg, Ontario. He was an ordained priest and had attended the University of Toronto and Columbia University. Prior to coming to the Mohawk Institute, Zimmerman had worked as a missionary on the Big Island Lake Indian Reserve in Saskatchewan. Zimmerman's appointment as principal coincided with the end of the Second World War. Indigenous soldiers had fought and served admirably in the war, and this made officials begin to reassess existing policies and embark on a new era of integration. This was a significant change from the policies of segregation that Duncan Campbell Scott had emphasized in the early years of the twentieth century. Increasingly, administrators were questioning the goals of the government's education policies for Indigenous peoples. In 1946, Hugh Castledon, a member of Parliament from Saskatchewan, claimed that only 16,000 of the 130,000 eligible Indigenous peoples in Canada that year received any educational training. Of that number, only 883 reached grade 7, 324 obtained grade 8, and only 71 completed grade 9.[124] In addition, this was a time when the Indian Department experienced financial difficulties and residential schools were very expensive to maintain and run.[125] In 1948, a special joint committee of the Senate and House of Commons on the *Indian Act* recommended significant changes. Moving forward, Indigenous children were to be taught alongside non-Indigenous children—integration rather than segregation.[126] In 1951 a new *Indian Act* stated that while the goal of "civilization" should be retained, it should not be "directed or forced," as it had been up to that point.[127] In the act the ban on Indigenous ceremonies and dances was lifted, as was the ban on pursuing land claims. More control was granted to band councils, particularly in the area of spending. New guidelines about the legal definition of an "Indian" were also made in the act. Despite these policy changes, many orphans and unwanted children still attended the Mohawk Institute. Government administrators said the Institute should primarily admit children who were orphans, destitute, or whose home conditions were poor. One student, for instance, was denied entry and told to go to a day school as he had two parents and a "suitable" home.[128]

Figure 2.3. Mohawk Institute trip to Christian Island, 1960s. Roberta Hill on the far left. Roberta recalls, "My fondest memories of the Mush Hole are leaving it. Occasionally, the supervisors took us on outings: hikes, a visit to the Welland Canal, trips to the cinema where we watched Elvis Presley movies. At the end of the school year, when most kids went home, my siblings and I went to summer camp on Christian Island, a reserve near Midland where we swam, camped and foraged for berries. It was the only time I felt like a regular kid. The joy of those summer months only made it more devastating when I had to return to the Mush Hole in September."
Source: Huronia Museum, 2006-0020-3690

Principal Zimmerman claimed to have made the school as appealing as possible by undertaking plans such as acquiring a skating rink and building a hockey team. Despite these changes, many conditions at the school still cried out for improvement. Bernard F. Neary, the superintendent of welfare and training for Indian Affairs, reported in 1946 that one teacher taught eighty-seven children in one room.[129] In addition, a doctor's report on the school disclosed many unsatisfactory sanitary conditions. For example, dishwater was not changed often enough and dishes were dried with dirty towels; the towels in the washrooms were filthy; the girls used reusable sanitary napkins; the flour and sugar were exposed to mice; and the bread

Figure 2.4. Summer camp at Christian Island, 1960s. From left, Donald Cooke, Baptist George, Hilton Sandy, and Robert Whiteye.
Source: Huronia Museum, 2006-0020-3694

was open and exposed to flies, while rats infested all of the outbuildings.[130] Another doctor found that milk was not being cooled properly and that the Institute was using ice made from canal water, which had been condemned for use.[131] Zimmerman also worried that children might contract sexually transmitted infections through the sharing of so many items including towels.[132]

Zimmerman's time as principal was a difficult period for students. Though he often wrote to the department about improving conditions in the school and began activities such as trips to the movie theatre and camping trips to Christian Island, he was seen as a strict and indeed violent disciplinarian.[133] Students have shared accusations of beatings and sexual abuse in which he participated. In 1946, not long after Zimmerman took over as principal, an investigation into conditions at the Mohawk Institute was launched by the Indian Affairs Branch. The investigation was in response to complaints from groups such as the Brantford Women's Council who were concerned about a "lack of sufficient clothing and educational facilities." Conditions in the school were described as "abysmal and below any standard suitable to human living."[134] The department claimed that conditions at the school had deteriorated as the NEC suspended their grants to the school after the outbreak of the Second World War.[135] In response, Archdeacon A. L. G. Clarke said that "the Indian Department is responsible for the buildings, upkeep and repairs," and that, while the NEC had "leased the buildings to the department," it had to stop paying a grant to the school since "its real estate in London had been reduced to rubble from bombings" during the war.[136] A newspaper article a few days later said the faults at the school rested with the federal government, which was not properly funding the Mohawk Institute: "it is difficult to make good bricks without straw, neither is it possible to run a good school without essential physical plant, equipment and educational accommodation."[137] The "Supreme Court Grand Jury" was thus tasked with making an inspection of the Institute (the first time this had been done). They reported that Principal Zimmerman provided a detailed tour of the school and that they found everything in "smooth running order" and commended him on "his capable management."[138] They did describe some areas of the school, however, as in desperate need of repair and recommended that chairs be purchased for the dormitories. The "Grand Jury" also said conditions at the school would need to be monitored closely via other investigations.[139] There is no indication that the inspectors spoke to any of the students to hear their opinion about life at the school. The Brantford Women's Council again expressed their ongoing concerns as well.[140]

Often students were unhappy with the situation they found themselves in, and during the 1950s numerous children ran away from the school. Some students left to meet up with boyfriends or girlfriends, but many others left in the hopes of returning home. Others claim they left because they were mistreated. Many simply felt that no one cared for them. In 1949, twenty-five girls ran away from the Mohawk Institute at the same time. They were caught, but within two weeks of their return ten ran away again. Several of the girls were committed to a reformatory and the individual who sheltered them on the reserve was charged under the *Juvenile Delinquents Act*.[141] The Institute permitted the dismissal of students who constantly ran away and warned parents that students could not be discharged "to suit their whims."[142]

The department set out specific punishment guidelines to ensure that children were not being abused, but when Zimmerman caught boys "in the act of homo-sex" (likely rape) while the other boys watched the "filthy business," he felt that spanking "their posterior ends . . . might do some good."[143] Many former students describe having experienced extreme abuse while in the Institute, not only from administrators, but at the hands of other students as well.[144] Former student Russell Moses recalls horrific disciplinary tactics used in this era as well: "I have seen Indian children having their faces rubbed in excrement, this was done by a gentleman who has now gone to his just reward." Flora Moore said she was severely punished simply for "playing around" in line: "The guy picked me up by the back of my neck, he kicked my butt, and then he took me to the room, and I don't know what happened there, but all I know was that I had strap marks on my body, and my hands were blistered. . . . I never told anybody. . . . That was the first I ever encountered physical abuse. . . . And I could never sleep after that."[145]

Not surprisingly, during the 1950s neither students and their parents nor the government were pleased with life at residential schools. Starting in the 1950s "there was a dramatic rise in Indian enrolment in Provincial school systems."[146] Little wonder given the conditions in many of the schools such as the Mohawk Institute. In 1957, Indian Affairs Branch Director H. M. Jones wrote that "No one can defend the salaries residential schools are presently paying their help nor in some instances the quality of the food and clothing."[147] A 1956 study revealed that 61 per cent of children in residential schools had attained the equivalent of grades 1 to 3, and less than 0.5 per cent had reached grade 12 levels.[148] An overreliance on children's physical labour in schools was still taking place.[149] The federal government began to encourage greater parental involvement in schools via school committees: "In 1963, the Department provided for the organizing and minimal funding of these Committees. By 1971 there were 215 such Committees in existence, with greatly increased areas of responsibility." By this time only fourteen teachers in residential schools in Canada were Indigenous.[150] In the 1960s the department made it clear that its view was that residential schools were to draw from a limited pool of children—"[those] from broken homes or whose parents [were] unable to provide the proper care," as well as "children of migrant hunters and trappers whose life makes day school arrangements impracticable."[151]

Closure of the Mohawk Institute

In 1966 government administrators undertook *A Survey of the Contemporary Indians of Canada: Economic, Political, Educational Needs and Policies*. This two-volume report, which came to be known as the "Hawthorn Report," claimed that the schooling of Indigenous peoples was necessary if they were to "fit properly and competently into our economic and social structure."[152] The report recommended, "without basic question," "the principle of integrated education."[153] The Caldwell Report of 1967 reiterated concerns with the number of students in residential schools for welfare rather than educational reasons.

In 1969, in what has become known as the White Paper, government administrators declared their plan to repeal the *Indian Act* and absolve themselves of responsibility for Indigenous affairs. In their minds, these actions would bring an immediate end to the "Indian problem" since Indigenous peoples would lose their status. As part of this new policy, the federal government planned to close residential schools, citing low attendance and high costs. This new approach did not differ from those of years past—the government was still forcing Indigenous peoples to accept the place that the government had designated for them. Indigenous reaction to the White Paper was swift and strong, with the government's actions "caus[ing] the reawakening of political consciousness and the emergence of provincial and territorial organizations [of Indigenous people]."[154] Indigenous groups, led by the National Indian Brotherhood, responded to the White Paper with their own plan entitled "Citizens Plus" (commonly referred to as "The Red Paper"). Moving forward, control of the education of Indigenous children became a key goal of such groups. The Brotherhood also wrote an important policy paper entitled *Indian Control of Indian Education*. Its message to church and state administrators could not have been clearer: Get out of the "business" of supposedly educating Indigenous children and youth and devolve that role to Indigenous nations. In the end, the government would not act on the White Paper, but the move to close the remaining residential schools was already well underway.

By the end of the 1960s, most of the children attending the Mohawk Institute were not from nearby, so the school's ostensible utility began to be challenged. Many Cree children from northern Ontario arrived in the early 1960s, and they generally spoke Cree and French as their first languages.[155] The experience of these children is a part of the school's history that is yet to be studied. By 1960, over one-quarter of Indigenous students in Canada were

Figure 2.5. An image from May 1966 in *The Toronto Star*. The original caption read, "Canadian birds are old hat to these Cree Indian children from the Mohawk Institute; a residential school in Brantford; who met some imports at Riverdale zoo. There were 27 on the trip sponsored by HMS Ajax Chapter; IODE."
Source: Toronto Public Library, TSPA_0116424F

enrolled in provincially controlled institutions rather than schools intended solely for Indigenous students.[156] By 1968, of 68,386 Indigenous students in Canada, only 9,071 were enrolled in residential schools.[157] At the Mohawk Institute, only 25 of the 96 students came from southern Ontario, the area the school was intended to serve, and enrolment was expected to drop to 25 students due to the opening of more reserve schools in Quebec and northwestern Ontario.[158] Rather than using the schools as welfare agencies, the department ensured that many children deemed to be in need of care were adopted primarily by non-Indigenous families during what has come to be known as the "Sixties Scoop." Additional day schools, improved roads and housing, and alternate boarding services also diminished the need for schools such as the Mohawk Institute. If the Mohawk Institute closed, the children could be placed in homes and sent to day schools in places such as Brantford, Caledonia, or Hagersville, or they could attend non-Indigenous schools in Brantford.[159] Since it cost $235,000 per year to run the Institute, it did not seem economically sound to keep the school running for a relatively small number of students who could be educated elsewhere.[160] As of 1969, residential schools were to exist as "a supplementary service provided by the Department to Indian Children who, for very special reasons, [could not] commute to federal day schools or provincial schools from their homes."[161] Finally, in June 1970, the government decided to close what had formerly been known as the "model" industrial school, which had been in existence for a century and a half—the longest of any residential school in Canada. By that time, over the school's long and dark history, over 21,000 children had spent time behind the bricks.[162]

The Mohawk Institute: 1970s to the Present

At the time of the closure, newspapers reported that few of the last residents of the Mohawk Institute were from Six Nations (only twenty-three of the final ninety-six)—most were from northern Ontario and Quebec.[163] The school was said to be housing "children from broken homes and reserves without schools." The government indicated that it was "holding [the school] at the request of the elected council" and that the school was being "constantly patrolled" in case of any violence.[164] The school was finally completely vacated in March 1971.[165] That year, the Six Nations Elected Council agreed to the provincial commemoration of the school through a plaque that was erected in 1972.[166]

After the Mohawk Institute closed, a battle over who would control the school ensued. In the end, the Department of Indian Affairs gave the school building to the Six Nations. McMaster University was keen to use it as a satellite campus, but instead in 1972 the school was turned into the Woodland Indian Cultural Educational Centre (now known as the Woodland Cultural Centre). The Woodland Cultural Centre focuses on the revitalization of Indigenous cultural heritage, directly combating the assimilationist ideologies of the Mohawk Institute Indian Residential School.[167] In these early years, the centre sought to preserve and revitalize Eastern Woodlands culture through exhibits, with a mandate to collect research materials and artifacts for its library and museum (now totalling over fifty thousand artifacts). In 1975, the centre expanded to encompass the arts, and in 1984, it launched a language program. Today, the Woodland Cultural Centre describes itself as "an organization with historic expertise and strong community connections" and with "a key role to play in knowledge and learning through its program offerings, including education, museum, language, library and arts."[168]

The school building built in 1904 still stands today. In 2013, after damage from a failing roof necessitated repairs, the Woodland Cultural Centre organized a consultation with the Six Nations community, among other First Nations and survivors, to see what they wanted to happen with the former school buildings. Some expressed a desire to tear down the buildings, but 98 per cent of the people who participated in the feedback process opted to undertake renovations and keep the Mohawk Institute building open as a site to teach people about the history of the residential school and its devastating impact on their community.[169] Former student Douglas George Kanentiio from Awkwesasne explains why he supported saving the school from demolition:

> I believe the (Mohawk) Institute should be preserved as a memorial. . . . My wife and I visited Buchenwald when we were in Germany which is, with the exception of the rat-infested inmate barracks, left just as it was when liberated by the Russians in 1945. When anyone connected with the residential school reconciliation process brings this issue up I tell them to go to the institute and stay there for a couple of nights. Sleep in our bunk beds, eat our food, listen to the floors creak and the slow walk of the night watchman as he makes his rounds from the basement to the upper floors. This takes it from being an intellectual exercise to actual appreciating our circumstances.[170]

The "Save the Evidence" campaign was launched in 2014. Originally, this started as a simple fundraiser to repair the school's roof, but it has since turned into a full-scale renovation project. Funding has come from several sources including the Six Nations Elected Council, the City of Brantford, and both the federal and provincial governments.[171] By 2022, the Save the Evidence campaign had reached its goal of raising $23.5 million.[172] The renovated museum and school will open in 2025. This is a marked departure from what has happened to most former schools in Canada: "For years as the school system was dismantled, former residential school buildings were disposed of as government assets and sold to private interests, returned to communities to be repurposed as band offices and administration buildings, or left to slowly crumble away with the passage of time."[173] In addition to the school renovation, survivors have created the Mohawk Village Memorial Park project to honour the children who attended the Mohawk Institute.[174]

Though the Mohawk Institute is Canada's first and longest-running residential school, only four schools have been named a National Historic Site: the former Shubenacadie Indian Residential School in Nova Scotia, designated in 2020; the former Portage La Prairie Indian Residential School in Manitoba, designated in 2020; the former Muscowequan Indian Residential School in Saskatchewan, which was designated in 2021; and, finally, the former Shingwauk Indian Residential School in Ontario, also designated in 2021. In addition, on 1 September 2020, under the National Program of Historical Commemoration, the Government of Canada designated the residential school system as a whole a National Historic Event.[175] These designations took place as part of the Canadian government's response to the Truth and Reconciliation Commission's Calls to Action—in particular, Call to Action 79. Parks Canada notes that "commemoration is not celebration—it is recognition and acknowledgement that history has shaped Canada." The goal of these commemoration projects has also been the "inclusion of Indigenous peoples' history, voices and perspectives in the National Program of Historical Commemoration and other public history activities."[176] In 2014 the Six Nations Elected Council named the Mohawk Institute a "Six Nations Historic Place."[177]

Life Behind the Bricks

With the school preserved, what about the stories of the people behind the bricks? No two students had the same experience at the Mohawk Institute. Even those who attended at the very same time have divergent and unique memories. Conditions varied over time and were affected by situations such as who was principal and what was transpiring in the larger Canadian society. Thanks to the efforts of groups such as the Woodland Cultural Centre, and historians such as Elizabeth Graham, who has interviewed dozens of survivors, these stories are not lost.[178] In them we hear repeated themes such as physical and sexual abuse, hunger, loneliness, and an inadequate education. Many stories describe loss—loss of language, family, safety, personal possessions, home, and, ultimately, loss of identity, as each student was assigned a number rather than a name. Many survivors still refer to the Institute as the "Mush Hole," in reference to the amount of oatmeal porridge they were served every day (a menu for the school from 1895 showed students had porridge for breakfast every day and for supper five days per week).[179] Some have positive memories to share as well. The "Concluding Voices" chapter in this book allows us to hear directly from the former students who experienced the Institute's harsh conditions. Likewise, historians such as Thomas Peace are finding creative ways to use documentary sources such as the Mohawk Institute register to tell us about the lived experiences of students.[180] Archaeologists like Sarah Clarke, Paul Racher, and Tara Froman are also discovering what artifacts can tell us about life at the Mohawk Institute.[181]

Government Inaction and Action Since the 1970s

Though it had closed down the majority of residential schools by the 1970s when the Mohawk Institute closed, the Canadian government did not immediately take any action to atone for its role in the residential school system. This era saw the development of the land claims process (both comprehensive and specific) and the continued push by Indigenous rights groups such as the National Indian Brotherhood for First Nations to be recognized as sovereign nations with the rights to self-determination, among other rights. John Leslie describes the 1980s as more "productive" in terms of government action:

> The Charter of Rights and Freedoms, proclaimed in the early 1980s, had a section providing constitutional protection for treaty and aboriginal rights. Indeed, the Royal Proclamation of 1763 was deemed to be one of Canada's constitutional documents. In November 1983, the Special Parliamentary Committee on Indian Self-Government presented its findings and urged expanded powers for first nations governments, which in some instances would go beyond the traditional municipal model.[182]

The 1990s heralded an era of more in-depth discussions about the inherent right of First Nations to self-government. This period also saw the residential school system become national news after Phil Fontaine, national chief of the Assembly of First Nations, spoke publicly about his experiences while a student at residential school. Fontaine spoke to media about the sexual, physical, and psychological abuse he suffered as a child and called for a public inquiry into the residential school system.[183] The Anglican Church of Canada named 1992 as "A Year of Reconciliation with Aboriginal Peoples," and in 1993 it formally apologized for its role in the Mohawk Institute and the residential school system.[184]

In 1991 the Royal Commission on Aboriginal Peoples was established to investigate and find solutions to the challenges affecting the relationship between Indigenous peoples (including First Nations, Inuit, and Métis), the Canadian government, and Canada. It would take until 1996 for the commission to submit its final, multi-volume report.[185] In an unprecedented fashion, the Royal Commission began to open up conversations in Canada about the residential school system, and also revealed the abuse and conditions faced in schools such as the Mohawk Institute for over a century and a half—concerns raised by Indigenous peoples from the start, who said the same thing but were ignored or dismissed. Central to this discussion were conversations about the intentions of church and state officials in the creation of the school system—namely, cultural genocide (sanitized by use of the term "assimilation"), land acquisition, and financial savings. Rather than learning places, schools were "sites of unlearning."[186] Historian John Milloy has called them a "National Crime."[187] As scholar Wendy Fletcher has indicated, when it comes to the residential school system, financial considerations always trumped concern for people: "The economics of enforcing an assimilationist monologue through a residential school system led to the dehumanization of indigenous children. How money is spent reveals much about what people value, speaking louder than any text about the philosophy of life and values. Such was certainly the case at the MI [Mohawk Institute]. The financial story demonstrates that aboriginal children were not valued as fully human nor their dignity respected."[188] Fletcher goes on to stress that neither the NEC nor the Canadian government can claim ignorance of conditions at the Institute. Besides several inquiries, court cases, and public stories about the school, described in this and the previous chapter, school inspectors and others regularly reported on the Institute's happenings. By the time of the school's closure, in addition to the Department of Indian Affairs, the following entities were regularly monitoring the school: the Children's Aid Society, a local mental health clinic, the National Health and Welfare Service, a Brant public school inspector, the Superintendent of Schools Regional Office, and the Six Nations Inspectorate of Schools.[189]

The Royal Commission report said that schools such as the Mohawk Institute were the cause of what some psychologists have deemed "residential-school syndrome" and linked the schools to alcohol abuse, suicide, and family violence. Residential schools were the leading issue raised by Indigenous participants in their presentations to the commission. Georges Erasmus, co-chair of the Royal Commission emphasized that "there probably has not been a hearing that we have conducted that has not, at one point or another, provided an opportunity for someone that either has themselves experienced residential school or else someone in their family has been involved in a residential school."[190] Canadians were beginning to realize the enormous negative impact that residential schools such as the Mohawk Institute had on Indigenous peoples and that their legacy was still being felt in Indigenous communities across Canada. No longer were Indigenous peoples going to be quiet about their experiences—they wanted change and justice. The residential school system was not something from the distant past with no relevance to the present. Issues plaguing some Indigenous communities, such as marginalization, financial disparities, poor parenting skills, addictions issues, intergenerational trauma and lateral violence, lack of housing, violence against Indigenous women and girls, over-incarceration in prisons, high rates of child apprehension, and systemic poverty, could be directly traced back to the schools. The TRC later described this as "disparities that condemn many Aboriginal people to shorter, poorer, and more troubled lives."[191] In 1998, the government responded to the Royal Commission with *Gathering Strength: Canada's Aboriginal Action Plan*. The plan discusses the need to renew the "partnership" with Canada's Indigenous peoples, strengthen Indigenous governance, develop a new fiscal relationship, and support people and economies. A $350 million "Healing Fund" was to help address the effects of the residential school system. Most felt this was far too little, far too late.

In the years since, more and more survivors of residential schools have turned to the court system to find recourse for what they had experienced. In 1998, former Mohawk Institute survivors launched a $900 million class action lawsuit on behalf of former students against the federal government and the Anglican Church of Canada. An additional $600 million suit was filed on behalf of the parents, siblings, children, and relatives of the students. At the time, it was estimated that more than one thousand students of the Mohawk Institute were still alive.[192] They would eventually claim $2.3 billion in damages.[193] It was fitting that a group of students from Canada's first and longest-running residential school, the Mohawk Institute, would lead the cause for redress. To address this rising tide of complaints—and in particular the court cases related to the Mohawk Institute—the Canadian federal government signed the Indian Residential Schools Settlement Agreement in 2006. The agreement includes five main elements:

- a Common Experience Payment (CEP) for all eligible former students of Indian Residential Schools;

- an Independent Assessment Process (IAP) for claims of sexual or serious physical abuse;

- measures to support healing such as the Indian Residential Schools Resolution Health Support Program and an endowment to the Aboriginal Healing Foundation;

- commemorative activities;

- the establishment of a Truth and Reconciliation Commission (TRC).[194]

Many survivors have opted to take the payment rather than go through a long and potentially harmful court case. To date, over $3 billion has been paid to school survivors across Canada, with an average payment per person of $111,265. Additional funds have been paid for commemoration, healing, and other activities.[195] Many have criticized this approach for, in the words of Andrew Woolford,

> offering one-time payments with one hand while threatening with the might of police, prisons, and economic rollbacks with the other. . . . In such circumstances redress is felt not as a decolonizing impulse pushing toward a new nonsettler society but as another form of . . . "transfer". . . . In this case, redress transfers the legitimate justice demands of Indigenous peoples into tiny boxes of repair, removing them as a challenge to the legitimacy of the settler colonial nation and potentially hiding the violence of settle colonialism within a language of reconciliation.[196]

In 2008, while the TRC's hearings were underway, the federal government finally issued a formal apology for its role in the residential school system. On 11 June 2008, Prime Minister Harper apologized and stated the following:

> Two primary objectives of the Residential Schools system were to remove and isolate children from the influence of their homes, families, traditions and cultures, and to assimilate them into the dominant culture. These objectives were based on the assumption Aboriginal cultures and spiritual

beliefs were inferior and unequal. Indeed, some sought, as it was infamously said, "to kill the Indian in the child." Today, we recognize that this policy of assimilation was wrong, has caused great harm, and has no place in our country. . . . The Government of Canada built an educational system in which very young children were often forcibly removed from their homes, often taken far from their communities. Many were inadequately fed, clothed and housed. All were deprived of the care and nurturing of their parents, grandparents and communities. First Nations, Inuit and Métis languages and cultural practices were prohibited in these schools. Tragically, some of these children died while attending residential schools and others never returned home. The government now recognizes that the consequences of the Indian Residential Schools policy were profoundly negative and that this policy has had a lasting and damaging impact on Aboriginal culture, heritage and language. While some former students have spoken positively about their experiences at residential schools, these stories are far overshadowed by tragic accounts of the emotional, physical and sexual abuse and neglect of helpless children, and their separation from powerless families and communities. The legacy of Indian Residential Schools has contributed to social problems that continue to exist in many communities today.[197]

Now that the apology had been made, Indigenous peoples waited for action and the results of the TRC. Several former Mohawk Institute students testified at TRC hearings when commissioners visited Six Nations in 2012. It was reported that "hundreds of survivors and family members gathered at the Six Nations community hall" to tell their stories.[198] Norman Lickers, for instance, a former Mohawk Institute student, told the commission the following: "When we got up in the morning we did chores, we had breakfast, and after that we went out and did whatever else we were told to do. There was no actual instruction about it. . . . We were given just enough instruction in school to know that we were dissatisfied when we went back to the reserve, and yet we never got enough instruction with which we could go on."[199]

It would take until 2015 for the TRC to issue its report.[200] By that time, over $72 million had been spent by the federal government to support the work being undertaken by the commission. In addition to hosting national events and conducting many studies, TRC commissioners spent six years travelling across Canada and hearing from more than six thousand witnesses. The TRC would assess over five million government records, which are now housed at the University of Manitoba. The commission's findings were released in a six-volume set. It also issued ninety-four "Calls to Action" for Canada. These calls are far-reaching and pertain to the ongoing impact of residential schools like the Mohawk Institute.[201] One of the key findings was that the residential school system amounted to "cultural genocide":

> *Cultural genocide* is the destruction of those structures and practices that allow the group to continue as a group. States that engage in cultural genocide set out to destroy the political and social institutions of the targeted group. Land is seized, and populations are forcibly transferred and their movement is restricted. Languages are banned. Spiritual leaders are persecuted, spiritual practices are forbidden, and objects of spiritual value are confiscated and destroyed. And, most significantly to the issue at hand, families are disrupted to prevent the transmission of cultural values and identity from one generation to the next. In dealing with Aboriginal people, Canada did all these things.[202]

Though Canadians professed to be shocked by the use of the term "genocide," this was not the first time the term had been utilized in this context. As early as 1954 a joint committee of the Senate and House of Commons said the situation of Indigenous peoples was akin to the "concentration camps of Nazi Europe," and in 1993 Elijah Harper, himself a residential school survivor, "told the *Winnipeg Free Press* that Residential schools are a 'prime example' of federal government policies whose purpose was deliberate assimilation and genocide of Canada's aboriginal people."[203] The Canadian government announced that September 30 would be National Day for Truth and Reconciliation. Many people also now recognize this as "Orange Shirt Day," started by Phyllis Webstad, a residential school survivor, who had the orange shirt her grandmother had bought her for the first day of school taken away when she attended the St. Joseph's Mission Residential School.[204] In 2022, the Canadian Parliament unanimously called upon the Government of Canada to recognize the residential schools policy as an act of genocide.[205]

As Canadians were grappling with their growing knowledge about the residential school system, shockwaves were once again sent across the country when the Tk'emlúps te Secwépemc community in British Columbia released a statement about 215 potential graves being found via ground-penetrating radar on the grounds of the former Kamloops Indian Residential School in 2021.[206] This grew into the Missing Children Project, whose goal is recording the deaths and burial places of children who died while attending residential school.[207] The Tk'emlúps te Secwépemc community's statement prompted a national outcry (in the summer of 2021 more than sixty churches in Canada were destroyed, desecrated, or vandalized in a wave of grassroots anger), and *The New York Times* called the site a "mass grave." Since that time, dissenters have said the findings do not pertain to the actual bodies of children and that the impact of residential schools has been sensationalized.[208] The Tk'emlúps te Secwépemc are now referring to the findings as "anomalies," rather than unmarked graves.[209] Despite this, over six thousand known child deaths in residential schools have been documented (records are incomplete, so the exact number will never be known).[210]

Survivors' Secretariat and the Mohawk Institute

After the news from the Tk'emlúps te Secwépemc, survivors of the Mohawk Institute began weekly meetings to determine how they would go about searching over six hundred acres of land tied to the school. That same year, Mark Hill, the elected chief of Six Nations, called on the federal government to provide funding for the search; at the same time, survivors of the Mohawk Institute encouraged police to launch criminal investigations into missing children and unmarked burials at the Institute, which ultimately led to the creation of a police task force. The Six Nations of the Grand River provided $1 million in funding to create the Survivors' Secretariat, and searches of the Mohawk Institute school grounds using ground-penetrating radar equipment began. In 2022, the government provided $10.3 million in funding over three years in support of the work of the Survivors' Secretariat.[211] In 2024, after a gathering in Thunder Bay, the secretariat released *A Time for Truth: Knowledge Is Sacred; Truth Is Healing*. This report included a list of demands that must be met to move toward truth and reconciliation. These include the release of "all 23 million documents identified but not released to the National Centre for Truth and Reconciliation, and all RCMP records related to missing children and unmarked burials associated with Indian Residential Schools." The secretariat is also seeking long-term funding to search for missing children and unmarked burials and has demanded that the Canadian government commit to "a complete account of the Indian

Residential School experience," create "spaces for sharing, learning and healing," and "include support for memorialization and public commemoration as a central part of funding."[212]

Conclusion

Initially, during the eighteenth and nineteenth centuries, the Crown sought out Indigenous groups such as the Six Nations as allies, but once the threat of war subsided after the War of 1812, Indigenous peoples were increasingly perceived as a "problem" that would supposedly be solved by the creation of schools like the Mohawk Institute. The schools evolved into a partnership between church and state. When they created the Mohawk Institute in the 1830s, NEC officials claimed to have sought the assimilation of the Six Nations, but by 1910, faced with increased racist sentiments combined with population growth and economic development of the larger non-Indigenous society, the Canadian government adopted a policy of reserve containment for Indigenous peoples. From the beginning of the First World War to the end of the Second World War, government officials largely retreated from Indigenous affairs. Beginning in 1945, however, the government took a renewed interest in "managing" Indigenous peoples through a policy of integration. This culminated in the White Paper, the Indigenous response to which eventually brought an end to residential schools, including the Mohawk Institute.

The school has left a lasting scar—not only on students who attended, but on the entire Six Nations community, both past and present. Six Nations responded positively to the Institute in early years because they valued off-reserve labouring jobs and employment related to the agricultural industry; they believed the Institute would provide them with the necessary skills and connections to obtain such positions. Six Nations began responding negatively to the Institute when its benefits to their community decreased and the real intentions of school administrators became clear: access to Indigenous land, cultural genocide, and cost savings. Since non-Indigenous people replaced Indigenous people as labourers by the turn of the century, the school no longer served as a conduit to jobs, and increasingly Indigenous people opposed the abuse and paternalism of administrators. By 1900, the majority of pupils were orphans and indigent children, often from outside communities.

Many writers and historians assume the Institute can be deemed a "success" since the school existed for almost a century and a half, while many other industrial schools stayed open only a few years or decades. Yet, upon closer examination, it becomes obvious that the Mohawk Institute can only be called a success for government and church administrators in the very early years of the school. The school did not quickly "civilize" the Six Nations as its administrators assumed it would. Neither the church nor the government were willing to properly finance the high costs of running the Institute, and both church and government administrators underestimated the strength of Six Nations traditions, values, and culture, which were a formidable force. Despite numerous formal and informal investigations, officials ignored the many forms of harm that went on in the Mohawk Institute. Clearly, the school also failed to meet Indigenous needs or goals—rather than obtaining jobs, children faced abuse, suffering, and, as is increasingly being uncovered, even death.

The refusal of the Six Nations and other Indigenous communities to succumb to the forced assimilation policy of church and state officials contributed greatly to the eventual demise of schools like the Mohawk Institute. It took many years, however, for the government to respond to Indigenous discontent, and even then, it only did so due to the rising fear of the cost of court cases brought forward by school survivors. Thankfully, the "school" that was designed for cultural genocide is now home to a place in which Indigenous culture is preserved and fostered—a far cry from what church and state administrators originally envisioned for the Mohawk Institute. Much work remains to be done and more stories about life "behind the bricks" need to be told, however, before reconciliation can occur and the "truth" of the Mohawk Institute is widely recognized and known. This book is a small step in that direction.

NOTES

I would like to thank the Social Sciences and Humanities Research Council for providing financial support for this research, and George Emery, professor emeritus at Western University, for supervising my 1993 master's thesis on the Mohawk Institute.

1. Frank Oliver, in Canada, *House of Commons Debates*, 11th Parl., 1st Sess., Vol. 1 (12 February 1909), 977. There are several secondary and primary sources quoted throughout this chapter that utilize the term "Indian." Otherwise, the terms "First Nations," "Indigenous peoples," or references to specific nations (e.g., Six Nations) will be utilized.
2. Frank Oliver, in Canada, *House of Commons Debates*, 11th Parl., 1st Sess., Vol. 1 (12 February 2009), 977.
3. Residential schools have been described in various ways over time, though most today use the term "residential." It would not be until the 1920s that the term "residential schools" was utilized. This chapter uses the terms "mechanics' institute," "manual labour," "industrial" and "residential" interchangeably, though, as this chapter will demonstrate, historically there were some differences between these types of schools. Boarding schools were seen as separate from industrial schools until 1923.
4. Jean Barman, Yvonne Hebert, and Don McCaskill, eds., *Indian Education in Canada*, vol. 1, *The Legacy* (University of British Columbia Press, 1986), 8.

5. Treaties and Historical Research Centre, "The Historical Development of the Indian Act" (PRE Group, Indian and Northern Affairs, 1978), 105.
6. David Laird, Indian Commissioner, to Superintendent General of Indian Affairs, *Annual Report of the Department of Indian Affairs for the Year Ended 30 June 1904* (S. E. Dawson, 1905), 204.
7. For example, Frank Pedley wrote that "it is clear that the present system with its large expenditure has not operated as was expected towards the civilization of the aborigines." See Frank Pedley to Joint Church Commission, 21 March 1908, File 1-1-1, pt. 2, Vol. 6001, Record Group 10 [hereafter RG 10], Library and Archives Canada [hereafter LAC].
8. Frank Pedley, Report of the Deputy Superintendent General of Indian Affairs, *Annual Report of the Department of Indian Affairs for the Year Ended 30 June 1906* (S. E. Dawson, 1907), xxxii.
9. See chapters 1 and 11 in this volume.
10. Frank Pedley, Report of the Deputy Superintendent General of Indian Affairs, *Annual Report of the Department of Indian Affairs for the Year Ended 30 June 1905* (S. E. Dawson, 1906), xxxiii.
11. Frank Oliver, in Canada, *House of Commons Debates*, 11th Parl., 1st Sess., Vol. 1 (12 February 1909), 977.
12. Frank Pedley, Report of the Deputy Superintendent General of Indian Affairs, *Annual Report of the Department of Indian Affairs for the Year Ended 31 March 1907* (S. E. Dawson, 1907), xxxiii.
13. Duncan C. Scott, Report of the Superintendent of Indian Education, *Annual Report of the Department of Indian Affairs for the Year Ended 31 March 1910* (C. H. Parmelee, 1910), 273.
14. David Hoffman, *A Summary of Findings from Departmental Files and Selected Secondary Sources Related to Indian Residential School Policy* (DIAND, 1993), 15.
15. Report of the Superintendent of Indian Education, *Annual Report of the Department of Indian Affairs for the Year Ended 31 March 1910*, 273.
16. Clifford Sifton in extract from *Hansard* of 18 July 1904, File 1-1-1, pt. 1, Vol. 6001, RG 10, LAC.
17. Duncan C. Scott, Superintendent of Indian Education Report, *Annual Report of the Department of Indian Affairs for the Year Ended 31 March 1913* (C. H. Parmelee, 1913), 305, and Duncan C. Scott, Superintendent of Indian Education Report, *Annual Report of the Department of Indian Affairs for the Year Ended 31 March 1915* (J. de L. Tache, 1915), 123.
18. Alison Norman, "The History of Education at Six Nations of the Grand River, 1828–1939," in *Ontario Since Confederation: A Reader*, 2nd ed. (University of Toronto Press, 2024), 97.
19. R. Ashton, Principal's Report on the Mohawk Institute, 10 August 1905, *Annual Report of the Department of Indian Affairs for the Year Ended 30 June 1905* (S. E. Dawson, 1906), 282.
20. There were a large number of well-established farms on the reserve. Sally Weaver claims the 1890s was the heyday of farming at Six Nations. See Sally Weaver, "The Iroquois: The Consolidation of the Grand River Reserve in the Mid-Nineteenth Century, 1847–1875," in *Aboriginal Ontario: Historical Perspectives on the First Nations*, ed. Edward S. Rogers and Donald B. Smith (Dundurn Press, 1994), 223.
21. W. F. Webster, *Report of Mr. W. F. Webster Upon His Visit to the Mohawk Institute, Brantford, and the Grand River Reserve, Canada* (Spottiswoode & Co., 1908), 11.
22. Committee to Investigate Schools to Superintendent General of Indian Affairs, 11 March 1904, Box 5, #5, records pertaining to missions to the Aboriginal People in Western Canada, Presbyterian Church in Canada Foreign Mission Fonds, United Church Archives.
23. P. H. Bryce, *Report of the Indian Schools of Manitoba and the NorthWest Territories* (Government Printing Bureau, 1907). In 1922 Bryce would go on to publish his findings in a book entitled *The Story of a National Crime, Being an Appeal for Justice to the Indians of Canada*.
24. Kathleen McKenzie and Sean Carleton, "Hiding in Plain Sight: Newspaper Coverage of Dr. Peter Bryce's 1907 Report on Residential Schools," *Active History*, 29 September 2021, https://activehistory.ca/blog/2021/09/29/hiding-in-plain-sight-newspaper-coverage-of-dr-peter-bryces-1907-report-on-residential-schools/.
25. See *Regulations Relating to the Education of Indian Children* (Government Printing Bureau, 1908).
26. New England Company Committee, 10 April 1905, B3, File 7928-5, Manuscript Group [hereafter MG] 17, New England Company [hereafter NEC], LAC; Indian Department Memorandum, 22 August 1903, File 7825-1B, Vol. 2007, RG 10, LAC.
27. Report of Rev. R. Ashton, Principal of the Mohawk Institute, Brantford, Ont., for the Year Ended 31 March 1910, *Annual Report of the Department of Indian Affairs for the Year Ended 31 March 1910*, 420.
28. S. H. Blake, *Memorandum on Indian Work* (Bryant Press, 1909).
29. Indian Board, 12 October 1905, File 7825-1B, Vol. 2007, RG 10, LAC.

30 "Indians Have a Grievance," *Globe*, 5 June 1906, 10.
31 Donald Purich, *Our Land: Native Rights in Canada* (James Lorimer & Company, 1986), 134.
32 *Globe*, "Indians Have a Grievance."
33 Letter from Six Nations Indians, *Haldimand Banner*, 22 March 1906.
34 New England Company Committee, 9 August 1905, B3, File 7928-5, MG 17, NEC, LAC.
35 *Globe*, "Indians Have a Grievance."
36 Duncan C. Scott, Deputy Superintendent General of Indian Affairs, 18 December 1930, *Annual Report of the Department of Indian Affairs for the Year Ended 31 March 1930*, 18.
37 The Report of A. Nelles Ashton, Principal of the Mohawk Institute Brantford, Ont., for the Year Ended 31 March 1911, in *Annual Report of the Department of Indian Affairs for the Year Ended 31 March 1911* (C. H. Parmelee, 1911), 521–2.
38 Report of A. Nelles Ashton, Principal of the Mohawk Institute Brantford, Ont. in *Annual Report of the Department of Indian Affairs for the Year Ended 31 March 1912* (C. H. Parmelee, 1912), 510–11.
39 See various letters to the Department of Indian Affairs in Elizabeth Graham, *The Mush Hole: Life at Two Indian Residential Schools* (Heffle Publishing, 1997), 107.
40 Memo from D. C. Scott, 28 November 1912, File 160-1, Pt. 1, Vol. 6039, RG 10, LAC.
41 Memo from the Deputy Superintendent General, File 150-9, Pt. 1, Vol. 6031, RG 10, LAC.
42 Duncan Campbell Scott to Hon. Dr. Roche, File 154,845, Pt. 1, 28 October 1913, Vol. 2771, RG 10, LAC.
43 See chapter 8 for a detailed analysis of the court case and settlement.
44 Sir John Winnifrith, *The New England Company, 1890–1992* (New England Company, 1993), 103.
45 Memo from D. C. Scott, 25 June 1917, File 160-1, Pt. 1, Vol. 6039, RG 10, LAC.
46 Deputy Superintendent General to F. W. Jacobs, the Secretary of the Grand Indian Council of Ontario, 29 March 1917, File 493106, Vol. 3195, RG 10, LAC.
47 Statement of Indian Industrial Schools, Tabular Statements, Year Ended 31 March 1918, *Annual Report of the Department of Indian Affairs for the Year Ended 31 March 1918* (J. de L. Tache, 1918), 95 of tabular statements section.
48 Duncan C. Scott, Report of the Deputy Superintendent General, 31 October 1918, *Annual Report of the Department of Indian Affairs for the Year Ended 31 March 1918*, 11.
49 "A History of the Mohawk Institute," *Wadrihawa, Quarterly Newsletter of the Woodland Cultural Centre* 17–18, nos. 4 and 1 (June 2003): 7.
50 "A History of the Mohawk Institute."
51 Graham, *The Mush Hole*, 10.
52 See File 466-1, Pt. 1, Vol. 6200, RG 10, LAC. These descriptions were taken from various years during the period 1919–21.
53 Duncan C. Scott, Report of the Deputy Superintendent General, The Visit of His Royal Highness the Prince of Wales, 1 December 1919, *Annual Report of the Department of Indian Affairs for the Year Ended 31 March 1919* (J. de L. Tache, 1920), 7.
54 Scott, 33.
55 Scott, 33.
56 Scott, *Annual Report of the Department of Indian Affairs for the Year Ended 31 March 1930*, 19.
57 See report by Boyce, September–October 1921, File 466-1, Pt. 1, Vol. 6200, RG 10, LAC, and Boyce to Department of Indian Affairs [hereafter DIA], 4 November 1922, File 466-1, Pt. 1, Vol. 6200, RG 10, LAC. See also chapter 4 of this volume.
58 Gordon J. Smith, Superintendent to DIA, 23 December 1921, File 466-1, Pt. 1, Vol. 6200, RG 10, LAC.
59 A. Boyce, 20 June 1921, File 466-1, Pt. 1A, Vol. 6200, RG 10, LAC; Boyce, May–June Report, 1921, File 466-1, Pt. 1, Vol. 6200, RG 10, LAC.
60 A. Boyce, July–August Report, 1921, File 466-1, Pt. 1, Vol. 6200, RG 10, LAC.
61 Emily Pheasant to Boyce, 9 August 1921, File 466-1, Pt. 1, Vol. 6200, RG 10, LAC.
62 Gordon J. Smith, Superintendent, 30 January 1922, File 466-2, Pt. 1, Vol. 6200, RG 10, LAC.
63 "A History of the Mohawk Institute."
64 See File 466-1, Pt. 1, Vol. 6200, RG 10, LAC for correspondence that describes these issues.
65 Ann Boyce, September–October Report, 1921, File 466-1, Pt. 1, Vol. 6200, RG 10, LAC.

66   Report of Reverend T. Ferrier, 24–25 April 1906, File 468-1, Pt. 1, Vol. 6205, RG 10, LAC. See also Inspector Gordon J. Smith to Secretary, DIA, 16 July 1908, File 468-1, Pt. 1, Vol. 6205, RG 10, LAC. Finally, see Mary Jane Logan McCallum's book *Nii Ndahlohke: Boys' and Girls' Work at Mount Elgin Industrial School, 1890–1915* (Friesen Press, 2022).

67   The principal of Wikwemikong reported in 1904 that only 126 children were in attendance at the school even though it could hold 160. See *Annual Report of the Department of Indian Affairs for the Year Ended 30 June 1904*, 311. Likewise, by 1904 only 57 were in attendance at the Shingwauk school; of these, 19 were motherless, 9 were fatherless, and 17 were orphans. By 1910 only 37 remained. See *Annual Report of the Department of Indian Affairs for the Year Ended 30 June 1904*, 308, and *Annual Report of the Department of Indian Affairs for the Year Ended 31 March 1910*, 423.

68   See *Annual Reports of the Department of Indian Affairs* for the early years of the twentieth century. By 1918 the Mohawk Institute had 140 children in attendance. See *Annual Report of the Department of Indian Affairs for the Year Ended 31 March 1918*, 95.

69   Indian Department Memorandum, 13 December 1922, File 466-9, Pt. 1, Vol. 6201, RG 10, LAC.

70   See correspondence in File 466-1, Pt. 2, Vol. 6200, RG 10, LAC.

71   Schultz Brothers Company, 12 October 1922, File 466-5, Pt. 1, Vol. 6201, RG 10, LAC.

72   Duncan C. Scott, 8 January 1923, File 466-1, Pt. 1, Vol. 6200, RG 10, LAC.

73   Rogers, Sydney, Marriage, 13 December 1922, BX, P. 16, Col. 1, Boyce, Alice Mary (wife), *Brantford Expositor*.

74   Russell Ferrier to F. R. Bush, Charter Clerk, New England Company, 21 October 1924, File 466-1, Pt. 1, Vol. 6200, RG 10, LAC.

75   Duncan Campbell Scott, 13 September 1924, File 166-1, Pt. 1, Vol. 6200, RG 10, LAC.

76   Russell T. Ferrier claimed in 1924 that "we have discontinued the use of the words 'Boarding' and 'Industrial' in connection with out [sic] residential institutions. Indian schools are now divided into day and residential." See Russell T. Ferrier to M. C. MacLean, Assistant Chief of Education Statistics, 18 November 1924, File 1-1-1, Pt. 2, Vol. 6001, RG 10, LAC.

77   *Brantford Junior Expositor*, 20 December 1924.

78   Extract from Inspection Report, 7 November 1923, File 466-1, Pt. 1, Vol. 6200, RG 10, LAC.

79   In his report for January of 1923, classroom work appears, but in the following reports it is seldom mentioned. See Rogers's reports in File 466-1, Pt. 1, Vol. 6200, RG 10, LAC.

80   "Sister of Pauline Johnson Explains Trouble at the Reserve, Sends Open Letter, Declares Mohawks Want Chance for Higher Education," *Toronto Sunday World*, 18 November 1923.

81   Cecil E. Moran, Superintendent of Six Nations, 19 November 1923, File 466-1, Pt. 1, Vol. 6200, RG 10, LAC.

82   Col. Andrew T. Thompson, *Report by Col. Andrew T. Thompson, B. A., LL. B. Commissioner to Investigate and Enquire into the Affairs of the Six Nations Indians* (Printer to the King's Most Excellent Majesty, 1924), 5.

83   Thompson, 6.

84   Thompson, 7.

85   See Thompson, Report, Supplementary Report, 20–5.

86   See student interviews from this era in Graham, *The Mush Hole*.

87   Sydney Rogers, 7 April 1924, File 466-1, Pt. 1, Vol. 6200, RG 10, LAC.

88   S. Tapscott and Co. order form, 29 December 1929, File 466-1-13, Pt. 1, Vol. 6202, RG 10, LAC; Ingram Bell statement, 9 January 1925, File 466-1, Pt. 1, Vol. 6200, RG 10, LAC.

89   Sydney Rogers, 8 October 1925, File 466-1, Pt. 1, Vol. 6200, RG 10, LAC.

90   Sydney Rogers, 5 January 1926, File 466-1, Pt. 1, Vol. 6200, RG 10, LAC.

91   Sydney Rogers, 30 June 1929, File 466-1, Pt. 2, Vol. 6200, RG 10, LAC.

92   Sydney Rogers, 10 April 1923, File 466-1, Pt. 1, Vol. 6200, RG 10, LAC.

93   Sydney Rogers, 19 May 1925, File 466-1, Pt. 1, Vol. 6200, RG 10, LAC.

94   A. Rogers in Thompson, Report, Supplementary Report, 22.

95   A. Rogers in Thompson, 22.

96   Alison Norman, "'True to My Own Noble Race': Six Nations Women Teachers at Grand River in the Early Twentieth Century," *Ontario History* 107, no. 1 (2018): 18, https://doi.org/10.7202/1050677ar.

97   Norman, 19.

98 New England Company Governor, 27 July 1928, File 466-1, Pt. 2, Vol. 6200, RG 10, LAC.
99 New England Company Governor, 27 July 1928, 14 January 1929, File 466-1, Pt. 2, Vol. 6200, RG 10, LAC.
100 Russell T. Ferrier, 9 April 1926, File 466-5, Pt. 2, Vol. 6201, RG 10, LAC.
101 See Wendy Fletcher, "A Canadian Experiment with Social Engineering, a Historical Case: The Mohawk Institute," *Historical Papers 2004: Canadian Society of Church History* (2004): 136, https://doi.org/10.25071/0848-1563.39276; and Report to D. C. Scott, 23 May 1929, File 466-1, Pt. 2, Vol. 6200, RG 10, LAC.
102 John L. Tobias, "Protection, Civilization, Assimilation: An Outline History of Canada's Indian Policy," in *As Long as the Sun Shines and Water Flows: A Reader in Canadian Native Studies*, ed. Ian A. Getty and Antoine S. Lussier (University of British Columbia Press, 1988), 51; Rev. H. W. Snell, "The Mohawk Institute," *The Eagle*, July 1930, in File 466-1, Pt. 2, Vol. 6200, RG 10, LAC.
103 Hoffman, *A Summary of Findings from Departmental Files and Selected Secondary Sources Related to Indian Residential School Policy*, 50.
104 See File 466-5, Pt. 4, Vol. 6201, RG 10, LAC, and File 466-1, Pt. 2, Vol. 6200, RG 10, LAC.
105 See File 466-5, Pt. 4, Vol. 6201, RG 10, LAC.
106 Russell Ferrier, 14 March 1930, File 466-1, Pt. 2, Vol. 6200, RG 10, LAC.
107 *Brantford Expositor*, 16 May 1936.
108 Rev. H. W. Snell, "The Mohawk Institute," *The Eagle*, July 1930, in File 466-1, Pt. 2, Vol. 6200, RG 10, LAC.
109 Truth and Reconciliation Commission, *Final Report of the Truth and Reconciliation Commission of Canada*, vol. 1, *Canada's Residential Schools: The History, Part 1, Origins to 1939* (McGill-Queen's University Press, 2015), 343.
110 Philip Phelan, Chief of Training Division, 20 October 1944, File 466-1, Pt. 3, Vol. 6200, RG 10, LAC.
111 James E. Deley, Indian agent for Walpole Island to DIA, October 1941, File 466-5, Pt. 3, Vol. 6201, RG 10, LAC.
112 Mohawk Institute Report, 13 October 1934, File 466-1, Pt. 2, Vol. 6200, RG 10, LAC.
113 Mohawk Institute Investigation Report, 12 November 1934, File 466-1, Pt. 2, Vol. 6200, RG 10, LAC
114 Rev. H. W. Snell, "The Mohawk Institute," *The Eagle*, July 1930, File 466-1, Pt. 2, Vol. 6200, RG 10, LAC2.
115 Horace Snell, 26 October 1936, File 466-1, Pt. 3, Vol. 6200, RG 10, LAC.
116 H. H. Craig, lawyer of Ross Chrysler, 29 July 1937, File 466-1, Pt. 3, Vol. 6200, RG 10, LAC.
117 Horace Snell, 11 August 1937, File 466-1, Pt. 3, Vol. 6200, RG 10, LAC.
118 R. A. Hoey to Reverend S. R. McVitty, 7 November 1941, File 1-1-1, Pt. 4, Vol. 6001, RG 10, LAC.
119 Truth and Reconciliation Commission, *Final Report of the Truth and Reconciliation Commission of Canada*, vol. 1, *Canada's Residential Schools: The History, Part 2, 1939 to 2000* (McGill-Queen's University Press, 2015), 49.
120 New England Company to the Department, 16 June 1943, File 466-1, Pt. 3, Vol. 6200, RG 10, LAC.
121 See Fletcher, "A Canadian Experiment with Social Engineering," 137.
122 R. A. Hoey, Superintendent of Welfare and Training, 9 November 1942, File 466-1, Pt. 3, Vol. 6200, RG 10, LAC.
123 See File 466-1, Pt. 4, Vol. 6200, RG 10, LAC for correspondence regarding the potential appointment of Hill as principal.
124 Canada, *House of Commons Debates*, 20th Parl., 2nd Sess., Vol. 5 (27 August 1946), 5489.
125 J. R. Miller, "The Irony of Residential Schooling," *Canadian Journal of Native Education* 14, no. 2 (1987): 9.
126 See Canada, Parliament, House of Commons, Special Joint Committee of the Senate and the House of Commons on the Indian Act, *Minutes of Proceedings of Evidence*, 1946–8, 20th Parl., 2nd Sess., Meeting No. 1, 1946.
127 Tobias, "Protection, Civilization, Assimilation," 52.
128 See Philip Phelan, 13 September 1950, File 466-1, Pt. 6, Vol. 6202, RG 10, LAC.
129 Report of Bernard F. Neary, Superintendent of Welfare and Training, 29 October 1946, File 466-5, Pt. 5, Vol. 6201, RG 10, LAC.
130 Harold Palmer to C. P. Randle, 20 July 1946, File 466-3, Pt. 1, Vol. 6200, RG 10, LAC.
131 W. L. Falconer, 2 June 1948, File 466-1, Pt. 5, Vol. 6200, RG 10, LAC.
132 Infections were so common that part of the admission process required that a child be tested for disease. See File 466-13, Pt. 2, Vol. 6202, RG 10, LAC.

133 "A History of the Mohawk Institute," 6.
134 *Brantford Expositor*, 22 February 1946.
135 "Probe Ordered into Affairs of Indian School," *Globe and Mail*, 23 February 1946, 5.
136 "Denies Anglicans Are Responsible," *Globe and Mail*, 25 February 1946.
137 See unidentified newspaper article "Church Not Responsible for Upkeep of Institute," hand-dated 23 February 1946, in File 466-1, Pt. 4, Vol. 6200, RG 10, LAC.
138 See unidentified newspaper article, "Say Criticism of Institute Unfounded," 20 March 1946, 7, in File 466-1, Pt. 4, Vol. 6200, RG 10, LAC.
139 *Brantford Expositor*, 15 March 1950.
140 See unidentified newspaper article, "L. C. W Reply Re Findings of Grand Jury," n.d., File 466-1, Pt. 4, Vol. 6200, RG 10, LAC.
141 Truth and Reconciliation Commission, *Final Report*, vol. 1, pt. 2:338.
142 E. Randle, Indian Superintendent, 25 March 1949, File 466-10, Pt. 6, Vol. 6202, RG 10, LAC; Bernard F. Neary, Superintendent of Education, 9 April 1949, File 466-10, Pt. 6, Vol. 6202, RG 10, LAC.
143 Punishment Regulations by Superintendent of Welfare and Training, 15 December 1947, File 466-1, Pt. 5, Vol. 6200, RG 10, LAC; W. J. Zimmerman to DIA, 6 December 1947, File 466-1, Pt. 5, Vol. 6200, RG 10, LAC.
144 See the experience recounted by one student, known to us only as Gary, in *Brantford Expositor*, 6 July 1991.
145 Truth and Reconciliation Commission, *Final Report*, vol. 1, pt. 2:368.
146 Hoffman, *A Summary of Findings from Departmental Files and Selected Secondary Sources Related to Indian Residential School Policy*, 47.
147 Truth and Reconciliation Commission, *Final Report*, vol. 1, pt. 2:19.
148 Truth and Reconciliation Commission, 111.
149 Truth and Reconciliation Commission, 137.
150 Hoffman, *A Summary of Findings from Departmental Files and Selected Secondary Sources Related to Indian Residential School Policy*, 47.
151 Hoffman, 39.
152 H. B. Hawthorn, ed., *A Survey of the Contemporary Indians of Canada: A Report on Economic, Political, Educational Needs and Policies in Two Volumes* (Indian Affairs Branch, 1967), 2:30.
153 Hawthorn, 2:12.
154 Deirdre F. Jordan, "Education and the Reclaiming of Identity: Rights and Claims of Canadian Indians, Norwegian Sami, and Australian Aborigines," in *Arduous Journey: Canadian Indians and Decolonization*, ed. J. Rick Ponting (McClelland and Stewart, 1988), 267.
155 Graham, *The Mush Hole*, 22.
156 Barman et al., *Indian Education in Canada*, 13.
157 See Hoffman *A Summary of Findings from Departmental Files and Selected Secondary Sources Related to Indian Residential School Policy*, 11.
158 Truth and Reconciliation Commission, *Final Report*, vol. 1, pt. 2:93.
159 *Brantford Expositor*, 10 June 1970.
160 *Brantford Expositor*, 3 November 1971.
161 Education Division letter in Hoffman, *A Summary of Findings from Departmental Files and Selected Secondary Sources Related to Indian Residential School Policy*, 48.
162 Donna Duric, Lynda Powless, and Chase Jarrett, "'Mush-Hole Kids' Finally Get to Tell Their Story to History," *Turtle Island News*, 29 August 2012, https://vitacollections.ca/sixnationsarchive/3247590/data; Michelle Ruby, "Save the Evidence Campaign Reaches $23.5-Million Goal," *Brantford Expositor*, 26 April 2002.
163 "Mohawk Institute," Engracia De Jesus Matias Archives and Special Collections, Algoma University, accessed 1 March 2024, http://archives.algomau.ca/main/?q=taxonomy/term/1022.
164 See "Institute Now History" article reproduced in "50th Anniversary of the Closure of the Mohawk Institute Residential School," Woodland Cultural Centre, 29 June 2020, https://woodlandculturalcentre.ca/50th-anniversary-of-the-closure-of-the-mohawk-institute-residential-school/.
165 "Mohawk Institute," Engracia De Jesus Matias Archives and Special Collections, Algoma University.

166 Letter from Six Nations Council, Office of the Secretary, signed by Council Clerk M. Bloomfield to the Department of Public Records and Archives, ℅ C. Thorpe, 10 March 1972, File—Mohawk Institute, 1831, Ontario Heritage Trust Archives. See Cody Groat's chapter in this volume for further information about the plaque and how the schools has been commemorated.

167 Naohiro Nakamura, "Indigenous Cultural Self-Representation and Its Internal Critiques: A Case Study of the Woodland Cultural Centre, Canada," *Diaspora, Indigenous and Minority Education* 8 no. 3 (2014): 148.

168 See "About Us," Woodland Culture Centre, accessed 31 October 2024, https://woodlandculturalcentre.ca/about/.

169 Numerous schools had been demolished, including the Lower Post Residential School, the Coqualeetza Institute, St. Michael's Residential School, and Isle La Crosse School, among others.

170 Douglas George Kanentioo in Mike Peeling, "Brant News' Community Hero Award: Save the Evidence Campaign," *Indian Time* (reprinted from *Brant News*), 5 January 2017, https://www.indiantime.net/story/2017/01/05/news/brant-news-community-hero-award-save-the-evidence-campaign/23414.html.

171 Peeling, "Brant News' Community Hero Award."

172 Ruby, "Save the Evidence Campaign Reaches $23.5-Million Goal."

173 See Ry Moran, "Tear Down Residential Schools, or Keep Them as Memorials? Communities Should Decide," *Tyee*, 12 January 2021, https://thetyee.ca/Analysis/2021/01/12/Community-Choice-Tear-Down-Or-Keep-Residential-Schools/; Carling Beninger, "Implementing TRC Call to Action #79: Commemoration of Indian Residential School Sites," *Active History*, 30 September 2017, https://activehistory.ca/blog/2017/09/30/implementing-trc-call-to-action-79-commemoration-of-indian-residential-school-sites/.

174 See chapter 7 for a more detailed analysis of preservation and commemoration at the Mohawk Institute.

175 Parks Canada, "Residential Schools in Canada," Government of Canada, last modified 23 July 2024, https://parks.canada.ca/culture/designation/pensionnat-residential.

176 Parks Canada, "Residential Schools in Canada."

177 "Mohawk Institute a Historic Site," *Turtle Island News*, 16 April 2014, 4, https://vitacollections.ca/sixnationsarchive/3247331/data .

178 See Graham, *The Mush Hole.*

179 Graham, 25.

180 See chapter 13 of this volume.

181 See chapter 14 of this volume.

182 Canada, 37th Parl., 1st Sess., Standing Committee on Aboriginal Affairs, Northern Development and Natural Resources, meeting 43, presentation by John Leslie, research consultant, 12 March 2002.

183 See, for instance, Fontaine's interview with CBC's *The Journal*, which aired 30 October 1990.

184 See Peter G. Bush, "The Canadian Churches' Apologies for Colonialism and Residential Schools, 1986–1998," *Canadian Journal of Peace and Conflict Studies* 47, no. 102 (2015): 47–70.

185 See Canada, Royal Commission on Aboriginal Peoples, *Report of the Royal Commission on Aboriginal Peoples* (Royal Commission on Aboriginal Peoples, 1996). The report comprises five volumes.

186 Facing History and Ourselves, *Stolen Lives: The Indigenous Peoples of Canada and the Indian Residential Schools* (Facing History and Ourselves, 2015), 11.

187 John Milloy, *A National Crime: The Canadian Government and the Residential School System, 1879 to 1986* (University of Manitoba Press, 1999). Milloy's title comes from Peter Bryce's 1922 work of the same name, which focused on the deplorable conditions in residential schools.

188 See Fletcher, "A Canadian Experiment with Social Engineering," 138.

189 See Fletcher, 145.

190 See Canada, Royal Commission on Aboriginal Peoples, *Round Table on Residential Schools* (CD-ROM record), George Erasmus, 18 March 1993.

191 Truth and Reconciliation Commission, *Final Report of the Truth and Reconciliation Commission of Canada*, vol. 5, *Canada's Residential Schools: The Legacy* (McGill-Queen's University Press, 2015), 3.

192 See Lynda Powless, "'Mush-Hole' $900 Million Survivor Suit Sparks Memories," *Turtle Island News*, 14 October 1998.

193 Truth and Reconciliation Commission, *Final Report*, vol. 1, pt. 2:568.

194   Crown-Indigenous Relations and Northern Affairs Canada, "Indian Residential Schools Settlement Agreement," Government of Canada, last modified 9 June 2021, https://www.rcaanc-cirnac.gc.ca/eng/1100100015576/1571581687074.

195   Crown-Indigenous Relations and Northern Affairs Canada, "Statistics on the Implementation of the Indian Residential Schools Settlement Agreement," Government of Canada, last modified 19 February 2019, https://www.rcaanc-cirnac.gc.ca/eng/1315320539682/1571590489978.

196   Andrew Woolford, *This Benevolent Experiment: Indigenous Boarding Schools, Genocide, and Redress in Canada and the United States* (University of Manitoba Press, 2015), 287.

197   Stephen Harper, on behalf of the Government of Canada, "Statement of Apology to Former Students of Indian Residential Schools," Government of Canada, last modified 15 September 2010, https://www.rcaanc-cirnac.gc.ca/eng/1100100015644/1571589171655.

198   Duric et al., "'Mush-Hole Kids' Finally Get to Tell Their Story to History."

199   Truth and Reconciliation Commission, *Final Report*, vol. 1, pt. 2:29.

200   See Brieg Capitaine and Karine Vanthuyne, eds., *Power Through Testimony: Reframing Residential Schools in the Age of Reconciliation* (UBC Press, 2017), for a discussion of whether the TRC will be able to change colonial thinking about residential schools and alter the relationship between Indigenous peoples and Canadian society.

201   See Crown-Indigenous Relations and Northern Affairs Canada, "Truth and Reconciliation Commission of Canada," Government of Canada, last modified 28 May 2024, https://www.rcaanc-cirnac.gc.ca/eng/1450124405592/1529106060525, and Truth and Reconciliation Commission of Canada, *Honouring the Truth, Reconciling for the Future: Summary of the Final Report of the Truth and Reconciliation Commission of Canada* (Truth and Reconciliation Commission of Canada, 2015). See also Arthur Manuel and Ronald Derrickson, *Unsettling Canada: A National Wake-Up Call* (Between the Lines, 2015), for a discussion of how Canada is grappling with the place of Indigenous peoples in Canadian society.

202   National Centre for Truth and Reconciliation, *A Knock on the Door: The Essential History of Residential Schools from the Truth and Reconciliation Commission of Canada*, edited and Abridged version (University of Manitoba Press, 2016), 4. Residential schools were only part of the policy of cultural genocide—other aspects include the pass system, treaties, and the ban on ceremonies such as the Sun Dance and potlatch, etc.

203   Agnes Grant, *No End of Grief: Indian Residential Schools in Canada* (Pemmican Publications Inc., 1996), 269.

204   See Marie Battiste, *Decolonizing Education, Nourishing the Learning Spirit* (Purich, 2013), for a discussion of the potential of new models of education.

205   Richard Raycraft, "MPs Back Motion Calling on Government to Recognize Residential Schools Program as Genocide," *CBC News*, last updated 28 October 2022, https://www.cbc.ca/news/politics/house-motion-recognize-genocide-1.6632450.

206   Tk'emlúps te Secwépemc (Kamloops Indian Band), Office of the Chief, press release, 27 May 2021, https://tkemlups.ca/wp-content/uploads/05-May-27-2021-TteS-MEDIA-RELEASE.pdf.

207   See Crown-Indigenous Relations and Northern Affairs Canada, "Missing Children and Burial Information," Government of Canada, last modified 24 May 2024, https://www.rcaanc-cirnac.gc.ca/eng/1524504992259/1557512149981.

208   See, for example, Crystal Gail Fraser, "Residential School Denialism Is an Attack on the truth," *Conversation*, 3 July 2024, https://theconversation.com/residential-school-denialism-is-an-attack-on-the-truth-233318, and Sean Carleton, "We Fact-Checked Residential School Denialists and Debunked Their 'Mass Grave Hoax' Theory," *Conversation*, 17 October 2023, https://theconversation.com/we-fact-checked-residential-school-denialists-and-debunked-their-mass-grave-hoax-theory-213435.

209   Tristin Hopper, "B. C. First Nation Now Referring to 215 Suspected Graves as 'Anomalies' Instead of 'Children,'" *National Post*, 28 May 2024, https://nationalpost.com/opinion/tkemlups-te-secwepemc-first-nation-graves-kamloops.

210   Daniel Schwartz, "Truth and Reconciliation Commission: By the Numbers," *CBC News*, 2 June 2015, https://www.cbc.ca/news/indigenous/truth-and-reconciliation-commission-by-the-numbers-1.3096185.

211   "Our Story," Survivors' Secretariat, accessed 30 October 2024, https://survivorssecretariat.ca/our-story/.

212   "New Report Urges Federal Government to Stay True to Its Commitment to the Missing Children of Indian Residential Schools," Survivors' Secretariat, press release, 30 September 2024, https://survivorssecretariat.ca/pressreleases/new-report-urges-federal-government-to-stay-true-to-its-commitment-to-themissing-children-of-indian-residential-schools/.

PART 2
Teachers, Curriculum, and Tools of Control

Figure 0.6. Mohawk Institute students
Source: Richard Hill Collection

3

The Indian Normal School: The Role of the Mohawk Institute in the Training of Indigenous Teachers in the Late Nineteenth Century

Alison Norman

This chapter will investigate how educating children to become teachers was a priority for Mohawk Institute principals the Reverends Abraham Nelles and Robert Ashton. Both identified high-performing students with an interest in education careers and helped them attend secondary school and sometimes post-secondary school. They supported their efforts to build a career in teaching at day schools in reserves across the province, as well as occasionally at the Institute itself. While Nelles helped students get funding for higher education, Ashton created a teaching certificate at the Mohawk Institute. Both actions resulted in students obtaining the necessary education and certification to teach, and the students' own efforts led to significant teaching careers for many of the graduates. Ashton's program was quite possibly the first and only teacher education program in a residential school in Canada. Teaching was a popular choice for graduates of the school, so much so that, at the end of the nineteenth century, the twelve day schools on the reserve were filled with teachers who had trained at the Mohawk Institute. The New England Company (NEC) and the Department of Indian Affairs (DIA) trusted these graduates to play an important role in the efforts to provide a Christian and Western education for Indigenous children.

The Early Decades, 1828–1850s

Initially, as the NEC was establishing the Mohawk Institute and the day schools on the reserve at Grand River, the Company hired mostly non-Indigenous male teachers to staff the schools. The teachers usually had experience in England and came to Upper Canada to work at the mission-run schools. However, over time, the Company realized that Haudenosaunee teachers from within Six Nations might be effective teachers at these schools. The reasons were practical: They believed Haudenosaunee teachers who spoke Haudenosaunee languages, and who understood the students, would be most efficient and effective in teaching them. These teachers were also more likely to stay in their jobs, whereas non-Indigenous teachers often left to return to England or other parts of the Canadas. The NEC had earlier used this strategy of training local students to become teachers in other Company schools in New England.[1] In general, graduates of the schools were seen as potential role models and people who could help with the Christianization of the community. For instance, when the bishop of Toronto visited the missions and schools on the reserve, he noted that "it was most gratifying to observe so many of the rising generation of this interesting people receiving instruction which qualifies them to impart the same to others; and to improve themselves and others in the social arts of a civilized and christian [sic] life."[2] Over time, an increasing number of graduates would become teachers, and the Mohawk Institute played a particular role in training and supporting its students to become teachers.

As early as 1837, on a tour of the Mohawk Institute, Hannah Nelles, wife of the Reverend Abraham Nelles, advised lay agent William Richardson from the NEC that some of the girls at the school "might become very useful in the education of children in their respective neighbourhoods." She believed that the girls should have more time to study and argued that they should be exempt from "menial duties," and that the school would "endeavour to qualify them for higher duties."[3] It does not seem that they actually became teachers, however, as the day schools and the Institute had non-Indigenous teachers in this period, and there is no evidence in the records that girls were provided with time for training.[4] In the early decades, Richardson spoke of admitting more girls to help with "instructing in the Institute."[5] He noted in 1838 that they were "very desirous of completing the education of at least a few [girls], that they may be qualified to instruct the younger children."[6]

Despite Richardson's suggestions, the school instead focused its efforts on training the boys for future careers. At the time, the school was known as the Mechanics' Institute, and boys were provided with training in things like shoemaking, cabinetry, wagon making, and blacksmithing. The school acquired funds from the NEC to supply these students with tools upon graduation, helped them find work as apprentices, and supported them in establishing their own businesses. While the Company had brought in girls around the same time with the aim of them becoming teachers, the records show that this did not actually happen. Nelles's report of July 1844 describes the lives and the careers of students who had left the institution. Seven female graduates are described, none of whom were teachers. While the idea had been brought forth, in reality, girls generally received an education in skills to be used within the home: "House-keeping, Needlework, Spinning and Knitting."[7] These skills were taught so that the girls could help produce clothing for students at the school, thereby keeping costs down.[8] They were also skills believed to be useful for a farmwife.

At the time, in the 1840s, there was one Haudenosaunee teacher working in a day school at Six Nations, Lawrence Davids. He was likely the first Haudenosaunee teacher to teach in the NEC day schools. It is unclear from the records if Davids had himself attended the Mohawk Institute, but it is very possible, as he would have had to have had an excellent command of the English language and the subjects to be taught in the day schools, as well as the respect of the NEC, in order to be employed by the Company.[9] In 1842, Nelles hired Davids, who had been teaching elsewhere on the reserve, to teach in a new school that had just been established in the Council House at the Delaware Settlement. Nelles noted that Davids was to "prepare the way for a white teacher; he is competent to instruct them in the rudiments of learning, and possesses advantages over any white man unacquainted with Indian habits, which qualify him for commencing a school among Indians who have scarcely given up their prejudices against Christianity."[10] Davids was seen as successful in his teaching, but Nelles believed his teaching knowledge was limited: "I think it probably [sic] that a white teacher will be required here before long."[11] Davids was seen as particularly useful as the first teacher when a new school was to be established. Nelles considered having him teach at a school being planned among the Cayuga: "If the Cayugas, who are becoming more favourably disposed, will consent to have a school, I will send Lawrence to them; the old man will do better to commence a school among them than a white person."[12] This did not come to pass, however. Davids retired in 1844, and the NEC granted him a pension of twelve pounds per year "in consideration of his past services as one of the Company's Schoolmasters."[13]

Less evidence is available about the schools in the late 1840s and '50s due to a lack of records, but by 1859, four graduates of the Mohawk Institute had become teachers. Nelles noted that having Indigenous teachers at local day schools aided in the success of the project to educate Haudenosaunee children on the reserve: "It is satisfactory to observe an increasing desire on the part of the Indians to have their children educated. . . . This improved state of feeling among the Indians is probably chiefly brought about by the influence of those who have been educated at the Company's schools, of whom four are now engaged as School Teachers, five as Catechists, besides many others who render much useful assistance both to Mr. Elliot and myself, by their advice and example."[14] Those teachers included James Styres (Cayuga), Thomas Thomas (Tuscarora), and Isaac Bearfoot (Onondaga), all of whom attended the Mohawk Institute as students.[15] In 1860, after Frederick Augustus O'Meara visited the Mohawk Institute and the day schools on behalf of the NEC, he commented on the effectiveness of the teachers he encountered there:

> I was struck by the difference between the schools which are taught by Indian-speaking masters, and those the teachers of which do not understand the language of their pupils. In the former the pupils evidently understood what they were learning, so as to give an intelligent account in their own language of the lesson that they were reading or learning in English; which was by no means the case in those of which the masters and pupils had no common medium of communication.[16]

The Company saw the value in having Haudenosaunee teachers who could effectively communicate with their students in both their native languages and in English. They also noted that they could sometimes pay Indigenous teachers less: "the best and cheapest teachers for them would be Indians brought up at the Institution; and perhaps sent afterwards for a year to a good school for teachers, like the Normal School in Toronto."[17]

Both the NEC and its local missionaries, including the Reverends Nelles, Elliott, and Roberts, believed in graduating students from the Mohawk Institute to become teachers in local day schools, and sometimes at the Mohawk Institute itself. But they also realized that further education for these students was needed. In 1870, the Company noted that teachers at the day schools and the Mohawk Institute should ideally take a course at the Toronto Normal School, but that such instruction should not be required, as it would be difficult for all current teachers to attend. Rather, gradually over time, students should be selected and sent to Toronto to train as teachers.[18]

In September 1870, the commissioner of the NEC, A. E. Botsford, toured Six Nations, and his comments provide information on the teachers working in schools at the time, the vast majority of whom had attended the Mohawk Institute.[19] James Hill (Mohawk) was teaching at the No. 2 School. Alexander Smith (Mohawk) was teaching at the No. 3 School. It had formerly been taught by Isaac Bearfoot, also an Institute graduate. The No. 4 School was taught by Elizabeth Martin Powless (Mohawk) who had attended a day school herself and then finished her education at the Institute.[20] The No. 5 School was taught by Daniel Simon (Lenape/Delaware) who had graduated from the Mohawk Institute and had previously been taught by Albert Anthony (Lenape/Delaware), another graduate. The No. 6 School was taught by Mrs. Yagoweia Loft Beaver (Mohawk), who was raised and educated at Tyendinaga and moved to Grand River to marry and work.[21] No. 8 School was taught by Isaiah Joseph (Tuscarora), a graduate of the Mohawk Institute who spoke Kanyen'kéhaka (Mohawk). Botsford noted that Bearfoot, Smith, Powless, Simon, Beaver, Joseph, and Hill "are capable of conversing with their pupils in their own dialects." He added,

> No doubt it is in some respects an advantage for the teacher to be able to explain to the children, when first sent to school, in their own language, what is being taught to them; still, as one of the first and most essential things to be taught the Indian pupils is to speak English, and in a manner to forget their own tongue, it is by no means absolutely necessary that the teacher should possess a knowledge of the dialects of the Six Nations Indians.[22]

So, while the schools had teachers who were from within the community, spoke the languages, and had attended school on the reserve themselves, often at the Mohawk Institute, most had not had additional training to become teachers. This began to change with the establishment of colleges in nearby London, Ontario.

Huron College, Hellmuth College, and Hellmuth Ladies' College and the Mohawk Institute

In 1869, the NEC began providing grants for a select few graduates of the Mohawk Institute, as chosen by the missionaries, to attend college in London, Ontario. These included Huron College, Hellmuth College, and Hellmuth Ladies' College, each school under the direction of Isaac Hellmuth and each a precursor to Western University, which was founded by Hellmuth about a decade later. The goal for these students was generally a career in either education or the ministry, jobs that would further the mission of the NEC. Sometimes graduates were chosen to receive further education to become a teacher, while other times, Mohawk Institute graduates who had already become teachers in reserve schools were chosen to be able to further their education, generally with the aim of joining the Anglican Church. The Reverend Abraham Nelles made recommendations to the NEC as to who should be provided with funding to further their education based on who he believed would benefit from such an education and was interested in going. As a result, discussions as to the academic careers and potential imagined futures of these students exist in the records of the NEC reports. Students were often chosen because they were seen to be "deserving" of higher education, but also because they were interested in a career as a teacher or minister, both callings of which the NEC and the Anglican Church were supportive.

Albert Anthony (Lenape/Delaware) was one of the first to receive such support. He attended the Mohawk Institute for some time; he is listed in the attendance records for 1859 as being nineteen years old.[23] He graduated that year, and began working as a teacher in a reserve school.[24] In the late 1860s, he taught at the No. 5 School.[25] Anthony might have been considering a career in medicine, as he took a twelve-month surgery course at the University of Toronto.[26] In 1869, though, he was chosen by the bishop of Huron, Benjamin Cronyn, to attend the newly created Huron College with an eye toward becoming a minister. After three years at the college, Anthony was ordained and became an interpreter to a reserve missionary before becoming a missionary himself and working for many years on the reserve, especially with the Lenape community. He no longer worked as a teacher, but later in life he published a Lenape dictionary, and education seems to have remained a part of his career.[27]

A year after Anthony was chosen to attend Huron, Mohawk Institute graduates Susannah Carpenter and Nelles A. Monture were chosen to

Figure 3.1 Albert Anthony
Source: Cronyn Archives, Diocese of Huron

attend, respectively, Hellmuth Ladies' College and Hellmuth College. Both became teachers in day schools in the community after graduating. Susanna (Mohawk) was the daughter of the interpreter for the Reverend James Chance at St. Paul's Anglican Church on the reserve; after Susanna's father passed away, Chance advocated for her education, and in particular, her efforts to become a teacher. He wrote that the goal of her education at Hellmuth was training "to qualify her . . . [as] an efficient and useful teacher among her own people on the Reserve."[28] She was fluent in Kanyen'kéhaka and English, which was seen as helpful for a teacher on the reserve.[29] After graduating, Chance wrote that she was "fully competent to undertake the duties of the best school on the Reserve." He added, "It is most reasonable to expect that, after Miss Carpenter has enjoyed all the advantages of Hellmuth Ladies College during a period of three years, from which College she has received valuable prizes, she is competent to teach school." By October 1872, she was teaching at the No. 8 School on the reserve.[30]

Nelles Monture (Lenape/Delaware) was a top student at the Mohawk Institute, and after attending Hellmuth College, he found a position as a teacher at the No. 5 School at Six Nations.[31] Monture was later a Delaware chief of the Six Nations who became well-known beyond the community when, in 1898, he addressed the Ontario Historical Society and spoke of the loyalty of the Six Nations to the British Crown.[32]

Isaac Bearfoot (Onondaga) was also chosen by the NEC to attend Huron College. Like Albert Anthony, he was a graduate of the Mohawk Institute who worked as a teacher and then acquired further education to become a minister. He attended the Mohawk Institute at the same time as Anthony, graduating from the school in the same year, 1859. A couple of years later, he went to Toronto to attend the Normal School.[33] He may have been the first Haudenosaunee person to do so. He then began teaching at a local reserve day school, No. 3.[34] In 1869, he was hired to teach at the Mohawk Institute, the first Indigenous person to do so. His language skills were recognized by the school, which continued to find it useful to have teachers who spoke local Indigenous languages.[35] Bearfoot held a senior teaching position at the Mohawk Institute for several years until 1876, when he attended Huron College, with NEC support, with the aim of becoming a minister. He was ordained a deacon in May 1877 and a priest in June 1878.[36] After working at several parishes across southern Ontario, he returned to Grand River to take charge of St. Paul's Anglican Church (Kanyengeh) in 1888.[37] In 1890 he became superintendent of education at Grand River, inspecting all of the day schools on the reserve, and reporting to the Six Nations School Board.[38] He held that position until 1907, when the board dismissed him and replaced him with a (non-Indigenous) inspector they deemed to be more qualified.[39] Given all of his experience as a teacher, clergyman, and superintendent, Bearfoot had perhaps one of the most influential careers in Anglican education at Grand River.

Figure 3.2. The Reverend Isaac Bearfoot, Christ Church
Source: Cronyn Archives, Diocese of Huron

Teaching Beyond Six Nations

The school also played a role in informally training students who wished to teach. Lydia Hill was a young Mohawk woman from the community of Tyendinaga. In the late 1860s, she spent six months at the Mohawk Institute "preparing herself for teaching."[40] Although there was no specific teaching training program at the time, this may have been the precursor to Ashton's teaching certificate, which was to come in the 1880s. After leaving the Mohawk Institute, Lydia Hill was hired to teach at what was known as the Upper Mohawk School in Tyendinaga in 1870.[41] Hill taught there for several years in the 1870s, but then her teaching career ended, perhaps because she was paid significantly less than non-Indigenous teachers on the reserve.[42] She travelled through Western Canada and to England, taught Sunday school, and was the organist for All Saints Anglican Church.[43]

While the Mohawk Institute generally housed children from Six Nations, children from other communities in the lower Great Lakes also attended in this period, and some of them also used their education to become teachers after leaving the school. In a 1930 list of "successful graduates," several students from the 1870s were identified as teachers, but it is unclear if they remained in the role for very long. For instance, Lucius Henry and Moses Walker both left the school in 1876. According to the 1930 list, Henry taught at the Ojibwe school in Munsey, and Walker taught at Moraviantown and at Chippeway Hill. John Schuyler and Louis Scanada also both left the Mohawk Institute in 1876, and both taught at Oneida. In 1876 Amelia Checkock taught at Muncey Town, at Stone Ridge, and at Shawanaga near Parry Sound.[44] Adam Sickles left in 1879 and taught at Moraviantown.[45]

Scobie Logan is perhaps the most well-known of this group of students.[46] He graduated in 1878 and initially taught at Muncey before beginning a career as a councillor and leader for the community.[47] In 1882, he travelled to England to petition Queen Victoria to settle a land claim for the Munsees of the Thames. A few years later, he served as secretary-treasurer of the Grand Council of Indians of Ontario, an important leadership role in an organization fighting against discriminatory Indian status legislation.[48] In 1920, Principal Boyce noted that Logan had written to the Mohawk Institute in 1920 when he was chief at Munsey to express his concern that the school could close down, and stated that he owed his start in life to the school; it is unlikely that one letter accurately conveys his potentially complex views on the school.[49] No other non-Haudenosaunee students are listed as becoming teachers in this period or later.

Policy Changes

Despite having several graduates attend Huron College and the Hellmuth Colleges, there was discussion in the 1870s among the NEC that perhaps the Company's money might be better spent on the Mohawk Institute itself, rather than on tuition for pupils at post-secondary schools beyond Brantford. A plan was thus developed for the use of Company money to fund the Mohawk Institute and send graduates to the Normal School in Toronto.[50] Though Nelles had been supportive of sending graduates to college, the Reverend James Chance, missionary at Six Nations, believed the money should be spent on the Institute itself, an opinion the NEC shared. An April 1872 NEC report notes that "the education given on the Reserve and at the Institution should be sufficient for all classes of Indian pupils, and that the practice of sending them to the highest schools and colleges in the Dominion as a general rule be discontinued; and that, for teachers, the Toronto Training School is the best preparation."[51] Nelles retired in late 1872; in the same year Bishop Cronyn passed away. He had been involved in the founding of Huron College and in having Mohawk Institute graduates attend. With the hiring of Robert Ashton as principal of the Mohawk Institute, the NEC had support for its idea to cease funding students to leave the school. Ashton worked to improve the education at the school, and then later developed a program whereby graduates could train as teachers at the Mohawk Institute itself.

New regulations for the school were developed by the NEC and published in 1872. The Institute's stated aim was "to impart such an education as shall fit its pupils for teachers amongst their own people, at the same time training them in the arts and practices of civilized nations."[52] Ashton, like Nelles before him, worked toward this goal, identifying students he thought would make good teachers. Ashton was not always successful in choosing new teachers. For instance, in March 1873, he noted in his journal that he helped Phoebe Snake, a nineteen-year-old graduate, find work as a domestic at an Anglican minister's home in Brantford. He wrote, "I am sorry to lose this girl as she is the best in the school & I had hoped to make a teacher of her but she does not like teaching."[53] But Ashton did continue to work toward helping Institute graduates succeed at becoming teachers. In July 1873, Ashton met with the local missionaries at Grand River and requested that the school board supply him with a list of subjects that the teachers on the reserve must know to pass an examination "so that I might be enabled to present some of the more advanced scholars for examination in those subjects from time to time, in order that they may ultimately obtain their own certificates. I believe this will be an incentive to greater exertion on the part of both pupils and teachers as they will have a definite object in view."[54] In the first three years of his time as principal, Ashton noted that two boys and four girls were engaged in teaching at one of the day schools.[55] The following year, an NEC report noted that "most of the teachers having been his former pupils, his influence over them is considerable. . . . Hence, Mr. Ashton practically controls the education of all the children on the Reserve."[56]

By December 1875, Ashton had come up with the idea to form a small class of reserve children at the Mohawk Institute to serve as a "practising class for pupils under special training for teachers." However, Ashton seemed to have some trouble inducing teacher trainees to stay at the school under this scheme. He noted that they left to become teachers without the training. The students knew some of the teachers on the reserve at the time

TEACHER AND PUPILS IN No. 3 SCHOOL.

Figure 3.3. "Teacher and Pupils in No. 3 School." The quality of this photo is the result of photographic technology from the 1880s. While the faces are blurry, very few photos exist of children and teachers at day schools in this period.
Source: William Land Carpenter, *Report to the New England Company of a Visit to Two of Their Missions Stations in the Province of Ontario, Canada, in the Year 1884* (London, 1884)

had no formal training, and they wanted to work as soon as possible.[57] Ashton believed that once standards were improved on the reserve for teachers, his students would be more interested in his training program. But over time, Ashton developed a more focused and successful program. As early as 1876, he mentioned in his journal creating a certificate, one with agreed-upon standards set by the NEC.[58] His goal was to professionalize teaching in schools where Indigenous children were taught.

In the late 1870s and early 1880s, Ashton continued to work toward educating students to become teachers. When the Six Nations School Board was created in 1878 to manage the day schools on the reserve, Ashton was appointed secretary, and he held significant power in this position until he retired decades later, in 1908. It was in this capacity that he inspected the

No. 3 School, with Pupils and Teachers, the Rev. Mr. and Mrs Caswell, and Others.

Figure 3.4. "No. 3 School, with Pupils and Teachers, the Rev. Mr. and Mrs. Caswell and Others." The quality of this photo is the result of photographic technology from the 1880s. While the faces are blurry, very few photos exist of children and teachers at day schools in this period.
Source: William Land Carpenter, *Report to the New England Company of a Visit to Two of Their Missions Stations in the Province of Ontario, Canada, in the Year 1884* (London, 1884).

schools on a regular basis and paid the salaries of the teachers (which were paid out of NEC funds). The board was responsible for hiring teachers and determining salaries. Many of the teachers it hired were graduates of the Mohawk Institute and were known to Ashton. By training teachers at the Mohawk Institute, the school was able to exert some influence over children in the day schools as well, or at least those taught by Mohawk Institute graduates.

One example is Sarah Davis, who graduated in 1880, and who passed the high school entrance exam with the highest mark in all of Brant County. She attended Brantford Collegiate Institute (BCI), and by 1884 was teaching at the No. 3 School. She taught for more than twenty-five years and passed away in 1923.[59] She was considered a successful graduate of the school by the

Figure 3.5. "Miss F. K. Maracle, 1905, Toronto."
Source: Richard Hill Collection

DIA. Englishman William Carpenter visited Six Nations on behalf of the NEC in September 1884 and produced a report on his travels.[60] He visited Davis's school and took a photograph of her with some students, as well as the school with the class outside. These are two of the few photos of a day school with its teacher and students from the nineteenth century. Davis is likely at the right in the first photo (figure 3.3).

Floretta Maracle was another top student who became a teacher. She attended the school at the same time as Sarah Davis, but she had a more varied career. She graduated in 1881 and attended Brantford Collegiate and then the Normal School.[61] She began teaching at the No. 2 School and taught successfully for nearly ten years. She then moved to Ottawa and, in January 1891, she was appointed to a DIA clerkship, becoming the first status Indian woman to be hired to a position in the department.[62] She worked in the federal Indian Accounts Branch, which was led by Duncan Campbell Scott, clerk in charge of accounts (and who later became deputy superintendent general of the DIA). She lived in the Home for Friendless Women in Ottawa, a boarding house for single women. In 1908, she married Allen Wawanosh Johnson, brother of Mohawk poet Pauline Johnson, a friend of Floretta's, and Evelyn Johnson, and lived in Toronto.[63] After the death of her husband in 1923, she returned to Six Nations, but it does seem that she taught again.[64]

The Mohawk Institute Certificate

While Ashton had been working to support Mohawk Institute graduates to become teachers by providing some training opportunities within the Institute, in 1882, he created a formally approved certificate for Indigenous teachers that could be used to teach across the country in on-reserve day schools controlled by the DIA. In March 1882, Ashton corresponded with the DIA about what he called "Indian Teachers' Certificates," intended for graduates of the Mohawk Institute and Brantford Collegiate so that they could work as schoolteachers beyond schools at Six Nations: "I am seeking the recognition and indorsement of approval of the Dep'y Superintendent General so that graduates from this Institution may more directly obtain schools in distant Indian Superintendencies."[65] A significant number of students from the Institute wanted to become teachers and thus chose this training, but there were a limited number of jobs in school at Six Nations. A certificate that could be used to teach at other day schools on reserves in Canada was a good idea.

There was some discussion between the deputy superintendent general of Indian Affairs, Lawrence Vankoughnet, and the department's superintendent of the Six Nations Agency, Jasper Gilkison, about the special certificate having a three-year term in order for candidates to acquire public school certification in that time, but the DIA was generally supportive of the program.[66] By the end of 1882, the certificate was a reality. Ashton noted that the new program would be awarded to students who met a specific set of conditions: "the Holder must be an Indian, not less than seventeen years of age, of good moral character"; they must have passed the examination for entrance into a collegiate institute in Ontario; and they must have completed "six months Special Training as a Teacher in the Schools of the Above Institution."[67] Ashton explained that "the Superintendent having certified the above, the Deputy Superintendent General accepts and endorses it as a certificate of competency to teach an Indian school for three years unless revoked."[68] It became known as the "Mohawk Institute Certificate," and the school became known as the Mohawk Institution and Indian Normal

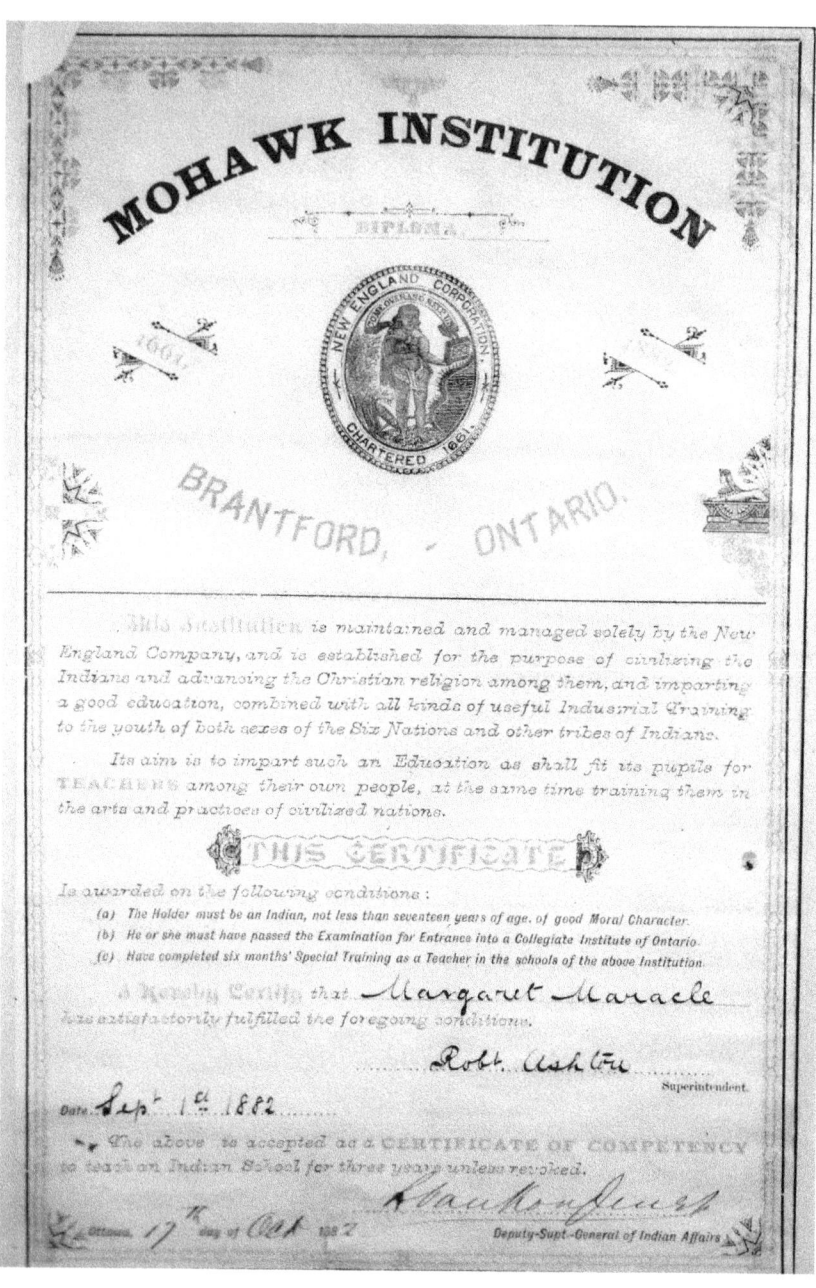

Figure 3.6. Margaret Maracle's certificate from 1882
Source: Don Smith Collection, Woodland Cultural Centre

School in 1885.⁶⁹ Those wishing to earn a certificate did not need to be graduates of the Mohawk Institute itself—some attended local on-reserve day schools, or came from other Indigenous nations—but most came from the Institute. During this same period, there was also a focus on ensuring that graduates of the school studied for and passed the entrance examination for BCI. Some of these students boarded at the Mohawk Institute while they attended BCI, given that the Institute was only a handful of kilometres away and much closer than the children's homes on the reserve.

Ashton supported having teenagers stay at the Institute, as it facilitated graduates achieving their higher-education goals. The NEC provided grants to the school to pay for the expense of having to board the teenagers there, even though they did not attend school at the Institute.⁷⁰ Ashton noted in an 1885 report, "During the last thirteen years I have done much to advance education among the Indians and have personally trained many as teachers, now I am endeavouring to bring them up to the standard of Provincial Certificates. . . . It is very desirable that we should have a supply of fully qualified teachers for our Indian Schools."⁷¹ And in fact, in 1885, all of the teachers at the day schools at Grand River had been trained at the Mohawk Institute.⁷² Ashton's efforts formalized a process that had been taking place for several decades and helped teachers who had graduated from the Mohawk Institute find work.

One of the first teachers to gain a certificate was honour roll student Jessie Osborne (Mohawk). Although Jessie's father was a Scottish immigrant, her mother was Mohawk, a descendant of both Joseph Brant and William Johnson and Molly Brant.⁷³ Jessie and her older sister Jane both attended the Institute, likely enrolling after their mother's death.⁷⁴ Both became teachers after graduating, but Jessie obtained one of the school's first certificates. Ashton was keen on Jessie's career, as he tracked her progress in his journal. In July 1883, he noted that she flew through her exams, and the plan was for her to study in Toronto, teach for a year, and then earn her certificate, although her training did not follow that exact schedule.⁷⁵

Osborne was a high-profile graduate and member of the community until she moved to Manitoba. In October 1884, she was one of three women from Six Nations who joined a delegation of Haudenosaunee people from Grand River travelling to Buffalo, New York, to attend the reinternment of the Seneca Chief Red Jacket. It was a large commemorative event, and Osborne attended along with about ten Haudenosaunee Confederacy chiefs, Pauline Johnson, Evelyn Johnson, the Reverend Albert Anthony (a missionary at Six Nations at that point), and Jasper T. Gilkison, the superintendent of Six Nations. Their attendance was noted in the commemorative booklet published by the Buffalo Historical Society the following year.[76]

In 1885, Osborne was employed as a governess at the Mohawk Institute, and by the following year she was teaching at the school.[77] She took part in a visit by several chiefs from Western Canada, part of a promotional tour organized by Prime Minister Sir. John A. Macdonald after the Northwest Resistance the year prior.[78] The chiefs visited the Six Nations, as the community was considered a showpiece for the DIA, and, on 14 October, they visited the Mohawk Institute. A newspaper report notes that "Each of the chiefs was presented with a pair of mittens made by the pupils under Miss Osborne's charge and Red Crow was so delighted with them that he wore his on the way home."[79] The following year Osborne attended the Toronto Normal School and obtained a grade A second-class professional certificate, possibly because she planned to go to Winnipeg and wanted to be able to teach there.[80] For Osborne, the Mohawk Institute did not provide enough training.

Osborne continued to teach after leaving Six Nations. Her father had moved to Winnipeg, and her sister Jane had moved there too (after graduating from the Mohawk Institute and working as a governess at the Toronto Young Ladies' College) and married in 1886. While it is unclear when Osborne moved, by 1891 she was living with her widowed father, an accountant, in Winnipeg.[81] She married John Young from Brandon, also an accountant, and the two were recorded in the census of 1901 as living in Rat Portage; it does not seem that she was teaching there.[82] Her husband died in 1906, at which time she likely moved back to Winnipeg. Little is known about her teaching career there, although it seems she did not teach in any on-reserve schools in Manitoba. Her certificate from the Toronto Normal School would have been useful there. She died in 1928, and Ferrier noted her as a prominent graduate of the school in 1930, having taught at the No 3. School, the Mohawk Institute, and in Winnipeg.[83]

Another important teacher to come out of this system, and perhaps the most well-known teacher at the Institute, was Susan Hardie (Mohawk). She passed the entrance examination to the Mohawk Institute at age eleven in 1878 and attended BCI several years later.[84] Ashton was very supportive of Hardie, advocating on her behalf to the Ontario Department of Education when she failed to obtain a second-class teaching certificate in 1885. In a letter to the department, Ashton argued that "As a pupil in this Institution her application & perseverance have been most commendable. She has therefore been permitted to continue her studies at the cost of the New

Figure 3.7. Bishop Appleyard, the Reverend Canon Zimmerman, David Wilson, and Susan Hardie in the Mohawk Chapel.
Source: Elliott Moses Fonds / Library and Archives Canada / e011206867

England Company in order that she may become a teacher to her people. It is desired to appoint her as a junior teacher in this Institution as soon as she has completed her training in the Model School."[85] Ashton had a plan for Hardie's career, but she had not done well in English composition and literature, which Ashton, in his letter to the minister of education, said "present almost insurmountable difficulties to an Indian. This you will more fully realize when you consider that an Indian must translate the question from English to Indian, think out the answer in Indian and then translate it into English." Ashton suggested that "unless the examinations are conducted in Mohawk, Ojibway etc.," they would lose Indigenous teachers because of their bilingualism, which he believed was a useful skill: "it is necessary that they should have a speaking acquaintance with the language spoken by the pupils."[86] Ashton was successful in convincing the Department of Education to approve of Hardie's application, as it responded with a letter saying that "under special circumstances," the department would approve of her receiving a second-class teaching certificate and return her third-class certificate.[87] She then took the training program at the Mohawk Institute, taught at the Mohawk Institute for a year, and then attended the Toronto Normal School for one year before returning to teach at the Institute.[88] Hardie went on to teach until 1936, for a total of fifty years, making her the longest-serving teacher there. She was especially proud of having taught and prepared students from the Mohawk Institute to take the entrance exam at BCI, all of whom apparently passed.[89] She retired with a pension from the NEC, and was honoured with a stained glass window in the Mohawk Chapel in 1960, although students did not report exclusively positive reviews of her teaching methods.[90] Hardie was only the second Indigenous teacher, after Isaac Bearfoot, to have a significant teaching career at the Mohawk Institute.

In his report of 1889, Ashton noted that sixteen past pupils were working as teachers in "Indian schools," thirteen of them "having special certificates of qualification for teaching Indian schools."[91] For example, Ashton reported that

> Josephine Good and Sarah Russell, having attended the Collegiate Institute at Brantford [BCI] for some time, and completed a course of six months' special training for teachers in our own schools, received certificates as Indian school teachers, and obtained appointments, the former taking charge of a school at Parry Island and the latter of School No. 7, on the Tuscarora Reserve. Their work has been most favourably reported on.[92]

Good had graduated in 1888 and earned the Nelles Medal for highest marks on a high school entrance examination.[93] She attended BCI and then taught in Parry Island (Wasauksing).[94] In the summer of 1891, Ashton noted in his journal that Good, after teaching for three years at that location, wanted more education to widen her teaching opportunities. He wrote, "she is very anxious to attend the high school again to enable her to obtain a certificate as a public school teacher." Ashton allowed her to return to the Mohawk Institute and provided room and board but noted that she would have to pay for her books and clothing herself from her savings.[95] She later found employment at the Bay of Quinte. Russell also received the Nelles Medal the same year as Good, and was hired to teach at No. 7 School on the reserve. She married William Smith and was seen as "influential for good on the Reserve" by the DIA.[96] Both women were top graduates who did the training program at the Mohawk Institute and had careers as teachers in day schools. Ashton clearly took pride in the production of teachers at the Mohawk Institute. It signified the success of the school as a place of education and training for Haudenosaunee youth who then went on to participate in the colonial education system.

Despite the success of the teacher training program at the Mohawk Institute, the formal certificate seemed to decline over time and the school shifted its focus away from being the "Indian Normal School." Over the late 1880s, despite the support of the NEC and the DIA, fewer students took advantage of the "students fund" that provided free room and board for teenagers at the Mohawk Institute while they attended BCI. The special Institute teaching certificate is not mentioned as often in DIA records or in Ashton's journals in the 1890s, and the school ceased to be known as the Mohawk Institution and Indian Normal School in 1893, shortening its name to the Mohawk Institution.[97]

However, students continued to receive training at the school, and some received certificates. While DIA official Martin Benson did not mention the certificate in his thorough report on the school in 1894, Ashton noted the following year that three students completed their course of training "as Indian school teachers."[98] Benson also noted that three ex-pupils, who were employed as teachers in day schools in other parts of Ontario, spent part of their summer holidays at the Mohawk Institute, including Josephine Good, who came from Tyendinaga.[99] At some point, the Institute stopped offering the "special certificate," but it is unclear when. Graduates of the school continued to become teachers, however, teaching in Six Nations day schools and in schools on reserves across the country.

In the early twentieth century, some of the children graduating from the Mohawk Institute attended BCI, where they took courses in business, telegraphy, stenography, and bookkeeping. A small number went on to agricultural college, medical school, and law school. Several young women found work as domestic servants and governesses, and some went on to train as nurses after the Great War.[100] And, as teaching requirements changed in this period, many graduates went to the Toronto or Hamilton Normal Schools to train as teachers. Teaching remained a popular career choice. By the early 1920s, the Six Nations School Board required all teachers to have a normal school certificate, which was the provincial standard, and teachers without one had to take a leave to attend normal school. By 1923, no teacher was employed on the reserve without one.[101]

Conclusion

The evidence presented in this chapter suggests that some graduates from the Mohawk Institute in the late nineteenth and early twentieth centuries were able to pursue their interests in secondary school and post-secondary education and thereby build careers, especially in education. While this was in part because the Reverends Abraham Nelles and Robert Ashton both worked to build programs to support students working to acquire further education and training in teaching, it was largely the result of the efforts and talents of children who faced enormous challenges living at the Mohawk Institute. They survived and had successful careers due to their own intelligence, skills, and determination. They were successful despite their residential school experience. It is also important to note that school officials supported their education because they wished for those graduates who became teachers to contribute to the DIA's assimilation agenda. As Mary Jane Logan McCallum has noted with reference to her mother, who taught at a day school in the postwar period, these teachers represented "an ideal model of assimilated youth—a way to show off the department's 'excellence' in Indian education programming, still underfunded and unequal today."[102]

NOTES

1. Margaret Connell Szasz, *Indian Education in the American Colonies, 1607–1783* (University of Nebraska Press, 2007), 104–106.
2. Bishop of Toronto to the Treasurer, 15 February 15 1841, in *Report by a Committee of the Corporation Commonly Called the New England Company, of Their Proceedings for the Civilization and Conversion of Indians, Blacks, and Pagans, in the British Colonies in America and the West Indies Since the Last Report in 1840* (J. P. Gibson, 1846), 14.
3. *Report by a Committee of the Corporation Commonly Called the New England Company* (J. Masters, 1840), 219–20.
4. For instance, in the 1840s, teachers included Thomas Howells, Henry Racey, R. Yeoward, and Henry Peatman. Appendix A, *Report by a Committee of the Corporation Commonly Called the New England Company* (1846), 95–99.
5. Elizabeth Graham, *The Mush Hole: Life at Two Indian Residential Schools* (Heffle Publishing, 1997), 47.
6. 12 February 1838 Report, from the 1846 NEC Annual Report, in Graham, 46.
7. 1 October 1844 Report, from the 1846 NEC Annual Report, in Graham, 52.
8. "The girls are required to make as much of the clothes as possible, and are also learning to knit. Mrs. Nelles intends introducing a spinning wheel among them this summer, so that in a year or two . . . they should be able to reduce the expense of clothing considerably." Nelles, 3 April 1840 Report, in Graham, 48.
9. It is unclear when he was first hired. Records from the 1830s rarely mention teachers in the schools. I searched the 1840 report, which covers the 1830s, and only two teachers are mentioned in an appendix, Mr. Ludlow and Mr. Senior, at the Johnson Settlement school and the Mohawk Institute. Appendix F, *Report by a Committee of the Corporation Commonly Called the New England Company* (1840), 251.

10 10 June 1842, Nelles to the New England Company, *Report by a Committee of the Corporation Commonly Called the New England Company* (1846), 30.

11 24 January 1843, Nelles to New England Company Treasurer, *Report by a Committee of the Corporation Commonly Called the New England Company* (1846), 36.

12 Nelles to the Treasurer, 22 February 1844, *Report by a Committee of the Corporation Commonly Called the New England Company* (1846), 45.

13 8 November 1844, *Report by a Committee of the Corporation Commonly Called the New England Company* (1846), 56. Nelles suffered from a similar fate as other people at Six Nations in this period in the form of non-Indigenous squatters and challenges to his lands. In a statement that Nelles put together in July 1844 regarding land issues at Six Nations, he wrote that "an old Indian of the name Laurence David's, the Company's first schoolmaster, has gone away as far as he can into the woods, on the South side of the river: he had an improvement on the North side, which he was not willing to quit; he was offered by white persons much more than the actual worth of it, but he refused to part with it: —his cattle and pigs were then stolen or destroyed; and, overcome by these calamities, he was induced to sell his improvement and go away." "Statement of Information furnished by the Rev. A. Nelles to the Members of a Special Committee of the Company, on the 19th of July, 1844," appendix B in *Report by a Committee of the Corporation Commonly Called the New England Company* (1846), 151–2.

14 Nelles Report, 9 February 1859, in Graham, *The Mush Hole*, 53. See also *Report by a Committee of the Corporation Commonly Called the New England Company, of Their Proceedings for the Civilization and Conversion of Indians, Blacks, and Pagans, in the British Colonies in America and the West Indies Since the Last Report in 1840* (J. P. Gibson, 1859).

15 In 1855, Thomas was described as "quite competent to teach, and so far has given satisfaction both to Mr. Elliott and the people." "1855 January 15th—Mr. Nelles Remarks," in *Report by a Committee of the Corporation Commonly Called the New England Company* (1859), 26.

16 O'Meara Report, 12 July 1860, in Graham, *The Mush Hole*, 54–5.

17 1868 New England Company Report, in Graham, 56.

18 "Report of the Hon. A. E. Botsford, Commissioner of the New England Company, on Their Missionary Stations on the Grand River, Near Brantford, Ontario," appendix VII in *History of the New England Company: From Its Incorporation, in the Seventeenth Century, to the Present Time: Including a Detailed Report of the Company's Proceedings for the Civilization and Conversion of Indians, Blacks, and Pagans in the Dominion of Canada, British Columbia, the West Indies and S. Africa, During the Two Years 1869–1870* (Taylor, 1871), 326.

19 Two other schools were taught by non-Indigenous women, Miss Crombie and Mrs. Hyndman. "Report of the Hon. A. E. Botsford," 318–32.

20 "Report of the Hon. A. E. Botsford," 320. Also see Alison Norman, "'Teachers Amongst Their Own People': Kanyen'kehá:Ka (Mohawk) Women Teachers in Nineteenth-Century Tyendinaga and Grand River, Ontario," *Historical Studies in Education / Revue d'histoire de l'éducation* 29, no. 1 (2017): 32–56.

21 Norman, "'Teachers Amongst Their Own People,'" 42–3.

22 "Report of the Hon. A. E. Botsford," 326.

23 "Institution Report, Thomas Griffiths," 30 June 1859, in Graham, *The Mush Hole*, 215.

24 *History of the New England Company* (1871), 121.

25 Canada, *Annual Report of the Secretary of State for the Year 1868* (Hunter, Rose & Co, 1869); Canada, *Report of the Secretary of State of Canada for the Year Ending on the 30th June, 1869* (I. B. Taylor, 1870).

26 *History of the New England Company* (1871), 75.

27 Ives Goddard, "The Origin and Meaning of the Name 'Manhattan,'" *New York History* 92, no. 4 (2010): 277–93.

28 *History of the New England Company, from Its Incorporation, in the Seventeenth Century to the Present Time: Including a Detailed Report of the Company's Proceedings for the Civilization and Conversion of Indians, Blacks, and Pagans in the Dominion of Canada, British Columbia, the West Indies, and S. Africa, During the Two Years 1869–1870, Volume 2* (Taylor & Co., 1874), 229.

29 "Missionaries and School Teachers in Canada," in *History of the New England Company* (1874), xvi.

30 The teachers all took an examination, and Susannah Carpenter was the top teacher; she beat Nelles Monture. *History of the New England Company* (1874), 146.

31 "Missionaries and School Teachers in Canada," in *History of the New England Company* (1874), xvi.

32 Michelle A. Hamilton, *Collections and Objections: Aboriginal Material Culture in Southern Ontario* (McGill-Queen's University Press, 2010), 126.

33   Upon his arrival in Toronto for normal school training in 1861, Bearfoot wrote to Principal Abraham Nelles, "I sincerely trust that the Supreme being may in his infinite goodness bestow a blessing upon my efforts in propagating civilization and enlightenment amongst my fellow country people." Bearfoot to Nelles, 14 January 1861, in Graham, *The Mush Hole*, 55.

34   Canada, *Annual Report of the Secretary of State for the Year Department of Indian Affairs for the Year 1868* (Hunter, Rose & Co., 1869); Canada, *Report of the Secretary of State of Canada for the Year Ending on the 30th June, 1869*.

35   In 1871, he published a book of hymns in Mohawk. Isaac Bearfoot, *A Collection of Psalms and Hymns in the Mohawk Language: For the Use of the Six Nation Indians* (New England Company, 1871).

36   Isaac Bearfoot, No. 276. Synod record series, sub-series: yearbook and clergy list sub-series, File 6. index and abstracts of the clergy register of the Diocese of Huron: volume 1. The Incorporated Synod of the Diocese of Huron Fonds, Verschoyle Phillip Cronyn Memorial Archives, London, Ontario.

37   Douglas Leighton, "A Calling that Straddled Two Cultures," *Anglican Diocese of Huron Church News*, February 2015. 10.

38   Canada, *Annual Report of the Secretary of State* (1869); Canada, *Annual Report of the Department of Indian Affairs for the Year Ended 31st December, 1890* (Brown Chamberlin, 1891).

39   Bearfoot was replaced with T. W. Standing, who was already the inspector for Brant County, and who they deemed to be more qualified. He passed away several years later, in 1911. Keith Jamieson, *History of Education on the Six Nations Reserve* (Woodland Cultural Centre, 1987), 8.

40   *History of the New England Company, from Its Incorporation* (1874), 396.

41   *History of the New England Company, from Its Incorporation* (1874), 390, 396.

42   Return F, "Statement of the Condition of the Various Indian Schools Within the Dominion, for the Year Ended 30th June 1875," *Annual Report of the Department of the Interior for the Year Ended 30th June 1875* (Maclean, Roger & Co., 1876), 87.

43   "Miss Lydia Hill," *Brantford Expositor*, 29 July 1927, 6. For more on Lydia Hill, see Norman, "'Teachers Amongst Their Own People,'" 44–5.

44   Amelia married a man from Cape Croker in 1889, Charles Kejedonce Jones, and had four children. She passed away at the birth of her fourth son at the age of forty-one in 1898. Her husband later became chief of the Chippewas of Nawash. Russell T. Ferrier, "History of the Mohawk Institute, Successful Graduates," File 466-1, Pt. 2, Vol. 6200, RG 10, Library and Archives Canada (LAC).

45   Ferrier.

46   Ian McCallum, "Family Story, a Heritage Home, and Munsee-Delaware Histories," *Active History*, 28 January 2022, https://activehistory.ca/2022/01/31492/; Mary Jane Logan McCallum, "Intentional, Articulate and Worldly: Archival Records of My Munsee-Delaware Ancestors," *Closer to Home: Locating and Retrieving Indigenous Heritage from Archives Outside Canada*, organized by the Indigenous Heritage Circle, Winnipeg, Manitoba, 5 March 2019; Mary Jane Logan McCallum, "Indigenous People, Archives and History," Shekon Neechie: An Indigenous History Site, 21 June 2018, https://shekonneechie.ca/2018/06/21/indigenous-people-archives-and-history/.

47   McCallum, "Indigenous People, Archives and History."

48   Norman D. Shields, "Anishinabek Political Alliance in the Post-Confederation Period: The Grand General Indian Council of Ontario, 1870–1936" (master's thesis, Queen's University, 2001.) See also Chandra Murdoch, "Act to Control: The Grand General Indian Council, the Department of Indian Affairs, and the Struggle over the Indian Act in Ontario, 1850–1906" (PhD diss., University of Toronto, 2023).

49   Boyce to Scott, 14 May 1920, File 466-1, Pt. 2, Vol. 6200, RG 10, LAC, in Graham, *The Mush Hole*, 122. Chief Logan also attended the closing day picnic at Mount Elgin on 1 July 1919 and gave words of welcome to returned soldiers. See Graham, 284. Logan was included in a 1920 description of graduates of Mount Elgin: "Scobie Logan, able writer and platform speaker, ardent supporter of the Anglican Church, ex-chief and secretary of the Muncey Council, a loyal Britisher and true friend of the Indian." Graham, 287.

50   "Report of the Hon. A. E. Botsford," 346.

51   Nelles, 6 April 1872 NEC Report, from the NEC 1874 Annual Report, in Graham, *The Mush Hole*, 64.

52   *Six Years' Summary of the Proceedings of the New England Company for the Civilization and Conversion of Indians, Blacks, and Pagans in the Dominion of Canada and the West Indies, 1873–1878* (Gilbert and Rivington, 1879), 136.

53   Ashton workbook 1872–6, 52, HCH-2003-43-05-20787, Verschoyle Phillip Cronyn Memorial Archives.

54   Ashton workbook, 85–6.

55   Ashton workbook, table VI, December 1875.

56   William Lant Carpenter, *Report to the New England Company of a Visit to Two of Their Mission Stations in the Province of Ontario in the Year 1884* (Spottiswoode & Co., 1884), 8–9.

57   Ashton's workbook notes the following (pp. 146–7): "The Committee were pleased to consider the admission of a few young and ignorant children to form a practising class for pupils under special training for teachers. I have not however availed myself of the permission to form this class at present, owing to the disappointments I have me[t] with, in failing to induce the most advanced scholars to place themselves under special training. They profess a desire to become teachers but fail when their energies are put to the test or else believing themselves to be more competent than they really are they persuade their friends to allow them to leave the Institution thinking they will be able to obtain situations as teachers at once. This latter idea has arisen from the fact that they know that the majority of teachers in Indian Schools are less qualified than themselves, and with the natural incredulity of Indians, they refuse the guidance of those best fitted to direct them. // After the Summer vacation, I selected the two most advanced girls and with the approbation of their friends, placed them in training for teachers, at first they displayed great zeal and application but within a month expressed a wish to change—I used all possible means to induce them to persevere, they do so till the end of the term and then left the Institution altogether. // When all teachers in Indian Schools are subjected to an Examination similar to that conducted by the Company's Missionaries or are required to hold certificates of qualification Indian Youths will exercise as much zeal in seeking the attainments as they now display in obtaining the emoluments of teachers."

58   Ashton workbook, 31 June 1876. He wanted the Company to agree to a standard by which a student would be considered to have obtained competency as a teacher with the correct credentials—namely, a teaching certificate.

59   Ferrier, "History of the Mohawk Institute, Successful Graduates"; Jamieson, *History of Education on the Six Nations Reserve*; Graham, *The Mush Hole*, 87, 140.

60   Carpenter, *Report to the New England Company*.

61   Ferrier, "History of the Mohawk Institute, Successful Graduates"; Wilma Green, personal communication, 31 August 2020.

62   *Our Forest Children* 3, no. 11 (February 1890): 141.

63   "Ontario Marriages, 1869–1927," Allen Wawanosh Johnson and Floretta Kathryn Maracle, 25 June 1908, Family History Library microfilm 1,871,864, Archives of Ontario, Toronto.

64   Floretta had a government pension. In addition, in Evelyn Johnson's will, she left a room at Chiefswood to Floretta, should she ever need a room. Personal communication with Wilma Green, 8 March 2022. In the 1881 census, she was listed as eighteen years old, an Anglican, a teacher, and was living with Charlotte Martin and William General. She was a good friend of Pauline Johnson, and they had a very close relationship.

65   Ashton Workbook, March 1882, HCH-2003-43-05-20787, Verschoyle Phillip Cronyn Memorial Archives.

66   Lawrence Vankoughnet to Gilkison, 2 June 1882; Jasper Gilkison to Robert Ashton, 5 June 1882, "Extracts from Annual Report of Robert Ashton, Esq., Superintendent of the Mohawk Institution, Brantford (Grand River), Ontario, for the Year Ending 31st December, 1882," Six Nations Agency—Reports, Correspondence and Memoranda Regarding the Mohawk Institute and Day Schools. Reports and Correspondence of the New England Company, File 154,845, Pt. 11, Vol. 2771, RG 10, LAC.

67   "Extracts From Annual Report of Robert Ashton," 92/478.

68   "Extracts From Annual Report of Robert Ashton," 92/478.

69   "Mohawk Institute Indian Residential School Narrative," p. 1, National Centre for Truth and Reconciliation, accessed 1 May 2025, https://archives.nctr.ca/NAR-NCTR-080.

70   Ashton to Hayter Reed, 5 February 1885, Six Nations Agency—Reports, correspondence and memoranda regarding the Mohawk Institute and day schools. Reports and correspondence of the New England Company, File 154,845, Pt. 11, Vol. 2771, RG 10, LAC.

71   R. Ashton Report, 29 September 1885, in Graham, *The Mush Hole*, 85.

72   According to Ashton, "all of the present staff of teachers in the Board schools, one teacher in this Institution and several on other reservations have received their education and training here, whilst the many who failed to reach the necessary standard as teachers have received a fair education in addition to the training necessary to make them useful citizens." Ashton to Hayter Reed, 5 February 1885, Six Nations Agency, File 154,845, Pt. 11, Vol. 2771, RG 10, LAC.

73   Edward Marion Chadwick, *Ontario Families: Genealogies of United Empire Loyalist and other Pioneer Families of Upper Canada* (1894; repr. Hunterdon House, 1970), 72–3. Census records always note her ethnicity as Scottish.

74   Both girls were born in Hamilton—Jessie in 1865, and Jane in 1863.

75   Ashton Workbook, July 1883.
76   Osborne's Mohawk name was recorded as "Sa-pa-na," meaning "The Lily." *Red Jacket. Transactions of the Buffalo Historical Society, Volume 3* (Buffalo Historical Society, 1885), 46.
77   Letter from Rev. Ashton, published in *Special Report by the Bureau of Education: Educational Exhibits and Conventions at the World's Industrial and Cotton Centennial Exposition, New Orleans, 1884–'85* (Government Printing House, 1886), 318.
78   See Donald B. Smith, "Chiefs Journey," *Canada's History*, 5 September 2017, https://www.canadashistory.ca/explore/first-nations-inuit-metis/chiefs-journey#72.
79   "The Brant Memorial. The North-West Chiefs Visit an Industrial Institution," *Toronto Globe*, 15 October 1886, 1.
80   Ashton Report, September 1887, in Graham, *The Mush Hole*, 86.
81   1891 Census of Canada, Census Place: Ward 5, Winnipeg, Manitoba, Family No: 337, Roll: T-6297.
82   1901 Census of Canada, Census Place: Rat Portage (Town/Ville), Algoma, Ontario, Page: 6; Family No: 60.
83   Ferrier in Graham, *The Mush Hole*, 220.
84   Her memories are shared in Jamieson, *History of Education on the Six Nations Reserve*.
85   R. Ashton to Secretary Education Department, 4 September 1885, in Graham, *The Mush Hole*, 84.
86   R. Ashton to G. W. Ross, Minister of Education, 29 September 1885, in Graham, 84–5.
87   Education Department to R. Ashton, 8 October 1885, in Graham, 85.
88   Hardies' memories, in Jamieson, *History of Education on the Six Nations Reserve*.
89   Standing to whom it may concern, 12 May 1921, File 466-1, Part 1, Vol. 6200, RG 10, LAC. T. W. Standing was the Brant County school Inspector from 1907 to 1932. See Jamieson, *History of Education on the Six Nations Reserve*, 15; Thelma Finlay, "Institute Teacher Is 90," *Brantford Expositor*, 9 October 1957.
90   See Alison Norman, "'True to My Own Noble Race': Six Nations Women Teachers at Grand River in the Early Twentieth Century," *Ontario History* 107, no. 1 (2015): 5–34.
91   R. Ashton Annual Report, 1 September 1889, in Graham, *The Mush Hole*, 87.
92   R. Ashton Annual Report, 1 September 1889, in Graham, 86.
93   The Nelles Medal was created in 1885 when the Reverend Nelles's widow donated a silver medal to be given annually to the pupil who obtained the highest marks at the entrance examination. Kelly Report, 15 July 1885, in Graham, 84.
94   Ferrier, *History of Education on the Six Nations Reserve*.
95   Ashton Workbook, 1890–3, 115.
96   Ferrier, *History of Education on the Six Nations Reserve*.
97   "Mohawk Institute Indian Residential School Narrative," p. 1.
98   Ashton calls them by their initials, P. W., H. B., and L. G. See R. Ashton Annual Report, 1 August 1895, in Graham, *The Mush Hole*, 95.
99   Graham, 93.
100 One report on the school in 1902 noted how many graduates were helped to find work as domestics by Mrs. Ashton, the principal's wife. Duncan Milligan to the New England Company, 1 October 1902, File 154,845, Part 1A, Six Nations Agency—Reports, Correspondence and Memoranda Regarding the Mohawk Institute, 1915–1921, Vol. 2771, RG 10, LAC. See also Alison Norman, "Race, Gender and Colonialism: Public Life Among the Six Nations of Grand River, 1899–1939" (PhD diss., University of Toronto, 2010), on teachers (63–7); on clerical training (122–5); and on domestic labour (132–6). See also Ferrier, *History of Education on the Six Nations Reserve*.
101 Julia L. Jamieson, *Echoes of the Past: A History of Education from the Time of the Six Nations Settlement on the Banks of the Grand River in 1784 to 1924* (self-printed, n.d.)
102 McCallum, "Indigenous People, Archives and History."

4

Teaching Control and Service: The Use of Military Training at the Mohawk Institute

Evan Habkirk

Figure 4.1. The Mohawk Institute Cadet Corps, displayed at the Central Canada Exhibition, 1896
Source: Richard Hill Collection

In 1896, at the Central Canada Exhibition in Ottawa, the militarization of the Mohawk Institute received national recognition when visitors were shown portraits of the victory of the Mohawk Institute Cadet Corps over their local rivals, the military-trained Brantford Collegiate Institute cadets, at Brantford's Dominion/Gala Day competition.[1] Throughout the 1900s, the Mohawk Institute cadets' fame continued to grow, especially after they were featured in the British military publication *Navy and Army Illustrated* in 1902.[2] For Principal Robert Ashton, these accolades marked the zenith of a twenty-year campaign to bring order and discipline to the Mohawk Institute, a mission he began immediately after his appointment as superintendent and principal in 1870. More importantly, what Ashton had created was a tool that he, and other administrators of the school, used not only to control Indigenous children, but to show the non-Indigenous public the positive effects the school was having on its Indigenous charges. No matter the internal failings of the school and the abuses and inadequacies of school administrators, to the Canadian public, the cadets and public displays of their drill showed the Mohawk Institute was fulfilling its mission to "civilize" and bring the school's Indigenous youth into Canadian society.

Ashton and Military Drill

When he first arrived at the Institute, Ashton described the school as in a "general appearance of neglect," noting that the boys of the schools were "the idlest and most disobedient boys I ever saw; they will not do a stroke of work but just when it pleases them."[3] He further noted that he

> had to keep them all out of school one week to hurry in the harvest, but they had no idea of work, and when I attempted to show some, the others took the opportunity to slip off and I had to fetch them back again; if I left the field for a few moments they would do nothing until I returned. . . . The boys have been *taught* that they have no right to be set to work of any kind against their will; it has been the practice to coax a boy to do any little thing required of him.[4]

Ashton concluded that the reason for this insubordination was due to the lax attitude of his predecessor, the Reverend Canon Nelles, toward the children. As he told his superiors at the New England Company,

> [Nelles] made the following remark to the boys in my presence on the night we celebrated our Harvest Home:—"That now the

Figure 4.2. Cadets at the Mohawk Institute, possibly 1890s
Source: Richard Hill Collection

harvest is gathered in or nearly so, there will be no further necessity for keeping any of you from school to work in the fields; and as the objects of your coming here is that you may be educated," etc.—"but now at harvest time, when there is a press of work, it is right that you should render what assistance you can, else the crops would spoil on the ground."[5]

When Ashton asked Onondaga teacher Isaac Bearfoot why Nelles needed to make such remarks to the students about fieldwork, Bearfoot explained "that the prevailing idea among the boys' parents was that the children came here to be educated only, and not to work unless they liked. He added that most of the boys would on leaving here follow farming, but that the manner of working this farm was so slovenly, they could learn how to farm better at home."[6]

Once in control of the Institute, Ashton began his mission to change the behaviours he deemed unacceptable. He modelled the Institute after a British reformatory/industrial school education, like he had previously known during his time at the Industrial School for Boys in Feltham,

4 | Teaching Control and Service

England. At the base of this education was drills, routines, and uniforms. This system was found to be popular among many child reformers and educators in Britain and within the Canadian public school system. Social reformers felt that drill, found in boys brigades, cadet corps, and the Boy Scout movement, combatted the negative influences found in city slums and promoted Christian and Victorian values like discipline, duty, loyalty, honour, punctuality, and precision, while educators found that these groups aided in ceasing the potential feminization of young boys due to the growing number of female teachers in the public school system.[7] These ideas would later meld with the growing patriotism and militarism found in non-Indigenous culture in the late nineteenth and twentieth centuries, making these movements very popular until the 1970s.[8]

At the Mohawk Institute, Ashton took these ideas and established strict routines and codes of conduct for his Indigenous charges. He instructed the children in drill and ensured that, every morning, students would fall into formation on the school's parade square and break into squads before beginning their daily chores.[9] When moving about the school, students were required to form lines and march to their destinations, be it the Mohawk Chapel, dining hall, or classrooms.[10] Ashton would also create a strict military-styled disciplinary system that included good conduct badges, black lists, and a solitary confinement cell for students who misbehaved.[11] Ashton hoped that the use of this military structure would control and change the behaviour of his Six Nations students into that of the surrounding Euro-Canadian population.

By the 1890s, the school was beginning to look and operate as a military camp. In 1894, Ashton required the boys of the school to wear polished boots and grey uniforms tailored by the girls at the Institute.[12] Older children were also appointed as corporals and sergeants to monitor students in their squads, ensuring their general good behaviour and that their assigned duties were completed.[13] Likely being drilled by his sons Ernest and Alfred,[14] who were both serving as officers of the local militia regiment, the 38th Dufferin Rifles, Ashton organized displays of the students' military drills for visiting officials and the Brantford public. A brass band was added to these shows in 1899.[15]

Distinguished guests were often introduced to displays of Ashton's uniformed students, demonstrating the "progress" that the school, and therefore the Ashtons, were making in "civilizing" their Indigenous charges. For instance, when the Marquis of Lorne and Princess Louise stopped in Brantford as part of their 1879 tour of Canada, the students of the

Institute were placed prominently on a grandstand erected for them and their teachers. This uniformed presence of the students showed the royal couple and the people of Brantford that "those dusky sons for the forest" were able to recognize and conform to the greatness of the British Empire.[16] This uniformed conformity further showed non-Indigenous viewers that these children no longer represented the "savage," but instead presented a picture of Indigenous people who could be trusted and employable upon leaving the school.[17] These uniformed students were not only meant to impress the viewer, but to show them that they were serious and controlled people.[18] Placing these students in uniforms for public events showed the non-Indigenous public a pacified and tamed image of Indigenous people, making them virtuous, aesthetically pleasing, and respected based upon Euro-Canadian and British values.[19]

The event that thrust the corps to fame, however, occurred when the cadets, drilled by Ernest Ashton, won top prize at Brantford's Dominion/Gala Day celebrations at Agriculture Park in 1896, beating the non-Indigenous and upper-middle-class Brantford Collegiate Institute Cadet Corps. The judges declared the drill of the Mohawk Institute cadets "to be the best of its kind ever seen in Brantford."[20] According to Robert Ashton, the cadets performed their drill "with a spirit which is found nowhere outside of the regular army. The marching was not quite up to the mark of former public performances, but at times the most complicated military movements were done with the utmost regularity."[21] On 7 July during a band concert in Brantford, the Mohawk Institute cadets were presented with a silver tankard for their drill by the city's mayor.[22] After this, the Institute's cadet corps became central features of royal and viceregal visits to Brantford and the Grand River Territory. At a local fair in fall 1896, the cadets formed the honour guard for the governor general and Lady Aberdeen and then performed an exhibition of their drill for the honoured guests and fair spectators.[23] In 1901, they formed part of the honour guard for the Duke and Duchess of York and Cornwall when they visited Brantford. The cadets were also featured at the Duke of Connaught's visit to the Grand River Territory in 1913 and were later inspected by the Prince of Wales when he visited Brantford in 1919.[24]

When the British journal *Navy and Army Illustrated* published a full-page article on the Mohawk Institute cadets, including a photograph originally taken for the 1896 Central Canada Exhibition in Ottawa, the article's title, "A Red Man's Cadet Corps: Civilised Sons of the Wild West," reinforced the school's goal of assimilating Indigenous children into Euro-Canadian

Figure 4.3 A. Nelles Ashton and Mohawk Institute cadets with the Brantford Gala Day Trophy, 1896. Ashton is wearing his 38th Dufferin Rifles uniform. The students are Senior Sergeant O. Planter, Junior Sergeant A. Peters, and Corporals O. Montour, C. Cusick, J. Moses, and A. Leween.
Source: Woodland Cultural Centre

culture and the British Empire. It also extended the use of military drill beyond these efforts, tying it to the absorption of the students into state and military service. As the article states, the goal of the Institute and the cadet corps was to "cultivate the martial predications of the young Indians, so that they may form part of the dominion defence," and that "after leaving the institute many of them enter the active militia, chiefly the 37th Regiment, Haldimand Rifles."[25]

Aside from the displays of the cadets, the Ashtons also used their connections at the school to place Indigenous students into local military units. In a December 1896 report to the New England Company, Robert Ashton "permitted" six senior cadets to attend extracurricular drill with D Company of the 38th Dufferin Rifles, commanded by Ashton's son, E. C. Ashton.[26] A review of the 38th Dufferin Rifles' nominal rolls from the period

1896–8 shows that the cadets who drilled with D Company were actually paid soldiers within the regiment.[27] This clearly was not an extracurricular activity bestowed on these cadets through the "goodwill" of Ashton or the regiment, but instead was a way to funnel students into military service for the Canadian state.

No. 161 Mohawk Institute Cadet Corps

When Robert Ashton retired in 1903, his son, A. Nelles Ashton, took over as superintendent of the school. In 1909, with the support of the Canadian government, Ashton officially established No. 161 Mohawk Institute Cadet Corps, which, through the Strathcona Trust, provided monies, uniforms, and equipment to schools with cadet and drill companies for physical training and education. By 1910, the Department of Indian Affairs began recommending drill and calisthenics exercises as physical education programs in Canada's residential schools, producing an eighteen-page calisthenics and drill manual accompanied with many breathing exercises.[28] According to the manual, these exercises and drills were designed to foster the health of the students, but could also be used to assimilate them into Euro-Canadian society since the drills "assist in obtaining the attention and prompt discipline so necessary before real work can be commenced."[29] As noted by sport historian Janice Forsyth, this regimen also retrained Indigenous children by teaching them the "proper" ways of moving their bodies in a "unified and orderly" manner for state service and manual labour.[30] This was publicly supported by *The Brantford Expositor*, which reported that "nowhere is the necessity for physical development along with the brain culture more readily recognized than in the Mohawk Institute, where drill and the cadet program taught Indigenous children 'a wholesome regard for authority.'"[31]

Although the students had these exercises imposed on them by leaders at the Institute, they seemed to excel at cadet drill. This has led scholars, including myself and Janice Forsyth, to hypothesize that some children may have used cadets much in the same ways some residential school survivors used sports—as a way of surviving their residential school experience. Cadets may have provided students with an outlet to succeed and be rewarded, with some survivors claiming their participation in cadets gave them something to do in the evenings, extra time on the playground, or took them away from the school grounds.[32]

Although the residential school system reinforced that Indigenous students were not equal to non-Indigenous people, cadet drill provided these students an outlet to prove themselves and outperform their non-Indigenous

Figure 4.4. A. Nelles Ashton and Mohawk Institute cadets in front of the Mohawk Institute, 1909
Source: Richard Hill Collection

counterparts.[33] During their 1908 inspection and drill demonstration, the inspecting officer claimed that the Mohawk Institute Cadet Corps made a "very credible showing" and further noted that the corps received a commendation from the minister of militia and the Canadian Militia Council for their good conduct.[34] In their 1912 inspection, the corps placed first in the Central Ontario Cadet Competition, with *The Brantford Expositor* reporting that the corps was "awarded the place of honor by the inspector over the cadet corps of Toronto, Hamilton and practically central Ontario."[35] That year they also won the No. 2 Central Ontario Military District rifle competition.[36] While the corps passed their 1913 inspection, their commanding officer, E. C. Ashton, hoped they could improve their score in the rifle competition.[37] This could easily be accomplished; by 1880, the Ashtons had established a rifle range on the grounds of the Institute that they regularly rented out to the Dufferin Rifles.[38] Positive accolades bestowed on the

Figure 4.5. A. Nelles Ashton and Mohawk Institute cadets on the front steps of the Mohawk Institute, 1909
Source: Richard Hill Collection

Mohawk Institute Cadet Corps from those who viewed their drill would continue into the 1920s, with their commanding officers noting that in advance of inspections or competitions, members of the corps would demand extra drill and practice time in order to outperform their non-Indigenous competitors.[39]

Wartime

The First and Second World Wars did little to change the militarization of the Mohawk Institute. There has been some debate whether the militaristic environment found within residential schools, especially at the Mohawk Institute, led them to function as feeders into the Canadian Armed Forces during the World Wars. Officially, this claim as it relates to the First World War, remains uncertain due to the changing recruitment policies of the Department of Indian Affairs, which would, at times, grant some recruiters access to certain schools, while denying access to other schools without clear explanation or cause.⁴⁰ Locally, however, this did not prevent school or local department administrators from helping guide Six Nations men, and quite possibly students from the Institute, to enlist.

It would have been easy for the now Lieutenant Colonel E. C. Ashton and Major A. Nelles Ashton to use their connections with the Mohawk Institute to obtain recruits when they were recruiting a local company of the 36th Battalion.⁴¹ After being appointed second-in-command of the Canadian Mounted Rifles Depot in Hamilton, Ontario, Gordon Smith, superintendent of the Six Nations Territory, was also known to use his connections to gather Six Nations men for enlistment.⁴² A preliminary survey of the Canadian Mounted Rifles nominal rolls found four Six Nations men from the Grand River Territory, with a potential seven more, among the ranks of the Canadian Mounted Rifles. In 1916, military authorities even requested that Smith transfer some of these Six Nations recruits to the newly formed 114th Battalion when they were looking for First Nations soldiers to fill its ranks.⁴³ Smith and his wife would later be appointed as representatives of a citizens' recruiting league in Brantford and Brant County.⁴⁴ It is no wonder that in a recent survey conducted for the Woodland Cultural Centre exhibit *Warriors, Veterans, and Peacekeepers*, Paula Whitlow and Tammy Martin found that 325 Haudenosaunee men and women enlisted in the First World War, with 86 of this total coming from the Mohawk Institute. Six of these former students were killed in action.⁴⁵

The militarization of the school continued in the wake of the First World War. As noted by historian Alison Norman, by the end of the 1920s, the Mohawk Institute was outfitted with Canadian Army hand-me-downs including cots, kitchen utensils, and clothing.⁴⁶ Residential school administrators purchased vast quantities of surplus materials, including bedding and uniforms that, with help of girls and the sewing room at the Institute, were cut down and refitted into dresses and uniforms for the children and other materials needed for the Institute.⁴⁷ In her July and August 1919 report, Boyce notes that the Militia Department gave the Institute "fifty-five returned men's suits, which we will remake into school and work suits." Students who attended the school in the 1940s recalled wearing these cut-down First World War uniforms to Sunday services at the Mohawk Chapel.⁴⁸ Ann Boyce, Ashton's daughter, who had become principal by this point, also notes that the Department of Militia sent two collar and cap badges for fifty-five boys, showing that the military structure and rank system for students first established at the school by Robert Ashton was still intact.⁴⁹

Advancing the militarization of the school further, Boyce also noted that now Quartermaster General E. C. Ashton presented the cadet corps with German war trophies in 1923.[50]

Although other cadet corps in Brantford disbanded in the 1920s due to the rise of anti-militarist sentiment in postwar Canada (especially within the Anglican Church),[51] the Mohawk Institute cadets continued to remain active until 1925 under the direction of the boys' instructor and Boyce's husband, Sydney Rogers, who was also an officer in the artillery. He started a boys' bugle band that was connected to the cadets in 1919. For girls, Boyce added Girl Guides and Brownies to the school's extracurricular activities.[52] This trend of replacing cadet corps with Boy Scouts and the establishment of Girl Guide troops was championed by many residential schools run by the Anglican Church. It was praised as a less militaristic alternative that still promoted British and Canadian citizenship among Indigenous students but continued the tradition of displaying Indigenous children in orderly uniforms, promoting their apparent acceptance of their place within Canadian society.[53]

The memory of the war was also used to introduce and assimilate students into the values of British and Canadian society. Along with participating in events during the Prince of Wales's tour of Brantford in 1919, there were many other reminders of the loyalty the students were required to show to the British Crown and its imperial order, manifested through military service. In July 1919, students took part in a reception for returned Six Nations soldiers at which, dressed in their school uniforms—girls in blue serge skirts, buff middies with blue trim, and blue straw hats with red bands, and boys in their cadet uniforms—they both marched and drilled for the veterans. After these demonstrations, the girls waited tables.[54] Later that month, they were also permitted to attend a military tattoo in Agricultural Park in Brantford.[55] Armistice and Empire Days were also readily celebrated at the Institute. Students and staff would assemble at the school and sing patriotic songs, while staff would also give patriotic addresses.[56] In 1923, Principal Sydney Rogers explained the effects this socialization was having on the children, reporting that during the school's Empire Day celebrations, "the Victrola Record of the King's speech was played. One interesting feature of this ceremony was the manner in which every boy stiffened to attention as soon as the record commenced playing the National Anthem."[57]

Outside organizations, seeing the good effect the school was having on its Indigenous students, were also willing to assist with these lessons of re-socialization. In 1924, the Remembrance Chapter of the Imperial Order

Daughters of the Empire (IODE) purchased the portrait *Canadian Foresters at Windsor Castle* as a memorial for the Institute's students to see and remember the role many Six Nations men played in pioneer and forestry corps during the war.[58] At the portrait's dedication ceremony, the children saluted the British flag and sang patriotic songs.[59] The IODE was also involved with organizing the Girl Guide program at the Institute, with the Sarah Jeanette Duncan Chapter presenting the Mohawk Institute's Girl Guide troop their flag in 1924.[60]

These and other events demonstrate that pre-war messages promoting Indigenous subservience to the British and Canadian states continued to be a central theme of student education at the Mohawk Institute. By using events that celebrated the British Empire, Canada's military, and the Institute's military past, administrators of the school hoped to teach students to reject their own culture in favour of the Euro-Canadian way of life. This was especially true during the dedication of the Mohawk Institute's honour roll for the First World War in 1925.[61] During the dedication, the bishop of the Diocese of Huron, the Right Reverend David Williams, instructed students that the deeds of the older generation—mainly First World War veterans—were "instrumental in the building of a better Canadian citizenship."[62] According to Bishop Williams, the British entered the war because they had pledged their word to do so. In his summation, he told the children, "it is of the primary importance that you keep your word than it is to save your life."[63] The bishop further instructed the students that they were

> to defend and preserve the life of the empire itself. This was eminently worth while, as the British Commonwealth had done what no other nation, empire, or agency had done toward civilizing and Christianizing the world. . . . Canada's life as a nation and as a constituent part of the empire was at stake. It is to your infinite credit and glory . . . that so many of your number took part in that great struggle against brute force. Remember the record of your countrymen made in the Great War and try to live up to it.[64]

The bishop stated he hoped commemorative services would "be conducted each year to keep alive in the hearts of the coming generation the remembrance of those who fought and the great ideas for which they had been willing, if need be, to give their all."[65] These lessons of continued military participation, assimilation, and obedience to the empire were further reinforced at this event with the students singing "Onward Christian Soldiers," "Fight the Good Fight," and "On the Resurrection Morning" during the dedication.[66]

This constant messaging primed generations of students at the Mohawk Institute to be ready to participate in the Second World War. Although no honour roll for the Mohawk Institute exists for the Second World War, testimonies from Six Nations and other Indigenous veterans reveal that the shared stories of their relatives' participation in the First World War influenced them to enlist in the war in both Canada and the United States.[67] Other studies show that Indigenous participation in the Second World War was influenced by the education and militaristic training Indigenous recruits received at Canadian residentials schools.[68] Unlike in the First World War, however, government officials were more than willing to recruit directly from residential schools, with a 1944 recruitment manual recommending this strategy to recruiters as the military-styled training and strict discipline students were subject to at residential schools was deemed to make the students great soldiers.[69] Due to racial biases and the limited education residential schools provided their students, most of these recruits were forced to serve in the army as opposed to other branches of service.[70]

Postwar Transitions

After 1945, the trends of the First World War were repeated. Although the Second World War sparked a resurgence of cadet corps in Canada, budget cuts by the federal government in 1947 saw many of these units disband, especially with the elimination of cadet programs for children younger than fourteen years old.[71] Although this elimination was unsuccessfully protested by the Department of Indian Affairs, the department still found ways to interject military drill into the schools by purchasing surplus copies of Ottawa's and the British War Office's manual, *Pre-Service Physical Training and Recreation for Army Cadets*, to serve as the basis for physical education programs in residential schools.[72] Military surplus also made its way into residential schools, but quantities are difficult to track since the War Assets Corporation—the governmental body established to sell surplus military goods to civilian organizations—only tracked individual sales over $5,000. Notably, the Department of Indian Affairs did purchase $7,067 worth of coats, underwear, shirts, boots, and blankets from the corporation in 1945–6.[73]

Like Ashton, postwar school administrators found that, even if the federal government was not going to provide as much funding or resources for cadet corps, they were still a visible way to ensure local and national publicity of the school's "civilizing" influence.[74] In 1949, the school's principal, the Reverend William Zimmerman, re-established the Mohawk Institute Cadet Corps. Although this organization—like many other cadet corps formed in the residential school system during this period—disbanded shortly after its formation, the school tried to again establish a cadet corps, this time a Sea Cadet Corps, in 1966.[75] Alongside the Sea Cadet program, the Mohawk Institute also ran Brownies, Girl Guides, Cub, and Boy Scout troops.[76] Although the Department of Indian Affairs provided limited funding for Girl Guide and Boy Scout programs, school administrators found that these programs—aside from having a hierarchical and military structure with uniforms, drills, and discipline—also provided lessons in the values of state service and citizenship, while also continuing the display of orderly and uniformed Indigenous children.[77]

Although these programs provided students some relief and escape from the repressive nature of the school,[78] the Canadian government had a more sinister motivation. By the 1960s, the schools and federal government used these cadet programs to integrate and assimilate students into the Canadian body politic through their employment in the Canadian Armed Forces. Not only could students be employed by the Canadian military through summer programs, but "Indian Affairs and Northern Development had reached an agreement with the Department of National Defence that the military would seek recruits from the cadet corps at residential schools."[79] As a result, many residential school survivors found their way to military service.[80] One student, who after leaving the Institute in the 1940s served seven years in the United States Marine Corps, stated that "the Mohawk Institute was a good training ground for the Marine Corps."[81]

As with most residential schools in Canada, the military structure and cadet corps embedded at the Mohawk Institute only ended when the school closed its doors in the 1970s.[82] For other schools, however, the military structure of the cadet corps remained a constant part of the residential school experience until 1996, Gordon's Indian Residential School, transferred its award-winning cadet corps to the community of Punnichy, Saskatchewan, after it closed its doors.[83] Today, in many Indigenous communities, the Canadian government continues the mission of residential schools by training and funnelling Indigenous youth into the Canadian military or other forms of state service through government-sponsored cadet corps and sports programming.[84] Through these programs, organizations like the Royal Canadian Mounted Police and the Canadian Armed Forces gain access to Indigenous children and train them for

Canadian citizenship, with many of these young people seeing their futures within these federal services.

Conclusion

For Robert Ashton and other residential school administrators, cadet corps were more than a way to organize and train Indigenous youth. These students became living displays to a skeptical non-Indigenous public of the immediate "progress" of the school's "civilizing" mission. Cadets and the military order they represent masked many of the inadequacies found in the school system and the abusive and other shortcomings found among school administrators. As seen in other chapters in this book, despite the evident realities that school buildings were insufficient, in disrepair, or crumbling and the standards of education and care were inadequate or non-existent, cadet corps were used to show any and all onlookers that the schools were supposedly working for the best interests of these students while instilling the ideals of duty, loyalty, patriotism, obedience, and the ability to submit to authority. These programs shielded the public from the emotional and physical trauma these children faced, while training Indigenous students to turn their backs on their culture and replace it with service to the Canadian state. For school administrators, the cadet corps and the military structure of the school were just two of the many tools created to control the school's narrative, hiding from the public the truth of what the students experienced behind the school's brick walls.

NOTES

1. Report of the Mohawk Institute to the New England Company, 16 September 1896, Truth and Reconciliation Files, Verschoyle Phillip Cronyn Memorial Archives, London, Ontario.
2. "A Red Man's Cadet Corp: Civilised Sons of the Wild West," *Navy and Army Illustrated* 15 (1902): 112.
3. R. Ashton, Report for the Mohawk Institute to the New England Company, 20 November 1872, in *Report of the Proceedings of the New England Company for the Civilization and Conversion of Indians, Blacks, and Pagans in the Dominion of Canada, South Africa, and the West Indies, During the Two Years 1871–1872* (Taylor and Company, 1874), 157.
4. Ashton, 157, 158.
5. Ashton, 158.
6. Ashton, 158.
7. Frank Dawes, *A Cry from the Street: The Boys' Club Movement in Britain from the 1850s to Present Day* (Wayland, 1974), and Evan J. Habkirk, "From Indian Boys to Canadian Men? The Use of Cadet Drill in the Canadian Indian Residential School System," *British Journal of Canadian Studies* 30, no. 2 (2017): 230–1.
8. Habkirk, "From Indian Boys to Canadian Men?," 230–1.
9. Other residential and boarding schools in Canada and the United States used military discipline and drill to organize and re-socialize Indigenous students, including the famed Carlisle Boarding School, founded by Richard Henry Pratt, in Carlisle, Pennsylvania. Ashton, Report for the Mohawk Institute to the New England Company, 158, and Martin Benson's Report, 1894, in Elizabeth Graham, *The Mush Hole: Life at Two Indian Residential Schools* (Heffle Publishing, 1997), 90.

10 Graham, 9, 23, and 40; Benson's Report, 1894, in Graham, 90.
11 Graham, 9–10, and 23; Benson's Report, 1894, in Graham, 94; R. Ashton, Annual Report, 26 August 1896, in Graham, 96.
12 Although it is likely that the girls of the Institute participated in calisthenic exercises and drills, the cadet corps was exclusively for the boys of the school. As noted by J. R. Miller, there is a deficit of information relating to extracurricular activities for girls at residential schools. The only records of similar training to cadets that the girls of the Mohawk Institute would have received was through the Girl Guide program, which was present at the Institute in the post–First World War years, but which really took off throughout the residential school system in the 1950s and '60s. See J. R. Miller, *Shingwauk's Vision: A History of Native Residential Schools* (University of Toronto Press, 1996), 217–50. See also Annual Reports of the Department of Indian Affairs, available at https://publications.gc.ca/site/eng/9.846380/publication.html.
13 Graham, *The Mush Hole*, 9; Benson, Report, 1894, in Graham, 93; and R. Ashton, Annual Report, 26 August 1896, in Graham, 96.
14 It is unclear who was drilling the boys at the Mohawk Institute until the 1890s. Rev. Robert Ashton probably drilled the boys of the school from the 1870s to the 1890s. His sons, Ernest and Alfred, probably took on these duties in the 1890s, when they enlisted in the Dufferin Rifles, with Ernest becoming a second lieutenant when he joined in 1893 and Alfred also becoming an officer when he joined in 1895. We know that by 1896, Rev. Ashton reported that Ernest was in charge of drilling the cadets.
15 Benson, Report, 1894, in Graham, *The Mush Hole*, 93; R. Ashton, Annual Report, 26 August 1896, in Graham, 96; and R. Ashton, Annual Report, 7 August 1901, in Graham, 97.
16 "Vice Regal Progress," *Brantford Expositor*, 16 September 1879.
17 Paul Fussell, *Uniforms: Why We Are What We Wear* (Houghton Mifflin, 2002), 3, 4, 34, and 106.
18 Fussell, 4, 34.
19 Fussell, 117–18.
20 Report of the Mohawk Institute to the New England Company, October 1896, Truth and Reconciliation Files, Verschoyle Phillip Cronyn Memorial Archives.
21 *Brantford Expositor*, 5 July 1898, in Graham, *The Mush Hole*, 96.
22 The following names are engraved on the tankard: E. C. Ashton, Senior Sergeant O. Planter, Junior Sergeant A. Peters, and Corporals O. Montour, C. Cusick, J. Moses, and A. Leween.
23 Report of the Mohawk Institute to the New England Company, 16 September 1896, Truth and Reconciliation Files, Verschoyle Phillip Cronyn Memorial Archives.
24 Evan J. Habkirk, "Charting Continuation: Understanding Post-Traditional Six Nations Militarism, 1814–1930" (PhD diss., University of Western Ontario, 2018), 170, 177, 267.
25 "A Red Man's Cadet Corp," 112. Although there were three companies of the Haldimand Rifles made up of Six Nations men during this period, more work needs to be done comparing the attendance rolls of the Mohawk Institute to the nominal rolls of the 37th Haldimand Rifles to know if this claim is correct.
26 Report of the Mohawk Institute to the New England Company, December 1896, Truth and Reconciliation Files, Verschoyle Phillip Cronyn Memorial Archives.
27 Nominal Rolls of the 38th Dufferin Rifles, Brantford Public Library Local Reading Room.
28 Department of Indian Affairs, *Calisthenics and Games Prescribed for Use in All Indian Schools* (Department of Indian Affairs, 1910), 3.
29 Department of Indian Affairs, 5.
30 Janice Forsyth, "Bodies of Meaning: Sports and Games at Canadian Residential Schools," in *Indigenous Peoples and Sport: Historical Foundations and Contemporary Issues*, ed. Audrey R. Giles and Janice Forsyth (University of British Columbia Press, 2012), 23 and 25. For more on health and the control and retraining of Indigenous bodies, see Mary-Ellen Kelm, *Civilizing Bodies: Aboriginal Health in British Columbia, 1900–50* (University of British Columbia Press, 1998). For more on how this training instilled British imperialism in children, see Anne Bloomfield, "Drill and Dance as Symbols of Imperialism," in *Making Imperial Mentalities: Socialization and British Imperialism*, ed. J. A. Mangan (Manchester University Press, 1990), 74–93.
31 "Souvenir Old Boys Reunion Edition," *Brantford Expositor*, 28–9 December 1898.
32 Truth and Reconciliation Commission of Canada (hereafter TRC), *The Survivors Speak: A Report of the Truth and Reconciliation Commission of Canada* (Truth and Reconciliation Commission of Canada, 2015), 197–8, https://ehprnh2mwo3.exactdn.com/wp-content/uploads/2021/01/Survivors_Speak_English_Web.pdf.

33 Habkirk, "From Indian Boys to Canadian Men?," 227–48; Evan J. Habkirk and Janice Forsyth, "Truth, Reconciliation and the Politics of the Body in Indian Residential School History," *Active History*, 24 January 2016, http://activehistory.ca/papers/truth-reconciliation-and-the-politics-of-the-body-in-indian-residential-school-history/.
34 R. Ashton, Annual Report, 29 April 1909, in Graham, *The Mush Hole*, 105.
35 *Brantford Expositor*, 6 January 1912.
36 A. Nelles Ashton, Annual Report, 31 March 1912, in Graham, *The Mush Hole*, 106.
37 A. Nelles Ashton, Annual Report, 31 March 1913, in Graham, *The Mush Hole*, 107.
38 Report of the Mohawk Institute, 1 April 1880, Truth and Reconciliation Files, Verschoyle Phillip Cronyn Memorial Archives; A. Nelles Ashton, Annual Report, 31 March 1913, in Graham, *The Mush Hole*, 107; Gordon J. Smith to the Secretary of the Department of Indian Affairs, 18 November 1920, File 547,596, Vol. 3224, RG 10, LAC. According to this file, Robert Ashton, who was also the chaplain for the Dufferin Rifles, would take the rent of thirty dollars given to him from the Department of the Militia for use of the range and donate it back to the Dufferin Rifles for regimental use.
39 "Mohawk Cadets Passed Inspection," *Brantford Expositor*, 2 July 1920.
40 For instance, although denying recruiters access to the Mohawk Institute and other schools in 1916, Scott would allow the commander of the 107th Timberwolf Battalion to recruit out of the Elkhorn and Brandon residential schools. See Department of Indian Affairs to William Hamilton Merritt, 26 May 1898, File 171,348, Vol. 2837, RG 10, LAC; Duncan Campbell Scott to Glen Campbell, 11 February 1916, File 452–13, Vol. 6766, RG 10, LAC; TRC, *The Final Report of the Truth and Reconciliation Commission of Canada*, vol. 1, *Canada's Residential Schools, the History, Part 1, Origins to 1939* (McGill-Queen's University Press, 2015), 372.
41 The author completed a survey of the 36th Battalion's nominal rolls found at the Brantford Public Library Local Reading Room. Although no known Grand River Six Nations people were found on the roll during this survey, a more detailed exploration may find the names of other First Nations people who attended the Mohawk Institute. See F. Douglas Reville, *History of the County of Brant*, vol. 2 (Hurley Printing Company, 1920), 465.
42 Reville, 2:601.
43 Nominal Rolls of the Canadian Mounted Rifles, Brantford Public Library Local Reading Room; "We Remember: WWI Records Search" [database], Great War Centenary Association of Brantford, Brant County, and Six Nations, accessed 12 March 2025, http://www.doingourbit.ca/records-search; Richard Holt, "First Nations Soldiers in the Great War," *Native Studies Review* 22, nos. 1 –2 (2013): 147n60.
44 Reville, *History of the County of Brant*, 2:469.
45 Mohawk Institute Honour Roll, St. Paul's Her Majesty's Royal Chapel of the Mohawks. In a 12 June 1925 edition of *The Brantford Expositor*, Privates Charles Wesley and Fredrick Doxtator were added to the honour roll, bringing the total number of staff and students who served in the war to 88, 86 of whom were students.
46 Alison Norman, "Race, Gender and Colonialism: Public Life Among the Six Nations Grand River, 1899–1939" (PhD diss., University of Toronto, 2010), 185.
47 Norman, 185; and Miller, *Shingwauk's Vision*, 298.
48 Acting Principal Boyce Report, July and August 1919, in Graham, *The Mush Hole*, 121. See also "The Russ Moses Residential School Memoir" in this volume.
49 Acting Principal Boyce, Report, July and August 1919, in Graham, *The Mush Hole*, 121.
50 Although it is not known what these items were, other war trophies at Six Nations and Brantford included mortars, machine guns, and field artillery pieces. Rogers's Quarterly Report, 30 September 1923, in Graham, *The Mush Hole*, 140.
51 "The Cadet Movement," Great War Centenary Association of Brantford, Brant County, and Six Nations, accessed 12 March 2025, http://www.doingourbit.ca/cadets; Evan J. Habkirk, "Masking the Support of War: The Anglican Church and the Expansion and Suspension of the Cadets in Brantford, Ontario," *Journal of the Canadian Church History Society* 57 (Spring-Fall 2019): 32–55; Miller, *Shingwauk's Vision*, 227.
52 Boyce to D. C. Scott, 7 September 1919, in Graham, *The Mush Hole*, 28 and 121.
53 Miller, *Shingwauk's Vision*, 227. In Boyce's July 1919 report, she briefly mentions students wearing a "scout hat," meaning that there may have been a Boy Scout troop established at the Mohawk Institute as early as 1919. See Acting Principal Boyce, Report, 2 July 1919, in Graham, *The Mush Hole*, 121.
54 Boyce to Secretary DIA, 2 July 1919, in Graham, *The Mush Hole*, 120–1.

55 Acting Principal Boyce Report, July and August 1919, in Graham, *The Mush Hole*, 121.
56 Boyce Report, November and December 1920, in Graham, *The Mush Hole*, 125.
57 Rogers' Quarterly Report, 30 June 1923, in Graham, *The Mush Hole*, 140.
58 Norman, "Race, Gender and Colonialism," 166.
59 Norman, 167.
60 The IODE also supplied the school children with books and other gifts at Christmas. See "The Russ Moses Residential School Memoir" in this volume; Norman, "Race, Gender and Colonialism," 168.
61 This honour roll was prepared and completed at the request of the New England Company in 1922. See Gordon Smith to Secretary of the DIA, 20 April 1922, in Graham, *The Mush Hole*, 135.
62 "Memorial Unveiled at the Mohawk Church," *Brantford Expositor*, 12 June 1925.
63 "Memorial Unveiled at the Mohawk Church."
64 "Memorial Unveiled at the Mohawk Church."
65 "Memorial Unveiled at the Mohawk Church."
66 "Memorial Unveiled at the Mohawk Church."
67 Tom Holm, *Strong Heart Wounded Souls: First Nations American Veterans of the Vietnam War* (University of Texas Press, 1996), 101, 102, 167; Jim Powless and Mina Burnham, Warrior's Symposium, 13 November 1986, Woodland Cultural Centre, tape 1; Austin Fuller, Warrior's Symposium, 14 November 1986, tape 4.
68 Although the TRC found, through interviews with former students, that students' lived experiences at these schools, including participating in cadet corps, led them to enlist in the Second World War and the Korean War, other studies have shown that the reasons for military participation by Indigenous people is more nuanced and based on their varied cultural understandings and historical experiences. TRC, *The Final Report of the Truth and Reconciliation Commission of Canada*, vol. 1, *Canada's Residential Schools, The History, Part 2, 1939–2000* (McGill-Queen's University Press, 2015), 484. For a Kainai (Blood) perspective, see Yale D. Belanger and Billy Wadsworth, "'It's My Duty . . . To Be a Warrior of the People': Kainai Perceptions of and Participation in the Canadian and American Forces," *Prairie Forum* 33, no. 2 (2008): 297–322. For a Haudenosaunee/Six Nations historical and cultural perspective, see Habkirk, "Charting Continuation."
69 R. Scott Sheffield and Noah Riseman, *Indigenous Peoples and the Second World War: The Politics, Experiences and Legacies of War in the US, Canada, Australia and New Zealand* (Cambridge University Press, 2019), 113.
70 See R. Scott Sheffield, "'Of Pure European Descent and of the White Race': Recruitment Policy and Aboriginal Canadians, 1939–1945," *Canadian Military History* 5, no. 1, (1996): 8–15.
71 TRC, *The History, Part 2, 1939–2000*, 485.
72 Letter to Mr. Driscoll from Bernard F. Neary, 21 January 1947, File 1/25/2010, Vol. 10245, RG 10, LAC.
73 Alex Souchen, personal communication, 26 May 2021. For more on the War Assets Corporation and the buying and selling of Second World War surplus, see Alex Souchen, *War Junk: Munitions Disposal and Postwar Reconstruction in Canada* (University of British Columbia Press, 2020).
74 TRC, *The History, Part 2, 1939–2000*, 485 and various editions of the *Indian School Bulletin*, 1946–57. For more on the *Indian School Bulletin*, see Janice Forsyth and Michael Heine, "'The Only Good Thing That Happened at School': Colonising Narratives of Sport in the *Indian School Bulletin*," *British Journal of Canadian Studies* 30, no. 2 (2017): 205–25.
75 Graham, *The Mush Hole*, 28, and TRC, *The History, Part 2, 1939–2000*, 485.
76 Graham, *The Mush Hole*, 28.
77 TRC, *The History, Part 2, 1939–2000*, 488.
78 TRC, 490; Kevin Woodger, "Whiteness and Ambiguous Canadianization: The Boy Scouts Association and the Canadian Cadet Organization," *Journal of the Canadian Historical Association* 28, no. 1 (2017): 117.
79 TRC, *The History, Part 2, 1939–2000*, 487.
80 TRC, *The Survivors Speak*, 197–8.
81 Albert Sault as cited in Graham, *The Mush Hole*, 399.
82 Igor Egorov, "General History of Cadet Corps in Indian Residential Schools 1879–1996," unpublished report (Ottawa, 2005), 34.
83 Egorov, 58.
84 For more on this, see Jordan Robert Koch, "'Iyacisitayin Newoskan Simakanisikanisak': The (Re)Making of the Hobbema Community Cadet Corps Program" (PhD diss., University of Alberta, 2015).

Figure 5.1. Calum Miller, from Six Nations, in 1936. Photograph taken by D. F. Kidd.
Source: Kenneth Kidd Collection, Trent University Archives

5

"New Weapons": Race, Indigeneity, and Intelligence Testing at the Mohawk Institute, 1920–1949

Alexandra Giancarlo

The history of the Mohawk Institute and its curriculum, and any evaluation of its legacy, rests on two seemingly contradictory facts: Its graduates and their successes were a point of major pride for Six Nations, yet the school also exemplified many of the worst assumptions about the presumed inferiority of Indigenous peoples. It is, therefore, important to separate the educational achievements of notable graduates from the experiences of the masses of children who passed through its doors without graduating or having received a meaningful education. The latter seemed to especially characterize the school in its later years, with one inspector in 1948 noting, "No-one knowing well the conditions of the Mohawk Institute can be happy or satisfied."[1]

In this chapter, I investigate how intelligence testing influenced the structure and curriculum of the Mohawk Institute in the period 1920–49. Records indicate that at least three rounds of IQ testing occurred in these decades at the school. Aside from the formally documented testing, Mohawk Institute officials also used vocabulary throughout this period that indicated a general familiarity with the sorting of pupils into intelligence categories, such as remarks that one boy in the hospital was "sub-normal."[2] The most notable tests were likely those conducted by Elmer Jamieson, himself a Mohawk from Six Nations, for his doctoral dissertation under the supervision of Dr. Peter Sandiford, who was a "self-proclaimed social

Darwinist."³ This research illuminates how discourses of race-based mental inferiority impacted the type and quality of education provided to Indigenous children at the Mohawk Institute and within Canada's residential schools more broadly. It adds to a growing body of scholarship that examines not only the prevalence of intelligence testing for racialized and immigrant students across North America in the early to mid-1900s, but also how the dubious "science" of intelligence was used to, at first justify, and later legitimize school segregation and "special" curricula.⁴ As the history of intelligence testing in moulding education for Ontario's children within the *non*-Indigenous school system is only now being fully written,⁵ it is hoped that the history and analysis offered here contributes to a more fulsome understanding of the society-wide effects of the intelligence testing movement from 1920 to 1949.

Intelligence Testing in Canada

Hereditary theories of intelligence, and their handmaid, eugenics, impacted Canadian society in the realms of educational policy, immigration, and public health.⁶ Ideas linking race and intelligence were not fringe thinking during this period. Beliefs about the inherited nature of intelligence and the general desirability of maintaining an Anglo-Saxon society were common in the early 1900s. During the 1920s, books such as *The Rising Tide of Color Against White World-Supremacy* (L. Stoddard, 1921) and *The Passing of the Great Race* (M. Grant, 1921) made for popular reading across North America.⁷ The conventional wisdom of the period aligned with Sandiford's main argument—that race had a direct relationship with intelligence.⁸

In fact, a general belief that Indigenous North Americans were less intelligent than Europeans had existed for several hundred years.⁹ Scores of studies in the early twentieth century seemed to confirm the "mental deficiency" of non-white groups, especially Black Americans and Indigenous peoples. In the eyes of intelligence testers, inter-group differences in intelligence were real and highly consequential, and widely publicized studies popularized the idea for the North American public that "everyone's intelligence was innate and inherited."¹⁰ Pearce Bailey, a physician, concluded in 1922 that "because mental deficiency is so profusely distributed among Africans and American Indians ... their average intelligence must be inferior to that of average European intelligence."¹¹ In their published reports on testing results, Terman (1916) and Garth (1922, 1923, 1925, 1927) focused on the relationship between intelligence and degree of "Indian blood."¹² These scholars' hypotheses—which their data, unsurprisingly, confirmed—posited that test scores would improve as the amount of white blood increased. It was on these same grounds that the Department of Indian Affairs (DIA) conducted intelligence testing in Manitoba and Saskatchewan residential schools and on-reserve day schools in the late 1920s.[13]

Sandiford, Jamieson's doctoral supervisor, was one of the founders of educational psychology and a proponent of the "mental hygiene" movement. He was a professor of education at the University of Toronto and desired widespread adoption of intelligence testing across Canada.[14] Sandiford had firm beliefs regarding the racial and cultural superiority of Anglo-Saxons. He openly espoused eugenicist beliefs, including sterilization of people deemed to fall outside the bounds of "normal," which was disproportionately extended to include immigrants, racialized peoples, and those of low socio-economic status. In his estimation, it was the duty of the school system to detect inferior children and to "segregate(e) the subnormal."[15] Sandiford's influence on educational policy should not be underestimated as he founded the first university department dedicated to educational research in Canada.[16] Sandiford oversaw Jamieson's study of intelligence among the children of the Six Nations reserve who attended local residential and day schools. This study, detailed below, was published in the *Journal of Educational Psychology* in 1928 and remains accessible in the records of the DIA School Files Series.

"A Complete Mental Survey": The Department of Indian Affairs and "Indian" Intelligence

Common throughout the history of the Canadian residential school system was discourse among administrators regarding the chronic underachievement of Indigenous students attending their schools. From 1890 to 1950, the children showed alarmingly poor grade progression. Across the whole period, more than 60 per cent—and, in some decades, greater than 80 per cent—of children in residential and day schools had not advanced beyond grade 3.[17] Out of more than nine thousand residential school students in 1945, slightly more than one hundred attended grades beyond grade 8 and *none* were enrolled beyond grade 9.[18] At the Mohawk Institute, Elizabeth Graham states that in 1953, about fourteen pupils attended high school.[19] What could account for this so-called "age-grade retardation"? Instead of pointing the finger at the real issues of higher-age enrolments of students who did not speak English fluently, the perennially poorly trained teachers,[20] or underfunding so severe that children regularly missed school to work on school farms, observers identified the children themselves as the main cause of the problem.

Administrators deemed Indigenous pupils "sullen" and "irresponsible" and averred that "you can't treat them like white children."[21] The authors of "Indian Education in Manitoba," an unsigned report found in the United Church of Canada's archives, proclaimed Indigenous people "a distinct sub-species of the human race."[22] According to one inspector, the blame lay in the students' home environments and supposedly hereditary racial traits. Another suspected that the schools were plagued by a large percentage of "sub-normals." He was not alone in this concern. At their 1923 convention, the Workers Among the Methodist Indians of Manitoba passed a resolution expressing approval of the DIA's proposed plan to investigate "sub-normal conditions, mental, moral, and physical, among our Indians."[23] The writer specifically requested that this study focus on, initially, the Brandon Industrial Institute—at the time under Methodist operation—and the boarding school at Norway House that they also ran. The superintendent of Indian education agreed, recommending that an even wider scope be adopted: "A complete mental survey of all Indian children of school age in Canada would be of real value in that the relative capacity of Indian children would be ascertained."[24]

Scholarly works on the Canadian residential schooling system are relatively silent on the role and impact of intelligence testing and scientific racism on both the curricula and outcomes of residential schools. J. R. Miller contends that no "scientific means" were used to confirm the apparently widespread view that Indigenous children were intellectually inferior, while John Milloy points to a dearth of social scientific knowledge as a possible reason for a "lack of agreement about the potential of the Aboriginal race."[25] This ambivalence about Indigenous people's "potential" is clear from the historical record of discussions and conferences that occurred in the early to mid-1900s. For instance, R. A. Hoey, the director of the DIA, wrote to his deputy minister in 1947 to ask for research assistance to better understand "Indian" traits such as a "lack of frugality" and "innate inertia."[26] Meanwhile, DIA Secretary T. R. L. MacInnes publicly claimed that the department did not believe that Indigenous people were mentally less endowed than other races,[27] yet in interdepartmental correspondence classified Indigenous people on a racialized hierarchy from "primitive" to "advanced" (the latter identified by one's length and degree of contact with white civilization).[28]

In Ontario, during the 1920s, intelligence testing was "an important bureaucratic response and strategy for creating an efficient, differentiated system of schooling based on 'scientific' methods."[29] While it is clear that the goings-on of the academic world were not always definitively linked to policy shifts at the DIA, social sciences research can be thought of as forming a general frame of reference for the DIA.[30] The DIA itself existed within a broader socio-political context in which Indigenous peoples and their cultures were seen as a hindrance to nation building. As the Truth and Reconciliation Commission (TRC) bluntly states in its final report, "successive governments considered Aboriginal people inferior."[31] Missionary teachers, Miller observes, largely "subscribed to the pervasive racism of Euro-Canadian society."[32]

Despite the schools' abhorrent educational record and limited genuine commitment to curricular improvements, policy-makers at the DIA could not claim ignorance of the pedagogical trends gripping the educational landscape of the time. A deeper look into the school system's archives suggest that "scientific" evidence linking race and intelligence circulated through the communication networks of the DIA and that officials sought out information from other educational contexts to inform their decisions. In devising his testing program for the industrial schools in Canada's West, one zealous school inspector referenced a study conducted at an "Indian" boarding school in Kansas in which test results showed a negative correlation between intelligence and percentage of "Indian blood."[33] Philip Phelan, chief of the Training Division, wrote to the Mohawk Institute's principal that he was travelling to Toronto to attend an Ontario Educational Association's meeting in 1944,[34] indicating that, at minimum, the DIA valued the association's professional insights. Furthermore, the DIA's files contain evidence that they had received publications on the topic of race and intelligence and were clearly conversant in these matters, or at least thought they ought to be. A copy of the article "How People Differ Mentally," originally printed in *Scientific American*, was found in DIA correspondence from 1929. There is also evidence that the article's conclusions about race and mental ability were not without challenge; the author's statement that "the newer generation of Negroes are more intelligent, due to an admixture of appreciable amounts of white blood" is accompanied by a marginal rebuttal of unknown penmanship: "No! Cultural."[35]

"New Weapons": Testing at the Mohawk Institute

As a large farm- and livestock-based institution that remained close to major urban centres, the Mohawk Institute during the second quarter of the twentieth century was emblematic of the contradictions and tensions at the heart of the residential school project. Its curriculum—such as it was—exemplified the system's multiple, and at times competing, purposes of education, manual training, and evangelization, in its later years increasingly serving as a child welfare institution. Across these decades, concerned parents, the public, clergy, and DIA officials themselves levelled complaints about the poor conditions at the institution. Many of these focused on educational provisions or lack thereof. The male students were regularly spoken about as a labour pool for the Institute, and while this work would have had some instructional worth, DIA officials themselves questioned the value of what was euphemistically called "manual training."[36] For example, officials engaged in discussion about the closure of the school's greenhouse, deemed of little value to the students who ran it, even as the principal argued for its necessity as a revenue source.[37] The Institute was able to reduce costs and, in all likelihood, keep its doors open, by pressing pupils into roles that should have been filled by paid labourers.

Under such conditions, the TRC's conclusions speak volumes: "the vocational training program too often degenerated into a student labour program."[38] At the Mohawk Institute, a 1944 inspection revealed that the Institute's inability to hire a qualified teacher meant that "the boys evidently receive little vocational training."[39] One student, Peter Smith, who attended in the 1930s explained that he "had to work all the time. We got up at 6 in the morning and we worked until 6 at night."[40] In 1946, outrage from the local Women's Council prompted an investigation into the "alleged lack of sufficient clothing and educational opportunities" at the school.[41] Two years later, an inspector still had cause to comment that a proper primary classroom needed to be added as he had seen a small child sleeping under one of the desks in the junior room (see image of the report in figure 5.2).[42] The problems of overworking students and a corresponding lack of educational opportunity clearly persisted for decades.

In a 1925 letter to the superintendent of Indian education, Elmer Jamieson set out his plan for intelligence and achievement tests to be administered to the students of the Six Nations School Board, from which permission had also been granted. Jamieson hailed from one of Six Nations' most well-known families with a deep interest in, and commitment to, education for Indigenous children. Two of his sisters were teachers on the reserve for many decades and were honoured by the DIA upon their retirements.[43] Their brother, Andrew, was the first Six Nations graduate of the Ontario Agricultural College (1931) and went on to become a school principal on the reserve.[44] Explaining that he was working under the supervision

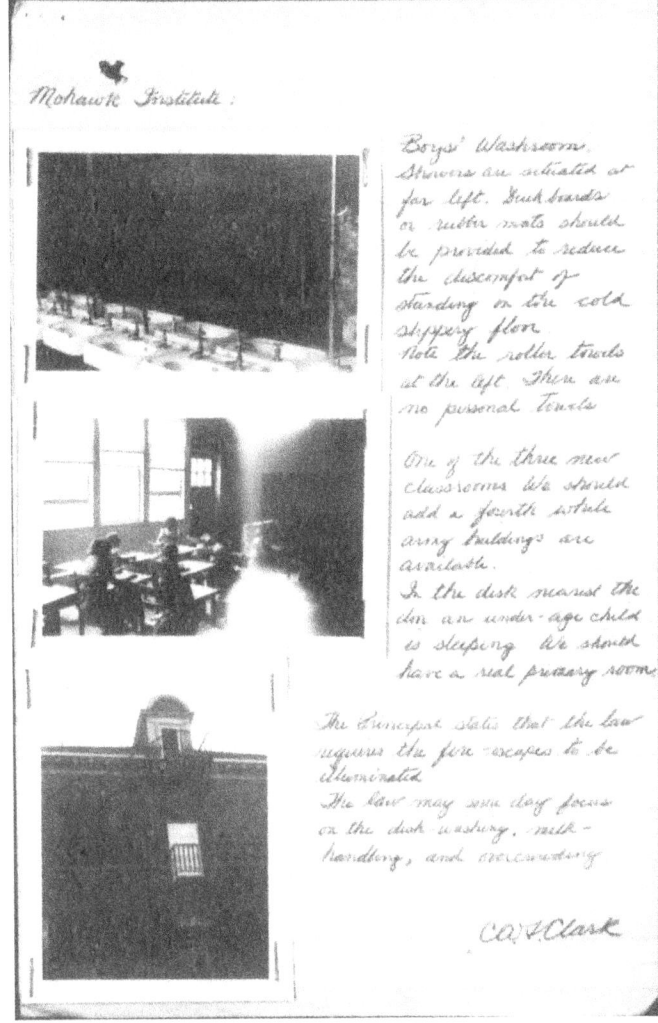

Figure 5.2. A page from C. A. F. Clark's report on the Mohawk Institute in 1948, with photos

Source: C.A.F. Clark, Report to Colonel Neary of conditions at the Mohawk Institute, 24 September 1948, File 466-1, Pt. 5, c-7933, Vol. 6200, RG 10, Library and Archives Canada

of Dr. Sandiford, Jamieson expressed the hope that his results comparing Indigenous, white, Asian, and Black students could be put to "practical uses."[45] Russell T. Ferrier, superintendent of Indian education, responded to confirm the department's approval of the research.[46] Separately, Ferrier wrote to the Mohawk Institute's principal to request the school's assistance,[47] and Ferrier's deputy wrote to the Brantford Indian superintendent requesting the same.[48] We know that the testing was undertaken later that month as reported by the principal.[49] According to the report on student activities up to the end of March 1926 compiled by Principal Sydney Rogers, Jamieson's research was rather extensive, as he had been spending many weekends "conducting his intelligence tests."[50] He returned in June to continue this work.[51]

It seemed that his efforts were already paying dividends as, according to Rogers, he was able to identify a "troublesome" girl in the senior class as having "the mentality of a child of five."[52] Indeed, low IQ scores were blamed for various behavioural problems at the Institute, such as pupils running away.[53] The links between bad behaviour and limited intelligence reflected beliefs about unchecked "mental deficiency" characteristic of the time period. Educational experts blamed what was then referred to as "feeblemindedness" for a range of social problems.[54]

As an indication of how the new science of intelligence testing had reached those on the periphery of the teaching profession, Principal Rogers already had familiarity with IQ categorizations by the time Jamieson arrived to conduct his research. He recounted in his quarterly report the previous year that "Mr. McFadden of the local Collegiate conducted some psychological tests upon our pupils . . . in order that he might compare children of Indian descent with others."[55] Patrice Milewski explains that, as part of a growing cadre of institutional experts in the science of education in Ontario, the local public-school inspector usually administered such mental tests.[56] Though the frequency of interactions between the DIA, its schools, and the Ontario Department of Education is not fully known (or it is not evident through the limited lens of the DIA School Files series), this chapter demonstrates that the students of the Institute were of interest to educators and educational researchers of the period who endeavoured to harness mental testing to "identify and sort students and arrange appropriate forms of schooling based on innate abilities (or inabilities)."[57]

Jamieson clearly understood the ramifications of such testing regimes on the opportunities provided to Indigenous students. In his article based on the tests conducted at the Six Nations schools, "The mental capacity of Southern Ontario Indians," he calls intelligence and achievement tests "new weapons in the hands of those who wish to compare the intelligence and achievement of different races."[58] While a cursory read of his results suggests they conform to the racialized conclusions about intelligence typical of the time period, his analysis subtly pointed researchers away from understanding test results as firm conclusions about race and intellect—surely no small feat under the tutelage of Sandiford. He cautioned readers to recognize that residential school pupils are likely to score less well owing to their half day of work. Their lack of proficiency in English, he reminded the reader, would also hamper pupils' abilities. He noted that "every one" of the children tested "suffered from a language handicap" in these types of tests.[59] He pointed out that lower socio-economic status and irregular school attendance also limited the achievement of some students. Jamieson advocated for further studies that could account for these "environmental" factors and asked that "deductions from the results" should be made carefully.[60]

While not offering an outright rejection of the race-based intelligence theories of the day, Jamieson is considerably more circumspect than many of his peers and certainly more so than his supervisor, Sandiford. After all, Jamieson understood that the stakes were high with these "new weapons." From his previous 1922 work, he also knew that Indigenous students were disadvantaged by a curriculum that did not follow the provincial guidelines and appeared to be "made simple and constructed differently" than that of white schools.[61] Though I have not been able to locate any first-hand accounts of Jamieson reflecting on this research, we know that he was deeply committed to education for Indigenous children and can surmise that he sought to disarm the "new weapons" of intelligence and achievement tests by emphasizing the external factors hampering pupils' scholarly achievements.

Given the heightened interest in classifying student populations according to "innate" traits during these decades, Jamieson's was not the only major round of testing to occur at the Mohawk Institute. Though relatively little contextual information is provided in the DIA School Files Series, documents that have been preserved at the Woodland Cultural Centre show that a teacher at the school conducted intelligence and achievement tests in the mid-1930s.[62] Kenneth E. Kidd gave the students the National Intelligence Test, the Pinter-Cunningham Primary Mental Test, and other supplementary testing instruments. He summarized his results in a manuscript, "A Study of the Mental Ability of the Indian Children in Mohawk Institute, 1934–1935."[63] It appears that it was unpublished, but the date given is June 1935. Although he employed distasteful and stereotypical language common to the time to describe students, in a manner similar to Jamieson's, he provided more analytical nuance than is typical. For instance, he identified students' language limitations and proposed that those more familiar with white culture have a testing advantage. He also stated that he does not believe that mental inferiority of Indigenous children has been proven.

Despite this seemingly more measured view, two publications about his teaching at the Institute tell a different story. In "The Education of the Canadian Indian" (1937), he expresses his low opinion of Indigenous culture, and in "The Basis of Indian Culture" (1936) he presents white "civilization" as the unquestioned goal for Indigenous people and comments on a student's "apparent stupidity."[64] It seems that when it came time to speak publicly about Indigenous education, his previously sympathetic tone had changed—perhaps to fall in line with the prevailing sentiments of the era. In the final analysis, it is difficult to know what to make of Kidd; his early works cited here, based on his testing of Mohawk Institute pupils, are unflattering in their assessments (though notably less so than those of many of his contemporaries). However, Graham states that Kidd remained lifelong friends with many of his students, and he went on to found Trent University's Indian-Eskimo Studies Program, which later became Native Studies.[65]

According to correspondence pertaining to the Mohawk Institute in 1948 and 1949, the changing student body warranted major curriculum alterations. To understand these changes and their significance for the educational opportunities provided to the Institute's students, a bit of context is warranted. A 1941 three-page report from the inspector of auxiliary classes for the Ontario Department of Education, C. E. Stothers, conveyed the results of a preliminary study of residential schools by a Miss Helen L. Delaporte, who was his assistant inspector of auxiliary classes. "Auxiliary classes," in the language of the early to mid-1900s, were "separate classrooms for children with learning difficulties or intellectual disabilities."[66] In her report, Delaporte explained that Indigenous students are currently given a full academic course load but, owing to intellectual deficiencies, should be given curricula for "dull-normal" and "retarded" children. Only "special cases of apparent brilliancy" warranted a full academic course load. Delaporte pointed out that Mr. Jamieson's studies showed an IQ between 80 and 85 for students at the school. These results, which Jamieson had intended to be interpreted cautiously, in Delaporte's view meant that "over half of the pupils have little chance of getting their entrance to high school."[67] While Jamieson had encouraged his results to be interpreted with care, Delaporte used the results of his educational testing with Six Nations students as part of her justification in recommending curricula equivalent to today's "special education" because of the apparent lower intellectual abilities of Indigenous children. It could be argued, in fact, that she used his results as the "new weapons" he spoke out against.

Correspondence between the church, the bishop, and the local board of education during the late 1940s centres on how to manage the Mohawk Institute's changing student body. The bishop of Huron stated that he had consulted with the Mohawk Institute's principal, the City of London's assistant school superintendent, a local school principal, and a member of the province's Royal Commission on Education. This bishop, C. A. Seager, noted that as the Institute increasingly came to serve a child-welfare purpose, the quality of students plummeted, due to emotional problems, delayed mental abilities, and, perhaps, "definite mental defectiveness." He determined that a survey of mental ability should be conducted and, if needed, "special opportunity" classes established. Seager also suggested that the handful of students found to be of high intelligence should be trained to assist school staff.[68] In response, the representative of the DIA, probably Superintendent of Indian Education Colonel Neary, concurred, writing that soon, "a great many of the pupils . . . will be backward and in the low intelligence classes." He asked the ODE to conduct intelligence assessments of the Mohawk Institute's students.[69] Though the results of the intelligence testing themselves are not found in the existing records, the evaluations were carried out by Brantford Public School Inspector J. O. Webster in late 1947 or early 1948.[70] A 1949 letter confirms that only 1 in 25 students were found to be of normal intelligence and 40 out of the total 155 students should be placed in "auxiliary" classes.[71] Intelligence testing, with its built-in class and race biases, led to fewer opportunities for Indigenous students by restricting their education to the vocational "crafts"-based curricula prescribed for "auxiliary" classes.

Conclusion

The point here is not to discount the genuine need for auxiliary education for some students in the residential school system, but rather to identify how race and class biases inherent to intelligence testing led to Indigenous students at the Institute—and beyond—being unfairly labelled as lacking in intellectual capacities. One of the foremost authorities on the Indian Residential School system explains that the system's teachers often held the belief that their students were incapable of completing a regular public-school course. This lack of confidence in Indigenous students' abilities "helped limit achievement and no doubt reinforced the negative stereotyping of the children."[72]

By the 1920s, intelligence testing was standard curriculum at the Ontario College of Education. As historian Jennifer Anne Stephen explains, such systematic testing was seen as "smart social and economic policy" that helped to limit "social malaise caused by mental deficiency."[73] Children were to be streamed early, ideally beginning at age seven, into academic or non-academic programs.[74] In the residential school system, it was not uncommon for students to enrol for the first time at age seven or older. Students, mostly older ones, attended class for only part of the day and were forced to work as the schools' main labour force. In fact, in a 1949 letter to DIA headquarters, one teacher candidate for a position at the Mohawk Institute offered her opinion that "the rule be established and enforced that Indian children attend school a <u>full</u> and not a half day at present."[75] The following year a letter from Principal Zimmerman to Colonel Neary, superintendent of Indian education, indicated that children from grade 5 onward still only had a half day of classes.[76] A great chasm separated what have since been called child labour institutions masquerading as schools from the modern school system so described, yet Indigenous students were judged by the latter standards and found lacking.

When their intelligence testing scores were considered in light of the prevailing "racial template of intelligence,"[77] inspectors, educational psychologists, school administrators, and DIA officials concluded that residential school students themselves, not the dysfunctional and degrading institutions they were forced to attend, were the cause of insufficient levels of achievement. The Mohawk Institute graduated many notable Six Nations students who went on to become educators and other professionals across Canadian society. Their successes challenged racial stereotypes. Yet they were the exceptions at an institution that was plagued by the same inadequacies that characterized the residential school system as a whole. Out of the thirty-six former students that Graham interviewed for her book published in 1997, not a single respondent credited the education received at the Mohawk Institute for their life successes.[78] From 1929 to 1969, no more than 5 per cent of students per year attended high school; during the period that the Reverend Horace Snell was principal (1929–45), some students left the Institute "barely literate."[79] Intelligence tests were used to justify a claim that Indigenous students possessed lower "mental powers," which was subsequently used to justify a reduced curriculum and in turn limit students' future potential.

NOTES

Small sections of this chapter were previously published in Alexandra Giancarlo, "To 'Evaluate the Mental Powers of the Indian Children': Race and Intelligence Testing in Canada's Indian Residential School System," *Historical Studies in Education / Revue d'histoire de l'éducation* 34, no. 2 (2022), https://doi.org/10.32316/hse-rhe.v34i2.5021.

1. E. P. Randle, to Superintendent, Indian Affairs Branch, 16 September 1948, File 466-1, Pt. 5, c-7933, Vol. 6200, RG 10, Library and Archives Canada (hereafter LAC).
2. S. Rogers to Medical Branch, Dept. Indian Affairs, Ottawa, 7 July 1929, File 466-13, Pt. 1, c-7935, Vol. 6202, RG 10, LAC.
3. Angus McLaren, *Our Own Master Race: Eugenics in Canada, 1885–1945* (University of Toronto Press, 1990), 62.
4. Carlos Kevin Blanton, "From Intellectual Deficiency to Cultural Deficiency: Mexican Americans, Testing, and Public School Policy in the American Southwest, 1920–1940," *Pacific Historical Review* 72, no. 1 (2003): 39–62.
5. Jason Ellis, *A Class by Themselves? The Origins of Special Education in Toronto and Beyond* (University of Toronto Press, 2019).
6. Ellis.
7. G. Thomson, "'So Many Clever, Industrious and Frugal Aliens': Peter Sandiford, Intelligence Testing, and Anti-Asian Sentiment in Vancouver Schools Between 1920 and 1939," *BC Studies* 197 (2018): 67–100.
8. Jennifer Anne Stephen, *Pick One Intelligent Girl: Employability, Domesticity, and the Gendering of Canada's Welfare State, 1939–1947* (University of Toronto Press, 2007), 68.
9. James Waldram, *Revenge of the Windigo: The Construction of the Mind and Mental Health of North American Aboriginal Peoples* (University of Toronto Press, 2004), 90.
10. Ellis, *A Class by Themselves?*, 56.
11. Quoted in Waldram, *Revenge of the Windigo*, 90–1.
12. Cited in Waldram, 91.
13. See, for example, Bartlett 1927[?] and Bartlett 1929. G. W. Bartlett, Notes, handwritten and signed by Bartlett, recording the results of the Otis Intelligence Test at the Haskell Institute, 1927[?], File 1/25-17, Pt. 1, c-9721, Vol. 8807, RG 10, LAC; G. W. Bartlett, Inspector's report on the Birtle Residential Indian School, 12 September 1929, File 511/23-5-014, c-13800, Vol. 8449, RG 10, LAC.
14. G. Thomson, "'So Many Clever.'"
15. Thomson, "'So Many Clever,'" 73.
16. Patrice Milewski, "The Scientisation of Schooling in Ontario, 1910–1934," *Paedagogica Historica* 46, no. 3 (2010): 348; Stephen, *Pick One*, 72.
17. See John S. Milloy, *A National Crime: The Canadian Government and the Residential School System* (1999; University of Manitoba Press, 2017), 171.
18. Milloy, 171.
19. Elizabeth Graham, *The Mush Hole: Life at Two Residential Schools* (Heffle Publishing, 1997), 17–18.
20. A 1948 departmental study indicated that although its teachers were supposed to have provincial certificates and follow the provincial curricula, 40 per cent had no professional training. Some had not even graduated from high school. See Milloy, *A National Crime*, 176. Occasionally, dissenting observers raised this very point, arguing that the substandard teaching endemic to the system was surely to blame for the students' poor progress, not any "racial" trait (school inspector H. McArthur, in Milloy, 180). At the Mohawk Institute, there were regular complaints about the quality of the teachers, which in turn reflected the insufficient operating grants common across the residential school system.
21. E. Stehelin, quoted in Milloy, 179.
22. No author, "Indian Education in Manitoba," ca. 1920, filed in the United Church of Canada's Archives, Winnipeg.
23. Rev. F. G. Stevens, Fisher River Indian Mission, to Department of Indian Affairs, 26 June 1923, File 1/25-17, Pt. 1, Vol. 8807, RG 10, LAC. Little detail in the file is provided about the convening body, the Workers Among the Methodist Indians of Manitoba; however, the Methodists had a substantial role in missionary efforts in what was then called Rupert's Land beginning in 1840. See Elizabeth Bingham Young and E. Ryerson Young, *Mission Life in Cree-Ojibwe Country: Memories of a Mother and Son*, ed. Jennifer S. H. Brown (Athabasca University Press, 2017).

24 Russell T. Ferrier, Superintendent of Indian Education, to Reverend F. G. Stevens, Koostatak, MB, 10 July 1923, File 1/25-17, Pt. 1, c-9721, Vol. 8807, RG 10, LAC.
25 Miller, *Shingwauk's Vision*, 179; Milloy, *A National Crime*, 153
26 Quoted in H. Shewell, "'What Makes the Indian Tick?' The Influence of Social Sciences on Canada's Indian Policy, 1947–1964," *Histoire sociale / Social History* 34, no. 67 (2001): 148.
27 A. G. Bailey, "Reviewed Work: The North American Indian Today by C. T. Loram, T. F. McIlwraith," *Canadian Journal of Economics and Political Science / Revue canadienne d'Economique et de Science politique* 10, no. 1 (1944): 110–12.
28 Jacqueline Briggs, "Exemplary Punishment: T. R. L. MacInnes, the Department of Indian Affairs, and Indigenous Executions, 1936–52," *Canadian Historical Review* 100, no. 3 (2019): 398–438.
29 Milewski, "The Scientisation of Schooling," 378; Ellis, *A Class by Themselves?*
30 Shewell, "'What Makes the Indian Tick?,'" 138.
31 Truth and Reconciliation Commission of Canada, *The Final Report of the Truth and Reconciliation Commission of Canada*, vol. 5, *Canada's Residential Schools: The Legacy* (McGill-Queen's University Press, 2015), 62.
32 Miller, *Shingwauk's Vision*, 186.
33 Bartlett 1927[?].
34 Philip Phelan to Horace Snell, principal of the Mohawk Institute, 31 March 1944, File 466-1, Pt. 3, c-7933, Vol. 6200, RG 10, LAC.
35 Donald A. Laird, clipping from *The Canadian Military Gazette* in which Laird's article from *Scientific American* was originally reprinted, 1929, File 1/25-17, Pt. 1, c-9721, Vol. 8807, RG 10, LAC.
36 For example, principal Horace Snell wrote to headquarters to confirm that the pupils repainted the "entire exterior" of the Mohawk Institute as well as painted and varnished the interior. Horace Snell, Principal of the Mohawk Institute, to Secretary, Department of Indian Affairs, 14 November 1930, File 466-5, Pt. 3, c-7934, Vol. 6201, RG 10, LAC.
37 Horace Snell, Principal of the Mohawk Institute, to Secretary, Department of Indian Affairs, 17 March 1936, File 466-1, Pt. 2, c-7933, Vol. 6200, RG 10, LAC; A. F. MacKenzie, Secretary of the Department of Indian Affairs, Letter from A. F. MacKenzie, to H. W. Snell, Principal of the Mohawk Institute, 26 February 1936, File 466-1, Pt. 2, c-7933, Vol. 6200, RG 10, LAC.
38 Truth and Reconciliation Commission of Canada, *The Final Report of the Truth and Reconciliation Commission of Canada*, vol. 1, *Canada's Residential Schools, the History, Part 1, Origins to 1939* (McGill-Queen's University Press, 2015), 331.
39 Philip Phelan to Horace Snell, Principal of the Mohawk Institute, 31 March 1944, File 466-1, Pt. 3, c-7933, Vol. 6200, RG 10, LAC.
40 Truth and Reconciliation Commission, *Final Report*, 1:343.
41 "Probe Ordered into Affairs of Indian School," *Globe and Mail*, 23 February 1946, 5.
42 C. A. F. Clark, Report to Colonel Neary of conditions at the Mohawk Institute, 24 September 1948, File 466-1, Pt. 5, c-7933, Vol. 6200, RG 10, LAC.
43 "Honor Two Indian Sisters on Retirement: Teaching Years Total 82 on Reservation," *Indian Record* 20, no. 1 (January 1957).
44 "Note Three Grads from Farm College," *Indian Record* 5, no. 4 (April 1962).
45 E. Jamieson to Mr. R. T. Ferrier, Superintendent of Indian Education, Department of Indian Affairs, 14 December 1925, File 1/25-17, Pt. 1, c-9721, Vol. 8807, RG 10, LAC.
46 Russell T. Ferrier to Elmer Jamieson, 16 December 1925, File 1/25-17, Pt. 1, c-9721, Vol. 8807, RG 10, LAC.
47 Russell T. Ferrier to S. Rogers, Principal of the Mohawk Institute, 16 December 1925, File 1/25-17, Pt. 1, c-9721, Vol. 8807, RG 10, LAC.
48 J. D. McLean to Lieutenant Colonel Morgan, Indian Superintendent, Brantford, File 1/25-17, Pt. 1, c-9721, Vol. 8807, RG 10, LAC.
49 S. Rogers, "Report on activities and progress of this Institute" (quarter ending 31 December 1925), 5 January 1926, File 466-1, Pt. 2, c-7933, Vol. 6200, RG 10, LAC.
50 S. Rogers, "Report on activities and progress of this Institute" (quarter ending 31 March 1926), 1926, exact date unknown, File 466-1, Pt. 2, c-7933, Vol. 6200, RG 10, LAC.
51 S. Rogers, "Report on activities and progress of this Institute" (quarter ending 30 June 1926), 3 July 1926, File 466-1, Pt. 2, c-7933, Vol. 6200, RG 10, LAC.
52 Rogers, "Report on activities and progress of this Institute" (quarter ending 31 March 1926), 1926.

53 Rogers, "Report on activities" (quarter ending 31 December 1925), 1926.
54 Ellis, *A Class by Themselves?*, 18–19.
55 S. Rogers, Mohawk Institute, Quarterly Report (quarter ending 31 December 1924), 1924, File 466-1, Pt. 1, c-7933, Vol. 6200, RG 10, LAC.
56 Milewski, "The Scientisation of Schooling," 347.
57 Milewski, 351.
58 Elmer Jamieson, "The Mental Capacity of Southern Ontario Indians" (repr., including original page numbers, from the May 1928 issue of *Journal of Educational Psychology*), 313, File 1/25-17, Pt. 1, c-9721, Vol. 8807, RG 10, LAC.
59 Jamieson, 325.
60 Jamieson, 326.
61 Quoted in Constance Barbara Thomas, "Indian Education in Canada" (master's thesis, McMaster University, 1972), 109.
62 Thank you to Rick Hill for flagging these documents and sharing copies with me.
63 Kenneth E. Kidd, "A Study of the Mental Ability of the Indian Children in Mohawk Institute, 1934–1935" (unpublished manuscript, June 1935).
64 Kenneth E. Kidd. "The Education of the Ontario Indian," *Canadian School Journal* (January 1937); Kenneth E. Kidd, "The Basis of Indian Education," unknown publication [probably *Canadian School Journal*] (September 1936): 253.
65 Graham, *The Mush Hole*.
66 Ellis, *A Class by Themselves?*
67 C. E. Stothers, Memorandum for the Superintendent of Indian Affairs, 6 February 1941, File 1/25-17, Pt. 1, c-9721, Vol. 8807, RG 10, LAC.
68 C. A. Seager, Archbishop of Huron Diocese, to the Minister of Mines and Resources, 10 February 1948, File 466-1, Pt. 5, c-7933, Vol. 6200, RG 10, LAC.
69 Unknown government official to Archbishop Seager, 13 February 1948, File 466-1, Pt. 5, c-7933, Vol. 6200, RG 10, LAC.
70 Bernard F. Neary, Letter from Neary, Superintendent of Welfare and Training, to J. O. Webster, Inspector of Public Schools, Brantford, 22 January 1948, File 466-1, Pt. 5, c-7933, Vol. 6200, RG 10, LAC.
71 Bishop Luxton to Colonel F. B. Neary 10 February 10, 1949, File 466-1, Pt. 5, c-7933, Vol. 6200, RG 10, LAC.
72 Miller, *Shingwauk's Vision*, 180.
73 Stephen, *Pick One*, 67.
74 Stephen, 72.
75 Alexandria How[?] to Philip Phelan, Chief, Education Division, Indian Affairs Branch, 17 September 1949, File 466-1, Pt. 5, c-7933, Vol. 6200, RG 10, LAC.
76 Graham, *The Mush Hole*, 193.
77 Stephen, *Pick One*, 68.
78 Graham, *The Mush Hole*, 17–18.
79 Wendy Fletcher, "The Canadian Experiment with Social Engineering, A Historical Case: The Mohawk Institute," *Historical Papers: Canadian Society of Church History* (July 2004): 133–49.

PART 3
The Building, the Grounds, and Commemoration

Figure 0.7. Undated photo, Mohawk Institute grounds
Source: Woodland Cultural Centre

170

6

A "Model" School: An Architectural History of the Mohawk Institute

Magdalena Miłosz

Looking "behind the bricks" of the Mohawk Institute means understanding the experiences of the children who lived there: the routines, interactions with staff, work, play, discipline, and resistance that happened inside and outside its walls. Yet the "bricks" themselves—the architecture of the institution and its role in these experiences—merit attention as well. How did the children perceive the walls that confined them? Who designed, built, and maintained the institution's buildings and landscapes? What were the practical and symbolic contributions of architecture in enacting an assimilative program? How did the architecture serve to shield the workings of the school from surrounding settler neighbourhoods? This chapter engages the built environment of the Mohawk Institute to explore these questions.

Industrial and residential schools for Indigenous children have not been extensively considered in the field of architectural history. Janet Wright mentions industrial schools in her study of Canadian federal architecture, *Crown Assets*, placing these "permanent and imposing symbols of the dominance and supremacy of white society" in the context of late nineteenth-century assimilation policy in Western Canada. "The design of these schools," she writes, "which was firmly rooted in white society, was clearly intended to support and reinforce the values, skills, and codes of behaviour in which the students were so rigorously indoctrinated."[1] For Geoffrey Carr, although residential schools bear a passing resemblance to building types like schools and prisons, they exist outside of these conventional typologies because "they cannot be understood apart from the distinct impressions of colonial power that required [their] construction."[2] Focusing on schools in British Columbia, Carr uses their architecture as a historical source to both broaden understandings of the residential school system and to address what he sees as a gap in Canadian architectural history—namely, the role of architecture in settler-state oppression against Indigenous peoples.[3] These histories interpret the architecture of industrial and residential schools as inseparable from their colonial purposes.[4]

Scholars in other disciplines have likewise used themes of space, place, and architecture to study residential schools. Like the architectural historians cited above, geographer Sarah de Leeuw links the physical spaces of residential schools to larger systems of power, arguing that these institutions existed in nested, "multidirectional and permeable" relationships with both "the smaller body-places" of students and "larger spatial colonial projects."[5] In other words, the architectural scale of the residential school functioned as an intermediary between the human scale of Indigenous children's bodies and the regional or national scale of settler-colonial acquisition of Indigenous territory. In the US context, historian Jacqueline Fear-Segal's work on the Carlisle Indian Industrial School in Pennsylvania examines how racial segregation was implicit in the buildings' uses and spatial relationships at the scale of the campus.[6] She argues that Carlisle's built environment served a dual purpose, that of enabling control and surveillance of students and that of conveying to non-Indigenous outsiders the benefits of assimilating Indigenous peoples.[7] As this chapter will show, a similar dynamic animated the architecture of the Mohawk Institute. Domesticity is embedded in the architecture of residential schools, and anthropologist Jo-Anne Fiske looks specifically at changing understandings of their domestic character in light of survivors' disclosures of abuse. She charts how survivor testimony catalyzed a "discursive shift" about residential schools from private to public, from the schools possessing a "mystique of domestic altruism" to becoming "the most poignant symbol of colonial violence."[8] This scholarship suggests that the architectural scale of residential schools can illuminate both the broader aims of the settler-colonial authorities who built them and the experiences of the children who were taken there.[9]

This chapter takes a similar, multi-scalar approach to the architectural history of the Mohawk Institute. The first three sections examine the institution's three main architectural phases: its beginnings at the Mohawk Village in 1828 and conversion into a residential institution in 1834, the yellow-brick building constructed in 1858, and the red-brick building of 1904, which still stands today. Although this periodization is based on the construction dates of new main buildings, it is important to note that the built environment of the Mohawk Institute was in fact undergoing continuous change through repairs, renovations, additions, and other modifications. Furthermore, the spaces of the institution extended far beyond the main buildings, encompassing many outbuildings within expansive agrarian and ornamental landscapes. Nonetheless, this periodization is useful because each of the three phases can be understood through an additional layer of historical evidence, from text only, to visual sources such as plans and photographs, through to the testimony of survivors.

This layering of evidence renders an increasingly complex view of the Mohawk Institute's built environment over time, moving from official viewpoints to the experiences of the children who inhabited and laboured within it. Some key themes that reappear throughout this long history are official perceptions of the school as a "model" or "pattern" institution, the use of architecture for segregation and control, as well as continual change through repairs, renovations, and additions, frequently using the children's labour. The fourth section of this chapter pays particular attention to how survivors understood the built environment of the Mohawk Institute, with a focus on segregation, discipline, labour, and play. The final section examines the extensive architectural changes of the post–Second World War period, associated with the government's attempts to reform the residential school system. Taken together, this chapter demonstrates how the architecture of the Mohawk Institute not only reflected, but also enacted, the goals of missionaries and the state. It was not a backdrop, but a key component of the daily struggles of power, assimilation, and resistance that took place at the school.

The Mohawk Institute at the Mohawk Village: Beginnings to Abandonment (1828–1858)

A predecessor of the Mohawk Institute was a day school established in the Mohawk Village in the 1780s by the Kanyen'kehaka (Mohawk) leader Thayendanegea, also known as Joseph Brant.[10] In his youth, Brant had been educated at Moor's Charity School in Lebanon, Connecticut, which aimed to train Indigenous and settler students as missionaries, diplomats, and translators.[11] Brant's time at the school was among the experiences that shaped his "cross-cultural belief systems," which Rick Monture argues "influenced not only his own life, but . . . also had considerable impact upon the rest of the Six Nations throughout the rest of the late eighteenth century."[12] The school stood across from the Mohawk Chapel, a small Carpenter Gothic Anglican church, in a settlement of about twenty-four houses as well as a council house.[13] Both the church and the school were part of the strategy of cultural syncretism by which Six Nations intended to maintain control of their lands and continue their distinct Haudenosaunee identity in the face of colonial pressures.[14]

This perspective of cultural exchange was reflected in a 1781 publication, *A Primer for the Use of the Mohawk Children / Waerighwaghsawe iksaongoenwa*, which contains lessons printed in English on one side and Kanyen'keha on the other.[15] It was written by Daniel Claus, who supervised the resettlement of the Six Nations at Grand River following the loss of their lands during the American Revolution. The second edition, published in 1786, features an engraved frontispiece by James Peachey depicting a classroom with Kanyen'kehaka students and their teacher (figure 6.1). It has been speculated that the teacher in the scene is a portrayal of Paulus Sahonwadi, a Kanyen'kehaka schoolmaster who was acquainted with Claus and was living at Grand River by 1785.[16] Likewise, it is tempting to conjecture that the engraving might represent the interior of the first Mohawk Village school as it actually existed. The artist, Peachey, was known for his watercolour views of Canadian places; he was also a surveyor and draughtsman associated with Governor Frederick Haldimand and would have had occasion to visit the Mohawk Village in person.[17] The high wood-beam ceiling, wood floorboards, and double-hung window shown in the engraving may well reflect the space in which young Kanyen'kehaka scholars learned during a time of great transition for their nation.

The beginnings of the Mohawk Institute itself came forty years later, a decade after the original day school was disrupted by the War of 1812. No visual sources or student testimonies exist from this early era, although some sense of what the institution looked like can be pieced together from settler-colonial texts, especially the reports of the New England Company (NEC), the missionary society which ran it. A short account by the notorious Indian Affairs bureaucrat Duncan Campbell Scott, written a century after the Mohawk Institute's founding, is also useful.

Scott writes that in 1822, Joseph Brant's son, John Brant (Ahyonwaeghs), travelled to England, with "one of his requests being the establishment of an Indian school."[18] What Scott does not mention is that Brant made this request in the context of a broader appeal for the Crown to take action on the "undue acquisition" and "encroachments upon" Six Nations territory.[19]

Figure 6.1. The Mohawk Village School, 1780s.

Source: Daniel Claus: *A Primer for the Use of the Mohawk Children / Waerighwaghsawe iksaongoenwa* (London, 1786)

While the land issue remained unresolved, the school was started in 1824 with twenty-one students attending.[20] Initially, it may have been located in the old school, a house, or other repurposed building. Two years later, Brant requested further funds for various building projects and, "although there is evidence that the materials for the Mohawk Village school were on the ground the same year, it was not until 1828 that the school building was ready for occupation."[21]

Brant played a part in establishing the Mohawk Institute, but did not necessarily have broad community support. The NEC initially "sought the approval of the Six Nations people for all educational undertakings" and the school was certainly viewed positively by some, with wait-lists at times.[22] However, as Susan M. Hill observes, Brant, like his father, was an ambiguous figure who held leadership roles within both the Haudenosaunee

Confederacy and the imperial government.[23] He actively promoted Christianity and education, but, according to Monture, "the Grand River community was reluctant to fully embrace such practices."[24]

Notwithstanding wavering community support, religious and secular colonial authorities regarded the Mohawk Institute with optimism, evident in the rapid pace at which it expanded in its early years. In 1829, the NEC missionary in charge of the school, the Reverend Robert Lugger, reported that Brant and Sir John Colborne, lieutenant-governor of Upper Canada, intended "to draw on the Treasurer for the sum allowed by the Company, for the purpose of advancing the children in various handicraft works, and for the residences."[25] The result was the addition, in 1830, of a "Mechanics' Institution" to facilitate industrial training for boys.[26] By the following year, the school comprised, besides the mechanics' shop, "four large rooms, in two of which girls might be taught spinning and weaving, and in the other two, the boys tailoring and carpentering."[27] In 1834, residences were added with accommodation for ten boys and four girls.[28] Both the industrial training and boarding facilities can be linked to the prevailing "Christianize and civilize" mission model, which used cultural re-education to support religious conversion.[29] Lugger himself expressed this perspective, writing that it would be impossible for the children to understand what they learned "until they are taken from their families and obliged to speak nothing but English."[30] Another NEC missionary, the Reverend Abraham Nelles, stationed nearby at Tuscarora, believed that "while the groundwork of improvement must be laid amongst the young, that can be but imperfectly done if they are left to live and grow up at home."[31] This missionary philosophy meshed with government views, as expressed in Colborne's proposal for "civilizing" Indigenous peoples through settlement in villages, agriculture, education, and religious instruction.[32]

Attention soon turned to increasing the institution's population. In 1835, the NEC treasurer wrote that "wishes were expressed that the number of children might be increased from fourteen to fifty."[33] By early 1839, there were about thirty children.[34] This number was apparently accommodated by altering the existing buildings, rather than expanding them, as the NEC reported that "it has been gratifying . . . to have been able, whilst the number of scholars was nearly doubled, so to alter the arrangements there, as greatly to increase the means of comfort and instruction to them all."[35] Later that year, however, Nelles, who had been appointed principal upon Lugger's death in 1836, received "the assent of the Company to the enlargement of the Mohawk Institution."[36] This addition, which would enable the accommodation of forty children in total, was completed in the summer of 1840.[37] The school's carpenters were employed to do the work, assisted by student apprentices, saving "the Company any advance in money for that portion of the labour, which would come under the heading of carpentering."[38] Whereas boys worked on building the structure, girls worked at the domestic labour of maintaining it. Several girls, however, protested having to perform "menial... household duties" by leaving the institution.[39]

The expansion of the Mohawk Institute's physical plant in the 1830s was clearly linked to missionary assimilation efforts, which in turn were tied to broader settler-colonial processes. Training young people "in the arts, habits and customs of civilized life," as the missionaries put it, was the best way to "remove... prejudices" and change the "irresolute and suspicious" attitudes of their communities, who viewed "all whites as intruders."[40] The missionaries did not consider, or else ignored, the fact that the Six Nations had legitimate concerns about the encroaching settler occupation of their territory. In the early 1840s, the Mohawk Village was largely, but not entirely, abandoned after the government relocated residents south of the Grand River due to an influx of non-Indigenous squatters on their lands.[41] Nelles remained undeterred, proposing in 1844 that the Mohawk Institute should be conducted "on a larger scale" and that "more land should be attached to it, in the cultivation of which the children might be employed."[42] The relocation seemed to present a justification for expanding the institution's residential facilities, since few families now lived in the village.[43] The physical separation of the school from the community could only have helped the missionaries' aim of producing graduates to "act as instruments in the hands of the Company, for the complete civilization of Indians generally."[44]

It was around this time that the Mohawk Institute became known as a "model" or "pattern" institution by Indian Affairs.[45] Specifically, the 1847 *Report on the Affairs of the Indians in Canada* recommended that Indigenous children should be given an education "on a uniform system, something similar to the New England Company's Establishment."[46] What was considered prototypical about the Mohawk Institute was not necessarily its precise architectural arrangement, but its combination of classroom and industrial work in a residential setting. However, the accommodation of these functions within its built environment would likely have drawn attention from those looking to establish similar institutions. A visitor around this time remarked that "the school... is upon a plan almost exactly the same as that adopted in the boarding and day schools for farmers' sons in England."[47]

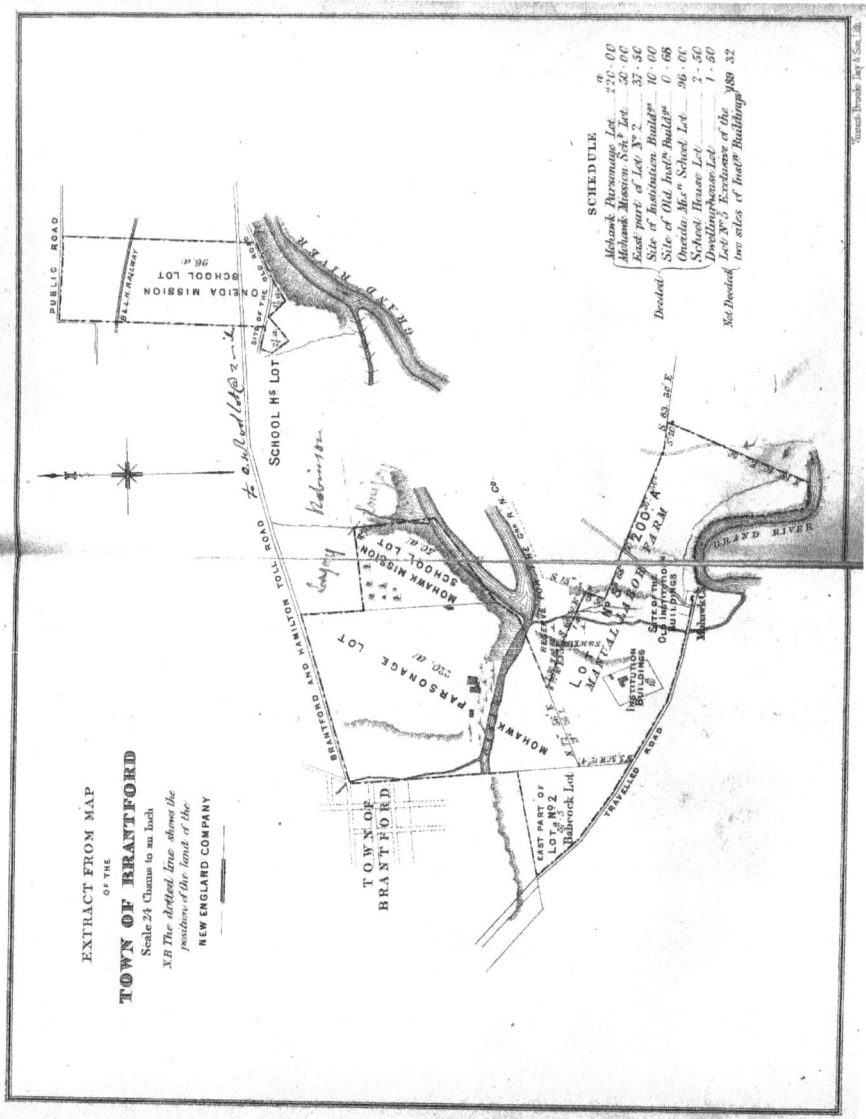

Figure 6.2. Map of Brantford showing "Site of the Old Institution Buildings" near the Mohawk Chapel. "Institution Buildings" indicates the location of the Mohawk Institute beginning in 1858. Source: General Synod Archives, Anglican Church of Canada

The previously consistent growth of the Mohawk Institute plateaued during the 1840s. In 1844, "the boarding school . . . numbered between 40 and 50 children," yet by the end of the decade, the population remained at fifty, with another fifty awaiting admission.[48] Despite an apparently lengthy waiting list, no building projects appear to have been initiated during this period. In 1853, the NEC finally agreed with Nelles that "more commodious buildings were necessary for extending the Institution."[49] Yet three years later, in 1856, the principal reported that "the Institution building was in very bad repair" and recommended converting it into workshops, constructing a new, larger building in its place.[50] However, a fire destroyed the existing school in 1858, prompting its move a few hundred metres away to its present location, where it was rebuilt on a larger scale (figure 6.2).[51]

In the absence of visual evidence or survivor testimony, an early architectural history of the Mohawk Institute can be gleaned from a variety of settler-colonial texts. These sources yield only a biased and partial view of the institutional built environment, but they nevertheless reveal several spatial themes that would reappear in each of its subsequent phases. These include the incorporation of residential and industrial spaces in its building program, as well as the gendered segregation of space; its role as a model institution, which would extend to refer more specifically to its architecture; as well as continual change, often through unfree student labour in building construction and maintenance.

The Yellow-Brick Building: Architectural Change and Destruction (1858–1903)

From the road, an elaborate white gate guarded a long lane leading to a boxy, two-storey Georgian building of buff-yellow brick.[52] This was the new Mohawk Institute, completed and occupied in April 1858 by fifty-five children and the staff. In September, Principal Nelles wrote that he "would probably make it sixty, which would be as many as the building would accommodate without some additions."[53] Like the first school, the new site would indeed be characterized by almost incessant expansion. The Mohawk Institute's second architectural phase is well-documented not only in text but also in visual sources such as photographs and plans, which enable a more fine-grained analysis of the institution's visual and spatial codes.

Although the new building lacked overt classical details such as columns, cornices, pediments, and arches, it nevertheless presented a stripped-down version of typical Georgian classicism: symmetry, chimneys on either side,

Figure 6.3. The Mohawk Institute, 1884
Source: Library and Archives Canada / PA-051882 / a051882-v8

a low hipped roof, and a row of five unpaired, double-hung sash windows on the upper floor (figure 6.3).[54] The style had arrived in Upper Canada during the late eighteenth century from the United States and Britain, when it was already considered old-fashioned in those places.[55] Georgian classicism was associated with a continuity of British traditions and in Upper Canada, specifically, the style "declared loyalty to the British Crown and British values."[56] It remained popular in Ontario through the mid-nineteenth century, a period often referred to as late Georgian or Georgian Survival.[57] At the Mohawk Institute, these architectural references connected the institution to British imperialism and Anglicanism, but also to Six Nations' historical relationship with Britain as sovereign allies.

The architectural historian Harold Kalman counts "many Mohawks who had remained loyal to the Crown, and whose land had been bartered away to the Americans" among the seven thousand Loyalists who influenced the profusion of the Georgian style in Canada.[58] Johnson Hall, the pre-revolutionary home of Sir William Johnson and Molly Brant (Konwatsi'tsiaiénni) in Kanyen'kehaka territory at Johnstown, New York, was another significant Georgian building in Haudenosaunee history.[59]

Figure 6.4. Edward Lamson Henry, *Johnson Hall (Sir William Johnson Presenting Medals to the Indian Chiefs of the Six Nations at Johnstown, NY, 1772)*, 1903, oil on canvas
Source: Albany Institute of History & Art Purchase, accession 1993.44

Built in 1763, it served as the site of councils among Haudenosaunee chiefs and colonial officials. Edward Lamson Henry's painting of one such gathering shows Haudenosaunee chiefs assembled in a circle in front of the house, with its rectangular form, pedimented entrance, five window bays, cornice, and double-hipped roof (see figure 6.4). The circle and the square suggest two distinct world views functioning side by side.[60] Johnson Hall demonstrates some of the ways that Georgian classicism may have worked as part of the Mohawk Institute's symbolism in the broader historical context of British-Haudenosaunee relations. If so, it was no longer in a geopolitical situation of two sovereign cultures, but one that stressed Britishness over Indigeneity.

The domestic scale and appearance of the 1858 Mohawk Institute was typical of first-generation residential schools. These were sometimes called "homes," and the Mohawk Institute was referred to as a "household" by the New England Company and staff.[61] The administrative hierarchy was modelled on the settler nuclear family: the principal, generally a man, was the head of the "household," while his female counterpart, often his wife, was the matron.[62] Although all residential schools were inherently *domestic* in that children and staff lived at the institutions, early missionary boarding schools, in particular, resembled single-family domestic architecture. This

Figure 6.5. The Mohawk Institute and its landscape, 1884
Source: Library and Archives Canada / PA-051881 / a051881

was related to the schools' teaching of habitus—socially ingrained habits and ways of life—as a form of assimilation, in addition to labour and religious, academic, and industrial training. Religious and secular authorities' removal of children from their family homes and placement within homelike environments modelled on settler culture were key to this philosophy.

The veranda that spanned the Mohawk Institute's front facade highlighted its domestic character in a public way, acting as a threshold between an idealized settler domestic interior within and the agrarian and natural worlds beyond. Robert Mugerauer writes of porches as mediating places between interiors and exteriors, both in social and environmental terms; grander houses with wealthier and more powerful inhabitants tended to have larger and more elevated porches.[63] The Mohawk Institute's veranda was elevated to accommodate the raised basement below the ground floor, but it also flagged the institution's importance, to both occupants and passersby. Ascending the veranda's thirteen steps may have been an intimidating experience, particularly for younger children arriving for the first time, but also for visitors who were not used to such large structures.

Beyond the veranda of the Mohawk Institute was a landscape characteristic of late nineteenth-century rural southern Ontario, whose rapid deforestation was being tempered by increased planting.[64] A dense stand of trees serving as a windbreak on the border of a field, orchards, and parallel rows of maples along the entrance road to the main building were typical of this type of landscape (figure 6.5).[65] The gate and fence added to the sense of order, conforming to "the regularity of the surveys and the land-division regime that had been gradually implanted since the first days of colonization."[66] This was a visual expression of mastery over nature, a fitting message for a colonial institution increasingly focused on transforming Indigenous children into farmers. In 1859, Six Nations allowed over two hundred acres of adjacent farmland to be held in trust by the NEC as long as it continued to operate the school.[67] Its landscape thus became a productive agricultural terrain that, through the children's labour, would sustain the institution, largely through the sale of these goods.

Congruent with its domestic character, the new building was used primarily as a living space in its early years, since classes continued to be held at the old school near the Mohawk Chapel. Describing his visit to the institution in July 1860, Anglican clergyman Frederick O'Meara wrote, "The buildings appear to me to be very commodious and suitable for the purpose for which they are intended; but I think that a good-sized school-house close to the building, is much needed—the one that is at present in use being that belonging to the old institution, and at a considerable distance from the new building."[68] The separation of the residences and classrooms created an expanded institutional landscape, marked by the children's regular walks to and from classes at the former site. O'Meara's suggestion that the institution should be expanded would be realized over the next two decades. A series of additions would transform the building, making it almost unrecognizable by the end of its forty-five-year existence. The NEC approved the first addition in 1864, based on a sketch provided by Nelles, and it was completed the following year.[69]

Criticism of the facility began to mount a few years later, when an NEC report recommended that each child should have a separate bed as "the dormitories seemed very clean and well ventilated, but there were only 16 beds for 37 boys so some contained three boys apiece."[70] Around the same time, Nelles had also "suggested that a school-house should be built with two apartments, one for boys and one for girls," to allow enough space in the existing building for each boy to have his own bed.[71] This suggestion, along with reports of overcrowding in the dormitories, persisted in the following years.[72] An 1872 report criticized the fourteen-year-old building in terms of overcrowding, health, and safety, citing the need for improved ventilation and heating, as well as a hospital.[73] In addition to persistently overcrowded dormitories, the lavatories were a point of contention that revealed the staff's racist perceptions of the children in the institution. When staff showed the girls' lavatory to John Martland, the master of Upper Canada College, he was told the children were given "tubs and pails" rather than wash basins, because they were "dirty in their habits."[74] For the boys, their classroom doubled as their recreation space and where they washed in winter: "The room was very little better than a cellar in an ordinary house; not so good as a laundry. . . . In summer the boys washed in a shed close by, in which he saw one tub and one pail. He asked about the privies, but could get no answer."[75] These observations documented the austere and unhygienic conditions prevailing at the school and suggested that the staff had different perceptions of what constituted an appropriate environment for the children than did outside observers. In a place supposedly conducted for their education and eventual absorption into settler society, the environment signalled to the children that they were inferior to the mainly white staff.

A new principal, the Reverend Robert Ashton, arrived at the Mohawk Institute with his family in 1872. His initial positive impression quickly gave way to a less favourable assessment: "It is very pleasantly situated, and from the public road has the appearance of being a newly and substantially built brick building, with a wooden veranda six feet wide across the front and level with the first floor. On passing the gate, however, from the general appearance of neglect and untidiness, I began to think the whole place deserted."[76] Ashton condemned the landscaping; the unfinished state of the building; poor ventilation; limited staff accommodation; ill-defined physical boundaries for children, parents, and other visitors; and the fact that he and his family had to dine with the staff, as there was no separate dining room for them.[77] Motivated perhaps in part by improving conditions for the children, and certainly those of his own family, he set about renovating the school and lands. Scott noted that "the new principal had an eye for beauty and he turned the uninteresting grounds in front of the building into lawns and planted shrubs and trees."[78] Ashton could thus take credit, at least in part, for the straight rows of trees and perfectly mowed lawns, both symbols and embodiments of nature tamed through settler-colonial industry. The principal also contemplated expanding the building in order "to admit children at the earliest age," while another official suggested that the Mohawk Institute should take children "even in infancy," though this was not common in schools.[79] The physical expansion of the institution can thus be linked to authorities' perceived capacity to remove more, and increasingly younger, children from their homes and communities in service of their assimilative agenda.

Efforts to improve the institutional environment reflected the dichotomy between appearance and reality that characterized the Mohawk Institute and other residential schools. On the one hand, the physical plan was there to enable the religious and cultural assimilation of Indigenous children who, despite progressivist rhetoric from some quarters, were not seen as the equals of settler children, and certainly not equals of the staff. The quality of the built environment as the setting "where the experiment to transform Indians was being conducted," as Fear-Segal writes of the Carlisle school in the United States, reflected this disparity.[80] On the other hand, the institution also served as a "living showcase, where the results of this experiment were displayed to the White public."[81] Another example, the Model Indian School at the 1893 Chicago World's Columbian Exposition, was the epitome of residential-school-as-display. Built as a functioning boarding school resembling those proliferating across the continent, it offered the exhibition-going public an up-close view of assimilation in progress using actual students as performers.[82]

Permanent institutions like Carlisle and the Mohawk Institute partook in similar practices of display. As the "model" institution for Indigenous children in Canada, the Mohawk Institute's functions included exhibiting the worthiness of the colonial assimilation project to visitors. Apart from NEC officials, the institution received members of the public and dignitaries like the Prince of Wales, who made an appearance in 1860 as part of his tour of British North America. These practices can be understood at the intersection of what Erving Goffman calls "institutional display" and the nineteenth-century "exhibitionary complex" described by Tony Bennett, a strong focus of which was the cultures of colonized peoples, put on display to strengthen popular support for imperial policies.[83]

In 1879, the Indian Affairs visiting superintendent reported that the grounds at the Mohawk Institute "have been much improved, with a large addition to the main building, rendering it a model establishment."[84] The new addition, at the rear of the existing building, doubled its size. Ashton also noted the construction of "a play-house for the boys" and "extensive improvements and repairs to the main building."[85] In plan, the original building continued the Georgian symmetry of the exterior with a central staircase hall aligned with the main entrance, while the new wing was

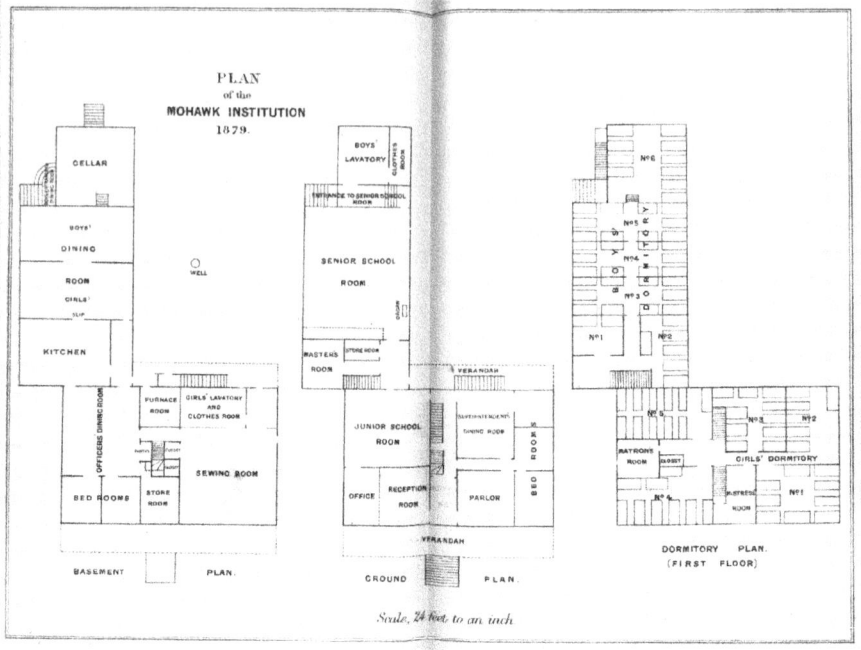

Figure 6.6. Floor plan of the Mohawk Institute, 1879
Source: General Synod Archives, Anglican Church of Canada

connected at its back left corner (figure 6.6). Immediately inside the front door were a parlour and reception room on either side, the latter probably where children could meet their parents and other visitors. A school regulation from the 1870s stated they could meet with family on Saturdays between 10:00 a.m. and 4:00 p.m. "in the room set apart for that purpose."[86] Adjacent to the parlour was the superintendent's dining room, likely created to address Ashton's complaint of having to dine with the staff. Beyond the parlour and dining room were three bedrooms, which together constituted the more private domestic sphere of the principal and his family. Across the central hall from the parlour, the reception room led to an office connected to the junior schoolroom, which in turn led to the new back wing with the senior school room and master's (teacher's) room.

Segregation of boys and girls, typical in residential school buildings, rigidly enforced colonial gender differences.[87] At the Mohawk Institute's newly expanded building, the separation was not as clearly inscribed as in later schools, but the main block could be understood as the girls' area,

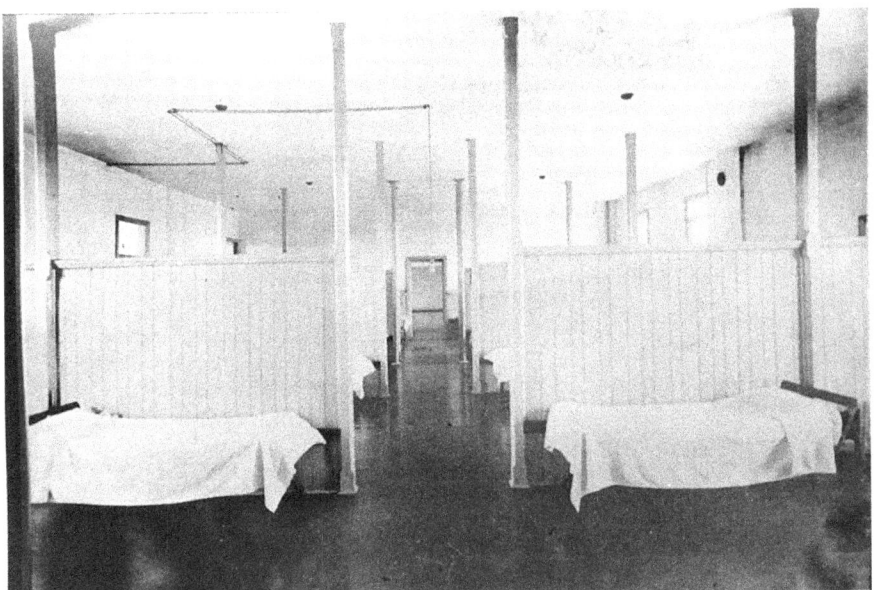

Figure 6.7. Boys' dormitory, possibly Mohawk Institute, before 1904
Source: Richard Hill Collection

while the new rear wing was for the boys. This division was most evident on the upper floor, where both the girls' and boys' dormitories were located but completely disconnected, with no passage between them—each was accessed separately from the floor below. Unlike the large, open dormitories of later residential institutions for Indigenous children, they were divided by wooden half-height partitions into smaller areas, each with space for between two and eleven children. These partitions created a minimal sense of privacy and may also have sorted students by age while enabling staff to monitor children through auditory and, to some extent, visual surveillance. The 1879 plan shows ninety-three beds, forty-eight in the boys' dormitory and forty-five in the girls'. Although they remained very close together, there were now enough beds for each child to have their own.

Circulation through and use of the Mohawk Institute's interior spaces were tightly controlled. From their dormitory, girls could descend the central stairs, past the ground floor, and into the basement, where their lavatory and clothes room were located. Here, also, was the sewing room, which would have been used exclusively by girls during domestic science lessons and while doing work, like mending, for the institution. Moving into the

Mohawk Institute for the Education of Indian Youth

Figure 6.8. This postcard was printed in the late nineteenth century, and while the image quality is poor, the photo shows the new addition to the school after 1886
Source: Toronto Public Library

new wing through the staff dining room and past the kitchen, they could reach their dining room, which was next to, but separate from, that of the boys. The boys, conversely, arrived at their dining area down a set of stairs at the back of their dormitory, which went past their ground-floor lavatory and clothes room, and through a separate door next to the cellar, marked "boys entrance to dining room."

Food was a strong mechanism of social control at residential schools. Spaces of food consumption at the Mohawk Institute were correspondingly arranged in a hierarchical way: In the basement were the children and staff, the former in gender-segregated group dining areas and the latter in a separate dining room on the other side of the kitchen, while the dining room for the principal and his family was on the ground floor. The internal organization of residential schools, writes J. R. Miller, "was a silent reminder of racial barriers as well as gender differences. Nowhere was this more dramatically revealed than in the separate dining facilities for staff and students."[88]

In addition to segregating girls and boys in the dormitories, lavatories, and dining room, the arrangement of space reinforced racial hierarchies in areas like the dining rooms as part of the school's "hidden curriculum."[89]

During the late 1880s and early 1890s, the Mohawk Institute underwent a series of dramatic renovations and additions. Its simple Georgian exterior was radically transformed into an elaborate Gothic Revival ensemble, a change that reflected architectural trends, Canadian nationalism tied to Britain, and the Anglican adoption of Gothic as a denominational style (figures 6.8 and 6.9).[90] The latter was connected to the ideas of the Ecclesiological Society, which was influential in promoting a return to medieval building practices for Anglican churches in England and its colonies.[91] More broadly, the Gothic Revival was intertwined with the maintenance of a British Protestant identity through architecture in the global "Anglosphere," connecting the Mohawk Institute not only to Britain itself but to Britain's global empire.[92] In this period, therefore, Georgian buildings were often reinterpreted with Gothic Revival detailing.[93] The Mohawk Institute's new "Gothic garb" consisted of elaborate trim, including decorative brackets on the veranda, scroll-shaped brackets (or corbels) at the eaves, and a new dormer window with a finial (an ornament at the apex of the roof).

The first major addition, in 1886, included a residence for the principal's family, probably the new wing resembling a single-family house, visible to the left of the main building (figure 6.8). It had a separate entrance at ground level, emphasized by a porch with intricate roof cresting, along with other Gothic Revival details like louvered shutters, an elaborate bargeboard, and a prominent finial capping the gable. The addition reflected the necessity for the principal to live on-site, but also his power to delineate private space for himself and his family within the institution. The renovations also included improvements to staff living areas and increased sleeping space for the children, doubling the size of the boys' dormitories. The new roof dormer, with twin arched windows, suggests that the attic was turned into usable space. The addition also created a picturesque irregularity, another feature of the Gothic Revival, that contrasted with the building's earlier symmetry.[94] Boys from the institution worked on the construction, completing most of the carpentry and painting.[95] It was thus the unfree labour of the children that aesthetically reinterpreted the building as part of an expanding imperial Gothic world.

Toward the end of the century, the Mohawk Institute was seemingly under constant construction. The mechanical and electrical systems were upgraded in 1891, and a brick basement was added to the boys' playhouse,

Figure 6.9. The Mohawk Institute, following 1893–4 addition
Source: Richard Hill Collection

which contained a "lavatory, hot and cold shower baths, dressing room, in which each boy has a separate locker, a boot shelf and towel rack."[96] Electrical lighting was also added to the classrooms and sewing room, the furnace moved from the dining hall into a new furnace room in the boys' wing, and new equipment for cooking, baking, and hot water were added to the kitchen.[97]

The second major addition was built in 1893–4, with slightly larger massing, but similar detailing, which balanced out the previous addition of 1886 (figure 6.9). A cupola, in the style of a widow's walk, crowned the roof. This feature had both practical and symbolic uses, as it may have been associated with a new ventilation system, but also communicated the authority of the institution and thus the supposed superiority of settler-colonial culture.[98] The new, three-storey wing contained a playroom for the girls in the basement, which also housed two furnaces for heating the building, as well as a classroom, dormitories, and staff bedrooms. By 1896, the third floor was used as a "hospital for contagious diseases."[99] The existing building was also renovated, and the institution was now capable of holding 30 additional children, for a total of 120.[100] This expansion in capacity coincided with an

Indian Act amendment in 1894 that empowered Indian agents to send children to residential schools if they believed parents to be unfit or unwilling to provide for their child's education. Thus, architecture was linked with the state's ability to carry out colonial policies of assimilation and cultural destruction.

Although confinement probably existed earlier in the Mohawk Institute's history, we get detailed descriptions of these spaces and practices from an 1894 account by Martin Benson, an Indian Affairs inspector from the Schools Branch. He described two rooms used to confine children: the dormitories, which were locked at night, and purpose-built rooms for solitary confinement. He wrote that "the pupils are all locked in their dormitories at night, but each lock has a pane of glass ... which can be broken in case of alarm and the bolt shot back."[101] He also described fire escapes and other safety measures, suggesting that confining the children in this way did not really pose a danger to them. A description of the solitary confinement rooms used for punishment included a similar rationalization:

> A room at the head of the landing leading to the rear of the Principal's house, is set apart for the solitary confinement of very refractory boys with a similar place on the girls [sic] side of the building. These two rooms are about 6 by 10 and are only lighted by a barred fanlight over the door. I asked the Principal if he ever had occasion to make use of these rooms, and he replied that he sometimes did so for short periods and that he found that this mode of punishment has a most salutary effect.[102]

If the confinement was "short," in the principal's eyes, and had the desired result of forcing children to modify their behaviour then perhaps, Benson might have thought, it was justifiable. Yet for a child, being locked alone in a dark room was likely a particularly distressing experience. It is also important to consider that these rooms were deliberately included in planning the renovations of the building. Nested within the larger institutional landscape, these small spaces of confinement operated as concentrated spaces of social control in the service of the church and government's colonial objectives.

Many outbuildings supported the operation of the Mohawk Institute in addition to the main building, forming a complex social and agricultural landscape. Barns and sheds were used to store crops that the students harvested from the farm, such as wheat, oats, and peas.[103] Boys milked cows and girls churned butter in another building with a "cold-storage room."[104] The trade shop was busy as well, with its resident carpenter employed in building maintenance, but Ashton complained that the boys did not want to stay long enough to gain "a fair knowledge of their trade."[105] In 1892, a greenhouse was built, where a gardener and the children cultivated flowers, fruits, and vegetables that were sold.[106] It is unclear if children benefited from the food they produced, but later testimony suggests they did not to any great extent.

The role of residential school students in building the very institutions that contained them has recently received more scholarly attention. In her research on children's work at the nearby Mount Elgin Institute, Mary Jane Logan McCallum draws a connection between the location of the school on reserve land and that fact that it "experienced the full brunt of the notoriously stingy federal government, which delayed necessary repairs, cut corners, and," as at the Mohawk Institute, "whenever possible offloaded building and maintenance labour onto students."[107] Alexandra Giancarlo notes that in 1902, the *Manitoba Free Press* reported that male students at the Brandon residential school "built their own buildings."[108] At the Mohawk Institute, boys were likewise employed. When the old buildings near the Mohawk Chapel fell into disrepair, some materials were taken from them to build "five large pig-sties" at the new location.[109] Students laboured on the construction of the pig sties under the supervision of the resident carpenter and did other work, like painting.[110] In their "spare time," they worked at paving the barnyard using stones gathered from the fields.[111] Benson noted that "the barns, sheds, stables, silos, barn-yards and grounds were neatness personified, while everything in and about the building was scrupulously clean and tidy."[112] Later on, the boys also built a new cottage for the gardener, and renovated the Mohawk Chapel.[113] Like the main building, the larger landscape of the Mohawk Institute bore evidence of the children's constant labour through its remarkable neatness and impressive appearance to outsiders.

The landscape also included elements of recreation alongside work. The upper floor of the boys' playhouse contained a reading room, clothes press, playroom, and trunk room. The principal thought, in a bit of foreshadowing, that this outbuilding could provide refuge in case there was a fire in the main building.[114] Here, the boys played draughts, dominoes, shuffleboard, and read magazines. Their wooden muskets were stored here as well, and used for military-style exercises that, along with a system of rewards and punishments, rendered the school "as well regulated and controlled as a piece of machinery, going on without stop or hitch from morning to night."[115] On a Sunday, the girls might be "walking along the avenue and about the grounds in front of the Institute while the boys were taking their Sunday recreation on the other side in rear of the building."[116]

Reading settler-colonial textual and visual sources largely elides the children's experiences, which is why the actions of several boys in destroying the Mohawk Institute buildings speak so loudly. Aside from running away, arson was one of the most explicit ways for children to protest harsh conditions at residential schools, because by destroying the institution's buildings, they directly affected its ability to function.[117] On 19 April 1903, a group of boys twice attempted to burn down the school. The second attempt was successful, and the building perished, just as the previous one had nearly fifty years earlier. The next day, *The Globe* reported that "the entire structure was burned to the ground, only the walls standing."[118] The blaze at the school was followed by the burning of barns, together with cows and horses, on 7 May. Finally, on 21 June, students set fire to the playhouse, which, as the principal had predicted, had become their temporary residence. Eight boys were arrested in connection with these incidents; four confessed to arson and received sentences of three to five years at the Mimico Industrial School and Kingston Penitentiary.[119]

The Red-Brick Building: Expansion and Continuity of the "Model" (1904–1970)

After the fires of 1903, the Mohawk Institute was rebuilt in 1904 as the imposing, three-storey red-brick building that still stands today. Constructed behind the building that burned down, it was set even farther back from the road. The year after it was completed, there were fifty-four boys and fifty-four girls living within its walls.[120] The new school was designed with elements of the Beaux-Arts style commonly used for public and commercial architecture in the first two decades of the twentieth century, a mode that was "grand and theatrical, monumental and self-confident."[121] The Mohawk Institute's new building presented a more modest interpretation of the style than the train stations and other large public buildings of the time, but its front elevation embodied this quality of grandiosity in its central, two-storey portico composed of four colossal Doric columns (figure 6.10). It also possessed characteristics of Edwardian classicism, such as the cupola, five arched dormers, balustrade, and quoins on the corners. Abandoning the domestic character, Gothic adornment, and irregularity of the previous

Figure 6.10. Mohawk Institute, 1917
Source: John Boyd Fonds / Library and Archives Canada / a071300

structure, the new building was characterized by order, symmetry, and a more daunting, institutional appearance that seemed to defy its precursor's destruction.

Like its Georgian and Victorian predecessors, the Mohawk Institute's new stylistic iteration signified connections to the British Empire and reinforced a colonial narrative of dominance and superiority through its size and classical references.[122] Its scale and monumentality were emphasized in school photographs that used the front facade as a backdrop, such as a 1930s image depicting students standing in ten variously sized rows on the stairs and porch, with staff seated in front (figure 6.11).[123] The columns appear gigantic, dwarfing the children standing between and in front of them. "At first glance," notes Sherry Farrell Racette, "many photographs of children in residential schools are indistinguishable from the broader genre of school photography."[124] Many of these images, however, reveal the measures used by these institutions to break students' individuality: identical uniforms, similar haircuts, and grouping children by age and sex. The Eurocentric architecture in the Mohawk Institute photograph emphasizes these strategies of conformity as well as signalling the institution's colonial purpose of transforming children into non-Indigenous subjects.[125]

194   BEHIND THE BRICKS

Figure 6.11. Students and staff in front of the Mohawk Institute, ca. 1934
Source: Richard Hill Collection

Survivors' recollections are key to understanding how the architectural spaces of the Mohawk Institute were experienced. These narratives are much more readily accessible for the post-1904 era than for earlier phases, thanks to written accounts and oral histories such as those collected in Elizabeth Graham's *The Mush Hole: Life at Two Indian Residential Schools*.[126] This testimony goes beyond official records and what can be gleaned from visual sources to convey students' perspectives on and lived experiences in the built environment. The overwhelming size of residential school buildings characterize the memories of many survivors, especially those who first arrived as small children. A survivor who was brought to the Mohawk Institute in 1940 as a four-and-a-half-year-old child relates, "All I remember is a great big building with great big walls. I remember crying. I was confused—scared."[127] To young children who had just been separated from their families, the "monumental" architecture appeared threatening, alluding to the power that staff and teachers would have over their lives.

Arriving at the Mohawk Institute and entering the building for the first time was a significant event for many children. Coming with siblings often meant being separated from them right away, particularly those of the opposite sex. In survivor Marie Hess's fictionalized account of her experiences, the young protagonist arrives with her brothers and sisters to the "towering" building, which she perceives as an "enormous house." But their older brother reminds them, "this is not our home," warning that "you must always remember to follow the rules here. I'm not sure if I'll be close enough to help you any more."

> He catches his brothers' and sisters' eyes one by one as they nervously climb the stairs to the front entrance. As they entered the heavy doors, they were quickly ushered away into different rooms. Noreen could hear her brother telling the woman in a white uniform and cap, "we don't have bugs, none of us do."[128]

Hess's account reveals the emotional resonance of the architecture: The school is an "enormous house" that is not a home, lacking the comfort and security of family and community. The enormity of the exterior yields to an immense interior, parts of which are off-limits, into which the siblings are swiftly sorted. When she can no longer see her brother, Noreen can hear his voice as he speaks to the school nurse, foreshadowing the fragmented relationship between many siblings inside the institution.

The segregation and surveillance of children within the main building of the Mohawk Institute was enabled by its plan, which was I-shaped and symmetrical, with a narrower central section flanked by two wings. When the building was first completed, children going through the main entrance would have encountered offices, the sewing room, and bedrooms for female staff on the ground floor. Down a corridor to the left, the west wing had a classroom, master's (teacher's) room, and farm men's bedrooms; to the right, the east wing comprised another classroom and an assembly room. Upstairs, the boys' and girls' dormitories were in the east and west wings, separated by the principal's family residence and two sickrooms in the central block.[129] The attic was left unfinished until it was partially renovated into dormitories in 1929.[130]

The origin of the building's design can be traced both to the Mohawk Institute's specificity as an Anglican residential school and the broader architectural culture of the time. According to Scott, the building was designed by Principal Ashton and his son, Ernest.[131] Given what was by that time the principal's thirty-year career at the Mohawk Institute, it is conceivable that he contributed detailed ideas about how it should be rebuilt and had significant influence over its final form, especially its program and layout. He was also, in all likelihood, influenced by his early experiences as schoolmaster at the Middlesex Industrial School at Feltham, outside London, England.[132] However, the NEC also enlisted the aid of an architecture firm called Stewart, Stewart & Taylor, which was active in Hamilton and Brantford from 1902 to 1904.[133] In this short time, the firm completed at least four projects in Brantford, including the Beaux-Arts Carnegie Library on George Street.[134] The library and the Mohawk Institute were vastly different in use and size, but their exteriors share many stylistic features, such as their symmetry, rusticated and raised first stories, monumental entrances with classical columns, pediments, and central domes. These aesthetic similarities are superficial, but they speak to the entanglement of the Mohawk Institute's architecture, and that of residential schools more generally, with broader settler-colonial architectural cultures.[135] These institutions' shared architectural symbolism referred to civic enlightenment and Eurocentric notions of progress, which in the case of the library helped increase public access to knowledge, but at the Mohawk Institute manifested as an active suppression of Indigenous ways of being and knowing.[136]

Consistent with the Mohawk Institute's history as a "model" or "pattern" institution, the 1904 building may have served as an architectural template for later residential schools. The school was built at the beginning of a transition period, lasting from about 1905 to 1923, when boarding and industrial schools were both now referred to by the government as "residential schools." In 1911, the government introduced contracts with the churches, which offered higher per capita grants to institutions that met certain criteria for their physical plant.[137] The Indian Affairs report for that year declared that "under the new contract arrangement improvements have been undertaken at the Mohawk Institute and at Mount Elgin, which are designed to make these institutions model ones in every respect."[138]

The centralization of government power over residential schools led Indian Affairs to assume increased involvement in the design of new buildings and additions. Two early government-built institutions that show the influence of the Mohawk Institute are the Portage La Prairie residential school in Manitoba, designed by Jean Dosithe Chene in 1914, and the Chapleau (St. John's) residential school in Ontario, designed by Roland Guerney Orr in 1919.[139] Orr became chief architect of Indian Affairs in 1921, and in the following decade and a half, designed around two dozen new residential

6 | A "Model" School   197

schools, often replacements for older buildings.[140] Although he moved away from Beaux-Arts and Edwardian exteriors, he kept the I-shaped plan and general interior arrangement found at the Mohawk Institute.

Just as the Mohawk Institute may have served as a prototype for the residential school system at large, its inclusion in this colonial network in turn influenced its own physical form. In 1913, D. C. Scott, then superintendent of Indian education, wrote that "the location of the dining-room in the basement is very objectionable" and asked the departmental architect to prepare plans for a new dining room, among other renovations.[141] Like most Indian Affairs construction projects, this addition was delayed by the First World War. It was not until 1922 that Orr designed a new rear wing for the building, a feature that brought its form in line with new government-designed residential schools elsewhere.[142] The plans included a dining room and service spaces in the basement, as well as an assembly hall above it on the ground floor (a de facto chapel, since it had a platform with an altar on one end) (see figures 6.12 and 6.13).

The ground-floor part of the addition was never built because the school continued to use the nearby Mohawk Chapel for weekly religious services.[143] As survivor Jennie Blackbird recalled, the existing senior classroom also doubled as a space for "chapel service every evening after supper."[144] Thus, despite the church being located away from the school, daily religious activities still took place in a room borrowed for the purpose. The new rear wing did incorporate a large, open dining room, laundry, kitchen, boiler room, coal bin, and small storage room in the basement. The renovations also included new boys' and girls' lavatories in the existing basement, as well as the installation of steam heating throughout the building. A survivor who attended the Mohawk Institute during the 1920s, Harrison Burning, remembered the construction, suggesting that the children saw the renovations as a significant event.[145] Orr, the Indian Affairs architect, visited the building site on several occasions while the project was being built and continued to correspond with the principal afterwards.[146] He also wrote to Scott about seemingly minute matters of repairs and alterations to the building, such as replacing ladders with steel stair fire escapes in 1930. The involvement of Scott—now the deputy superintendent general of Indians affairs—suggests the tight control he wielded over the department and individual residential schools, as well as the Mohawk Institute's increasing enmeshment with a centralized government bureaucracy.

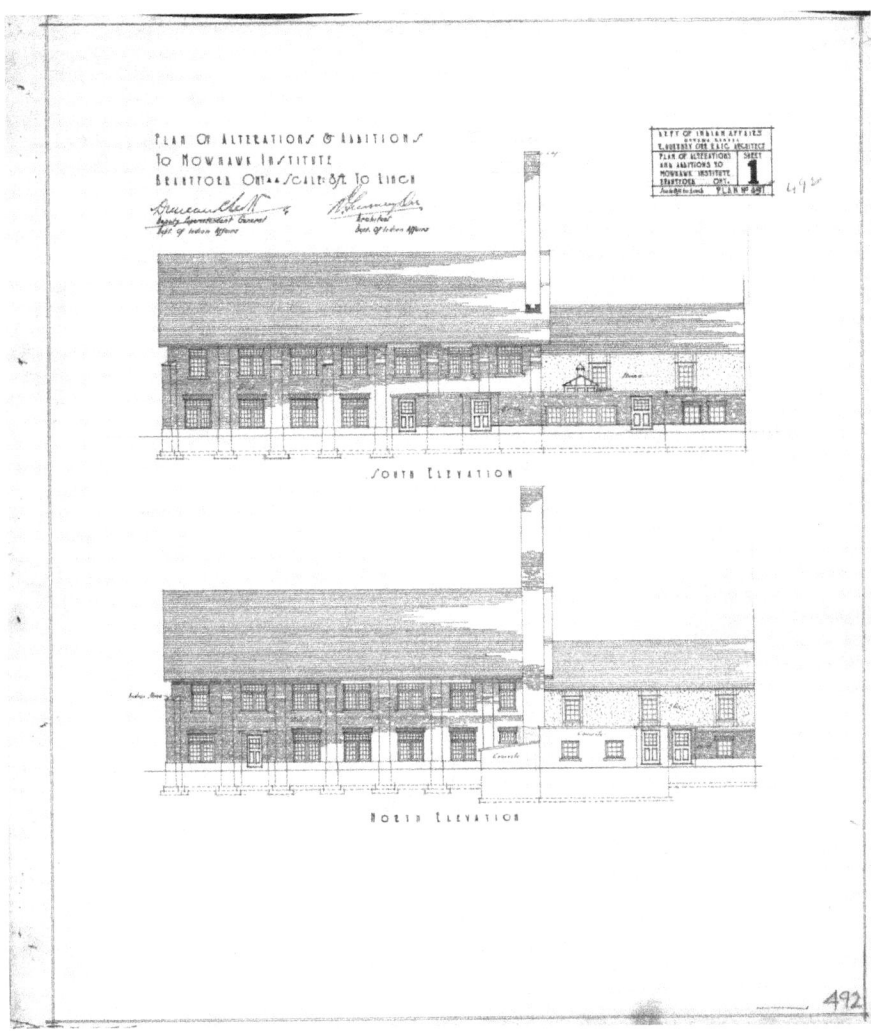

Figure 6.12. Elevations of proposed addition to the Mohawk Institute, 1922. R. Guerney Orr, architect.
Source: Library and Archives Canada / Department of Indian Affairs and Northern Development Fonds / NMC 178261

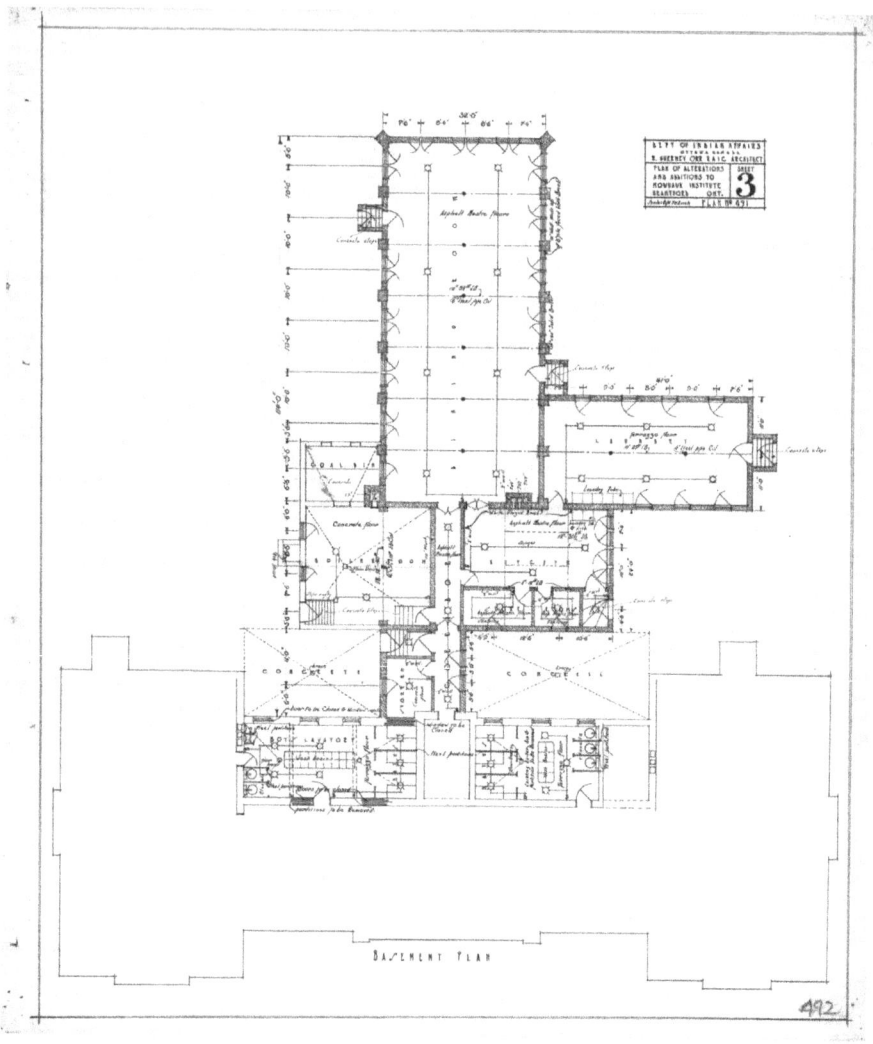

Figure 6.13. Plan of alterations and additions to the Mohawk Institute basement, 1922. R. Guerney Orr, architect.

Source: Library and Archives Canada / Department of Indian Affairs and Northern Development Fonds / NMC 178263

Survivors' Experiences of Segregation, Discipline, Labour, and Play

The built environment, from the smallest room to the institutional landscape as a whole, was an inextricable part of children's experiences at the Mohawk Institute. Learning through survivors' own words how they understood and navigated this environment offers an invaluable perspective on the institution's architectural history. Gender segregation was a remarkably consistent feature of survivors' memories, even those who attended decades apart, and not only in architecturally separated spaces like the dormitories. Martha Hill, who was at the school from 1912 to 1918, related that "the girls played with the girls over here, and the boys played with the boys. The only time you might say we was mixed together was when we went into church, because there wasn't enough seats. . . . But even our dining-rooms—our dining-room was here—the boys dining-room over there."[147] Vera Styres recounted that, in the 1940s, the institution constituted two distinct spheres: "I don't know too much about what happened on the boys' side, as the boys and girls were kept separate. Even in the classroom the girls sat on one side and the boys sat on the other side."[148] The one exception to this strict segregation, aside from church, was the visitors' room, where brothers and sisters could talk for a short time at designated times. In the 1940s, "once a month the brothers and sisters were allowed to visit in the visiting room on a Wednesday night," recalled Jennie Blackbird. "I was allowed to visit with the three I went there with, which was nice."[149] Marguerite Beaver remembers that, around the same time, "we could speak with our brothers—on Thursday nights, in turn when your name came up. . . . We used to have to go up in the front—we used to call it the Visitor's Room and I think we could talk to them three minutes, or five minutes."[150]

As in earlier phases of the institution, official records and visual sources such as photographs and plans leave out how staff used certain spaces to subject children to extremes of institutional discipline: incarceration and physical violence. These hidden or informal uses, though not listed in reports or marked on plans, were integral to the social control enacted at the Mohawk Institute. Spaces of confinement were in use not long after the school was rebuilt, as a government official detailed in 1907: "I cannot say that I was favorably impressed with the sight of two prison cells in the boys [sic] play house. I was informed, however, that these were for pupils who ran away from the institution, confinement being made for a week at a time when pupils returned."[151] The phrase "prison cells" indicates that the purpose of these spaces for confinement was clearly legible. Martha Hill describes a similar space in the main building during the 1910s:

> They had one little room—it had just had room to crawl in and go in the bed if you done anything wrong. That's how [the principal would] punish you—he'd make you go in that room. No light—shut the door and lock it from the outside. You couldn't get out of there and you had to stay in there for so many hours. Of course, after Turnell took it over he just closed that room up for good.[152]

Despite Hill's recollection that the room was no longer used once Cyril Turnell became principal in 1915, survivors of later periods continued to be confined in other ways. One survivor, who was at the Mohawk Institute from 1940 to 1945, remembers being "thrown in the clothes closet" with another young student. "I guess we were thrown in there for speaking Indian," she recalled.[153] This punishment reinforced the genocidal aim of depriving children of their Indigenous languages, associating their use with confinement and isolation. Blackbird did not experience confinement but remembered hearing of such practices: "While there I did hear of rumours, if some child did something really wrong, they was put in solitary confinement and was locked up for three days, no lights in the room. A room—I believe four by four?—with only water three times a day. It was a dark room."[154]

In addition to confinement and food deprivation, many survivors remembered frequent physical punishments. Blackbird recalled leaving the institution with some other girls and getting as far as the orchard before they were caught and "strapped" by the principal: "The strappings were always in the visiting room."[155] Blackbird's account has a haunting resonance with the earlier account of prison cells in the boys' playhouse: punishments were enacted in spaces that also held positive associations. As they enjoyed their rare leisure time in the playhouse, boys may have been reminded of the severe consequences of absconding from school; as they spoke with siblings during short meetings in the visiting room, children may have remembered a punishment meted out to them or others in the same space. On arriving at the Mohawk Institute from Walpole Island in 1943, Sylvia Soney remembered "getting an orientation—going into the visitors' room and being told what the rules were."[156] This spatial overlap between discipline and recreation (or time with family) no doubt created an atmosphere of constant

Figure 6.14. Girls in the sewing room, Mohawk Institute, ca. 1943
Source: General Synod Archives, Anglican Church of Canada

vigilance, cautioning students to ensure that their behaviour followed staff expectations at all times.

The children's labour, as with other parts of the Mohawk Institute, was spatially segregated by gender. The girls were largely restricted to the main building, working in the laundry, kitchen, and sewing room, as well as cleaning throughout. A photograph from 1943 shows five girls in front of a wood-panelled wall with a grid of "cubbyholes" in the sewing room, which was on the ground floor of the girls' wing (figure 6.14). On Soney's first day at the school, she recalled, "my sister and I were taken over to the sewing room and my brother went wherever he went, and there was a lady there and she gave us our number and showed us where our little box would be where every Saturday we'd get clean clothes."[157] The photograph shows neatly folded items in the boxes, which are labelled with the numbers the institution used to identify each child. The built-in cabinetry echoes the girls' dress: identical and anonymous. The image is clearly staged, with sewing machines angled so that the girls are visible and naturally lit from the window to their right. Such photographs of sewing rooms at residential schools promoted the idea that what female students learned in their half day of work had practical value. As Racette observes, "while photographs of both genders focus on the acquisition of useful skills, images of girls emphasize docility, industry, and neatness. Girls were most often photographed in the sewing room, and less often in the kitchen. They were never photographed in the laundry room or scrubbing floors, which actually constituted the bulk of their work."[158]

Though absent from the photographic record, the ceaseless cleaning done by girls at the Mohawk Institute is well-documented in survivors' oral histories. While doing this work, they often transgressed physical boundaries into parts of the building that were normally off-limits. Marjorie J. Groat, who entered the Mohawk Institute in 1928, remembered working "in the Principal's department" on the second floor, a space that was accessed by its own stairwell and thus isolated from the rest of the building.[159] The principal's private apartment included a living room and den that opened onto the second-storey veranda over the main entrance, a dining room, a small kitchen with a dumbwaiter connected to the staff dining room below, a lavatory, and four bedrooms.[160] Doors on either end of the hallway led to the children's sleeping areas. Referring to the girls' domestic work in the principal's home, survivor Edward S. Groat declared that "they had built-in servants."[161] Another normally restricted area that girls entered in the course of their work was the boys' side of the building, as Soney experienced during the 1940s: "One of my duties was to scrub either the dormitory or a section of the boys' dormitory, and when I was over there I could look out of the window and see the boys a couple of storeys below, and oftentimes in the spring or fall they would be like little dustballs, fighting.... Another job I had was to scrub a row in the junior schoolroom or senior schoolroom."[162] Domestic labour such as laundry, cooking, serving, sewing, mending, and cleaning was largely done by female students and defined their spatial experience of the Mohawk Institute. Many of these activities had dedicated spaces within the building, but cleaning extended throughout the interior, even to places that were usually inaccessible. Although scrubbing and washing are visually absent in archival photographs of the Mohawk Institute, these were integral to the functioning of the institution and constituted some of the most common activities remembered by women survivors.

Like earlier in its history, the Mohawk Institute's landscape of labour extended well beyond the confines of the main building, which sat at the centre of 350 acres of agricultural land. It was mainly boys who worked in the fields and outbuildings, including barns for crops and livestock, horse stables, chicken coop, greenhouses, and carpentry shop. The farm and trades

Figure 6.15. Mohawk Institute fields looking northwest, with the school and farm buildings in the background, 1917
Source: John Boyd Fonds / Library and Archives Canada / a071299

structures were largely grouped behind the main building, an arrangement that implied the importance of classroom learning over manual labour. In this context, the school building could be seen as a kind of disguise, an image the church and government projected to shield the working landscape from the view of passersby. A side view of the grounds from 1917, however, reveals that the farm structures rivalled the main building in size, reflecting the importance of this landscape to the half-day labour system. The vast fields in the foreground, accentuated by the diminutive ploughman and team of horses, evoke the ceaseless work demanded of the children. Peter Smith recalled, "we worked on the farm, we were hungry all the time."[163] Many survivors remembered hard labour, with the products of their efforts rarely ending up on their plates.

The Mohawk Institute's productive landscape was represented by Russ Moses, who attended the institution from 1942 to 1947, in a detailed site plan drawn from memory in 1999 (see figure 0.4 in "Russ Moses Residential School Memoir," near the beginning of this book). The circle at the end of the drive is at the centre of the image, alluding to its significance in arrivals at and departures from the institution. The main building is adjacent to the circle, and these two elements act as a kind of fulcrum around which other parts of the landscape revolve. Yet the circle and the school are small compared to the apple orchards, vegetable gardens, and farmlands surrounding them, suggesting that these were even more significant in the children's experience of the place. Indeed, Moses recalled that everyone worked the land: children under Grade 5 "worked in the market garden in which every type of vegetable was grown and in the main sold," while "the senior boys worked on the farm—and I mean worked, we were underfed, ill clad and out in all types of weather."[164] The orchard between the main building and the street continues to be a distinguishing feature of the site, but its apples were as inaccessible to the children as other produce. Soney remembered that "there was an apple orchard next to our playground, and the only way you'd get any of them was to climb the fence, and then it was considered stealing and you'd get into trouble. But they were the Mohawk Institute's orchards."[165] As Moses's and Soney's testimonies show, children were often alienated from the food they grew, generating an added sense of injustice about the institution's theft of their labour.

Despite the hard physical work and deprivation that children endured at the Mohawk Institute, they also occasionally experienced this usually harsh environment through play. A few areas of the institution were designated for recreation, either purpose-built or appropriated by children for their amusement. In Moses's drawing, we see that boys' and girls' experiences of play were as spatially segregated as their labour. West of the driveway circle was the girls' fenced playground, which, as indicated by Soney, bordered the orchard in front of the main building. Smith remembered that the girls were mostly limited to this area: "the girls were kinda restricted—in a fenced-in playground. If they went out some place they took 25 of them in a bunch."[166] By contrast, the open "play area" behind the main building, presumably for the boys, appeared to have no defined boundaries. Smith recalled playing hide-and-seek throughout the grounds in the 1920s and '30s:

> Right after supper you'd take right off and you had till 8 o'clock. We'd run right off and go some place. . . . One night we were playing by the Mohawk lake, and we were being chased and they saw them coming from all three sides, and we jumped right in the Mohawk lake, and there were water snakes, and everybody swam right across the lake—with all their clothes on!!! We really laughed about that. We used to swim back of the chapel at noon time. At the weekends we'd go right back on the Henry property, and the water was deep back there.[167]

Soney remembers similarly unsupervised time to play, but her recollection lacks the expansiveness and exuberance of Smith's testimony, suggesting a more confined experience:

> We spent a lot of time that was unsupervised, just entertaining ourselves in the playroom or outside. Whatever we did there we basically entertained ourselves. There was nothing down there—it was a cement floor playroom and there were lockers around the edges, or boxes, but there was really nothing there—you know how a basement looks with those columns. We'd play tag and hide-and-go-seek, and go into another room and tell ghost stories.[168]

While some boys found respite in moving throughout and even beyond the grounds, the girls used the spaces provided to them, where "there was nothing," and reappropriated them for playing games and telling stories. Though starkly different, both boys' and girls' spatial reimagination of the Mohawk Institute for play demonstrates the children's resilience and inventiveness in surviving its harsh institutional environment.

Postwar Reforms

Reforms to the residential school system following the Second World War manifested, in part, as an extensive government construction program to renew the system's aging building stock. Even after a special joint committee of the Senate and House of Commons recommended integrating First Nations children into public schools, new, modernist residential schools replaced dilapidated buildings, while many existing schools were renovated and had new additions built.[169] These projects can be seen in terms of the progressive, liberal image the government wished to cultivate as it, in theory, moved away from paternalism toward integration and citizenship—a change many First Nations saw as continued efforts at assimilation. At the Mohawk Institute, postwar reforms to the built environment were influenced partly by these larger national trends, but also by more localized circumstances. In 1946, the number of children at the institution increased because of the closure of the Mount Elgin residential school 120 kilometres west.[170] The NEC also withdrew financial support, leading to local concerns about poor conditions. In February 1946, *The Windsor Daily Star* reported that the Brantford Women's Council had lodged a complaint with Indian

Affairs about inadequate clothing and educational facilities at the school, followed by the promise of "a full investigation" from the government.[171]

Indian Affairs made incremental improvements to the Mohawk Institute in the following years based on two reports detailing substantial deficiencies. The first revealed major problems with the electrical system, particularly in the 1904 building, which posed significant safety hazards.[172] Plans for an overhaul were prepared in July 1948.[173] The second report contained a scathing account of the children's living conditions. In several hand-written pages, an Indian Affairs official, C. A. F. Clark, described washrooms with no partitions between toilets, broken or missing toilet seats, and communal roller towels instead of personal towels—conditions under which "dignity and decency aren't getting much consideration" and which "would by ordinary white standards be called degrading."[174] The accompanying photos showed narrow beds crowded together, as well as toilets open to the children's sleeping spaces. Clark recommended improving the washrooms and expanding the dormitories into the central attic space, which was still unfinished, to alleviate overcrowding. Yet aside from improving the physical environment, he made these recommendations with the aim of transforming the children within it, suggesting that the dormitory "should approximate more the home bedroom if it is to train pupils in looking after their own things and leaving other people's things alone."[175] He summed up his aim: "to create a physical environment which will help rather than hinder the process of conditioning the inmates, many of whom constitute a challenge to the abilities of such staff members as we can attract. . . . The conditions are not good enough for a school whose objective is to raise the cultural and moral level of children who have already had a lower-than-average start."[176] Although the report implied that a better physical environment would assist staff in "improving" and assimilating the children under their care, it also brought to light the derelict state of the building and forced government action.

The architectural remnants of the Second World War played a role in postwar change in some First Nations communities and institutions like residential schools, which minimized government costs in providing infrastructure.[177] By the time of the Clark report, huts from the No. 20 Canadian Army (Basic) Training Centre, which operated in Brantford from 1940 to 1945, had been moved to the grounds of the Mohawk Institute. Located directly south of the main building, the huts were connected and renovated into a classroom block (figure 6.16).[178] Clark included a photograph of one of the three classrooms in his report, suggesting that "we should add a fourth

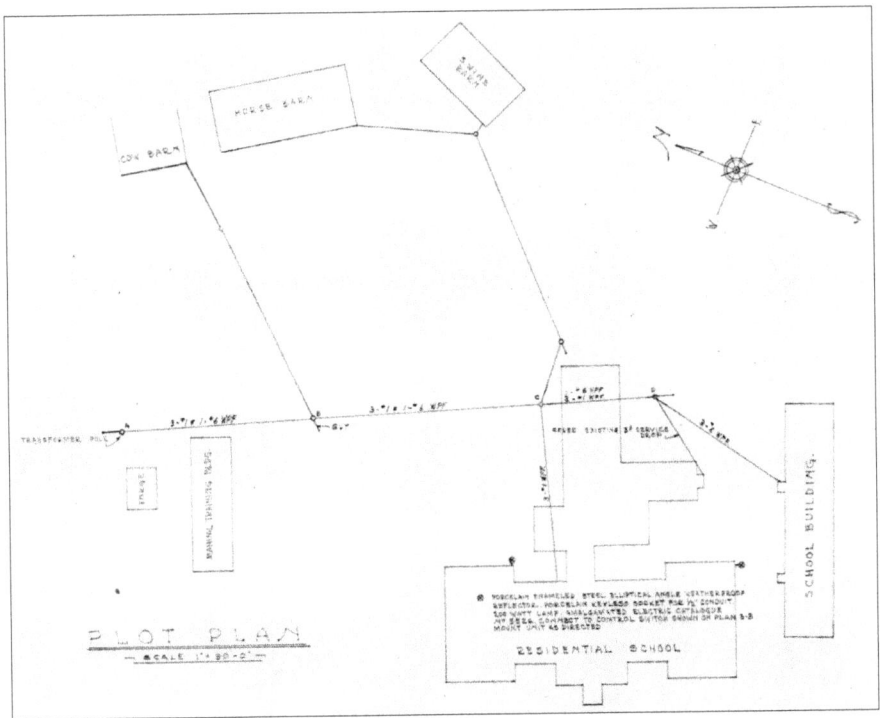

Figure 6.16. Detail of site plan showing the main building of the Mohawk Institute ("residential school"), classroom block built of army huts ("school building"), and other outbuildings, 1948
Source: Library and Archives Canada / Department of Indian Affairs and Northern Development Fonds / NMC 180189

while army buildings are available" (figure 6.17). Yet he also noted that in the photo, "in the desk nearest the door an under-age child is sleeping. We should have a real primary room."[179] In addition to generally inadequate conditions, the report thus revealed a lack of proper facilities for very young children who were taken to the institution. In 1949, another former military building, an army camp chapel, was moved to the front of the property, close to the driveway entrance on Mohawk Street. The chapel was converted into a two-classroom block, and, by 1953, all classroom activities were taking place in these former military buildings.[180]

The principal's accommodations also changed significantly in the mid-twentieth century. Clark's report recommended expanding the children's dormitories into the unused central attic space, which was located above the principal's apartment. The supervisor of vocational training for

6 | A "Model" School   209

Figure 6.17. Children in the army-hut classroom at the Mohawk Institute, 1948
Source: Copyright Government of Canada. Reproduced with the permission of Library and Archives Canada (2023). Library and Archives Canada / Department of Indian Affairs and Northern Development Fonds / e011864903_s1

Indian Affairs, A. J. Doucet, noted that "there is a great deal of space lost in the middle of this school. This is due, I believe, to the fact that the Principal would be reluctant to have dormitories above his own living quarters."[181] The crowded conditions in the children's dormitories were thus created, at least partly, to maintain the principal's comfort—a spatial inscription of racial hierarchies similar to those of the dining areas noted in earlier parts of the institution's history. Nevertheless, plans for expanding the dormitories were prepared in 1949, and the design provided for finishing the central attic space as well as renovating the existing dormitories. Also added at this time were the two octagonal windows visible in the pedimented dormers on the exterior of the building. The renovation included a new staff bedroom with its own toilet, as well as a nurse's room. These rooms increased surveillance by installing staff on the attic floor, as well as providing a buffer between the new boys' and girls' dormitories.[182] The principal's residence was finally moved to a detached house on the grounds in 1952 and the vacated space on the second floor was converted into nine staff bedrooms with a shared washroom.[183] The new house, still extant on the site, had a two-car garage and could be accessed by a driveway off the road leading to the main building. As part of this reconfiguration, the main building's two-storey porch, formerly accessed from the principal's apartment on the second floor, was reduced to one storey.

The plans of the 1952 renovations are of note because they refer to the visiting room near the entrance as the "Indian reception room."[184] This terminology complements survivors' testimonies of their experiences visiting siblings in this room by revealing it as a space that was explicitly racially segregated. Although parents and other visiting family members would have entered through the front door, their physical and visual access to the building would have likely stopped at the reception room.[185] The addition of a small washroom with a single sink and toilet, despite an existing staff washroom down the hall, suggests the importance that Indian Affairs and school authorities placed on preventing family members from moving beyond the reception room. The washroom played into the creation and maintenance of racial hierarchies through segregated facilities, which occurred in various contexts in twentieth-century Canada.[186]

The incremental changes of the immediate postwar period were followed by several significant projects at the Mohawk Institute in the late 1950s and '60s. These included a new classroom building, kitchen addition, and an outdoor pool. As with many architectural changes since the 1920s, these modifications related to Indian Affairs' centralized approach to residential school design, bringing the physical plant in line with that of other institutions in the federal system. However, they can also be read in the newer context of efforts toward equality, if not equity, between Indigenous peoples and settlers in Canada. The government saw investments in education, including architecture, as advancing these aims, even if the system itself continued to be inequitable given the ongoing separation of children from their families and communities, as well as its Eurocentric curriculum. The 1956 report of a commission on federal educational facilities for Indigenous children exposed a system that was physically crumbling, and its recommendations amounted to an extensive, national building program intended to facilitate integration.[187] The new four-classroom block completed at the Mohawk Institute in 1959 was a direct result of this report. Built to the north of the main building, the one-storey, flat-roofed classroom building contained two regular classrooms and two specialized classrooms for manual training and domestic science, along with a gymnasium, locker rooms, and offices.[188] The minister of the Department of Citizenship and

Immigration officiated at the inauguration of the new building, signifying the political utility of such investments.

The major projects of the 1960s fed into the government's "modernization" narrative with regards to its relations with Indigenous peoples. The renovation of the Mohawk Institute's dining room and the construction of an extensive kitchen addition in 1961 was a subject of such modernization discourse. In its annual report, the government declared that "the Mohawk Institute at Brantford benefitted from the first phase of extensive alterations designed to make it a modern residential school. The new kitchen and dining-room alterations which cost more than $100,000 provide facilities for feeding all students."[189] The theme of modernization was also emphasized in a photograph published in *The Brantford Expositor*, staged to show a staff member and student preparing food at a stainless-steel island with a variety of kitchen implements (figure 6.18). Behind them hovers Principal Zimmerman, who was quoted as saying that the project was part of efforts to create a "homey atmosphere" at the institution. According to the accompanying text, the new kitchen was "gleaming and efficient," "well-equipped and completely fireproof," with "many of the latest automatic facilities." Such descriptions were intended to show off these improvements to a larger public. The text made sure to specify that the renovations were "financed by the federal government," and Zimmerman stated in the article that he intended to hold an "official open house" when the project was completed.[190] Recalling Goffman's notion of "institutional display," the architectural and technological improvements showcased at the Mohawk Institute doubled as government propaganda.

While the classroom building and kitchen addition still exist today, only a trace remains of another postwar addition: an outdoor swimming pool tucked into the corner formed by the dining room and laundry. According to survivor testimony, this pool was used once a week by children who did not go home but remained at the institution over the summer.[191] Two square-format snapshots from June 1965 show a group of girls playing in the pool, then lining up in the water and on the deck to pose for the camera.[192] Behind the girls is a short fence, which probably wrapped around the entire pool. These images suggest that the use of the pool, like so many other aspects of the institution's constructed environment, was segregated by gender. It was, nevertheless, a source of enjoyment and respite for those who were forced to stay throughout the year. Kelly Curley, who was at the Mohawk Institute in 1969, right before it closed, recalled that going swimming "was one of the things we looked forward to in the summertime."[193]

Figure 6.18. The back of this photograph, taken on 21 January 1961 reads, in part, "admiring the kitchen are Canon W. J. Zimmerman, Mohawk Institute principal, one of the kitchen staff and several of the girl pupils who assist in the kitchen after school."
Source: *Brantford Expositor* / Library and Archives Canada / Department of Indian Affairs and Northern Development Fonds / e011308096

In 1969, the federal government took operational control of residential schools away from the churches and turned them into residences, from which children were sent to schools in nearby settler communities.[194] This change also occurred at the Mohawk Institute and came with programs in Indigenous languages and traditions that had once been suppressed by the schools. The federal ownership did not last long; control of many schools was relinquished to nearby Indigenous communities, regardless of the community's relationship to a particular school. The Mohawk Institute reverted to Six Nations of the Grand River, whose elected council still owns the building today. At its foundation, the school operated to serve children from Six Nations, but in 1965, only fifteen residents from that community remained. The rest, including over one hundred from Quebec, came from sparsely populated northern areas where day schools had not yet been built.[195]

Upon the full-fledged closure of the Mohawk Institute in 1969, G. D. Cromb, director of the Education Branch of Indian Affairs, commented that "it is the firm opinion of this Department that the children will receive better care in their own homes under the guidance of their parents than they would in residence."[196] This attitude was an about-face from the views expressed throughout the Mohawk Institute's entire history, with no special explanation or acknowledgement. The same year, the former Mohawk Institute was repurposed by the Association of Iroquois and Allied Indians as the Woodland Indian Cultural Education Centre (known since 1988 as the Woodland Cultural Centre), which has developed a museum and library and offers programming in arts, Indigenous languages, and education. The community's takeover of the building and transformation of its purpose—from a site of cultural genocide to one of cultural resurgence—is an exemplar of what Māori planning scholar Hirini Matunga describes as "quiet narrative" Indigenous architecture: an "architecture of necessity" and "of retrofit and repurpose" that relates a "poignant story of Indigenous survival in the modern era."[197] The structure's new identity as a cultural centre was opposed to its original use as a residential school, yet the site's complex history has continued to inform the understanding and interpretation of its built environment.[198]

Conclusion

The architecture of the Mohawk Institute has a history as long as the institution itself, as well as over five decades since the closure of the residential school. An important phase of its spatial history, which merits its own historical study, is its reuse as the Woodland Cultural Centre by nine original member communities in 1972 and the current support communities of Wahta, Tyendinaga, and Six Nations of the Grand River. This history, as well as the restoration and commemoration of the former residential school's main building, represent two major directions for future study. The community-led Save the Evidence campaign has recognized the importance of the built fabric of the institution as a form of testimony that, alongside that of survivors, will help ensure that the tragic history of the Mohawk Institute is never forgotten.

This chapter has shown that the study of the Mohawk Institute's architecture can reveal much about the experiences of the children who were taken there, as well as the intentions of government and church officials in the fine-grain operation of the residential school system. While serving as a model for residential schools across Canada, the Mohawk Institute was itself influenced by its inclusion in this national system. The built environment played a significant role in the school's program of cultural genocide, enabling punishments, social control, and reinforcing gender and racial hierarchies. Many similarities persisted in the creation and organization of the built environment across the different phases of the institution's history, despite their distinct architectural identities. Gender segregation, uncompensated child labour on construction and maintenance, spaces of confinement and punishment, and an expansive but segregated landscape of work were some of the spatial continuities throughout the Mohawk Institute's history. With each architectural phase, we can interpret the built environment using an additional type of evidence, from textual sources, to visual sources such as photographs and plans, to survivor testimony. Children's experiences of the institution, not unexpectedly, emerge most clearly through the oral histories of survivors. These experiences were highly spatial, and survivors' recollections are often firmly situated within the complex constructed environment that contained them.

The Mohawk Institute's architecture is a crucial vessel for these stories, standing as a silent witness, alongside the testimony of survivors, to the hardships of the residential school era. Perhaps the most poignant aspect of the institution's built environment in the present are the many inscriptions by students of names, dates, and other messages on the bricks of the main building and hidden places inside. These marks, inscribed into the very material of the former residential school, speak to descendants and visitors of the presence, resistance, and survival of the children and honour those who did not survive. As the transformation of the Mohawk Institute continues into the future, it will serve as an important "site of conscience"[199] that concretizes residential school history more broadly and commemorates the struggles of the children who were there.

NOTES

An early version of this chapter was part of my master's thesis completed at the University of Waterloo. A more recent version was workshopped in Professor Itohan Osayimwese's "Race and Architecture" course at Brown University in fall 2021. I would like to thank Dr. Osayimwese, Dr. Felipe Hernández, and the students for their thoughtful feedback. Thank you also to the editors of the present volume for their invitation to participate in the project and their support in completing this chapter.

1   Janet Wright, *Crown Assets: The Architecture of the Department of Public Works, 1867–1967* (University of Toronto Press, 1997), 61.

2   Geoffrey Paul Carr, "'House of No Spirit': An Architectural History of the Indian Residential School in British Columbia" (PhD diss., University of British Columbia, 2011), 12. See also Geoffrey Carr, "Atopoi of the Modern: Revisiting the Place of the Indian Residential School," *ESC: English Studies in Canada* 35, no. 1 (2009): 109–35; Geoffrey Carr, "Educating Memory: Regarding the Remnants of the Indian Residential School," *Journal of the Society for the Study of Architecture in Canada* 34, no. 2 (2009): 87–99.

3   Carr, "'House of No Spirit,'" 43.
4   For further scholarship on the architecture of residential schools in Canada and the United States, see Hugh James Bitz, "School-House: Additions and Renovations to White Calf Collegiate; Lebret, Saskatchewan" (master's thesis, University of British Columbia, 1997); Sandra U. Dielissen, "Teaching a School to Talk: Archaeology of the Queen Victoria Jubilee Home for Indian Children" (master's thesis, Simon Fraser University, 2012); Christopher T. Green, "A Stage Set for Assimilation: The Model Indian School at the World's Columbian Exposition," *Winterthur Portfolio* 51, nos. 2–3 (2017): 95–133; Emily Elizabeth Turner, "Mission Infrastructure Development in the Canadian North, c. 1850–1920" (PhD diss., University of Edinburgh, 2018); Jennifer N. Harvey, "Landscapes of Conversion: The Evolution of the Residential School Sites at Wiikwemkoong and Spanish, Ontario" (master's thesis, Laurentian University, 2019); Trina Cooper-Bolam, "Workhouses and Residential Schools: From Institutional Models to Museums," in *Cybercartography in a Reconciliation Community*, ed. D. R. Fraser Taylor and Stephanie Pyne (Elsevier, 2019), 143–66; Émélie Desrochers-Turgeon, "On the Silence of the Colonial Archive: Examining Sensorial Agency Through the Archival Drawings of Indian Residential Schools in Canada," in *The Routledge Companion to Architectural Drawings and Models*, ed. Federica Goffi (Routledge, 2022), 460–75.
5   Sarah de Leeuw, "Intimate Colonialisms: The Material and Experienced Places of British Columbia's Residential Schools," *Canadian Geographer* 51, no. 3 (2007): 343.
6   Jacqueline Fear-Segal, "Carlisle Campus: Landscape of Race and Erasure," in *White Man's Club: Schools, Race, and the Struggle of Indian Acculturation* (University of Nebraska Press, 2007), 184–205.
7   Fear-Segal, 185–6.
8   Jo-Anne Fiske, "Placing Violence Against First Nations Children: The Use of Space and Place to Construct the (In)Credible Violated Subject," in *Healing Traditions: The Mental Health of Aboriginal Peoples in Canada*, ed. Laurence J. Kirmayer and Gail Guthrie Valaskakis (UBC Press, 2009), 152.
9   Mary Louise Pratt describes contact zones as "social spaces where disparate cultures meet, clash, and grapple with each other, often in highly asymmetrical relations of domination and subordination." Mary Louise Pratt, "Introduction: Criticism in the Contact Zone," in *Imperial Eyes: Travel Writing and Transculturation* (Routledge, 1992), 7.
10 Frank Eames, *Pioneer Schools of Upper Canada* (reprinted from Ontario Historical Society Papers and Records, vol. 18 [1920?]), 5.
11 The school, conducted by the Reverend Eleazar Wheelock, was later moved to New Hampshire, where it became Dartmouth College. Isabel Thompson Kelsay, *Joseph Brant, 1743–1807: Man of Two Worlds* (Syracuse University Press, 1984), 71–2.
12 Rick Monture, *We Share Our Matters = Teionkwakhashion Tsi Niionkwariho:Ten: Two Centuries of Writing and Resistance at Six Nations of the Grand River* (University of Manitoba Press, 2014), 31–2.
13 The British Crown built the Mohawk Chapel in 1785 in thanks for the Kanyen'kehaka's support during the American Revolution and as a replacement for the place of worship built by Queen Anne in 1711 in the Kanyen'kehaka homelands of the Mohawk Valley, which were taken over by the American rebels. Originally called St. Paul's, the chapel is known today as Her Majesty's Royal Chapel of the Mohawks. It is a National Historic Site and currently the oldest surviving church building in Ontario, as well as the only standing remnant of the village. Violet M. Holroyd, *Foundations of Faith: Historic Religious Buildings of Ontario* (Natural Heritage, 1991), 58.
14 Monture, *We Share Our Matters = Teionkwakhashion Tsi Niionkwariho:Ten*, 32. Brant's Kanyen'kehaka name, Thayendanegea, reflected a synthetic approach to culture in its meaning: "Two sticks of wood bound together" or "Two arrows bound together." The first definition is found in Kelsay, *Joseph Brant*, 43, and the second was provided to me by Dr. William Woodworth / Raweno:kwas.
15 This philosophy is, of course, also embodied in the Two Row Wampum. See Monture, *We Share Our Matters = Teionkwakhashion Tsi Niionkwariho:Ten*, 13–14.
16 Camille Prevost and Sam Russell, "A Primer for the Use of the Mohawk Children," Edith and Lorne Pierce Collection of Canadiana, Queen's University Library, 2021, https://piercecanadiana.omeka.net/exhibits/show/mohawk-primer; Gus Richardson, "SAHONWAGY," in *Dictionary of Canadian Biography*, vol. 4, University of Toronto/Université Laval, 2003–, http://www.biographi.ca/en/bio/sahonwagy_4E.html.
17 W. Martha E. Cooke and Bruce G. Wilson, "Peachey, James," in *Dictionary of Canadian Biography*, vol. 4, University of Toronto/Université Laval, 2003–, http://www.biographi.ca/en/bio/peachey_james_4E.html.
18 Duncan Campbell Scott, "The Mohawk Institute," in *Annual Report of the Department of Indian Affairs for the Year Ended March 31, 1930* (F. A. Acland, 1931), 15.
19 Aborigines Protection Society, *Report on the Indians of Upper Canada* (William Ball, Arnold, and Co., 1839), 5.

20 Scott, "The Mohawk Institute," 15.
21 Scott, 15. The possible use of a repurposed building early in the Mohawk Institute's history reflects common practice in nineteenth-century institution-building for reasons of economy, but which may also have been advantageous by locating an unfamiliar institution in a familiar physical setting. See Marta Gutman, *A City for Children: Women, Architecture, and the Charitable Landscapes of Oakland, 1850–1950* (University of Chicago Press, 2014), 30–1; Sara Honarmand Ebrahimi, *Emotion, Mission, Architecture: Building Hospitals in Persia and British India, 1865–1914* (Edinburgh University Press, 2023), 52–6.
22 Jennifer Pettit, "From Longhouse to Schoolhouse: The Mohawk Institute 1834–1970" (master's thesis, University of Western Ontario, 1993), 55.
23 Susan M. Hill, *The Clay We Are Made Of: Haudenosaunee Land Tenure on the Grand River* (University of Manitoba Press, 2017), 278n143.
24 Monture, *We Share Our Matters = Teionkwakhashion Tsi Niionkwariho:Ten*, 58.
25 "November 1829 NEC Report: Lugger," in Elizabeth Graham, *The Mush Hole: Life at Two Indian Residential Schools* (Heffle Publishing, 1997), 44.
26 The phrase "Mechanics Institution" (or "Mechanics' Institute") may have been used interchangeably to refer to one specific building that was used for industrial or trades training, as well as to the school as a whole. Graham, *The Mush Hole*, 7, 44–5; Pettit, "From Longhouse to Schoolhouse," 50.
27 "29 April 1831 NEC Report," in Graham, *The Mush Hole*, 45.
28 Scott, "The Mohawk Institute," 16; "26 April 1834 NEC Report," in Graham, *The Mush Hole*, 45; Cf. Miller, who writes that the residences were opened in 1833 and accommodated ten boys and ten girls. J. R. Miller, *Shingwauk's Vision: A History of Native Residential Schools* (University of Toronto Press, 1996), 73; See also Pettit, "From Longhouse to Schoolhouse," 54.
29 Emily Elizabeth Turner, "Mission Infrastructure Development in the Canadian North, c. 1850–1920" (PhD diss., University of Edinburgh, 2018), 16–19.
30 "June 1833 NEC Report: Lugger," in Graham, *The Mush Hole*, 45.
31 "26 April 1834 NEC Report," in Graham, 45.
32 Robert S. Allen, "The British Indian Department and the Frontier in North America, 1755–1830," *Canadian Historic Sites: Occasional Papers in Archaeology and History*, no. 14 (1975): 89, 99–100.
33 "23 May 1835 NEC Report," in Graham, *The Mush Hole*, 45.
34 "1 February 1839 NEC Report," in Graham, 47.
35 "1839 NEC Report," in Graham, 47.
36 "29 August 1839 NEC Report: Treasurer to Nelles," in Graham, 47.
37 "29 August 1839 NEC Report: Treasurer to Nelles," in Graham, 47.
38 "26 May 1840 NEC Report"; "26 August 1840 NEC Report: Nelles," in Graham, 48.
39 One official recommended that the NEC exempt certain girls from this work and "allow them to be treated ... as boarders at a white school are treated" so that they could be trained as teachers. "18 November 1837 Richardson to Busk," in Graham, 46. See the chapter by Alison Norman in this volume for more on training girls to be teachers.
40 "8 September 1834 NEC Report: Lugger Nellis [sic] Richardson," in Graham, 45.
41 Scott, "The Mohawk Institute," 16.
42 "22 February 1844 NEC Report: Nelles"; "19 July 1844 NEC Report," in Graham, *The Mush Hole*, 51.
43 Pettit, "From Longhouse to Schoolhouse," 55.
44 "8 September 1834 NEC Report: Lugger Nellis [sic] Richardson," in Graham, *The Mush Hole*, 45.
45 Scott, "The Mohawk Institute," 16; James Douglas Leighton, "The Development of Federal Indian Policy in Canada, 1840–1890" (PhD diss., University of Western Ontario, 1975), 237.
46 This recommendation was made by the chief superintendent of Indian Affairs. "Report on the Affairs of the Indians in Canada; submitted to the Honorable the Legislative Assembly, for their information," Section III, Appendix (T.) in *Journals of the Legislative Council of the Province of Canada*, vol. VI (John C. Becket, 1847), n.p. [3].
47 James Beaven, *Recreations of a Long Vacation; or a Visit to Indian Missions in Upper Canada* (James Burns; H. and A. Rowsell, 1846), 52–3.
48 "Evidence of Mr. Superintendent Winnett, (respecting the Six Nations of the Grand River.)," Appendix No. 17 in "Report on the Affairs of the Indians in Canada," n.p. [118].
49 "NEC Report," in Graham, *The Mush Hole*, 53.

50   "NEC Report."
51   The fire goes unmentioned in the NEC reports republished in Graham's *The Mush Hole* and Scott's 1930 text. The Anglican Church of Canada's web page on the Mohawk Institute, since removed, mentions a fire around 1854–9, while Jennifer Pettit writes that the fire occurred in 1858. Scott, "The Mohawk Institute," 16; "10 June 1844 Six Nations Indians to NEC," in Graham, *The Mush Hole*, 51; "The Mohawk Institute—Brantford, ON," Anglican Church of Canada, 23 September 2008, accessed 23 March 2021, http://www.anglican.ca/tr/histories/mohawk-institute/; Pettit, "From Longhouse to Schoolhouse," 59; Jennifer Loretta Pettit, "'To Christianize and Civilize': Native Industrial Schools in Canada" (PhD diss., University of Calgary, 1997), 25.
52   This colour of brick was common in the area and known regionally as "white brick." Dominion of Canada, *Annual Report of the Department of Indian Affairs for the Year Ended 30th June, 1896* (Printed by S.E. Dawson, Printer to the Queen's Most Excellent Majesty, 1897). See also Harold Kalman, *A History of Canadian Architecture*, vol. 1 (Oxford University Press, 1994), 289.
53   "NEC Report," in Graham, *The Mush Hole*, 53.
54   Kalman, *A History of Canadian Architecture*, 1:146–60.
55   Kalman, 1:146.
56   Kalman, 1:139.
57   John J. G. Blumenson, *Ontario Architecture: A Guide to Styles and Building Terms, 1784 to the Present* (Fitzhenry & Whiteside, 1990), 5.
58   Kalman, *A History of Canadian Architecture*, 1:139.
59   Johnson was an Irish colonial administrator, enslaver, and influential British superintendent of Indian Affairs in the province of New York, while Brant was a Kanyen'kehaka leader and the stepsister of Joseph Brant. Some historians have evaluated Johnson in a less-than-favourable light vis-à-vis his relationship with Indigenous peoples; for instance, Gwyn writes that "he was indeed one of their principal exploiters." Julian Gwyn, "Johnson, Sir William," in *Dictionary of Canadian Biography*, vol. 4, University of Toronto/Université Laval, 2003–, http://www.biographi.ca/en/bio/johnson_william_4E.html; Heather Conn, "Mary Brant (Konwatsi'tsiaiénni)," in *Canadian Encyclopedia*, 20 August 2019, https://www.thecanadianencyclopedia.ca/en/article/mary-brant.
60   Thank you to Dr. William Woodworth / Raweno:kwas for teaching me about Johnson Hall and drawing my attention to its significance in the Haudenosaunee narrative.
61   See, for instance, "23 December 1872 NEC Report: Committee," in Graham, *The Mush Hole*, 74.
62   This was more so the case at Protestant institutions like the Mohawk Institute; Roman Catholic residential schools were usually run with a gender-segregated administration, depending on the religious order running the school.
63   I consider verandas here as a type of porch. Robert Mugerauer, "Toward an Architectural Vocabulary: The Porch as a Between," in *Dwelling, Seeing, and Designing: Toward a Phenomenological Ecology*, ed. David Seamon (State University of New York Press, 1993), 111.
64   Ron Williams, *Landscape Architecture in Canada* (McGill-Queen's University Press, 2014), 136–7.
65   Martin Benson noted that the trees were maples in his 1895 report. Martin Benson, "Report on the Mohawk Institute and Six Nations Board Schools," 1895, n.p., File 7825-1A, C-11133, Vol. 2006, RG 10, Library and Archives Canada (hereafter LAC).
66   Williams, *Landscape Architecture in Canada*, 136.
67   "NEC Report"; "3 August 1859 NEC Report: Nelles," in Graham, *The Mush Hole*, 53–4.
68   "12 July 1860 NEC Report: O'Meara," in Graham, 54.
69   No further details on this addition are provided. "NEC Report," in Graham, 56. See also Province of Canada, *The Indian Affairs, Province of Canada Report for the Half-Year Ended 30th June, 1864* (Printed by Hunter, Rose & Co., St. Ursule Street, 1865), 27.
70   "Autumn 1868 NEC Report: Lister"; the recommendation is in "25 February 1869 NEC Report," in Graham, *The Mush Hole*, 56–7.
71   "23 November 1869 NEC Report," in Graham, 58.
72   "December 1870 NEC Report: Botsford"; "2 March 1872 NEC Report: Blomfield"; "6 April 1872 NEC Report: Nelles," in Graham, 59, 62, 64.
73   "The accommodation in point of lodging is not sufficient. The ventilation and heating are defective, and require improvement according to modern approved plans. A commodious room, which will fully serve all the purposes of an [sic] hospital for the sick, is much needed. They have separate beds.... A new

school-room, built, arranged, and furnished on some good modern plan is much needed. . . . The rooms . . . now occupied for school purposes would be then available for sleeping accommodation." "16 May 1872 NEC Report: Nelles, Elliot, Chance, Roberts," in Graham, 65–6.

74   "NEC Report: Martland notes of verbal statement," in Graham, 68–9.
75   "NEC Report: Martland notes of verbal statement," in Graham, 69.
76   "20 November 1872 R. Ashton to NEC," in Graham, 71.
77   "20 November 1872 R. Ashton to NEC," in Graham, 71.
78   Scott, "The Mohawk Institute," 17.
79   "1877 NEC Report: R. Ashton"; "30 July 1877 Gilkison," in Graham, *The Mush Hole*, 78.
80   Fear-Segal, "Carlisle Campus," 185.
81   Fear-Segal, 185.
82   See Christopher T. Green, "A Stage Set for Assimilation: The Model Indian School at the World's Columbian Exposition," *Winterthur Portfolio* 51, nos. 2–3 (2017): 95–133, https://doi.org/10.1086/694225.
83   See Erving Goffman, *Asylums: Essays on the Social Situation of Mental Patients and Other Inmates* (Aldine Pub. Co., 1962), 104–5; Tony Bennett, "The Exhibitionary Complex," in *Culture/Power/History: A Reader in Contemporary Social Theory* (Princeton University Press, 1994), 123–54.
84   "29 September 1879 Gilkison," in Graham, *The Mush Hole*, 82. J. T. Gilkison reported in both 1877 and 1879 that an addition had been built, although it is not clear whether he was referring to the same addition in each instance. See also "30 July 1877 Gilkison," in Graham, 78.
85   "1878 NEC Report: R. Ashton," in Graham, 78.
86   "NEC Report: Six Years Summary," in Graham, 75.
87   On gender and gender segregation in residential schools, see J. R. Miller, "'The Misfortune of Being a Woman': Gender," in *Shingwauk's Vision*, 218–50; John S. Milloy, *A National Crime: The Canadian Government and the Residential School System, 1879 to 1986*, anniv. ed. (University of Manitoba Press, 2017), 238; de Leeuw, "Intimate Colonialisms," 345, 349–52.
88   Miller, *Shingwauk's Vision*, 193.
89   Miller, 193–4.
90   On the Gothic mode as "a statement of political and cultural allegiance to Britain," particularly in relation to Canada's first Parliament Buildings, see Wright, *Crown Assets*, 109. On the rejection of classicism due to its associations with American republicanism, see Ryan Ferko, "The Value of Regionalism in Assessing Canadian Architectural Heritage: An Examination of the Historical Context of Maritime Collegiate Classicism," *Journal of the Society for the Study of Architecture in Canada* 36, no. 2 (2011): 61.
91   The Ecclesiological Society published a widely read journal and influenced the design of churches for other denominations as well as buildings of all kinds. See Kalman, *A History of Canadian Architecture*, 1:279–80; Leslie Maitland, Jacqueline Hucker, and Shannon Ricketts, *A Guide to Canadian Architectural Styles* (Broadview Press, 1992), 51–2; Barry Magrill, "'Development' and Ecclesiology in the Outposts of the British Empire: William Hay's Gothic Solutions For Church Building in Tropical Climates (1840–1890)," *Journal of the Society for the Study of Architecture in Canada* 29, no. 1 (2004): 15–26.
92   See G. A. Bremner, *Imperial Gothic: Religious Architecture and High Anglican Culture in the British Empire, c. 1840–70* (Yale University Press, 2013); Alex Bremner, "Colonial Architecture and its Global Contexts," *Architecture Australia* 104, no. 4 (July–August 2015): 53–6.
93   See Kalman, *A History of Canadian Architecture*, 1:264, 269, 276.
94   Kalman, 1:277.
95   "29 September 1886 R. Ashton Annual Report," in Graham, *The Mush Hole*, 85.
96   "11 September 1891 R. Ashton Annual Report," in Graham, 87.
97   "11 September 1891 R. Ashton Annual Report," in Graham, 87.
98   Cupolas were used on other residential schools remodelled in a similar period. See, for example, the Birtle residential school renovated around 1909. Magdalena Milosz, "'Don't Let Fear Take Over': The Space and Memory of Indian Residential Schools" (master's thesis, University of Waterloo, 2015), 92–3.
99   "Mohawk Institute Indian Residential School IAP School Narrative," National Centre for Truth and Reconciliation, 31 May 2013, 8, https://archives.nctr.ca/NAR-NCTR-080.
100   "14 September 1893 R. Ashton Annual Report"; "6 September 1894 R. Ashton Annual Report," in Graham, *The Mush Hole*, 89.
101   "1894 Benson," in Graham, 91.

102 "1894 Benson," in Graham, 92.
103 "December 1879 NEC Report: Botsford," in Graham, 60.
104 "1894 Benson," in Graham, 90.
105 "11 September 1891 R. Ashton Annual Report," in Graham, 88.
106 "20 September 1892 R. Ashton Annual Report," in Graham, 88.
107 Mary Jane Logan McCallum, *Nii Ndahlohke: Boys' and Girls' Work at Mount Elgin Industrial School, 1890–1915* (Friesen Press, 2022), 17.
108 Alexandra Giancarlo, "Indigenous Student Labour and Settler Colonialism at Brandon Residential School," *Canadian Geographer* 64, no. 3 (2020): 466–7.
109 "December 1870 NEC Report: Botsford"; "NEC Report: Six Years Summary," in Graham, *The Mush Hole*, 60, 75.
110 "NEC Report: Six Years Summary," in Graham, 79.
111 "1894 Benson," in Graham, 91.
112 "1894 Benson," in Graham, 90.
113 Dominion of Canada, *Annual Report of the Department of Indian Affairs for the Year Ended June 30, 1903* (S. E. Dawson, 1904), 327.
114 "11 September 1891 R. Ashton Annual Report," in Graham, *The Mush Hole*, 87.
115 "1894 Benson," in Graham, 90.
116 Benson, "Report on the Mohawk Institute and Six Nations Board Schools," n.p.
117 On arson as a form of resistance at residential schools, including the Mohawk Institute, see Miller, *Shingwauk's Vision*, 368–70. See also de Leeuw, "Intimate Colonialisms," 353.
118 "Blaze at Brantford: The Mohawk Institute Totally Destroyed," *The Globe*, 20 April 1903, 9.
119 "25 April 1906 Cameron to McLean," in Graham, *The Mush Hole*, 104. On the carceral history of the Mimico Industrial School, currently the site of the Toronto South Detention Centre, see Magdalena Miłosz, "Ghosts of Prisons Past: A Prehistory of the Toronto South Detention Centre," *Scapegoat* 7 (2014): 47–67.
120 Dominion of Canada, *Annual Report of the Department of Indian Affairs for the Year Ended 30 June 1905* (S. E. Dawson, 1906), 282.
121 Maitland et al., *A Guide to Canadian Architectural Styles*, 111.
122 See G. A. Bremner, *Building Greater Britain: Architecture, Imperialism, and the Edwardian Baroque Revival, 1885–1920* (Paul Mellon Centre for Studies in British Art, 2022).
123 This type of composition was common in residential school photography. See de Leeuw, "Intimate Colonialisms," 345.
124 Sherry Farrell Racette, "Haunted: First Nations Children in Residential School Photography," in *Depicting Canada's Children*, ed. Loren Lerner (Wilfrid Laurier University Press, 2009), 49.
125 De Leeuw, "Intimate Colonialisms," 345.
126 On photography and oral history in research on residential schools, see also J. R. Miller, "Reading Photographs, Reading Voices: Documenting the History of Native Residential Schools," in *Reflections on Native-Newcomer Relations: Selected Essays* (University of Toronto Press, 2004), 82–103.
127 "Lorna's Sister with Lorna, 1940–1945," in Graham, *The Mush Hole*, 379. For a further discussion of the size of institutional architecture in children's experiences, see de Leeuw, "Intimate Colonialisms," 343.
128 Marie Hess, *Going Back Home* (BookLand Press, 2019), 55.
129 "10 August 1905 R. Ashton Annual Report," in Graham, *The Mush Hole*, 103.
130 "Mohawk Institute Indian Residential School IAP School Narrative," 9–10.
131 Scott, "The Mohawk Institute," 18. In 1903, Ernest Charles Ashton was a major in the Dufferin Rifles, which he had joined in 1893. He went on to have an illustrious military career, becoming head of the Canadian Army in 1935. Reverend Ashton's other son, Alfred Nelles Ashton, became principal of the Mohawk Institute upon his father's retirement in 1911 but resigned to enlist in the military in 1914. He was known as a particularly cruel administrator. See chapters 1, 8, 11, and 12 for more information about the Ashtons.
132 A closer comparison between the Mohawk Institute and the Middlesex Industrial School may reveal a more detailed architectural genealogy. On industrial schools in the United Kingdom, including Middlesex, see John A. Stack, "Reformatory and Industrial Schools and the Decline of Child Imprisonment in Mid-Victorian England and Wales," *History of Education* 23, no. 1 (1994), 59–73, https://

doi.org/10.1080/0046760940230104; Peter Higginbotham, *Children's Homes: A History of Institutional Care for Britain's Young* (Pen & Sword History, 2017).

133 "The Mohawk Institute: New Plans Are Being Drawn Up," *Brantford Weekly Expositor*, 9 July 1903; Robert G. Hill, "Stewart, William," *Biographical Dictionary of Architects in Canada 1800–1950*, 2022, http://www.dictionaryofarchitectsincanada.org/node/1332. Lewis H. Taylor acted as the local representative for the firm, which was headed by father and son William and Walter Stewart in Hamilton.

134 Hill, "Stewart, William." The firm's other projects included a private residence on Brant Avenue in 1902 and an office and factory for Buck Stove Works on Elgin Street in 1903. The Carnegie Building, as the library is now known, is part of Wilfrid Laurier University's Brantford campus. Although Stewart, Stewart & Taylor dissolved in 1904 upon the elder Stewart's retirement, Walter Stewart and Lewis H. Taylor continued to practise together and separately in a succession of firms, with projects located primarily in southwestern Ontario.

135 Lewis H. Taylor, as part of a firm he formed with his nephew, J. Albert Taylor, also worked on two churches the New England Company intended to build "on the Indian reserve," presumably Six Nations of the Grand River, in 1907. Further research is needed to ascertain the fate of these projects and what relationship they may have had with the Mohawk Institute. "Contracts Open," *Canadian Contract Record* 18, no. 11 (15 May 1907): 6; Robert G. Hill, "Taylor, Lewis H.," *Biographical Dictionary of Architects in Canada 1800–1950*, 2022, http://www.dictionaryofarchitectsincanada.org/node/1351.

136 Carnegie libraries were philanthropically funded institutions that were built in towns and cities across North America. Over sixteen hundred libraries resulted from Andrew Carnegie's building program. On the relationship between classicism and the design of Carnegie libraries, see Abigail A. van Slyck, "'The Utmost Amount of Effectiv [sic] Accommodation': Andrew Carnegie and the Reform of the American Library," *Journal of the Society of Architectural Historians* 50, no. 4 (1991): 372.

137 On the consolidation of industrial and boarding schools, see Miller, *Shingwauk's Vision*, 148; Milloy, *A National Crime*, 71. The contract between government and churches can be found in *Correspondence and Agreement Relating to the Maintenance and Management of Indian Boarding Schools* (Government Printing Bureau, 1911).

138 Dominion of Canada, *Annual Report of the Department of Indian Affairs for the Year Ended March 31, 1911* (C. H. Parmelee, 1911), 314.

139 The former Portage La Prairie Indian Residential School now belongs to Long Plain First Nation and is home to the National Indigenous Residential School Museum of Canada. It is a National Historic Site. The residential school in Chapleau was demolished soon after it was sold in the late 1950s. See also Robert G. Hill, "Chene, Jean Dosithe," *Biographical Dictionary of Architects in Canada 1800–1950*, 2022, http://dictionaryofarchitectsincanada.org/node/912; Robert G. Hill, "Orr, Roland Guerney," *Biographical Dictionary of Architects in Canada 1800–1950*, 2022, http://dictionaryofarchitectsincanada.org/node/123.

140 For a list of Orr's residential school projects, see Milosz, "'Don't Let Fear Take Over,'" 12–13.

141 "3 December 1913 Scott to Roche," in Graham, *The Mush Hole*, 109.

142 Although a rear wing with a different configuration appears to be visible in a photograph of the building from 1917, it is not mentioned in NEC reports, nor is a demolition. See LAC, John Boyd fonds, accession number 1971-120 NPC, "Mohawk Institute Farm in Brantford, [Ont.]," 14 November 1917, photograph by John Boyd, copy negative PA-071299. Scott himself, as deputy superintendent of Indian Affairs, signed the drawings for the 1922 project, suggesting his involvement in the design process and the importance of architecture in the department's activities.

143 Scott, "The Mohawk Institute," 19.

144 "Jennie Blackbird, 1942–1946," in Graham, *The Mush Hole*, 389.

145 "I was there when they renovated the buildings, and put up the new barn." "Harrison Burning, 1920–1928?," in Graham, *The Mush Hole*, 357. The barn was also likely designed by Orr, as numerous drawings of barns for other residential schools are credited to him in the Indian Affairs archive. See LAC, Finding Aid for RG22M 912016, pages 1–83, a copy of which is in the author's possession.

146 "31 December 1922 Rogers Quarterly Report"; "31 March 1923 Rogers Quarterly Report," in Graham, *The Mush Hole*, 138, 139. In 1924, Orr wrote to Rogers to let him know there were no funds to complete the requested work of painting and sheathing the boys' and girls' playrooms. R. Guerney Orr to S. Rogers, 3 April 1924, File 466-5, Pt. 2, Vol. 6201, RG 10, LAC.

147 "Martha Hill, 1912–1918," in Graham, *The Mush Hole*, 355. Hill's observation about girls and boys being "mixed together" at church is interesting as it contrasts with an earlier phase in the Mohawk Chapel's history, when its interior was "divided into open seats, one side for the men, the other for the women." See Beaven, *Recreations*, 51.

148 "Vera Styres, 1942–1943, 1946–1947," in Graham, *The Mush Hole*, 391.

149 "Jennie Blackbird, 1942–1946," in Graham, 389.
150 "Marguerite Beaver, 1940–1948," in Graham, 385.
151 "23 December 1907 Ramsden to McLean," in Graham, 105.
152 "Martha Hill, 1912–1918," in Graham, 356.
153 "Lorna's Sister with Lorna, 1940–1945," in Graham, 380.
154 "Jennie Blackbird, 1942–1946," in Graham, 389.
155 "Jennie Blackbird, 1942–1946," in Graham, 389.
156 "Sylvia Soney, 1943–1947," in Graham, 392.
157 "Sylvia Soney, 1943–1947," in Graham, 392.
158 Racette, "Haunted," 65.
159 Groat refers to it as the third floor, but I write "second floor" for the sake of consistency with descriptions in other parts of this chapter. Some architectural plans refer to it as the first floor. To clarify, the principal's apartment was in the central block above the ground floor. "Edward S. (a.k.a. Russell) Groat and Marjorie J. Groat (nee Smith), Ruth Jamieson Seneca, 1930–1939 and 1928–193?, 193?," in Graham, *The Mush Hole*, 363.
160 Description based on Chas H. Buck, architect, "Mohawk Institute, Brantford, Ontario, Plan No. 876, Sheet No. E - 3, Ground & First Floor Plans," scale ⅛" = 1 - 0", July 1948, item number 2407, RG 22M 912016, LAC.
161 "Edward S. (a.k.a. Russell) Groat and Marjorie J. Groat (nee Smith), Ruth Jamieson Seneca, 1930–1939 and 1928–193?, 193?," in Graham, *The Mush Hole*, 363.
162 "Sylvia Soney, 1943–1947," in Graham, 393.
163 "Peter Smith, 1926–1935," in Graham, 361.
164 See "Russ Moses Residential School Memoir" in the opening material of *Behind the Bricks*.
165 "Sylvia Soney, 1943–1947," in Graham, *The Mush Hole*, 393.
166 "Peter Smith, 1926–1935," in Graham, 361.
167 "Peter Smith, 1926–1935," in Graham, 361.
168 "Sylvia Soney, 1943–1947," in Graham, 392.
169 The special joint committee of the Senate and the House of Commons made these recommendations as part of its review of the *Indian Act* between 1946 and 1948. This review led to the 1951 *Indian Act* amendments, the first to be made with First Nations' consultation. Canada, *Department of Mines and Resources, Report of the Indian Affairs Branch for the Fiscal Year Ended March 31, 1949* (Edmond Cloutier, 1950), 199. See also Zach Parrott, "Indian Act," in *Canadian Encyclopedia*, 16 December 2020, https://www.thecanadianencyclopedia.ca/en/article/indian-act. On modernist residential schools, see Magdalena Milosz, "Settler-Colonial Modern," *Canadian Architect* (September 2021): 12–14, https://www.canadianarchitect.com/settler-colonial-modern/.
170 "Mission Work to be Pushed," *Windsor Daily Star*, 13 May 1947, 17.
171 "Indian School Investigated: Pupils at Brantford Lack Clothing, Facilities," *Windsor Daily Star*, 23 February 1946, 9.
172 V. G. Kosnar, "Report on Electrical Installation, Mohawk Institute, Brantford, Ontario," n.d., File 466-5, Pt. 5, Vol. 6201, RG 10, LAC.
173 Chas H. Buck, architect, "Mohawk Institute, Brantford, Ontario, Plan No. 876, Sheet No. E - 1 to E - 4," various scales, July 1948, item numbers 2405–08, RG 22M 912016, LAC.
174 C. A. F. Clark to Colonel Neary, 24 September 1948, File 466-1, Pt. 1, Vol. 6200, RG 10, LAC.
175 C. A. F. Clark to Colonel Neary.
176 C. A. F. Clark to Colonel Neary.
177 Examples include the Charles Camsell Hospital in Edmonton, which was opened in 1946 on the site of a former American army base and served Indigenous patients. Temporary wartime housing was also repurposed in some First Nations following the war. See Magdalena Miłosz, "Simulated Domesticities: Settings for Colonial Assimilation in Mid-Twentieth-Century Canada," *RACAR: Revue d'art Canadienne / Canadian Art Review* 45, no. 2 (2020): 84–5, https://doi.org/10.7202/1073940ar.
178 "Mohawk Institute Indian Residential School IAP School Narrative," 10.
179 C. A. F. Clark to Colonel Neary, 24 September 1948, n.p.
180 "Mohawk Institute Indian Residential School IAP School Narrative," 10. For a site plan showing the location of this structure, see "Department of Public Works of Canada, Fire Prevention Branch, Ottawa,

Mohawk Institute, Indian Residential School, Brantford, Ontario, Drawing No. 60-1-C," scale 1 inch = 50 feet, January 1960, File 479/6-1-001, Pt. 9, Vol. 8253, RG 10, LAC.

181   A. J. Doucet to Colonel Neary, 23 November 1948, File 466-1, Pt. 5, Vol. 6200, RG 10, LAC.

182   See Chas H. Buck, architect, "Alterations to Attic Floor, Mohawk Institute, Brantford, Ontario, Plan No. 876-A, Sheet No. 1, Plan & Details," scale as noted (various), November 1949, item number 2409, RG 22M 912016, LAC.

183   Canada, *Department of Citizenship and Immigration: Report of Indian Affairs Branch for the Fiscal Year Ended March 31, 1953* (Edmond Cloutier, 1953), 70. According to Rick Hill, local oral history also relates that the principal, the Reverend Canon William John Zimmerman, was moved into the new house to remove him from the principal's residence in the main building, which was connected to the girls' dorms and "where he was known to wander in the night from time to time." For the new staff bedrooms built in the former principal's space, see "Mohawk Institute, Brantford, Ontario, Alterations to Main Bldg., Sheet No. 2," scale as noted, May 1952, reproduction number NMC180196, item 2415, RG 22M 912016, LAC.

184   "Mohawk Institute, Brantford, Ontario, Alterations to Main Bldg., Sheet No. 2," scale as noted, May 1952, reproduction number NMC180196.

185   On the so-called "Indian parlour" in residential schools, see Carr, "'House of No Spirit,'" 99–105.

186   See, for example, Matthew Barager, "'No Indians Allowed': Challenging Aboriginal Segregation in Northern British Columbia, 1945–1965" (master's thesis, University of Northern British Columbia, 2016), 37, 69–72; Peter Millman, "African Nova Scotian Youth Experience on the Island, the Hill, and the Marsh: A Study of Truro, Nova Scotia in the 1950s and 1960s" (master's thesis, University of Lethbridge, 2017), 64–71.

187   C. G. Brown, G. J. Buck, and B. O. Filteau, *Survey of the Educational Facilities and Requirements of the Indians in Canada*, 2 vols. (Department of Citizenship and Immigration, Indian Affairs Branch, 1956), https://publications.gc.ca/site/eng/9.839390/publication.html.

188   Canada, *Department of Citizenship and Immigration: Report of the Indian Affairs Branch for the Fiscal Year Ended March 31, 1959* (Queen's Printer and Controller of Stationery, 1960), 82.

189   Canada, *Report of Indian Affairs Branch for the Fiscal Year Ended March 31, 1961* (Roger Duhamel, 1962), 90.

190   Photograph caption, "The Mohawk Institute Boasts An Efficient Modern Kitchen," *Brantford Expositor*, 20 January 1961, 13. See also "[Canon W. J. Zimmerman, principal of the Mohawk Institute, examines the new kitchen facilities]," 21 January 1961, Ottawa, photograph by *Brantford Expositor*, copy negative PA-185878, item number 3638, accession number 1976-281 NPC, Department of Indian Affairs and Northern Development fonds, LAC.

191   See "Kenneth George, 1953–1960" and "Bill Monture and Kelly Curley, 1963–1969 and 1969," in Graham, *The Mush Hole*, 411, 426.

192   The photographs are part of the collection "Mohawk Institute Student Photos, 1965" in the larger archive of the Mohawk Institute Histories project initiated and coordinated by Rick Hill.

193   "Bill Monture and Kelly Curley, 1963–1969 and 1969," in Graham, *The Mush Hole*, 426.

194   "Government Takes Over Schools," CBC Television News, 1 May 1969, CBC Digital Archives, video, 3:32, http://www.cbc.ca/player/Digital%2BArchives/Society/Education/Residential%2BSchools/ID/1423591585/.

195   Milloy, *A National Crime*, 204.

196   G. D. Cromb, Memorandum to File, 6 March 1970, INAC File 479/1-1, in Milloy, 205.

197   Hirini Matunga, "A Discourse on the Nature of Indigenous Architecture," in *The Handbook of Contemporary Indigenous Architecture*, ed. Elizabeth Grant et al. (Springer, 2018), 320.

198   For a discussion of the relationship between the identity of the cultural centre and the history of its site as a residential school, see Christina Cecelia Hovey, "Planning for the Memorialisation of the Indian Residential School System: A Case Study of the Woodland Cultural Centre, Brantford, Ontario" (master's thesis, Queen's University, 2012), 90, http://hdl.handle.net/1974/7462.

199   The International Coalition of Sites of Conscience defines a site of conscience as "a place of memory—such as a historic site, place-based museum or memorial—that prevents this erasure [of the past] from happening in order to foster more just and humane societies today." See "About Us," International Coalition of Sites of Conscience, accessed 9 November 2022, https://www.sitesofconscience.org/about-us/about-us/.

7

The Stewardship, Preservation, and Commemoration of the Mohawk Institute

Cody Groat

The Woodland Cultural Centre was established in 1972 at the site of the former Mohawk Institute Residential School and celebrated its fiftieth anniversary in 2022. This milestone is appropriate for considering the public memory of the site and how local, provincial, and federal bodies have interpreted the narratives that they deem to be significant. Throughout the past five decades, the Mohawk Institute has been recognized as a site of remembrance for the Six Nations of the Grand River Reserve, as seen through the Save the Evidence campaign and the Mohawk Village Memorial Park. It has also been recognized as a representative example of the entire residential school system by the Ontario Heritage Trust (OHT) and the Historic Sites and Monuments Board of Canada (HSMBC). By comparing the public narratives associated with the former Mohawk Institute, it is possible to not only understand how it has been perceived over the past five decades but also to conceptualize the role that the site may have into the future.

Save the Evidence and Mohawk Village Memorial Park

The 2006 Indian Residential Schools Settlement Agreement (IRSSA), which established the Truth and Reconciliation Commission of Canada (TRC), also included an appendix classified as Schedule J. This was a commemoration policy directive stating that, in part, "commemoration is honouring, educating, remembering, memorializing, and/or paying tribute to residential school former students, their families and their communities, and acknowledging their experiences."[1] Recognizing this, the IRSSA allocated $20 million for commemorative projects, including projects "that promote Aboriginal languages, cultures, and traditional spiritual values."[2] Between 2011 and 2014, 144 projects were approved by Aboriginal Affairs and Northern Development, the disbursement agency for the commemorative funding.

The Woodland Cultural Centre was not approved for funding through Schedule J of the IRSSA, but the Mohawk Institute was referenced in alternative proposals, such as one submitted by the Assembly of First Nations (AFN). In this document, the AFN proposed to install commemorative plaques at every former residential school, attempting, as some have argued, to "reinscribe the Canadian memorial landscape . . . as an historical corrective to the near absence of physical markers of a cultural genocide."[3] The proposal suggested identical plaques at each school with relevant contextual information including years of operation and the denomination that oversaw the institution. The first plaque proposed by the AFN was for the Mohawk Institute, and it stated, "on this site stood one of the 139 federal government-funded church-operated Indian Residential Schools designed to assimilate Aboriginal children into mainstream Canadian society."[4] The Mohawk Institute was likely chosen for the first proposed plaque as it was the longest continually operated residential school in Canada, and one of the few schools that remains standing. The AFN project received $1,609,068 in funding through the IRSSA, but its ultimate goals were never fully realized as criticisms were soon levied that a plaque-based program was rooted within Western conceptions of cultural heritage. It was further noted that the IRSSA funds could be reallocated toward community-driven initiatives.[5]

The communities responsible for stewarding the former residential school, including Six Nations of the Grand River, the Mohawks of the Bay of Quinte, and the Wahta Mohawks, have ensured that the site remains a place of remembrance for survivors and intergenerational survivors. The Woodland Cultural Centre launched a restoration initiative called Save the Evidence in 2013. The first phase, a replacement of the original roof, took place between 2015 and 2017 at an expense of $1.6 million. The second phase, costing nearly $11 million, included upgrading the HVAC system, electrical and plumbing systems, and work on the floors, walls, and windows. The final phase addressed masonry repairs and the development of an interpretive plan that reflects the history of the Mohawk Institute and its transition to the Woodland Cultural Centre in 1972.[6]

Survivors have also established the Mohawk Village Memorial Park, located adjacent to the school and the cultural centre, as a commemorative space to honour the children who attended the Mohawk Institute. This park actively combats the assimilationist ideologies that were inherently associated with the residential school system. Survivors envision the park as a place where "children can play in the presence of their families and [have] loving experiences and form happy memories," and also as "a place where ceremonies, cultural teachings, and family nurturing can take place in order to restore and reconcile some of what was lost by the Survivors."[7] These objectives indicate that the Mohawk Village Memorial Park is based upon the recognition of intangible values, or those that do not relate to the physical structure of the former residential school. This differs significantly from the commemorative strategies of the OHT and the HSMBC.

The Mohawk Institute and the Ontario Heritage Trust

The Mohawk Institute was the first residential school commemorated by the Archaeological and Historical Sites Board of Ontario, which eventually became the Ontario Heritage Trust. This recognition followed a recommendation made by the Brant Historical Society (BHS) in 1969. The BHS expressed its concern that "a plaque [was] required to keep alive the story of the [Mohawk Institute]," as the Government of Canada had recently announced the school's imminent closure citing poor attendance from the local Six Nations of the Grand River Reserve.[8] Nineteen sixty-nine was a significant year for the entire residential school system as the Department of Indian Affairs (DIA) formally concluded its partnership with religious denominations including the Anglican Church of Canada, which had administered the Mohawk Institute in various capacities since 1885.[9] This closure was part of a broader process beginning with amendments to the *Indian Act* in 1951 that favoured the full integration of First Nations children into provincially operated school boards.[10] Several critics argued that this was based on the same concept of cultural assimilation that guided First Nations education since the early nineteenth century, with the federal government failing to transition to alternatives such as the Cree School Board of Quebec, which was established in 1978.[11]

Survivors of the Mohawk Institute were not consulted regarding the initial commemorative proposal, much as they were excluded from discussions regarding the school's closure by the DIA. The BHS primarily worked alongside Canon W. J. Zimmerman, who was the principal of the Mohawk Institute when it closed in 1970. Zimmerman, a minister of the Anglican

Church, had also served as chair of the BHS from 1958 to 1959.[12] His opinion was highly regarded by the society, and the BHS notified the OHT that it would only propose a provincial commemoration if it had the full endorsement of Zimmerman.[13] This demonstrates the significant influence that school administrators had over the public interpretation of the schools that they ran.[14] The OHT notified the BHS that "representatives of the Indian community" should also be consulted in the preparation of a commemorative plaque.[15] Instead of preparing this collaboratively, however, the BHS and Canon Zimmerman wrote a version that they felt was appropriate and then sent this to the Six Nations Elected Council for approval.[16]

In the interim, the OHT approached the DIA regarding the future of the Mohawk Institute once it formally closed in 1970. They focused on the built infrastructure itself, noting that if the building was demolished, it was unlikely that a commemorative plaque would be erected elsewhere on the property.[17] The assistant deputy minister noted that the property was being transferred to the Six Nations of the Grand River, who were "giving consideration to a number of proposals concerning the use of the facilities, including the possibility of an Indian college."[18] Alternatively, the Association of Iroquois and Allied Indians established the Woodland Cultural Centre through a partnership with the Six Nations of the Grand River, the Mohawks of the Bay of Quinte, and the Wahta Mohawks. The Woodland Cultural Centre is now focused on the revitalization of Indigenous cultural heritage, directly combating the assimilationist ideologies of the Mohawk Institute Indian Residential School.[19]

The Six Nations Elected Council passed a resolution supporting the provincial commemoration in 1971.[20] The plaque was unveiled a year later by Norman Lickers, the first status First Nations person called to the bar in Ontario, who represented the former student body. It was then dedicated by Canon Zimmerman, who had served as the school's principal for twenty-six years. The text on the plaque offered what was primarily an institutional history, noting that the Mohawk Institute "was the first residential school in Canada to complete 100 years of service to the Indian people . . . and, from its inception in 1831, offered academic and vocational training to children of the Six Nations Reserve."[21] The plaque remained in place for nearly twenty years until it was mysteriously removed in 1991.

The plaque's removal came at a pivotal time in the history of residential schools. A year earlier, Phil Fontaine, a vice-chief of the Assembly of Manitoba Chiefs (he became grand chief in 1991), had publicly disclosed abuses that he had suffered while attending the former Fort Alexander

Figure 7.1. Plaque unveiling at the Mohawk Institute, 17 June 1972
Source: Ontario Heritage Trust's Provincial Plaque Program Records

Indian Residential School. Historian J. R. Miller has noted that this disclosure brought an unprecedented level of public attention to residential school abuses, with several Indigenous organizations calling for a federal inquiry.[22] Fontaine noted that "it wasn't just sexual abuse; it was physical and psychological abuse. It was a violation."[23] This disclosure led to a greater recognition of cultural assimilation and systematic abuse that were inherently associated with the residential school system.

Unbeknownst to Fontaine, this also had an impact on the provincial commemoration of the Mohawk Institute. With the plaque gone, a company called Shanahan Research Associates assisted in the first round of revisions for the OHT plaque in 1992. They interviewed Ken Raymer (who had been a teacher in the 1960s) and Sally English (a student in the 1930s and house mother in the 1960s). Shanahan Research Associates did not propose any revisions and there are no existing records associated with the remarks of

Figure 7.2. Current plaque in front of the Woodland Cultural Centre
Source: Ontario Heritage Trust

Raymer or English.[24] A second round of revisions took place between 1995 and 1996, the same year that the Royal Commission on Aboriginal Peoples (RCAP) released its final report condemning the Indian Residential School system. Mary Ellen Perkins and Paul Litt were hired as consultants and worked alongside Joanna Bedard, who was serving as the executive director of the Woodland Cultural Centre.[25] The revised plaque was revealed in 1996 and reads, in part, "the Mohawk Institute tried to assimilate its students into the rapidly growing Euro-Canadian society. To that end, it disregarded native cultural traditions and stressed instead Christian teachings, English-language instruction, and manual labour skills. . . . The Institute closed in 1970. . . . It then became a centre for the renaissance of First Nations cultures."[26]

This new text differed significantly from the interpretation that was advanced by the former principal of the Mohawk Institute twenty years earlier. An OHT press release further condemned the assimilationist ideologies of the residential school system by noting that "the lack of success this attitude engendered is evident in official reports of the times and, more heart-breakingly, in the oral histories of First Nations people who, in the later years of the 20th century, began to speak openly about the spiritual and psychological pain they suffered."[27]

It is notable how far behind the HSMBC was in relation to its provincial counterpart, the OHT. The revised plaque for the Mohawk Institute was unveiled the same year that the DIA stalled the federal commemoration of St. Eugene's Indian Residential School in Cranbrook, British Columbia. Instead of learning from the RCAP, as the OHT had, the HSMBC followed the advice of the federal government and chose not to commemorate a former residential school structure. This was based on concerns in the DIA that a negative interpretation of St. Eugene's could be used in litigation against the Government of Canada as the HSMBC, per the *Historic Sites and Monuments Act*, was a federal advisory body.[28] It is possible that the provincial government did not exert similar pressure on the OHT because Indigenous education is a federal responsibility, and therefore, the Government of Ontario did not have the same level of legal culpability.

The Mohawk Institute and the Historic Sites and Monuments Board of Canada

Building on Schedule J of the IRSSA, the *Final Report of the Truth and Reconciliation Commission of Canada* contained five Calls to Action (CTA) relating to commemoration. CTA 79 focused on the HSMBC and its role in designating National Historic Sites of Canada, with 79(iii) calling for the development and implementation of a national strategy for recognizing former residential schools.[29] While the TRC had a significant influence on the commemoration of these structures, the Mohawk Institute had actually been considered by the HSMBC as early as 1987. In the ensuring decades, however, the HSMBC had still not recognized the Mohawk Institute as a National Historic Site as of 2025. Regardless, the perspectives of the HSMBC demonstrate how the national narrative regarding the residential school system is still being actively shaped by the Government of Canada.

The HSMBC first considered the commemoration of Indian Residential Schools in 1987 while evaluating a six-volume study called *Historic Schools of Canada*, which, it was argued, allowed the HSMBC to commemorate school structures as "a crucial element of childhood [and as] a part of social development."[30] The author of volume 1 of the study, Dana Johnson, wrote that *Historic Schools of Canada* "[attempted] to examine the changing role of formal schooling within the totality of socialization by looking at the changing role of family, church, community and state . . . at various points in time."[31] Johnson felt that this contextual information was vital when commemorating former school structures as these buildings often had little in the way of physical or tangible evidence associated with their use or significance, including the education of children, or, in the context of residential schools, the forced assimilation of Indigenous children.

Historic Schools of Canada included a list of structures from specific eras that could be considered for commemoration as National Historic Sites. These were classified as urban and rural schools, but the HSMBC had also requested that Indian Residential Schools be included as a category for consideration. Johnson noted several problems associated with the inclusion of residential schools in a study focusing on non-Indigenous educational provision. He wrote, for instance, that "federal officials argued that the destruction of the native way of life was a necessary and desirable consequence of changing economic circumstances."[32] Johnson still felt, though, that the commemoration of residential schools could achieve the HSMBC's objective of recognizing the intangible values of childhood socialization through built structures. In order to effectively identify the differences between Indigenous and non-Indigenous education through architectural analysis, Johnson prepared a separate study that specifically focused on the structural legacy of Indian Residential Schools. This was presented at a later meeting of the HSMBC and was not included within *Historic Schools of Canada*.

The agenda paper prepared by Johnson was based on a specific case study—that of the Red Bank Day School in New Brunswick, proposed for commemoration as a National Historic Site by the Elected Council of the Red Bank Reserve in 1985.[33] Johnson wrote that the school "was built in 1916 and provides a convenient, if limited, point of reference from which the whole of native education in Canada can be seen."[34] The Red Bank Day School was based on architectural plans developed by Robert M. Ogilvie for use on reserves across Canada. It was noted that these were structurally similar to early twentieth century non-Indigenous rural schoolhouses that were being considered by the HSMBC as part of *Historic Schools of Canada*, but Johnson argued against any comparison as "the purpose of the former was very different from the later, and the reasons for possible commemoration of rural and native day schools would therefore presumably be dissimilar."[35]

The agenda paper proposed three commemorative strategies for the HSMBC to consider. The first was the commemoration of a day school building as a National Historic Site. Johnson wrote that "the [DIA] reports that only ten structures of more than 50 years of age remain in use under band control."[36] Five of these were located on the Six Nations of the Grand River Reserve, including S.S. #3, S.S. #5, S.S. #7, and S.S. #11, all built in 1910. The agenda paper observed that it was rare for older day schools to remain standing as they represented assimilationist ideologies that were increasingly "the source of much debate and controversy."[37] As with rural schoolhouses, it was noted that choosing one representative day school as a National Historic Site would prove problematic as "one structure appears to be very nearly like many others, and it is difficult to conceive how one building's claim to suitability can be reasonably weighted against any others."[38]

The second strategy proposed to the HSMBC was the recognition of a single residential school building as a National Historic Site. Two options were proposed for the HSMBC to consider—the Mount Elgin Industrial Institute and the Mohawk Institute Indian Residential School.[39] These were recognized as "the earliest, and by general agreement, the most important boarding schools" funded by the DIA.[40] The agenda paper encouraged the HSMBC to consider the Mohawk Institute as more than just the extant structure of the school building. It was noted that this was a 380-acre working farm that included a recreation hall, a hospital, stables, greenhouses, a carpenter's workshop, a fruit cellar, and a grain silo.[41] As with other structures recommended in the *Historic Schools of Canada* report, it was noted that the Mohawk Institute was destroyed and rebuilt on numerous occasions, most recently in 1904. This led to questions about the commemorative integrity of the structure, demonstrating the significance that the HSMBC placed upon the tangible architectural aspects of the building itself instead of the intangible values associated with the broader landscape.[42]

The final strategy proposed to the HSMBC in 1987 was the commemoration of "Indian Education" as a National Historic Event without the specific recognition of an individual school structure.[43] Further consideration of all three strategies was deferred until 1988, when they were considered by the Historic Buildings Committee of the HSMBC. It was agreed that education itself was an aspect of social history that was worthy of commemoration by the Government of Canada, but members of the HSMBC debated if this theme could be appropriately interpreted through the commemoration of specific school structures as National Historic Sites. The Historic Buildings Committee developed four criteria for the evaluation of specific schools based on recommendations in *Historic Schools of Canada*. These were based in turn on the concepts of interpretive integrity and architectural significance that made a structure such as the Mohawk Institute, which was rebuilt in 1904, difficult for the HSMBC to consider for recognition as a National Historic Site. This reflected deeply engrained beliefs within the conservation movement that architectural values were more inherently significant than intangible or social values associated with a structure, meaning that the overarching beliefs associated with the Mohawk Institute, such as the forced assimilation of First Nations children, were viewed as less significant than its structural status.[44]

The criteria developed by the Historic Buildings Committee was used once again in 1996 when the HSMBC considered the status of St. Eugene's Indian Residential School in Cranbrook, British Columbia. St. Eugene's was nominated for consideration by the Ktunaxa/Kinbasket Tribal Council, which was overseeing a thorough renovation of the property as a band-operated golf course and casino. It was recognized that federal commemoration as a National Historic Site would help to attract external investments for the renovation project while also making the structure eligible for financial assistance through the National Cost-Sharing Program, a funding mechanism aimed at preserving the architectural integrity of structures recognized as nationally significant by the HSMBC.[45] The HSMBC did not support the renovation plans and voted against the commemoration of St. Eugene's after stating that the original architectural values associated with the structure had been lost.[46]

The HSMBC was also influenced by the imminent publication of the RCAP's report. HSMBC minutes record that Indian and Northern Affairs Canada (INAC) was concerned about Parks Canada undertaking any further research for the HSMBC relating to St. Eugene's as this "would invite speculation about the ... overall context of the government's relations with Native groups," adding that "INAC officials felt that this speculation could be potentially harmful because of the imminent release of [the RCAP report]."[47] Johnson, who wrote the agenda paper considered by the HSMBC in 1987, informed the board that RCAP would be calling for "a public inquiry into the residential school system and its effects on Native individuals and society."[48] As a result, the HSMBC passed a resolution to defer the commemoration of Indigenous education and specific residential school structures for a period of five years, or until 2002.[49]

It was not until the *Final Report of the Truth and Reconciliation Commission of Canada*, released in 2015, that the HSMBC considered the federal commemoration of residential schools once again. The HSMBC focused on CTA 79(iii), which calls for the development of a national commemorative strategy.[50] Richard Alway, who was then serving as the chairman of the HSMBC, said that there was no institutional memory of the 1987 report prepared by Dana Johnson that had considered the commemoration of the Mohawk Institute.[51] In 2017, the HSMBC met with Paula Whitlow, the executive director of the Woodland Cultural Centre, and Ry Moran, the director of the National Centre for Truth and Reconciliation (NCTR). Whitlow discussed the adaptive reuse of the Mohawk Institute as the Woodland Cultural Centre and further discussed the community-driven Save the Evidence campaign. She noted that "the community is dedicated to saving the former Mohawk Institute as part of history," adding that, "when restoration is complete, the former Mohawk Institute Indian Residential School will be a fully interpreted historic site, dedicated to the history of the Indian Residential School system in Canada."[52]

Whitlow and Moran stressed that the federal commemorative strategy had to be driven by survivors and intergenerational survivors of the residential school system, a notable shift from the architectural criteria that was developed in 1987. Recognizing this, the HSMBC passed a resolution calling on Parks Canada to work with the NCTR to "[develop] a report that presents the complex history and legacy of the residential school system."[53] It was further recommended that the HSMBC, Parks Canada, and the NCTR collaborate on a nomination to recognize the Indian Residential School system as a National Historic Event, which was one of the recommendations made by Dana Johnson in 1987.[54]

A further shift away from the HSMBC's architectural focus emerged in 2019. That year the HSMBC considered a recently published report called *Places of Memory and Indian Residential Schools: An Options Analysis*. This discussed former schools that were engaged in adaptive reuse, such as the Mohawk Institute and its transformation into the Woodland Cultural Centre, and schools that were no longer physically standing, including the former Shubenacadie Indian Residential School, destroyed in 1986. After endorsing this report, the HSMBC evaluated the national significance of Shubenacadie in Nova Scotia and the former Portage La Prairie Indian Residential School in Saskatchewan. These were both designated National Historic Sites in 2019, the first residential schools to receive this designation from the Government of Canada. In describing the commemorative intent for Portage La Prairie, the HSMBC recognized that "the school has been readapted by [Long Plains First Nation] to serve a number of community purposes."[55] Similarly, it recognized that "although the [Shubenacadie] school building is no longer standing, the site of the former school is a place of remembrance and healing for some of the survivors and their descendants."[56]

A central focus of these commemorations was the recognition that the holistic health and well-being of Indigenous people, rooted within cultural revitalization, was more significant than the mere commemoration of a building based on architectural determinants. A similar concept has been recognized through a report by the Indigenous Heritage Circle, a national not-for-profit, regarding the opportunities of embedding the United Nations Declaration on the Rights of Indigenous Peoples into heritage legislation such as the *Historic Sites and Monuments Act*. In considering the adaptive reuse of these structures, the report recognized that "many communities want to create heritage facilities that will serve multiple goals—as places to hold and share historical materials, ancestral remains, and cultural belongings while also serving to protect and reinvigorate languages and cultural practices."[57] It is certain that these ways of perceiving former residential schools, and the affirmative commemorations of Portage La Prairie and Shubenacadie in 2019, will influence the future evaluation of the Mohawk Institute, as discussed by the HSMBC.

Conclusion

Public memory of the Mohawk Institute has changed significantly since its closure. Before the school was even closed, the BHS approached the OHT in 1968 to see if the school could be provincially commemorated to "keep alive the story" of the Mohawk Institute. This was achieved in 1972, when the Institute became the first residential school to be recognized by the Province of Ontario through a heritage designation. Twenty years later, shortly after Phil Fontaine publicly disclosed the abuse that he had experienced at Fort Alexander Indian Residential School, the celebratory plaque prepared by Canon W. J. Zimmerman, the Mohawk Institute's former principal, was removed by community members. The OHT plaque was revised following the publication of the RCAP's report in 1996 with the support of Joanna Bedard, the executive director of the Woodland Cultural Centre. The new plaque, which remains standing at the time of writing in 2025, recognized both cultural assimilation at the Mohawk Institute and cultural revitalization at the Woodland Cultural Centre, reflecting the strength of survivors and the intangible significance of the site. These intangible aspects are similarly reflected through commemorative spaces including the Mohawk Village Memorial Park, which celebrates and upholds positive familial relationships.

These local and provincial commemorations differ from the work of the HSMBC, which emphasizes the concept of architectural significance. The HSMBC first considered the Mohawk Institute in 1988, with Parks Canada employee Dana Johnson calling for the recognition of intangible values, including cultural assimilation. The HSMBC chose to defer any commemoration as the school had been rebuilt in 1904 and allegedly lacked architectural integrity. It was only after the publication of the *Final Report of the Truth and Reconciliation Commission* in 2015 that the HSMBC followed the example of the OHT and began recognizing the intangible significance of former residential schools. This will likely impact any future consideration of the Mohawk Institute as a National Historic Site of Canada.

The communities responsible for the stewardship of the former Mohawk Institute recognize the site as a significant part of their own history. Only time will tell if the Government of Canada perceives it as a part of the country's own history as well.

NOTES

1. See "Schedule 'J': Commemoration Policy Directive," Indian Residential Schools Settlement Agreement (2006), 1, https://www.residentialschoolsettlement.ca/Schedule_J-CommemorationPolicyDirective.PDF.
2. "Schedule 'J,'" 1.
3. Trina Cooper-Bolam, "Healing Heritage: New Approaches to Commemorating Canada's Indian Residential School System" (master's thesis, Carleton University, 2014), 70.
4. Cooper-Bolam, 70.
5. Trina Cooper-Bolam, "On the Call for a Residential School National Monument," *Journal of Canadian Studies* 51, no. 1 (June 2018): 72.
6. Michelle Ruby, "Save the Evidence Campaign Entering Final Phases," *Brantford Expositor*, 10 June 2021.
7. Personal correspondence with Rick Monture via email, 13 January 2022.
8. Richard Pilant to Richard Apted, 19 December 1969, File—Mohawk Institute, 1831, Ontario Heritage Trust Archives, Toronto, Ontario.
9. John Milloy, *A National Crime: The Canadian Government and the Residential School System, 1879 to 1986* (University of Manitoba Press, 1999), xvii.
10. J. R. Miller, *Shingwauk's Vision: A History of Native Residential School* (University of Toronto Press, 1996), 390.
11. See Billy Diamond, "The Cree Experience," in *Indian Education in Canada*, vol. 2, *The Challenge*, ed. Jean Barman, Yvonne Hebert, and Don McCaskill (UBC Press, 1987), and Jean Barman, Yvonne Hebert, and Don McCaskill, "The Challenge of Indian Education: An Overview," in Barman et al., *Indian Education in Canada*, 2:86.
12. Zimmerman was also the chaplain of Her Majesty's Royal Chapel of the Mohawks, designated as a National Historic Site by the HSMBC in 1981, the final year of his chaplaincy.
13. Richard Pilant to Richard Apted, 19 December 1969, File—Mohawk Institute, 1831, Ontario Heritage Trust Archives.
14. Isabelle Knockwood has also written of how the principal of Shubenacadie Indian Residential School played an active role in creating a celebratory interpretation of this residential school in Nova Scotia. See Isabelle Knockwood, *Out of the Depths: The Experiences of Mi'kmaw Children at the Indian Residential School at Shubenacadie, Nova Scotia* (Fernwood Publishing, 2015).
15. W. Rutherford to Carl Thorpe, 19 December 1969, File—Mohawk Institute, 1831, Ontario Heritage Trust Archives.

16   Carl Thorpe to the Secretary, Six Nations Council House, Ohsweken, Ontario, 6 January 1970, File—Mohawk Institute, 1831, Ontario Heritage Trust Archives.

17   Richard Apted, Director, Historical Branch, to J. W. Churchman, Director, Indian and Eskimo Affairs, Department of Indian Affairs and Northern Development, 29 April 1970, File—Mohawk Institute, 1831, Ontario Heritage Trust Archives.

18   Apted to Churcman, 29 April 1970.

19   Naohiro Nakamura, "Indigenous Cultural Self-Representation and Its Internal Critiques: A Case Study of the Woodland Cultural Centre, Canada" *Diaspora, Indigenous and Minority Education* 8, no. 3 (2014): 148.

20   Letter from Six Nations Council, Office of the Secretary, signed by Council Clerk M. Bloomfield to the Department of Public Records and Archives, % C. Thorpe, 10 March 1972, File—Mohawk Institute, 1831, Ontario Heritage Trust Archives.

21   Press Release: Historical Plaque to be Unveiled Commemorating the Founding of the Mohawk Institute, 8 June 1972, File—Mohawk Institute, 1831, Ontario Heritage Trust Archives.

22   Miller, *Shingwauk's Vision*, 328.

23   Miller, 328.

24   Rough Notes: Shanahan Research Associates "Re: Mohawk Institute," January 1992, File—Mohawk Institute, 1831, Ontario Heritage Trust Archives.

25   Rough Notes: Paul Litt and Mary Ellen Perkins, Provincial Plaque Consultants, undated, File—Mohawk Institute, 1831, Ontario Heritage Trust Archives.

26   Press Release: Provincial Historical Plaque Marks the History of the Mohawk Institute, 1996, File—Mohawk Institute, 1831, Ontario Heritage Trust Archives.

27   Press Release: Provincial Historical Plaque Marks the History of the Mohawk Institute, 1996.

28   Minutes of the Historic Sites and Monuments Board of Canada, June 1997. Received via email from Parks Canada on 13 February 2019.

29   Truth and Reconciliation Commission of Canada, *Honouring the Truth, Reconciling for the Future: Summary of the Final Report of the Truth and Reconciliation Commission of Canada* (James Lorimer and Company, Toronto, 2015), 334.

30   Dana Johnson, *The History of School Design in Canada Before 1930*, vol. 1, *An Introduction* (Architectural History Branch, Ottawa, 1987), 3.

31   Johnson, 5.

32   Johnson, 84.

33   Dana Johnson, *Indian Schools in Canada, Including the Red Bank Day School, Red Bank Reserve, New Brunswick* (Architectural History Branch, 1988), 306.

34   Johnson, 306.

35   Johnson, 305.

36   Johnson, 330.

37   Johnson, 330.

38   Johnson, 330.

39   Johnson, 331.

40   Johnson, 331.

41   Johnson, 321.

42   Johnson, 321.

43   Johnson, 331.

44   Cooper-Bolam, "Healing Heritage," 62.

45   Geoffrey Carr, "Difficult Inheritances: Canadian Commemoration Policy and the Indian Residential School," in *Des Couvents en heritage / Religious Houses: A Legacy*, ed. Luc Noppen, Martin Drouin, and Thomas Coomans (University of Quebec Press, 2015), 464.

46   Minutes of the Historic Sites and Monuments Board of Canada, June 1996. Received via email from Parks Canada on 13 February 2019.

47   Minutes of the Historic Sites and Monuments Board of Canada, June 1997. Received via email from Parks Canada on 13 February 2019.

48   Minutes of the Historic Sites and Monuments Board of Canada, June 1997.

49 Minutes of the Historic Sites and Monuments Board of Canada, June 1997.
50 Truth and Reconciliation Commission of Canada, *Honouring the Truth, Reconciling for the Future*, 334.
51 Interview with Richard Alway, 1 November 2021
52 Minutes of the Historic Sites and Monuments Board of Canada, December 2017. Received via email from Parks Canada on 25 February 2019.
53 Minutes of the Historic Sites and Monuments Board of Canada, December 2017.
54 Minutes of the Historic Sites and Monuments Board of Canada, June 2018. Received via email from Parks Canada on 21 June 2019.
55 Minutes of the Historic Sites and Monuments Board of Canada, December 2019. Received via email from Parks Canada on 16 November 2020.
56 Minutes of the Historic Sites and Monuments Board of Canada, December 2019.
57 Indigenous Heritage Circle, *Indigenous Heritage and the United Nations Declaration on the Rights of Indigenous Peoples* (Indigenous Heritage Circle, 2022), 25.

PART 4
Survival and Resistance

Figure 0.8. Mohawk Chapel confirmation, 1918.
Source: Canada, Department of the Interior / Library and Archives Canada / PA-043609

8

Ten Years of Student Resistance at the Mohawk Institute, 1903-1913

Diana Castillo

Survivors of the Mohawk Institute speak of the importance of resiliency in helping cope with what took place inside the brick walls. Resistance and rebellion in the face of state-sponsored racism, a core part of that resilience, was often the only option available for Indigenous children at the school. The accounts described in this chapter tell of the extraordinary bravery of students at the Mohawk Institute who pushed back against school authorities and were cruelly punished for doing so. The first example occurred in 1903 when several boys between the ages of twelve and sixteen started the first of three fires that would destroy the entire structure of the Mohawk Institute. A police investigation ensued shortly after the third fire and resulted in the young boys being arrested, charged, and convicted. The boys were to serve their sentences at the Mimico Industrial School, a reformatory school known for its extreme corporal punishment, and the Kingston Penitentiary.[1] Ten years later, in 1913, two sisters, Ruth and Hazel Miller, ran away from the Mohawk Institute. Upon the girls' return, they were severely punished by the school principal. The girls were put in a small cell-like room and given minimal food and water rations for three days. Ruth was whipped with a rawhide strap thirteen times on her back. This resulted in Ruth and Hazel's father suing the school and the principal in court a year later. After a lengthy trial filled with testimony from multiple individuals, the jury awarded Ruth and Hazel damages. This was a unique win in the Canadian legal system, both for the young girls and for Indigenous people as a whole. The case provided a stark contrast with section 141 of the 1927 amended *Indian Act*, which made it a punishable offence for any legal counsel to receive payment by any First Nation or band.[2] As the legacy of residential schools remains in the public eye, accounts such as these remind Canadians that Indigenous children and youth often advocated on their own behalf.

Fire at the Mohawk Institute

On the night of 19 April 1903, the Mohawk Institute was set on fire. By the time the fire was extinguished, only the walls remained standing.[3] The extent of the damage meant that the school had to be rebuilt a year later. The estimated cost of the new building was reported to be $30,000.[4] On 25 June 1903, Frank Winney, a thirteen-year-old boy from Stony Creek, was arrested on charges connected to the fires.[5] Winney pleaded guilty and implicated Roy Wilson in the burning of the barns.[6] Shortly after, Wilson, Jesse Debo, Isaiah Antoine, and a fourth boy, Alexander Maracle, from Six Nations, were arrested and charged. They pleaded not guilty through their lawyer, L. F. Hyde. Consequently, all the boys were scheduled for trial.

According to newspaper reports, Isaiah Antoine and Jesse Debo helped Roy Wilson climb into the attic, where he left an old coat stuffed with wood shavings that were saturated with coal oil from a lamp.[7] Wilson set fire to the bundle and placed it in the corner of the attic. The boys then returned to their dormitory and stayed there until the fire alarm sounded. There were about eighty students in the building when the fire broke out.[8] Fortunately, the fire began on the west side of the building, allowing the children and staff time to escape.[9] In addition to the main building and the barn, the barn of Mr. Alexander, whose farm was in "the vicinity of the Mohawk Institute," was also destroyed. Several students testified that Antoine and Wilson set fire to Mr. Alexander's barn "to divert suspicion from themselves."[10] They added that this information was known among the students but was kept a secret.[11] Mr. Alexander filed a petition with the Indian Department and the New England Company for compensation of his losses.[12] He argued that, because the students were not being properly looked after, the Mohawk Institute was liable for his damaged property and that he was owed compensation due to the Company's negligence.[13] His petition was denied.[14]

Trial and the Law

The boys' trial was presided by Justice A. D. Hardy, sibling of A. S. Hardy, who had served as premier of Ontario from 1896 to 1899. Justice Hardy served the Brantford area for thirty-eight years, many of them in juvenile court. During the boys' trial, evidence was presented by both the Crown and defence counsel to determine if the boys had committed all of the essential elements of arson. *The Globe* reported that the first witness was Sergeant Wallace, who stated that the young boys had confessed to him that they had burned the building.[15] Additionally, the newspaper reported that various students were held as material witnesses and testified for both Crown and defence counsel.[16]

Without the court transcripts, it is difficult to ascertain what other evidence was presented by the Crown counsel to prove their case. *The Globe*, however, reported that Wilson confessed only to the first fire and implicated another student, Alexander Maracle.[17] The newspaper also reported that Debo and Antoine testified that they helped Wilson climb into the attic, but that they did not know what he intended to do.[18]

In the end, the boys (Wilson, Winney, Debo, and Antoine) were found guilty of arson and were sentenced by Justice Hardy. Wilson was sentenced to five years at Mimico Industrial School, a reformatory school located at what is today the location of the Toronto South Detention Centre. This sentence was especially harsh given that at twelve years of age Wilson should have been exempt from criminal responsibility. Jesse Debo and Frank Winney were both sentenced to three years at the Mimico Industrial School.[19] Due to his age (sixteen), Isaiah Antoine was sentenced to three years at the Kingston Penitentiary, where teenagers served their sentences alongside adult men.[20] Prior to the *Juvenile Delinquents Act, 1908*, it was possible for children and adults to serve their sentences together.[21] Alexander Maracle was let off on a suspended sentence.[22]

It is important to recognize that systemic racism has been prevalent in the Canadian legal system since its establishment and likely contributed to the boys' severe sentences. Government officials also recognized that the deliberate burning down of school property was a form of protest.[23] This likely meant that the severity of the boys' sentences was also aimed at deterring other students from participating in similar acts of rebellion. This is especially concerning given that in 1875, the Canadian government passed *An Act to Amend the Act Respecting Procedure in Criminal Cases and Other Matters Related to Criminal Law*, which determined that juvenile offenders were to be sentenced to a reformatory for terms of no less than two years and not more than five.[24] In other words, there were legal grounds for giving each of the young boys leaner sentences.

Reformation School or Jail?

The Mimico Industrial School promised to reform young boys through an education program that centred on drills, industrial training, farming, education, religion, and athletics.[25] Similar to the Mohawk Institute, inmates at the Mimico Industrial School suffered from violent and capricious penalties as well as calculated psychological manipulation.[26] Bryan Hogeveen has documented that punishments and penalties experienced by boys at the Mimico Industrial School exceeded what can reasonably be grouped under the notion of corporal punishment, institutional grouping, or force.[27] It is likely that Wilson, Maracle, and Debo suffered this fate during their stay.

While the historical record is incomplete regarding what happened to these young boys, there is evidence that their families tried to retrieve them from the school. Jesse Debo's father, Mathew Debo, wrote a letter to the deputy superintendent of Indian Affairs on 7 April 1906.[28] This letter was written after his son had not been allowed to depart the school even though he had served his three-year sentence. Debo requested that the department use its influence and power to return his son to him. He added that his son had "been punished enough" and that he was able to look after him.[29] While it is unknown if Debo and his father were reunited, there exists an internal letter from Superintendent Chester Ferrier of the Mimico Industrial School in which he confirmed that Jesse Debo had been working with a gentleman for three months.[30] Mr. Ferrier added that Jesse was extremely anxious to take the position and that it would be in his best interests to allow him to continue working with the gentleman, who he was providing him with work and good wages. Mr. Ferrier added, "I think the father should not be allowed to interfere with the boy."[31]

The stories of Wilson, Antoine, Maracle, and Debo are not unique. During the residential school era, children and youth deliberately set fires to schools across Canada as a form of resistance. The Truth and Reconciliation Commission indicated that at least twenty-five school fires were either suspected or proven to have been deliberately set by students.[32] In the aftermath of the fires at the Mohawk Institute, Indian Affairs official Martin Benson concluded that the fires in 1903 were evidence of an underlying failure in the system.[33] He would later write, "even an Indian will not set fire to buildings, destroy valuable property and endanger life from pure cussedness.

There must have been some real or imaginary grievance which led some boys to commit incendiarism."[34] Despite these comments, there was more interest in punishing these children than finding the underlying cause that led them to burn down the Mohawk Institute.

The Great Escape from the "Mush Hole"

Resistance to the horrors of the Mohawk Institute did not only take the form of fires. In fact, ten years after the 1903 fire, four brave girls took legal action against their principal for his severe abuse.

Like the setting of fires, running away from the Mohawk Institute was a common occurrence. The historical record shows that children at the Institute were often fed meals without enough sustenance. In fact, the Mohawk Institute earned its nickname, the "Mush Hole," after years where children were fed oatmeal porridge for breakfast and cornmeal porridge for supper.[35] On more than one occasion, students were served spoiled food, even food with worms in it.[36] This is why, on the evening of 7 August 1913, four girls decided to run away. Tired and hungry due to the lack of nutritious food at the Mohawk Institute, Ruth Miller, her sister Hazel, and their two family friends, Emma and Edith Isaac, planned their escape. Ruth, who was only thirteen, sewed clothes out of white bedsheets for the four girls so that they would not be recognized in their school uniforms out in public after their escape.[37] The girls then waited until midnight to jump out of a window and then walked for three hours before reaching their home in Ohsweken. Though the girls reached home safely, their father, Chief George Miller, drove them back to the school the very next morning.[38] The girls' mother had passed away years before, and as a result, Chief Miller likely felt that he had no choice but to return the girls to the school. Chief Miller was close with his daughters, but his work hours prevented him from taking care of them full-time. Chief Miller himself had been a student at the school decades before.

Punished Like Criminals

The Mohawk Institute was known for its harsh discipline, which many students likened to the treatment of prisoners.[39] On the girls' return, Principal A. Nelles Ashton ordered that Ruth be whipped with rawhide on her bare back thirteen times. After that punishment, she was placed in a small cell, three feet by six feet, for a minimum of twenty-four hours.[40] *The Brantford Expositor* subsequently reported on Ruth's testimony at trial: "There was no light, no bed, and no chair. In this, she remained for three days, getting bread and water on Sunday. Her hair was cut off on Monday. She was put on the blacklist, having to walk in a ring in place of playing and not allowed to talk to the other girls."[41] The rest of the girls who had run away were put in a small room and were given minimal food and water rations for three days. To make matters worse, all the girls' hair was cut short to humiliate them.[42]

The punishment the girls received was so severe that, upon telling their parents, Chief George Miller and Jefferson D. Isaac made a complaint to the Six Nations Council (SNC). Concerned about the welfare of Indigenous children at the Mohawk Institute, the SNC asked the New England Company to hold an impartial investigation into the matter.[43] Principal Ashton expelled Ruth and Hazel from the school in response to the request for an investigation. The SNC sent a letter to Education Superintendent Duncan Campbell Scott requesting a reason for the girls' dismissal.[44] It would take more than four months for the girls and the SNC to receive an answer.

An Informal Investigation of the Mohawk Institute

While the girls' punishment was severe, their resistance led to an informal investigation of the Mohawk Institute by Deputy Superintendent General Duncan Campbell Scott. Scott reported that the children were given separated milk, that there had once been worms in their oatmeal, and that they were often served boiled meat. With respect to discipline, Scott found that the rules regarding disciplinary action were antiquated, but he said a formal investigation was not warranted and that there was a lengthy waiting list of eighty parents who sought to send their children to the Mohawk Institute and who were waiting due to a lack of vacancies.[45]

The Trial

Following a long wait and no response from the government or the Mohawk Institute regarding their claim, the families pursued legal action against Principal Ashton. Ruth, Hazel, and Chief Miller sued Principal Ashton for $5,000, alleging several forms of mistreatment.[46] They filed a civil suit, which was heard on 1 April 1914 at the High Court of Brantford.

The trial lasted for twelve hours, ending at one in the morning. The court heard testimony from all the parties, including Principal Ashton, the four girls, Chief Miller, and other staff and students. Ruth and Hazel gave clear testimony demonstrating the school's abuse of power and maltreatment of the students.[47] Justice Hugh Thomas Kelly, who presided over the case, noted that, "someone should receive praise for the brightness shown by the school children giving their evidence."[48] Justice Kelly advised the jury that although the school principal "had the power to punish the child in a reasonable way, the institution was not a penal institution."[49] In addition, the all-white male jury (standard at the time) were instructed to consider whether the school had been legally entitled to cut the girls' hair, whether Ruth was whipped too severely, and whether the girls were fed spoiled food.[50]

Ultimately, the jury dismissed the claim regarding the girls' humiliation from having their hair cut off. It was dismissed because it had been a customary practice for many years to cut students' hair short when they misbehaved.[51] The jury also dismissed the claim for damages for the risk to the girls' health posed by the Mohawk Institute's food. It was admitted by Principal Ashton that the students were served spoiled food and separated milk. Both Ruth and Hazel expressed in their testimony that it was their main reason for running away.[52] This dismissal is demonstrative of how concerns raised by Indigenous children and youth were ignored by a justice system that was supposed to protect them. Out of the four girls, Ruth was the only one whose harsh treatment was deemed worthy of compensation. Her father was awarded $300 for her being whipped with rawhide and $100 for her being locked up in a cell.[53]

The SNC initially agreed to provide funds to cover the legal fees on behalf of Ruth and Hazel; however, by the end, Ottawa officially disapproved of the SNC's decision to fully support the litigation and refused to release band funds to cover the grant the council had authorized for legal expenses.[54] The family was left to pay the lawyer on their own. It is important to note that only thirteen years later, in 1927, an amendment to the *Indian Act* would subsequently make it an offence for First Nations people to raise money to hire legal counsel. Without legal representation, it would have been impossible for Ruth and Hazel to have their claim heard in court.

Aftermath of the Trial

Ruth, Hazel, Emma, and Edith left their mark on the Canadian legal system because of their courage to speak out against the horrific treatment they and fellow students received from the principal of the Mohawk Institute. Principal Ashton resigned from the school and enlisted in the Canadian Expeditionary Force, as the First World War began months after the trial ended. After being expelled from the Mohawk Institute, Ruth and Hazel attended a day school near their home, like most children at Six Nations.

The Miller sisters continued to be trailblazers for the rest of their lives, with Hazel becoming one of the only Indigenous women to work as a missionary.[55] In later years, Hazel moved to Toronto and attended the Toronto Bible College. She graduated in 1932, at age twenty-one, and then focused her life on Christian mission work among her own people.[56] Hazel eventually started teaching Sunday school out of her father's home, and later out of her own cottage.[57] Hazel's mission was cut short when she died at the age thirty-six due to bronchial pneumonia.[58] However, her work would be commemorated by her siblings, who founded the Bethany Baptist Mission, with Ruth supervising the building. The Bethany Mission Church still stands today.[59]

Legacy

These are just two stories among many concerning the brave Indigenous children who resisted the very people and policies that were trying to destroy their culture, language, and sense of self. While resistance was expressed in different forms, both stories have something in common: the miscarriage of justice perpetrated by the staff of the Mohawk Institute, the Department of Indian Affairs, and the Canadian government. And, while the students documented in this chapter survived the Mohawk Institute, many did not. While both events were highly publicized at the time, one can only wonder about all the other untold stories of resistance that occurred during Principal Ashton's eleven-year tenure. It goes without saying that the bravery of these children changed the lives of many. Consequently, this chapter is dedicated to them.

NOTES

1. Bryan Hogeveen, "Accounting for Violence at the Victoria Industrial School," *Histoire sociale / Social History* 42, no. 83 (2009): 148.
2. *Indian Act*, S.C. 1926–7, c. 32, and R.S.C. 1927, c. 98, s. 141; repealed by S.C. 1950–1, c. 29 s. 123.
3. "Blaze at Brantford," *The Globe*, 20 April 1903, 9; "Mohawk Institute Fire," *The Globe*, 11 July 1903, 5.
4. "Brantford," *The Globe*, 3 September 1903, 2.
5. "Committed for Trial; Four Indian Boys Charged with Arson," *The Globe*, 26 June 1903, 5.
6. "Committed for Trial."
7. "Boys Started Fires, Indian Lads Arrested at Brantford," *The Globe*, 23 June 1903, 1.
8. "Blaze at Brantford."
9. "Blaze at Brantford."
10. "Bad Crowd of Boys," *The Globe*, 4 July 1903, 22.
11. "Bad Crowd of Boys."
12. John R. Alexander to Superintendent General of Indian Affairs for the Dominion of Canada, File 154,845, Pt. 11, Vol. 2771, RG 10, LAC. The petition is undated but was completed between 25 July 1903 and 18 September 1903.
13. John R. Alexander to Superintendent General.

14 The Indian Department replied that while they regretted Mr. Alexander's loss, they were in no way responsible for the destruction of his property, and that there were no funds that could be applied to assisting Mr. Alexander. Deputy Superintendent General of Indian Affairs to C. B. Heyd, 18 September 1903, File 154,845, Pt. 11, Vol. 2771, RG 10, LAC.
15 "Fire Loss 1," *The Globe*, 11 July 1903, 5.
16 "Boys Started Fires: Indian Lads Arrested at Brantford," *The Globe*, 23 June 1903, 1.
17 "Boys Started Fires."
18 "Boys Started Fires."
19 "Firebugs Sentenced," *The Globe*, 21 July 1903.
20 "Firebugs Sentenced."
21 *Juvenile Delinquents Act*, S.C. 1908, c. 40.
22 "Firebugs Sentenced."
23 Truth and Reconciliation Commission of Canada, *Final Report of the Truth and Reconciliation Commission of Canada*, vol. 1, *Canada's Residential Schools: The History, Part 1, Origins to 1939* (McGill-Queen's University Press), 483.
24 *An Act to Amend the Act Respecting Procedure in Criminal Cases and Other Matters Relating to Criminal Law*, S.C. 1875, c. 43, s. 1.
25 Hogeveen, "Accounting for Violence at the Victoria Industrial School," 152.
26 Hogeveen, 148.
27 Hogeveen, 148.
28 Mathew Debo to the Deputy Superintendent of Indian Affairs, 7 April 1906, File 154,845, Pt. 11, Vol. 2771, RG 10, LAC.
29 Debo to the Deputy Superintendent.
30 Superintendent Chester Ferrier to R. Ashton, 17 August 1906, File 154,845, Pt. 11, Vol. 2771, RG 10, LAC.
31 Ferrier to Ashton.
32 Truth and Reconciliation Commission of Canada, *Final Report*, 1:483.
33 Truth and Reconciliation Commission of Canada, 483.
34 Truth and Reconciliation Commission of Canada, 483; Martin Benson to Deputy Superintendent General, Indian Affairs, 24 June 1903, File 154,845, Pt. 11, Vol. 2771, RG 10, LAC.
35 Elizabeth Graham, *The Mush Hole: Life at Two Indian Reservation Schools* (Heffle Publishing, 1997), 503.
36 "Miller v Ashton Case: Girls Too Severely Punished," *Brantford Expositor*, 1 April 1914, File 154,845, Pt. 11, Vol. 2771, RG 10, LAC.
37 Alison Elizabeth Norman, "Race, Gender and Colonialism: Public Life among the Six Nations of Grand River, 1899–1939" (PhD diss., Ontario Institute for Studies in Education, University of Toronto, 2010), 143.
38 "Miller v Ashton Case."
39 Kelly and Porter to the Superintendent of the Department of Indian Affairs, 29 September 1913, File 154,845, Pt. 1, Vol. 2771, RG 10, LAC.
40 "Miller v Ashton Case."
41 "Miller v Ashton Case."
42 "Miller v Ashton Case."
43 Ohsweken Council House Minute Book by Josiah Hill, 3 September 1913, File 154,845, Pt. 1, Vol. 2771, RG 10, LAC.
44 Ohsweken Council House Minute Book by Josiah Hill, 24 September 1913, File 154,845, Pt. 1, Vol. 2771, RG 10, LAC. Scott was appointed deputy superintendent general of Indian Affairs in 1913.
45 Duncan Campbell Scott to Hon. Dr. Roche, 28 October 1913, File 154,845, Pt. 1, Vol. 2771, RG 10, LAC.
46 "Miller v Ashton Case."
47 "Miller v Ashton Case."
48 "Miller v Ashton Case."
49 "Miller v Ashton Case."
50 "Miller v Ashton Case."
51 "Miller v Ashton Case."
52 "Miller v Ashton Case."

53   "Miller v Ashton Case."
54   J. R. Miller, *Shingwauk's Vision: A History of Native Residential Schools* (University of Toronto Press, 1996), 357.
55   Julia L. Jamieson, *The One Hundredth Anniversary of the Ohsweken Baptist Church* (n.p., 1940); "Ohsweken Baptist," File 5, Box 470, Accession 89/55, Sally Weaver Collection, Canadian Museum of History, Ottawa: 11. Thanks to Alison Norman for these sources on the Miller sisters.
56   Jamieson, *The One Hundredth Anniversary*.
57   Jamieson.
58   Hazel Miller, Tuscarora, Brant County, Province of Ontario Certificate of Registration of Death, 15 March 1938.
59   Ruth "[accumulated] enough money from her savings to pay for all the labour. The mission was built at a cost of $500 and has a seating capacity of eighty-five." Jamieson, *The One Hundredth Anniversary of the Ohsweken Baptist Church*, 12.

9

ęhǫwadihsadǫ ne:ʔhniʔ gadigyenǫ:gyeʔs ganahaǫgwęʔ ęyagǫnhehgǫhǫ:k / They Buried Them, but They the Seeds Floated Around What Will Sustain Them

Teri Lyn Morrow, Bonnie Freeman, and Sandra Juutilainen

Introduction

Nê togyę́: niyódǫhǫ:k ǫgwânigǫ́hâ (so be it in our minds) is a common phrase that is used in our Ganǫhǫnyǫhk (Thanksgiving Address) in the Gayogoho:nǫ nigawęno:dęʔ (Cayuga language), a language that was denied to many who attended the Mush Hole in Tganadahae:ʔ (where the town sits up on something, later named Brantford). Our words become the foundation of how we see ourselves and how we see our connection to the world around us. Intrinsic and extrinsic and the bridge that flows between, this is how our language speaks to us; it is relational gyǫnhehgǫh odiyaęnaʔ (what we all live on; our sustenance). When we understand our connection to the living world around us, we speak to it as if it has the same value as any human being that we may encounter in our time here on ohwęjadeʔ (existing earth, land). Although there has been over one hundred years of engagement for our children and families with residential schools, this seems small in comparison to the thousands of years that Ǫgwehǫ:weh (Original peoples of this land) have been existing upon our traditional lands. When we think of who bore the brunt of these horrific engagements with non-Native peoples, it was our children. Children who carry our legacy, culture, and language with them as dęyagodawęnyehahk (they walk about).

This chapter presents a case study based on a Social Sciences and Humanities Research Council–funded research project entitled "Truth Telling: Gardens, Farming and Food Experiences at the Mohawk Institute Indian Residential School." The case study shares the experience and perception of gardens, farming, and food of participants who attended the Mohawk Institute Indian Residential School located in Brantford, Ontario, and how this has impacted their lives and families after their attendance in residential school. The aim of this research study is to understand and improve the food access and food sovereignty of Indigenous community-led programs, as well to advance the understanding of reconciliation through the Call to Action 65 of the Truth and Reconciliation Commission: "We call upon the federal government, through the Social Sciences and Humanities Research Council, and in collaboration with Aboriginal peoples, post-secondary institutions and educators, and the National Centre for Truth and Reconciliation and its partner institutions, to establish a national research program with multi-year funding to advance understanding of reconciliation."[1]

First Nations, Food, Nutrition, and Environment

The 2012 First Nations Food, Nutrition and Environment Study, completed in collaboration with Six Nations of the Grand River residents, found that it is more nutritious for our people—physically, emotionally, mentally, and spiritually—when we can eat the traditional foods of our territory and ancestors. These traditional foods included sustenance from the land, water, and natural environment (plants and animals) we lived among. Our sustenance also included how we grew and attended to our heritage foods, such as corn, beans, and squash (Three Sisters). The results from this study reveal how today's dietary intake among Six Nations residents strayed from the traditional natural foods we were accustomed to and veered more toward foods with higher-than-recommended amounts of fat and salt. While important nutrients such as iron, vitamin B12, riboflavin, niacin, thiamine, zinc, and phosphorus were present in adequate quantities, vitamins A, C, and D, calcium, magnesium, and fibre were lacking according to modern dietary standards.[2] The number one source of saturated fat consumed by Six Nations was from beef and processed meats such as cold cuts and sausage. Saturated fat is a fat source that can raise the low-density lipoproteins in our bodies, and too much of this type of fat can increase the risk of heart disease or stroke.

The study also found that the common traditional foods in Six Nations were gathered, hunted, fished, and gardened. When we examined the nutritional value set of the commonly eaten traditional foods in Six Nations, we found that deer, corn, beans, walleye, and perch were the top traditional foods eaten. These foods provide lower amounts of saturated fats and higher amounts of omega-3, -6, and -9 fats, which contribute to healthy brain development; vitamins D, B12, and B6 are also increased when these foods are eaten. Plants in this diet produce multiple varieties of Haudenosaunee seeds that draw out specific vitamins. During processing, we make a lye for the corn with boiling water and wood ashes, in the traditional Haudenosaunee way. Doing so increases the calcium, fibre, and zinc content.[3]

In contrast, Western perspectives about food are derived from a food system that only respects nutritional value. These perspectives are void of the *ceremonial value of these recommended traditional foods*. The ritual, respect, and reciprocity of hunting, gathering, and tending responsibility to these natural foods is required to gain a holistic and ancestral ecological knowledge of the Haudenosaunee food system that has been imperative to our survival. Our people also understood the "nutritional" value of these foods as they paid attention to when they were given to us by creation. Once we followed the moon and sun cycles to learn when these foods would honour us with their presence, we began a reciprocal relationship that continues to be practised today.[4] When food is streamlined into its vitamin and mineral counterparts without looking at the holistic and reciprocal relationships embedded in the language, land, and ceremony associated with particular foods, it results in a disconnected relationship with food.

Two Row Research Paradigm

The framework of Indigenous inquiry engages a holistic paradigm that integrates the epistemology of land and is built upon a relationship with the spiritual and natural worlds.[5] The relationship between the spiritual and natural worlds is reflected through interactions people have with the natural environment and expressed through the discourse of Indigenous languages and cultural practices.[6] The Two Row research paradigm has been developed to "decolonize Western presumptions and re-establish healthy and productive research partnerships."[7] These principles are based on the philosophical tenets of the Kahswenhta and the support of an Indigenous methodological approach to understanding the experiences of residential school survivors, their families, and the traditional knowledge associated with gardens, farming, and food experiences.

The foundation of this research paradigm is based on Kaianere'kó:wa (Great Law of Peace) and calls upon all researchers (Indigenous or non-Indigenous) to adopt a Good Mind in working with and guiding those relationships in a peaceful and respectful way.[8] The researchers and authors of this research have respectfully guided their research methods according to the five principles of this research paradigm: (1) establishing and maintaining relationships and trust with Indigenous people and communities; (2) Indigenous knowledge, language, and understanding is at the core of this research; (3) researchers honour Indigenous epistemology, methods, and practices; (4) the research honours the distinctness of Indigenous knowledge and methods without blending with other methods of knowledge in doing research; and (5) the research adheres to the First Nations Information Governance Centre's OCAP principles (ownership, control, access, and possession) as it relates to data and information collected on Indigenous people and communities remain with Indigenous communities.[9] The following research is guided by these principles as they relate to the Two Row research paradigm. The next section highlights the stories and experiences of a mother and daughter through the Indigenous framework of storytelling.

Indigenous Storytelling Methodology

This case study draws on two semi-structured interviews that were conducted by Sandra Juutilainen between January and February 2020 as part of the research project "Truth Telling: Gardens, Farming and Food Experiences at the Mohawk Institute Indian residential school." We chose an interview with a mother and daughter from twenty-three interviews that were conducted for this study to highlight the intergenerational link between parent and child. The case study explores the experiences the mother and daughter have had with gardens, farming, and food during and beyond the Mohawk Institute Indian Residential School experience. The data is explored through two different time frames: (1) as an attendee of the Mohawk Institute Indian Residential School; and (2) as a daughter of an attendee. Both interviewees were asked open-ended questions about their experiences with gardens, farming, and food at the Mohawk Institute and traditional food systems revitalization. Consent from both mother and daughter was obtained in sharing their names and stories presented within this chapter. While research often anonymizes the identity of study participants, as

Indigenous scholars we see our study participants as both collaborators in research and on a deeper level as our extended family. As such, we would never refer to a member of our family with a pseudonym.

Sharing Stories and Experiences—Findings

This case study is a reflection of the experiences of Beverly Albreight, a Cayuga woman, Turtle Clan, who attended the Mohawk Institute from 1966 until 1970. Beverly is from Six Nations of the Grand River. She first entered through the daunting school doors of the Mohawk Institute as a seven-year-old. Interjected alongside the lived experiences of Beverly are those of her adult daughter, Elizabeth Maracle. Elizabeth grew up primarily in the urban settings of Brantford and St. Catharine's, Ontario. She shares her experience growing up with a parent who attended residential school. She had many family members who attended the Mohawk Institute, including her mom, grandmother, and all of her aunts and uncles. One of the key themes during our interviews was not being fully connected to the community of Six Nations, since she had a predominantly urban upbringing. Elizabeth iterated that "the women in my mom's part of the family, like her and her sisters, her sister did not get any land. So, none of the women have any lands in our family. So, it's been a bit of a struggle. So, yeah. I would like to live down here, but I don't. I have not been able to do that yet." Elizabeth's comment refers to the sexist and racist policies that impact Native women as a result of the *Indian Act*, whereby these Indigenous women lost their rights to land.[10] There are well-documented intergenerational impacts for women who attend residential school and marry non-Native men.[11] It is therefore important to have an understanding of the experiences of both attendees and their family members. The findings from this case study highlight what children knew of and/or understood about their food sources prior to going into the residential school system. The research also examines what children were fed while they were at the Mush Hole and how this impacted and changed the way they ate and fed their own families. In addition, this study explores how these experiences influence the relationships with food among family members.

Language, Land, and Our Connection

Haudenosaunee food systems are deeply shaped by ceremony. As we practise these ceremonies collectively in our homes and at our Longhouses, we are passing on the words and traditional ecological knowledge that our ancestors have shared from time immemorial. We have a reciprocal relationship with this ecosystem and a duty to be mindful and respectful to keep its presence in the front of our minds and to ensure that our children are taught the same. When the children were taken from their homes, denied their language and specific cultural values, as mentioned above, this resulted in the present-day chronic health conditions and limited access to language and Haudenosaunee food ways.

We have been taught to sadę'nigǫhahni:ya:t (keep your mind strong) and put forth the words or ideas of our hędwaihwadihę:to' (Knowledge Keepers in our ceremonies). The Hwihs Nihonǫhwęjage (Five Nations) have ahsęh skae' (thirteen ceremonies) that we offer as families. These ceremonies follow the ęhni'da:gye's (phases of the moon) on the dihsgo:wah (thirteenth or first moon of the lunar calendar). The Haudenosaunee ceremonies associated with the lunar calendar include the following:

Gaya'dago:wah: The Month of Big Dolls (January)

- Mid-winter ceremony, usually second week in January, lasting for approximately eight days

Ganrahdahgah: Rustling Leaves (February)

- Haditsehsdǫda:s (The males are putting sap in the tree around the second week in February for approximately one day)

Ganęsgwaǫta:'ah: A Few Frogs Month (March)

- Ęhadiyaǫdata't Drying up the Trees

Ganęsgwaǫ:ta'go:wah: A Lot of Frogs Month (April)

- Hǫwadiwęnǫgohta' Hadiwęnodagye's (Thunder ceremony around the first week in April)

Gana'gaht: Budding Leaf Month (May)

- Ęhǫwaddiwanǫ:goth Ędehgeha:' ga:gwa:' (Sun ceremony around the first week of May)

- Ęshagodiwęnǫ:goth Ahsǫhehka:' Ęhni'da:gye's (Uplifting the stature of the moon around the second week of May)

- Dęyetiya'tahahgwadę' (We will walk the seeds around the middle of May)
- Gotędihs'anhǫ' (Finishing planting ceremony around end of May)

Hyai:kneh: Berry Ripening Month (June)

- Adahyaohǫ:' (Gathering of fruit ceremony around middle of June and last approximately one day)

Hyaiknehgo:wah: Many Berry Ripening Month (July)

Jihsgęhneh: Corn Silk Month or Firefly Month (August)

- Ęhęnadehsahe'daohe:k (They gather the green beans ceremony around the first week of August for one day)

Sa'gęhneh: Cough Month (September)

- Adekwao:hǫ:' (Gathering of the foods, both green corn ceremonies around the middle of August/September)

Sa'gęhnehgo:wah: Big Cough Month (October)

- Tsa'degohsrahęh Gaihwayaǫni: (Mid-winter ceremony around the middle of October lasting about four days)

Jo:to:': Cold Weather Month (November)

- Hǫwadiwęnǫgohta' Hadiwęnodagye's (Thunder ceremony in November lasting one day)

Jo:to:'go:wah: Really Cold Month (December)

For over one hundred years, our children who attended these schools had an unstable relationship with food, often going hungry and very seldom having access to the traditions of hunting, harvesting, and fishing and the passing on of procuring, processing, and sharing practices at the dining tables of these schools. Many survivors today express the limited ability they have to access this system of ceremony, language, and land; to know how to bring these foods back into their diet. According to Beverly, "the

Figure 9.1. *Katsian[:ionte Hanging Flower*, Jake Thomas print
Source: Jake Thomas Learning Centre

only traditional foods I knew was beans, corn and squash. That's all I know. Um, because I didn't go to the Longhouse or anything like that. And my mom didn't take us. So, that's why I didn't really know about (traditional) foods."

The importance of traditional foods is why in our Creation Story we are told our Mother, the Earth, has brought these gifts specifically for us. She brought us traditional tobacco to help heal our minds. She brought us corn grown from her breast to nourish our babies. As corn silk is nutrition for the baby, the squash grows from her stomach; it contains fibre and vitamin A that helps us to digest and connect a healthy mind with gut health. The beans grow from her pelvis and kidneys and help us to replenish the Earth within a reciprocal relationship. Out of her feet grows the sunflower or Jerusalem artichoke. The root is deep and helps keep us grounded to the soil and water that flows beneath us.

The Six Nations community was lucky enough to hear this story and teaching presented along with the visual painting done by Chief Jake

Figure 9.2. Christine Skye, Six Nations Mohawk
Source: Richard Hill Collection

Thomas and shared by Christine Skye (cant),[12] who has passed on to the sky world, but who has left a legacy of knowledge and food responsibilities to her family and those she shared within Six Nations. The resilience of us as Haudenosaunee has been maintained and passed on through our stories and through working alongside our Knowledge Keepers. While residential schools tried to bury us, they didn't know we are created from seeds.

Before Indian Residential School

Many residential school survivors are unaware of traditional Haudenosaunee food. For many Haudenosaunee families, growing and harvesting food was very common in the days before residential schools. These relationships were not categorized as "traditional food." Regarding food, Beverly stated, "I remember before I went to residential school, we had cow's milk." While she was aware that her family consumed corn, beans, and squash, as well as other healthy foods from the garden, forest, and their farm, Beverly did not have a conceptualization of traditional Haudenosaunee foods. Many of the survivors, though they also sometimes lacked a conceptualization of traditional foods, shared the important social and familial values that were central in their homes before being placed in residential school. Beverly remembers, for example, that, as a child, the dinner table was so important within her family, and she explained that this value continued to resonate into her adulthood as she established her own family:

> Because a lot of people, they eat in front of the TV. And I think, well, if you have a table, you should get together and eat. See, when we were at home that's what we did with my mom. Like even before I went to the residential school. And so, to me what's the use of having a table if you don't use it? So, I think that stayed with me.

Even though attendees were children, they were still able to draw on previous memories of what a healthy food environment entailed and had an innate sense of the horrific nature of the food environment within the Mohawk Institute.

During and After Indian Residential School

The children attending the Mohawk Institute had the worst possible food environment.[13] The name "Mush Hole" was a moniker used by the children survivors to refer to the residential school because of the mushy oatmeal they were served. Beverly recounts the "mush" she ate: "The only thing I remember is oatmeal. Yeah. And that was even—not even thick, it was watery." In addition, Beverly remembers that much of the food that was served was plain and did not have any seasoning or spices added to it. Also, "no healthy fruit or vegetables." She remembers that the boys and girls were always segregated and were not allowed to interact during mealtimes, except on Sundays. "On Sundays they . . . would let us eat, um, dinner together." Beverly compares the food she had prior to being in the Mush Hole—for example, fresh cow's milk—to what she was served while in residential school: "When we had milk, it was powdered milk mixed with water. . . . There was nobody that was fat when we were in residential school. We were all thin. Like even with cows [at the Mush Hole], I don't remember them even giving us cow's milk or anything."

Mealtime for children survivors was very rigid and strict. Beverly remembered that "when we had to go to the meals, we had to be like the military, in a straight line and you had to be straight. They used to put books on our head to make sure we walked straight." During meals children were expected to eat a certain way, chew their food a specific number of times, and eat slowly. Beverly shares that they were not allowed to talk to other children, even their own siblings, while sitting for a meal, or they would be yelled at or punished:

> All I remember is, they told us that we had to count our food. They usually say about fifty or sixty [times]. Yeah, so . . . take your time. . . . During meals we weren't even allowed to talk to each other. Like even with my brothers, even though we saw them, we never talked across the table or anything because we'd get hollered at. We're supposed to be there to eat.

Though Beverly had positive memories of the dinner table with her family before residential school, her experience at the Mush Hole was not good, and it left a lasting impression. She expresses how this affected her: "I think too with how they were saying that you couldn't even associate with anybody? To me that's not a mealtime. It's not a happy time to eat. And, like I said with us being so thin, to me I felt like this wasn't a good time."

Beverly and her fellow residential school survivors were treated according to the old adage that "children are to be seen and not heard." Children in residential school were not to question what they were given to eat at mealtime, regardless of whether they wanted to eat what they were given. Beverly shares this experience:

> Like I said with residential school, they just gave it to us because we're children and we're not supposed to argue or talk back and say, "I don't want that." Because I remember, um, some children if they didn't go eat their oatmeal, they would save it for the next meal and make them eat it then. See, that's forcing people to do that even though they don't want to eat it. They stand there and make sure you eat it, and I don't think that's right either.

For Beverly, the dominant theme of punishment was related to her food environment and continued after her time at the Mush Hole. While in foster care she was still exposed to authoritarian figures who used food as a weapon, whether by withholding food or by forcing foods that she did not want to eat. Even trying to eat those foods today brings her reminders of when food was used as a punishment: "The only thing I won't eat now is when I was in foster care, how they used to punish us. They'd say, 'Go to your room.' But, they would withhold food from us. And one thing that I think they forced us to eat was mushroom soup. I won't eat mushroom soup. ... I tried to eat mushrooms, but I still can't. It just seems to come back to me."

As Beverly shared her experiences in the Mush Hole with her children, her daughter Elizabeth iterates similar experiences to those of her mom at the Mush Hole, describing her relationship with food as one of deprivation as she thinks back to the poverty she experienced growing up with her mother and grandmother. The Truth and Reconciliation Commission reports many similar survivor accounts of seeing foods that were not available to the children in residential school.[14] Elizabeth remembers her mother talking about the food she rarely, if ever, had,

> [or] stuff she couldn't have. There were apples there, but I couldn't have that, or I would get an orange at Christmas, but just that one time. And she hated certain foods. Like, she couldn't eat Jello, or she didn't like oatmeal, or like mushy foods. She didn't know how to cook with spices and didn't seem to have any cooking experience really. And didn't find joy in preparing food. It was kind of like a dead zone for her.

Beverly was hesitant to share her residential school experiences with her children. She remembers talking with her adult son about what she went through and explaining that she could not use her name and instead had to refer to herself by the number she was assigned. She said that her son was shocked and told his mother it was like she was in jail. In her interview, Beverly recounts in her words the conversation she had with her son:

> Beverly's son: Mom, you know what? You were in jail. You couldn't use your name, you had to use your number.
>
> Beverly: I've never been to jail.
>
> Beverly's son: That's how a jail is, they will go by a number. That's how you were, but you were children.
>
> Beverly: I never thought about it like that. I never thought about it like being in jail and having to use that number. It's

true. That's why it's good to get other people that listen to you and get their feedback.

Beverly's sense-making of her experiences, along with her son's interjections, highlight the legacy of wrongdoing that occurred within the Mohawk Institute and the ways in which survivors and their families are re-traumatized when recounting their experiences at the Mohawk Institute.

Legacy of Indian Residential School

Today's Indigenous people carry the historical legacy, shame, and pain of their parents', grandparents', and their own experiences regarding the psychological trauma inflicted upon them through residential schools. Children as young as two years of age were forcefully taken away or hesitantly given up by their families because of government policies that indicated that First Nations children were to be civilized and assimilated into non-Indigenous culture.[15] The system was, as Vine Deloria Jr. and Clifford Lytle have observed, "one of the major weapons of forced assimilation since the establishment of colonies."[16]

Brad McKenzie and Vern Morrissette identify three forms of trauma experienced by former students of residential schools.[17] The first is the lack of love, which damages a child's self-esteem. The second form of trauma is the stripping away of cultural expression through language, clothing, hair, ceremonies, and food, which relates to the establishment of identity. The third trauma is the loss of family and the collective experience as a people. This last type of trauma inhibits a child's ability to connect and establish important kinship relationships. Adult residential school survivors would often turn their negative experiences inward, therefore affecting their self-esteem. Many adult children reported an inability to walk in either their Haudenosaunee or non-Indigenous worlds.

This loss of culture had a great impact not only on Indigenous families, but also on the whole community.[18] Haudenosaunee communities who lost their children to residential schools also experienced this sense of loss. When those children returned home to their communities and became parents, they transferred what was taught to them in residential school to their children. As a result, subsequent generations of Haudenosaunee children were doomed to experience what their parents and grandparents experienced, not at the hands of nuns and clergy, but from their own mothers and fathers.

It is not surprising that this experience would have lifelong impacts in terms of survivors' and intergenerational survivors' relationship with food. Beverly's daughter Elizabeth shares some of her observations from her childhood of her mother's relationship with food: "She's not connected to it very much other than processed food or easy food, or a lot of takeout. She seems to enjoy food when she goes to gatherings, but she hoards. I noticed that she'll take home like plates and plates of food and then doesn't really eat it. But, she has to have it. So, yeah, there's a big hoarding piece that's been in my childhood." Elizabeth also realizes how her mother's experience with lack of food has contributed to her overproduction of food and the centrality of food at gatherings, rather than enjoying the relationships of family: "I over-nurture . . . I make too much food. I realize that we don't seem to do things outside of food. I think about our holidays and our events and our family gatherings. I think food should be there, but I notice . . . I think food is the centre versus it being present. And I worry about that sometimes." The centrality of food and the disconnect from family and friends stems from Beverly's experiences of mealtime during her time at residential school. She shares what it was like: "You had to sit up or you'd get punished if you didn't. And when I say punished, I mean the belt. So that's why, um—like to me that's extreme. Because when you have a meal, you're supposed to enjoy yourself. Enjoy your foods."

Beverly's account of a military-style food environment refers back to how her prior mealtimes before residential school occurred; she knew that mealtimes were supposed to be a time where you enjoy your food and spend time with your family. Both Beverly and Elizabeth discussed the value they place on returning to food sharing as a repudiation of the idea of food being used as a weapon in favour of seeing food as the way to live a good life.

Return to Food Sharing

> *If education and food can be used as a weapon, to take away culture, to harm people, then the opposite must be true: education and food can also be used to relearn the good way, to live a good life.*
>
> Chandra Maracle[19]

Chandra Maracle's reflections as part of the Earth to Table Legacies project are embodied in the way Beverly has reflected on her personal experiences and how this has influenced her adult life and her interactions with her own children and grandchildren, with an emphasis on eating together as a family, being allowed to choose their own foods, and talk at the dinner table. She iterates, "Now that I'm older, I've changed that with my children. . . . They used to say, 'children should be seen and not heard.' When I had children, I let them talk to me whenever they can. That's why they're assertive, and my grandchildren are more [so]. That's because I didn't tell them to be quiet all the time." Elizabeth spoke about her observations of her mother in ceremony as having a "tiny" voice after being taught to sing some songs. "I know she has a booming voice . . . but I noticed how hard it was for her to express, and I realized—to me that represented [that] someone had taken her voice." Elizabeth further acknowledged how thankful she was for the resistance her mother showed in not continuing the dysfunctional cycle of "children should only be seen and not heard," as she had the freedom to always express herself, and this healthier way of being was also passed on to her children.

In the return to food sharing both Beverly and Elizabeth recounted family- and community-focused food environments, which include the food you grow yourself and share with others in the community. Beverly talked about how she had opportunities to learn from friends and grow food in their gardens. Elizabeth shared how her mom would take her and her siblings to the homes of family members who had hobby farms so they would get a better understanding of where food comes from, in addition to community gatherings where food would be talked about in a more holistic manner. Since they lived primarily in urban areas, Friendship Centres were also an important site for learning about traditional foods. Elizabeth stated, "I know that white corn was ours. . . . Growing up mom would buy the white corn that was shaped like a round disk (cornbread)."

The importance of seeds and their relation to Indigenous food sovereignty was also highlighted by both Beverly and Elizabeth. Beverly had strong opinions on seeds and a non-GMO standpoint that stemmed from the knowledge passed down to her by her family: "When we grew up, we always had seeds. How are you going to make things if you have no seeds? And now the government tried to tell you how to grow your seeds and what you put in it." She shared how sustainable seeds are and how this benefits the community, and, recognizing that not everyone has knowledge of seed keeping and growing, she emphasized the importance of seeking out those who have this community knowledge. Elizabeth discussed how her mom gathers seeds and understands their importance. "We need to keep our seeds because there's sovereignty in that."

Elizabeth talked about relearning after participating in a predominantly Western food system that is disconnected from the land. She talked about her struggles with gardening and not knowing how the whole cycle is interconnected but iterated how gardening resulted in her feeling "joyous and happy" when she produced some of her own foods and herbs. She explained further how not having land in the community of Six Nations was a barrier for gardening. Elizabeth learned a lot about canning from her husband's family, in particular his grandmother, who is "Oneida and lived off-reserve, but she had land and they gardened." She talked about how she learned about cycles of food within ceremonies.

Elizabeth shared a personal experience of attending a community project taught by Elder Jan Longboat specifically for residential school survivors and with a focus on the intergenerational impacts on their children. She participated in a lot of circles with her mother there and was exposed to a lot of the traditions, such as Rite of Passage, that have been lost. "I decided to do a Rite of Passage as an adult and then I decided I was going to raise my kids with that." Elizabeth described this as an emotional endeavour as her mom "cried" when watching Elizabeth and her grandchildren participating in ceremonies. Elizabeth reflected on this, feeling that this is something her mom would have wanted—that is, to have a relationship to ceremony as a Haudenosaunee woman "and to have her power."

Elizabeth recounts her ongoing learning about women's social representation within Haudenosaunee culture, in particular with respect to food. She described hearing the Kaianere'kó:wa / Great Law of Peace at Akwesasne and how the totality of culture was embedded in how traditional foods were served: "That it was getting our cultural content, our languages, knowing the wampums, our creation . . . like our stories of how our Confederacy is and how it came to be. But, food was present too, and people were engaging. And all different levels of that, so that was something I found really, really powerful."

Conclusion

This case study is the first to use a Haudenosaunee food-based lens to investigate the historical and contemporary vulnerabilities and resiliencies related to food, farming, and gardening experienced by those who attended the Mohawk Institute. In Beverly's words, "I don't really know anybody who talks about what kind of food they had there . . . so, it's good that people are finding out. . . . It's important that you know about it. Like I said, with you doing this [study] about residential schools, you're probably learning a lot too." Beverly was correct. The stories that were gathered during this study informed and confirmed what many of us as family members and as a community have experienced through the loss of our children to residential schools. We as researchers learned a lot from the individuals and family members that participated in this study. While this research assumes a community-based focus, it holds to account Indigenous epistemologies as well as the relationality of the participants as collaborators. It is our responsibility not only as researchers but more importantly as Haudenosaunee women to share what we learned in ways that are meaningful and relevant.

Since Ian Mosby published his research on nutritional testing in residential schools, Canadians have been informed of the unethical food-based practices that occurred in some Canadian Indian Residential Schools.[20] Every aspect of Indigenous life and livelihood has been affected by the colonial history of Canada.[21] Settlers have attempted to implement policies, such as residential schools, to remove Indigenous hunting, fishing, and gathering narratives under the notion of *terra nullius* that persists within the "monocultures of the mind."[22] This strategy has fragmented the complex systems of Indigenous biocultural heritage regarding the land and food systems in North America.[23] Food has become one of the tools of colonialism,[24] and Indigenous people have been resisting and fighting for their sovereign rights to continue to connect and maintain their spiritual relationship with what sustains them as a people and as a nation. An Indigenous Knowledge Keeper once shared that "what we do today will have an impact on our next seven generations."[25] Therefore, Indigenous people must be food sovereign in order to be sovereign as nations. According to Oneida scholar Leni Sunseri, "For true liberation from colonial oppression to occur for all members of the nation, decolonizing governance practices must be inclusive and should follow the traditional principles of governance found in the Great Law of Peace: peace, power, and righteousness."[26] In doing so, we must ultimately uphold our long-standing sacred responsibilities to nurture our own health and well-being, and carry on with our relationships with land, plants, and animals.[27] The same Knowledge Keeper also shared that "the earth, plants, and animals have a role and responsibility and can exist without humans; however, humans cannot exist without the earth, plants, and animals. Therefore, our creator has provided us with knowledge, teachings, and practices to honour our relationships with the natural world."[28]

Indigenous food sovereignty is a tool to protect Indigenous food systems that have specifically evolved in different communities and therefore depend on a community's own social, political, historical, and cultural context. As such, it is best defined by the community itself.[29]

NOTES TO CHAPTER 9

1. Truth and Reconciliation Commission of Canada, *Calls to Action* (Truth and Reconciliation Commission of Canada, 2015), 8, https://ehprnh2mwo3.exactdn.com/wp-content/uploads/2021/01/Calls_to_Action_English2.pdf.
2. First Nations Food, Nutrition and Environment Study, *Summary of Key Findings for Eight Assembly of First Nations Regions 2008–2018* (University of Ottawa, Université de Montréal, Assembly of First Nations, 2019).
3. Tania M. Ngapo, Pauline Bilodeau, Yves Arcand, Marie Thérèse Charles, Axel Diederichsen, Isabelle Germain, et al., "Historical Indigenous Food Preparation Using Produce of the Three Sisters Intercropping System," *Foods* 10, no. 3 (2021): 524.
4. "13 Moons Turtle Island," Oneida Language and Cultural Centre, accessed 13 May 2025, https://oneidalanguage.ca/oneida-culture/oneidalanguage-symbols/13-moons-turtle-island/.
5. Kathleen Absolon King, *Kaandossiwin How We Come to Know* (Fernwood Publishing, 2011); Linda Tuhiwai Smith, *Decolonizing Methodologies: Research and Indigenous Peoples* (St. Martin's Press, 1999); Margaret Kovach, *Indigenous Methodologies: Characteristics, Conversations, and Contexts* (University of Toronto Press, 2009); Sandra A. Juutilainen, Melanie Jeffrey, and Suzanne Stewart, "Methodology Matters: Designing a Pilot Study Guided by Indigenous Epistemologies," *Human Biology* 91, no. 3 (2020): 141–51, https://doi.org/10.13110/humanbiology.91.3.06; Shawn Wilson, *Research Is Ceremony: Indigenous Research Methods* (Fernwood Publishing, 2008); Vanessa Watts, "Indigenous Place-Thought and Agency Amongst Humans And Non-Humans (First Woman and Sky Woman Go on a European World Tour!)," *Decolonization: Indigeneity, Education & Society* 2, no. 1 (2013): 20–34.
6. Bonnie M. Freeman, "The Spirit of Haudenosaunee Youth: The Transformation of Identity and Well-Being Through Culture-Based Activism" (PhD diss., Wilfrid Laurier University, 2015), https://scholars.wlu.ca/etd/1697/.
7. Richard W. Hill and Daniel Coleman, "The Two Row Wampum-Covenant Chain Tradition as a Guide for Indigenous-University Research Partnerships," *Cultural Studies ↔ Critical Methodologies* 19, no. 5 (2019): 339–59, https://doi.org/10.1177/1532708618809138.
8. Freeman, "The Spirit of Haudenosaunee Youth."
9. Freeman; Hill and Coleman, "The Two Row Wampum-Covenant Chain"; Bonnie Freeman and Trish Van Katwyk, "Navigating the Waters: Understanding Allied Relationships Through a Tekéni Teyohà: ke Kahswénhtake Two Row Research Paradigm," *Journal of Indigenous Social Development* 9, no. 1 (2020): 60–76.
10. Mackenzie Deschambault, "An Exploration of the Colonial Impacts of the Indian Act on Indigenous Women in Canada" (PhD diss., Carleton University, 2020).
11. Amy Bombay, Kimberly Matheson, and Hymie Anisman, "The Intergenerational Effects of Indian Residential Schools: Implications for the Concept of Historical Trauma," *Transcultural Psychiatry* 51, no. 3 (2014): 320–38, https://doi.org/10.1177/1363461513503380; Amy Bombay, Kimberly Matheson, and Hymie Anisman, "Appraisals of Discriminatory Events Among Adult Offspring of Indian Residential School Survivors: The Influences of Identity Centrality and Past Perceptions of Discrimination," *Cultural Diversity and Ethnic Minority Psychology* 20, no. 1 (2014): 75–86, https://psycnet.apa.org/doi/10.1037/a0033352; A. Bombay, R. J. McQuaid, F. Schwartz, A. Thomas, H. Anisman, and K. Matheson, "Suicidal Thoughts and Attempts in First Nations Communities: Links to Parental Indian Residential School Attendance Across Development," *Journal of Developmental Origins of Health and Disease* 10, no. 1 (2019): 123–31, https://doi.org/10.1017/S2040174418000405; Donna L. Feir, "The Intergenerational Effects of Residential Schools on Children's Educational Experiences in Ontario and Canada's Western Provinces," *International Indigenous Policy Journal* 7, no. 3 (2016) https://doi.org/10.18584/iipj.2016.7.3.5; Kimberly Matheson, Amy Bombay, Kaylyn Dixon, and Hymie Anisman, "Intergenerational Communication Regarding Indian Residential Schools: Implications for Cultural Identity, Perceived Discrimination, and Depressive Symptoms," *Transcultural Psychiatry* 57, no. 2 (2020): 304–20.

12 "Cant" is a phrase Haudenosaunee use when we speak about someone who has passed on.
13 Elizabeth Graham, *The Mush Hole: Life at Two Indian Residential Schools* (Heffle Publishing, 1997), 7–40; Arja Rautio, Ruby Miller, Sandra A. Juutilainen, and Lydia Heikkilä, "Structural Racism and Indigenous Health: What Indigenous Perspectives of Residential School and Boarding School Tell Us? A Case Study of Canada and Finland," *International Indigenous Policy Journal* 5, no. 3 (2014): 1–18, https://doi.org/10.18584/iipj.2014.5.3.3. See also Alison Norman, "'Our Strength Comes from the Land': the Hybrid Culinary Traditions of the Six Nations of Grand River in the Early Twentieth Century," *Cuizine* 6, no. 2 (2015), https://doi.org/10.7202/1033506ar.
14 Truth and Reconciliation Commission of Canada, *The Survivors Speak: A Report of the Truth and Reconciliation Commission of Canada* (Truth and Reconciliation Commission of Canada, 2015), https://nctr.ca/records/reports/#highlighted-reports.
15 Robert Gary Miller, "Mush Hole Remembered: R. G.," Woodland Cultural Art Exhibit, 2008; J. S. Milloy, *A National Crime: The Canadian government and the Residential School System* (University of Manitoba Press, 2017).
16 Clifford M. Lytle and Vine Deloria Jr., *American Indians, American Justice* (University of Texas Press, 1983), 240.
17 Vern Morrissette and Brad McKenzie, "Social Work Practice with Canadians of Aboriginal Background: Guidelines for Respectful Social Work," *Envision: The Manitoba Journal of Child Welfare* 2, no. 1 (2003): 13–39.
18 Bill Lee, "Colonialization and Community: Implications for First Nations Development," *Community Development Journal* 27, no. 3 (1992): 211–19.
19 Chandra Maracle and Ian Mosby, "The Mush Hole: Colonial Food Legacies Among the Haudenosaunee," Earth to Tables Legacies, accessed 6 June 2021, https://earthtotables.org/essays/mush-hole/.
20 Ian Mosby, "Administering Colonial Science: Nutrition Research and Human Biomedical Experimentation in Aboriginal Communities and Residential Schools," *Histoire sociale / Social History* 46, no 1 (2013): 145–72, https://doi.org/10.1353/his.2013.0015.
21 Priscilla Settee and Shailesh Shukla, "Introduction," in *Indigenous Food Systems: Concepts, Cases, and Conversations*, ed. Shailesh Shukla and Priscilla Settee (Canadian Scholars, 2020), 6–13.
22 Vandana Shiva, "Monocultures of the Mind—Understanding the Threats to Biological and Cultural Diversity," *Indian Journal of Public Administration* 39, no. 3 (July 1993): 237–48, https://doi.org/10.1177/0019556119930304.
23 Dawn Morrison, "Reflections and Realities: Expressions of Food Sovereignty in the Fourth World," in *Indigenous Food Systems: Concepts, Cases, and Conversations*, ed. Shailesh Shukla and Priscilla Settee (Canadian Scholars, 2020), 17–38.
24 James Daschuk, *Clearing the Plains: Disease, Politics of Starvation and the Loss of Indigenous Life* (University of Regina Press, 2019); Ian Mosby, "Administering Colonial Science," 145–72.
25 John L. Cayer (Indigenous Knowledge Keeper and grandfather) in discussion with author Bonnie Freeman, February 1979.
26 Lina Sunseri, *Being Again of One Mind: Oneida Women and the Struggle for Decolonization* (UBC Press, 2011), 2–3.
27 Dawn Morrison, "Indigenous Food Sovereignty: A Model for Social Learning," in *Food Sovereignty in Canada: Creating Just and Sustainable Food Systems*, ed. H. Wittman, N. Wiebe, and A. A. Desmararais (Fernwood Publishing, 2011), 97–113.
28 Harvey Longboat (Six Nations Knowledge Keeper) in discussion with author Bonnie Freeman, October 1995.
29 Settee and Shukla, "Introduction," 6–13.

PART 5
The New England Company and the Mohawk Institute

Figure 0.9. Boys farming at Mohawk Institute, 1943.
Source: General Synod Archives, Anglican Church of Canada

10

A Model to Follow? The Sussex Vale Indian School

Thomas Peace

It is common to hear the Mohawk Institute referred to as "Canada's first residential school." Though this statement may be technically correct, it cultivates a misunderstanding that obscures rather than illuminates the broader history of residential schooling in Canada. In addition to early French, Catholic proto-residential schools, which laid the groundwork for later Catholic residential schools during the nineteenth and twentieth centuries, on the anglophone, Protestant side there was also, in fact, a school that preceded the Mohawk Institute, and, from its failure, the Mohawk Institute—among several other New England Company initiatives—was built. Known as "The Academy for Instructing and Civilizing the Indians," the school, built in 1787 in Sussex Vale, New Brunswick, could also be considered the first residential school in Canada. Though the residential school system's Catholic roots share a very different lineage—anchored in Récollet, Jesuit, and Ursuline missionization during the seventeenth century—understanding Sussex Vale and the New England Company helps explain why residential schools became such problematic and pervasive institutions in English Canada.[1] If we want to understand how the Mohawk Institute was created, we must first look to the Protestant missionary efforts that shaped northeastern North America leading up to the school's founding. These efforts originated in New England in the early to mid-seventeenth century.

The New England Company

The New England Company (NEC) was founded in England by an act of Parliament in 1649. Its purpose was to build upon the work of English

275

Congregationalist missionaries, such as John Eliot and Thomas Mayhew, who had been proselytizing among the First Peoples of Massachusetts for nearly two decades. Seeing fruit in such work, the Company sought to extend these ecclesiastic labours by building "universities, schools and nurseries of literature, settled for further instructing and civilizing" Indigenous populations into English culture, society, and faith.[2] Based in England, the NEC's incorporation empowered sixteen men to make the Company's key decisions. Their purpose was to acquire land and solicit subscriptions to support the Company's missionary work in North America. In its 1661 charter, the Company was likewise empowered to appoint commissioners based in North America to oversee local operations.[3] By the late seventeenth century the local commissioners comprised the colonial elite. Often chaired by the governor of Massachusetts, the other commissioners were prominent businessmen, officials, and clergy from the colony.[4]

The reporting network for the early Company was anchored in English university culture and laid the groundwork for settler-colonial systems of control. From the early 1660s, funds for two missionary teachers were to be disbursed through the president's office at Harvard College and reported through the president's office of Trinity College at Oxford.[5] Though funded through other structures, and never very successful, Harvard itself during these years aspired to welcome Indigenous students, founding a short-lived "Indian College" in 1655; it continued to disburse NEC funds through to the American Revolution. According to Jean Fitz Hankins, the majority of NEC missionaries were Harvard graduates, as were several members of the local board in Boston.[6]

Structured in this way—through a nascent university system—the NEC itself was much more focused on evangelism and day schooling than it was interested in concerns about higher education. Initially targeting Massachusetts, Pawkunnakut, Nipmuc, and Montauk populations, the Company met only marginal successes as many First Peoples were reluctant to engage with the English newcomers.[7] What "gains" the Company might have seen were mostly found in John Eliot's fourteen "praying towns,"[8] each with a school; in some ways these communities served as precursors to the development of the reserve/reservation system. As is well-documented, these advances were not just Eliot's to claim; throughout his work, Eliot collaborated with Indigenous men such as the Montauk Cockenoe, Massachusetts men Job Nesuton and Montequassum, and the Nipmuc Wowaus (James Printer), each of whom helped Eliot learn, print, and otherwise use the languages of the land.[9] Where church and school may have made a long-lasting impact, it was more immediate circumstances and local actors than NEC influence that facilitated how Indigenous peoples interacted with these institutions.

It was not until the eighteenth century, however, that the Company began to expand geographically. Over the course of New England's evangelical Great Awakening, the Company's work extended its scope to target westward nations. During the 1740s, the NEC began to pursue the Haudenosaunee as potential prospects. Though the Society for the Propagation of the Gospel (SPG) was already active in Kanien'kehá:ka (Mohawk) communities, the roots of the NEC-Haudenosaunee relationship were slowly developed alongside these efforts; the Company sent two itinerant preachers to them after 1745.[10] By the 1760s, as a child, well-known Kanien'kehá:ka leader Thayendanegea (Joseph Brant) attended Moor's Indian Charity School, run by Eleazar Wheelock in Lebanon, Connecticut, and partially funded by the NEC; though his son Tekarihogen (John Brant) did not attend the school, Tekarihogen's two older brothers, Joseph and Jacob, attended between 1800 and 1803.[11] Although missionary-supported schooling for the Haudenosaunee was primarily driven by the SPG in its early years, the NEC's own involvement with the Confederacy dates back to the 1740s and '50s. Specifically, the relationship between the Brant family and the NEC remains one that requires additional research.

The important point here is to recognize that the NEC is the longest-serving Protestant missionary organization in the northeastern part of North America. The structures upon which it sought to build—namely, the university, printed books, and segregated praying towns—continued to underpin its work for well over two centuries. The Harvard Indian College and Moor's Indian Charity School excepted, these early efforts were mostly local in nature and centred upon Christian missionary work in Indigenous communities and nations. Though more work is needed here, the organization's relationship with the Haudenosaunee Confederacy dates to before the American Revolution and the subsequent relocation of some of the Haudenosaunee Confederacy to the Grand River and Bay of Quinte. The Company's more direct involvement with the Haudenosaunee did not really begin until the 1820s, when Tekarihogen, whose family was deeply involved with colonial schooling, approached the NEC about supporting a school in the community.

How Sussex Vale Operated

What happened with Sussex Vale marks a significant transition from the NEC's earlier history in New England. Unlike its more localized efforts on the Indigenous territories that the English increasingly saw as southern New England, at Sussex Vale the NEC sought to meet its broader evangelical and assimilationist goals by establishing a residential facility that would remove Indigenous children from the influence of their families. Unlike in New England, the school was located in the borderland between the Mi'kmaw and Wolastoqiyik homelands, where the Company had never worked before. With these nations tightly allied with the Catholic Church—a legacy of nearly two centuries of alliance with the French—the goal of the school was to convert these children to Protestantism, as well as teach them English and a skill set that would prepare them for the society that early New Brunswickers hoped to build. With their "education" complete, the Company's commissioners hoped, these students would return to their families, affecting similar religious, cultural, and linguistic changes in their home communities.

Sussex Vale was managed by the who's who of New Brunswick society. At various times the local NEC Board of Commissioners included Lieutenant-Governor Thomas Carleton, George Leonard, Ward Chipman, Edward Winslow, Joshua Upham, William Hazen, and George Proulx. These men were some of New Brunswick's most significant early leaders. Many of them were instrumental in lobbying for New Brunswick to be partitioned from Nova Scotia, becoming its own separate Loyalist colony. They served on the Legislative Council, in the militia, and in key administrative positions. Chipman was a Harvard graduate (like Winslow and Upham) and acted as the colony's first solicitor general; he also prepared the charter for the city of Saint John and was instrumental in setting up the colonial legal system.[12] With several additional responsibilities, the amount of time members of the NEC's board could allocate to the school was minimal. The actual operation of the school, therefore, was overseen by Oliver Arnold, the school master and local Anglican missionary, and—after reorganization in 1807—Major General John Coffin, the school's superintendent. NEC oversight of Arnold and Coffin was minimal.[13]

The school was located along the upper banks of the Kennebecasis River in the community today known as Sussex Corner. There, Loyalists from the American Revolution settled in the late 1780s, moving upriver from Saint John as the population grew. Some settler children also attended the school. The location was chosen because George Leonard, treasurer of the local commissioners, resided there, and he soon took Arnold under his wing.[14] In 1804, Edward Winslow described the setting with these words: "The academy being placed in the centre of a fertile tract of country, and surrounded by wealthy & independent inhabitants, the Indians could not fail to observe their manners and to profit by comparing the comfortable effects of the industry of the white people with the miserable consequences of their own indolent folly."[15] In addition to describing the school site, another point drawn out by Winslow's letter was the association of the school with the hoped-for removal of the Mi'kmaq and Wolastoqiyik from their lands. Though Micah Pawling has demonstrated that this removal was never complete,[16] the purpose of the school was to equip these people for the world early New Brunswickers planned to build. There was no place for either of these nations in this vision. The plan was to have Mi'kmaw and Wolastoqiyik families reside permanently near the settlement, adopt agriculture, and send their children to school, eventually assimilating into the settler society developing around them.

Arnold shared much in common with British missionaries working in New England and New York in the decades before the revolution. Like Eleazar Wheelock, Samuel Kirkland, and other prominent New England missionaries, Arnold was educated at Yale, completing his studies just as the revolution began. Like them, he saw school as a useful tool to help Indigenous peoples peacefully navigate the foreign occupation of their land. Little is known about Arnold's activities during the war, but by 1783 he had arrived in Saint John and was working with George Leonard. Four years later, he had moved to Sussex Vale to take up his teaching position. In recognition of his role with the NEC, he was ordained by Anglican Bishop Charles Inglis, receiving a government salary, a stipend from the SPG, as well as his NEC income and a Company home. Over the course of his career, Arnold also served as a justice of the peace.[17] Though he sometimes claimed otherwise, he was compensated handsomely for his efforts.

At first, the Sussex Vale school served to consolidate isolated local schools that had popped up across the colony in the intervening years. We only know about these early schools because of their relationship to the plans for consolidation, though it seems like a few day schools were up and running by the time the Sussex Vale plan was hatched.[18] With the opening of Sussex Vale, for example, Frederick Dibblee, who had been teaching as many as twenty-two Wolastoqiyik adults and children at Fredericton, had his salary removed; the freed-up funds were used to support two other missionary teachers at Miramichi and Memramcook.[19] There were clearly more efforts to school the Mi'kmaq and Wolastoqiyik than there is evidence that has withstood the tests of time. The prospect of these schools should not be forgotten. In fact, it was not until the mid-1790s that plans to consolidate efforts at Sussex Vale were cemented.[20]

In 1797, the local NEC board drafted instructions for the schoolmaster.[21] The routine at the school was clear. Six days per week were to be spent in exercises of reading and writing, with the school master responsible for attendance, while on Sundays (when the missionary was present) the children were to attend church. The schoolmaster was under relatively strict supervision. He was to keep detailed records of the students, including their arrival and departure, and present it to the board each February; quarterly, the board was also to receive a report on each student's academic progress. Few of these procedures seem to have been followed, and according to historian Judith Fingard, the school—such as it was—remained more oriented to a segregated group of colonial children than the school's Mi'kmaw or Wolastoqiyik charges;[22] the records I have consulted are not good enough to closely detail the differences between how Indigenous and colonial children experienced the school.

Unsurprisingly, with hindsight, Sussex Vale's early years resulted in utter failure. Few students attended, and following the resignation of three commissioners, the decision was made in 1804 to close the school. This failure, in the eyes of the commissioners who left, stemmed from the fact that there was little Wolastoqiyik or Mi'kmaw interest in the school, while its operation cost the Company significant money (about £800 per year) to entice families to send their children. Furthermore, the three men felt that the school could only do its work if the children were removed from their homes.[23]

In 1807, a new plan arose. Blending elements that we would later see in the residential school system and the Sixties Scoop, the local commissioners planned to remove young children—some in their infancy—from their families and place them in English families under indenture, a type of bound labour determined by contract with the student's parents. Using cash payments and clothing given to the children's parents, the Company was able to recruit just over fifty children before the school closed in the late 1820s. In its first year of operation, the Company sent over £1,000 in cash and goods to support this work.[24] Given the associated pressures on Mi'kmaw and Wolastoqiyik populations during these years—whereby the expansion of settler private property increasingly restricted access to land

and resources—it seems likely that families of the children indentured made such difficult decisions in hopes of better times to come.[25] Judith Fingard notes that most of the students came from families who were relatively isolated from other Mi'kmaw and Wolastoqiyik communities; students in later years were often the children of the students who had attended earlier.[26] White children also attended the school. They were taught separately, however, and were not removed from their families. An 1815 report claimed thirty-five Mi'kmaw and Wolastoqiyik children attended the school.[27] The relationship between the white, Mi'kmaw, and Wolastoqiyik children at the schools is not clear from the documentary record that has survived.

By this point in time, Arnold and his family used the "school" for their own financial and personal benefit. According to Fingard, Arnold made somewhere between £130 and £190 annually for his work with the Company, and kept between four and seven indentured children to run his household.[28] In Fingard's words, "the indentured children became virtual slaves to the leading families of Sussex Vale."[29] These abuses, and others, brought systemic funding of Arnold's work to a halt in 1816, though some funds continued to flow into the project for well over a decade more.[30] No matter what perspective one takes about the school, it was never on solid ground, and almost always harmful to its charges.

The School Routine and Its Failure

The relationship between the Company's board and the local commissioners was always somewhat rocky. From the outset of the revised 1807 scheme, board members in England expressed concern about the age at which children were removed from their families, their inability to learn their own language, as well as the general safety of children indentured to specific families.[31] In the early 1820s, the NEC commissioned Walter Bromley, a prominent social reformer in Nova Scotia, to investigate the school. Much of what we know about the school's operation comes from his report. A few years later, in 1825–6, Anglican missionary John West was charged with investigating the school as well. Both reports were damning, providing insight into what daily life must have been like for the children.

It is difficult to determine Sussex Vale's curriculum but it is clear that there were several aspects of school life that hindered student learning. In addition to the manual labour expected of students, many children also lived far away. In 1822, for example, seven children lived several miles from the school; the closest of these students lived three miles away, the farthest lived twenty-two miles away. For the students who did attend regularly,

Bromley explained that they were proficient in bookkeeping, basic arithmetic and multiplication, the reading of religious texts and catechism, and some basic spelling and writing.[32] Four years later, West believed that the quality of schooling had improved in more recent years.[33]

Formal curriculum, though, was not the school's primary focus. Rather, by the 1810s, the NEC commissioners turned their attention to indenturing Mi'kmaw and Wolastoqiyik children. In 1822, for example, the school's superintendent was given responsibility to select "Indian Children and place them out in English Families as Apprentices and to report to the Commissioners and through them to the Company the employment and conduct of each child separately."[34] Four years later, West claimed that settlers "purchased" these children at ages between one and three, their parents having been "unnaturally induced to part with their children" by a weekly allowance and some additional money from the NEC.[35] West did not mince words. The school might have been an effective academy for general teaching and learning, but—in his words—whatever gains made were "counteracted by the generally bad examples they witnessed [and] the degradation which they naturally feel under an involuntary and indented servitude."[36]

These were not idle allegations either. West's report is absolutely damning. Abuse of the school's charges was rife. In recounting the experiences of two young girls, who upon leaving their apprenticeship wandered "the roads with loss of character," West claims that this was the case for almost all the girls who attended the school. The evidence that the Anglican missionary put forth was the "bastard children by the white men." To be cautious, it is important to note that West frames these children as mostly born because of sex out of wedlock, rather than the result of sexual assault. The issue of consent goes unaddressed. In 1809, for example, one of Arnold's indentured servants, the Wolastoqiyik girl Molly Ann Gell, claimed that someone had carried her "into the Bushes and Against her Will forced her to Comply with his Wishes." She bore a son—who was also indentured to Arnold—and later recanted this story, claiming it was Arnold's own son who had seduced her in his home.[37] Another woman complained to West during her pregnancy of having been seduced by a local white farmer.[38] It is hard today to read West's report and not see in it a sickening culture of racialized sexual abuse condoned by the settler community at Sussex Vale.

The school was a complete disaster. Both Bromley's and West's reports demonstrate that few students left Sussex Vale with the skills for which the NEC had hoped. Furthermore, and foreshadowing some of the real horrors of the residential school system, some students returned home and—if we can trust West's account—were complained about as burdens in their own communities.³⁹ The difficulties for many Indigenous students in returning home is a well-documented result of this type of schooling, seen clearly in early seventeenth-century Récollet and Jesuit efforts to school First Peoples and right up until, and beyond, the closure of the residential school system.⁴⁰

Though Sussex Vale closed in 1826, eighteen apprentices were left behind in the community.⁴¹ Even though Bromley critiqued the school's work in 1822, and John West did so again in 1826, as late as 1831, some children remained indentured. The latter years of their contracts were deemed the most profitable and their masters were unwilling to forgo their labour.⁴² A nineteenth-century Company history claimed that the NEC's role in New Brunswick ended in 1836.⁴³

The New England Company Looks West

Bromley's and West's reports were followed by changes in procedure but not in emphasis. No longer would the Company work through local boards, nor would they use the apprenticeship model. That noted, upon receiving Bromley's report, the board in England shut down Sussex Vale and instead cast their gaze further westward, where Protestant missionaries were seemingly having greater success. Immediately, the Company began supporting missionary work at Grand River, Rice and Chemong Lakes, the Bay of Quinte, and Garden River. All four missions were locations where we can trace the roots of the Canadian residential school system. The banks of the Grand River became the home of the Mohawk Institute, on Rice Lake was built the Alderville Industrial School, and Garden River was where the Shingwauk and Wawanosh Homes began. Though no specific colonial school was built on the Bay of Quinte, it is a place of long-standing significance in the contest and negotiation over colonial schooling; it was also the site of a Methodist mission village during the 1820s and '30s, and day schools built later in the century.⁴⁴

Of these efforts, the Mohawk Institute's roots, in particular, anchor tightly into the closing of the school at Sussex Vale. Rather than imposing its school on an unsuspecting and relatively distant society, the NEC's arrival at Six Nations was, at least partially, at their request. In 1822, while in England lobbying for Six Nations' land rights, Tekarihogen requested that the Company build a mission and school in his community.⁴⁵ It was in this context that, after he visited Sussex Vale, John West travelled to the Six Nations at Grand River to investigate the possibility of beginning a new mission. There, with the support of Tekarihogen, he visited several day schools.

Although the NEC arrived on the Grand River with plans to try assimilative schooling again, the structure of the Mohawk Institute looked very different than Sussex Vale. Rather than being imposed from the outside, the NEC work at Six Nations was much more collaborative. Tekarihogen, for example, acted as agent for the Company, filing reports and drawing on their funds.[46] The school also operated in a broader context where day schools were much more common and established. In 1753, the Kanien'kehá:ka man Sahonwagy was appointed by the SPG missionary at Fort Hunter as the community day school teacher at nearby Canajoharie; he replaced Paulus Petrus, another Kanien'kehá:ka schoolteacher from the community.[47]

Sahonwagy was appointed to this position at a time when the British-Haudenosaunee alliance was tightening. Two years after he took up his position, William Johnson, a fur trader and large landholder in the region, was appointed British superintendent of Indian Affairs. Johnson, who had been previously married, entered into a long-term relationship with Konwatsi'tsiaiénni (Molly Brant), Thayendanegea's sister. Anglicanism, in addition to kinship—as Elizabeth Elbourne's work demonstrates—formed an important part of this alliance.[48] Given their missionary ties, schools might be considered through a similar strategic lens. In these early days, schools were institutions of negotiation and alliance.

It was within this context that Thayendanegea first attended school. Growing up in Canajoharie, it seems likely that the well-known Haudenosaunee leader attended the school taught by Sahonwagy before he went down to Eleazar Wheelock's Charity School. These early experiences shaped Thayendanegea's perspective about the value of schooling. When he negotiated his community's move to the Grand River, schooling remained a core requirement. In Frederick Haldimand's instructions to his officers, the governor made it clear that he had promised the Haudenosaunee that the government would build a school and provide "an allowance of £25. Sterlg. pr. annum for a School Master (whom they are to choose themselves)."[49] By 1787 there was a school established in the Mohawk Village with about sixty students in attendance, though it seems like the teacher ("an Old Yanky") was probably not from the community.[50] In 1810, a school was also noted in the community, though this document raised concerns that the school fostered "idleness" and bad manners, indicating that not everyone in the Confederacy was supportive of these initiatives.[51] Sixteen years later, George Ryerson (Egerton Ryerson's brother) wrote to Lieutenant-Governor

Peregrine Maitland "that the Mohawk School taught by William Hesse is faithfully conducted and attended, I cannot say one word in favour of the School in the Village by David Lawrence."[52] John West also visited that year and filed this report concerning the two schools:

> There were about twenty present, who were taught by a Mohawk named Laurence Davis [David Lawrence], some of them were just beginning to read, and of the thirty-four, who were said to belong to the school, twelve could read in the English Testament. Within a few miles of this school in the Mohawk village, is a school supported by the Society for the Propagation of the Gospel, which Mr. Brandt informed me consisted of about twenty children, with their schoolmaster William Hess.[53]

What becomes clear when all of this is taken together is the relatively continuous history of schooling at Grand River, from its establishment through to the founding of the Mohawk Institute. By the 1820s, in addition to the Kanien'kehá:ka schools, there were also schools attended by Skaru:reh (Tuscarora) and Onyata'a:ka (Oneida) children.

Although this chapter focuses on residential schools, what this trajectory shows is the need to understand the history of day schooling in order to adequately contextualize the development of the Mohawk Institute. In 1827, Robert Lugger, a Cambridge graduate, arrived on the Grand River as the first NEC missionary at Six Nations. Lugger's mission—like those of his counterparts at Rice and Chemong Lakes, the Bay of Quinte, and Garden River—was not focused on building boarding schools as much as it was to promote the assimilation of the peoples around these places through schooling. Within two years, the Company had built four schoolhouses at Six Nations; each had 100 acres of land associated with it, which—according to the Company—had been granted by Six Nations to the government for the NEC's use. These grants were accompanied by several others that—the Company feared—would lead to the gradual erosion of Six Nations' control over the land. A Company history, published in the 1870s, argued that it, along with Six Nations' leadership, opposed these alienations, although the NEC also acquired considerable land over this period (about 350 acres).[54]

The emphasis on day schools and the gradual erosion of Six Nations' land on the north shore of the Grand River are important to understand because they help frame how we think about the Mohawk Institute. By the late 1840s, after the Institute was established, few people from Six Nations were crossing from the south side of the river (where most people lived) over to the north, where the school was located.⁵⁵ The reserve was consolidated in 1847 after the loss of much of the Haldimand Tract, and lands were subsequently sold off. Community members who lived on lands to the north and south had to move to the newly defined reserve. The Mohawk Institute was now several kilometres away from the reserve. Perhaps because the school was farther away, in 1853, a decision was taken to expand the Institute to accommodate more children.⁵⁶ At the mission itself lived only about forty adults, most of whom had attended the Institute during its early years; there was hope within the Company that a larger building could serve children living too far from the day schools. A new building was opened in 1859, and the student population was capped at sixty.⁵⁷

Though the history above suggests a culture of schooling had developed at Six Nations by the end of the 1820s, this does not mean that colonial schooling went uncontested at Six Nations. In addition to the 1810 report, noted above, many members of the Haudenosaunee Confederacy resisted and rejected the Company's work. These lines in an 1834 NEC report resonate with sentiments that were likely widespread, but seldom shared with the missionaries responsible for creating the archival record: "in many instances the Indians show themselves insensible to these advantages, and continue irresolute and suspicious, and look upon all whites as intruders."⁵⁸ The solution to this problem, the NEC plotted, was to take ten boys and four to six girls away from their families and instruct them in the "arts, habits, and customs of civilized life."⁵⁹ Though the policy of indenture was not part of the emerging plan for the school, the removal of children from their families had returned to the Company's plan for Six Nations.

A big difference, however, from the plan at Sussex Vale was that the some leaders at Six Nations were involved in these decisions. In 1844, Henry Brant and "forty chiefs of the Onondaga Council Fire" expressed a hope to the NEC that "those of our youth who are educated at your institute, may hereafter, upon their assimilating themselves to the habits of the whites, receive each a farm for their good conduct. . . . The Chiefs are now anxious that 300 acres of the flats, in front of your Institute may be set apart for a farm."⁶⁰ Today, these words make little sense to us. When we remember, though, the long-standing practice of alliance, and the way it intersected with both Christianity and schooling, as well as the reality that, by 1844, land pressures were becoming even more acute at Six Nations than they were in the past, this decision becomes a little easier to understand. We must also remember that the "Onondaga Council Fire" was not necessarily representative of the Confederacy. In their report the following month, the NEC noted—in reference to their potentially gaining control over Six Nations' funds—that "the Indians themselves would have a good deal to say about their own funds, and would not like other persons to interfere, particularly the Pagan Indians, who do not approve of the Company's plans for civilization.... The Indians generally can manage their own affairs; they might perhaps make a better use of their money themselves, than agents appointed to act for them."[61] These words are perhaps some of the most accurate in the historical record about the early school. They call attention to the contested place of the NEC at Six Nations, as well as the reality that the important decisions were made by the Confederacy, not an outside body.

In thinking about this period in the school's history, I have found Rick Monture's work on Thayendanegea useful. In his book *We Share Our Matters*, Monture posits that Thayendanegea's goals in navigating Anglicanism and schools were always focused on ensuring that the Haudenosaunee would remain "sovereigns of the soil."[62] Taken with the concerns others in the Confederacy expressed about the NEC, we can see in these divergent approaches a common goal that sought the Confederacy's well-being in a time of rapid change.

The Mohawk Institute in Its Early Years

Originally designed to house a Mechanics' Institute, the first Mohawk Institute buildings were erected between 1829 and 1830 on land granted by the Six Nations' Council to the government for NEC use.[63] The school, whose focus was to be the teaching of "all sorts of handicraft trades,"[64] had four rooms initially. In two of these, girls were to be taught spinning and weaving, while in the remaining two boys would learn tailoring and carpentry.[65] Over the course of the decade, shoemaking, wagon making, and blacksmithing were important parts of the boys' curriculum, while girls—who were harder to recruit—focused on domestic tasks with an eye toward early childhood education. By 1839, the school was selling goods made by the students, though with little success.[66]

Though it was initially called a "Mechanics' Institute," the school at Six Nations never lived up to its name. The first Mechanics' Institutes were created just five years earlier in Glasgow, Liverpool, and London. In Canada, the first Mechanics' Institutes were founded in Montreal (1828) and Toronto (1830) at the same time as the school was being built at Six Nations.[67] Broadly, the aim of these new schools was "the instruction of their members in the principles of the Arts they practice, and in the various branches of Useful Knowledge."[68] Most Mechanics' Institutes had libraries and reading rooms and were focused on the continuing education of mostly professional adult men. What was built at Six Nations was nothing like this. Instead, the school there targeted children and—at least from the Company's perspective—always looked toward a day where children might be removed from their families. Here is Lugger's description of the school from June 1833, when the school was attended by thirty-six children: "The upper class read well in the Bible, repeat Scripture, Hymns, Catechisms, (Dr. Watts,) write a good round hand, cypher as far as division, and say all the tables. . . . As to understanding what they learn that is quite out of the question, and will be for years, until they are taken from their families and obliged to speak nothing but English, as I had proposed and planned for the proposed Institution."[69] This was a Mechanics' Institute in name only, and what Lugger reveals here is that the boarding school structure used at Sussex Vale was never far from mind. Removing children from their families was a recurrent strategy in the NEC's tool box to re-educate Indigenous children.

It is always difficult to assess the conditions in which the children lived. Reports tend to focus on the scholastic and vocational work of the school, as well as financial concerns, rather than its more day-to-day lived realities. What we do know from these early years is that, for the most part, the students were cared for by the "mechanic" and his family. Together, Mr. Smith, his wife, and daughters provided for the children's board, in addition to teaching them their trades and skills.[70] In 1841, vocational instruction was separated from housekeeping—because neither was going well—and the Smiths were replaced in their housekeeping responsibilities by an elderly couple without children.[71]

Given that the reports indicate that the Smiths had too much work to do initially, it did not take long for concerns to arise about the school's treatment of students. In October 1837, several parents complained, causing the NEC to revisit the school's operations.[72] Nearly a year later, a report to the Company noted that "the boys at the Institution are happy and contented; not one of them has attempted to depart the school for a long time," suggesting that earlier, the school had a problem with truancy.[73] Similarly in 1839, a report back to the Company offered the following observation: "It has been additionally gratifying, to find both the youths and their parents becoming every day, more and more contented with the treatment received; more sensible of the expediency of closer attention and stricter discipline; more inclined and better qualified, to take a juster view of the importance of knowledge imparted."⁷⁴ The implication here was that, in the past, students' desire to leave the school had posed problems. Though the root cause of student and parent concerns is unknown, that they were unhappy signals some problems at the school.

Lugger died in 1837 and was replaced by Abraham Nelles. Under Nelles's direction, the school doubled its student population in 1840, from twenty to forty students, the Company renovating the building to accommodate the increased numbers.⁷⁵ A report from the mid-1840s described the school's curriculum in this way:

> The mode of teaching is the same as that among the Common Schools for the Whites, and the Text-Books . . . are those recommended by the Provincial Board of Education, videlicet:—the Bible, Mavor's Spelling Book. English Reader, Daboll's Arithmetic, Murray's Grammar and a Geography. The instruction is carried on altogether in English. The children show as much aptitude in acquiring knowledge as the Whites.⁷⁶

Though far from what Mechanics' Institutes were becoming elsewhere in North America, by the end of its first decade, the structure of the Mohawk Institute had taken root. Blending manual labour and academic study, the school held promise as an institution that prepared its students for the settler society Anglo-Canadians were building around Six Nations. As the 1840s turned to the 1850s, however, farming came to occupy a much more prominent place in students' daily lives.

Overall, the success of the school was uncertain. Reports at this time emphasized that there was more demand from prospective students than there were spaces.⁷⁷ Front and centre in the NEC reports for these years was John Obey, who, upon leaving the school, ran a successful woodworking shop where he produced wagons, sleighs, tables, bedsteads, and chests.⁷⁸ There were also a handful of others noted. Most, though, seem to have been less enthusiastic in living up to the Company's vision. In 1844, Nelles observed, "I think all who have learned trades work a portion of their time at them. Though some may appear to adopt the indolent careless habit of their friends when they return home I feel sure the instruction they receive will be a benefit to them when those, perhaps, who have assisted in imparting it will not be here to observe it."⁷⁹ Even here—at Six Nations—where the school seems to have been far less physically damaging for its students than Sussex Vale, the degree of influence from the school remains unclear.

Nelles's proposed solution to this problem was further investment and a move toward farming. Rather than identify the boarding school approach as a flawed model, reinvestment and revision were the order of the day, as they would be for the next 150 years.

Conclusions

In many ways, the New England Company's work at Six Nations was fundamentally different from what took place at Sussex Vale. Though in the future the Mohawk Institute took on many of the characteristics of Sussex Vale—especially in terms of violence and sexual assault—in its early years, the Mechanics' Institute, and the boarding school that developed from it, were very distinct institutions. Where few Mi'kmaw and Wolastoqiyik families were interested in the Company's efforts along the Kennebecasis River, at Six Nations, the NEC had been invited into the community (at least by some) and—over time—dozens of families sent their children to the school. Where the curriculum at Sussex Vale can hardly be discussed using those words—it was unambiguously focused on exploiting the forced labour of children—at the Mohawk Institute the curriculum was discernible and comparable with that offered in nearby settler schools. Though there were obvious problems, by the end of the 1840s, the school was clearly part of the fabric of colonial schooling in a way never seen at Sussex Vale.

These differences ought not distract us from seeing the structural common ground between these schools. Though the history of the Mohawk Institute's founding was radically different from that of Sussex Vale, we can see that in the NEC, the two schools shared a common lineage, anchored as it was to the early history of Christian evangelism in New England. In the Mohawk Institute, the abuses of Sussex Vale might have been mitigated by early structures of community involvement and oversight, led initially by Tekarihogen, but over the school's nearly two centuries of operation this was not always the case. Survivor testimony by people like Bud Whiteye, who outlines the brutality of life at the twentieth-century Mohawk Institute, resonate strongly with the experiences of Molly Ann Gell and her early nineteenth-century Mi'kmaw and Wolastoqiyik peers.[80] As the chapters in *Behind the Bricks* demonstrate, it is important to understand this common foundation. As an organization founded to support Europe's resettlement of North America by engaging Indigenous societies in cultural, linguistic, and religious re-education, the New England Company—and the culture of residential schooling that developed from it—could never fully escape Sussex Vale's legacy.

NOTES

1. Good overviews of the school at Sussex Vale can be found in the Truth and Reconciliation Commission of Canada, *The Final Report of the Truth and Reconciliation Commission of Canada*, vol. 1, *Canada's Residential Schools: The History, Part 1, Origins to 1939* (McGill-Queen's University Press, 2015); and Judith Fingard, "The New England Company and the New Brunswick Indians, 1786–1826: A Comment on the Colonial Perversion of British Benevolence," *Acadiensis* 1, no. 2 (Spring 1972): 29–42. I have only cited specific material from these sources, though the general historical narrative here has been deeply shaped by these works. For a good understanding of early Catholic missions as they relate to residential schools, see Emma Anderson, *The Betrayal of Faith: The Tragic Journey of a Colonial Native Convert* (Harvard University Press, 2007).
2. The Company was renewed by charter after the restoration of Charles II in February 1661 with a similar mandate. New England Company, *History of the New England Company*, vol. 1 (Taylor and Co., 1871), 1. Henceforth cited as NEC, *History*.
3. NEC, *History*, 7.
4. Jean Fitz Hankins, "Bringing the Good News: Protestant Missionaries to the Indians of New England and New York, 1700–1775" (PhD diss., University of Connecticut, 1993), 43.
5. NEC, *History*, 12.
6. Hankins, "Bringing the Good News," 44.
7. Margaret Connell Szasz, *Indian Education in the American Colonies* (University of Nebraska Press, 1988), 107.
8. "Praying Towns" were places created by English missionaries for the purposes of religious conversion, but also acculturation toward English systems of law and culture. For someone like Eliot, religious conversion was deeply intertwined with cultural and political assimilation. Jean O'Brien's *Dispossession by Degrees* examines one of these communities—Natick—to demonstrate how the town's Indigenous residents navigated and resisted these efforts for well over a century. See Jean O'Brien, *Dispossession by Degrees: Indian Land and Identity in Natick, Massachusetts, 1650–1790* (Cambridge University Press, 1997).
9. Szasz lays out this history of collaboration well on pages 111–20. For a more complex discussion see O'Brien, *Dispossession by Degrees*, and Lisa Brooks, *Our Beloved Kin: A New History of King Philip's War* (Yale University Press, 2018).
10. NEC, *History*, 15.
11. Colin Calloway, *The Indian History of an American Institution: Native Americans and Dartmouth* (Dartmouth College Press, 2010), 70.
12. Phillip Buckner, "Ward Chipman," *Dictionary of Canadian Biography*, vol. 6 (henceforth *DCB*), University of Toronto/Université Laval, 2003–, http://www.biographi.ca/en/bio/chipman_ward_1754_1824_6E.html.
13. Fingard, "The New England Company," 41.
14. Fingard, 30.
15. Edward Winslow, "Notes Respecting the Indians and Acadians of New Brunswick," 1804, vol. 12-111, Winslow Papers, University of New Brunswick Libraries, accessed 13 May 2025, https://web.lib.unb.ca/winslow/pdf.cgi?img=./data/12/12_111_01_04.jpg.
16. Micah Pawling, "Wəlastəkwey (Maliseet) Homeland: Waterscapes and Continuity Within the Lower St. John River Valley, 1784–1900," *Acadiensis* 46, no. 2 (2017): 5–34, https://journals.lib.unb.ca/index.php/Acadiensis/article/view/25946.
17. Judith Fingard, "Oliver Arnold," *DCB*, http://www.biographi.ca/en/bio/arnold_oliver_6E.html.
18. A day school is an institution where the children attend during the day and return home to sleep.
19. "Instructions to be observed at the Academy established at Sussex Vale for the purpose of teaching and civilizing the Indian Nations; and by the missionaries appointed by the Board in the several districts," Leonard Family Fonds, New Brunswick Museum, Saint John, NB. See also George Leonard, 22 March 1791, letter 2, item 2, Historical Documents: Indian Academy Sussex, F242, New Brunswick Museum, and Darrel Butler, "Fredercik Dibblee," *DCB*, http://www.biographi.ca/en/bio/dibblee_frederick_6E.html.
20. Fingard, "The New England Company," 30.
21. "Instructions to be observed at the Academy established at Sussex Vale for the purpose of teaching and civilizing the Indian Nations; and by the missionaries appointed by the Board in the several districts."
22. Fingard, "The New England Company," 38.
23. Fingard, 30–2.
24. NEC, *History*, 23.

25   Fingard, "The New England Company," 34.
26   Fingard, 34.
27   NEC, *History*, 30–1.
28   Fingard, "The New England Company," 36.
29   Fingard, "Oliver Arnold."
30   Fingard, "The New England Company," 37.
31   Fingard, 34.
32   "General Report to the New England Company by their Committee appointed by Resolutions of the 9th May 1822 concerning the Company's affairs at home and abroad," Historical Documents: Indian Academy Sussex, F242, New Brunswick Museum.
33   Copy of the Report made to the New England Company by the Rev. John West M. A. after his visit to the Indian Academy at Sussex N.B. in 1825 and 1826 [26 September 1826], Historical Documents: Indian Academy Sussex, F242, New Brunswick Museum.
34   "General Report to the New England Company."
35   Copy of the Report made to the New England Company by the Rev. John West.
36   Copy of the Report made to the New England Company by the Rev. John West.
37   The Examination of Molly Ann Gell, 6 January 1809, Sussex Indian Academy Fonds, S65A-8, New Brunswick Museum. See also L. F. S. Upton, "Molly Ann Gell," *DCB*, http://www.biographi.ca/en/bio/gell_molly_ann_6E.html.
38   Copy of the Report made to the New England Company by the Rev. John West.
39   Copy of the Report made to the New England Company by the Rev. John West.
40   See Anderson, *The Betrayal of Faith*; Truth and Reconciliation of Canada, *The Final Report of the Truth and Reconciliation Commission of Canada*, vol. 5, *Canada's Residential Schools: The Legacy* (McGill-Queen's University Press, 2015).
41   Copy of the Report made to the New England Company by the Rev. John West.
42   Copy of Draft of letter by Judge Chipman, 25 February 1831, Historical Documents: Indian Academy Sussex, F242, New Brunswick Museum.
43   NEC, *History*, 40.
44   For more on this see Thomas Peace, "Indigenous Intellectual Traditions and Biography in the Northeast," *History Compass* 16, no. 4 (2018): 6.
45   Truth and Reconciliation Commission of Canada, *Final Report*, 1:70.
46   "History of the New England Company on the Grand River," in *The Valley of the Six Nations: A Collection of Documents on the Indian Lands of the Grand River*, ed. Charles M. Johnston (Champlain Society, 1964), 257. See also Major General H. C. Darling's report on the Six Nations, 24 July 1828, in Johnston, 292.
47   Gus Richardson, "Sahonwagy," *DCB*, http://www.biographi.ca/en/bio/sahonwagy_4E.html.
48   Elizabeth Elbourne, "Managing Alliance, Negotiating Christianity: Haudenosaunee Uses of Anglicanism in Northeastern North America, 1760s–1830s," in *Mixed Blessings: Indigenous Encounters with Christianity in Canada*, ed. Tolly Bradford and Chelsea Horton (University of British Columbia Press, 2016), 38–60.
49   Haldimand to de Peyster, November 1784, in Johnston, 52. See also "Means Suggested as the Most Probable to Retain the Six Nations and Western Indians in the King's Interest" in Johnston, 53.
50   See Sir John Johnson to Claus, 19 October 1787, in Johnston, *Valley of the Six Nations*, 236; and A Visit with Joseph Brant on the Grand River, 1792, in Johnston, 60.
51   The Educational Problems of the Confederacy about 1810, in Johnston, 245.
52   George Ryerson to Maitland, 9 June 1826, in Johnston, 252.
53   The Rev. John West's Description of Religion and Education among the Six Nations, 1826, in Johnston, 254.
54   NEC, *History*, 78–81. For a clearer discussion of the politics of land along the Grand River, see Susan M. Hill, *The Clay We Are Made Of: Haudenosaunee Land Tenure on the Grand River* (University of Manitoba Press, 2017).
55   NEC, *History*, 83.
56   NEC, 84.
57   NEC, 85.

58 NEC Report, 8 September 1834, in Elizabeth Graham, *The Mush Hole: Life at Two Indian Residential Schools* (Heffle Publishing, 1997), 45.
59 NEC Report, 8 September 1834, in Graham, 45.
60 Six Nations to NEC, 10 June 1844, in Graham, 51.
61 NEC Report, 19 July 1844, in Graham, 51.
62 Rick Monture, *We Share Our Matters: Two Centuries of Writing and Resistance at Six Nations of the Grand River* (University of Manitoba Press, 2014), chap. 1, 60.
63 NEC Report, 14 May 1829, in Graham, *The Mush Hole*, 44; NEC Report, 29 April 1831, in Graham, 45.
64 NEC Report, 8 July 1830, in Graham, 44.
65 NEC Report, 29 April 1831, in Graham, 45.
66 NEC Report, 1839, in Graham, 47.
67 Chad Gaffield, "Mechanics' Institutes," *Canadian Encyclopedia*, last modified 16 December 2013, https://www.thecanadianencyclopedia.ca/en/article/mechanics-institutes.
68 T. and E. Kelly, *Books of the People: An Illustrated History of the British Library* (Andre Deutsch, 1977), 67, as cited in Martyn Walker, "'For the Last Many Years in England Everybody Has Been Educating the People, but They Have Forgotten to Find Them Any Books': The Mechanics' Institutes Library Movement and Its Contribution to Working-Class Adult Education During the Nineteenth Century," *Library & Information History* 29 no. 4 (November 2013): 273.
69 NEC Report, June 1833, in Graham, *The Mush Hole*, 45.
70 NEC Report, 26 May 1840, and NEC Report, 24 November 1840, in Graham, 48.
71 NEC Reports for 1841, in Graham, 49.
72 NEC Report, 15 October 1837, in Graham, 46.
73 NEW Report, 3 July 1838, in Graham, 47.
74 NEC Report, 1839, in Graham, 47.
75 NEC Report, 24 February 1840, in Graham, 47.
76 Commissioners' Report, in Graham, 53.
77 NEC Reports, 6 January 1842 and 24 January 1843, in Graham 50.
78 NEC Report, 22 May 1843, in Graham, 50.
79 NEC Report, 22 February 1844, in Graham, 51. Nelles's report on 23 July 1844 lists children who have left the school and describes their current work. See NEC Report, 23 July 1844, in Graham, 52.
80 Bud Whiteye, *A Dark Legacy: A Primer on Residential Schools in Canada* (Woodland Cultural Centre).

11

Robert Ashton, the New England Company, and the Mohawk Institute, 1872–1910

William Acres

Roughly three decades after the Mohawk Institute's inception in the 1830s, church administrators decided to "modernize" the school. This work was to be completed under the leadership of Robert Ashton, the Mohawk Institute's third principal, who managed the Institute from 1872 until 1910, an important and lengthy period in the school's history. This chapter examines Ashton's influence on the Mohawk Institute, focusing on how he changed the school to a much stricter environment than had existed when Abraham Nelles, his predecessor, oversaw the Mohawk Institute. Robert Ashton modelled the supposedly improved Mohawk Institute after the industrial school at Feltham in England, where Ashton had worked; Feltham was intended to be a reformatory school for young offenders. This chapter's focused examination of Ashton's time as principal highlights several themes such as the significant influence a principal could exert and the impact he could have on the school, and, at times, the power struggles between school administrators and the church. In the end, Ashton's reforms were spurned, especially by students and community members, and likely greatly contributed to the burning down of the school in 1903 and the removal of Ashton as principal in 1910.

Consultation with English social reformer Florence Nightingale (best known as the founder of modern nursing) and others led the leadership of the New England Company (NEC) in the 1860s to seek out a new vision for the education of Indigenous peoples. Part of their motivation was to bring new ideas about industrial schooling on the English model to bear on schools such as the Mohawk Institute, together with new theories about physiology and mental discipline. Rather than industrial training, the emphasis would be on farming. Hence, the NEC planned for the cultivation of all their properties, including the two-hundred-acre Manual Labour Farm near the Mohawk Institute, which, to date, it had not utilized. The plan was to have these properties cultivated and tended by the students at the Institute. It was believed by authorities at the NEC that participation in farm and domestic labour would quell the children's instinct to return to the culture of their origins and that the work would instil new discipline and values in the students. If students were entirely engaged in this work, it was hoped, the "Indian" in the children would be replaced by a domestic, industrious labouring population, capable of earning a living, with a strong Christian component.

Another innovation promoted by some members of the NEC, among others, was the goal of removing what was sometimes referred to as the "contagion" of Indigenous culture through the application of hygienic principles and properly ventilated and secured residential facilities, bathing facilities, dry manure latrines, and other sanitary ideals. These ameliorative changes were frustrated by the 1858 Mohawk Institute building, which, by the early 1870s, was no longer fit for purpose. Mary Carpenter (1807–77), the sister of two Company members and a leading advocate of what were called Ragged Schools for indigent children in Bristol and elsewhere, visited the Mohawk Institute in 1873 with her brother and sister-in-law. The Carpenters, like Nightingale, were interested in cleanliness in all parts of the school, proper lavatories, bathing facilities, and the eradication of disease. While not all their reforms were possible—given that the 1858 structure did not meet any of their principal criticisms—the new head of the Mohawk Institute, Robert Ashton, was to try his hardest to ensure that the best British and imperial methods were put in place.

Before arriving at the Mohawk Institute, Ashton was influenced by another NEC member, Edward Mash Browell. Browell was a member of the Board of Visitors at the Middlesex Industrial School at Feltham, Middlesex, where a young Robert Ashton had been employed since 1861. The purpose of the Middlesex Industrial School was to reform the nearly criminalized, impoverished youth of some of London's worst neighbourhoods. Browell and others of the Company saw the benefit of importing into an Indigenous community the Middlesex school's designs and purposes.

The enactment of new ideas such as these meant new leadership for the Mohawk Institute would need to be recruited, as the current principal, Abraham Nelles (1805–84), the chief missionary of the Company's Grand River Station, was considered incapable of steering the radical changes proposed by Browell. Nelles's older mission was primarily Anglican, and his role was carried out almost independently of outside counsel. The Company replaced Nelles to minimize the Anglican influence so heavily promoted by the older missionaries of the NEC. By the spring of 1872, after interviews and consultation, the Company leadership settled on Robert Ashton (1842–1930) as the new superintendent, alongside his wife, Alice Turner Ashton (1840–1920). The Company's efforts were experimental but served as the foundation of what would be nearly forty years of the Ashtons' service at the Mohawk Institute. From his earliest days as superintendent, Ashton took his counsel almost entirely from the leadership of the NEC, following their directives and budgets and their decisions on how to expand the farm, work the children, and create a model school.

Some of the Ashtons' reports and journals remain.[1] Robert Ashton maintained an extensive correspondence with the NEC leadership on a wide variety of business: lands, money, expansion of farming, the admission and discharge of students, curricula and academic progress, and relations with the Canadian government. Much of the material in this chapter is drawn from these sources, which are found largely in the NEC's records, housed at the London Metropolitan Archives. As well, there are papers in the V. P. Cronyn Archives of the Diocese of Huron, at Huron University College. These materials ended up at the diocese due to litigation carried out between 1996 and 2006 by survivors of the Mohawk Institute, which meant the contents of historic superintendents' and principals' papers were released from the iron safe at the Institute and preserved by the last principal, William John Zimmerman, and his wife, Gladys. I treat these sources here primarily as NEC directives to Ashton, as they informed his very long tenure. What actually emerged from the execution of those directives from the NEC is yet another story.

Robert Ashton's four-decade tenure as superintendent of the Mohawk Institute began in November 1872 and concluded with his retirement on 31 December 1910. By that time, the men who sat on the Special Committee for Missions of the NEC were relieved when he departed. A successor had been chosen in 1907, but Ashton remained until he was replaced by his son, Nelles Ashton, during a visit by the Company's governor, John Walker Ford, and Herbert Henry Browell in 1910 to the NEC's Grand River Station. The

Ashton dynasty was saved only by an increase from the Department of Indian Affairs in the per-head capitation grant for students at the Institute in 1910. It was, nonetheless, a controversial decision to retain Nelles Ashton.

Ashton senior had become rigid and difficult to manage from London, England, the headquarters of the NEC's charitable work. The system he imposed on the Institute, with decades of support from the Special Committee and the members of the ancient charity, gained very lukewarm reviews. In 1908, when Company member W. F. Webster visited, he noted, in his very confidential report, that if the NEC was pleased with a "reformatory," then so be it. Clearly that was not the Company's intention; they had already planned different approaches to expending their influence on Canadian Indigenous populations, but Ashton was at the end of his usefulness to them.[2]

Ashton had been deaf alike to the politics of the Six Nations over the Company's claims to title on Six Nations lands and to the policies of both the government and the Anglican Church. Without diplomatic skills, he caused strife and bitterness. His power and severity in dealing with the leadership of the Confederacy Council, parents, educational interests, and students alike came from having created what amounted to a personal fiefdom at the Mohawk Institute. His exertions were met with three cases of arson in 1903. In April of that year, the Institute was razed and rebuilt at minimum expense. Three years later, a Company missionary, the Reverend James Leonard Strong at St. Paul's Kenyengeh, on the Six Nations, was met with glowing approval by the NEC for his suggestion to recast their mission by building new churches on the Tuscarora Reserve. Ashton's proposal for a hospital for contagious diseases was received with little enthusiasm, despite the fact that his son, Dr. Ernest Charles Ashton, was locally respected for his treatment of tuberculosis and other maladies devastating Indigenous peoples. Clearly, in the end, Ashton did not meet the goals of either the NEC or the Six Nations for the Mohawk Institute.

The Feltham Model: Ashton's Early Years

Ashton was hired as the school's principal in the spring of 1872 with a clear remit. He planned to impose a smaller version of the Middlesex Industrial School at Feltham, where he had previously been a schoolmaster. He brought his two small children to the Mohawk Institute, which he described as an unprofitable wreck of a place, with the children running the show.[3]

The industrial school model in place at Feltham, England, where Ashton worked as a schoolmaster from 1861 until his appointment at the Mohawk

Institute in the spring of 1872, was designed to cure the "sins" that were endemic in poor, urban families in Victorian London. Feltham's strict work schedule prepared young boys, aged eight to fourteen, for trades, the navy, or other work. Parents of these children were either absent, criminal, or incapable of controlling their children. While the boys were not entirely criminalized, they were there at the behest of the local justices of the peace acting under parliamentary statutes, most remanded for vagrancy and destitution. These "inmates"—a term also used at times by Ashton to describe the children at the Mohawk Institute—lived within a walled institution of immense size and complexity. There was a working farm designed for profit, a tailor's shop where all uniforms and repairs were done, a band for musical training, singing, and a long series of prayer times and double Sunday church services, strict (and parsimonious diets), and daily work and educational schedules on the half-day model. Work teams and distribution of all manner of work was enforced. Good conduct was rewarded.

These elements of Feltham would be adapted and used for the children at the Mohawk Institute. Ashton was to find the Feltham-style model entirely unknown at the Mohawk Institute when he arrived. Abraham Nelles, his predecessor, had subscribed to the view that the children were at the school to be educated. Nelles knew the community intimately; Ashton, though virtually ignorant, was keen to impose a new model for running the school. The overwhelming majority of Feltham boys were Church of England followers. Most of the Six Nations children at the Institute were within a Church of England—and later Anglican—system, but their acculturation was entirely different. The boys at Feltham lived communally. After the most recent dispossession of the Tuscarora Reserve in the early 1840s, the politics and culture at Six Nations were undergoing significant challenges. Sweeping legislation imposed the surveillance of resources, lands, and governance, and communal pressures, which a common educational system could only partly address. The children, by and large, lived with their families, and no legal authority had found these families incapable of raising their children. Feltham had been built for eight hundred boys, whereas the 1858 rebuilt Mohawk Institute, although enlarged over the years, was capable of housing a maximum of eighty "inmates." In addition, the Feltham standards and organization were inspected and subject to rigorous statutory requirements; this rarely happened at the Mohawk Institute.

The NEC was concerned that their chief missionary, Abraham Nelles, was unsuited to so modern a task as creating an Anglocentric universe designed for rapid "civilizing and Christianizing" of Six Nations children. It was their hope that Robert Ashton would instead design this new model. Moreover, it was an economic model dependent on farm production, rather than the trades and vocations of the English model. The success of Ashton's venture relied on a steady, and increasing, enrolment of students capable of sustained, hard physical work, on about 430 acres of property. Nelles's school had operated only about 70 acres of farmland. Ashton entered the politically fraught world of the NEC's Grand River Station, an agglomeration of properties—and policies—that the Company hoped in the later 1860s to meld into a thoroughly modern community with full surveillance, standards of behaviour, and model work.

When Ashton arrived, he confronted a situation entirely different from the conditions and students at the publicly funded, hugely staffed institution at Feltham—none of his charges were under the remand of justices of the peace. While there was no outright use of the justice system at the Institute, the Ashton regime would operate on intensive land cultivation, including orchards and a quasi-military discipline for both sexes. Indeed, Ashton's doctrine was that the children of the Six Nations had to adapt to the Feltham model, rather than the other way around.

In his prime, Robert Ashton had been a *force majeure*: he had imported the latest British ideals of the industrial school model and brought them to bear on a population of Indigenous children with whom he had no prior experience. These children were of mixed tribal and linguistic identities, both boys and girls, and ranged in ages from seven to eighteen. By the mid-1880s, he was considered something of an expert in Canadian Indigenous child education. At first, he followed the NEC line at every turn, most particularly in adapting the industrial school model. Ashton's vision was not a model that was universally approved, nor was it one derived from Canadian experience in Indigenous communities and education. But Ashton's increasing primacy within the NEC's Grand River Station allowed him funds and latitude to organize the institute as he saw fit. Now fifteen miles away from the Tuscarora Reserve, it was nonetheless an integral, not to say integrated, part of the "station" as a whole.

Quarrels among NEC missionaries had broken into open conflict by 1870–1 over attempts to create new mission "stations" on the Tuscarora Reserve. Where some members of the NEC wanted an innovative model of mission complete with public health rules, closely watched students, and a generally organized community, there was fierce resistance to this change among the older missionaries, such as Abraham Nelles and the Reverend Adam Elliott, as well as among the Confederacy chiefs, who were the

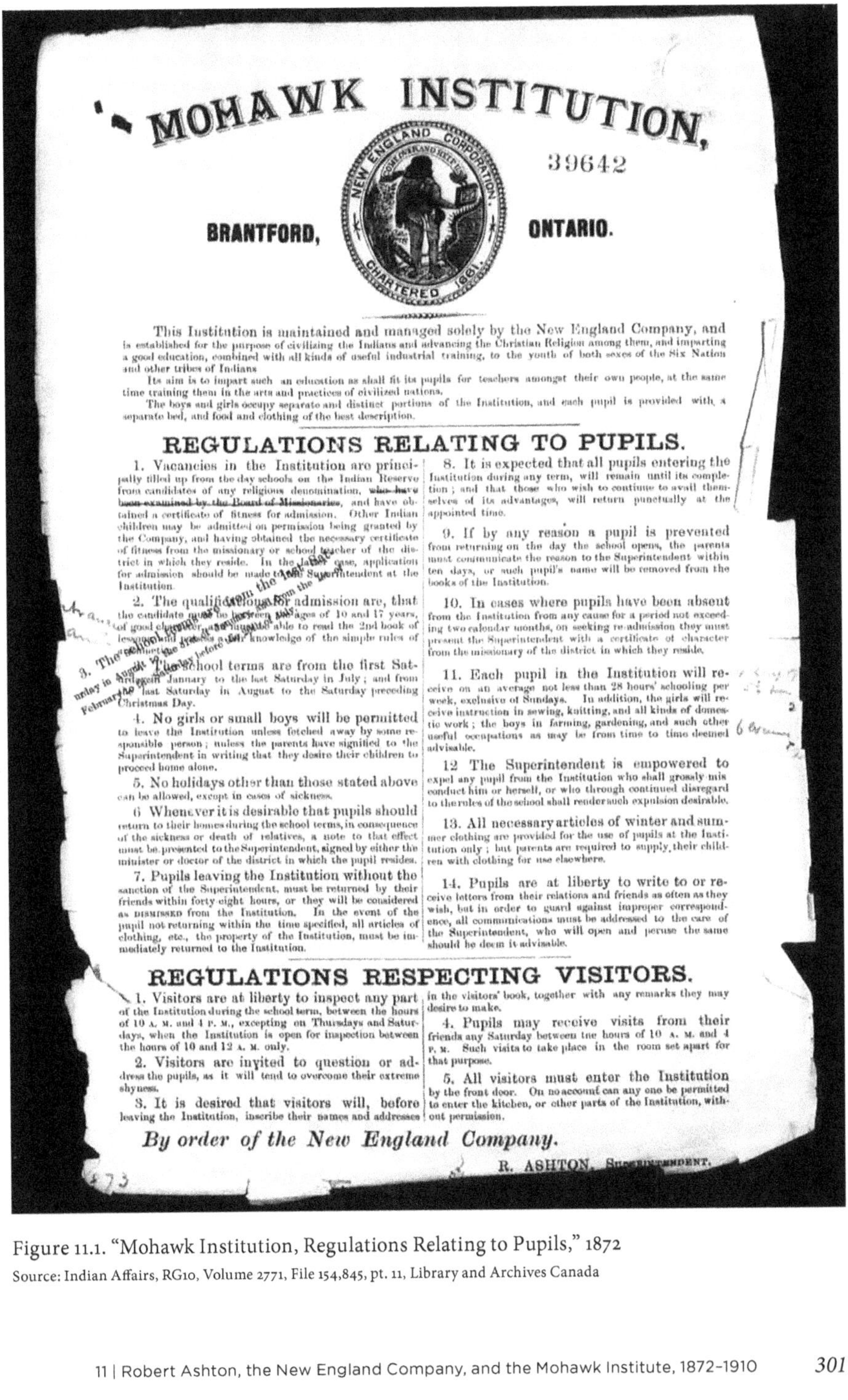

MOHAWK INSTITUTION,

39642

BRANTFORD, **ONTARIO.**

This Institution is maintained and managed solely by the New England Company, and is established for the purpose of civilizing the Indians and advancing the Christian Religion among them, and imparting a good education, combined with all kinds of useful industrial training, to the youth of both sexes of the Six Nation and other tribes of Indians.

Its aim is to impart such an education as shall fit its pupils for teachers amongst their own people, at the same time training them in the arts and practices of civilized nations.

The boys and girls occupy separate and distinct portions of the Institution, and each pupil is provided with a separate bed, and food and clothing of the best description.

REGULATIONS RELATING TO PUPILS.

1. Vacancies in the Institution are principally filled up from the day schools on the Indian Reserve from candidates of any religious denomination, who have been examined by the Board of Missionaries, and have obtained a certificate of fitness for admission. Other Indian children may be admitted on permission being granted by the Company, and having obtained the necessary certificate of fitness from the missionary or school teacher of the district in which they reside. In the latter case, application for admission should be made to the Superintendent at the Institution.

2. The qualifications for admission are, that the candidate must be between the ages of 10 and 17 years, of good character, must be taught to read the 2nd book of lessons, and possess a fair knowledge of the simple rules of arithmetic.

3. The school terms are from the first Saturday in January to the last Saturday in July; and from the last Saturday in August to the Saturday preceding Christmas Day.

4. No girls or small boys will be permitted to leave the Institution unless fetched away by some responsible person; unless the parents have signified to the Superintendent in writing that they desire their children to proceed home alone.

5. No holidays other than those stated above can be allowed, except in cases of sickness.

6. Whenever it is desirable that pupils should return to their homes during the school terms, in consequence of the sickness or death of relatives, a note to that effect must be presented to the Superintendent, signed by either the minister or doctor of the district in which the pupil resides.

7. Pupils leaving the Institution without the sanction of the Superintendent, must be returned by their friends within forty eight hours, or they will be considered as DISMISSED from the Institution. In the event of the pupil not returning within the time specified, all articles of clothing, etc., the property of the Institution, must be immediately returned to the Institution.

8. It is expected that all pupils entering the Institution during any term, will remain until its completion; and that those who wish to continue to avail themselves of its advantages, will return punctually at the appointed time.

9. If by any reason a pupil is prevented from returning on the day the school opens, the parents must communicate the reason to the Superintendent within ten days, or such pupil's name will be removed from the books of the Institution.

10. In cases where pupils have been absent from the Institution from any cause for a period not exceeding two calendar months, on seeking re-admission they must present the Superintendent with a certificate of character from the missionary of the district in which they reside.

11. Each pupil in the Institution will receive on an average not less than 28 hours' schooling per week, exclusive of Sundays. In addition, the girls will receive instruction in sewing, knitting, and all kinds of domestic work; the boys in farming, gardening, and such other useful occupations as may be from time to time deemed advisable.

12. The Superintendent is empowered to expel any pupil from the Institution who shall grossly misconduct him or herself, or who through continued disregard to the rules of the school shall render such expulsion desirable.

13. All necessary articles of winter and summer clothing are provided for the use of pupils at the Institution only; but parents are required to supply their children with clothing for use elsewhere.

14. Pupils are at liberty to write to or receive letters from their relations and friends as often as they wish, but in order to guard against improper correspondence, all communications must be addressed to the care of the Superintendent, who will open and peruse the same should he deem it advisable.

REGULATIONS RESPECTING VISITORS.

1. Visitors are at liberty to inspect any part of the Institution during the school term, between the hours of 10 A. M. and 4 P. M., excepting on Thursdays and Saturdays, when the Institution is open for inspection between the hours of 10 and 12 A. M. only.

2. Visitors are invited to question or address the pupils, as it will tend to overcome their extreme shyness.

3. It is desired that visitors will, before leaving the Institution, inscribe their names and addresses in the visitors' book, together with any remarks they may desire to make.

4. Pupils may receive visits from their friends any Saturday between the hours of 10 A. M. and 4 P. M. Such visits to take place in the room set apart for that purpose.

5. All visitors must enter the Institution by the front door. On no account can any one be permitted to enter the kitchen, or other parts of the Institution, without permission.

By order of the New England Company.

R. ASHTON, Superintendent.

Figure 11.1. "Mohawk Institution, Regulations Relating to Pupils," 1872

Source: Indian Affairs, RG10, Volume 2771, File 154,845, pt. 11, Library and Archives Canada

hereditary governing body of the Six Nations. Another resistant missionary, the Reverend James Chance, recently displaced by the NEC's closure of their Garden River mission near Sault Ste-Marie, arrived in the summer of 1871. In that same year, Nelles left for a surprise visit to the NEC to urge them to remove a fourth missionary, the Reverend Robert J. Roberts, about to undertake a new "station" at Cayuga, in the eastern portion of the Six Nations. Roberts was the NEC's up-and-coming man in the 1860s who had established the new mission church at Kenyengeh (taken over by Chance). He, like Ashton, enjoyed the support of leading modernizers in the NEC.[4]

Superintendency and Consolidation of Power

NEC Members and political luminaries Sir James Carter and Senator Amos Edwin Botsford had constructed a system where missionaries at parishes had superintendency of particular schools; Ashton was one of five school superintendents. He was not considered a missionary and, thus, had no place on the Board of Missionaries devised in the regulations. These new regulations of November 1872 saw admissions to the Institute managed by the Company's Board of Missionaries, headed by Nelles, and assigned to school districts mapped by the Reverend Robert J. Roberts (of the Cayuga Station). Ashton's role as superintendent was set down in detail. Carter's regulation had rules for the missionaries as well, but Ashton's extensive duties, printed in the Company's report of 1871–2, envisioned sweeping responsibilities.[5] As the Special Committee outlined in a letter on 12 September 1871, there were to be "certain changes to the management of the Mohawk Institution which were in the contemplation of the New England Company, having for their object to bring the Institution to a state of efficiency and usefulness to the Indian races on the Reserve."[6] Efficiency was to be Ashton's forte. The instructions were as follows:

> The Superintendent
>
> 1. The Superintendent shall have the control, and be responsible for the management of the Institution, Manual Labour School, and Farm, and upon him shall devolve the due exertion of the directions of the Company, or Special Committee in relation thereto;

2. The School Teachers at the Institution shall be independently recommended to the Company by the Superintendent, and the Board of Missionaries, and appointed by the Company.

3. Vacancies in the Institution will be filled up from the Day Schools on the Indian Reserve, from candidates who have been examined by the Board of Missionaries, and have obtained a certificate of fitness for admission. Other Indian children may be admitted on permission being granted by the Special Committee of the Company, and having passed an examination by the Board of Missionaries and obtained the necessary certificate of fitness.

4. The Superintendent is to keep a list of all of the children in the Institution, showing the dates of their admission, their age when admitted, the names and occupations of their parents, and from what school on the Reserve or elsewhere they came; together with a note of the state of knowledge at the time of admission.

5. He is to keep a list of the children as they leave the Institution; to keep up a communication with them, and to chronicle their progress in life, as far as is practicable for four years afterwards.[7]

6. He is to forward every quarter to the Special Committee a report of the actual state of the Institution, in the form required by the Committee.

7. He is to provide for the daily board of the establishment according to a dietary sanctioned by the Special Committee; also to be responsible for the cleanliness and good order of the dormitories and other rooms inhabited by or used by the children; also to advance with all diligence the industrial, moral, and religious education of the establishment; and is expected to interest himself in all that may conduce to the good of those that are placed under his care. He will conduct family Prayer night and morning with the children, and attend with them Public Worship every Sunday.[8]

The superintendent and the board were meant to work closely together. Students were recruited from the day schools under the missionary stations at Kenyengeh, Tuscarora, Mohawk, and Cayuga under examination/approval by these clergy. Various models, including Indigenous trustees for each school, were tried. But in effect, all were run by Anglican clergy with "superintendence" of NEC schools under the licence of the bishop of Huron. By the late 1870s these men were fully enmeshed with others in the Six Nations School Board; by the 1880s, the NEC jointly funded the latter body, though the Board of Missionaries continued to exist.[9]

When Ashton arrived, the new regulations meant the Board of Missionaries approved all admissions to schools falling within its various districts. Thus, Ashton had to rely almost entirely on these men for his admissions to the Mohawk Institute. Even more oversight was exercised by the Special Committee in London, where recommendations had to be sent for their final approval. In this way, there was an entirely new set of politics and personalities at the Grand River Station. The Board of Missionaries itself was a fractious and occasionally controversial group, although individually they were more amenable. They were also remarkably self-obsessed and incurious about what they were examining students for. When they first met at the Institute after Ashton's arrival, he tried to offer board members a tour: "At the conclusion of the sitting, as they had not inspected the school or Institution I requested them to do so, but only Mr. Roberts, & Mr. Chance accompanied me & they only visited the girls' dormitories & wash room & stated that that was far more than they had ever seen of the Institution before. No note respecting their inspection was entered in their minutes I presume."[10] The missionaries' obliviousness indicated that the Institute was not particularly important to them in 1873. Soon after, each missionary was ordered to inspect the Institute each year to see for themselves how well Ashton was doing. By 1875 this system was cumbersome and prey to the jealousies—which were many—among the board. The NEC leadership eventually honed the system until it was only Ashton admitting and discharging students. Where Carter's 1872 regulations had seen the superintendent as separate from the Board of Missionaries, disputes and quarrels among them were damaging admissions to both day schools and the Mohawk Institute. Over time, Ashton gained supremacy in these councils, superseding the Board of Missionaries and becoming the honorary secretary of the Six Nations School Board in 1878, from which office he exercised great influence in the training and appointment of day school teachers.

Over the subsequent few years, Ashton and Nelles were the sole survivors of the bitter controversies among the missionaries. At first Ashton attempted to tar his predecessor, Nelles, as lazy. In reality, Nelles's family had been favoured by the Mohawks for several generations, since before the American Revolution in the 1700s.[11] Indeed, while Nelles was seen to be beloved due to his advocacy against colonial administrators regarding the 1840s removals of the Six Nations to Tuscarora, he was no man of business.[12] Nelles's once dominant authority over the Grand River Station was being seriously eroded by NEC leadership; their chief missionary was rendering the entire mission into a personal fiefdom.

When the NEC proposed new churches in the early 1860s, Nelles and his junior missionary, the Reverend Robert J. Roberts, acted together to fundraise and work with the new Diocese of Huron. But when St. Paul's Kenyengeh was to be built in 1868–9, the NEC entrusted these affairs entirely to Roberts. As a result, Nelles was furious and aggressive. He petitioned the diocese's Bishop Benjamin Cronyn to remove Roberts. This demand was met with equal rage from the NEC. Since the NEC was funding everything, management of the accounting was taken from Nelles, who fumed that this "secular" work was being done by a missionary instead of a "lay agent," or by a secular person whose sole oversight was in lands, their conveyancing, and other property matters.

This system of lay and clerical agents had been in place from the 1833–53 period, before Nelles took control. Where others, including NEC lay agent William Richardson (1833–47), were keen land speculators, and were felt to have betrayed the Six Nations, Nelles claimed to have proved ceaselessly loyal over the 1840s and '50s.[13] This was a great exaggeration on Nelles's part. He had proved obstreperous in NEC business, and by the time of the dismissal of a second lay agent, William Clark, in 1853, he had gained sole control of the annual NEC grant to the entire mission.

Nelles's accounting methods proved suspicious. Nelles was also known for his interference and campaigns of disinformation in the 1860s about government policies. By the time of Ashton's arrival, Nelles's control had been stopped with individual "station" missionaries managing their own accounts. Ashton, of course, maintained his own budget for the Institute and the farm. The Institute received larger shares of the total subvention during these early years. Nelles had tried to manipulate the Board of Missionaries—and various allies among Anglican Mohawk chiefs—to stop the NEC's attempts to remove him.

When Ashton took over the Mohawk Institute from Nelles, with the advice of an excellent boys' schoolmaster, Isaac Bearfoot, and others, he learned to keep quiet in the missionaries' quarrels. For most of his first decade he confined his energies to the strictest, most disciplined form of student life.

Figure 11.2. Mohawk Institute staff, with Robert and Alice Ashton standing in the centre, Isaac Bearfoot on the left next to Jennie Fisher, and likely Mr. Thomas, the notorious boys' master, on the right, who was always intoxicated

Source: William Lant Carpenter, *Report to the New England Company of a Visit to Two of Their Mission Stations in the Province of Ontario, Canada, in the Year 1884* (London, 1884)

This was an abrupt and disquieting reversal of Nelles's relative ease with the students and his concentration on their studies. Nonetheless, Ashton came out on top and was able to become honorary secretary of the revised Six Nations School Board from 1878 until the early 1900s. From Nelles's death in 1884 until about 1906, Ashton was considered to be a skilled NEC employee.

Most of Ashton's days were spent maintaining a constant presence on the farm, paying bills, planning improvements, working as man-of-all-business on properties, conveyances, and trustee work.[14] The NEC's properties were all under trusts. Ashton's role was as both agent—negotiating land deals and sales, working with surveyors and local politicians—and trustee, maintaining an official legal capacity of signing into law the deals he had already done as an agent for the NEC. A distant set of English trustees relied increasingly on Ashton's long-term tenure as superintendent to know how to manage, insure, and maintain a variety of buildings, parsonages, schools, and the Institute in its many parts. Everywhere, it seemed, Ashton's organization and efficiency gave sufficient defence against criticism of the NEC, although he occasionally served as an irritant through his intractable attitudes toward the Department of Indian Affairs. Despite these numerous roles, it was the running of the Institute that gave him almost complete power.

Scholastic Life

When Ashton arrived, he found the boys better able to read compared to the girls. He summarized and reported all academic progress. Each student was graded precisely and administered by the boys' or girls' heads. Ashton also reported on the results of the regular examinations by the Board of Missionaries, with detailed summaries of each student's progress in each subject. This practice continued throughout his tenure. After 1891, he augmented the NEC admissions with similar certificates sent to the Indian Office at Brantford. Since the Institute was now receiving "capitation" monies, these were for the use of the Department of Indian Affairs, which was now financing student enrolment. From 1878, Ashton could also control students' provisional admissions from the Six Nations' day schools and others, but only with NEC approval. A direct role for the missionaries in Institute admissions was removed, although they, too, sat on the Six Nations School Board.

The results of examinations were posted at the end of the reports to the NEC.[15] These reports show that for the years 1872–6 most students were drawn from the day schools; their religion, nation, and origins were recorded. Additional students from Muncey Town, Sarnia, Walpole Island, and Tyendinaga at the Bay of Quinte were also admitted, continuing a pattern begun under Nelles. The geographical catchment was largely unchanged, despite a few more students from Walpole Island and the Sarnia reserves. According to Ashton's journals, some students who died were recorded as being buried in the "pagan" or Longhouse traditions, so perhaps the fact of baptism was not considered solely binding; the same was true, it would seem, for Methodist, Baptist, or other students, though the NEC refused to fund Roman Catholics. This was a matter of some debate that resulted from moments of alliance or quarrel with other missionary societies operating on the Six Nations. Only in 1917 did then-Principal Cyril Mae Turnell record an increase in "pagan" students attending, although stricter Anglican regulations could not be enforced in 1877, for example, when there were many empty spaces.

The NEC wanted five-year progress reports on every graduate, a stipulation Ashton tried as best he could to fulfill. As much as they measured the advancement of students, these progress reports assisted in the Department of Indian Affairs' repeated "morality" surveys, such as that carried out in 1908, which included the quantity of couples who were married in church (Anglican) and had children within wedlock. Great pride was taken in the achievements of many graduates, including Mohawk Institute graduates who were admitted to the Brantford Collegiate Institute for advanced studies in preparation for teaching, nursing, engineering, and medicine. But many more students seemed to go back to the world to which the administration incessantly feared they would return.

Student Labour

Ashton kept a full fourteen-month workbook of reports, correspondence, and daily journal entries in compliance with the NEC's new "regulations." As previously discussed, the regulations set out the duties and obligations of the superintendent of the Mohawk Institution. As part of these requirements, the Company demanded rigorous reporting—bimonthly, with quarterly accounts, annual reports, and accounting.[16] Through these sources we learn about the extent of Ashton's role as the NEC's chief man of business. In this capacity, he exercised significant influence over Six Nations education, but it came at the expense of the day schools in NEC ledgers and was achieved almost entirely through what the Truth and Reconciliation Commission's 2015 *Final Report* termed "institutionalized child labour."

Ashton's radical utilization of child labour was a complete reversal of the Nelles regime. He parsed the children's efforts with much precision. For instance, this is an example of his reporting: "The cost of Maintenance and Management for the past year inclusive of supplies received from the farm amounts to $6381.89 or $176.13 less than in 1874 whilst the average number of pupils boarded was 9 more than in that year."[17] Ashton's epitaph might have been his own words: "I have laboured anxiously to promote the happiness and insure [sic] the progress of those intrusted to my charge and whilst setting them examples of industry and order worthy of their imitation. I have greatly improved the Company's property and exercised the strictest economy."[18] It appears that the students' "happiness" was, of course, meant in a long-term sense, rather than in the immediate world of grinding labour that they were subjected to while at the Mohawk Institute. The word "study," for example, does not appear once in his journals and reports of his first year, whereas "work" or "working" get 141 mentions.

So radical was the immediate impression of abrupt change at the school that over the course of Ashton's first year, every staff member departed. The previous head teacher, Mr. Bouslaugh, and his wife retired. Thomas Griffiths, who was called "superintendent" by the NEC, and his wife, the boys' and girls' teachers, respectively, left. Robert Park, the highly competent farmer, also departed.[19] Isaac Bearfoot, an Onondaga teacher, who had once attended the school and was mentored by Nelles, was the sole remaining employee, but he had only been working part-time. Ashton came to rely on Bearfoot heavily. He quickly appointed Bearfoot as boys' master,[20] as well as Miss Jennie Fisher of Toronto. As head male and female teachers, respectively, Bearfoot and Fisher were two of the best.[21]

Owing much to his previous experience at Feltham, Ashton's preoccupation with work systems was obvious from the outset. By 1876, the environment under Nelles's tenure had changed considerably:

> The farm has borne the expense of very considerable improvements. The stables were entirely refitted, a barn and granary removed and thoroughly repaired and improved besides other extensive repairs. We also dug a ditch 1000 feet long with an average depth of 3½ feet, built 800 feet of new board fence, removed and rebuilt 350 feet of closely boarded fence (girls' yard) and 300 feet of board fence and graded and gravelled grounds and roads to the value of upwards of $300. We have also sown about 35 acres of fall wheat and fall ploughed 40 acres of land additionally—with this I can hardly consider that the working of the farm for the past year has resulted in any loss to the Company.[22]

To facilitate these changes, Ashton introduced work teams. This model was developed from his experience at Feltham and was consistent with English industrial schooling more generally. Students were to spend half days in the classroom and half days in work activities such as doing laundry, baking, cleaning, or in the fields, with sections alternating throughout the year. Ashton modified this system, alternating days, rather than half days, for each team in the fields or other labour. The immediate effect of Ashton's new system on the children must have been jarring:

> During the Winter so little can be done out of doors that the boys are mostly at School. But as the warmer weather sets in

> I think it will be desireable [sic] to divide them into two divisions having one out of school on alternate days. This arrangement will make me to employ them in gardening, road-making, draining etc. whilst at the same time it will only leave two classes in school & these having the undivided attention of the Master will be in a position to make greater progress in their studies than could be expected when the teacher is compelled to divide his attention among four classes.[23]

It was only through the military organization of these divisions or teams that the system worked. What appears entirely natural in photographs taken soon afterwards—the ditches and fencing—was all done by the boys. This was intense, manual, back-breaking work, unremitting under Ashton's supervision via a hired man.[24]

Most of the time this was "routine" work; but, occasionally, Ashton's designs for improvements or alterations saw immediate policy change. After an extended trip to England between July and September 1877—when Alice Ashton was left in charge of the Mohawk Institute, with Tom Green sometimes acting as the farm foreman and Isaac Bearfoot sometimes as superintendent—he returned with plans for regrading and settling the rear of the school structure. Surveyors were summoned. On 13 December his wife recorded that Ashton had "spent all day drawing plan of farm, and house buildings, going continually out to get measurements—and two days later, 'several teams' [of male students] were carting sand, work continuing the 17th, 18th, and 20th, of 'teams grading.'" A few weeks before, school was cancelled for the heavy work of husking corn and drilling fifty-five acres of winter wheat; similarly, when threshing went slowly, the boys were released from school to help complete it. Potatoes were picked, peas were cut.[25]

Much of this farm production was for profit, not consumption, although the NEC leadership rejected the idea that their charity could operate as a business—this would have been in total violation of charitable law in the United Kingdom, for any surpluses recorded had to be reinvested immediately in the operations of the Institute and that accounting had to be approved by the Charity Commission. But the impression that profit was being made off the children was strong, as was the knowledge that until 1841 these were lands that had been farmed by Mohawks adjacent to the village; the children were working hard to cultivate crops on their ancestors' farms in some cases. Just prior to the first sales or expropriations of NEC lands in 1891, Ashton reported to the superintendent general of

Indian Affairs a harvest of 1,275 bushels of wheat, 1,495 bushels of oats, 200 bushels of peas, 150 tons of hay, 990 bushels of corn, and 600 bushels of corn—a particularly excellent crop, together with corn fodder and a market garden. Consequently, it was very doubtful that students, particularly the senior male students, were present in class for much of that autumn.[26] School Inspector Martin Benson noted that in 1895 there was now a farm of some 430 acres, significant growth from the 70 acres that existed during the 1860s, just prior to Ashton taking over the Mohawk Institute. Moreover, a rigorous accounting for food, and sales of food, are absent from the 1873–6 lists, but it must be presumed that a great deal of excess food was intended for market.[27] These materials would have been submitted in the bimonthly reports to the NEC as the farm expanded to its final extent. Here, again, the idea of sales of produce was explicitly derived from the for-profit farm at Feltham. In addition to calculating the cost of maintaining each pupil each year, it was a primarily economic model with philanthropic motives undercut by constant heavy child labour.

Students also worked beyond the school's walls. When inspector Benson made his extensive report for the Department of Indian Affairs in 1895, he did not mention children working outside of the school specifically, but it was not policy to stop students from seeking outside employment in the summer breaks, and, it would appear, students were sometimes farmed out for labour. As early as 1877, Alice Ashton was constantly arranging "situations" for the girls, often in positions as maids and cooks. In addition, the weekly "fatigue" students, teams of boys and girls, took their orders and supplies on Thursday evenings: for blacking, polishing, and scrubbing, ironing, and outdoor labour. Principal Turnell mentioned in 1917 that a neighbour was put out because boys from the Mohawk Institute were no longer available for threshing. The year before, the NEC had put an end to the practice encouraged by Ashton of children working beyond the school's walls. This did not stop Mohawk Institute Principal Ann Boyce (who assumed the position after it was vacated by Robert Ashton's son) from running a domestic finishing school of sorts at the Mohawk Parsonage. Her girls worked in the great houses of Brantford's finest families. Eventually, she and her husband, Sydney Rogers, were themselves dismissed for using the labour of the children at a horse farm they had purchased adjacent to the Institute in 1929. If the boys' work was measured in acreage, milk output, and the prizes for livestock received at various fairs, the girls' endeavours were measured in carefully recorded piecework. Each student was given equipment to be cleaned, inspected, and their work meticulously recorded.

The need to keep children's energy up led to dietary changes at the school. In 1873 Ashton instituted the NEC's idea of a "dietary," presumably garnered from the Company members' significant charitable and philanthropic connections in England and elsewhere. "Formerly the children had potatoes and bread & butter or cornmeal porridge alone on alternate nights for supper their drink being cold water. For breakfast they had bread & milk."[28] But the new diet contained too much meat and had to be changed.[29] While students disliked an excess of meat, and Ashton cut back on this, it may be presumed he instituted something like an English industrial school diet. At Feltham, supper consisted more or less of cocoa and bread. Later two suppers with meats were instituted. At lunch, or "dinner," the fare was far more substantial, beef or mutton with vegetables. In 1895, inspector Martin Benson recorded the "Dietary."[30] The sparse evening meal corresponded nearly exactly to the Feltham fare, with "gravy" doubtless considered a filling meat derivative. "Dinner," or lunch, was the more substantial meal. Presumably the potatoes could be grown easily, with porridge and bread made from oats, cornmeal, and wheat cultivated on the Mohawk Institute properties.

Additionally, Ashton immediately ordered new beds as there had been a serious shortage in Nelles's day. Bedclothes, clothing, hats, boots, walking attire, and church clothes all had to be made, sorted, stored, and accounted for. This was exactly the Feltham regime. All repairs to clothes, boots, shoes, and working attire were done in-house. Presumably, this was now the work of the girls in the sewing room. The following account describes the boys' attire at the school:

> The boys have each one good suit of Tweed many of the coats being quite new, they are not supplied with vests & most of them find their own caps—the same suit is generally worn Sunday & week days—excepting in a few cases where the old suit is not entirely worn out. They have all one good pair of boots or shoes but no second pair. Those who wear boots pay one dollar towards the expence [sic], the Company only supplying shoes—boots are best adapted for the Winter, and are generally worn outside the trousers to protect them from the snow. Every boy will be supplied with a pair of stout worsted socks this week—They wear home during the summer months. We have not sufficient shirts belonging to the Company to supply every boy with two—but as several of them find their own we are able

to make what we have do for the present. In the Summer the boys are supplied with Coats and Pants of Cotton, tween and straw hats.[31]

Similarly, girls' attire had to be made, along with almost everything else; such was the state of want Ashton found: "I will get some coarse aprons made at once for girls to work in but though I think all should have either aprons or pinafores I do not like to buy them without your instructions—for so many things are required in every department that I am quite afraid to purchase until I am instructed."[32] The girls would make all their own clothes, including their outfits for summer and Christmas holiday. Constant supplies and materials had to be bought, such as "12 pairs of blankets. 28 towels 1½ yards long. About 60 cords of fire-wood, 12 bags for farm use. 46 yards of serge at 40 cents per yd. Sundry cooking utensils. 6 lamps & glasses. 42½ yds. of calico for sheets but before we have two sheets for each bed & be able to give each child a clean pair once a fortnight we shall require 450 yds. at 14 cents per yd. as we are obliged to put a width & a half in each bed."[33]

Every expense had to be noted and approved by the NEC, then accounted. Everything was NEC property, and the auditors were very picky. In addition to keeping all the accounts, Alice Ashton ran an inventory of pieces of clothing, bedclothes, and other items considered standard. No detail appears to have been overlooked. The surveillance extended to every reach of a child's life; privacy was non-existent.

Maintaining Order

Achieving all this labour mandated the creation of a tight schedule. What appears below in table 11.1 is the schedule from January 1873, but extant later journals do not show amendments to it.[34]

To keep to the schedule, bells were rung, and promptness was always necessary. Ashton's world operated around this schedule. The electricity, for example, was entirely controlled on a master switch by the principal (as Ashton was now called). In addition, the infractions or merits of every student in every class were visible to them by way of a notice board with moveable markers in each class, and badges for merit were awarded and worn. All matters physical and economic were within Ashton's immediate surveillance, a horse and cart available always for his use.[35] It was an entire school run for maximum efficiency on very tight budgets in every department. Presumably Ashton was also in charge of intellectual, spiritual, and emotional needs; however, virtually none of this appears in any of his reports, correspondence, or, indeed, in any inspection, thus telling us a great deal about his priorities and goals for the Mohawk Institute.[36]

Ashton worried about the students not conforming to his vision of proper gendered behaviour. At first, the girls were too spirited and boisterous, not bowing to a senior male leader. In his journal Ashton lamented, "I have long since seen the great necessity of having a female with the girls as they are extremely rough and vulgar and greatly require the constant supervision of well mannered and cheerful females."[37] Classes were integrated immediately, boys and girls together, but there was to be rigid physical separation outside the classrooms. Ashton fretted about the comingling of the sexes. In his journal, he notes, "To prevent the boys & girls from having almost unlimited communication, has been a source of much difficulty & anxiety to me."[38] Ashton insisted that the young girls maintained incessant productivity in the laundry and other domestic tasks such as cleaning, sewing, scrubbing, and polishing. Not only was there a strict daily routine following the new "regulations," but there were also additions to the curricula: evening and morning prayers were printed out, scriptural history (an Ashton obsession), singing (another Ashton obsession), and weekly service, usually ran by Nelles at the Mohawk Chapel down the road, or evening or morning prayers said by Ashton in bad weather at the Institute in a classroom with a chancel reserved for the purpose.[39] Recreation for the boys included games, lacrosse, and cricket, and for the girls a regime of long walks was instituted. This was far more intensive, regulated, and severe than in the Mohawk Institute in the era when Nelles was principal. The insolence of students in those years was replaced by a constant hum of quiet activity noted by Inspector Benson in 1895.

Six Nations voiced objections immediately. According to Ashton's journal, "The Indians generally do not appreciate the great advantages of the Institution and consequently do not second my efforts to instruct and control their children, in fact at present they appear to offer me every possible opposition."[40] In a way, the NEC and Ashton anticipated that parents would be reluctant to contribute to the general upkeep and maintenance of their children:

> Subsequently, I have seen the Superintendent of Indian Affairs [David Laird], respecting the interest money of orphans & he at once suggested that the Interest money of all children in the school be paid by the Department directly to the Company, to be applied to their benefit—and offered to further the subject

Table 11.1. Mohawk Institute daily schedule, January 1873

Time	Summer	Winter
5:30 a.m.	Rise, wash, and prepare for breakfast	–
6:00 a.m.	Breakfast	Rise, wash, and prepare for breakfast
6:30 a.m.	Boys: school or work if weather permits; girls: clean house, make beds, etc.	Breakfast
7:00 a.m.	–	Boys: school or work if weather permits; girls: clean house, make beds, etc.
8:00 a.m.	Recreation	Recreation
8:30 a.m.	Prayers, distribution for work and school	Prayers, distribution for work and school
10:00 a.m.	Fifteen-minute intermission	Fifteen-minute intermission
12:00 p.m.	Leave work and school	Leave work and school
12:05 p.m.	Dinner and recreation	Dinner and recreation
1:30 p.m.	Distribution for work and school	Distribution for work and school
3:15 p.m.	Fifteen-minute intermission	Fifteen-minute intermission
3:30 p.m.	Boys: school or work if weather permits; girls: needlework until 5:00 p.m.	Boys: school or work if weather permits; girls: needlework until 5:00 p.m.
5:00 p.m.	Recreation	Recreation
6:00 p.m.	Supper	Supper
6:45 p.m.	Boys: school; girls: needlework	Boys: school; girls: needlework
7:45 p.m.	Prayers	Prayers
8:00 p.m.	Bed	Bed

Source: Compiled from William Acres, ed., "Documents of the Mohawk Institute: The Journals and Reports of Robert Ashton, 1872–76 and the Diary of Alice Ashton, 1877," special issue, *Journal of the Canadian Church Historical Society* 59, nos. 2021–2 (2024).

both with the Department & Indian Council, if approved by the Company. I am afraid that at present the advantages of the Institution are not sufficiently appreciated by the Indians to induce them willingly to adopt this suggestion.[41]

The lack of "appreciation" and parental financial support were constant refrains. But as teacher Isaac Bearfoot reminded Ashton, "the New England Company could not require the Indians to pay anything towards the support of the schools as they [the NEC] were a board of Trustees appointed to take charge of a fund collected for the express purpose of educating the children of the Six Nations."[42]

Generally, Ashton worried little about student experiences, though he was concerned about their outward appearances. Students were locked in crowded dormitories at night—Ashton deplored the free movement of students during the Nelles regime. When hiring a governess, he required her to "use her best endeavours to train them in habits of cleanliness, order, and propriety of demeanour—to carefully check any approach to vulgarity & lightness of conduct, & as far as possible to prevent them from communicating with the boys."[43] Ashton also did not seem particularly interested in the young men, save as constant labourers. Alice Ashton, on the other hand, seemed to have had her favourites: She was particularly fond of Thomas Green and Obadiah Sickles, the former a superb academic and the latter a gifted artist.

A rigid internal system of favourites prevailed. Ashton retained a remnant of Robert Lugger's 1828 "Bell School" system of paid monitors to enforce his rules: "I have appointed Monitors from amongst the pupils and trust that with a little judicious training they will become very useful & ultimately fitted for Assistants if required." This was especially so when a single farmer was in charge, and a student was needed to superintend in Ashton's absence: "I am therefore prompted to solicit the favour of being permitted to expend a small amount annually in remunerating the monitors according to their deserts—this would greatly encourage them and I trust prove an incentive to others."[44] Good conduct badges were awarded, also following a Feltham custom.

Six Nations' Response

On the Six Nations side, a decade of Ashton's control of the Institute had very little effect on his popularity. Indeed, Ashton's reputation continued to be very poor. Absalom Dingman, Indian inspector, signalled Ottawa on 20 June 1888 with a telegram to his superior, Robert Sinclair, acting deputy superintendent general of Indian Affairs, stating, "There is bad feeling of Six Nations chiefs against Mohawk Institution here and schools generally." A pointed 1888 attack by the "Education Committee" of the Confederacy Council on Ashton made a strong case for the Six Nations and other

Indigenous children to have more "theoretic" learning at the Institute instead of incessant labour:

> this Committee is of the opinion that the time is now past when there was any necessity of teaching Indian children common farm work, and whereas the class of work seems to be the exclusive industrial training that pupils receive at the Mohawk Institution, and whereas parents seem to expect that when placing their children in the said Institution their time during the school hours of five days in the week should be wholly devoted [to] the acquirement of theoretic knowledge and that the practical part of it should be confined to the hours before and after school.[45]

A rather brutal Six Nations School Board policy of forbidding late students, Ashton's design, from entering the reserve day schools after the morning bell was also cause of considerable distress among parents, for it applied in all conditions and weathers. Ashton's emphasis on extreme punctuality at the Mohawk Institute was reflected in this refusal of a request for more lenience: "It seems to be a step backward towards the primitive barbarism instead of an advance towards civilization and improvement. The School Board therefore is unwilling to take the backward step."[46] The Indian Department could not support Ashton in this approach. This long-standing grievance remained a constant.[47] Six boys absconded immediately on arriving in 1877. Ashton was not bothered. His axiom: The model was brittle, arranged against the constant fear of "fallenness" to which lay agent William Richardson had referred to in 1847 as the Six Nations' default position; it was believed that without unceasing labour, students would descend, equating Indigenous life with a kind of original sin.[48]

The failure to resolve these issues lingered. At the Cayuga mission Ashton was in open conflict with many members of the Confederacy Council, and further disputes over land claims rose in importance when questions began to be asked about Ashton's methods of accounting for NEC profits from lands and their reinvestment.

All of this may have provoked the fires set in 1903, which destroyed outbuildings and the Mohawk Institute itself. The bricks used for the school's reconstruction were sourced from the Workman and Watts brickyard, an operation producing two million bricks a year on the Babcock Lot near the school. Watts, like Ashton's daughter Minnie, had married into the

Cockshutt family, making the renovation all too much a family affair for Ashton.

After the Mohawk Institute was rebuilt, student movement became even more restricted in the new building. Vacations were entirely suspended unless a student leaving was able to reapply within thirty days at the beginning of the vacation. In 1908, Ashton tried to forbid the Christmas vacation despite NEC apprehension; the families' great attachment to their children was well-known in England, a fact perhaps not appreciated by Ashton. Thus, it was not attempted. Ashton's main objections to children leaving the school to go home were students' loss of English, the possibility of their returning with disease, and the supposed lack of sanitary habits among students' families. None of these restrictions suggested or imposed by Ashton were backed by the NEC.

These lingering issues were very difficult to make right and were exacerbated by disputes over land. The NEC's Cayuga mission quitclaims of 1871–5, received from prominent Anglican members of the Six Nations, continued to rankle at the Confederacy Council, for example. Indigenous persons were forbidden sales of land. The only purchaser could be the government. It was possible to transfer property by quitclaim to another Indigenous person by literally quitting a property, for a financial consideration, with due paperwork. These were settled only in 1912. Dispensation of properties owned by John Beaver, hotly contested by heirs, led to a lingering debate in which Ashton was publicly humiliated. Ashton took vengeance by refusing to obey the ruling of the Department of Indians Affairs that the NEC must vacate the property in 1903. The affair aggravated officials and gained widespread notice, even in the House of Commons. The land deals on the Six Nations, but also the development of properties adjacent to the Institute, created a legacy of bad faith, not only with Ashton, but also with the NEC as a whole. It was Ashton's absolute refusal to return these properties in 1903 after the Indian inspector ordered a fifteen-year tenure that may well have provoked the three fires set by students in 1903, as may have the vast industries begun in that year next door to the Institute on the so-called freehold of the Babcock Lot, which followed its sale to the wealthy Cockshutt family in 1902.[49]

Barrister and Company member W. F. Webster visited the Mohawk Institute in October 1908, for cordial meetings with the Confederacy Council. He found Ashton in better physical condition than reports had suggested, able to continue if the Institute continued along the present "lines." Changes were anticipated, but the NEC was at variance over the next directions.⁵⁰

But a more private visit to the Mohawk Institute by the governor of the NEC, John Walker Ford, and its treasurer, Ernest Mathews, in the summer of 1910 ended with Robert Ashton's son, Nelles Ashton, being appointed principal of the school. When criminal charges of abuse at the Institute—and Nelles Ashton's severe alcoholism—surfaced in 1913, the NEC's reputation sat at its lowest point. Perhaps the Company already knew of the difficulties with Nelles Ashton and alcohol from earlier visits, but this was far from the major difficulty at the school. As Webster's visit showed, the continued deteriorating relations with the Six Nations could not be allowed to continue. Changes were also coming with the appointment of Duncan Campbell Scott as deputy superintendent general of Indian Affairs. In the end, neither the New England Company nor the Six Nations were pleased with Ashton. Though he did not fully live up to initial expectations, Robert Ashton had a significant influence on the Mohawk Institute during his time as principal, albeit negative according to many. Focused studies such as this one demonstrate how much individual principals shaped and influenced the experiences of the students who lived behind the bricks of the Mohawk Institute.

NOTES

1. William Acres, ed., "Documents of the Mohawk Institute: The Journals and Reports of Robert Ashton, 1872–76 and the Diary of Alice Ashton, 1877," special issue, *Journal of the Canadian Church Historical Society* 59, nos. 2021–2 (2024). My pagination from the originals at CH-2003-43-05, HCH-2003-43-C 20787, V. P. Cronyn Archives, London, Ontario, for Robert Ashton is used here. The edition includes Alice Ashton's journal of 1877, HCH-2003-43-01, Cronyn Archives, Diocese of Huron, also in my pagination, as it uses dates rather than page numbers. The edition preserves the original pagination for all documents in square brackets for clarity. I have used these original page numbers throughout this chapter.

2. *Report of Mr. W. F. Webster Upon His Visit to the Mohawk Institute, Brantford, and the Grand River Reserve, Canada, October 1908* (Spottiswoode & Co., 1908).

3. All parts of the building were upgraded as far as possible, including better ventilation, windows, a system of "dry" closets in the rear of the building replacing damp pits for toilets, new carpets, flooring, and paint. Ashton saw the entire building, outdoor privies, waste, and garbage management as clearly ripe for epidemic.

4. Acres, "Introduction" in "Documents of the Mohawk Institute," 143–59.

5. *Report of the proceedings of the New England Company for the civilization and conversion of Indians, Blacks and pagans in the Dominion of Canada, South Africa, and the West Indies during the two years 1871–1872* (London, 1874), 9 October 1872, 136–7, where the full text of his duties on appointment, dated 9 October 1972, are listed.

6. *Report of the proceedings of the New England Company*, 132–3.

7. I do not have evidence of such annual five-year running reports, although Ashton records filing one, for example, in 1883. The originals do not exist in the London Metropolitan Archives collection.

8. *Report of the proceedings of the New England Company*, 9 October 1872, 136–7.

9. In the annual report of the superintendent general in 1871, all eleven day schools on the Six Nations were said to be under the "New England Society"; by 1891, none of the schools were so named in the report to the superintendent general. An elaborate system of trustees per school, mirroring the committees of the *Gradualization Act* (1869), were changed to trustees representing the New England Company (two), another denomination, with elections from the Confederacy Council. Ashton was honorary secretary from 1878 to 1908.
10. Robert Ashton, Report, p. 31, in "Documents of the Mohawk Institute," 212. See also, Acres, "Introduction," 159–66.
11. Douglas Leighton, "Nelles, Abraham," *Dictionary of Canadian Biography*, vol. 11, University of Toronto/Université Laval, 2003–, http://www.biographi.ca/en/bio/nelles_abram_11E.html.
12. "I enquired of Mr. Nelles how much land each of them had but he was unable to say or to point out the boundary of the Company's land, in fact he is not sure of any of the boundaries." Robert Ashton, Report, November 1872, first report, p. 16, in "Documents of the Mohawk Institute," 201.
13. Adam Elliott was second missionary for the NEC, appointed in 1837 by Edward Busk, and his wife, Charlotte, daughter of the Reverend Racey, incumbent of St. John's Tuscarora from its consecration in 1835. She died at the Tuscarora mission parsonage in 1893. The church was originally at the Onondaga section north of the Grand River, where Nelles had lived for some years as well (1833–7). Elliott had very little to do with the Institute but did a great deal of pastoral work on the Six Nations as well as examinations of day schools until ill health led to his complete retirement in 1874. The little church was moved in 1883 by the Reverend Albert Sequakind Anthony (d. 1896), a Company assistant missionary and sometime assistant to Elliott and David Johnstone Cazwell at Cayuga. St. John's was badly damaged by arson in June 2021 in the wake of revelations about Indigenous children's unmarked graves on Indian Residential School properties—the investigation into the Mohawk Institute began formally in November 2021.
14. Alice Ashton's journals for 1877, in "Documents of the Mohawk Institute," *passim*. She invariably refers to her husband as "the Super," and records for each day his work, the students' work, and other news.
15. Each annual report included a full set of statistics on classes, progress, reading, arithmetic, writing on slates, writing with pens, as well as English proficiency, and tables on the students' religion, tribe of origin, and the day school they had attended. From 1874 the students studied "Physiology," at the specific behest of the Company leadership. The term may have referred to human biology, temperance, and other forms of bodily continence and function; these innovations were certainly sanctioned in conjunction with Dr. Peter Martin, Oronhyatekha, who was an NEC stalwart and who received his medical education fees from the NEC. See Acres, "Introduction," in "Documents of the Mohawk Institute," 148.
16. *Report of the proceedings of the New England Company*, 136–7.
17. Robert Ashton, Report, December 1875 p. 148, in "Documents of the Mohawk Institute," 302, my pagination from the original at CH-2003-43-05, HCH-2003-43-C 20787, V. P. Cronyn Archives, Diocese of Huron.
18. Robert Ashton, Report, December 1876, p. 163, in "Documents of the Mohawk Institute," 313.
19. *Report of the proceedings of the New England Company*, 134, for Nelles's rather vague summary of the purpose of the Manual Labour Farm.
20. He went on to a distinguished career, ending as rector at Cayuga, Christ Church, for a time in the 1880s he was superintendent of the Six Nations School Board. He was in charge of the Junior School at the Institute from 1872 to 1876, thence to Huron College, where he received his divinity degree and then priestly ordination by Bishop Isaac Hellmuth, but was retained as needed by Ashton to help at the Institute. He was acting superintendent in 1877 when Ashton went to England for three months. He died at Cayuga in May 1911, after a bitter struggle between the bishop and Company over pensions.
21. "I have to recommend Miss. Jennie M. Fisher to fill the post of Governess vacant by the removal of Mrs. Barefoot to the Boys School on the 1st May next. Miss Fisher is 22 years of age and at present a student for the second term in the Normal School at Toronto. She is in possession of a Certificate & has been teaching for upwards of 2 years but left her situation to re-attend at the Normal School during the present Sessions." "Documents of the Mohawk Institute," p. 56 in the original, my pagination of the original.
22. Robert Ashton, Report, December 1876, pp. 162–3, in "Documents of the Mohawk Institute," 312–13.
23. Robert Ashton, Report, February 1873, in "Documents of the Mohawk Institute," 225, pp. 48–9 in the original manuscript.
24. "Documents of the Mohawk Institute," p. 293 in Ashton's original. "I have a man now working on the farm who thoroughly understands ditching and draining and with the assistance of the boys he will carry out the work without I think engaging additional labour."
25. "Documents of the Mohawk Institute," p. 58 in the original manuscript.

26 Dominion of Canada, *Annual Report of the Department of Indian Affairs for the Year Ended 31st December 1891* (S. E. Dawson, 1892), 95, https://www.bac-lac.gc.ca/eng/discover/aboriginal-heritage/first-nations/indian-affairs-annual-reports/

27 As the reports contained detailed budgets for the Institute, it can only be surmised that the Ashtons kept separate farm accounts. These farm accounts are not included in the reports for 1872–77. Indeed, only three registers for the 1890s have anything like these calculations.

28 Robert Ashton, 2 June 1873, p. 75, in "Documents of the Mohawk Institute," 245.

29 Ashton, 245.

30 Martin Benson, Clerk of the Indian Schools, "Report, Indian Affairs on the Mohawk Institute," 1895, File 7825 1A, Vol. 2006, RG 10, Library and Archives Canada (LAC).

31 Robert Ashton, Report November 1872, report 2, pp. 26–7, in "Documents of the Mohawk Institute," 210. H. J. Lister's inspection in 1870, as well as Archdeacon O'Meara's in 1860, found overcrowding and more beds needed.

32 Robert Ashton, Journal and Reports, "Documents of the Mohawk Institute," p. 28 in Ashton's original.

33 Robert Ashton, Report No. 2, p. 28, in "Documents of the Mohawk Institute," 211.

34 Ashton noted, "I do not approve of the early hour for breakfast but as I found it the custom here I have not altered it."

35 Martin Benson, Clerk of the Indian Schools, "Report, Indian Affairs on the Mohawk Institute," 1895, File 7825 1A, Vol. 2006, RG 10, LAC.

36 *Report, Indian Affairs on the Mohawk Institute*, File 7825 1A, Vol. 2006, RG 10, LAC.

37 Robert Ashton, Report No. 3, n.d., p. 41, in "Documents of the Mohawk Institute," 220.

38 Robert Ashton, Report, March 1873, p. 58, in "Documents of the Mohawk Institute," 233.

39 Ashton, Report, 1871–2, pp. 136–7.

40 Robert Ashton, Report, October 1873, p. 104, in "Documents of the Mohawk Institute," 266.

41 Laird (1833–1914) was minister of the interior under the Liberal government of Alexander Mackenzie. Robert Ashton, Report, March 1873, p. 59, in "Documents of the Mohawk Institute," 234.

42 Robert Ashton, Report, December 1873, p. 114, in "Documents of the Mohawk Institute," 274–5.

43 "Documents of the Mohawk Institute," p. 50 in the original manuscript.

44 See Charles M. Johnson, "Robert Lugger," *Dictionary of Canadian Biography*, vol. 7, University of Toronto/Université Laval, 2003–, http://www.biographi.ca/en/bio/lugger_robert_7E.html, as using the Scottish educational reformer Andrew Bell (1753–1832), *The Madras System* (London, 1808), where he developed the system of monitorial oversight in Church of England Schools in India. *Ashton Workbook*, 1872–6, 51–2.

45 David Seneca Hill, seconded Chief Benjamin Carpenter, and other members signing, 23 June 1888, File 75,494, Vol. 3202, RG 10, LAC.

46 Chief James Styres and the Reverend David Caswell Johnstone signed this letter, but as Honorary Secretary Ashton here dictated the substance and tone of it. The Six Nations School Board approved the letter, 29 October 1888, File 75,494, Vol. 3202, RG 10, LAC. Note that "the" is crossed out in the original document.

47 Dingman, October 1888, File 75,494, Vol. 3202, RG 10, LAC.

48 Acres, "Introduction," in "Documents of the Mohawk Institute," 108–27. I treat the various scientific theories current in the 1860s and '70s related to this relentless labour.

49 The Cayuga mission quitclaims reached a crisis point in 1903, which may have led to the arsons at the Institute; sentiment was running high against Ashton and the school at that juncture. The issue of the twenty-acre quitclaim at the Cayuga mission was part of Chisholm's statement of claim on behalf of the Six Nations in 1918, immediately following D. C. Scott's release of the second Mohawk Glebe tranche for the purchase by the Six Nations. See File 268, item no. 3, Litigation fonds, V. P. Cronyn Archives, Diocese of Huron.

50 *Report of Mr. W. F. Webster Upon His Visit to the Mohawk Institute*; CLC 540 MS 07920/8/pp. 149, 154–5, London Metropolitan Archives. Webster's report of his 12 October meeting, where he refused to commit the Company to the "reform" party—presumably those in favour of an elected council—at the Six Nations; but he discussed the lands at length. The meeting went particularly well, and the Company moved to follow his recommendation not to use the word "pagan" in the future in describing the non-Christians, but rather "Deist."

12

The Lands of the Mohawk Institute: Robert Ashton and the Demise of the New England Company's "Station," 1891–1922

William Acres

Under the guidance of the New England Company (NEC), a Protestant missionary society that founded the Mohawk Institute in the 1830s, Robert Ashton served as superintendent and principal of the Mohawk Institute from 1872 to 1910. In addition to these two roles, Ashton had the additional role of NEC agent and trustee of lands and properties for the Company.[1] While his power derived from the educational side of his work, particularly at the Institute and Six Nations School Board, Ashton performed a great deal of hidden work—and exerted considerable influence—related to the lands and properties of the NEC's "Grand River Station." The "management" of these lands by the Company reveal that it had an interest not only in educating the Six Nations but in appropriating their lands as well.

These "objects," as they were called, were managed under trusts held by the NEC, governed according to its charitable status in England under the Charity Commission (from 1853). Oversight of Ashton's daily work was generally fulfilled by the NEC's governor and treasurer. There was copious additional correspondence going through the Company's charter clerk—who was always a trained lawyer, skilled in English trusts. This was necessary. In addition to a yearly journal, bimonthly reports, and budgets and accounts, the NEC thought they were exercising sufficient control over their superintendent and the disposition of properties. Over the course of decades, the farm at the Mohawk Institute was expanded on the entrusted properties. These properties had been accumulated over time, specifically between 1836 and 1845, in the form of grants, with purchase, on what NEC minutes invariably referred to as "Indian Lands."

Primarily, it was the 1845 grant of 9.93 acres where the old Mechanics' Institute had stood, and on which the new Institute of 1858 was constructed, that is of most importance for understanding the school's history. Adjacent to the northwest, crossed by the Grand River Navigation Company's canal cut (1845) sat the Mohawk Glebe, given in surrender (by deeds held in London) in 1828, on which sat a substantial parsonage for a missionary "doing service" for the Six Nations.[2] According to their sights, each property near the Institute was held on "absolute title," a recurring phrase in the archival record. These properties were augmented by a large plot of 200 acres, always referred to as the Manual Labour Lot. It was acquired in 1859 on the condition that the NEC occupied the land. That large, farmed property was not under trust, but the conditions for it were set down by the government. Thus, it was a hybrid estate in which the legal differences and expectations blurred during Ashton's forty years of service. In total, there was a 430-acre property overseen by Ashton.

When Ashton arrived with his wife, Alice Turner Ashton, and their two small children in November 1872, his instructions were to report fully on the Institute. He was tasked with intensifying and expanding the farming operation by using as his base the existing seventy-acre farm with other pasturage areas long used by the farmer employed by the NEC, Robert Park. During Ashton's tenure, the expansion of Brantford—especially after its 1891 annexation—virtually abutted the lands to the northwest and north. This greatly increased the land values and caught the interest of the wealthy NEC members and encouraged them into a kind of speculation. Ashton was instructed by the Company to fence and determine the exact extent of these lands. Brantford town officials wanted these properties for urban expansion and leisure areas and had begun sales. These were refused by Ashton as the protector of the Six Nations through the NEC with high government connections through NEC member Senator Amos Edwin Botsford.

But, as Brantford grew during the 1890s into a major manufacturing centre for the production of agricultural implements—mainly plows—the fenced fortress of the NEC lots of land became more porous.[3] In large degree this was because the so-called Babcock Lot, a property not under the trust arrangement for "Civilizing and Christianizing" the Six Nations, consisting of thirty-three acres, was purchased in 1864 from an intestate farmer's family and, as such, was freely and clearly the NEC's to sell. Manufacturers

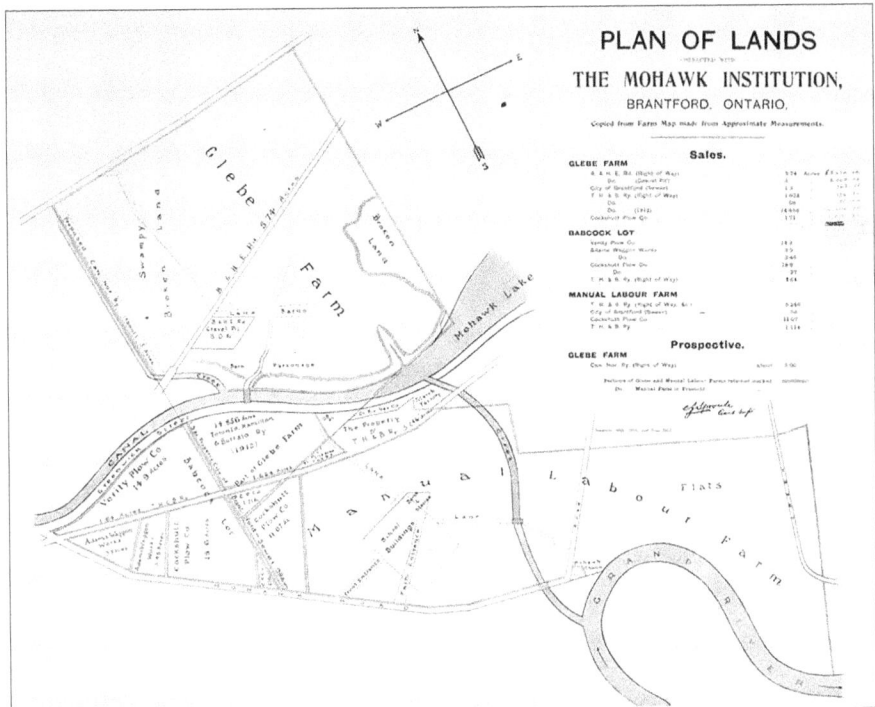

Figure 12.1. Glebe Farm Reserve no. 40B. Plan of lands connected with the Mohawk Institution, Brantford, Ontario.
Source: Library and Archives Canada / e008316815-v8

saw this land as highly desirable for the construction of large factories as it ran along what became Mohawk Road with city and water access, close to the railway and the extension of urban utilities. Other than housing workers' cottages, the Babcock Lot was never a part of the running of the school.

In the 1870s, several small strips of land running south of the Grand River Navigation Company's canal were given to the NEC through high political intervention in Ottawa to solidify the whole area—the whole area as shown on Ashton's 1910 "tracing map."[4] In 1902 the Babcock Lot was sold to the Cockshutt family, with additional acreage to their subsidiary, Adams Wagon, and partner Verity Plow, all within the ambit of the massive Massey-Harris consortium. By the beginning of the First World War, literally thousands of Brantfordians worked at these enterprises in shift work, many of them living in new adjacent neighbourhoods built in expectation of a complete annexation of the NEC properties.

Thus, the still visible extent of the Institute farming properties, as well the vast brownsite vacated by Brantford's major industries sat beside each other, emblematic of differences in progress, wealth, and race. The situation put Robert Ashton in a dilemma. His daughter Minnie married a Cockshutt, William Foster. Foster was a member of Parliament and one of four sons of Ignatius Cockshutt, Brantford's greatest capitalist and father of the hugely successful, internationally renowned Cockshutt Plow Company in 1877. The Cockshutts and their partners expanded operations requiring utilities, hydro, gas, railway spurs, and other industrial amenities of which the Institute was a secondary recipient—all of it organized by Ashton under the growing suspicion of the NEC over his involvement in these land transactions.

The lands of the Mohawk Institute were divested of the NEC by sales to the Six Nations in 1915 and subject to government litigation between 1919 and 1934. In part, these conflicts arose over disputed claims to title initiated by the Confederacy Council of the Six Nations; these conflicts were exacerbated by Ashton's running of the school, which one member of the NEC described in 1908 as a "reformatory." The tension between the city, the industrialists, the Six Nations, and the extraordinary burden of child labour required to keep it all going was, in effect, Ashton's undoing.

Conflicts of Interest

Most of the population of the Six Nations was removed to reserve land before Ashton's arrival. What he saw when he first arrived was about ten acres under cultivation where the 1858 Institute was built, with an additional sixty acres nearby. Ashton soon began to intensively farm the two-hundred-acre Manual Labour Lot as well. In addition to the farm operations on land under trusts, the Company had absolute title on the Babcock Lot. Over the 1890s and 1900s a contradictory policy, examined here, would be attempted: The Babcock Lot became a site of heavy industry. New legislation compelled expropriations for railways and other services needed by the new factories. All of it was complex and managed with increasing difficulty by an aging Ashton. At the same time, the reason for the Institute's existence was the farm. By the 1900s, the Six Nations, especially the Confederacy Council, which had long questioned Ashton's methods with their children, now began a serious questioning of the NEC's right to title on all their properties, including the lands of the Mohawk Institute.

In 1889 a sizeable deputation of NEC members came to what they called their Grand River Station—schools, churches, parsonages, and the Mohawk Institute itself—and issued their superintendent, Ashton, a series of commands. Ashton was to get electricity brought to the Institute and was instructed to sell the Babcock Lot (32.9 acres). Further, the 1889 policy they drafted instructed Ashton to make inquiries to the deputy superintendent general of Indian Affairs about "what conditions, if any, a capitation grant similar to those allowed to the Shingwauk Home and other Indian Industrial Schools would be made by the Dominion Government." Moreover, the Glebe itself, of which Ashton was one of the Company's trustees, was to be divested. Ashton was to commence "transferring the Mohawk Glebe, exclusive of the brick yard, to the Department of Indian Affairs with a view to it being sold and the proceeds invested for the purposes of the trust." The legality and process of this direction forms the spine in the ensuing problem of breaking an English trust for the use of the Canadian government. It would form the basis for litigation and claims to title for the next forty years.

Clearly, with talk of sales, the Mohawk Institute and adjacent properties were being eyed with a view to the NEC's departure, sooner or later. At the very least, Ashton was to get the best financial settlements possible. All profits, by law, had to be put directly into the NEC's so-called objects. The assumption was that sales and other expropriations would go back directly into the Institute—or in the case of the Mohawk Glebe, in accord with the original terms given by the Six Nations in 1828, to a missionary "doing service on the Six Nations." But English trusts were slippery. Although American, Canadian, and German trusts were—even at this time—becoming far more precise about their terms, the NEC, as an English trust, could dispense their profits in the service of any—or new—"objects," as long as the purpose was "Civilizing and Christianizing" the peoples for whom the objects were intended. By the end of Ashton's tenure, a change in Company policy saw the Mohawk Institute be of far less importance than it previously had been to the NEC. Ashton, an agricultural dynamo based at the Mohawk Institute, was soon joined by an industrial dynamo immediately next door.

Today, the railway spurs, rights of way, and various urban extensions Ashton negotiated for the NEC, and for his son-in-law William Foster Cockshutt, can still be seen at the Woodland Cultural Centre in Brantford, located on the grounds of the former Mohawk Institute. Indeed, the extensive forty acres of industrial brownsite abutting the northerly end of the centre's property was one of the largest manufacturing facilities in the British Empire. All of this was accomplished by Ashton—as agent and trustee of the NEC—more or less following the Company's general directions.

In 1906, the NEC's misgivings over the Mohawk Institute, and their work on the "Tuscarora Reserve," came to a head: They had realized a significant profit on the sale of the Babcock Lot and, by English charitable law, now had to reinvest all of it in missions—but amendments in 1899 to the Company's charter widened the geographic scope. Now, the Company could look to the West. Moreover, the NEC's disenchantment with Indian residential and industrial schools meant their focus was increasingly on missions, perhaps day schools, on other reserves. In 1906, they talked with church leaders from Saskatchewan. At that time the questions opened for consultation included:

1. Having regard to the numbers, probable future, and state of civilization of the Indians in Canada is the money now spent at the Company's Mohawk Institution and on the Tuscarora Reserve, being used to the best possible advantage?

2. Would you recommend any increased expenditure on the Tuscarora Reserve?[5]

What appeared nearly certain was a re-evaluation of the Institute and a move to build further churches on the Tuscarora Reserve. This was done on the recommendation of the Reverend James Leonard Strong, rector of the mission parish at Kenyengeh. It was a rebuke to Ashton's Mohawk Institute. How had matters reached such a low ebb in the minds of the NEC where the Institute was concerned?

Industry, Mission, and Conflict

The industrial development of NEC lands marked an unexpected turn of events. Members of the Company in England were against any manner of industrial development on their freehold Babcock site, strongly recommending to Ashton that the Mohawk Glebe property be returned to the Six Nations if such a development were to be proposed. Ashton was to "take precautions against the land being used for an obnoxious manufacturing or other purpose which might become a nuisance."[6] By 1910–1912, massive industrial development had taken place. Between 1894 and 1912 the Company sold thirty-seven acres of the Glebe, slivers of the Manual Labour Lot, as well as the entire Babcock Lot.[7]

The encroaching city, the demands of the industrialists, and mounting complaints from   Six Nations over lands and conditions at the Institute were all difficulties, any single one of which might have been met with negotiation, diplomacy, and resolution. But coming all together, with the First

World War interrupting, the question of the NEC's lands became a decisive issue in the history of the Mohawk Institute. Ashton had already made connections with Brantford residents who had great designs on the Babcock Lot. Whether or not the Company had full understanding of the desires and demands of the industrialists of Brantford remains open to speculation. Their presence would have benefits to the Mohawk Institute: electricity derived from the grid connecting the Canada Starch Company on the former Great Northern Railway Company canal; and a gas line from Dominion Natural Gas soon followed, albeit fitfully and inefficiently owing to problems with the companies and lines from Selkirk on Lake Erie. Subsequently, it would be replaced by gas wells on the southern edge of the Glebe supplying Brantford. Available, cheap power, gravel (for drainage), and a sound water table commended the neighbourhood to industry.[8]

In 1902, the Cockshutts bought the Babcock property and developed it quickly. Seven years later, another section of NEC land was purchased by Verity Plow Company with Adams Wagon, a Cockshutt subsidiary. These purchases indicate that the Company had been completely persuaded about the increasing value of their adjacent properties at the Mohawk Institute, Manual Labour Lot, and the Mohawk Glebe, should their sale ever be realized. The companies on the Babcock Lot were giants in the making, partners of the Massey-Harris manufacturing consortium. W. F. Cockshutt, Ashton's son-in-law through marriage to his daughter Minnie, had been critically important in making the Company's properties exempt from further political struggles.[9] Four days after their marriage, the first "capitation" monies of sixty dollars per student were granted by the Department of Indian Affairs (DIA) to the Mohawk Institute. Cockshutt's action was not selfless. The DIA's tenders for machinery as part of westward expansion in Canada's relatively new "reserved" lands may have added impetus to the Brantford efforts.[10] With increasing unease, through Ashton, the NEC fell under the influence of various wealthy Canadians.

Forced sales to service the massive factory shops with railways and other necessities, sewers, further power and gas, sidewalks, and other modes of transportation soon followed. The *Railway Act* of 1904, and expropriations of "Indian Lands" in 1906, were not done with NEC cognizance or approval. These sales were, in effect, beyond Company control, as responsibility for them had passed into the hands of the manufacturers who owned the Babcock Lot. Cockshutt, for example, forced expropriation of 11.07 acres of the Manual Labour Lot in 1909, with a further 14.6 acres going to Cockshutt off the Glebe Lot. Here were the first glimmers that the

Canadian government was going to exercise a heavy hand in Brantford and at Six Nations.

The NEC had no legal right to any such movement on the unceded Manual Labour Farm. On every conveyance, Ashton was scrupulous in notifying the NEC of terms, so the Company's officers could perfect the leases for signing by the trustees in the form of indentures. On each deal, Ashton notified the local land registry. He provided the calculation of "Indian Interest" monies on the expropriations, which were duly paid to the Indian Office at Brantford. All of this he found legally sufficient.

But slivers of land were also sold to complete the railway spurs on the southern Mohawk Glebe and Babcock Lot to service Cockshutt's factories. Only NEC members knew the exact contents of the various leasing arrangements Ashton had made on their lands.[11] By 1910, most of the southern part of the Glebe had been open to expropriations of this kind, following federal *Railway Act* stipulations, with legal rulings by A. D. Hardy.[12] Hardy, alas, approved the expropriation of this section of the Manual Labour Lot to the Municipality of Brantford for a sewer. The monies received went to support St. George's, the NEC-run residential school at Lytton, which was part of the NEC's mission in British Columbia. This caused serious misgiving with C. Augustus Webb, the NEC's charter clerk.[13] He wrote the following to the Company's treasurer, Herbert Henry Browell: "I am far from happy about the £1463 received by sale of part of the Manual Labour Farm."[14] These properties were directly under the Indian Office jurisdiction and should have gone to the Institute for purely moral reasons. But the NEC could disperse funds under trust "objects" as it saw fit—it could not be dictated to by outside forces, not even by the Government of Canada—so long as no laws were broken.

There was obvious dissent among the NEC members about the decision to support the Lytton school in British Columbia, although it was never openly articulated. Perhaps the British Columbia mission's priority suggested an exit from the difficulties at Brantford.

Ashton was obviously furious, unwilling to touch the matter or this money, perhaps intuiting that his legacy was coming to an end: "for some reason best known to himself, Ashton does not want the dividends paid [from a related sale of lands on the Mohawk Glebe] to himself . . . so if you authorize me to request that he should receive the dividends in the same way as he receives the rents for the various houses and land—paying the proceeds through the accounts—I would act accordingly."[15] He must have known in the Company's special meetings and conversations about what to do with these windfalls that none of the financial proceeds were coming to the Mohawk Institute.

Such expropriations for railways were impossible for the NEC to reject; they were under federal statute. They were symbolic of the Company's loss of control. The extent of properties needed by the industries reached a worrying extent with a further "forced" sale of property to Verity Plow of 14.886 acres for a railway spur under the 1904 *Railway Act* and 1906 amendment from "Indian Lands." Lacking Cockshutt's close connection to the government, Verity's deed was secured externally through lobbying by the Verity family's adviser, Sir Melvin Jones, a man of great influence who had lobbied the government separately, pausing only for a courtesy visit to the members of the NEC when he was in London. The Company's shocked response was that this conveyance had taken place largely without their knowledge.[16]

Normally, the fund's sales or expropriations would have been applied directly to the Grand River Station, to the Mohawk Institute, or Six Nations parishes, "for the purposes of the Trust." But Company intentions were wearing thin with the Mohawk Institute and with Ashton. The funds were certainly plentiful and required immediate reinvestment in charitable "objects." Only now, without any local knowledge, the focus was on the West, on British Columbia—specifically St. George's, the NEC-run residential school at Lytton—as well as building new churches for the Six Nations.

The NEC mission at Lytton began in the 1890s following an earlier fledgling mission at Kuper Island. It was begun by the Reverend R. J. Roberts, a missionary who went west after working at Cayuga Station on the Six Nations' territory. There was an idea that a girls' school, All Hallows, might be joined to it, so new buildings and resources were needed. Lytton had the additional advantage of not having difficult conditions on lands; nor was there an activist Indigenous community nearby. Rising NEC interest in the Lytton school paralleled Ashton's demise at the Mohawk Institute. This caused mounting troubles within the NEC.

A Point of Crisis: The End of the NEC

It is not entirely clear that even Ashton grasped at the end of 1910 the full extent of what the NEC was then contemplating. They wanted permission to do one of three things: (1) sell the Glebe (this could have only been to the Six Nations); (2) buy ten acres of the Manual Labour Farm adjacent to the Institute lot; or (3) leave the Institute entirely. This is clear from barrister W. F. Webster's private communication on 7 February 1911 to the

NEC governor, John Walker Ford, calling for an emergency meeting of the members. Both men seemed willing to withhold the full extent of the NEC's plans:

> At any rate it is a matter which the Company should decide. All that has been decided up to date is that Blake [a lawyer] should be asked to obtain powers for the [NEC] to buy or sell the remainder of the Mohawk Glebe and the Manual Labour Farm. The Company has not decided that full information should be given of materials which do not appear to be connected with their proposal nor as to their intention to make the Mohawk less "permanent."[17]

The NEC had not abandoned their view of leaving the Institute entirely. Instead, they wanted to push up the value of the Mohawk Institute lot itself in a proposed sale—to be affected when the ten acres of the Manual Labour Lot were added to the ten acres of the Mohawk Institute, a twenty-acre parcel the NEC could buy, and, more importantly, sell, freehold. A 1909 note made clear what was being withheld from all but the NEC members: "That as lately as 1903 the Company have seriously considered the desirability of buying the Glebe themselves."[18] As the governor wrote to charter clerk Webb, in strictest confidence, "The bit we want is part of the Manual Labour Lot which we should want in selling the Institute but which probably the Government would be unwise to sell us & so enhance the price of our freehold against themselves."[19] Ashton's empire had already, in NEC minds, been divided into small pieces. The more pressing question was whether any of these plans were legal.

To address this, the NEC actively pursued lawyer Blake's counsel on how the Mohawk Glebe could be released or sold. Blake was very pessimistic when he eventually saw the full panoply of the trusts. He refused to engage. Blake realized that all the accounting, past and present, done on all NEC properties would have to be precisely tabulated. He knew the NEC wanted out of the Mohawk Institute, yet the trust was another matter. By 22 February 1911, barrister W. F. Webster clearly felt that the Company was "under attack." Canadians, he mused, writing to NEC Governor John Walker Ford, were intractable over the Glebe: "in case after your time or after Ashton's death" another such attack was mounted; at least there had been a dress rehearsal.[20]

Blake's refusal to assist was seen by the NEC as the action of an enemy. The Company saw themselves as victims of political aggression by the Six Nations and abandoned by the DIA. What they did not fully appreciate was the depth of the mess Ashton had got them into over the deals he had transacted over the twenty years since the Cockshutt connection had been made. Ashton had achieved the NEC's supreme position. When briefing Blake in December 1910 on the prospect of selling the Mohawk Glebe (he demurred), Ashton's encyclopedic knowledge of their arrangements over the last forty years was thought to be airtight: "they have so high [an] opinion of his knowledge of the conditions which govern the questions affecting Indian Lands, they feel clearly of [the] opinion that you ought to see the letter [outlining all land deals on the Glebe and Manual Labour Lot] in case you desire to communicate."[21]

The reality was not as certain: By 1908 Ashton had serious health issues. His signature was barely legible. His son Nelles was sent as his power of attorney as trustee to London in 1909 for important conveyances as his father was unable to sign.[22] Now, pressing legal questions about NEC land holdings around the Institute demanded precise answers the NEC were unable to provide. The Company was clearly anxious. After only five official visits between 1837 and 1889, a further five were made in 1902, 1903, 1904, 1908, and 1910.[23] In 1913, taking full measure with hindsight of their predicament, Webb wrote the following to Governor Ford: "No doubt we are suffering the sins of our Fathers and it is amazing the Rev. R. Ashton should not have taken every precaution in getting the consent of the Indian Department before the Sales took place."[24]

Ashton never felt he had needed the DIA's approval on anything. Framing his position on the land deals now as a sin of omission rather than of commission, Ashton was, thus, immediately relieved of his charge at St. Paul's, H.M. Chapel of the Mohawks. While he stayed on as an NEC trustee, his power lapsed. Cockshutt, in turn, failed to gain any support for a fledgling parliamentary bill in 1913 that would have allowed NEC trustees to sell the lands if all proceeds were invested immediately in Canadian missions.[25] This was the signal for the bishop of Huron, David Williams, to "ride rough-shod" over the NEC pressing a (false) claim as trustee on all of the Company's entrusted lands.[26] In short, the Company's time as sole actor was over.

The new deputy superintendent of Indian Affairs, Duncan Campbell Scott, seized his advantage in 1913 by personally taking up the cause of the Confederacy Council, which in 1912–14 proposed a plan for purchase of the

Mohawk Glebe through their legal counsel, primarily A. G. Chisholm. They radically altered the complexion of the Mohawk Institute, a long-standing project, and introduced a counteroffensive to the NEC's incessant stonewalling over the production of the right to title on properties past and present. Here began the unravelling of what had begun a century before. Duncan Campbell Scott, in his first address to the Six Nations as deputy superintendent general, on 2 December 1913,

> stated that he felt the responsible position of deciding this matter, and now that he was adopted as one of the Six Nations they could count on him to do the fair thing with their matters, he wants them to feel that they have a friend at Headquarters and hoped that when Providence [had] seen fit to take him from office it would be better and he intended to leave the Six Nations better than he found them.[27]

The chiefs reciprocated this sentiment, and supported Scott entirely.[28] But, they put direct conditions on their Glebe purchase:

> they also desire that some change might be made in the workings of the Mohawk Institute so as to bring about better results for the amount of money spent on the Institution, as they were doing far more for the advancement of their people, by giving them Education on the Reserve with much less expense and would suggest that the Government take over this School and conduct it as an Orphan School for Indian Children of Ontario, also provide a home for pupils attending the higher schools at Brantford.[29]

By 14 April 1914, they had concluded the following:

> The Council after carefully reconsidering the matter of the Glebe lot at Brantford originally containing 220 acres, and in view of the use by the missionaries, and the New England Company during the long period of 87 years they must have derived enormous benefits and profits from these lands, moreover they have disposed of some 45 or 46 acres to various companies and got some $22598.90.[30]

The Canadian government, not seeing the Charity Commission as higher in authority, began an "amicable" dispute over this amount. The number was calculated from proceeds the Company had received from expropriations on the Glebe lands already, and subtracted from an arbitrary sale price of $50,000 fixed by Scott at the DIA.[31] The NEC's solicitor, Willoughby Staples Brewster, protested that the Company had never offered the Glebe for sale, nor did they want any money for it. As Webb told new Mohawk Institute principal, C. M. Turnell, "surely it follows that if the Company have a good title to <u>sell</u> they have at least a good one to <u>keep</u>."[32] Scott's agreement with the Six Nations forced the NEC quitclaim of $50,000 in the autumn of 1915. Cockshutt's abortive proposed bill of 1913 would have seen the Company be allowed release, to sell and buy. But this merely drew further bad odour around the NEC at the Six Nations; it was, in effect, twenty years too late.

Facing the Government of Canada, members of the Company deemed the prospect of litigation unwise, complex, trans-imperial, and very expensive. The third option—for the NEC to leave the Mohawk Institute entirely—was probably their longest-held desire. But, after many consultations with lawyers in both Canada and England, it was deemed impossible by legal means without political support. It appeared, then, that the Canadian government's plan would be to remove the properties from the NEC's jurisdiction with or, as it happened, without due regard whatsoever to the Company's legal trust position under the English Charity Commissioners.

Such a move would erode the NEC's ability to support the Mohawk Institute. There had never been a moment when the students' labour was absolutely necessary to run the school, especially after the capitation grants began in 1891. The NEC was being forced out of its charitable "object," the lands returning to the Six Nations in right of the Crown, thus bringing the running of the farm—and, thus, the Mohawk Institute—under complete oversight. This was antagonistic to NEC thinking, as well as a violation of their trusts. Without such objects—lands, buildings, teachers, equipment, supplies, food, etc.—they were unable to serve the people for whom the "objects" were intended.

There was a very practical dilemma here. In 1915, during the Reverend Cyril Mae Turnell's first year as superintendent of the Mohawk Institute, he put it succinctly: Without the Glebe, the school could only expand eastward onto freehold farms.[33] Constant development was eroding the farmland: "New land will have to be acquired if the Institution is to justify its existence as an Industrial School"; and among the Confederacy Council the "party in power" did not favour the Church of England, regarding them as a patriarchal artifact.³⁴ There were thoughts of a boys' school, separate from the twenty-acre Mohawk Institute, possibly retained for the girls' school, given the likely loss of all of the farm properties. This was never done, despite various schemes.³⁵

Matters did not go straightforwardly for the Six Nations with Scott in charge. The chiefs' condition that all NEC titles be searched and made good before the balance was paid was never met. Scott acted alone and released the second tranche in 1919 to the balance of $50,000 by making sure to keep this knowledge from the Six Nations Council of Chiefs. Chief Asa Hill, secretary of the Council at Six Nations, replied to A. G. Chisholm's query on 5 June 1920, referring to the release of the final funds from the sale for the Mohawk Glebe, paid to the NEC, that "Mr. Scott has at no time written me concerning the settlement of the Mohawk Institute Lot" (meaning the Glebe).³⁶ None of the Glebe funds the NEC received went to the Mohawk Institute, nor to the maintenance of a missionary at Six Nations.

Scott, the bishop of Huron, and many others wanted to know what the NEC was going to do with the proceeds from the Glebe sale "on the subject of the possible enlargement of the Institute." Rumours against the NEC flew when the monies from the Glebe sale went largely to the new mission at Lytton. Turnell was $3,500 in debt at his dismissal, a sum easily cleared by the monies.³⁷ An important link between Six Nations' demands about conditions at the Mohawk Institute and the future of the Company's lands was fractured.

Filling the Vacuum Left by the NEC: Ashton's Legacy

Bad faith abounded. Urban expansion, and the sheer political will required to continue the Ashton system, conflicted. The intensive child labour practised on the Institute farm, and the demands of industrialists—especially in Ashton's own family—met headlong with the litigation arising from the Confederacy Council in 1913. It was a body uniquely ignored at every turn throughout Ashton's entire tenure. No example of negotiation or capitulation to their wants and policies is recorded in Ashton's work. The aftermath of the Ashton years was characterized by far worse than mere stubbornness. The cruelty and severity that lay behind his endlessly optimistic accounts of expansion, cultivation of lands, and student achievements were revealed in a series of events before the Institute was finally leased to the DIA in February 1922.

Running the Institute as a massive farm, based on a for profit-framework imported from the English industrial school system, had beggared the energies and resources of the students. It had strained the patience and temper of the Confederacy Council, which despaired of the lack of education and advancement the Mohawk Institute and day schools were able to provide. This was a far larger, Canadian policy issue. But, on the Six Nations it found a local target with plenty of obnoxious examples on which to focus. Ashton's militaristic ideal of perfect order, efficient production, and a heavy emphasis on work over education had irritated and incensed leaders of the Six Nations Confederacy Council and parents alike. Conditions at the Institute were very poor. The building in 1903 had been done without any "extras," stretching the $18,000 in insurance to its capacity and very little beyond.

The combination of ill-treatment of students, poor rations, and bad living conditions only drew further ire. The Six Nations Confederacy Council's demands over conditions at the Institute were of great moment—and their records, and that of a dissenting NEC principal, Reverend Cyril Mae Turnell, furnished evidence of a grave situation. The Institute had essentially become a Victorian agricultural reformatory under which Ashton descended further into cruelty. Documents created between Ashton's retirement on 31 December 1910 and the lease to the Department of Indian Affairs in 1922 expose much about the facts of his regime, especially the human cost hidden beneath the photographs and balance sheets, which did so much to sustain the endeavour.[38]

Ashton would not have known of this; his dementia was already advancing in 1912. But Scott's immediate plan was to cultivate alliances against the NEC, an easy task given the legacy of Ashton and his son Nelles. After all, given Ashton's approach to Indigenous education and policies more widely, this medieval trust under an English charity can only have seemed an unwelcome and occasionally noisome relic of vanished world. But Scott did like Turnell. The men became friendly with each other, which provoked hostility and mystification among the Company members, who might have been otherwise disposed to help Turnell further had war, politics, and the problem of the Glebe not been on the table.

When the bishop of Huron, David Williams, was invited by the NEC to inspect Turnell's Mohawk Institute in 1917, he noted that everything had changed from the previous Ashton regime. Earlier, Williams criticized the management of the school as lacking in pastoralia: "the essence of the change is that severity has been replaced by kindness," the attitude was "free and open, and even smiling countenance, and pupils no longer are eager to run away."[39] There were smiles, laughter, and a general light-heartedness to the place. Turnell's unpalatable reflections on his predecessors in the Ashton family were too grim. Their "chronic alcoholism" could be overlooked, but the "severity" of their ways could not. The "cheesepairing policy of my predecessors was not real economy."[40]

Bishop Williams found little evidence of training, but masses of endless, pointless "Drudgery." The students were working—for what amount is never stated—at outside farms, for the boys, and, for the girls, as maids in great Brantford houses, including the Cockshutts'. These concerns resonated with Chief Josiah Hill and others who had written to the NEC on 11 September 1913 complaining that students were "poorly fed" and "suffering indignities from the staff," demanding "an impartial investigation."[41] This was determined to be criminally actionable on Nelles Ashton's part. With Turnell, as Colonel Andrew Thorburn Thompson reported in 1923, there was a conscious rejection of previous methods, solitary confinement, for example, having been abandoned about "a decade before."[42]

It was not long before Turnell was accused repeatedly of financial mismanagement. This rankled the NEC, but his popularity with the government and the Six Nations authorities rose. Turnell was simply unable to stay within the amounts budgeted by the NEC. He was constantly asking for more and more resources. Within this context, Alice Ashton Boyce supplied background information to Company charter clerk C. Augustus Webb. Boyce sketched a slovenly and poor agricultural practice on all fronts—corn left in the fields all winter, now rented from Verity Plow Company—an affront to the legacy of her father Robert Ashton's enviable farming methods. The children at the Institute were apparently released somewhat from the endless labours required to keep up the farming. They were seen out of uniform in town. Students were, according to Alice Ashton Boyce, running the place. Webb therefore had asked her to "let us know generally how the Mohawk Institution is being carried on, and whether in your opinion the children are being educated too extravagantly for their future life on the Reserve, taking into account their future life there, and whether Mr. Turnell is employing too many teachers."[43]

Boyce's cousin William Foster Cockshutt backed everything she said. Doubtless, information was also coming from the sewing mistress, Susan Hardie, who was very critical of Turnell's management. No one, it appears, directly addressed Webb's question about the teaching. As the NEC's Canadian commercial agent since 1913—meant to serve as a brake on Ashton Nelles—Cockshutt's word carried enormous weight with the Company. Discipline, the NEC lectured Turnell, had to be maintained on all fronts: "But you must understand that the Indians are a very different class of boy: their ideas of morality are peculiar; and therefore, while we want you to be kind to them, as far as possible—you must maintain discipline—which is a factor in every well-regulated school."[44]

Against these loaded accusations, implying luxurious training, Ernest Mathews, NEC treasurer, was mentoring Turnell in expensive agricultural methods, many of which were from the perspective of a major landowner on an English estate. The state of farming had fallen badly behind contemporary practices and needed to be revised drastically. The cost was prohibitive, however, and there was a disagreement among NEC members as to whether "experimental" farming was a waste.

The NEC was, justifiably, upset by a series of damning events indicative of poor regulation. Niblock, the boys' master, had just been dismissed in June 1916 for "unjustifiable and excessive corporal punishment" after an altercation where it had been "considered necessary to import a constable into the school." This occurred while the Turnells were on an unannounced holiday in Bermuda. Two deaths in rapid succession left Turnell open to serious questions. The NEC was furious they had not been informed by Turnell of the drowning of a boy, Edward Smith, on 29 March 1916. Was a responsible adult present? The drowning of Robert Gibson in the unfenced pool of water at the starch factory a few months later was a worse shock, and there were criminal proceedings against the owners for negligence. "You are succeeding to the headship of a school which has been carried on under a too severe standard of discipline," Turnell was instructed, but the "Indian" boys, Turnell was informed, could not be considered the same as the boys in "Public Schools" here, with honour and other privileges given by their "Masters."

Turnell countered that the Ashton method was obsolete. It was beyond his ethics "to tax the children beyond what I know, from my training, that they have physical and mental ability to do."[45] By the end of 1917, Turnell's demise was inevitable. To Scott's initial consternation, the Company fired Turnell in early 1918. It was unclear if the Institute could continue without having to rely on profits from agriculture.[46]

Wrangling to Control the Mohawk Institute

This was the situation when the London, Ontario, barrister Andrew Gordon Chisholm advanced. His vast compilation of primary materials on the Grand River Navigation Company and other work gave him some facility with the archives at the DIA relating to the Six Nations.[47] He was, thus, great friends with important Confederacy chiefs, particularly Asa Hill. With his preliminary findings he persuaded the DIA and the Secretary of State and Minister of the Interior Sir Arthur Meighen to pursue litigation against the NEC in 1919 over the Manual Labour Lot—the loss of which, in February 1922, by Chief Justice Audette at the Exchequer Court of Canada, was based on a faulty grant of 1859, the two-hundred-acre plot farmed so intensively under Ashton, apparently void *ab initio* (from the beginning).[48] Further, by 1916 the NEC had realized the Glebe was no longer theirs; and the "occupation of use" of the two hundred acres of the lot, critical to the far-reaching farming under Ashton's design, was under even more scrutiny. Schemes for new ways forward were hatched. Not surprisingly, the NEC was relieved about the fact that everything might be purchased by the DIA, including the ten acres, the Institute, and outbuildings, as long as they retained "control."[49] The word "control" was never defined.

These terms exposed a crisis of sorts. If the government would not buy the Mohawk Institute, the NEC was left with the extremely expensive prospect of both capital improvements and daily maintenance—all on reduced land holdings. While the lands adjacent were being divested, the Canadian government refused to purchase the Mohawk Institute and the surrounding ten acres, thus compounding the NEC dilemma: "That by the sale of the Mohawk Glebe Farm the most profitable land for supplying the produce to the Institute and for farming has been taken away." Experimental farming was to cease, immediately. It might be suitable elsewhere, "where the Indians are not in the advanced state of civilization as the districts from which the pupils of the Mohawk Institute were drawn."[50] Typically, this paradox of the "peculiar" morality of the boys contrasted with constant refrains of "advancement" among the Six Nations; the blandishments of Brantford were "detrimental to the missionary work of the Institution," and Turnell's efforts "too extravagant." Was twenty acres enough for a market garden at a girls' school on the existing site from the Institute and a bit of the Manual Labour Lot? Could two hundred acres be found elsewhere for a boys' school?[51] These were the ideas mooted by the NEC and their friends. The uncertainty continued until 1921, when, in the summer, Principal Alice Boyce had no idea under whose management the new school term would begin.[52] Odd as it appears, with Ashton's demise, the NEC lost its compass at the exact moment it lost use of the lands.

Duncan Campbell Scott wanted the entirety of the Mohawk Institute properties returned to the Six Nations, while refusing to allow the NEC to sell anything more than the Glebe. The church would assume some manner of oversight, spiritual and material, of Six Nations' mission and the Grand River Station. But DIA control moved forward once Scott supported Chisholm's documentation for a case to remove from NEC the Manual Lot, the unceded portion in 1919. The department took up exactly where the NEC's weakness left them exposed financially. On the legal side, Scott forbade the Six Nations from making an adjoining legal motion through Chisholm from Ohsweken in the Manual Labour Lot case in 1920. Then Scott agreed to Chisholm's taking the case forward, but only on behalf of the Department of Justice and the DIA, not the Six Nations. In this way, every document and letter were under Scott's surveillance.[53] Moreover, at no juncture were the Six Nations allowed into, or notified of, any legal proceedings from 1918. Chisholm's anger over the exclusion from legal action by the Confederacy Council of the Six Nations galvanized his anger against the NEC. What was being established was Scott's and the DIA's authority in deciding what was to the "benefit" of the Six Nations.[54] As Blake remarked in 1911, "The matter seems to me to be broadening out much beyond what was contemplated when the matter was first entered upon."[55] This was an understatement.

The years 1919–22 were studded with legal land mines over NEC properties. Seeing the potential for dire financial loss, the bishop of Huron tried sweeping in to collect and manage his own "Residential School." He did so with the reluctant assistance of the field secretary of the Missionary Society of the Church of England in Canada (MSCC), Canon Lewis Gould.[56] Together they tried to obtain the Institute for the Anglican Church of Canada, which managed in some form another seventeen or eighteen schools. But on inspection, in the fall of 1920, the two men found the school in appalling condition.[57] Henry Weld, the NEC's English solicitor, coached by Alice Boyce, had meanwhile reported cheerily a few months before that all looked well.[58] The financial costs were beyond the capability of either the diocese or the MSCC to take over. Immediate repairs were estimated at $40,000.[59] But the shortfall was already so severe that the DIA had taken over financial management beginning on 1 October 1920.[60]

Williams remained stubborn over the Institute: As chair of the Anglican Church's "Forward Movement," whereby the residential schools became the focus of Anglican mission, he was furious at this juncture. He accused the NEC of double-crossing him as he waited for the MSCC and internal diocesan approvals on a June 1920 arrangement to take over running the Mohawk Institute on condition no lands or properties were disposed of;

this set him against Scott.⁶¹ Thereafter, he continued to insert the diocese's claims despite their being groundless.

In the summer of 1921 Sir James Lougheed, superintendent general of Indian Affairs, intervened in the chaos. He ordered Scott to go to London to meet with the NEC, where he was entertained at the House of Lords in August 1921. Everything was on the table. Litigation over the Manual Labour Lot had been already scheduled at the Exchequer Court on historical evidence provided by Chisholm; leases for St. George's, Lytton, and the Mohawk Institute were negotiated. An arrangement was made whereby an "Anglican" or Church of England presence would be maintained, the NEC paying a stipend of £1,000 for a chaplain, or principal, who would celebrate as needed at the Mohawk Chapel.⁶² The Mohawk Institute itself would be leased for $1,000 a year to the DIA. The bishop's insistence that he enjoyed an *ex officio* trusteeship as gained in some manner of inheritance from an original trustee, Bishop John Strachan of Toronto, was later found to be false. But it did mean that the bishop installed a notion in the minds of subsequent principals that the bishop of Huron was a person of some consequence in the operations of the Institute, all without basis.

An attempt by the bishop of Huron to take over all the NEC's work—including the Mohawk Institute—had met with the disquieting and potentially extremely expensive problem of unsettled land titles. In this, no doubt, the DIA seemed far better positioned to answer and administer issues. It must be noticed, almost surreptitiously, that the initial legal campaign, lodged with Chisholm by the chiefs and put in strategic execution from 1912 beginning with the Glebe, had passed entirely from the latter's hands in these years. Extensive litigation against the Company on lines anticipated by Webb over failure to notify the DIA of sales of "Indian Lands" and other financial lapses dating back to the 1870s effectively removed the NEC from direct oversight of any mission between 1922 and 1934. Decades went by with annual NEC assistance to the parishes, forming new relationships with clergy at Six Nations to the present day.

The Six Nations, on the other hand, would have no say in the matters they had raised with the NEC over the conduct of the Ashton regime at the Mohawk Institute, culminating in the 1913 conviction of Nelles Ashton, and expanding into other properties and purposes of the English charity. This was largely an attempt by Scott and the DIA to subdue and control the politics of the 1920s. It would be Duncan Campbell Scott and the Indian Department who would succeed the NEC in providing oversight of Indigenous children at the Mohawk Institute.

The Manual Labour Lot was, thus, not really open to adverse possession by occupation, at least once Chisholm contested it.[63] When the Institute finally sold its remaining 9.93 acres in 1965, after much wrangling, for $100,000, the NEC was still pressing its historical accounting over improvements, buildings, and other "objects" directed by its trusts dating back beyond Canadian Confederation. Other than minor involvement over the renewal of their lease between 1945 and 1947, and occasional visits, the NEC dissolved its Special Committee for Missions in 1932 when it paid the tax penalty to the Department of Indian Affairs. All of it had been accomplished entirely without the "concurrence" of the Six Nations.

NOTES

1. This was not unusual—his predecessor, the Reverend Abraham Nelles, and local merchant William Richardson and others had taken on these positions acting as land agents as well as trustees. In practical terms, all legal surveys, conveyances, and other sales were done by the agent. When transferring funds or signing indentures for the sales etc. these men were acting as trustees.

2. The sole repository for all the materials relating to the historic sales, conveyances, deeds, and indentures referred to in this chapter is at the London Metropolitan Archives (LMA) in the New England Company's holdings—CLC 540/MS. A box of five bundles, LMA CLC/540/MS 08005 of uncatalogued materials has been reconstructed for the Company's trusts and accounting of them by the author and Matteo Clarkshon Maciel on a SSHRC Insight Development Grant, 2018–21. These papers were in large part gathered in 1928 for the Government of Canada's litigation against the New England Company by Gower Edwards, an agent bonded for archival legal searches by the Charles Russell Company of London, England, hired by the Departments of Indian Affairs and Justice. As that litigation never went to trial, as settled in 1928, no judgment was given by the Exchequer (now the Federal) Court of Canada and the materials remained sealed there. The complexity of these materials has been reduced to a few salient examples of sales between 1908 and 1912 (below) for the sake of brevity and clarity.

3. From the 1870s leases were given to Workman and Watts brickyard off the Mohawk Glebe on the southern edge, as well as a lease to the Canada Starch Company. There were gas wells sunk in 1907 near these concerns. This chapter does not investigate the full extent of these leases.

4. Robert Ashton's tracing map for the Company relating to land sales and expropriations, 1891–1910, CLC 540/MS 08005, LMA, based on the original properties of the Institute Lot, the Manual Labour Lot (1859), the Mohawk Glebe (to the upper end, 1828, 1845), and the so-called freehold of the Babcock Lot (1864) purchased by Abraham Nelles for the Company. The industrial developments on the Babcock began in the 1890s and reached their zenith after the Cockshutt Plow Company purchase in 1902 and subsequent improvements thereafter to 1910.

5. "Committee appointed to consider and report upon the matters of the disposal of Surplus Income and Possible Future Spheres of work," minutes, 10 June 1908, CLC/540/MS 07940, LMA. The questionnaire had been sent out to interested parties in late 1906—clearly Strong's view was the favourite; so was the lobbying being done by Archdeacon G. E. Lloyd of Saskatchewan.

6. "With regard to the remaining portion of the Glebe, I have been instructed to write to Mr. Van Koughnet and inform him that the Company are prepared to adopt the course which was suggested by him at your own and the Commissioners' interview with him at Ottawa on the 24th Sept. last, viz. to advise the trustees to transfer the property to the Indian Department to be dealt with in the Company's interest. You will no doubt forward the amended draft deed of transfer, which you were instructed to have prepared as soon as it is ready for the consideration of the Company." Charter Clerk W. J. Venning to Ashton, 18 December 1889, fol. 783r, CLC 540/MS07928/004, LMA.

7. Benson in 1895 thought the Babcock was 59 acres; the actual size was 32.9 acres. Already in 1894, the very important railway right-of-way had gone through allowing the construction of massive manufacturing works. *Report, Indian Affairs on the Mohawk Institute*, File 7825, Pt. 1A, Vol. 2006, RG 10, Library and Archives Canada (LAC).

8   Flooding continued to be a problem on the properties. In the 1910s, the Company agreed to have a five-acre stretch of the old canal near the gravel pit filled in for this purpose; and Brantford's leading industrialists lobbied for a large series of dykes to be built along the edge of the properties, without success. CLC MS 540 07920/9, LMA.

9   The Cockshutts applied for a building permit in 1902, with about twenty further permits granted by 1909 for the expansion of their factories. All of the expropriations for rail spurs and rights-of-way followed. See the documents for these expropriations and purchases, CLC 540/MS 080050, LMA, which contains the discovery materials for litigation against the NEC between 1908 and 1934.

10 Douglas J. Leighton, "A Victorian Civil Servant at Work: Lawrence Van Koughnet and the Canadian Indian Department," in *As Long as the Sun Shines and the Water Flows*, ed. Ian Getty and Antoine Lussier (UBC Press, 1983), 114n52. Leighton is especially illuminating on the decline of J. T. Gilkison in the 1880s, pp. 112–13.

11 The Company kept notoriously poor records of these properties.

12 See, for example, a railway expropriation of 10.88 acres in 1908 for Verity Plow off the southern edge of the Glebe, dated 6 March 1908, CLC 540/080050, LMA, as it appears on Ashton's tracing map.

13 Webb had been charter secretary following the very long service of W. J. Venning—a relation of many Company members—and was not entirely clear himself on the precise nature of the properties. At one time he panicked because he thought the Mohawk Glebe expropriations were not under trust—but they were. These many conveyances created financial intricacies in the form of new sub-trusts necessary to wrap up profits from expropriations whereby monies were sent for expenditures within the Company's normal remit.

14 Herbert Henry Browell (1856–1915), treasurer, barrister, related to many Company members through his mother, Charlotte Busk. His father Edward Mash Browell, a Company member, had been instrumental in hiring Ashton as he was one of the Board of Visitors at Feltham Industrial School, where Ashton was a schoolmaster between 1861 and 1872.

15 Correspondence, p. 423, CLC 540/07928/6, LMA. G. A. Ditcham, principal of St. George's Lytton wrote to the Company stating he could purchase four hundred acres of land for $2,000 at that exact juncture. Correspondence, p. 438, CLC 540/07928/6, LMA. Webb seems to have felt the profit should have gone directly to the Institute or the missions to the Six Nations. Clearly Ashton felt very strongly that the profits should have been reinvested into the Institute, but he had virtually no say in the matter, even after forty years of service.

16 Jones travelled to London to lobby the Company personally on behalf of Verity in 1910. The sale realized $15,000 off the Glebe with an additional 1.144 acres off the Manual Labour Farm of about $1,000. David Roberts, "Sir Melvin Jones," *Dictionary of Canadian Biography*, vol. 14, University of Toronto/Université Laval, 2003–, http://www.biographi.ca/en/bio/jones_lyman_melvin_14E.html.

17 Webster to John Walker Ford, 7 February 1911, CLC MS 540/080050, LMA. Webster was willing to divulge all the trusts and properties and their terms to Blake but was certain it would be voted down by the members.

18 Undated fragment of note by W. F. Webster on what are probably notes sent by Blake to the Company on trust documents. Blake enjoyed very close relations with Company charter clerk Augustus Webb and his wife, Mary Hoare Webb. CLC MS 540/080050, LMA.

19 Ford to Webb, February 1911, CLC MS 540/080050, LMA.

20 John Walker Ford to Augustus Webb, February 1911, CLC MS 080050, LMA.

21 C. Augustus Webb, Company charter clerk, to S. H. Blake, 4 December 1910, CLC MS 540/080050, LMA

22 On 22 April 1909 Ashton Nelles was sworn to witness the conveyance of 10.88 acres for a railway right-of-way and gravel pit for a consideration of $2,184.50 authorized by Judge A. D. Hardy on 13 February 1909 from the Mohawk Glebe. The conveyance was taken to London by Ashton Nelles already with his father's signature. CLC MS 540/080050, LMA.

23 CLC 540 MS 07928/008, p. 71, LMA.

24 CLC 540 MS 07928/008, p. 71, LMA.

25 16 April 1913, CLC 540 MS 07920/10, 1913–25, LMA. "Unexpected opposition" from the secretary of the interior, T. W. Crothers. At about this exact time charges were made against Nelles Ashton, and these went through Duncan Campbell Scott, newly named deputy superintendent general of Indian Affairs, directly to Crothers's office. 11 October 1913, typed insertion at p. 69 in the minutes, CLC 540 MS 07920/10, 1913–25, LMA.

26 CLC 540 MS 07928/pp. 707, 758, 766, LMA; Williams's attempts, p. 872, 10 October 1913. Webb's was an entirely accurate characterization of Bishop Williams.

27 Extracts taken by the Reverend R. B. Farney of Simcoe, Ontario, from materials gathered 1 December 1922, at the Brantford Indian Office, Council Minute Books of the Six Nations, 1912–15, sent in 1925 to Chancellor F. P. Betts of the Diocese of Huron, noted Bay 20, Shelf 368, Box 3 [file 2], PREC-2011-18-02, CH-2011-43-02, Chancellors' Papers, Huron Diocesan Archives, Huron University College.

28 CLC 540 MS 07920/10, 1913–25, p. 69, LMA, notifying Cockshutt of the chiefs' concurrence with Scott over the Glebe, 15 December 1913.

29 CLC 540 MS 07920/10, 1913–25, p. 4 of brief, included by Farney. This may have been a pointed criticism of the new regime under Nelles Ashton (1879–1956), whose criminality and alcoholism are discussed elsewhere.

30 CLC 540 MS 07920/10, 1913–25. This full resolution was printed and presented in its entirety to the Company on 19 May 1913, dated 17 April 1914, CLC 540 MS 07920/10, 1913–25, p. 82, LMA.

31 Throughout, the DIA and NEC used words like "amicable," "friendly," or Webb's "devoid of antagonism." CLC 540 MS 07928/9, p. 124, LMA.

32 14 June 1916, CLC 540 MS 07928/9, p. 691, LMA.

33 The Reverend Cyril Mae Turnell was an English clergyman who was hired in short order in 1914 to replace Nelles Ashton following his conviction for cruelty to children at the Institute. After Nelles Ashton's stint in rehabilitation in Virginia for severe alcoholism, Cockshutt wanted to reinstate his cousin; Nelles's sister, Alice Ashton Boyce, refused to work with him. The Company would not entertain his coming back. Turnell was a graduate of St. John's College, Cambridge, and came highly recommended. He was fired in late 1917 for financial reasons.

34 Turnell's correspondence was rife with such unwelcome comments. See CLC 540 MS 07920/9, p. 165, LMA: his report of 26 June 1916; on Six Nations politics, to Webb, 10 July 1916.

35 Company lawyer Harry C. Weld following his visit to Ottawa and Brantford, November 1919, CLC MS 540/07920/9, LMA.

36 Chief Asa Hill, secretary of the council at Six Nations wrote Chisholm, 5 June 1920, that of the release of the final funds of sale for the Mohawk Glebe, paid to the Company the year before from their funds, no one had been informed of anything by Scott. See Hill to Chisholm, File 134, 275, Pt. 1IA, Vol. 2670, RG 10, LAC.

37 CLC MS 540/07928/9, pp. 904–5, LMA. In 1920, Scott received notice of the amount sent from the NEC for their new girls' school at Lytton: $20,661 in direct (from sale of Glebe) and a further grant of over $4,000. CLC MS 540/07928/9, pp. 904–5, insertion by date, on receipts from Louis Laronde, new Principal at Lytton, which he sent to Webb, 25 November 1920, printed and sent on to Scott.

38 Turnell's correspondence relating to Ashton's decline is found in CLC/540 MS 07920/9, LMA *passim*, see following notes. A comprehensive book of newspaper clippings, photographs, and other material is found in a scrapbook possibly kept by Ann Ashton Boyce [Rogers], 1906–22, CLC/540 MS/FO2/004, LMA.

39 Winnifreth, 1992, p. 107; original report at CLC MS 540/07920/9, LMA, by date of insertion in the minutes, inspection 13 April 1917, report 26 April 1917.

40 26 September 1916, CLC MS 540/07920/9, LMA. For a more balanced view of Susan Hardie, cf. Alison Norman, "True to Our Own Noble Race: Six Nations Women Teachers at Grand River in the Early Twentieth Century," *Ontario History* 107, no. 1 (Spring 2015): 5–34, especially 17–22. For Alice Boyce's attempt to replace Hardie because of her older ways and limited views having been at the Institute since the age of twelve, see 20n68.

41 11 September 1913, CLC 540 MS 07920/10, 1913–25, LMA.

42 *Report by Col. Andrew T. Thompson, Commissioner to Investigate and Enquire Into the Affairs of Six Nations Indians* (F. A. Ackland, 1924), 22, https://epe.lac-bac.gc.ca/100/200/301/pco-bcp/commissions-ef/thompson1924-eng/thompson1924-eng.pdf. Hardie said she had to whip all the girls; Alice Mary Ashton Boyce Rogers, assistant principal, said whipping was rarely used. Hardie said darkened rooms were not used for solitary confinement: "This practice was abolished more than ten years ago." But, in 1914, Boyce asked for more such cells to be constructed in the aftermath of ill-discipline following her brother's trial, which means they had been added for such a purpose in the new school building of 1903. October 1914, CLC MS 540/07290/9, 1913–25, LMA.

43 This was also recorded the same day the Company asked Boyce to replace Turnell. 14 March 1918, CLC 540 MS 07928/9, p. 970, LMA.

44 22 June 1916, CLC 540 MS 07928/9, p. 700, LMA.

45 CLC MS 540/07920/9 by date of insertion in the minutes, report of 28 February 1917, LMA.

46 CLC MS 540/07920/09 minutes, *passim*, unpaginated insertions of Company typed exhibits within the Minute Book, 1913–25, LMA.

47 Vol. 268, nos. 3–10, V. P. Cronyn Archives, Huron University College, known as Chisholm's "Extracts" from a larger set of documents of about one hundred pages; these were sent by the Department of Indian Affairs to the Reverend R. B. Farney at Simcoe, 7 February 1922, unsigned, sent from Scott's office. Vol. 268, nos. 3–10, V. P. Cronyn Archives, Huron University College, File 2, Chancellors' Papers, CH-2011-18-02, PREC 2011-11-02 by date. The preliminary précis of the various NEC holdings from 1919 were later hugely augmented, but Farney's immediate concern was the legal implications ahead on the lands during Williams's haste to rush into assuming a lease from the NEC. It is assumed that Chisholm used papers compiled in 1919–21 by G. M. Matheson, registrar of the Department of Indian Affairs, "Quantities of Land held by New England Company on Grand River, 1849," pp. 182–4, no. 51, Vol. 10023, RG 10, LAC. Chisholm's compilation would serve as the basis for all future litigation, 1922, and 1924–32, but would be amended significantly by hundreds of further documents.

48 *R v The New England Company*, [1922] 63 D.L.R. 537, https://epe.lac-bac.gc.ca/100/205/301/ic/cdc/aboriginaldocs/court/html/rvnewengcomp.htm, is the judgment by Audette, C.J., of the 1922 Exchequer Court against the Company over the Manual Labour Lot. No financial penalties were included, hence Chisholm's further "instrument of Intrusion," which began wider historical accounting claims against the NEC on behalf of the Six Nations beginning in 1924. Exchequer Court of Canada, B-4015-B (case was settled, 1932).

49 CLC MS 540/07920/9 by date of insertion in the minutes, February 1917, LMA.

50 CLC 540 MS 07928/09, pp. 975–6, LMA. Both quotations are from the same resolutions, passed 22 March 1918.

51 Weld's report, CLC MS 540/07920/9, LMA.

52 Insertion in the minutes, by date, August 1922, CLC MS 540/07920/9, LMA. The legal uncertainties over lands attached to the Institute were also *sub judice* during these years, which augmented the stress.

53 29 November 1920, File 510,305, Pt. 1, Vol. 3202, RG 10, LAC. Scott refused to recognize Chisholm as acting for the Six Nations or "any other Indians," either in the general claims against the NEC or in the Manual Labour Lot case before the Exchequer Court. On 5 November 1920, he instructed Chisholm to relay the message to the council that he was no longer in their service and was instead working on behalf of the Departments of Justice and Indian Affairs. See File 134,275, Pt. 1A, Vol. 2670, RG 10, LAC.

54 These are given at great length, with lawyerly debate over every single item in File 510,305A, Vol. 3202, RG 10, LAC; charter clerk Webb signed an affidavit on 9 January 1919 attesting to the accounting sent on behalf of the Company by auditor W. B. Peat. See File 134,275, Pt. 1A, Vol. 2670, RG 10, LAC.

55 File 134,275, Pt. 1A, Vol. 2670, RG 10, LAC. G. M. Matheson's file on a single property, the Manual Labour Lot (RG 10, Vol. 10023) was begun 1919 and completed in 1921.

56 The Anglican Church's successor body, established in 1902 to replace the foreign missions of the Church Missionary Society, which had announced its intention to leave Canada entirely in 1910.

57 Indeed, in all but trusteeship, the Mohawk Institute, having had solidly Church of England instruction and chaplaincies since its inception, was considered, rightly, to be an Anglican school, just not under the umbrella of the MSCC.

58 Weld had relations in London, Ontario, which allowed him slightly more time to investigate the legal side, and his report was primarily on the titles of the church and parsonage properties on the Six Nations in addition to the Institute lands; for which, until 1919 there had been no concerted effort either by the diocese or the Company to organize these papers into a single archival group. While the Six Nations Confederacy had asserted control over the parish properties in 1906, this was not acknowledged by the Company.

59 This was the exact figure given by the Indian Department architect, Ogilvie, in June 1917, by date of insertion in the minutes, CLC MS 540/07920/9, LMA.

60 By date of insertion in the minutes, CLC MS 540/07920/9, LMA. Duncan Campbell Scott's correspondence noted in the September 1920 meeting of the Company at p. 373 of the minutes.

61 Report of the meeting with the bishops of Huron and New Westminster, 23 June 1920, CLC 540 MS 07920/9 by date, LMA. Williams even had the diocesan synod held in Brantford in that year to strengthen the campaign to take over the NEC's work at the Institute and Six Nations mission.

62 In practice, the incumbency of the chapel rested with the bishop from 1922, but Nelles and Ashton had such long tenures—combined they ran from 1837 to 1913—that the bishop of Huron's right had never been exercised or, indeed, tested. Thus, the practical solution was to have the officer at the Institute who was in Anglican orders become the incumbent of the chapel. The possibility of a legal transfer of trust from the NEC to the Incorporated Synod of the Diocese of Huron was first mooted in 1920, specifically the parishes on Six Nations, but also including the Institute.

63 The essence of Chisholm's case was that, left unchecked, the NEC would have received fee, full freehold, of the two-hundred-acre Manual Labour Lot, by "adverse possession," on 5 April 1920. His case lasting from 1919 to 1922, which began the final unravelling of the Institute properties under the NEC, is detailed for those years, as noted above, in File 134,275, Pt. 1A, Vol. 2670, RG 10, LAC. Audette, C.J., of the Exchequer Court of Canada ruled in January 1922 that the occupation of use was void *ab initio* by reason of the unceded lands.

PART 6
Student Experiences and Voices

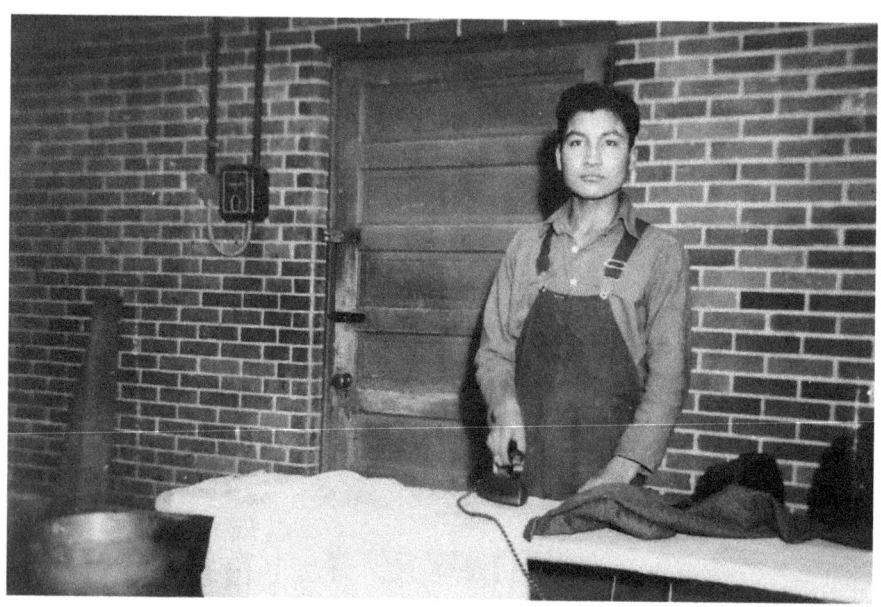

Figure 0.10. Elwood Burnham, Mohawk Institute, 1934
Source: Kenneth Kidd Collection, Trent University Archives

13

Life at the Mohawk Institute During the 1860s

Thomas Peace and the 2018 Huron University College Students in HIS 3201E

In 1859, the Mohawk Institute reopened with a newly constructed building, and the decade to come offered much promise for the school's principal. Anglican missionary Abraham Nelles, who had overseen the school for nearly two decades, saw in these years a moment for institutional expansion. Though the number of teachers remained just a few, the 1860s saw the school's population more than double from between forty and fifty students to near one hundred by the early 1870s. Reflecting on the work of the New England Company (NEC) at Six Nations, the school principal was convinced "that the most, if not only effectual way of imparting a useful education is by taking the children entirely under our own control, as is done at the Mohawk Institution; and therefore I hope the Company will not think me unreasonable in indulging the hope that I may see the Institution enlarged so as to accommodate a much larger number of children."[1] For Nelles, success in this work was marked not only by increasing student numbers, but also the achievements of his students, who trained to replicate the mission's work. Throughout the decade he pointed to the handful of children, such as Isaac Powless and Isaac Bearfoot, who left the school to become teachers, clergy, or prosperous farmers. By the time of his retirement in 1872, Nelles had overseen one of the school's most significant periods of expansion and growth.

Much of what we know about this period in the school's history comes from the reports Nelles filed with the NEC. We therefore know much about the school's general operation, administrative structures, and students who

Nelles or the Company considered successful, or sometimes, troublesome. The experiences of most students at the school remain difficult to recover, however. Few students recorded their memories about the school during these years and the institutional records that have stood the test of time focus more on the operational nature of the school than the day-to-day lives of the students and staff.

In 2018 and 2019, my students and I were involved in the Social Sciences and Humanities Research Council–funded Documenting Early Residential Schools project. In partnership with the Woodland Cultural Centre, the Shingwauk Residential Schools Centre, and the Verschoyle Phillip Cronyn Memorial Archives at Huron University College, we studied and transcribed the Mohawk Institute's only surviving nineteenth-century attendance register. The document spans the years 1860–73, which corresponds with the opening of the school's second building and the end of Abraham Nelles's superintendence. The book provides us with periodic glimpses into everyday life at the school during this decade. What follows is a summary of the findings in the register, combined with information filed in the NEC annual reports. Taken together, these documents paint a more specific picture about what life was like for children at the school during this transformational decade in the Institute's history.[2]

Though imperfect, both in its recording and its authorship (likely by Nelles or teacher Thomas Griffith), the register provides unique insight into daily life at the school just after its second building opened in 1859. Within the register's pages we find recorded the days that students were absent from their classes, when they got sick or died, some of the activities in which they participated, how they performed academically, and when they ran away from the school. In addition to the day-to-day log, the book also contains records related to boys' examinations, as well as observations made by visitors to the school. Taken together, the information transcribed and studied by the students in this class provides a window into what life was like for the over four hundred boys and girls who attended the school during the 1860s. Though upon his retirement Nelles might have celebrated the successes of his expanding school, the pages of the register reveal a much more complicated picture of everyday life at the Mohawk Institute during the mid-nineteenth century.

The Register

The register has four distinct parts. The core of the document is the daily attendance register, listing students by name and annotating each date when something unusual happened to them. Annotations include basic school-related activities, such as when a student missed their classes, received new equipment, or were sick, as well as more exceptional circumstances such as when a student ran away or was vaccinated. In addition to this daily log, the book also records students' entry into the school, their departure, and their age. In most years, the register also takes account of student examinations and their level of achievement. Each of these three sections are periodically annotated with tidbits of additional information about life at the school. The register's final section is a record of remarks left by visitors, revealing several of the broader networks in which the school was situated during this decade. Though more detailed than any other source from the period, the information in the register was not kept in a systematic way, making it difficult to draw firm conclusions.

Though carefully laid out, the differences between these attributes of the register demonstrates well its own weaknesses. The log of students' arrival and departure at the school records fewer students, for example, than the daily attendance records. In the daily records, 415 students are noted as having been present in classes at the school, while the enrolment information in the register records only 323 students. Part of this can be explained because the first page of the enrolment list is missing, suggesting that there were as many as 47 more students enrolled at the school than we have enumerated using this part of the register. Even so, without any explanation, there remain 45 students in the day-to-day records who do not appear in the other records. More research needs to be done to explain this discrepancy, but it seems likely that this was the result of inconsistent record keeping.

There is another major discrepancy between the enrolment log and the day-to-day attendance register. According to enrolments, only thirty-one students ran away from the school. In our analysis of the day-to-day register, nearly four times as many students ($n = 104$) are listed as having run away at some point during their time at the school. We must therefore assume that the information in the register provides us with a window into life at the school but not one that is complete or transparent. However, though an imperfect source, given the absence of other documents from this period in the school's history, the register is an important one with which to engage and understand.

Figure 13.1. A page in the register, April 1868

Source: Cronyn Archives, Diocese of Huron

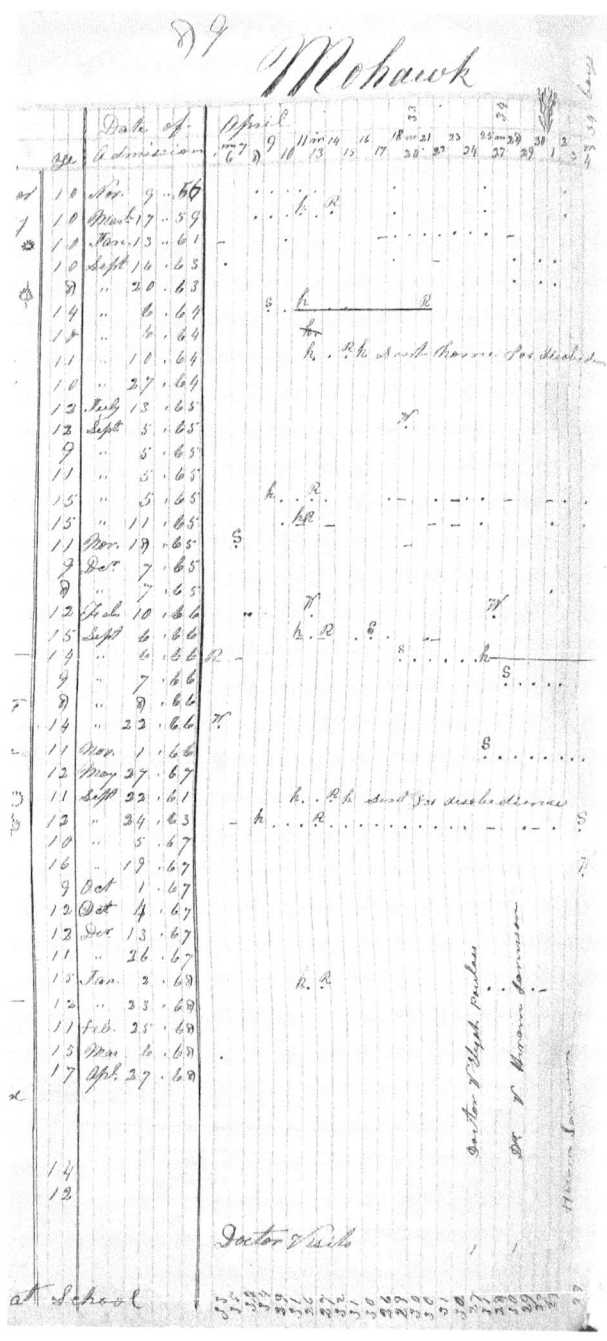

Attendance

Perhaps the most important window this document can provide onto the school's operation is its recording of student enrolment and attendance. Over its entire span, from late 1859 to early 1873, 415 children attended the school. For the most part, children were selected from day schools at Six Nations, but some children also came from much farther away. In the register, there are children from Munsee-Delaware Nation, just west of London, Ontario, and Bkejwanong Unceded Territory (Walpole Island) on the St. Clair River.[3]

Students stayed at the school for varying lengths of time. In the mid-1860s, Florence Nightingale surveyed schools for Indigenous children across the British Empire. The information provided to her about the Mohawk Institute suggested students stayed between five and six years.[4] The information seems to be misleading, though. Of the 235 students for whom the register provides arrival and departure dates, the average length of stay was just over two and a half years. Even this statistic masks significant differences between students. Only 100 students (one-quarter) stayed longer than this, with 69 students staying less than one year. Most children during this period stayed only for a few years, choosing to leave themselves or departing after being called home by their parents. A handful of students (2 in 1868) were sent home for disobedience. The successes Nelles pointed to in his reports, whereby students completed the school's curriculum and then moved on to further study, were not typical of the average student who attended the school.

Nonetheless, as Nelles hoped, the overall school population increased significantly over this decade. In fact, while his reports to the NEC indicated rising student numbers, often there were more students listed in the register than were filed in Nelles's reports. Between January and March 1860, someone has noted in the register that 40 boys and 19 girls were at the school. The year before, Nelles applied to the NEC to increase the school's enrolment from between 40 or 50 to 60 students.[5] Even after this approved expansion, he continued to lobby for further growth. By September 1867 there were about 80 students, according to the report filed with the NEC, but there are 104 names listed in the daily log of the register. Indeed, generally, there seem to have been about 100 or more children recorded annually at the school during the late 1860s and early 1870s, despite the NEC capping enrolment at 90.[6] In any given year, enrolment could be variable. On average, the school enrolled about 20 new students per year, with outlying years, such as 1867, seeing the enrolment of as few as 12, and the year following 44.

Students came to the school at all ages. The enrolment log notes the ages for 294 students. If we assume that this entry marks a student's age on entry, the average age that students arrived at the school was about 11.6 years. The youngest students, though, were 8 years old ($n = 23$) and the oldest were 19 years old ($n = 3$); only 18 students began their studies when they were 15 years or older. Even if they met the age threshold, the school's physical requirements could send them home, as it did for a student who, in 1866, was sent home for "being thought too small."[7] The student returned to the school in 1868 and remained until at least 1871.

Like the duration students spent at the school, absences are similarly variable. If we look at the aggregate data there were 12,965 full-day absences noted in the register, or about 1,000 per year; broken down over the eleven-month school year, this amounted to about 91 absences per month. Though it is hard to determine the exact number of students at the school in any given year, this works out to be about one or two days absent per student per month.

It was not unusual for students to run away. The school's administration considered these students as "fugitives" and noted an "f" on the days when they had run away. Generally, running away was more common in the first three months of the school year than during other times of the year, though May was the second most common month for students to leave the school. It is important that these cases be treated carefully. What caused students to run away is never clearly stated. Some students likely missed their families, while other students likely sought relief from the school's relatively harsh living conditions. Testimony from later survivors of the school also testify to cultures of abuse at the school, which may have also caused students to run away.

Not all "fugitive" students resented the school, though. One boy, who attended the school for eight years between 1859 and 1867, for example, ran away on three occasions, once in 1860 and twice in 1863, but he also went on to study at the Brantford Grammar School and returned to Six Nations to teach "school in the woods during vacation."[8] Though it is clear that the student was motivated to leave the school without permission—especially in 1863, when he ran away twice within two weeks—his continued attendance at the school and later teaching work suggests some degree of nuance is needed when thinking about these "fugitives."

This nuance noted, it seems most likely that students who ran away were missing their families and/or using their bodies to express displeasure with how the school was being run. It is hard not to think that there was some sort of crisis at the school in the fall of 1860, when, between late September and early October, sixteen students ran away, some of them more than once, and eight of them ran away on 6 October. In addition to these "fugitives," six students were also sent home, or kept home by their parents, during these weeks; one student is noted on October 1 as having died. All of this suggests there were visceral problems at the school during these months.

The incidents in 1860 point to an additional consideration about students who ran away. Though sometimes students would be listed as running away alone, it was not uncommon that groups of students would leave together, as did two separate groups of three students in mid-October 1863 and in 1867. Though it is impossible to know for sure, it seems reasonable to conclude that such collective action was a symbol of friendship or kinship between specific students.

Routine at the School

The schedule of classes was not recorded in the register and is somewhat difficult to piece together. The information provided to Nightingale claimed that students attended classes five and a half days per week. Their days were roughly broken into six hours of instruction, two hours of play, and four hours of outdoor work; a noted contrast with the well-known "half-day system" that came to define the Indian Residential School system.[9] Reports to the NEC set out the following daily schedule a little more specifically: School began at 9:00 a.m. with prayer; it adjourned at 12:15 p.m. for a forty-five minute lunch period; at 4:00 p.m. school closed with the reading of Christian scripture, catechism, and prayer.[10] On Sundays this routine was broken up by church. Usually, the students attended at the Mohawk Chapel, which was only a short distance away; in the early 1870s, however, the church was closed for repair and Christian services were likely held at the school and led by the teacher Thomas Griffith.[11] All of this, of course, must be read with the recognition that survivor testimony often points to ways in which the official schedule—drawn on here—was not actually followed in practice.

The language of instruction at the school was English. A December 1859 report, however, indicates that it was difficult for the children to practise the language. It seems likely that, among the students, their first languages were more commonly used.[12] By 1868, however, the NEC reported that "Both boys and girls talk more English among themselves than they ever did before."[13] Contrary to this assessment, in 1872, one former student was praised for their fluency in "five Indian dialects";[14] another report that year emphasized that students' first languages were used outside of class time and that English was encouraged but "without compulsion."[15] When Upper Canada College master John Martland visited the Institute in 1872, he reported that the boys "did not wish to speak English."[16] It is important to note—as Alison Norman has—that for much of the nineteenth century, teachers' use of Haudenosaunee languages in the classroom was encouraged in order to support student learning.[17]

The curriculum was varied. Examinations, however, were regularly held every June or July. For the most part, the students were examined by Nelles, under the supervision of clergy members or the Indian agent. More work needs to be done to understand the curriculum. Based on the students' examination records, the school was divided by sex and into five different classes. In the second class, students studied reading and spelling as well as multiplication. In the third class, students would focus on similar tasks, though geography was added. In some years, at this level, familiarity with the Anglican catechism and Lord's Prayer was also noted. The fourth class seems to have been similar. One student, though, was noted as having satisfactory "ciphering and book keeping," suggesting that some degree of accounting knowledge was being taught at the school. The fifth class is harder to determine. When examined, the girls in that class in 1868 could "read & spell very well and answer question in Roman history" as well as ciphering in fractions. In 1872 the girls were noted as "writing & ciphering satisfactory answers in grammar & geography . . . this class also study Ancient and Modern History & human physiology."

This trajectory is a little different from what was described to the NEC in June 1869 by teacher Thomas Griffith. By that time Griffith had taught at the school for eighteen years.[18] In this report he breaks down the boys into six classes and the girls into five. Table 13.1 lays out his description of their studies.[19] One of the subjects missing in this description is physical education, which, according to Nightingale, was part of the school's curriculum; it and the Jesuit school at Wikwemikong were the only schools in Canada mentioned in her report to provide physical education curriculum for Indigenous students. Contrary to Nightingale's report, in 1872, the school claimed to the NEC that "no special gymnastics are provided," suggesting that perhaps physical education was more aspirational than a curricular reality.[20]

Table 13.1. Mohawk Institute Curriculum, ca. 1869

Level	Ages	Girls	Boys
First class 3 boys; 11 girls	Boys: 15–19 Girls: 11–16	English history, grammar, geography, arithmetic to compound rules and fractions, explanatory catechism, Testament readings, needlework and spinning	Arithmetic to cube root, algebra, bookkeeping
Second class 4 boys; 6 girls	Boys: 17–20 Girls: 11–16	Reading, first principles of grammar, arithmetic to compound rules, explanatory catechism, Testament reading, needlework	English history, grammar, geography, arithmetic to compound proportion, and fractions
Third class 13 boys; 10 girls	Boys: 12–18 Girls: 10–16	Reading, simple multiplication and division, church catechism, Testament reading, needlework	Grammar, verb conjugation, compound rules and fractions, geography, catechism, Testament reading
Fourth class 7 boys; 8 girls	Boys: 12–14 Girls: 11–16	Reading, simple addition and subtraction, multiplication tables, catechism, needlework	Arithmetic as far as compound division, church catechism, etc.
Fifth class 14 boys; 7 girls	Boys: 10–18 Girls: 9–14	Reading and needlework	Spelling, reading, writing, multiplication tables, simple catechism, ciphering as far as simple addition
Sixth class 6 Boys	Boys: 9–12	N/A	Reading

Source: Compiled from Nelles, NEC Report, 18 May 1872, in Elizabeth Graham, *The Mush Hole: Life at Two Indian Residential Schools* (Heffle Publishing, 1997), 67.

The information in this table is a bit misleading because just a few years later the school reported five classes of boys and seven classes of girls.[21] There seems to have been considerable variation in the school's structure from year to year. Progress was not necessarily by year. As you can see by the range of ages in table 13.1, there was quite a spread between the students' ages in each class. Some students remained in the same class for several years. One, for example, was enrolled in the second class in 1864 but was only in the fourth class by 1868.[22]

There does not seem to be a significant difference between what the boys and girls learned in their studies. Far less attention, though, was paid to the girls in the register. Generally, school administrators were more interested in boys' progress than they were that of the girls. The records here, therefore, are quite incomplete.

All the instruction focused on book learning, though one source describes the school's walls as covered with illustrations and maps.[23] The books were numbered (first book, second book, third book, etc.) and paralleled the class in which the student was enrolled. The handful of books noted in the register are as follows:

- Canadian Series (Old and New)[24]
- Watt's First Catechism
- Sangster's "Elementary arithmetic"[25]
- Possible: Carpenter's Spelling Assistant
- Lovewell's General Geography[26]

It is unclear just how many books the school had in its possession. In late September 1861, Nelles took receipt of 12 copy books, 10 slates, 356 hymn books, and 12 grammars; the hymn books, I suspect, were for his work at the chapel. More work needs to be done comparing these texts with those used in the public school system. Though these texts do not align entirely with those approved in 1870 for use in the Ontario public school system, the common use of the *Canadian National Series of Reading* books and *Lovell's General Geography* suggests the school tried to follow the new province's curriculum.[27]

The academic curriculum was paired with training in agriculture and other skills. Farmland was only acquired in late 1859, and much of the food at that time seems to have been purchased rather than grown; Nelles expressed hope, however, that the school would become self-sustaining.[28] In an 1870 report, Nelles claimed that the school "teaches the large boys general farming."[29] According to the register, students mostly spent time digging potatoes, turnips, and other root vegetables.[30] In 1860, the school produced 1,000 bushels of potatoes, 1,000 bushels of turnips, 200 bushels of wheat, and 200 bushels of oats and peas.[31] Much of this was likely produced for sale, rather than consumption at the school. There are occasional references to students tending other crops, such as two days of pulling flax in late July 1866, threshing in 1867 and 1871, and husking corn.[32] These activities were mostly carried out by the boys, though in late July 1866 both boys and girls were involved in pulling flax. The only livestock mentioned was the periodic "washing of sheep," and one later reference to hogs. At various times of the year, these activities were all-consuming. From 16 October to 6 November 1872, for example, it is clear that every boy was working in the fields rather than completing their academic work, except when "this day being wet boys at school." As would become common at the school, it seems that even in these early years, agricultural work took priority over classroom learning.

Girls' work was focused mostly on domestic tasks. One of their biggest responsibilities was making and mending the children's clothing. In 1872 it was reported that all the clothing, except winter coats, was made at the school by female students.[33] This was significant. Over the year prior, the girls had made 155 smocks and coats, 212 pants, 193 shirts, 140 socks, 205 dresses, 104 chemises, 43 skirts, 46 petticoats, 105 stockings, 14 aprons, 87 sheets, 74 pillow slips, 22 bed ticks, 37 towels, 2 suits, 2 pairs of drawers, and 2 night dresses. At that time there were about thirty-eight girls at the school, meaning that if evenly distributed, each girl had produced about thirty-eight items each over the prior fifteen months.[34] All of this work was conducted under a guise of skill building, but, ultimately, it saved the school money by drawing upon the students' unpaid labour.

Religion was pervasive and thoroughly Anglican. Confirmation and baptisms of children were commonly noted.[35] Students studied the Anglican catechism.[36] In 1872, in a report to the NEC, the school claimed that Anglican teachings were part of daily instruction and that, though "there are some Roman Catholics and some pagans . . . , happily, no objection to the religious teaching has ever yet been made by any."[37]

Other types of activities at the school were variable and seem to have been carried out on an idiosyncratic schedule likely timed around the agricultural and material needs of the school. For example, on 11 June 1860 four girls were noted as spinning wool, while six boys were busy cleaning up the graveyard, likely at the Mohawk Chapel (though this is unspecified). On 25 April 1867, seven students went with a "Mr. Wilson" to have their photo taken as a group.[38] On 8 December 1871 there was a "concert in Brantford . . . to buy an organ for the Tuscarora church"; it is unclear whether the students participated in or attended the concert. A few months later, in April, the students and teachers visited the "menagerie" in Brantford. All these activities are typical of later student experiences at the school whereby students visited the nearby town for fundraisers and other events.

It is hard to think that the students were well supervised. In his report on the school in 1870, NEC Commissioner A. E. Botsford reported that the school accommodated ninety students in residence, as well as the superintendent and his wife.[39] That said, space was tight in the building. Martland's inspection reveals how rooms in the school building served several purposes: "Mr. M was shown the room in which the boys had their classes, and in which they sat in the evening, and in which also, in the winter time, they washed. The room was very little better than a cellar in an ordinary house; not so good as a laundry."[40] The space, it seems, was crammed and, given the large number of students—and minimal adult supervision—poorly supervised, at least by today's standards.

Students had time away from the school. The information provided to Nightingale claimed that the students had forty days of holiday each year.[41] Generally, the school closed for the month of August, with most students returning home, while a handful remained to tend the fields.[42] One student, in 1871, is noted as having gone to "camp," though it is unclear what exactly the word "camp" means in this context.

During the school year, students would also take breaks. Sometimes students would have a day's vacation down to the river or a trip into Brantford.[43] Other times, the students were given a free morning or afternoon to play.[44] Holidays were also observed. On Victoria Day 1863, for example, the following is noted: "Kept in memory of the queen's birth no school no thought—a day for nought."[45] Christmas was also a day without classes, though it seems that most students stayed at the school rather than returning home.[46] An important caveat here, though, is that in the 1870 NEC report, a break for Christmas was noted, with two girls remaining with Nelles over the holiday.[47]

Sickness and Health

Student health and well-being are hard to determine from this source because entries related to this aspect of student life seem to have been somewhat haphazard. For example, in 1870, hair cutting is noted in both early January and mid-March. Though it only appears here and a few times elsewhere, we can assume that this activity happened regularly at the school, perhaps in the two-month interval noted here.

Periodically, students were injured while at the school. There are seldom specific details about the injuries; usually just "sore" body parts are listed. Occasionally, though, we get a glimpse into the type of work the students were doing. One student, for example, ran a pitchfork through their foot in July 1867; another, in July 1870, cut off the top of one of his fingers. Given how the school capitalized on student labour, it is hardly surprising that many of the injuries noted can be linked to manual and agricultural work.

Disease visited the school from time to time. The experiences of the students can only be inferred from the records. One of the most common sicknesses in the school was "sore eyes." It is also tempting to think about this as the common childhood ailment of "pink eye" (conjunctivitis). We must be careful, though, not to rule out more serious illnesses. Trachoma, a bacterial infection that can lead to blindness, was a well-documented health issue in residential schools. It spread in overcrowded conditions where children shared water, towels, and bedding.[48] In July 1871 at least sixteen students were afflicted with "sore eyes." Even more seriously, a girl who attended the school in 1869 stayed home with "sore eyes" for September and October but died later that month or in early November. It seems that whatever was causing her eye problems was more serious than either conjunctivitis or trachoma.

Occasionally we catch a glimpse of how disease spread through the school. In January 1872, scarlet fever and diphtheria were noted;[49] a few days after this annotation a local doctor—Egerton Griffin—visited, noting that "Almost every boy and girl is ill with cough and sore throat."[50] Measles was another common ailment that threatened student well-being, with outbreaks recorded in 1867 and 1870. Other periods of widespread disease can be inferred from the annotations. Between April and June 1868, for example, the doctor attended the school on twenty occasions, visiting at least five students. What is important about these visits is that some students are marked as having mumps, another student with St. Vitus's dance (Sydenham's cholera), and two students were noted as having died. Several other students, including one of the students who died, were only noted with a generic "s" for sickness, a symbol that was also used for injury. Given the gravity of the situation, it seems like the school was facing some sort of outbreak, though the specific cause is unclear from the records.

It is easy to understand how disease could have travelled quickly through the school. In the fall of 1868, a report filed with the NEC claimed that for the thirty-seven boys at the school, there were only sixteen beds, requiring three boys to share a bunk. Because of this report, Nelles was authorized to purchase ample beds to ensure that each student could sleep alone.[51] A year later he reported that he had separate beds for each girl, but his facilities were not big enough to accommodate a bed each for the boys.[52] Mattresses were filled with straw and, at least on one occasion in the register (29 February 1867), the students are noted as having to replace the straw themselves. It seems baffling today to know that Nelles pushed to increase the number of students at the school knowing full well there was not enough space for all to safely sleep. More students, however, meant more funding for the school and greater approval from the NEC.

As we saw earlier in reference to the classroom that tripled as a social space and winter wash house, the general hygiene in the school seems to have been poor. In Martland's inspection of bathing facilities he noted that the girls had only tubs and pails, no wash basins. He was told that "Indian children were dirty in their habits, and if supplied with basins, etc. would use them improperly."[53] In that same report, Martland found that in the summer the boys washed in a shed with a single tub and pail. This claim is interesting because a month before Martland visited, the register marked 5 June as the "first day for the boys to bathe in the river," suggesting that this is where the boys bathed in summer. Later that year, just after a serious bout of scarlet fever, a visitor to the school reported that its heating was also insufficient.[54] No answer could be given when Martland asked about the "privies."[55] Taken together, it seems that the overall health and well-being of the children was not a very high priority at the school.

Despite these crowded and poorly built conditions, some medical care was provided to prevent disease from spreading. Students were vaccinated periodically against smallpox.[56] It is unclear exactly how this was carried out, and it seems that only some students received vaccinations, but in 1862 (two), 1864 (twenty-four), 1871 (eleven), 1872 (ten) some students received their inoculations at the school. The 1871 vaccination was conducted by Dr. Robert Dee, a full-time and long-serving physician at Six Nations.[57]

Death was not uncommon. Between 1860 and 1873, 24 students out of 415 (5.7 per cent) are listed as having died, though it is not clear that all died while attending the school. Few details were recorded about students who died. Rarely, it seems, did a student die at the school itself.[58] Only a single student, in 1869, is noted as having died on the school premises. Others, though, clearly went home to die. An eleven-year-old boy—part of the possible outbreak in 1868—"went home and died on Saturday"; he had only been at the school for three and a half months.[59] A girl had died three months earlier, in April, under similar circumstances. Another girl in 1872 was noted in a Company report as "dying of consumption" (tuberculosis).[60] At the time of writing, only 7 of the 24 children whose deaths are noted in the register have been included in the National Centre for Truth and Reconciliation's Memorial Register.[61] More work needs to be done to reconcile these lists.

All of this supports the conclusions Florence Nightingale reached in her study of student health at boarding schools across the British Empire. Supported by the British Colonial Office, Nightingale was charged with determining "the precise influence which school training exercised on the health of native children."[62] The celebrated nurse found that, across the empire, the mortality rate in colonial schools was about twice as high as it was in England; in Canada the mortality rate was about 12.5:1,000 for boys and 25:1,000 for girls.[63] Most children in these schools died of tuberculosis (consumption) or scrofula, which is a related symptom of tuberculosis. Neither disease appears prominently in the register. For her study, Nightingale received information from the Mohawk Institute for the period 1856–61. There were fifty-five students included in her study, one of whom—a boy between the ages of ten and fifteen—died. Echoing what we find in the register and reports to the NEC, Nightingale blamed these elevated statistics on students not being given enough time outdoors and the problem of overcrowding and poor ventilation in the buildings.[64]

As Nelles focused on expanding the school, he created unsanitary conditions that likely made day-to-day life unusually difficult and unsafe for the children entrusted to his care. Sleeping two to three to a bed, with little access to washing—and perhaps toilet—facilities, it is surprising that children were not sick more often.

Visitors

Visitors to the school were relatively common and seldom critical of the school. Over the thirteen years covered in the register, almost ninety people left a record of their visit. Many were from the area around Brantford, but others came from overseas; places like England, Ireland, and New Zealand. Almost all of them were men—though there were a few women too—and most adhered to the Anglican, or an allied Protestant, faith. Each of these people left short comments in the back of the register. Their comments followed a common theme: Visitors applauded the school for its sense of order and the progress that the students had made in their studies. As it belonged to a model institution, this guest book of sorts was not the place for criticism.

That there is little sign of critique is hardly surprising. Being responsible for the Institute's reputation, it is unlikely that Nelles would have permitted someone critical of the school to write their comments in the book. We would expect, therefore, that the perspective on the school provided in this document is rosier than what the students or faculty might have experienced; it likely worked to support Nelles's efforts toward school expansion. When read alongside the rest of the attendance register, however, we can develop a deeper and more critical understanding of what it was like at the school during the mid-nineteenth century.

A good illustration of just how misleading these visitor comments can be is the report by James H. Vidal, who was visiting from England in September 1872. In his comments, Vidal wrote, "I am much pleased with a brief inspection of the writing and ciphering books of the scholars in the Mohawk Institution." Reviewing the daily attendance register for the day he visited, however, reveals a more nuanced picture of what Vidal might have encountered. On the day that he reviewed the students' academic work, a student had run away from the school, and several others were busy "cutting corn." On these activities, about which he probably had no knowledge, Vidal is silent. Similarly, earlier that year, in May, a person named Shogesjowaueh from Stratford complimented Nelles on his "untiring kindness" and the "comfort and prosperity of the institution." Meanwhile, according to the register, the students spent the day "picking up stones off the meadow." It is clear, when the day-to-day records are compared with visitors' observations, that life at the school involved much more than the academic pursuits recorded by outsiders.

Perhaps more to the point, one wonders exactly what visitors must have experienced at the school. Was the Reverend James McDowall being ironic, for example, when—as two runaway students had still not returned to the school at the time of his visit—he wrote that "the school is well attended and the conduct of the boys of [goodness] and attention is to me a matter of agreeable wonder, considering that they are naturally of restless temperaments"? Another runaway student had been gone for three days when visitor Alex H. Heron observed that he was much pleased with the school's scholarly attainment; a student also ran away the day that F. C. Gamble and F. C. Stanton visited in 1871. It seems odd to hear of the school's successes while the attendance records list some students as "fugitives or runaways" on the very days these visitors were present. Although it is likely that visitors were not informed about "fugitive" students, the absence of comments about this suggest that there was little sign of disruption to school routines.

Though mostly straightforward and alike, occasional entries shed light on other important aspects of life at the school. When Major General Burrows visited in February 1867, for example, he noted the challenges with which teachers contended "as regards the Indian language." Five years later, four Americans stopped at the school and "were entertained by the young ladies of the institution with several songs both indian + English." Both comments demonstrate that students continued to use their first languages at the school in addition to English; a point that historians Elizabeth Graham and Alison Norman have elaborated on in their respective work about the Mush Hole and schooling at Six Nations. This was a reality that ended following the close of Nelles's tenure in 1872.

On a more concerning note, R. Doherty painted a carceral picture of the school three months earlier when he expressed his pleasure with the "order, neatness, and comfort which prevailed" in the boys' dormitory after passing through it "after the boys had retired." It is important to take a moment and think about the implications of these comments. Though his comments place a greater emphasis on order in the boys' sleeping accommodations than the comments of other visitors, as a stranger to the school, we must ask why Doherty was invited into the children's quarters as they slept. The stranger's comments suggest that he felt his surveillance was a good and natural thing for a visitor to do at the school. Given what we know about the horrors of residential schooling, his comments about visiting the boys while they slept point to—at the very least—an unwillingness to ensure student privacy and safety from visitors.

Two former students left their own comments in the book:

> Having spent four years at this School. I am glad to record my gratitude for the instruction received from Mr. Griffith [his teacher] also my thankfulness to the Revd Canon Nelles for his untiring kindness to me whilst here.

> My first five years were spent at this School from '64 to '69, I am now in my third year at the Hellmuth College. L. O. and during vacation I always consider this place as only second to my own father's home. Every time I come here thoughts of the past occur to me. I am glad to see so much improvement in the place, and the children seemingly so contented and happy.

Written within five months of each other, these entries feel more contrived, and for privacy reasons I will not name the students here. Unlike the other entries, for these, lines have been drawn onto the page on which the students could write their letters evenly. In the first entry, the student—though noted as absent for much of 1871—had not yet departed from the school. His formal date of departure was the same day, in April 1872, that the other entry was written, suggesting some degree of connection between the two entries. Also, reviewing his student record, it is interesting to note that the second student, who attended Hellmuth College in London, Ontario, after leaving the Mohawk Institute, had initially run away after his first two months at the school; his subsequent academic career serves as an interesting contrast with this event early in his life. Though it is important to honour the memories these students recorded, we might also ask why they are the only two student voices included in the book and why they were written so closely together.

What is important to note, relative to these two students, is that, of the register's thirteen-year span between 1860 and 1873, 78 per cent of the comments were written either during or after 1870. There seems to have been a reason for adding comments after 1870. In his comments about how neat the school was kept, Shogesjowaueh alluded to concerns about the school that might have been raised during the late 1860s. He began his 1872 comments by expressing his "utmost gradification [sic] for the improvement made in this Institution since A.D. 1868." Further, most of the names listed during 1870 were for journalists visiting the school from Bowmanville, Guelph, Hamilton, Kingston, Listowel, Petrolia, and Strathroy, suggesting that Nelles was trying to promote the school's work through the media. It seems likely that these two student reflections were part of a broader effort to potentially rehabilitate the school's reputation.

These two students were not the only Indigenous voices to comment on the school. Based on his name, it seems likely that Shogesjowaueh from Stratford was Anishinaabe or Haudenosaunee. The well-known Anishinaabe Episcopalian (Anglican) priest Enmegahbowh also visited the school in 1868, though he did not leave any additional comments in the book aside from his signature. Mi'kmaw Baptist and linguist Basamai Nachecallassootmamk, also known as Benjamin Christmas, visited eight years earlier, leaving these words in the visitors' log (preserving the original spelling): "My heart his overflowen with gratitude for the progress the Indian boys have made in this school. This school may be the origin of their everlasting blessing. My prayers will be continually offered for them, and for those who have taken so much interest in their wellfare. Some of these boys may meet with my students, and they will mingle their prayers, and offer them to God." Nachecallassootmamk's words are interesting because he is often referred to as a helper to the settler Baptist missionary Silas Rand. His life is mostly defined in the historical record by his association with Rand.

Here, though, he alludes to being a teacher in his own right, suggesting that the colonial record may mislead us about the life this man led.

The educational credentials of some of the other visitors are also important to note. Martland, for example, visited the school from Upper Canada College in 1872 at the request of the NEC directors. Earlier that year, Henry Newman visited from Balliol College at Oxford University. Spencer A. Jones was listed as a headmaster at the Grammar School in Smiths Falls in 1858 and at Vankleek Hill in 1862. These latter two visitors made interesting comparative observations. Newman noted that the Institute compared favourably with English elementary schools, while Jones made a similar comparison with Canadian students. Their comments indicate that any analysis of this period should be cautious in devaluing the education that was taking place at the Institute as being of a poorer quality than what was available to settlers elsewhere in the province. As Alison Norman's chapter in this book demonstrates, there was a concerted effort at the school to train students to become teachers.

Leaving School

The Mohawk Institute was not a terminal institution for some students' education. Several students went on to more advanced studies. The best-known alumni from this period are George Martin and George Hill, brothers-in-law who attended medical school after leaving the Institute.[65] It was more common, though, for students to leave the school to become teachers or clergy members, usually furthering their studies in colonial schools or colleges.

As Norman's chapter develops in greater detail, the most common path for students leaving the Mohawk Institute for further studies was teaching. Several students left the Institute to attend the Brantford Grammar School.[66] One of these students returned in 1867 to teach "school in the woods during vacation."[67] Another began to work as a teacher in 1869 at one of the day schools at Six Nations.[68] A third took a similar "teaching" path in 1871, beginning to teach at the Institute itself in 1871.[69] This path was expected for graduates of the Institute. The 1868 NEC report on the school noted that "The best and cheapest teachers for them would be Indians brought up at the Institution; and perhaps sent afterwards for a year to a good school for teachers, like the Normal School in Toronto."[70] Another former student, Isaiah Joseph, who spent most of the 1860s at the Institute, taught school at the "Ojibway Settlement" in the early 1870s.[71]

In addition to these boys, who seem to have remained closer to home, others travelled further afield. Susannah Carpenter and Nelles Monture, who were fourteen and fifteen years old at the time, were selected to attend Isaac Hellmuth's colleges in London. Both teenagers were chosen by Nelles because of their good character. In recommending the two for Hellmuth's schools, Nelles made it clear that bilingualism was seen as an asset; he asked the NEC whether "it shall be a necessary qualification that the child should speak the Indian language."[72] The following year, three students were similarly being prepared to head to London to study under Hellmuth, while another student two years later attended the Canadian Literary Institute, a Baptist college in Woodstock.[73] Nelles claimed that seven or eight other students had made applications to be sent to "superior schools."[74]

The connection to London was important. While Carpenter and Monture were heading to Hellmuth's colleges, Albert Anthony and John Jacobs, who attended the Institute during the early 1860s, were studying for the Anglican priesthood at Huron College, also in London and run by Hellmuth. Upon their ordination, Anthony returned to Six Nations, while Jacobs became a priest serving the Chippewa communities around Sarnia, Kettle, and Stoney Point.[75]

Neither path to becoming a teacher or priest was particularly unique. Nelles's report to the Company in June 1859 claimed that "Four of the school teachers at present employed are Indians, who have been educated at this Institution; and another, through the liberality of the Company is pursuing his studies with a view to entering the ministry."[76] One of those people was Isaac Bearfoot. Bearfoot attended the Institute in the 1850s and then taught there for several years before attending the Toronto Normal School for accreditation as a teacher. After teaching for many years at Six Nations, Bearfoot was given a teaching appointment at the Institute in August 1869.[77] In the late 1870s, he attended Huron College and was ordained an Anglican priest.

The experiences of the other students upon leaving the school are more opaque. This is especially the case for girls. Aside from the young women who went to Hellmuth's Ladies College, we know little about where girls ended up after their time at the school. An 1872 report to the NEC, though, demonstrates that some ended up "sought after as servants by some of the most respectable people at Brantford."[78] More work needs to be conducted using census records or family histories to follow the life course of the students about whom the register is silent after they left the school.

Conclusions

What becomes apparent after working with this document is the uneven nature of student experiences during this time in the Mohawk Institute's history. For many—likely most—the school had little attraction. They stayed a short time and appeared only briefly in the register's pages. A handful of students met their deaths within the school's walls. For other students, however, their time at the school was different. Though we cannot be certain about their feelings toward the school, we might interpret the decision by some to return to Six Nations to teach as a tacit agreement with the school's missions. There was no singular experience that defined life at the Mush Hole during this period.

Despite this diversity of experiences, we can point to two aspects of school life that were common. First, as the subsequent careers of some students demonstrates, Nelles was interested in ensuring that the children in his care were educated at a standard that would allow them to participate in higher forms of education. Though only a minority of students took this path, the register's attentiveness to examinations points to a scholarly mandate that was not always present in residential schools before or after this period. Second, Nelles's desire to expand the school took priority over student comfort and health. As Florence Nightingale's study revealed so starkly, health outcomes at this school were worse than those for children in comparable English schools; we might assume the more positive situation was also similar in Canadian schools.

These contrasting common experiences help explain how the school evolved from the partnership with Six Nations that first brought it about. Absent from the register is any sign of engagement with Six Nations as a political community. Rather than meeting the needs of the community (as was the goal when the school was initially envisioned by prominent community members like Tekarihogen), by the 1860s institutional life at the Institute was being shaped by people like Nelles. With a strong desire to expand, the school put students at risk, focusing more on the institution itself than the well-being of the children or community it purported to serve. In many ways, this is what the register symbolizes. In its idiosyncratic but bureaucratic documenting of these children's lives, the register points to the developing institutionalization and growing systematization of Indigenous schooling dawning in Canada by the end of the 1870s.

NOTES

1. Nelles, NEC Report, 13 August 1860, in Elizabeth Graham, *The Mush Hole: Life at Two Indian Residential Schools* (Heffle Publishing, 1997), 55.
2. A table and biographical dictionary were produced as part of this project and turned over to the Woodland Cultural Centre. There remains some discrepancy between these documents. I have also caught a few transcription errors while working on this essay. The most important is that seven students were transcribed as having run away on 1 July 1871. Upon revisiting the register, it is clear that these students are listed with a "t" for "town" and not an "f" for "fugitive" beside their name. More work is required on this document. The discussion in this chapter should be considered preliminary.
3. Botsford, NEC Report, December 1870, in Graham, *The Mush Hole*, 59; Mohawk Institute Attendance Register, 2 August 1886, Verschoyle Phillip Cronyn Memorial Archives, London, Ontario.
4. Florence Nightingale, *Sanitary Statistics of Native Colonial Schools and Hospitals* (London, 1863), 39.
5. NEC Report, 1859, in Graham, *The Mush Hole*, 53.
6. NEC Report, 9 April 1870, and NEC Report, 16 May 1872 in Graham, 59, 65.
7. Woodland Cultural Centre, *Documenting Early Residential Schools*, Student Biographies, Student #9.
8. Student Biographies, Student #21.
9. Nightingale, *Sanitary Statistics*, 39.
10. Institution Report, 30 June 1859, in Graham, *The Mush Hole*, 54.
11. Nelles, NEC Report, 15 July 1870, in Graham, 59.
12. Institution Report, 31 December 1859, in Graham, 54.
13. NEC Report, 1868, in Graham, 56.
14. A. Stewart, NEC Report, 2 May 1872, in Graham, 64.
15. Griffith, Institution Report, 30 June 1872, in Graham, 68.
16. Martland notes of verbal statement, NEC Report, in Graham, 69.
17. Alison Norman, "'Teachers Amongst Their Own People': Kanyen'kehà:ka (Mohawk) Women Teachers in Nineteenth-Century Tyendinaga and Grand River, Ontario," *Historical Studies in Education* 29, no. 1 (Spring 2017): 32–56.
18. Botsford, NEC Report, December 1870, in Graham, *The Mush Hole*, 59.
19. NEC Report, 30 June 1869, in Graham, 57.
20. Nightingale, *Sanitary Statistics*, 39; Nelles, Elliot, Chance, Roberts, NEC Report, 16 May 1872, in Graham, *The Mush Hole*, 65.
21. Nelles, Elliot, Chance, Roberts, NEC Report, 16 May 1872, in Graham, *The Mush Hole*, 65.
22. Student Biographies, Student #7.
23. Botsford, NEC Report, December 1870, in Graham, *The Mush Hole*, 59.
24. Botsford, NEC Report, December 1870, in Graham, 59.
25. Botsford, NEC Report, December 1870, in Graham, 59.
26. Botsford, NEC Report, December 1870, in Graham, 59.
27. *Annual Report of the Normal, Model, Grammar and Common Schools of Ontario* (London, 1871), appendix D.
28. NEC Report, 3 August 1859, in Graham, *The Mush Hole*, 54.
29. Nelles, NEC Report, 15 July 1870, in Graham, 59.
30. See Mohawk Institute Attendance Register, 20 June 1860; 10 October 1860; 16 October 1860; 15 November 1860; 10 November 1862; 28–9 September 1863; 11 November 1863; 1869; 1870; 9 October 1871.
31. NEC Report, January 1860, in Graham, *The Mush Hole*, 54.
32. Mohawk Institute Attendance Register, 30 and 31 July 1866; 26 and 28 February 1867; 6 January 1871; 18 October 1871; 27 October 1871; May and June 1872.
33. Nelles, NEC Report, 18 May 1872, in Graham, *The Mush Hole*, 67.
34. Griffith, Institution Report, 30 June 1872, in Graham, 68.
35. See Mohawk Institute Attendance Register, 6 April 1862; 5 April 1863.
36. Mohawk Institute Attendance Register, 26 October 1866.
37. Nelles, Elliot, Chance, Roberts, 16 May 1872, NEC Report, in Graham, *The Mush Hole*, 66.
38. Mohawk Institute Attendance Register, 25 April 1867.
39. Botsford, NEC Report, December 1870, in Graham, *The Mush Hole*, 59.

40 Martland notes of verbal statement, NEC Report, in Graham, 69.
41 Nightingale, *Sanitary Statistics*, 39.
42 Mohawk Institute Attendance Register, 2 August 1866.
43 Mohawk Institute Attendance Register, 25 June 1860; 14 September 1860; 1 July 1871.
44 Mohawk Institute Attendance Register, 2 January 1863.
45 Mohawk Institute Attendance Register, 25 May 1863.
46 Mohawk Institute Attendance Register, 25–6 December 1863; 25 December 1867.
47 Nelles, NEC Report, 5 February 1870, in Graham, *The Mush Hole*, 58.
48 Truth and Reconciliation Commission of Canada, *The Final Report of the Truth and Reconciliation Commission of Canada*, vol. 1, *The History, Part 1, Origins to 1939* (McGill-Queen's University Press, 2015), 446.
49 Nelles, NEC Report, 1 March 1872, in Graham, *The Mush Hole*, 62.
50 Mohawk Institute Attendance Register, 24 January 1872.
51 Lister, NEC Report, Autumn 1868, in Graham, *The Mush Hole*, 56; NEC Report, 25 February 1869, in Graham, 57.
52 NEC Report, 23 November 1869, in Graham, 58.
53 Martland notes of verbal statement, NEC Report, in Graham, 69.
54 Blomfield, NEC Report, 2 March 1872, in Graham, 62.
55 Martland notes of verbal statement, NEC Report, in Graham, 69.
56 Nelles, NEC Report, 1 March 1872, in Graham, 62.
57 Sally M. Weaver, "The Iroquois: The Grand River Reserve in the Late Nineteenth and Early Twentieth Centuries, 1875–1945," in *Aboriginal Ontario: Historical Perspectives on the First Nations*, ed. Edward S. Rogers and Donald Smith (Dundurn Press, 1994), 227–8.
58 There are a handful of exceptions to this. See Mohawk Institute Attendance Register, 2 October 1860.
59 Student Biographies, Student #96.
60 Roberts Journal, NEC Report, 13 March 1872, in Graham, *The Mush Hole*, 63.
61 "Memorial Register," National Centre for Truth and Reconciliation, accessed 17 January 2022, https://nctr.ca/memorial/national-student-memorial/memorial-register/.
62 Nightingale, *Sanitary Statistics*, 2.
63 Nightingale, 3.
64 Nightingale, 14.
65 Botsford, NEC Report, December 1870, in Graham, *The Mush Hole*, 59. On Martin, see Keith Jamieson and Michelle Hamilton, *Dr. Oronhyatekha: Security, Justice, and Equality* (Dundurn Press, 2016).
66 Some include Alex Smith, George Bomberry, and Youel Carryer.
67 Student Biographies, Student #36.
68 NEC Report, 31 December 1869, in Graham, *The Mush Hole*, 58.
69 Student Biographies, Student #58.
70 NEC Report, 1868, in Graham, *The Mush Hole*, 56.
71 Nelles, NEC Report, 5 February 1870, in Graham, 58–59. George Powless and Daniel Simon were also teachers. See NEC Report, June 1871, Graham, 60. James Powless was considered a candidate for attending the Toronto Normal School in 1872. See Clerk to Missionaries, 6 June 1872, NEC Report, in Graham, 68.
72 Nelles, NEC Report, 30 June 1869, in Graham, 57–8.
73 A. Stewart, NEC Report, 2 May 1872, in Graham, 64.
74 Nelles, NEC Report, 5 February 1870, in Graham, 58–9; Nelles, NEC Report, 9 April 1870, in Graham, 59.
75 For more on these students, see Natalie Cross and Thomas Peace, "'My Own Old English Friends': Networking Anglican Settler Colonialism at the Shingwauk Home, Huron College, and Western University," *Historical Studies in Education* 33, no. 1 (Spring 2021), https://doi.org/10.32316/hse-rhe.v33i1.4891.
76 Graham, *The Mush Hole*, 54.
77 Nelles, NEC Report, 30 August 1869, in Graham, 58.
78 Nelles, Elliot, Chance, Roberts, 16 May 1872, NEC Report, in Graham, 65.

14

Collecting the Evidence: Restoration and Archaeology at the Mohawk Institute

Sarah Clarke, Paul Racher, and Tara Froman

While sources such as written documents and interviews with former students of the Mohawk Institute have a great deal to tell us about life at the school, objects also have much to reveal. Drawing on materials recovered from the Mohawk Institute building during interior restoration, and artifacts unearthed during concurrent archaeological assessments performed on the grounds, this chapter explores the lived experience of children at the Mohawk Institute through objects.

The current building on the site of the Mohawk Institute—or "Mush Hole" as it was known locally—was constructed in 1903 after the previous 1858 structure was destroyed by fire. It is one of only two remaining Indian Residential Schools still standing in all of Ontario and serves as a "site of conscience" for that dark chapter of Canadian history.[1]

In 2017, water damage to the building's structure meant that extensive renovations were required if it was to continue to stand. The construction requirements of those renovations meant that considerable work had to be undertaken both within the Mush Hole and on its grounds. The possibility that the latter could impact either human or archaeological remains became a serious concern; particularly because the grounds had never been explored archaeologically. As it is situated within the limits of the Six Nations of the Grand River Reserve, the project is not covered by provincial planning legislation; were such work to take place off-reserve, this would have triggered an archaeological assessment in advance of construction.

Unfortunately, this latter point was not noted until the renovation process was well underway. In the absence of any available funding, and in the interests of just "getting the thing done," the necessary archaeological work was supported by volunteers from Archaeological Research Associates, the Ontario Archaeological Society, other firms and organizations, and Indigenous community members. The volunteer project has been a collaborative effort, from fieldwork to artifact processing, with participation from both Six Nations of the Grand River community members and Mississaugas of the Credit First Nation community members. The Mohawk Institute archaeological site has been registered with the Ministry of Heritage, Sport, Tourism and Culture Industries (archaeological site registration number AgHb-608).

Part 1: The Archaeology

Archaeological assessment services were provided to the project, sometimes with very little notice, as construction crews worked to repair damage to the school that was more extensive than had previously been supposed. As the crews worked, it became clear that the building, despite having stood for over a century, had not been particularly well-constructed. The front porch was structurally unsound, and the foundation needed significant repairs. Archaeological investigations were required in both locations, as well as in the apple orchard at the front of the building, an area that has been proposed for the construction of the Mohawk Village Memorial Park, a survivor-led commemoration project. Established in the mid-2010s by survivors of the Mohawk Institute, the Mohawk Village Memorial Park Board of Directors has been raising funds for the construction of a memorial park to honour the children who attended the school on approximately two hectares (five acres) on the grounds of the former Mohawk Institute. Construction for the park began in 2019.

In an unexpected twist, and to the delight of volunteers, the artifacts identified over three seasons of archaeology at the property span the pre-colonial Indigenous occupation of the area, through to the property's association with the residential school, and right up to the present day. To date, more than 35,000 artifacts have been collected during the archaeological assessments conducted at the Mohawk Institute property. Preliminary analysis suggests that as much as 25 percent of the archaeological assemblage dates to the period of Indigenous occupation prior to the arrival of settlers in the eighteenth century. The remainder of the artifacts appear to be associated with the use of the property as a residential school through the late twentieth century.

Artifacts recovered during the archaeological assessments at the Mohawk Institute property referred to herein will be housed at the offices of Archaeological Research Associates until they can be transferred to the Woodland Cultural Centre. As the project is both large and ongoing, comprehensive analyses have yet to be undertaken. Even a preliminary look at some of the objects recovered, however, can offer insights into the history of the Mush Hole and its grounds.

ARCHAEOLOGY BEFORE THE MUSH HOLE

The Mohawk Institute is situated in an area that was clearly favoured by Indigenous groups in the era prior to European influence, as evidenced by a large number of archaeological sites close by. The property is located in an area with fertile floodplains. With its location close to the Grand River, providing easy access to water, the site was an attractive place to settle. Archaeological evidence of Indigenous presence at the Mohawk Institute property extends across 9,500 years, stretching from the Archaic period, which dates from 9,500 to 2,900 years ago, to the Woodland period, which dates from 2,900 to 550 years ago.

During the test-pitting assessment of the property, various stone tools and by-products of stone tool production were recovered. Concentrations of these stone tool by-products or chipping "detritus" is typically interpreted as an indication of the presence of early Indigenous peoples' temporary camps or tool production sites (see figure 14.1, image A). Formal tools recovered from the site, particularly projectile points, are stylistically dateable and, as such, provide an indication as to when particular archaeological deposits/occupations occurred. Indigenous-made pottery that dates to the Woodland period was also found at various stages of the archaeological assessment (see figure 14.1, image B). Although fragmentary in nature, this pottery provides evidence of more permanent village settlement prior to the arrival of Europeans.

These early finds were followed by archaeological remains that date to the time of the return of the Haudenosaunee to the area following the American Revolutionary War and the Haldimand Grant for lands along the Grand River corridor in the early 1780s. During the investigations at the girls' (west) side of the building, part of a trade silver earring was found in a mixed soil context that also included more recent objects relating to the use of the property as a residential school (see figure 14.1, image C).

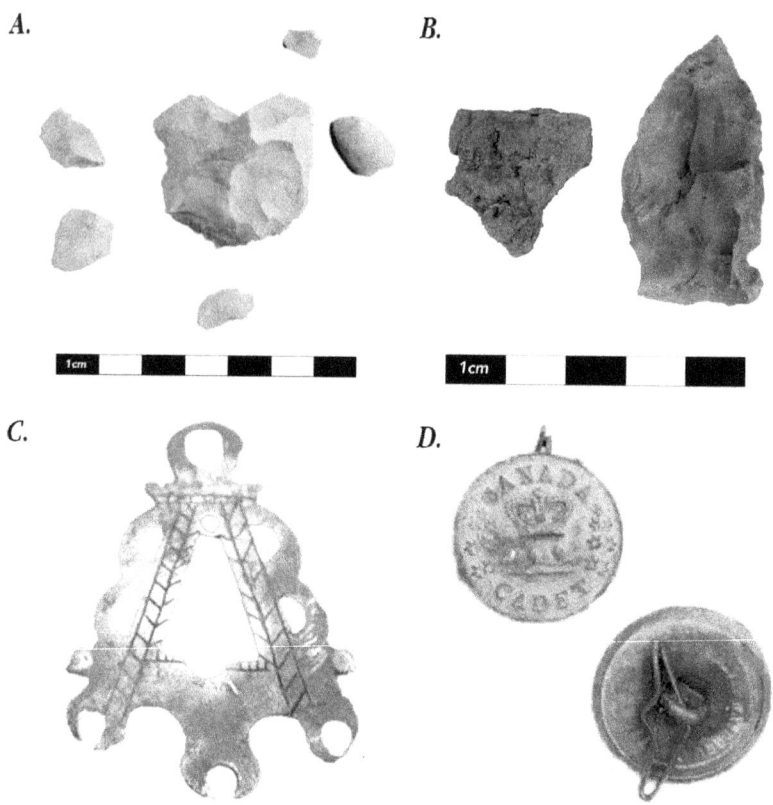

Figure 14.1. (A) Onondaga chert chipping "detritus" from the production of stone tools by an Indigenous person prior to the arrival of colonial settlers; (B) Indigenous-made pottery from the Woodland period and a bifacially flaked projectile point; (C) silver earring; (D) cadet uniform button (obverse and reverse) with "CANADA" at the top, "CADET" at the bottom, a beaver and crown at the centre, and maple leaves on either side of the beaver and crown.
Source: Dove Clarke and Archaeological Research Associates Ltd.

Trade silver was initially used during the fur trade between the French and Indigenous trappers. Silver continued to be in use as a trade item until the early 1800s. In Canada, it was produced from coin silver by silversmiths in Quebec City, Montreal, London, and several American cities. Beginning in the mid-nineteenth century, trade silver was popular as a medium for Indigenous craftspeople, which continued into the twentieth century.[2] The presence of these artifacts in the archaeological record further illustrates the continuous Indigenous and Haudenosaunee settlement on the lands of the Mohawk Institute.

ARTIFACTS OF ASSIMILATION

Evidence of the assimilation of students attending the Mohawk Institute is prevalent in the archaeological record at the school. Artifacts related to farming such as garden implements and school-related materials, including slate pencils and tablets, are ubiquitous.

After Robert Ashton was appointed principal and superintendent of the Institute in the early 1870s, he introduced disciplinary measures modelled after the military system that would eventually see male students drilled as the Mohawk Institute Cadet Corps (see Evan Habkirk's chapter in this volume). This tradition continued under the tenure of Ashton's son, A. Nelles Ashton, from 1911 to 1914, during which the program was recognized by the federal government's cadet program.[3] During the archaeological assessment in the former apple orchard, after the trees were cut down in preparation for the Mohawk Village Memorial Park installation, a military button was recovered that dates to the period that A. Nelles Ashton was principal. The button is made of brass with an embossed beaver and crown at the centre, with "CANADA" embossed above the crown and "CADET" embossed below the beaver on the obverse or button face (see figure 14.1, image D). The reverse of the button has a metal loop and fastener with illegible text. While the button may have adorned a piece of formal clothing, it doubtless was worn by a student attending the Institute.

During the initial stages of the restoration project, it was periodically necessary for construction to occur below the ground surface around the building. Although most work below ground was to take place within soils that had been disturbed by previous construction activities on the property, Archaeological Research Associates monitored and photo-documented the construction work to ensure any located archaeological materials were recovered. During the excavation of the foundation, down to the footings for the installation of flood protection and the installation of a new sewer line, enamelled tinware pitchers, plates, and cups provide tangible evidence of objects that would have been used within the walls of the residential school (see figure 14.2, images E and F).

The fact that they were found within the material (soil and debris) that was used to backfill the foundation of the laundry room addition can help infer the date of the deposit based on the circa 1922 construction date of the addition. Of particular interest are the number of cups found within

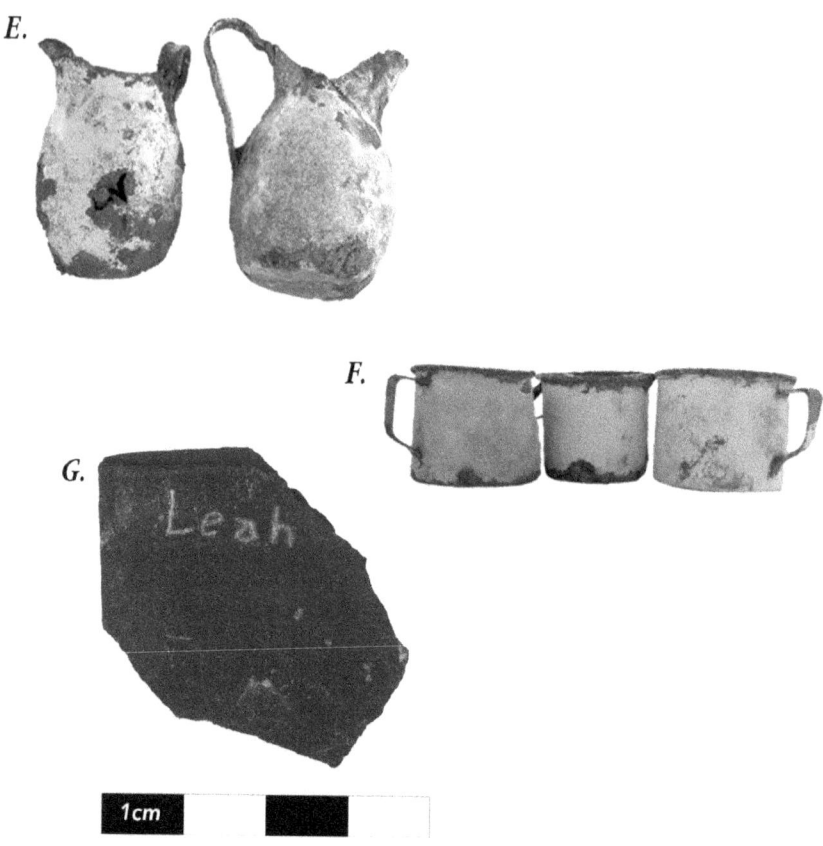

Figure 14.2. (E) enamelled metal pitchers used as fill along the foundation of the laundry room at the rear of the building; (F) enamelled metal cups found during the installation of a new sewer line through the former girls' play yard; (G) slate tablet with the name "Leah" inscribed into it.

Source: Dove Clarke and Woodland Cultural Centre

the girls' (south) side of the property that were recovered during the sewer installation, as they appeared to have been scattered near the extant tree line that formed a boundary within the girls' outdoor play area. These objects also provide a tangible connection to the school. It is more than probable that students residing at the school used the enamelled dishes during meals. These pieces of inexpensive, utilitarian, and durable tableware may have been in use at the Institute for many years.

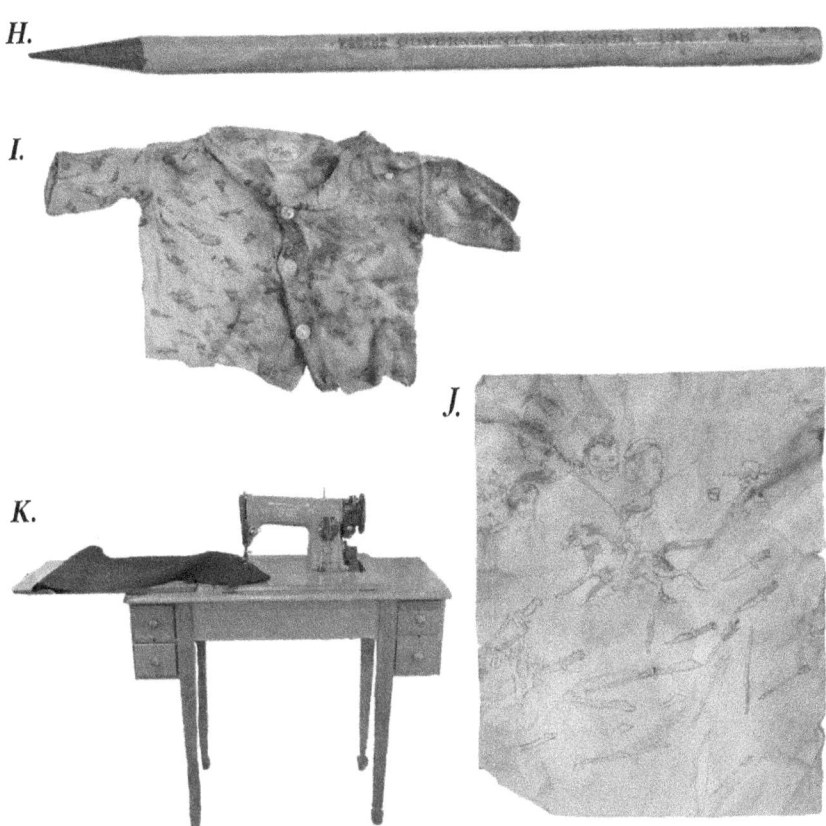

Figure 14.3. (H) "Government of Canada 1917" pencil found during interior restoration; (I) child's pyjama shirt found around window casing to prevent drafts; (J) pencil sketches of Indigenous men, knives, a gun, axes, bows, and arrows; (K) Singer sewing machine used at the Mohawk Institute.
Source: Dove Clarke and Woodland Cultural Centre

Assimilation through education, as noted earlier, is evidenced through the recovery of school-related materials such as slate tablets and pencils. During the archaeological assessment in the former apple orchard, a piece of slate tablet was recovered with the name "Leah" inscribed on it (see figure 14.2, image G). Prior to paper and graphite pencils, slate tablets and slate pencils were used. The transition to graphite pencils occurred in the early twentieth century, partially due to hygiene concerns relating to the method of cleaning the tablets between use, often with saliva. It is unclear how long slate pencils and tablets remained in use at the Institute, though a graphite pencil found during the interior restoration of the building labelled "Government of Canada—1917" suggests that they were being used at the Institute in the early 1900s (see figure 14.3, image H). The "Leah" tablet fragment likely predates the circa 1900 installation of the apple orchard on the property.

Part 2: The Building Restoration

ARTIFACTS OF RESISTANCE

Objects indicating student agency and resistance at the Mohawk Institute have been infrequently found during the archaeological assessments undertaken on the property. The fact is that there are likely many expressions of resistance to be found in the archaeological record, but further research is necessary to tease out these objects of agency.

In 1903, the 1858 brick residential school building was destroyed by a fire that was later determined to have been set by students attending the school. During the 2017 archaeological assessment, under the front porch, evidence of the previous building fire was identified below the ground. Yellow bricks from the previous building were used to backfill the foundation of the new building, many of which exhibit evidence of burning. It is possible that other evidence of burned features in the ground can be traced back to acts of student resistance.

Also discovered during the assessment at the front porch were names written in pencil on the wooden window casing located below the porch. Like the names found at the rear of the building inscribed in brick, these names were written as an act of agency and resistance, as students faced limited opportunities for self-expression. The names written on the window casing under the porch were hidden from plain sight by the porch. In addition to being an act of agency and resistance, the names found around and inside the Institute building have provided a tangible connection to students who attended the school.

With the onset of internal restoration in 2016, construction and trade specialists regularly discovered objects hidden, lost, or forgotten within the walls of the dormitory building that were original to the residential school and the students. From the expected (pencils, buttons) to the unexpected (baby clothes, farm ledger), these objects exemplify the students' daily lives, their struggles, their acts of resistance, and, ultimately, their pride of self (see figure 14.3, images H and I).[4]

OBJECTS OF IDENTITY

While the Canadian Indian Residential School system was developed to create a disconnect between children and their Indigenous identity, objects found within the walls of the former Mohawk Institute dormitory building show that the child residents of the Institute were still very connected to their homes, families, and cultures. These objects tell a story of homesickness, the missing of relatives, and traditional lives interrupted.

A plethora of holiday cards and everyday letters from home were found during the restoration process. Female relatives of the students were very attentive to sending wishes and love from home. "Wesley" regularly received letters and cards "From Mom."[5] The cache of correspondence between Wesley and his mother was obviously of great value to this student as he took the time to hide it away within the walls, where he could revisit the letters and cards while keeping them safe from discovery by school staff or other students. "Mom" did not date her cards and letters, but, based upon a letter to "Dear Cousin" from Wesley found among these objects, the bundle dates to 1947.[6]

An envelope sent to "Fredrick [redacted for privacy], Mohawk Inst., Brantford, Ont.," on 20 December 1950 contained a card.[7] This card conveyed Christmas greetings to "Freddie [redacted for privacy]" from "Aunty Velma" and "Uncle Joshua."[8]

Of particular interest is a letter written 30 March 1949 to "Dear Mother" from a son who was a student at the school.[9] In the missive, the son thanks his mother for sending money to him at the Institute. He then adds that she should throw out "the stinky hides" he presumably left at home. Is this letter evidence that the student had successfully completed a hunt but had not had time to finish tanning the hides before leaving for the Mohawk Institute the previous fall? The use of English as the language of correspondence is also interesting and may have been the result of the reviewing of letters by school staff before they were sent. It is likely in 1949 that "Mother" was able to read and write, at least somewhat, in English. The personal details of the letter, the thank you for sending money and throwing out "the stinky hides," also makes it likely that this letter, instead of being a school assignment, was a genuine letter home. Sadly, the fact that this letter was found within the walls means that it was never posted to "Mother."

A packet of pencil sketches spread over eight pages also provides evidence of a continued attachment to the unknown artist's Indigenous identity.[10] Mixed in with sketches of animals, race cars, pugilists, soldiers, and people smoking are well-drawn depictions of Indigenous people (albeit with cowboys as well) (see figure 14.3, image J). The young artist also showed a fondness for the Lone Ranger and Tonto. Perhaps this is more an indication of what was trending in popular culture at the time than an homage to the student's own Indigenous identity, but certainly the artist would have been aware he was Indigenous and felt a sense of commonality with these pop-culture drawings. The irony of a school built to destroy Indigenous identity having to combat a popular culture that was beginning to depict Indigenous people in minor heroic roles (Tonto) cannot be overlooked.

OBJECTS OF ASSIMILATION

With the Mohawk Institute's clear objective of assimilating Indigenous children into broader Canadian society, it is not surprising that many of the items found in the restoration provide evidence of the regimented indoctrination process employed at the school. Carpentry tools, sewing and farm equipment, numbered clothing, gun cartridges and bullets, institutional forms, and the copious number of toothbrushes and hair combs all indicate institutional living with an emphasis on manual trades over classroom learning (see figure 14.3, image K). Of the 754 objects found within the school's walls, only 73 (or less than 10 per cent) were related to academic schooling (worksheets, notebooks, a textbook, and a workbook). In comparison, 259 (approximately 34 per cent) items were work related (tools, equipment, and fragments of each). If objects such as uniform remnants, cafeteria ware, school admission forms and correspondence, and items needed for daily life at the Institute are added to this total, the overwhelming majority of found objects were related to the assimilation goals of the Mohawk Institute.[11]

The first assault to their Indigenous identity experienced by newly arriving students was the loss of their names. In the place of their personal identity each student was issued an identifying number.[12] This number not only replaced their personal names but also marked all their possessions—clothing, toothbrush, towel, shoes, etc. Found within the walls of the Mohawk Institute, a pair of boy's underpants with the handwritten label "12" provides evidence of this dehumanizing practice.[13]

New arrivals also experienced further trauma with the cutting of their hair. Ostensibly for the purpose of eliminating lice, these haircuts were

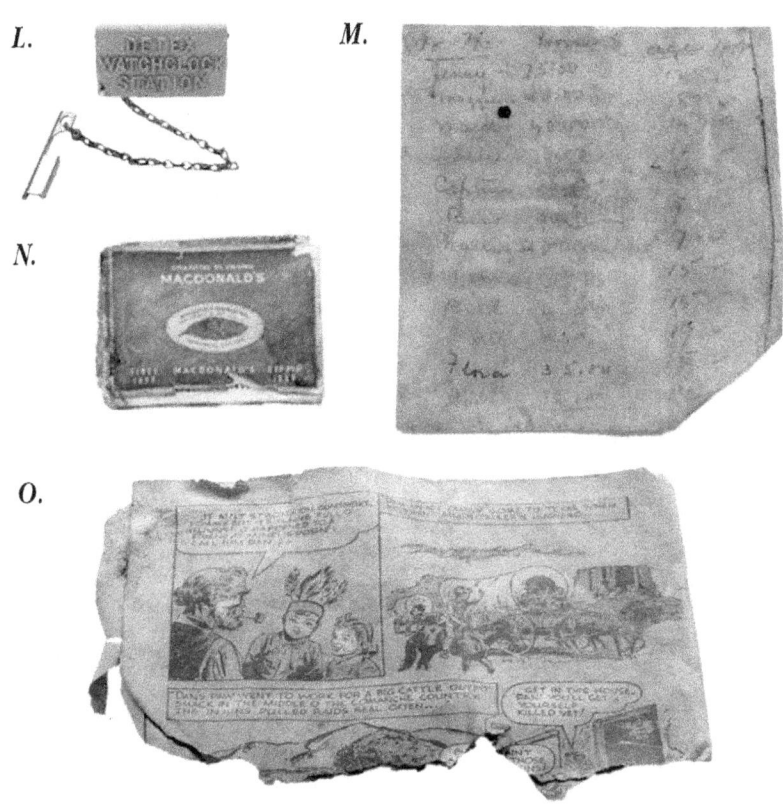

Figure 14.4. (L) "DETEX WATCHCLOCK STATION" watch clock key; (M) list of student names, ages, and hours of labour contributed to the school for a period of time; (N) MacDonald's cigarette package; (O) Torn comic strip describing the settlement of the West.
Source: Dove Clarke and Woodland Cultural Centre

a further attack on the child's humanity and identity. Masses of cut hair were found within the walls of the Mohawk Institute. Faded from time, these piles of hair were not accessioned to the collections of the Woodland Cultural Centre due to the sacred and sensitive role hair plays within Haudenosaunee culture.

Another dehumanizing practice levied on the students by the administrators of the Mohawk Institute was the literal imprisonment of children. Found on the corridor-side wall of the girls' dormitory was a mechanical clock.[14] This mechanical clock required a key to be inserted at set times by a school official who would be conducting the rounds, acting as a watchman (see figure 14.4, image L). If the key was not inserted at the set time, or the door to which it corresponded was forced open, an alarm bell would sound to indicate that something was amiss at a particular location. The mechanical clock found outside the girls' dormitory still had its key attached by chain to the mechanism. This alarm system suggests that school administrators were actively locking students in at night and making systematic rounds to ensure they were kept inside until released.

Maintaining a sufficient number of students to perform work tasks was necessary for the Mohawk Institute to function. A farm ledger found in the crevice between the school's outer wall and its balcony attachment covers the years 1899 through 1903.[15] Page after page, year after year, the ledger documents crop and farm animal accounts, including a range of details from growing/raising costs to selling prices (see figure 14.4, image M). Additionally, a detailed chart of labour put in by the students was also maintained on a monthly basis. Each student was listed; his/her age was recorded; and the hours of work he/she put into the school farm was logged. There was no accounting for received wages as the labour of the students was categorized either as teaching or apprenticeship and not seen as true work. The hours of free labour provided by the students (girls laboured away in the cafeteria, cleaning the school, picking garden crops, or over sewing machines, while boys maintained the livestock and fields in addition to groundskeeping and carpentry) kept the school operating both practically and financially.

OBJECTS OF RESISTANCE

The messages of love seen in objects of identity are a stark contrast to the dehumanizing objects of assimilation. It is not surprising that many of the students at the Mohawk Institute resisted all efforts to remove their identities and enslave them in a system of forced labour, with no payment and little bodily upkeep. Beyond the expected acts of youth rebellion, smoking and associated paraphernalia was overly represented in the hidden finds; more subtle signs of resistance to the school, its cultural annihilation policies, detrimental physical neglect, and all-encompassing attempts at assimilation, are evident in the objects found within the Mohawk Institute residence (see figure 14.4, images N and O).

The Mush Hole was not in the practice of feeding the children within its walls much of any nutritional or substantive value. Subsisting on a diet

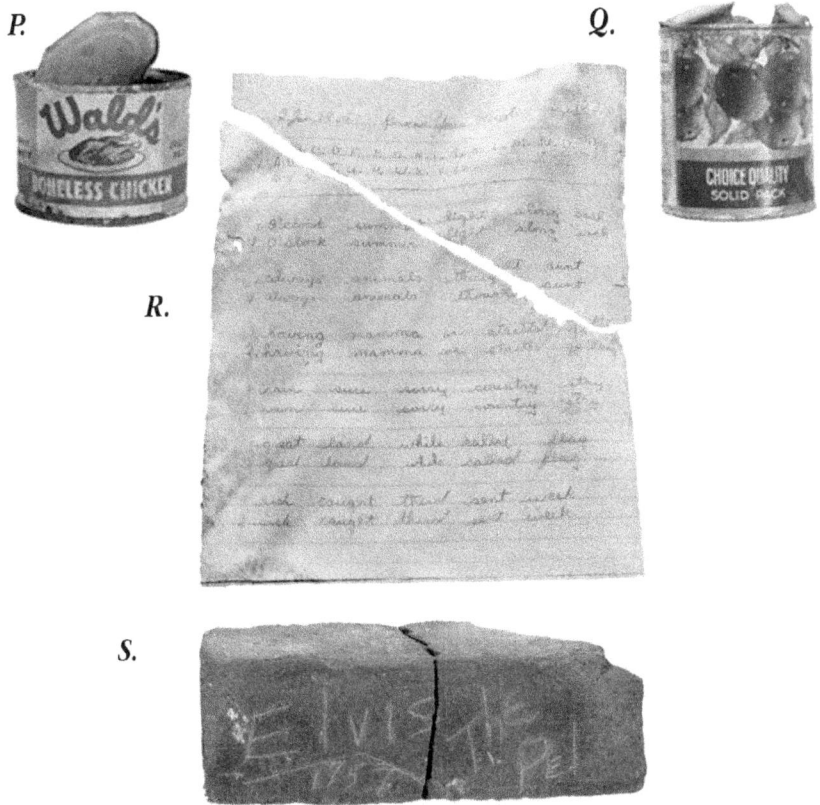

Figure 14.5. (P) "Wald's Boneless Chicken" can found during the building restoration; (Q) "Choice Quality Solid Pack" canned apples; (R) "2 Jan. 1951, Know Your Words" assignment, torn in half; (S) "Elvis the Pel, 1957" brick found during the interior restoration.
Source: Dove Clarke and Woodland Cultural Centre.

mainly comprised of oatmeal (mush), overworked and hungry students were forced to pilfer food from the staff pantry. In caches throughout the walls, tin cans, mangled in the attempt to open them for their caloric payload without the proper equipment to do so, are accompanied by torn wrappers, empty containers, and lidless jars, all once having stored an assortment of food ranging from sugarless pudding powder to an entire jellied chicken (see figure 14.5, image P).[16] Oddly, for an institution with an apple orchard

14 | Collecting the Evidence   387

maintained and harvested by the students, numerous cans and peeled labels were discovered that show the school was purchasing large tins of apple sauce rather than using the fruit on hand (see figure 14.5, image Q).

The quantity of food packaging, secreted away so well it took decades and a demolition to bring them to light, is evidence that the students were actively supplementing their institutional meals with whatever they could take from the school and the staff. Money received from home likely went to purchasing the sugary treats that were stashed in order to protect them from others or from confiscation. Paper evidence of candy, chocolate, and ice cream were found on all levels of the residential school building. The students clearly resisted the physical neglect they were forced to labour under while attending the Mohawk Institute.

A stash of school assignments, discovered in a walled-in fireplace chimney, show overt signs of resistance to the authority of the Mohawk Institute.[17] Written on the lined pages of notebook paper, the assignments are neatly signed spelling lists on one side and mathematical equations on the other (see figure 14.5, image R). All the sheets bear the date "Tuesday, January 2, 1951"; all have been torn in half. Stuffed into an unused nook of the school, it is obvious that the assignments were once a stack of papers waiting to be marked. This suggests some student took the stack of ungraded assignments, ripped the stack across the middle, and deposited them in the chimney. The tear was so clean and exact it was possible nearly seventy years later to match the halves of all the individual pages to their mates. It cannot be known what led to this act—whether anger, mischief, rebellion, boredom, or some other emotion was the cause—but the boldness required to do such a thing under the threat of extreme and disproportionate corporal punishment if caught exemplifies a spirit of resistance.

The most enduring physical evidence of resistance to the residential school's assimilation tactics cover the entirety of the residence, its inner and outer walls. Buried under layers of plaster, paint, and wallpaper, or openly etched into the red brick of the outer facade, generations of students and survivors of the Mohawk Institute left their names for all to see (see figure 14.5, image S).[18] Proudly and boldly signing their given names, "Amy," "Pauline," "Robert," "Minnie," "Vera," "Elmer," and many more courageous students made a stance.[19] Rejecting their status as faceless numbers, these students proclaimed their resistance and reclaimed their humanity. These names bravely left for posterity are not mere graffiti, covertly left to mar and disfigure; they represent the inherent warrior spirit of these Indigenous children. Just as their ancestors once learned the skills and tools of survival as children on the very same plot of land, the students of the Mohawk Institute fought for survival with the skills and tools they had at hand. Armed with pencils and nails—not the projectile points of their ancestors, as discussed earlier—these Indigenous children proclaimed that they mattered; that their spirits would not be broken; and that their identity as Indigenous people was not a sin but a strength.

Reflections

It is an axiom in archaeology that objects have the ability to tell a story, and indeed, a story that complements and adds richness to oral and written narratives. Archaeologist Gary Warrick has drawn parallels between this aspect of archaeology and the collection of physical evidence at crime scenes. Archaeological evidence may support oral testimony or contradict it. Events, activities, and meanings may or may not be discernible in the archaeological record. Objects may be misinterpreted, but they do not and cannot "lie."

The crime scene parallel in this case feels all too true as the testimony of survivors makes it clear that the Mush Hole was a place of human misery that extended from immorality through to outright illegality. The official records of the Mohawk Institute ("plentiful food," "contented children," etc.) were produced by the same people who were responsible for the criminal abuses perpetrated at the school. Establishing a counter-narrative to the official record is no easy feat. A place of horror and terror is apt to contain many of the same prosaic material objects as a happy one. Students at the Mush Hole had the same material needs as any other children, and those needs had to be served, however poorly. Nuance in this case is everything, however, and the fact that these children were not properly cared for is clearly attested to by the oral narratives/testimonies of the survivors. In the disconnect between the written/historical records of the school and the survivors' oral narratives/testimonies, the material-archaeological record *clearly* supports the latter.

The Indian Residential School system was an example of colonial history at its worst. In 1883, Canada's first prime minister, Sir John A. Macdonald, explained the system to the Canadian Parliament in the following terms:

> When the school is on the reserve the child lives with its parents, who are savages; he is surrounded by savages, and though he may learn to read and write his habits, and training and mode of thought are Indian. He is simply a savage who can

read and write. It has been strongly pressed on myself, as the head of the Department, that Indian children should be withdrawn as much as possible from the parental influence, and the only way to do that would be to put them in central training industrial schools where they will acquire the habits and modes of thought of white men.[20]

The Mush Hole was a place where Macdonald's goals for Indigenous peoples were translated into action. Children there were worked like slaves, physically and sexually abused, underfed, alienated from their languages and cultures, and isolated from their families and communities. As a "site of conscience" or counter-monument, the building and grounds serve as a place of memory for one of the darkest chapters in Canadian history.

On 21 July 2021, amid news from Tk'emlúps te Secwépemc First Nation in Kamloops, British Columbia, regarding the identification of potential student burials at the former Kamloops Indian Residential School, Six Nations of the Grand River Elected Council Chief Mark Hill held a press conference at the steps of the Mohawk Institute, surrounded by survivors of the school, at which he announced that a search of the school grounds should take place as part of a criminal investigation.[21] A Survivors' Secretariat was established in 2021 by a group of survivors to oversee the search for student burials on the Mohawk Institute property being undertaken by the Police Task Force comprised of Six Nations Police, Brantford Police, Ontario Provincial Police, cultural monitors, and Indigenous Human Rights Monitor Dr. Beverly Jacobs.[22] Since the announcement by Chief Hill in the summer of 2021 and the creation of the Survivors' Secretariat and Police Task Force, a ground-penetrating radar assessment has been initiated at the Mohawk Institute. At this time, the assessment has not been completed, and the results to date are unknown.

Canadians seem to be masters at navigating the complex logical contortions necessary to think of their society as "nice" or "polite" while simultaneously ignoring the abysmal ways in which the settler society has treated, and continues to treat, the Indigenous peoples who live within their country's borders. With little apparent irony, Canadians think of themselves as having usually landed on the right side of history: as a destination for the Underground Railroad; as a champion of women's suffrage; as a bulwark against Nazism; as a vigorous campaigner against apartheid; and more recently as a global proponent of LGBTQ2S+ rights. Despite these laudable (but, frankly, debatable) achievements, Canada has yet to fully reckon with its history as a colonial nation—one founded on the dispossession of Indigenous peoples from their traditional lands, a denial of the privileges and services extended to settler Canadians, and an attempt to erase Indigenous identity from the Canadian social fabric. Until such time as a reckoning with these sins can transpire, any thoughts of reconciliation between the settler society and Indigenous communities will remain elusive.

NOTES

1. See Office of the Independent Special Interlocutor, *Sites of Truth, Sites of Conscience: Unmarked Burials and Mass Graves of Missing and Disappeared Indigenous Children in Canada* (Office of the Independent Special Interlocutor for Missing Children and Unmarked Graves and Burial Sites Associated with Indian Residential Schools, 2024), https://osi-bis.ca/historical-report/.
2. Sandra Gibb, "Trade Silver," *Canadian Encyclopedia*, last modified 27 August 2020, https://www.thecanadianencyclopedia.ca/en/article/indian-trade-silver.
3. E. Habkirk, personal communication with the authors, 4 June 2021.
4. Collection of Six Nations Elected Council, Woodland Cultural Centre, 2017.8; 2018.1; 2019.5.
5. Collection of Six Nations Elected Council, 2017.8.67; 2017.8.68.
6. Collection of Six Nations Elected Council, 2017.8.82.
7. Collection of Six Nations Elected Council, 2018.1.98.
8. Collection of Six Nations Elected Council, 2018.1.97ab.
9. Collection of Six Nations Elected Council, 2017.8.88.
10. Collection of Six Nations Elected Council, 2017.8.149–56.
11. Collection of Six Nations Elected Council, 2017.8; 2018.1; 2019.5.
12. It is not clear when exactly students began to be referred to by number.
13. Collection of Six Nations Elected Council, 2017.8.2.
14. Collection of Six Nations Elected Council, 2018.1.46.
15. Collection of Six Nations Elected Council, 2017.8.224.
16. Collection of Six Nations Elected Council, 2017.8; 2018.1; 2019. See also Elizabeth Graham, *The Mush Hole: Life at Two Indian Residential Schools* (Heffle Publishing, 1997), 353–423.
17. Collection of Six Nations Elected Council, 2018.1.139ab–200.
18. Collection of Six Nations Elected Council, 2017.8; 2018.1; 2019.5.
19. Collection of Six Nations Elected Council, 2017.8.324; 2017.8.372; 2017.8.373; 2017.8.72.
20. Canada, *House of Commons Debates*, 5th Parl., 1st Sess., Vol. 2 (9 May 1883), 1107.
21. Bobby Hristova, "Search of Former Mohawk Institute Grounds Should Be a Criminal Investigation, Survivors Say," CBC News, 21 July 2021, https://www.cbc.ca/news/canada/hamilton/ground-search-mohawk-institute-1.6110935.
22. See the Survivors' Secretariat website at https://www.survivorssecretariat.ca/.

15

Collective Trauma and the Role of Religion in the Mohawk Institute Experience

Wendy Fletcher

Many years ago, when I first engaged with the story of the Mohawk Institute (MI) as a researcher, I was asked to explore the church's involvement. The school had closed in 1970. No one in the Diocese of Huron (the ecclesiastical area where the Institute was geographically located) remembered anything about it. Various questions about the school and its relationship with the church circulated: Had the church actually been involved? Who owned the school? What were the relationships that governed it? From that narrow structural lens my findings showed very little. Residential schools were usually administered through a partnership between the Canadian government and a Canadian denominational church body. The Anglican Church had been less connected to this residential school than to others. The place of religion in the daily lives of students appeared to be quite marginal.

In the early 2000s a group of survivors from Six Nations asked me to join them to talk about what I had found. I met with them and articulated these findings. The outrage was strong. As survivors, they stressed that they had been abused by the church. To suggest that the church was less responsible for the harms done to them than the government did not fit their experience, and they shared this view with me in the most direct terms.

I was puzzled about the dissonance between my findings and their experience. Eventually, understanding dawned. Symbols are important. Daily, the survivors experienced their life mediated through an authority structure headed by a man wearing a clerical collar. Daily they were fed a diet

Figure 15.1. *Trauma* by R. G. Miller, depicting the artist as a young boy at the Mohawk Institute.
Source: Used with permission of the artist

of Christianity through prayers and religious knowledge education. Those parameters defined the structure of all else that transpired at the Mohawk Institute.

A growing awareness of the theory of collective trauma expanded my understanding. I gradually came to see that although the structural relationships that managed the school were peripherally related to the church, and the religious content quantifiably small, the Anglican Church was in fact the symbolic conductor of trauma and thereby definitive of survivors' experience. This truth is reflected in the following vignette.

Some years ago, Renison University College in Waterloo, Ontario, held an exhibition entitled *The Mush Hole* that consisted of a collection of the artwork of R. G. Miller, a survivor of the Mohawk Institute. Renison is a college connected to the Anglican Church of Canada. The commitment to sponsoring the exhibition grew from the college's commitment to post–Truth and Reconciliation Commission healing work. This astonishing collection of paintings reflected R. G. Miller's experience at the Mohawk Institute, beginning at the age of three, and lasting until well into his adolescence.

When the artist arrived with his paintings, he asked that the most graphic of them, which had never been exhibited before, be displayed in the college's Chapel of St. Bede's. These paintings depict the sexual abuse of children by clergy and reflected the heart of his own trauma. For him, displaying the paintings in the chapel communicated a central message: At the centre of the harm done to him was the experience of religious trauma—or trauma experienced in connection to the Anglican identity of the Mohawk Institute.

Collective Trauma Theory

Traditionally, the idea of trauma has been understood as something that happens to disrupt the experience of individuals. More recently, theories of trauma have been broadened to take account of shared disruption—in other words, traumatic events that affect a collectivity rather than a lone individual. Illustrations include the Holocaust, ethnic cleansing in Rwanda, and other communal traumas designed to eradicate group identity, if not the group itself.

Collective trauma theory is an appropriate vehicle for understanding the experience of residential school survivors, including those children who lived all or part of their childhoods at the Mohawk Institute. We will proceed using the following definition: Collective trauma occurs "when members of a collectivity feel they have been subjected to a horrendous event that leaves indelible marks upon their group consciousness, marking their memories forever and changing their future identity in fundamental and irrevocable ways."[1] As implied with this definition, experiences that disrupt core aspects of a collective's identity and its stability are determinative. All identity engages matters of cultural reference. The residential school project, designed as a social engineering experiment in assimilation, was intended not only to disrupt Indigenous core identity but to replace it with another—the transformation of the Indigenous child into a child modelled on a Euro-descent settler citizen. The entire structure of the residential school model for Indigenous children dislocated traditional culture, language, parenting forms, and other socialization practices, replacing these with a highly structured regimen of different language, education, religion, routine, food, and discipline through the *in loco parentis* (in place of the parents) oversight of the government moderated by Christian leaders. It is the moderation of the message through the medium of church leaders that creates the most significant contribution by religion to the discourse of this collective trauma. Given that authority was placed in the hands of religious leaders, everything associated with the residential school experience for the children became de facto a religious experience, even though the weight of time and energy spent on actual religious observance and teaching may have been small in relation to other aspects of the children's daily lives.

In an experience of prolonged institutional trauma, symbols carry a heavy weight. In the case of the Mohawk Institute, the symbolic weight of things like a clergy collar, a cross, the chapel, and the Bible were magnified through the harming behaviours of individuals. The wider assimilationist context stripped away one world and its meaning and replaced it with another mediated through daily encounter with these symbols. Our primary thesis about the place of religion at the Mohawk Institute, then, is this: Religion became the framework for the collective traumatization of Indigenous children through the stripping away of their culture in favour of a process of "civilization" managed in a Christian context.

Collective trauma theory further argues that experienced trauma can be understood as a sociological process that "defines a painful injury to the collectivity, establishes the victim, attributes responsibility, and distributes the ideal and material consequence."[2] Through this multi-step process, the journey toward collective action and the reclamation of collective identity is possible.

In our exploration of the story of the Mohawk Institute, we are moving into the necessary next step in a collective trauma experience that seeks to participate in the resolution of, or at least a moving beyond, the traumatic experience. Documenting the story in a post–Truth and Reconciliation Commission era not only requires documentation of the trauma itself, but works to attribute responsibility and, in that, distribute consequences. Toward that end, understanding the role of organized religion in the trauma becomes paramount.

Unpacking the Narrative

In this chapter, we will attempt to explore two distinct threads that the preceding vignette raises: What was the connection of the Mohawk Institute to organized religion? And what was the role of religion in the experience of the children who lived there? These two threads then lead to a third theme that answers to the question of "So, what?" What was the impact of religious identity and practice on and in the stories and lived experiences of those who survived the Mohawk Institute?

Any attempt to explore the role of religion in the story of the Mohawk Institute must grapple with several things. We begin with a definition of religion: what it was and what it was used for in the context of colonial practice. We will also consider structural relationships as they relate to organized religion, the specifics of daily life in the context of religious practice, and, finally, the impact of that practice on the children who lived at the school. Our exploration of the impact of religious practice and identity on the children will lead us to consider the idea of collective trauma as it applied to survivors of the Mohawk Institute. Given the close link between discipline and religious values as practised by the school's leadership, we will also consider the control and terrorization of bodies as a tactic of assimilation assisted by the theoretical frame of biopower as articulated by Foucault.

Religion and Colonization

In its organic form, religion rises from the community that it reflects. There is a symbiotic relationship between the people who practise the religion and the ongoing development of religious practice. Religion is a structure/system (a product of culture) that reflects the attempt by human beings to address the larger questions of meaning, purpose, belonging, and transcendence in their lives and from which they derive an ethical and moral framework, ritual practice, and philosophical perspectives to guide their daily lives.

This was not the case in relation to the residential school experiment. As religion became embedded as an arm of colonial practice, it was used as a tool of racial and cultural assimilation. In the project of colonization broadly construed, the religion of the colonizer becomes an expression of colonial power and enforcement. Practices, meaning frameworks, ethics, and rituals connected to the religion of the colonizer, are used to suppress and ultimately eradicate the organic religious practice of Indigenous culture and replace them with those of the colonizer.

Famed early twentieth-century philosopher Antonio Gramsci theorized that everything of culture, including religion and education, is a product of the economic relations that lie beneath them. The economic drivers of any culture (substructure) determine the forms of our "civilization." They in turn enter an ongoing two-way conversation with the substructure as needs and capacities evolve.[3]

Colonization is primarily an economic activity. One group assumes control over another group or land with an economic imperative to expand and enrich itself. The colonization projects by which England, France, and Spain assumed control over what we know as the Americas had common strategies for expanding interests. The arrival of the colonizer was sometimes welcomed and at other times resisted. For their part, however, the colonizer saw the Indigenous persons already inhabiting lands they wished to assume as subjects to be managed, controlled, civilized, and used in support of their broader project of colonization. The assimilationist agenda was grounded in the racializing assumptions of the era, which developed a hierarchy of value for human beings based on skin colour, facial features, capacity, temperament, and more. Indigenous persons were considered less than those deemed as "white" (the colonizer) and thereby as in need of "civilization"—remaking the Indigenous person in their own image. It should be noted that this usually did not include the notion of equalization. People were civilized for service, not for equity.

An extremely pointed quote from the bishop of the Diocese of Huron circa 1970 will serve to illustrate the point. Upon learning that the Department of Indian Affairs (DIA) intended to close all residential schools, including the Mohawk Institute, he wrote an outraged letter to the department in opposition: "We must persist in our efforts among the Indian people. Of course, we know that there is no hope for this current generation, but if we persist in our efforts, perhaps, we will be able to raise up the grandchildren of this current generation to the level of a servant class in Canadian society."[4] What does this have to do with religion? The preceding quote shows us the issue. From the beginning, modern colonization efforts have understood that state religion is an essential arm of assimilating the subject population. The state religion of the English colonizer was Anglicanism.

Referencing Gramsci's perspective, the religious leadership of a culture is vested with authority by the state, through which it in turn contributes to the project of recreating the social norm of any society in the bodies of its citizens. The linkage of religion with state power sets the stage for church-state partnerships that have little to do with the content of religious teaching and much to do with the project of socialization. Our interest, then, is to understand the parameters of the church-state partnership in the work of the Mohawk Institute and how that partnership was experienced by the children who were subject to their authority.

Structural Connection to Organized Religion

In the case of the Mohawk Institute, as we saw in preceding chapters, the founding colonizing institution was the New England Company (NEC). While the NEC was an ecumenical body (members came from different Protestant denominations), its face at Six Nations was predominantly Anglican or Church of England.[5] The school's attachment to religion varied over time and by principal. For instance, under the Reverend Horace Snell, a priest of the Diocese of Huron of the Church of England in Canada, the focus on religion intensified. Regardless of who was principal, though, the Christian identity of the school linked to Anglican practice was a part of the children's daily experience throughout the Mohawk Institute's history.

The early beginnings of the Institute under the NEC meant that the school was set up differently than many other Canadian residential schools. This led to a slightly different set of structural relationships with organized religion. As the sole owner of the Mohawk Institute, the NEC had sole proprietorship. This began to change with the introduction in Canada of government and church partnerships in the development and management of residential schools. When the DIA (variously named over the years) set up most of its schools, the model was clear—the government owned and funded the schools through a per capita and capital grant system and the denominational church partner provided the management of the schools through provision of personnel. Usually, the principal of the school was a designated clergy person from the denominational partner.

In 1891 the NEC applied to the DIA for the Mohawk Institute to become one of its schools. This meant that from 1891 the NEC received a per capita grant toward the operation of the school. This grant was insufficient to fully cover the costs of caring for children. As such the NEC offset this cost and covered all costs of the maintenance of the property.[6] No significant changes in the administration of the school happened at this point in relation to religious affiliation and inputs.

In 1911 with the introduction of a series of new management agreements, the NEC remained the signatory partner with the government in the administration of the school. This distinguished it from other Anglican schools, which, for the most part, were run by the Mission Society of the Church of England in Canada. The principalship of the MI remained in the hands of the family originally appointed by the NEC. At times this leadership was clerical and other times not. However, the lease agreements between the Government of Canada and the NEC never stipulated that the principal should be a clergy person, although most leases of residential schools did.[7] This made the structural religious connection different for the Mohawk Institute. Those Anglican schools that were run by the Mission Society named clergy as their senior administrators, who in turn were accountable both to national and diocesan (local) church bureaucracies' input and oversight. In other words, the administrative connection to organized religion was different than in other cases in the first long segment of the Mohawk Institute's history.

The NEC had not come through the First World War well, financially. As such, it was hoping to sell the Mohawk Institute to the Canadian government and step back from its involvement. No agreement was reached for a sale. The result was the negotiation of a new lease agreement between the NEC and the DIA. Under the terms of the new lease, the DIA would assume all financial and management responsibilities for running and maintaining the school. The NEC in turn handed over all authority to the DIA. However, as part of the lease, it was stipulated that there would be an ongoing dimension of religious instruction in the "faith of the Church of England" as part of the Institute's educational work. As well, the NEC would also send the annual sum of fifteen hundred pounds sterling to cover the cost of the principal's salary and the upkeep of the Mohawk Chapel.[8]

Although, from 1922 through the new lease, the DIA became the de facto managing partner of the MI, the principal previously appointed by the NEC remained in charge of the school until 1929. That year, the DIA removed Sydney Rogers from this role for poor administration. Here, then, in terms of the narrative of religious partnership, comes an important turning point. The lease for the school's management did not stipulate that the principal should be an Anglican priest. However, the DIA assumed that it did and in June 1929 asked Archbishop David Williams of the Diocese of Huron to nominate a local Anglican clergyman for the role. Archbishop Williams named a Canadian priest by the name of Horace Snell to serve as principal. Snell then ran the Mohawk Institute from 1929 to 1944.[9]

This action set a direction that would last for the remainder of the Mohawk Institute's story. There was some greater involvement of the school with local Anglican churches, particularly the Women's Auxiliaries, who often sent gifts in kind to the Institute. As well, the bishop of Huron, from that point, did understand himself to have a certain authority over the Institute through the accountability mechanisms of the diocesan structure and the principal. This sense of authority surfaced strongly when it was time for the subsequent lease to be negotiated with the NEC.

Horace Snell approached retirement in 1944, as the lease was coming to an end. A new lease should have been negotiated, but the world was consumed with the Second World War, and a new agreement was not reached until 1946. Through those conversations, the NEC again asked that the DIA purchase the Mohawk Institute. Through these talks the Diocese of Huron expressed an interest in assuming full responsibility for the Institute. However, when it became evident that the NEC expected that the diocese would purchase the property, rather than receive it, both backed away from the deal. The DIA also declined to purchase. The new lease, which was signed in 1946, did not give the diocese any part of the management of the school. However, on the way to a formal agreement, the church stepped in on the matter of appointment of a new principal. In other words, the diocese stepped away from legal authority through ownership but assumed for itself the moral authority to exercise oversight through the principal's appointment.

By the 1940s the DIA was aware that the lease with the NEC did not require the appointment of an Anglican priest. Through its own internal discernment processes, and on the recommendation of the local Indian superintendent at Six Nations, the DIA wanted to appoint a man who had taught in the reserve day school for many years. Joseph Hill was well regarded by the Six Nations Band Council and had excellent qualifications. The government was confident that his leadership was what the Mohawk Institute and its students needed. Joseph Hill was Indigenous, not Anglican, and not clergy.

The bishop of Huron and other church leaders were vocal in their opposition to this idea. Church objections appear to have been twofold: that such an appointment would undermine the religious character of the school, and that an Indigenous person was not desirable in this role. Extensive correspondence on this matter exists. In a letter to DIA Director Hoey on 21 June 1945, Archbishop Seager wrote the following:

> We offered strong objection [to the terms of the revised lease] as the effect of it was to radically alter the whole religious character, atmosphere and purpose of the school.... The proposal stirred practically the whole Church of England in Canada into disapproval.... Our committee is of the opinion that the appointment of an Indian as head of the institution is definitely undesirable.... The supervision of staff and other officers of the

Figure 15.2. Photo of clergy in front of the Mohawk Chapel, ca. 1925.
Source: Richard Hill Collection

School is . . . likely to be much more successful in hands other than an Indian, however well qualified he might be.[10]

The overt racism of the church's perspective, while not atypical for the time, seems to outweigh that of the DIA at this juncture. The DIA leadership was strongly supportive of appointing Joseph Hill. They felt that his Indigenous identity and experience as a leader among his people would assist him in directing the work of the Institute. The DIA's proposal had been that the religious identity of the Mohawk Institute could be safeguarded through the hiring of a chaplain to teach religious knowledge as part of the curriculum and as part of his duties caring for the Mohawk Chapel. The church's representatives felt that this would be inadequate in safeguarding the Christian identity of the school and the church's interests in it.

Prior to the end of the war, Bishop Seager proceeded to appoint one of his clergy, the Reverend John Zimmerman, as principal. He had no authority to do this. However, the confusion of the war era meant that the DIA did not intervene in the matter, and Zimmerman subsequently served as principal of the Mohawk Institute until it closed in 1970.[11]

Education and Mission

To understand the place of religion in the lives of students at the Mohawk Institute, it is important to grasp the broader context of theories of missionization (outreach to non-Christian populations) as well as the broader context of Church of England education for children that was at work in the background. The NEC constructed their mission work with two basic prongs: religious practice (liturgical worship) and education. Wherever the NEC went, they carried the idea with them that to take the gospel (Christian faith) meant providing spaces and opportunities for worship, as well as education. The education they offered in support of mission was basic literacy in the English language, as well as basic math and social studies, skills training, and religious knowledge.

In principle (though not always in practice), this mission model was not notably different from the type of education that was offered in England during the period. The idea was that residential or boarding schools offered a more comprehensive opportunity for children to learn than those offered through day schools. At home in England, only the children of the wealthy had the opportunity for residential education. It was considered an optimal vehicle for education. NEC mission work usually set up both day schools and residential schools configured for slightly different constituencies. Both models, however, included the religious knowledge component, as well as daily exposure to Christian faith practice through such things as daily Bible readings, prayer, and religious instruction, predominantly, in the case of the NEC's work in North America, in the Anglican tradition.

At the invitation of the Mohawks, the NEC journeyed to Six Nations. They first built a church, Her Majesty's Royal Chapel of the Mohawks (1785), and then later schools. The chapel would continue to figure prominently in the life of the students at the Mohawk Institute. Religious worship, as well as education in Christian teaching and Anglican ways, meant that the chapel, its chaplaincy, and the Institute would live a close and symbiotic relationship. As we see, for many students it became a symbol of their oppression at the hands of the church rather than a beacon of hope, which theoretically it was likely intended to be.

The theory of mission that the NEC brought with them to the Six Nations of the Grand River was clear: conversion of the "heathen" to Christianity both as a means of saving their souls and of helping them assimilate to the ways of Anglo culture. These aspects of mission were understood as a good. The rightness of this course was never questioned. When this missiology became linked with the assimilationist agenda of the Canadian government circa 1890, the Mohawk Institute experience of the twentieth century was catalyzed.

Religion, Daily Life, Annual Cycles

As discussed above, there was a recognizable pattern to the life of the Anglican school of the day. This pattern had annual, seasonal, weekly, and daily cycles. These cycles were framed around repeating events in the church's calendar. Each part of the year had a rhythm of services and celebrations: Advent, Christmas, Epiphany, Lent, Easter, Pentecost, Trinity. As well, Anglicans of that period had an annual event known as confirmation, which involved children roughly around the age of twelve or thirteen. Annually children in every congregation around this age were asked to prepare to confirm their faith.

Life for children at the Mohawk Institute was built around these ritual Christian observances. One of the regular markers on which principals from the Institute reported, first to the NEC and then between 1929 and 1970 to the Diocese of Huron, was the number of services, the number of attendees, and the number of confirmands (children preparing for and participating in the ritual of committing to Christian faith).[12] This practice reflects a broader practice within the British Empire. Everywhere British colonizing agents went, they reported back to church and government officials with statistics. Numbers of converts, baptisms, attendees at services, and numbers of confirmands were all seen as measures of the progress of civilization by the empire through the church.[13]

Services were held at the Mohawk Chapel usually only through the summer season, given the difficulties with heating the building. Through the rest of the year, services were held at the Mohawk Institute itself, sometimes in the classrooms, and at other times in the refectory and the playroom. Attendance was mandatory at weekly Sunday service as well as daily prayer services in the morning and evening.

In addition to regular attendance at worship, children received religious instruction in the Christian faith and Anglican practice offered by either the principal or the chaplain, depending on the year and the season.[14] The content of the religious knowledge instruction appears to have been loose and variable. Basic exposure to prayers including the Lord's Prayer and other basic Anglican prayers gave some orientation to the history of Anglicanism and the practice of Anglican worship. Some orientation to basic biblical stories through a non-critical lens reinforced key messages: To be a good person was to be a Christian. Memorization of Bible verses was obligatory. Other aspects of the messaging included the idea that Christianity was the only path to salvation. Other religions were to be set aside. A Christian was hard-working, respectful of authority and the rules authority prescribed. God was communicated as an omnipotent and omnipresent authority figure. Priests in their role as principal represented God's authority. It appears that theology (faith teaching) that talked about this ever-present God as loving was at times discussed, but this depended on the perspective of the person transmitting the message. However, the overarching message received was that an authoritarian God was in charge. This God punished those who did not follow the designated path adequately. A heavy emphasis on sin and forgiveness through repentance attended the admonitions to live as prescribed.[15]

None of these teachings were notably different from the theology expressed in the broader context of either missionary endeavours or of the local Anglican congregations of the day. The significant challenge presented by this messaging in the context of the residential school was that it was presented within the framework of a racialized world view. At the core of Christian theology is the idea that all human beings are made in the image of God. Contrary to the intent of such a theology, which is to affirm the dignity of all, the messaging for children at the Mohawk Institute was nuanced with common forms of verbal abuse such as, "You worthless dirty Indian."[16] The assumption that Indigenous children were less than their Euro-descent counterparts was implicit in the very work of the residential school project. Changing Indigenous children so that they resembled settler children through their assimilation into that culture, in tandem with the loss of Indigenous culture, created the context for multi-generational harm and trauma in a way that was unique to the residential school enterprise and experience.

Religion, Worship, and Discipline

Survivors speak more about their memory of worship service than they do of religious instruction. The memories shared are rarely fond, and quite often include experiences of corporal punishment for falling asleep, not knowing prayers, and not singing loudly enough.[17] This leads, then, to one of the most difficult aspects of life at the Mohawk Institute—the use of discipline and corporal punishment as a civilizing agent, often linked to Christian admonition. We are familiar with the biblical adage "spare the rod and spoil the child" (Proverbs 13:24). This adage had a central place in the philosophy of child management employed at the Institute. Of course, until fairly recently most educational systems in the Western world had some form of corporal punishment as a child-management practice. Certainly, this was the case in British boarding schools. Such a child-rearing philosophy was not known in Indigenous cultures prior to European contact. The broader issue is that the extremity of how corporal punishment was used at the Mohawk Institute greatly exceeded even the comparatively brutal ethic of the time.

Biopower and Biopolitics

Toward the end of his life, French philosopher Michel Foucault coined a pair of interlocking terms that are helpful for us in understanding the subjugation of the body as a primary tactic in the assimilation work implicit in residential schools. Although his writing is dense, his meaning is quite straightforward: The modern era has used control and subjugation of the body in various ways as a means of ensuring social control, enforcing normativity as defined by power holders, and limiting diversity. He calls this the use of biopower.[18] He applies this to an exploration of things like the development of the modern prison system, regulation of human sexuality in Western cultures, and the definition of mental health and abnormality in our societies. His theory applies well to an analysis of the residential school system, although he himself did not live in an era where such an analysis had yet been considered.

The term he develops in tandem with biopower is biopolitics. This term expands the understanding of physical restraint of the body to broader political strategies for social control. Although he wrote little about race and racialization, the idea of biopolitics (systems using their authority to develop and implement political policies of subjugation as a normalizing strategy) applies in the assimilationist agenda of the early Canadian experience with reference to Indigenous people and their children.

Government policies defined the lives of the children at the Mohawk Institute. Policy allowed Indian agents, with the Royal Canadian Mounted Police, to remove children from their homes and place them at the Institute. Policy regulated what they should eat, wear, learn, and do while at the Institute. As well, the use of corporal punishment was defined by policy. The containment of their bodies using physical force to ensure conformity to daily routine, to prevent or punish runaways, and to punish children for failure to conform in many ways (including religious practice) was regulated by policy. However, as we shall see, the regulation of that policy was loosely monitored so as to lead to a more aggressive application of physical force on the bodies of the children than even the policy allowed. It was understood that the use of physical force was necessary not only to contain the children in the school (prevent runaways), but also to ensure their conformity to the behavioural norms the government and its church mediators had defined.

As noted, the DIA had corporal punishment policies. These evolved over time. During the period of 1929–70 it was the case that corporal punishment was to be administered by the principal of the school only. Each school, including the Mohawk Institute, had a strap of regulation size that was kept in the principal's office. Strapping was to be only on the palm of the hand and the number of strokes was proscribed by government policy. A register was kept in the principal's office of every act of discipline (supposedly), signed both by the principal and the student in question. However, it appears that at the Mohawk Institute the use of physical oppression through corporal punishment lived outside the prescribed parameters. The fact that it was the religious authority figure who administered corporal punishment linked religion and pain in a way that left deep scars on the psyche of the children, not least because it appears that at the Institute the use of corporal punishment was much more indiscriminate than advocated by the policy.

From the beginning of his time as principal at the Institute, John Zimmerman expressed the view that harsh physical punishment was necessary to control and retrain the "savage" children who lived at the school. In a letter he wrote to the DIA superintendent on 6 December 1947, Zimmerman asked for permission to use more extreme forms of corporal punishment as a means of managing the children. Zimmerman reports that one evening the maintenance man went up to the boys' dormitory and found two boys sexually assaulting a teenager who suffered from developmental challenges. He asked the superintendent his thoughts on the use of appropriate punishment as a means of correction: "What form of punishment will you permit for boys who persist in this filthy business? I have tried to reason with them and employ various approaches. For the lad who will not respond to the normal decencies of life through the normal approaches is there any other way that [sic] to resort to the pleasure pain principle?"[19]

Further on in the same letter he wrote about a boy stealing. Again, he asked to be able to use more extreme corporal punishment: "I may be of the old school but I believe that if we were permitted in these extreme cases to spank their posterior ends it might do some good. If you strap them on the hands they go down to the playroom and say they were not strapped hard. What do you think?"[20]

The DIA was not supportive of increasing the extremity of corporal punishment. The superintendent wrote back to Zimmerman on 15 December reaffirming that the only corporal punishment allowed was that mandated by DIA policy: "We have corporal punishment regulations which we recommend to Principals who are having difficulty with this matter.... You will find in the long run that it does not pay to strap pupils anywhere but on the hands. The above regulations 'systematize' the administration of corporal punishment and the very form which the pupil has to go through is a deterrent."[21]

There is no record of Zimmerman ever writing again to ask for exception to the corporal punishment policies of the department. However, the witness of the students and some staff demonstrate that he made the decision to apply physical punishment to the students in the manner he felt would create a culture of intimidation sufficient to control the population and achieve the school's ends. "Sado-masochism" would be another way of naming what resulted.

The witness of survivors of the Institute tells a story of often capricious physical punishment outside the parameters prescribed by policy. In the collection of first-hand accounts of life at the Mohawk Institute collected by Elizabeth Graham, there are repeated references to severe beatings and random use of corporal punishment, connected to many "provocations." Bob White Eye failed to pay attention in chapel: "I fell asleep in church. Zimmerman was preaching, and they dragged me back to the school and threw me in the dressing room, and they just beat me like a—if my older brother didn't jump in, I imagine they would have killed me."[22] Albert Sault was sent to work on a local farm whose owner brought him back ten minutes late and he was punished:

> Skin [Principal Zimmerman] was a nasty character—he flogged us. I stayed clear of him. If we were late we were flogged by the personnel.... The farmer brought us back 10 minutes late and he explained that it was his fault and they flogged us anyway. We'd be made to drop our pants and lie across a table and we were beaten with the wide strap. I heard he was as bad with the girls.[23]

Calvin Sault tried several times to run away: "I didn't really know where to accept any help or get any help. Every time I run away and got a beating I got the skin ripped right off my leg by Mr. Wilson—the boys' master."[24]

Lee Snake remembered lining up for everything including the beatings: "It seemed you lined up for everything. You lined up to get a beating. I got fifty-two beatings that I counted—from Zimmerman—whatever. . . . They wouldn't pick you right out in church—what they would do is make a note. After we'd get back from church they'd line us up downstairs and call your name out. If your name was called you knew you were in for it. . . . It was everyday too. I did something wrong on average once every two weeks."[25]

Some years ago, I conducted an interview with an Anglican priest who had worked at the Institute as acting principal during the summer of 1956, while a theological student at Huron College in London, Ontario. His name was Ken Jagz. It was Principal Zimmerman who hired him as a replacement for himself while he and his family spent the summer elsewhere. There were only about thirty students in residence that summer. The representation of the summer he gave was relatively positive, with one chilling exception. When Jagz arrived for his training, Zimmerman told him that he would be required to wear a strap on his belt at all times. The strap, he said, resembled a short cat-o'-nine-tails with several straps attached to it. He then observed that all staff members wore such straps, at all times. Although Jagz did not want to wear it, Zimmerman insisted. He instructed that the children must be in fear of the possibility of punishment at all times, as a way of keeping them in line. The threat of physical punishment was a daily reign of terror, used in the most dramatic Foucauldian terms to intimidate and constrain the children's behaviours.[26]

Jagz's reflective words illustrate the point regarding the role of religion in the trauma of the Institute's survivors: "I didn't want to wear that strap. How could it be that the threat of violence could communicate the meaning of the gospel? I thought we were there to love the children. Instead we presided over a reign of terror."[27]

Only a small portion of the children's daily life was given over to religious practice and teaching. However, the vesting of authority through which the entire experience of residential school trauma was mediated, in the hands of the religious leader as a symbol of ultimate authority, meant that the church itself mediated and presided over the collective trauma induced through the Mohawk Institute.

Religion and Sexual Abuse

We need to explore one more difficult dimension of the place of religion at this school. Other than the case of Nelles Ashton in the early 1900s (see Diana Castillo's chapter in this volume), criminal charges were not laid against any member of staff who worked there. This makes addressing the misuses of authority through corporal punishment (assault) and any allegations of sexual assault difficult to engage from the vantage point of this present. However, a significant dimension of the traumatic memory of many Mohawk Institute survivors was their experience of having been physically and sexually assaulted while at the Institute.

Over the course of the Institute's history, the forms and faces of sexual abuse were many. Among this current generation of survivors, abusers are named. Given the importance of religious symbolism in this narrative we need to note that students identify two Anglican priests as having participated in violating them sexually: one preyed on the boys and the other assaulted the girls.

Here we circle back to the exhibition *The Mush Hole*, created by survivor R. G. Miller. In his words, it was critical for his healing journey that the Anglican Church be confronted with harms he had experienced by placing his witness to that violation at the centre of the institution he understood to be responsible for it. If we revisit our understanding of collective trauma, we recall that after victimization has been named, attributing responsibility is the necessary next step in any movement beyond harm to collective action toward resolution of the past. Situating the graphic witness of harm within the context of the symbolic world of those who held authority, and thereby served as mediators of trauma, takes that step.

It is widely agreed that sexual abuse has more to do with power than it has to do with sex. In fact, over the course of history we have observed the use of sexual abuse and assault as a tactic for the diminishment of people particularly with reference to their collective identities. The feelings of shame and powerlessness that attend experiences of sexual assault and abuse reinforce messages of low self-esteem and lack of worth, not only for individuals, but also for carrier groups with a shared identity.[28] Messaging that contributed to low self-esteem and self-worth already abounded at the Mohawk Institute.

Survivors talk about the impact of this on their long-term trauma first as individuals but also with regard to how it impacted the group: "It wasn't just me. He came for a lot of us. You would be lying there awake in your bed wondering is it my turn tonight. It didn't make it better that I was the only one. We all felt powerless—he was like God. What could we do?"[29]

Conclusion

The collective trauma of survivors of the Institute was mediated through an authority structure that had an Anglican priest as its head and Anglican religious culture as its framework for daily life and experience. This trauma had many faces: It was cultural, it was physical, it was sexual, it was religious. In the end it was ultimate; it shook the identity structure of these children and their culture to the core, communicating a message of worthlessness. Value could only be found through the loss of individual and collective self in favour of a second-rate place in the settler's taxonomy of value. This was the project of assimilation through colonization. Abuse by clergy and others, laid on top of the basic practices of assimilation, worked to reinforce and exacerbate trauma at all levels.

When Foucault wrote about biopower he was addressing the use of force and containment to achieve a social end. The gathering up and incarceration of Indigenous children for the purpose of assimilation at the behest of the Canadian government reflects this. When Foucault wrote about biopolitics he addressed the use of policy to regulate the containment and direct processes of "normalization." The DIA tended this through their development of policy designed to regulate the children's life at the schools in every aspect. What will you wear? What will you eat? What will you do? What will you think?

If the government directed and the DIA regulated, what was the role left for religion? The churches administered the schools. They were the enforcement agency by which the model was implemented daily. The use of extreme discipline, as well as physical, emotional, and sexual abuse at the hands of authority figures in the daily life of the children at the Mohawk Institute pushed control, regulation, and enforcement into the realm of terror. For Foucault, tactics of terror meant crossing over: from use of power for social utility, into power as gross use/misuse of power for its own sake. [30]

When we are always afraid, we comply or resist. When the terror is great enough and the power overwhelming enough, we give ourselves up as a means of survival. Children at the Mohawk Institute lost their identities in the face of a harsh assimilationist agenda. Those who survived the collective trauma speak into history today as witnesses to what was lost, demanding through their very survival consequences, accountability, and the return of what was lost.

NOTES

1. Jeffrey C. Alexander, *Trauma: A Social Theory* (Polity, 2012), 6.
2. Alexander, 26.
3. In his *Prison Notebooks*, Gramsci develops the idea of hegemony as a modification of pure Marxist thought: Although the economic substructure is determinative in any society, the idea of a dialectic interaction between the substructure and its culture (superstructure) is developed as a nuance. Antonio Gramsci, *Prison Notebooks* (Columbia University Press, 2011).
4. Bishop George Luxton to Superintendent Davey, March 1970, File 479/24-13-001, Pt. 2, Vol. 8798, RG 10, Library and Archives Canada (LAC).
5. The Church of England and its broader religious group, known as Anglican, is a Protestant tradition begun as a breakaway from the Roman Catholic church during the Reformation in sixteenth-century England. It has ordained clergy known as bishops, priests, and deacons. With reference to the residential schools, most principals of Anglican schools were priests who reported both to the DIA but also to the Mission Society of the Anglican Church and to their appointing local bishop.
6. *NEC Minute Book*, 1896, Guildhall Library, London, England.
7. There were exceptions to this with the appointments of Canon Nelles in the nineteenth century, the Reverend Robert Ashton in the early 1890s, and then the Reverend Cyril Turnell, who was sent from England to serve as principal. His principalship lasted only three years (1915–18). After his time, management of the school returned to lay leadership within the family until 1929. The point is that the lease did not require the principal be a priest, and the priests who served at the MI were not connected to the local religious infrastructure in the way that subsequent clergy would be.
8. *NEC Minute Books*, 1919–22, Guildhall Library, London, England.
9. DIA to NEC Board of Governors, *NEC Minute Books*, 1929, Guildhall Library, London, England.
10. File 466-1, Pt. 3, Volume 6299, RG 10, LAC.
11. During this last era of the Institute's life John Zimmerman also brought two other clergy to work with him at the school: Laverne Morgan as assistant principal in 1946 and the Reverend George Boyce during the last decade of the Institute's history. Boyce had been ordained in a different Protestant tradition, but while at the MI was ordained as an Anglican priest. Both Morgan and Boyce served as master of the boys' dormitory (i.e., house father) and helped with worship and taught religious knowledge.
12. *NEC Minute Books*, 1922–69.
13. The most striking illustrations of this are in the decades-long reports that go from India to the British Crown under the name "The Moral and Material Progress Reports." In these reports you see the church listed as a department of the British government. Although the reporting with reference to the MI is not so direct, it is in the same vein and form.
14. At times the principal served as teacher of religion for the children, while at other times a chaplain was in place for this purpose. For example, George Boyce served both as house father for the boys and as chaplain in the latter part of his time at the Institute.
15. *NEC Minute Books and Correspondence*, 1922–69. Little is written about the religious curriculum followed at the MI during the period under consideration. I have formulated this summary of key aspects of religious knowledge teaching through a review of Church of England curriculum used in other forms of education for children, interviews with George Boyce, Ken Jagz, and Laverne Morgan, as well as interviews with the survivors themselves. I also reviewed the NEC minute books and correspondence from principals regarding religious instruction as detailed in their accounting to the NEC.
16. Roberta Hill, Mohawk at Six Nations, interview with author, August 2017. Hill attended the Institute in the early 1960s.
17. R. G. Miller, interview with author, November 2017.
18. Vernon W. Cisney and Nicolae Morar, eds., *Biopower: Foucault and Beyond* (University of Chicago Press, 2016). In this collection of essays, the idea of biopower and biopolitics in Foucault's work is applied to several recent events and contexts. Although the work does not address the North American Indigenous case, the arguments developed lend themselves to that application.
19. Zimmerman to Colonel Neary, 6 December 1947, in Elizabeth Graham, *The Mush Hole: Life at Two Indian Residential Schools* (Heffle Publishing, 1997), 188.
20. Zimmerman to Neary, in Graham, 188.
21. Zimmerman to Neary, in Graham, 188. Details of the proscribed policy are then given and included the following: strap is rubber, fifteen inches; maximum four strokes for boys fourteen or older—younger students less; a register of punishments must be kept.

22 Interview with Bob White Eye, who attended the school from 1955 to 1964, in Graham, *The Mush Hole*, 419.
23 Interview with Albert Sault, 194? (exact date unknown), in Graham, 399.
24 Interview with Calvin Sault, 194?–53 (exact admission year unknown), in Graham, 399.
25 Interview with Lee Snake, 1963–5, in Graham, 422.
26 The Reverend Ken Jagz, interview with author, 11 February 1999.
27 Jagz, interview.
28 Christina Lamb, *Our Bodies, Their Battlefield: War Through the Lives of Women* (William Collins, 2020). Lamb reflects on the use of sexual violence as a weapon of war and more narrowly of genocide designed to undermine social cohesion within collective identity groups.
29 R. G. Miller, interview with author, 4 April 2018.
30 Michel Foucault, *Discipline and Punish: The Birth of the Prison* (Vintage Books, 1975), 35–59. Foucault explores the role of torture in processes of conformity.

16

Concluding Voices: Survivor Stories of Life Behind the Bricks

Richard W. Hill, Sr.

"We, the boys of the Mohawk Institute desire to take this opportunity to gratefully acknowledge the services rendered by you to us," begins a handwritten memorial presented to Mr. O. R. (Roy) Pengelley, boys' master at the Mohawk Institute in the 1930s. "We have always expected and received fair treatment from you, in right or in wrong," the memorial goes on. Seventy boys signed the memorial to express their appreciation for Pengelley's interest in sport and sportsmanship.[1]

It is a brief and shining moment that stands in contrast with the majority of the memories of other survivors whose time at the Mush Hole was not so rewarding. This memorial reminds us that not everyone who worked at the Mohawk Institute was a sexual predator or mental punisher. Yet, for many, their memories of the hard times at the school have lasted a lifetime. Most of the children who attended the Institute did not leave a record of their time at the school. The current generation of survivors, however, have informed us of their experiences. Their recollections tell of a very different story than that which was reflected in sources such as New England Company reports, Anglican Church records, or federal government documents. While some students have positive memories, such as skills learned, or the shelter provided by the Mohawk Institute when their own families were unable to do so, most of the interviews with former students consist of stories about negative experiences and even abuse.

When reading the testimony left by some survivors, remember that they were children when these things happened to them. Until recently, many carried their stories in silence, afraid or ashamed to share what really

415

happened. Some were punished by school officials or even their own parents for telling their truth. Except for a court conviction of excessive punishment for Principal Nelles Ashton in 1914, no one was ever publicly condemned for the abuse they committed on the wards under their care at the Mohawk Institute.

Collecting Stories

One of the very best sources for stories from former students is *The Mush Hole: Life at Two Indian Residential Schools*.[2] Compiled by Elizabeth Graham, the book is an invaluable source that includes transcriptions of many primary documents and interviews with over thirty former Mohawk Institute students. This chapter cites many of the interview transcripts in *The Mush Hole*, but for a complete picture readers are encouraged to consult Graham's work. In addition to the interviews in *The Mush Hole*, since 1986 the Woodland Cultural Centre has been recording the recollections of the Mush Hole "survivors." There were three survivor gatherings during which interviews were conducted. I interviewed a number of survivors between 2018 and 2020. While every student had their own experience, and experiences varied over time, several themes emerged from these recordings.

First and foremost, students recalled that they were always hungry, never having enough food, and the food they did get tasted terrible. Consequently, they learned to steal food from the local dumps, from the kitchen, or the farm fields. Other themes include:

- *Feelings of loneliness*: They speak of the lack of love or affection within the Institute, leading to countless nights of crying, wondering why they were left alone in this foreign place.

- *Sexual abuse*: Some tell of their own abuse or witnessing it happening to others. The staff, principals, and older students committed these crimes. This kind of trauma affects a person their entire life, and creates fear and distrust, which can affect ongoing relationships.

- *Fist fighting and abuse from other students*: Sometimes the staff forced students to fight one another. Other times, student "gangs" would use violence to obtain favours. One way or another, students had to learn how to fight.

- *Extreme discipline*: Punishment at the Institute was often brutal and unnecessary. Strappings top the list, but there were many forms of violence used on children, sometimes causing bodily scars, hearing loss, and emotional abuse.

- *Resiliency*: Students learned to make the best of the situation or ran away to express discontent. Students learned how to survive. Sometimes these lessons would be internalized, and students stoically took their punishments. However, not all survived their time at the Mohawk Institute, and there were stories of fellow students or babies that disappeared, no one knowing what happened to them.

Taken together, these interviews shed considerable light on the more recent history of the Mush Hole. Below, I have grouped excerpts from these interviews by theme to provide a sense of what life was like at the school in the decades leading up to its closure in 1970. They are not meant to be exhaustive, but rather to give a sense of what life was like behind the bricks of the Mohawk Institute.

On Arriving[3]

"We're put into a dorm. We're not sure where we're going, but we realize it's full of sleeping people, and we're put into a bunk bed, and then we were there still trying to get some rest or sleep, and at six o'clock, the lights are switched on, and there's this heavy bell that rings, like a school bell, and then suddenly we're awake—and as we look on either side of us, there's these dozens of six-, seven-, eight-year-old boys, who we don't recognize, that are surrounding us, and they're just staring at us, because they didn't know who we were, where we came from, why we were there." **Doug George**, Akwesasne Mohawk, 1967–70[4]

Sara Jane Cromarty (1968–9) finally remembered her first day, after she had blocked out her recollections, when she began to see a series of flashbacks of a young girl being transported to a strange place with big pillars and massive front steps. After being drawn to the Mush Hole, her memories of what took place came rushing back to her: *"As soon as I went in, the lady was standing there already. Right away they grabbed me, took me to the washroom, totally just ripped my clothes off, and threw me in the shower. That's when I first felt, I must be very dirty. Seems like she acted as if I'm really dirty.*

Figure 16.1. Doug George

Source: Richard Hill Collection

She even cut my hair short. That's when I knew I lost myself, cause I had the long black hair, and I remember my kokum used to say, 'Don't ever cut your hair.' I just cried, cried, and cried, cause I was very homesick. Cause I didn't know where I was. When I went home, it was so different. I didn't feel at home at all. I wanted to leave, I cried every night, because I didn't know what was happening. I didn't even feel, you know, the love and care, what I had before. They get mad at me because I couldn't speak their language. My mom used to get mad at me because I couldn't understand her. So, I didn't know what to do, and then I just left. There was a big void in me that I was searching. I was looking for somebody to care for me. To love me. Somebody to give me a hug, cause my mom and dad never gave me a hug when I came back."[5]

"I was very lonely. You think you'd get over it, but you never do. I just felt so alone, and I thought, 'Oh my gosh, this is going to be my life now.'" **Geraldine Maness Robertson**, Aamjiwnaang Anishinaabekwe, 1947–50[6]

"I was three years old when I arrived here in the middle of the night. I can still remember when I woke up in a strange woman's arms, only to see my mother disappear into the night. I lived here for eleven years. My mother never came to visit." **Robert Gary Miller**, Tyendinaga Mohawk, 1953–64[7]

"I remember the first day I went there were steps that you go up into the Institute. I remember there was a little boy sitting on the steps, and I was waiting for someone to come and get me to tell me where I had to go. He gave me a hug and gave me a kiss on the cheek, and he goes, 'You're going to be all right.' I didn't even know this boy." **Beverly Albrecht**, Grand River, 1966–70[8]

On Crying

"When I first went there, I cried and I cried and I cried, but it didn't help any. . . . None of the rest of the kids are going to pity you or nothing. . . . It didn't matter you could cry to the Principal, you cried and they never even heard you." **Harrison Burning**, Grand River, 1920–8(?)[9]

"My sister was there too with me when I was there. To hear her lonesome cries—my goodness! It would have been better if I was there by myself. She was my father's baby. She had turned five when she went. To hear her cry and to hear her holler "Daddy," was worse than my lonesomeness. I used to put my arms around her and say "Don't cry, don't cry," and I'd be crying. Then we'd both be crying." **Lorna**, Grand River, 1940–5[10]

"I remember my brother crying really loud that night they took us, and even at that young age I was, I just told him 'There's no need to cry—they don't care about us. If they did, they wouldn't be sending us away.'" **Name withheld**, 1953–60[11]

On Hair Cutting

"I still remember the first day I went there. They took me downstairs and into the boys' playroom, and it was just like they put a cereal bowl on everybody's head and shaved right around it. That really scared me." **Bill Monture**, Grand River, 1963–9[12]

"The second day I was there I got in a big fight. I had beautiful long hair and because I was new, they hadn't cut it off, and the other girls were jealous and pulled my hair. The day they cut my hair—short like a boy's—I cried." **Peggy Hill,** Grand River, 1955-7[13]

On Hunger

"You'd get a bowl of porridge and a slice of bread in the morning, then at noon you'd get bread and soup, and at night biscuits and potatoes. It was a treat if you got meat . . . we were hungry all the time." **Peter Smith,** Grand River, 1926-35[14]

"We was hungry all the time we was there. . . . I was so determined that I'm going to eat it I don't care what it tastes like. Even with that I couldn't eat it—you had to starve. The food—the whole supper or three meals anyway—you couldn't eat it—don't care how hungry you were—how determined you was that you was going to eat it—the taste greets you—you couldn't—you couldn't eat it." **Harrison Burning,** Grand River, 1920-8(?)[15]

"They sold the cream, and gave us the skim milk. Not very often we got whole milk—never, that I can remember. . . . The porridge was just like glue in the morning. . . . One of the senior girls used to sneak me sandwiches. . . . The food there in the summertime was as terrible as in the winter." **Emmert General,** Grand River, 1932(?)-8(?)[16]

Lorna recalled stealing turnips with a group of girls and being forced to eat them for several days, causing them all to be sick. She also said that she couldn't eat apple pie anymore, as the stress over stealing apples for older girls, and the fear of being caught, caused negative associations in her mind that have lasted decades.[17]

"One time they brought us cereal in the morning and the darn stuff was moving—it had maggots in it. They expected us to eat it." **Lonnie Johnson,** Grand River, 1948-56(?)[18]

Figure 16.2. Drawing of Emmert General, 1934, by Richard Hill
Source: Richard Hill Collection

On Fist Fighting

Mush Hole survivor **Tony Bomberry** remembers being forced to fight. He said that they would often fight in teams of two. Once, his brother was on his team. During the initial shoving and roughhousing he got knocked out because someone grabbed him from behind and he fell backwards on his head. He just remembers waking up in the dispensary. While fighting was against the rules, the staff would often let boys fight.[19]

"I lived here for eleven years. I spent the first three years on the girls' side and they pampered me. Then I went over to the boys' side, but it was a very different experience. Because I have blue eyes, the boys said I looked white, and they would beat me up. The older boys would wrap towels around my head and turn me around until I choked on the towels and almost passed out. They would hang me on the hot water pipes and make bets on how long I could stand it." **R. Gary Miller**, Tyendinaga Mohawk, 1953–64.[20]

"Because they didn't want us to get along with the other girls, they [house mothers] would have boxing matches to make us fight just so that we wouldn't like the other girls. They thought if we fight with each other we'll end up taking our anger, or whatever we have, out on the other girls. I remember fighting with my sister. She's two years younger than me, but we never beat each other. We just did it. You don't do it just because you want to." **Beverly Albrecht**, Grand River, 1966–70[21]

"By the time you came out of the Mohawk you were a scrapper. Your culture was taken away—you were nothing. All you knew how to do was fight. You had a chip on your shoulder." **Salli General**, Grand River, 1940–5[22]

On Love and Hate

"The Mush Hole did not teach us how to love. I didn't think I had a heart, and it was because of this school." **Harrison Burning**, Grand River, 1920–8(?)[23]

"All I learned in there was to hate people—I learned you never have friends, because I had two friends and all they do is squeal and get you in trouble, and I learned you never have friends." **John Martin,** Grand River, 1949–54[24]

Imagine never seeing your mother for eleven years. **Geronimo Henry** (1942–53) experienced just that. *"All the time that I was there, my mom never even come to see me, and she never come and took me out for the summer holidays either. And there was always eight, or ten, sometimes fifteen kids that wouldn't go home. I remember like the last day of school we'd run around from our classrooms, and go down the playroom and look out these two windows, and you could see right down the laneway, right down to the street, you know, and you could see the people coming up to get their kids. But we were all at that window just waiting for my mom to come and get me, but she never did. So, I had to stay there all summer, so actually I was one of the guys that stayed there 365 days of the year."*[25] Geronimo spent eleven years looking out that window, watching his classmates going home. He stood there so often the other children called it "Geronimo's Window." Once I asked Geronimo how he felt about his mother given what happened. He looked down at the floor and took a few moments to collect his thoughts, then he said that he hated his mother for abandoning him there. *"I spent my whole childhood there, right from six till sixteen. So, you don't get no parental guidance from*

Figure 16.3. Geronimo Henry at age fifteen at the Mohawk Institute

Source: Courtesy of Geronimo Henry, Richard Hill Collection

like your parents. So, nobody told me they loved me. I imagine that's about the most important part of your life. Nobody hugs you, and nobody tells you they love you. There's no bonding. . . . When I left there, I had a lot of anger, resentment. Just kinda started drinking. I just drank more, and that lasted about twenty-five years. Finally, I sobered up, and I wanted to help other survivors of the residential school."[26] Today, you can find Geronimo at the Mush Hole, sharing his story, healing from doing so, one day at a time.

"You were basically alone. And your family wasn't there, you weren't encouraged to be with your family. It was just lonely. It was a very lonely place. . . . You weren't allowed to grow the way you should have been able to grow as a child. There was no love. There's no nurturing. You don't have that ability to sit on your mother's lap, to get those hugs, to get those stories. You can't get that love that's missing in your life, and the only thing that you got was . . . somebody like the minister, who was very abusive in many ways." **June Shawanda**[27]

On Being Punished

"They had one little room—it had just had room to crawl in and go in the bed if you done anything wrong. That's how he'd punish you—he'd make you go in that room. No light—shut the door and lock it from the outside. You couldn't get out of there and you had to stay in there so many hours." **Martha Hill**, Grand River, 1912–18[28]

Lorna and her sister **Salli** entered the school in 1940. Lorna recalled a girl who was caught out of bounds in the dorm because she was having her period and wanted privacy. The girl was nineteen years old, but still in grade 5. Principal Horace Snell sent for her to come to his office, but she refused. The principal then went to the girls' playroom and strapped the teenager in front of the others. The girl was beaten so severely that she had an epileptic seizure. When the other girls intervened because the principal kept strapping her, Snell became enraged and began shoving and knocking the girls down. When he recovered the strap, he began to beat all of the girls. The principal's wife came down and threatened the girls that if they told anyone what took place, they would "get worse." The other girls asked the girl, who was covered with welts on her back, head, face, legs, and rear end, why she refused to go with Snell. She replied, *"I don't know, but I didn't want to get raped."*[29]

Frank Hill (1945–7) recalled how older boys suspended a little boy from the hot overhead pipes, just to see how long he could hang there. Some boys would hang themselves with their towels from those same pipes until they passed out. Boys would steal potatoes, cabbage, and carrots from the root cellar. Boys would convince the kitchen help to become their girlfriends so they could get extra food. On a sad note, Frank, who worked in the barn, found a collie that he called Lassie. The dog would help him round up the cows. One of the staff members, always trying to break the boy's spirit, shot and killed the dog out of spite.[30]

Vera Styres, attended twice, first in 1942–3 and again in 1946–7. Vera recalled that captured runaways were punished by the other students by crawling through a lineup in which each student would give them a whack on their behind. The girls wore handmade striped work aprons and denim tunics. Button-up underwear was made of stiff, itchy cotton from recycled sugar bags or flour sacks. Vera said she was punished if she got sick, and that the nurse would not treat the students. She got so sick and skinny that her mother, who visited once a month, marched up to Principal Zimmerman and punched him right in the face for letting her daughter get in such a condition. In response, he began to force feed Vera.[31]

"*I ran away once and when I got back there I really got the strap—right to (forearm)—cut my wrist open. I seen a lot of them like that, getting the strap, and they wouldn't even cry. They punished us for practically nothing. . . . I couldn't even go and talk to my sister. . . . I'd get the strap just for talking to my sister.*" **Emmert General**, Grand River, 1932(?)–9(?)[32]

Peggy Hill (1955–7) recalled her life behind the bricks as a series of fights with other students, or punishments from the principal. "*Our only crime was being poor—our parents couldn't feed us the way the Indian agent thought we should be fed.*" Two runaways got caught and were strapped in front of all the students. Peggy got caught stealing food to sneak to her brothers, who were also in the school. For that she got strapped. Once a teacher knitted her a sweater, but a jealous student cut a big hole out of the back. Peggy got blamed and was strapped.[33]

Blanche Hill-Easton (1943), tells of a time when a teacher who she thought was a friend beat her and damaged her back when she was ten years old: "*I was in the sewing room when the teacher got really upset with me because I was crying, and the more she told me to not cry, the harder I cried—and she grabbed me by the hair, and grabbed me by the back, and we were on the bench, and she pulled me right over onto the floor, and then started beating me with the strap. They had a big strap, it looked like those straps that they do with the razors, the men's razors straps. But it had a point on it, and when she hit me with that, she hit me in the middle. Struck me from behind and wrapped around the front of my head and everything, but she kept right on beating me. I hit my head, and hit my shoulder on this side, and I passed out. To this day, I still have that problem, I have a fused vertebrae in the back, and now this whole side has gone.*"[34]

Jo-Bear Curley was a student twice, from 1955 to 1958 and from 1962 to 1964. She used to sneak out of her dorm to watch television in the girl's playroom in the basement. She was punished for stealing apples and getting caught kissing her boyfriend. For her punishment, she had to scrub the floor with a toothbrush. Jo-Bear recalled some darker moments. The girls would challenge each other to choke themselves with the scarves that

Figure 16.4. Blanche Hill-Easton by Greg Staats
Source: Greg Staats

they would wear on their heads. She choked herself until she blacked out. One girl was being punished by an Indigenous staff person and was beat so badly with a strap that her arms and shoulders turned black and blue, yet she would not cry out in pain.³⁵

I interviewed **Pat Hill**, an eighty-two-year-old survivor who lives in Buffalo, New York. She supplied this photo of herself (she is on the right) with an unknown school mate. She attended from 1946 to 1950. Pat had worked at cleaning the principal's apartment, which was next to the girls' dorm. She also had to serve food in the officers' dining room in the basement. She recalled that Principal Zimmerman was brutal, and he beat her repeatedly, for which she confesses that she never knew why. *"He had no mercy on anybody. . . . I often wonder, after I left, that whatever possessed him—how he could do it and get away with it, but he did. . . . He knew you couldn't go anywhere, even if you told somebody. Didn't make any difference."*³⁶ Once she was locked in the third-floor attic for a few days as a punishment. When Zimmerman tried to punish her, he insisted that she drop her pants so he could strap her bare bottom: *"I used to have to fight with him, cause he*

Figure 16.5. Pat Hill (on the right)
Source: Courtesy of Pat Hill, Richard Hill Collection

wanted me to take my ... dresses, he wanted me to take it down."[37] Pat found it ironic that Zimmerman would always preach to the students about the sins of sex at the Mohawk Chapel every Sunday, yet his own conduct made that seem hypocritical. Pat ran away but was caught by Zimmerman. *"I had had so many beatings, I wanted to get out of there. You know when you're a kid and somebody is beating you all the time, you try to get away as far as you can."*[38] One night a couple dozen girls ran away. Pat recalled how the girls used to scale the outside of the building, at the corners with small ledges in the brickwork, to sneak in and out of the second-floor dorm. Inside, there was constant fighting. Her younger sister was always fighting, and sometimes she would have to jump in to defend her. When asked what she would say to Zimmerman after all these years, she replied as follows: *"I don't think I'd ever talk to him. He ruined my life. He made me a hateful person when I was younger, and as you got older, it stayed with you. Never goes away. I never forgot those years. But like I said, I'm a survivor."*[39]

16 | Concluding Voices

"When we little kids wet our bed, we'd really get it. We had to wear the sheet like a diaper during lunch, and then had to wash the sheets. They used to march us into breakfast with these sheets around us." **R. Gary Miller**, Tyendinaga Mohawk, 1953–64[40]

Beverly Bomberry (1943–6), Mohawk, now Beverly Albrecht, recalled her worst memory: "*We were running around the bunk beds and we got caught [by the house mother]. And so, we got sent downstairs, and they had the playroom, and then there was a little office, and in the office was lockers, and they put us in the lockers. I was screaming and screaming to get out. . . . I don't even know how long I was in there, but to me it seemed like a long time because I'm young. And then I realized, oh if I stop screaming, they'll let me go. But to this day, I can't leave a door locked. Like, in my bedroom, I gotta have it open, because I always think I'm trapped. I know I'm not, but that's just in my mind.*"[41]

Marguerite Beaver (1940–8) recalled that a female student had a baby that was rumoured to have been fathered by one of the teachers. While Marguerite suffered no sexual abuse, likely because her mother, also a graduate of the school, worked for the Crown attorney, she was caught smoking and had her hair cut short as punishment. She also recalls getting the strap several times for offences such as running away: "*The strap was about a foot long and about four inches wide, and they hit you with that and naturally it stings for the first two or three times and after that it goes numb.*"[42]

On Language Loss
"*The thing that shocked me most was when I was told I could not speak my native language. I was birthed into this language, yet was told I was being rude. . . . My inner emotions could not accept this, but I could not express myself enough to say what was in my heart in the English language.*" **Jennie Blackbird**, 1942–6[43]

"*I remember this teacher, she had a big clock and she was asking me what time it was, and I must have been speaking my language instead of English, and she really smack[ed] me around with a ruler. I finally realized I was speaking my language, so after that I didn't speak my language.*" **Kenneth George**, 1953–60[44]

"When we went there we used to talk Mohawk, and when they caught us talking our own language they'd give you a strapping and you'd end up losing it—at a young age. You never got to talk it to nobody else. You never got to talk it to nobody else." **Lonnie Johnson**, Grand River, 1948–56(?)[45]

"There were three boys who came down from Bala and they spoke very little English . . . the smaller boy . . . he couldn't speak English at all. His worst experience was the boys teasing him. . . . He got to the point in the end where he learned the English language and they didn't pick on him anymore." **Edward (Russell) S. Groat**, Grand River, 1930–9[46]

"I lost my language. They threatened us with a strapping if we spoke it, and within a year I lost all of it. They said they thought we were talking about them." **Raymond (Ross) Hill**, Grand River, 1929–37[47]

"W] weren't allowed to talk Indian at all, we couldn't say a word in Indian, just speak English, and these children would come in and maybe have no English at all and they would get in groups like cattle, trying to understand English, because they would give them a licking—or they'd give you a scolding or something like that for not being able to say it in English, and they just wiped out the entire Indian language. . . . If we could have utilized our language, probably we would still have our language today. . . . The seniors today are dying off on the reserve and taking the language with them." **Peter Smith**, 1926–35[48]

On Running Away

"The first day I was there I ran away. I ran away about a hundred times. I literally hated that place. . . . I got a scar on my back where that guy—Reverend Zimmerman—strapped me. . . . He couldn't make me cry so he hit me on the back. He even strapped the girls and he wasn't supposed to do that—he would strip them and strap them. . . . I told him one day I was going to kill him, when they sent me to the training school. . . . My stepfather said the guy before him was even worse than that—I said nobody could be worse than Skin [student nickname for Zimmerman]." **John Martin**, Grand River, 1949–54[49]

Figure 16.6. Raymond Hill by Greg Statts
Source: Greg Staats

John R. Elliott arrived at the Mush Hole with two siblings in 1947. John was sent there because he was always truant at the reserve school. John and one of his brothers ran away soon after their arrival and made their way back to their grandfather's house on the reserve, only to hear their grandfather say that it was the government that sent them to the school, not him. Sadly, the grandfather had to take them back to the school again. That did not stop John from running away again. Even though he knew he would get a strapping, he risked it. *"They threw me in the hole.... [It] was two by twelve, about eight feet long, and that was your bed, and then there was a slop pail. You didn't get nothing to eat, no water or nothing. So that wasn't bad, it was only a day the first time. But the next time, they threw me in there for two days. But my buddy knew, and then he shoved me a couple of lavs, that's what they called a slice of bread."* John told me he still gets shivers when he walks past that small cubbyhole under the stairway where he was imprisoned.[50]

John made a point of running away every Christmas Eve. In fact, he ran away so many times, when the kids would see an old green panel

Figure 16.7. John Elliot by Greg Statts
Source: Courtesy of John Elliott, Richard Hill Collection

truck leaving the grounds, they would say, *"John's on the loose again."* John recalled, *"That one time we just got there [to a friend's house in Muncey] and his mother had just cooked a big supper for us and everything, in come that damn green Mush Hole truck. They got us, but they let us finish eating anyway."*[51] Then one time, in 1952, he ran away again, and they simply stopped looking for him. He was finally free of the abuse that he suffered at the Mohawk Institute. His recollections of the strappings he took from Principal Zimmerman are chilling. John had resolved not to cry, not to give Zimmerman that satisfaction, no matter how hard he was beaten. When you look at the photo of John as a student, it brings home the reality that these kinds of things happened to young children.

"It was corporal punishment by humiliation. They'd take your clothes off in front of everyone and bend you over in a chair and strap you. . . You'd have to cry right away, in which case you'd be a wimp, or you had to tough it out, in which case you'd be bruised . . . and severely. . . We were brought up to feel

16 | Concluding Voices   431

guilty or ashamed, ugly. To this day, I have feelings of shame." **R. G. Miller,** 1953–64[52]

The famed long-distance runner **Tom Longboat** ran away from the school twice. The first time he was caught and punished. Then he witnessed another student getting beat so severely that he ran away again. This time, a sympathetic uncle took him in and protected him. The truant officers stopped looking for him. Once he became famous, he was asked to return and give a pep talk to the students. He refused, saying, "I wouldn't even send my dog to that place."[53]

On Dead or Missing Students

With the recent discovery of unmarked graves at other residential schools, the question has come up about how many children died, or went missing, at the Mush Hole. The Survivor's Secretariat has identified at least ninety-seven children who died at the school or because of being at the school.[54] Some survivors talk about children getting hurt or ill and being taken away and never being seen again. Some children were sent away to other schools because they were considered incorrigible, not to be heard of again. Some runaways kept on running, making their way to places like Buffalo, New York, never to return.

One of the most-discussed deaths at the Mohawk Institute was that of thirteen-year-old student Effie Smith on 11 May 1936. Mohawk Institute teacher Susan Hardie described the event as follows: *"The May-Pole swing had not been in use for nearly a year. A new wheel [made from a car wheel] was put up on a Friday. On Monday noon, some new ball bearings were put in & the accident took place that eve after supper. There were four chains & the girls had put a plank into three of the seats & five girls were on it. The wheel fell & struck poor Effie on the diaphragm. She herself pushed it off of her. One girl immediately came to report which came to me & I at once called for Mr. Lager who was still at tea, to help carry her up. Then Mrs. Smith was notified who immediately sent for Dr. Palmer who came in very few minutes. As soon as he saw her, he sent for Dr. Morrison who also came in a few minutes. They then sent at once for the ambulance which took her to the Brantford hospital where she passed away, half an hour after her arrival. The doctor found it was internal hemorrhage. The poor child looked deathly from the first."*[55]

The official report of Smith's death noted that Miss Hardie reported the accident at 6:15 p.m., the doctor was called at 6:20, and Effie was taken to the hospital at 7:15. Principal Snell reported that five girls were playing on the "giant stride or maypole" to which they added boards through the chains and were being pushed around, "throwing all the weight toward one side of the pole. This caused the . . . wheel to spit a piece out of the side of the pole at the top allowing the wheel to fall to the ground where it struck Effie Smith in abdomen causing the injuries from which she died." Snell included a drawing to show the wheel as fairly large. Dr. Palmer reported that he treated Effie from 6:20 to 8:46 p.m. and that she died from bleeding caused by the rupture of the pancreas.[56]

A newspaper story said that the wheel weighed about one hundred pounds and fell from a height of between fifteen to eighteen feet. Other riders included Velma Powless, Laura Davis, and Hazel Van Every. Powless said that all the girls fell to the ground when the piece broke, and she was hit on the shoulder. When she stood up, she saw Effie, who had been sitting next to her, lying on the ground. At an inquest, Principal Snell said the pole had been there for nine years. The Crown attorney pointed out that the pole had an older break. Snell said that the maypole was of a makeshift nature. "I don't think any of us ever thought of danger in connection with it," testified Turnell. C. H. Lager, the boys' master, testified that he had just erected the wheel days before the accident and that he did not notice the crack. Molly Johnson testified that she, Effie, Velma, Laura, and Hazel Van Every had put a two-by-six through three of the loops. She said the wheel fell as they started. The jury, while calling the equipment unsafe, ruled it to be an accident, but recommended that the playground equipment be inspected every three months. Effie's mother did not blame the school, and in fact requested a spot for her younger son in her daughter's place.[57] Over the years this maypole was used in various ways, sometimes as a form of peer punishment. An unpopular child was strapped by the arms to the device and swung round and round until they vomited.[58]

Leander Snake (1963–5) lost track of his older brother, who was picked on by the other students. *"My brother was five years older than me. . . . And he wasn't like me. He was meek. I can remember him out there, and all the other boys would pick on him. . . . I think he got kicked in the kidneys or something, because around Halloween they took him to the hospital in Toronto, and he never came back."*[59]

Martha Albert, Chippewa of the Thames (1950–8), says her worst memory was about two girls who committed suicide in 1956: *"We're on the second dorm, and there my bed was in the far corner, and these little girls, I seen* *them standing in the window, I thought I was seeing shadows. You know, I never forgot those little girls, to this day, I never forgot those little girls. . . . They took their lives. . . . They jumped from the second floor there, hanging on hands. They hit the cement, just where the staircase used to come down. . . . Their names was Cookie and Tammy. . . . They keep bothering me, all the time. For the longest time, I had to go to therapy, to see a psychiatrist, over this, for all those years, for many years. . . . I just couldn't seem to get over that part, of these children, losing these children.*"[60]

Martha also witnessed another girl who tried to hang herself: "*She put the thing [around] her neck, and she was hanging there. So, I just run out and got the nurse, cause the nurse's station was just outside of our door. And they got her. They said she survived. You had to keep your eye on her because she was always trying to commit suicide in there.*" Finally, Martha recalled another girl, Myra, who fell from the maypole and split her head on the cement. The girls carried Myra into the school, and she was eventually taken to the hospital. The girls were told that Myra was taken by her relatives, but they never saw her again. Images of these events kept flashing in Martha's mind over the years.[61]

In early September 1968, after making it sixty miles toward his home in Golden Lake, thirteen-year-old runaway **Joey Commanda**, who was Pikwakanagan Anishinaabe, was struck and killed by a CN Dayliner train in Oakville. Joey had run away with his older brother Rocky. They were both caught by police, but Joey escaped from the police car. Six hours later his life came to an end. A train conductor testified that Joey crossed one set of tracks to avoid a westbound train, only to slip as an eastbound train struck him. In 2021 his community, including his brother Rocky and sisters Loretta and Jacqueline, led his spirit from the Mush Hole to his burial place on a three-day walk.[62]

On Sexual Abuse

Stories of sexual abuse were also prominent. Some survivors, like R. G. Miller, Bud White Eye, Roberta Hill, and Paul Dixon, were explicit in sharing their recollections. They all highlighted that such abuse was not always at the hands of the teachers or staff but also came from fellow students as well.

From 1963 to 1967, she was known as Number 33. **Mary Ann (Marguerite) Cooper** was from Waswanipi, a Cree community in central Quebec, about 1,040 kilometres from the Mohawk Institute. Mary Ann recalled her first night at the Mush Hole: "*It was lonely. Sometimes I would cry. In the evenings, they put us to bed, I'd be afraid to go to the washroom*

Figure 16.8. Bud Whiteye by Greg Staats
Source: Greg Staats

because I was afraid to go to the bathroom. I used to pee a lot on my bed. Afraid to go to washroom, get a strap. That's how it was. And I would crawl in her [sister's] bed sometimes, and we would sleep together, but the counsellor wouldn't catch us. And sometimes it was hard, to not sleep with her, and not be near her. We tried to be close to each other, and it was hard to face that every night. I guess I was nervous, or I was scared, I don't know. That's how it was." Her worst memory was of the night when she became paralyzed by what was happening to her as she was being sexually abused. *"For two years it happened to me, but the first time it happened, I didn't know, I didn't want to, I didn't want anybody to touch me. . . . After the sexual abuse, I didn't know how to handle it. I knew how to write. . . . When everybody left [the swimming pool], I carved something. It was only a small, light carving. I just wrote 'please help me,' cause I didn't know where to take it. . . . I walked away, but every time it happened to me, I carved it more, and more, and more. I carved deeper into it."*[63] That brick can still be seen on the back wall of the Mush Hole. Eventually, Marguerite, after some counselling, returned to see her words on the brick. Her healing journey allowed her to not only read

Figure 16.9. "Help me" brick
Source: Richard Hill Collection

the words she once carved, but to reclaim her original French name, not worrying about getting into trouble over using it.

"I can remember laying in bed wondering when it was my turn, at night. One of the staff was gonna come around, and I was wondering when it was my turn to take me down that aisle and back. My turn came but I never went. I wouldn't get out of bed, and I kicked and screamed and cried, and the guy just left." **Kelly Curley**, Grand River, 1969[64]

"I remember laying in my bunk, I was on the top bunk. All of a sudden, I felt a hand, like, touch me. I'm a fighter. I remember just turning, using my heels and my feet and just started kicking. Nobody came back. They prayed on the weak. I wasn't weak." **Leander (Lee) Snake**, 1963–5[65]

Mush Hole survivor **Tony Bomberry** remembers being in the boys' dorm at night. One of the housekeepers was waking him up, taking him to the room where they kept the shoes. That's where they would abuse him. To this day, when he smells the odour of new shoes, he recalls what happened to him when he was a child.[66]

"I felt imprisoned by the thoughts of other boys finding out about that furnace room 'thing' [where he was molested], and at nine, I felt I had no choice but to return again and again to keep the secret. I can't wash those moments or those feelings from my mind or off my body. We were lost, lonely, scared, and confused, but our biggest battle was to keep our secrets." **Bud White Eye**, 1955–61[67]

"A lot of the abuses—sexual—came from the older kids. A lot of the older kids would steal from the younger kids, and make the younger kids steal. If you didn't come back with what you were sent out to get, or if you were to tell, you'd get worse. A lot of the younger kids lived in fear and terror of the older boys—it was a way of life to us." **Delbert Riley**, 1950-5[68]

Paul Dixon came to the Mohawk Institute in 1963 from the Cree community of Waswanipi, Quebec. "There were times when some of the older boys forced the younger ones to do things to them sexually. I saw that happen many times. I didn't understand any of it and I'm still very angry when I remember those times. Nothing could have prepared us or any Indian child for what was going to happen to us in those years," Paul recalled. "I didn't know right from wrong as far as sexual abuse. How was I supposed to know what an adult can and cannot do to me as a child? . . . When you go through something like that you become very scared of intimacy and sharing your feelings," he said.[69]

Number 34, **Roberta Hill**, Grand River Mohawk, wipes tears away after describing her memories of Principal Zimmerman, now long dead, who had sexually abused her twice, once in his office and once inside the white, clapboard Mohawk Chapel down the road. At one point, her mother came to visit: "Zimmerman welcomed her at the front door, transforming from a Machiavellian monster into a genial host, the miracle worker responsible for moulding neglected children into polite young adults who opened their mouths only to say 'Yes, sir' and 'No, ma'am.' The charade worked. No one doubted or questioned him. As an Anglican priest, he lived on a pedestal, one step closer to God."[70] Roberta details what happened after this visit: "When the visit ended, Zimmerman warmly bade my mom farewell and then, as soon as she was out of earshot, he took me by the hand and brought me into his office, a barren room with a desk, a chair and sickly green walls. He closed the door and got uncomfortably close. Then he reached his hand up my dress and placed it inside my underwear. I couldn't breathe. I felt frozen in place. I was only seven or eight years old, and I didn't understand what was happening, but I knew something wasn't right. I don't remember how I got out of his office, just that I never wanted to go back in."[71]

The second time was even more devastating: "I lined up with the rest of the girls and marched to the chapel. I sunk into the pew, trying to avoid his gaze. In a haze of incense, I dozed off. When I awoke in a start, Zimmerman's eyes were fixed directly on me. My heart started pounding. I knew I was in trouble. After the other girls left church, Zimmerman kept me behind. He took me to a separate room and closed the door. This time, there was no surprise.

Figure 16.10. Dawn and Roberta Hill in their first foster home after leaving the Mohawk Institute
Source: Courtesy of Roberta Hill, Richard Hill Collection

Figure 16.11. Roberta Hill in 1972
Source: Courtesy of Roberta Hill, Richard Hill Collection

Figure 16.12. Roberta Hill more recently
Source: Courtesy of Roberta Hill, Richard Hill Collection

I knew what he was going to do. I don't remember if he ordered me to take off my clothes or if he took them off himself. I just know that I was naked and terrified. Then he molested me again, more roughly this time. Just like before, I was paralyzed, helpless against his hulking body and violating hands."[72]
When Roberta got out of the Mush Hole in 1960, she was sent directly to a foster home. She eventually made her way back to Six Nations after she graduated from high school, but she felt out of place, a stranger. She tried to forget what had happened to her. It was when she met other survivors after the class-action lawsuit was launched that she realized many others had suffered the way she had.

On Memories and the Road to Recovery

"*Looking back on it now, seeing this man beat up this girl, I lost my identity. I think not only seeing her get beat up was a denial of my own self, but not having a role model. There was a lot of feeling of being abandoned—aloneness. . . . That feeling of not having anybody, of being so lonesome. . . . The more counselling I've had, the more I realise the traumas—the effect the residential school had on me.*" **Lorna,** Grand River, 1940–5[73]

"*When you're a child, and . . . whatever it be, a grown woman, or a grown man picking you up, they give you some affection, and that, you know, makes you feel good. And then, they beat the crap outta you, and they do things to you, and it, like, confuses you. I guess with myself, it affected me in a way where I basically didn't deal with any of it, and I carried that shit with me. I didn't really start dealing with it till about six years ago. And still, you know, like today I'm still seeing a therapist. That's probably what I'll be doing for the rest of my life.*" **Johnny** (last name withheld)[74]

"*The harsh truth was that the beatings led to a lessening of empathy toward those who were victims because the expression of sympathy led to more cruelty, more strappings. We had no mentors, no adult protectors. We saw kids desperate for affection who willingly allowed themselves to be molested. We learned to position our bodies in places where the older boys could not attack. We learned quickly that the threat of violence and the resulting fear was the most effective way of controlling others.*" **Doug George,** Akwesasne Mohawk, 1967–8[75]

Figure 16.13. Newspaper photograph of Roberta Hill and Rev. Zimmerman

Source: Photo by Richard Hill of news clipping in Richard Hill Collection

"The little girl whose long braids were hacked off before a delousing and whose pretty white dress was thrown in the trash by the nurse at the Mush Hole will always be there, making sure I don't forget." **Ramona Kiyoshk**, 1956–60[76]

"I still have suicidal thoughts. My psychiatrist calls them suicidal idealizations. I have a tendency to ponder the dark side. I suppose it cannot be helped; all things considered. . . . When I drink, I drink too much. Or I just float in self pity. I'm on the dark side a lot. But that's also where I do my best work. My best work is found on the dark side. You have to get down and dirty with the devil to go to those dark places." **R. G. Miller.**[77]

His number was 73, and this was his "name" from 1967 until 1970, when the Mohawk Institute closed. His real name is **Doug George** (now known as Kanentiio) and he and his brother Deane came from the Mohawk

Figure 16.14. Ramona Kiyoshk, of Walpole Island, at the Mohawk Institute in July 1959. The Department of Indian Affairs noted that this photos shows "Ramona Kiyoshk, a grade 7 student at the Mohawk Institute, [who] has been writing poetry since before she started school, and just naturally puts her experiences into verse."

Source: Library and Archives Canada / Department of Indian Affairs and Northern Development Fonds / e011308265

Community of Akwesasne, about 540 kilometres east from Brantford. He calls his thoughts "photo memories" because he can recall in explicit detail what took place fifty years ago. His total recall keeps the wounds fresh. They arrived at the Brantford train station late at night, with no one to greet them. They did not know where they were headed. Someone called the Mohawk Institute, and they were finally taken behind the bricks, into an altered state of being. He returned to the Mush Hole only to dredge up painful memories: *"I thought that I had reconciled with it, intellectually, you know, that I [had] written about it, I commented about it, I've done interviews about it. I thought that I made some kind of accommodation with it. . . . The first time I remember seeing it, it looked like it was bringing you in, because of that long driveway with those beautiful trees and orchards on either side, and outwardly it looked like an attractive place. But behind the walls . . . there's things we left there. There's a DNA trail, there's semen stains, there's excrement, there's* urine. *That saturates that building. Our DNA is in there, it's not just benign walls. . . . I've been back to the institute maybe a half dozen times. . . . and I thought, I'll put this intellectually in a place where I can understand it. But I can't. I go there and I feel like physically as though I wanna climb back into a shell, I wanna vomit, I want to scream at the spirits that are in that building, 'I understand you, I'm with you.'"* One part of Doug wants to see the building obliterated. Another part wants it to stand in testimony to what really took place: *"We realize there's a very powerful spiritual presence inside that building, and on the grounds, that people have heard kids going up and down, either playing, yelling, or screaming, or crying, and you just want to enter into that. Maybe by entering into that, by being enveloped into that, you can help them, and lead them to a place of peace, so they can continue on with their journeys. But that's not possible—and so once again you're confronted with this thing, you're almost helpless against it again."*[78]

Conclusion

I also interviewed **Geraldine Maness Robertson** from Aamjiwnaang First Nation, Sarnia, Ontario, who attended the Mohawk Institute from 1947 to 1950. Geraldine, small in stature, faced big violence and extreme punishment almost daily. This photo was one of two photos she had of herself when she was young (standing on the right with Violet Riley). It was taken while at Mount Elgin, and given to her seventy years later by Marie Strapp, a former worker at the school.[79]

When she was seven years old, her white teacher told her that she was too stupid to learn anything. Her father then enrolled her and her sister in the Mount Elgin Residential School, near London, Ontario. She did well and returned to her home community, but was picked up by an Indian agent and shipped to the Mohawk Institute when she was eleven years old as her father, himself a residential school survivor, had recently died and her mother was suffering from tuberculosis.[80] *"That began my life in hell,"* Geraldine recalled in a newspaper interview.[81] She remembered that her time was spent working, getting beat up by other students, or trying not to get strapped by Principal Zimmerman. *"From the moment I first saw that man, I didn't trust him,"*[82] she told the reporter. She had good reason. When Zimmerman began strapping children, he did not stop at the four-strapping limit imposed by Indian Affairs rules. Instead, he often hit the children ten to fifteen times on each hand or across the arms. *"I was always afraid I would faint. I would put my back against the door so I could feel the doorknob at my back. I thought if I got close to fainting, I would just turn that knob and run,"*

Robertson recalled. "*I was afraid of what [the principal] might do if I passed out.*" She says she did not know why she would get the strappings. "*Maybe he was just trying to break my spirit,*"[83] she concluded. If you were to meet her, tiny and somewhat frail, you can tell those beatings wounded her spirit, but it was never broken. Emotionally, Zimmerman would constantly tell the students that as Indigenous people, they were "evil" and "were good for nothing, meant to burn in hell for eternity."[84]

Geraldine had toughened up so as not to cry when she was strapped. She said that if she did, the older girls would catch her, surround her, and force her to fight another girl. If she refused, the older girls would attack her. She learned how to fight. "*When I first came here, there were two girls who used to beat me up every day, and sometimes several times a day. . . . It started my life here on a very bad footing. So, it coloured my outlook a lot, until I was strong enough that they couldn't beat me anymore, then they didn't bother me. But it was a miserable first three months, until I toughened up.*"[85]

By the time she got out of the Mush Hole, she was angry with everyone and everything. "*I had to work hard, learn to be introspective and sort out my feelings, to get my life back in order,*" she says. Geraldine turned to reading and music, two things she did not experience at the Mohawk Institute. Yet she still dropped out of high school. She was employed at a local medical clinic, and she experienced such kindness and goodness that she made a career of it. Eventually, she moved back to her home community but could not help but notice the community dysfunctions, which she saw as directly attributable to residential school experiences. Geraldine then dedicated her life to telling the truth of what happened, to revealing the harsh treatment, sexual abuse, the constant hunger, and the mental abuse that took place. She started conversations that most were reluctant to engage in, bringing back too many bad memories.[86] "*People were asking me, how come their parents were so mean to them? I had to explain to them what it was like living here, and how you become so angry, and don't have role models to follow, and it's so completely opposite to what you learn when you're at home. You don't learn the values that you should. You learn to steal, to lie, to cheat. All the bad things that are not conducive to being a good human being. . . . They say one thing, but you're treated another way, so there was a conflict of what's right, and what's wrong. And when you're a very young child, to be exposed in that environment, you don't have the benefit of a home atmosphere at all. . . . They still needed to find that forgiveness, to be at peace with everything, and to go on with their life, and not to blame their parents with how they were raised,*

Figure 16.15. Geraldine Maness with Violet Riley

Source: Courtesy of Geraldine Maness Robertson, Richard Hill Collection)

they needed to know that it was beyond their capacity to show love, and to treat them in a gentle, kind way."[87]

Geraldine later returned and had tea with Principal Zimmerman. I asked her what she said to him. *"Not much,"* she said. *"I just wanted him to see me, to see that he had not beaten me."* She told the reporter that she wanted to show him that she forgave him. But no words were exchanged to that effect.[88]

Figure 16.16. Geraldine Robertson by Greg Staats.
Source: Greg Staats

Geraldine was one of the reasons that I wanted to write this piece. Her story really struck me in the heart. As she talked, her tears would come and go. I realized that the pain she suffered left lifelong wounds. She had become an advocate for survivors and lectured young children about residential schools. In 2018 she was awarded the Order of Ontario Lifetime Achievement Award for her advocacy. From this tiny powerhouse of a woman, the life within the bricks of the Mohawk Institute became real. The abuse against children was real. Their memories are real. Sadly, Geraldine passed away on 4 December 2020, while I was conducting research for this book. She once told a reporter, *"If you don't learn about history, you tend to repeat it."*[89] Knowledge of her and the other survivors' experiences are retold through this publication. We owe it to them to never forget. Geraldine, you have earned your rest, and we will never forget how you overcame your experiences and retained all that the Mush Hole tried to take away. Let these stories serve as a testament to the resilience of the survivors who, despite all odds, shared their stories with us so that we can better understand what took place behind the bricks of the Mohawk Institute.

NOTES

1. Tara Froman, *Wadrihwa*, vol. 29, no. 1, artifact collection, Woodland Cultural Centre, 2020.
2. Elizabeth Graham, *The Mush Hole: Life at Two Indian Residential Schools* (Heffle Publishing, 1997).
3. Some quotes in this chapter have been condensed for readability.
4. Doug George, interview with Rick Hill, 2018. The dates listed after each student's name refer to the period—if known—when they attended the Mohawk Institute.
5. Jane Ash Cromarty, interview with Rick Hill, Survivors' Gathering, Thru the Red Door, 2018.
6. Geraldine Maness Robertson, interview with Rick Hill, 2018.
7. *Brantford Expositor*, 6 June 1991.
8. Beverly Albrecht, interview transcript, Legacy of Hope Foundation, accessed 1 July 2024, https://legacyofhope.ca/wherearethechildren/stories/albrecht/.
9. Interview with Harrison Burning in Graham, *The Mush Hole*, 358-9.
10. Interview with Lorna (last name withheld) in Graham, 377.
11. Interview with anonymous in Graham, 409.
12. Interview with Bill Monture in Graham, 423.
13. Interview with Peggy Hill in Graham, 413-14.
14. Interview with Peter Smith in Graham, 361.
15. Interview with Harrison Burning in Graham, 357.
16. Interview with Emmert General in Graham, 374-5.
17. Interview with Lorna (last name withheld) in Graham, 376, 383.
18. Interview with Lonnie Johnson in Graham, 396.
19. Tony Bomberry, interview, Survivors' Gathering, Thru the Red Door, 2017.
20. *Brantford Expositor*, 6 June 1991.
21. Beverly Albrecht, interview transcript, Legacy of Hope Foundation, accessed 1 July 2024, https://legacyofhope.ca/wherearethechildren/stories/albrecht/
22. Interview with Salli [Lorna's sister] in Graham, 382.
23. Interview with Harrison Burning in Graham, 357.
24. Interview with John Martin in Graham, 403.
25. Geronimo Henry, interview, Survivors' Gathering, Thru the Red Door, 2016.
26. Geronimo Henry, interview with Rick Hill, 2019.
27. June Shawanda Richard, interview, Survivors' Gathering, Thru the Red Door, 2017.
28. Interview with Martha Hill in Graham, *The Mush Hole*, 356.
29. Interview with Lorna in Graham, 375-6.
30. Frank Hill Interview, Woodland Cultural Centre transcription, 1986.
31. Interview with Vera Styres in Graham, *The Mush Hole*, 390-1.
32. Interview with Emmert General in Graham, 374.
33. Peggy Hill, interview, Survivors' Gathering, Thru the Red Door, 2017.
34. Blanche Hill-Easton, interview with Rick Hill, Survivors' Gathering, Thru the Red Door, 2018.
35. Jo-Bear Curley Interview, Woodland Cultural Centre transcription, 198?.
36. Pat Hill, interview with Rick Hill, Buffalo, NY, 8 December 2019.
37. Pat Hill, interview with Rick Hill, Buffalo, NY, 8 December 2019.
38. Pat Hill, interview with Rick Hill, Buffalo, NY, 8 December 2019.
39. Pat Hill, interview with Rick Hill, Buffalo, NY, 8 December 2019.
40. Vicki White, "Breaking the Spirit," *Brantford Expositor*, 6 July 1991, 5.
41. Beverly Albrecht, interview, Survivors' Gathering, Thru the Red Door, 2017.
42. Interview with Marguerite Beaver in Graham, *The Mush Hole*, 384-7.
43. Interview with Jennie Blackbird in Graham, 388.
44. Interview with Kenneth George in Graham, 410.
45. Interview with Lonnie Johnson in Graham, 396.
46. Interview with Edward Groat in Graham, 364.

47 Interview with Raymond Hill in Graham, 368.
48 Interview with Peter Smith in Graham, 360.
49 Interview with John Martin in Graham, 401.
50 John Elliot, interview, Survivors' Gathering, Thru the Red Door, 2016.
51 John Elliot, interview with Rick Hill, Survivors' Gathering, Thru the Red Door, 2018.
52 White, "Breaking the Spirit," 5.
53 Gerry Burnie, "Tom Longboat," In Praise of Canadian History, 9 January 2014, https://interestingcanadianhistory.wordpress.com/2014/01/09/tom-longboat/.
54 Stephanie Villella and Daniel Caudle, "Survivors' Secretariat Identifies 97 Deaths in Connection to Former Brantford Residential School," CTV News, 1 September 2022, https://www.ctvnews.ca/kitchener/article/survivors-secretariat-identifies-97-deaths-in-connection-to-former-brantford-residential-school/.
55 Susan Hardie to Mr. Kidd, 25 May1936, Archival Collection of Woodland Cultural Centre.
56 See File 466-23, Pt. 1, Vol. 6202, RG 10, Library and Archives Canada (LAC).
57 *Brantford Expositor*, 16 May 1936; Snell to Secretary of the DIA, 25 May 1936, File 466-1, Pt. 2, Vol. 6200, RG 10, LAC.
58 Internal school memo, File 451/1-13, Pt. 1, Vol. 8605, RG 10, LAC.
59 Leander Snake, interview, Survivors' Gathering, Thru the Red Door, 2017.
60 Martha Albert, interview, Survivors' Gathering, Thru the Red Door, 2017.
61 Martha Albert, interview, Survivors' Gathering, Thru the Red Door, 2017.
62 The information from this paragraph is based on notes from Doug George, classmate of Joey at the Mohawk Institute. For further information see Ka'nhehsi:io Deer, "Family to Follow Footsteps of 13-Year-Old Who Died Fleeing Mohawk Institute Residential School," CBC News, last modified 9 August 2021, https://www.cbc.ca/news/indigenous/joseph-commanda-memorial-walk-runaway-mohawk-institute-1.6132242.
63 Mary Ann (Marguerite) Cooper, interview, Woodland Cultural Centre transcription, 1984.
64 Interview with Kelly Curley in Graham, *The Mush Hole*, 424.
65 Leander (Lee) Snake, interview, Survivors' Gathering, Thru the Red Door, 2017.
66 Tony Bomberry, interview, Survivors' Gathering, Thru the Red Door, 2017.
67 Bud White Eye, interview, Survivors' Gathering, Thru the Red Door, 2017.
68 Interview with Delbert Riley in Graham, *The Mush Hole*, 404–5.
69 Paul Dixon as quoted in Steve Bonspiel, *Nation* Archives, 18 February 2005, http://www.nationnewsarchives.ca/article/residential-school-one-mans-story/.
70 Roberta Hill, "Survivor," *Toronto Life*, 27 July 2021, https://torontolife.com/life/how-i-survived-canadas-residential-school-system/.
71 Hill, "Survivor."
72 Hill.
73 Interview with Lorna in Graham, *The Mush Hole*, 377.
74 Johnny, interview, Survivors' Gathering, Thru the Red Door, 2017.
75 Doug George, interview with Rick Hill, Survivors' Gathering, Thru the Red Door, 2018.
76 Ramona Kiyoshk, "Why White Guys Shouldn't Be Writing Native Stories," *NOW*, 17 May 2017, https://nowtoronto.com/news/why-white-guys-shouldnt-be-writing-native-stories/.
77 Mark Bonokoski, "The Injury-Packed Road of Indigenous Artist R. Gary Miller," *Toronto Sun*, 19 July 2021, https://torontosun.com/opinion/columnists/bonokoski-the-injury-packed-road-of-indigenous-artist-r-gary-mille
78 Doug George, interview with Rick Hill, Survivors' Gathering, Thru the Red Door, 2018.
79 Colin Graf, "This Residential School Survivor and Worker Reunited 70 Years Later," *Buzzfeed News*, 21 July 2017, https://www.buzzfeed.com/colingraf/this-residential-school-teacher-and-survivor-reunited-70.
80 Mary Alderson, "Geraldine: Her Life Story and Her Achievements," *Entertain This Thought*, 17 March 2017, https://www.entertainthisthought.com/geraldine-robertson/.
81 Graf, "This Residential School Survivor and Worker Reunited 70 Years Later."
82 Graf.
83 Graf.

84 Alderson, "Geraldine."
85 Interview by Woodland Cultural Center staff and Thru The Red Door, 2017.
86 Alderson, "Geraldine."
87 Geraldine Robertson, interview with Rick Hill, 2018.
88 Graf, "This Residential School Survivor and Worker Reunited 70 Years Later."
89 Barbara Simpson, "Aamjiwnaang First Nation Elder Finds Healing in Sharing Her Residential School Story," *Sarnia Observer*, 10 April 2017, https://www.theobserver.ca/2017/04/10/aamjiwnaang-first-nation-elder-finds-healing-in-sharing-her-residential-school-story.

Closing Poems

There is a place I know far, far away
Where we get mush and milk three times a day

Oh Canada do you think we should be proud
Oh Canada to sing your name out loud
The forgotten ones you scattered in the wind
Have come back to haunt you now my friend
Oh Canada your home upon my home

I grew up in the school of racial genocide
Self-hate and shame always walking by my side
You stole my tongue tried to chain my mind
To turn me into a different kind
Oh Canada your home upon my home

Many scars covered over many here to stay
On our children now and those who are on the way
Many struggle each day trying to find the door
To Grandmother's voice as we did before
Oh Canada your home upon my home

The so-called men of God who gave us care
Many were perverts and I'm sure you were aware
They preyed on us both girls and boys
Fulfilling their fantasies but left us destroyed
May you hang your head in shame Oh Canada

So many brothers gone now, so many sisters too
Who were chained in the mind from the residential school
When you broke our families you sealed our fate
We hope for our children that it is not too late
Oh Canada your home upon my home

Reconcile with you I cannot do
You have everything now how your wealth grew
What we have broken treaties and church crap
Many men, women, and children who will never come back
Oh Canada your home upon my home

When I came home I knew no one there
Ten years in the Mush Hole but a lifetime of despair
Still I struggle each day trying to find the door
To speak in Grandmother's tongue as we did before
May your God forgive you, Oh Canada, for I cannot

Jimmie Edgar, Anishnaabe, Scugog Island
Mohawk Institute (Mush Hole), 1950–60

***

Lonely are these frightening spaces
Dark and dreary, evil places
Babes of innocence and gentle ages
Soon are gone as pedophilia rages

Silence cut deep by unmuffled wailing
Guiltless progeny asleep yet waiting
Upon them leapt the dauntless rout
The child fights to no account

Tears and sweat are the boys' reward
For having fought to no accord
The bigger foe filled with lust
He penetrates the boy's sacred trust

Tho' the child no longer weeps
He's still afraid and longs for sleep
Stillness of the dorm's dark chamber
T'is again roughed by cries of pain and anger

Time stood still for students yearning
For release from this unclean dreaming
Tears still fall from rustic faces
Yet still move with youthful graces

> Bud Whiteye, Delaware-Turtle Clan, Moraviantown
> Mohawk Institute (Mush Hole), 1955–61

Appendix 1

History of Six Nations Education

Keith Jamieson

This essay was originally published as a booklet by the Woodland Cultural Centre in 1987. It has been included here, with light revisions, in recognition of the significant contribution Keith Jamieson has made to the understanding of history and education at Six Nations.

As it is with any civilization, the Iroquois peoples had an effective process for preparing children for active participation in the society. The society and the concepts of participation were founded in the Great Law of Peace, the very principles of which united Mohawk, Onondaga, Oneida, Cayuga, Seneca and later the Tuscarora, in the formation of the Iroquois Confederacy. The mother-child relationship in tandem with all the women of the longhouse, shared in the task of developing in the child, an appreciation for the home and family, language, values and beliefs. As the child entered adulthood, the leaders and elders of the Nations began to influence the youth, instilling an understanding of the laws, government, morality and individuality of the young adult, as a member of a clan, a Nation and a Confederacy.

Basically unstructured and non-coercive in nature, the child acquired knowledge through experience of participation, and by the examples and environment in which they lived. The entire community shared in this responsibility and had an interest in its form. The issue of control over the process did not arise in this environment, nor did the issue of priority, for it was interwoven with the political, economic, social and cultural components essential to the survival of the people.

There was a need to develop the skill, abilities and knowledge required to ensure the continuation of the culture, yet there was no concept of failure, nor differentiation between gifted and ungifted, fit and unfit.

Specialization and structured training occurred in only a few instances, relating primarily to religion, health, fortification for security purposes and house-construction. The reciting of long ceremonies required a period of training, as an example.

The elements of cooperation, competence, coexistence and individuality were the basis of the process used by the Iroquois peoples. Appreciation of all the things which was their experience was the only real benchmark.

These elements were in place before the arrival of the European. And it was with the arrival and subsequent settling of the European that the structured, formalized process of "education" was introduced. Through the classroom environment, a designated instructor was charged with the responsibility of transmitting facts, skills and knowledge to the child, separated from the parents, family and community.

In this manner, education was a matter of itself, separated from other facets of life and controlled by various religious, political and economic concerns. Control was a major issue in this situation, and priority for it placed by the concern which was most pressing at the time, be it economic, political and/or religious.

For this "educative" process, the Iroquois peoples had no real understanding or appreciation.

The period between the arrival of the Europeans and the eventual migration of the Six Nations from their homelands, in what is now upstate New York, to the Grand River Valley in 1784, tells of a time of alliance and conflict, of compromise and transition, extending over 300 years.

While the Iroquois sought to understand and coexist with the European, the first missionaries sent to educate the Iroquois sought allies and converts.

> French policy in Indian relations grew directly out of economic interest in winning Indian allies against England. . . . National political and economic concern overshadowed education which was woven marginally around the government's objective and confined to religious instruction and the imparting of the simplest French customs and manners.[1]

While the colonial government of New France made attempts to establish influence over the Iroquois through Jesuit missionaries/diplomats, the British attempted to reverse the trend:

In cooperation with the Anglican Church, the British tried to convert the Iroquois into the Protestant faith to secure their loyalty and attachment to Great Britain. Various missionary organizations and colonial governments attempted to educate the Iroquois children as well.[2]

As will be demonstrated in this history of education at Six Nations, the compromise and transition are issues of the present, and may well be into the future.

Settlement at Grand River, 1784

Following the successful negotiations for the Grand River Valley tract, Captain Joseph Brant and Chief David Hill were able to secure a commitment from Sir Frederick Haldimand, then Governor-in-Chief of Canada, concerning the provision of educational services to the people at Six Nations.

In a letter from Haldimand to A. S. De Peyster, De Peyster is apprised of the promise to Capt. Brant and Chief Hill in providing

> An allowance of £25 Sterg. per annum for a School Master (whom they are to choose for themselves) will be made and paid every six months by Warrant upon the Receiver-General of the Province.[3]

By the next year, 1785, the government had erected a school house at Mohawk Village, "the teacher chosen and appointed by the Chiefs and other members of the bond interested in education."[4]

The school at Mohawk Village was to be the first school built at the Grand River Valley tract, however, it was not the first school amongst the Iroquois people. They had had numerous others built by and for them in their previous homelands, of which Captain Joseph Brant had been a product.

The efforts of Joseph Brant before and at the time of settlement at the Grand River impacted on activities in education, and for this reason, a little about Joseph Brant should be reviewed.

Brant's Influence

Due to the ambitious Margaret, Joseph's mother, his life would benefit in a large way by "being in the right place at the right time," for by the age of ten, Margaret would marry Brant Canadgaranuncka, a Mohawk Sachem. Joseph's new stepfather,

had no problem of loyalty or of what to do or think. Thanks to
the influence of William Johnson, the friendly Irishman who
operated a store across the river from the chief's former home,
Brant was heartily pro-British.... Chief Brant had long been
won over and, indeed, Johnson was by this time firmly installed
as the best friend of the whole Mohawk Nation.[5]

The connection of William Johnson to the Brant family would result in
Joseph's experience of the formal education process of the European. In
July of 1761, the 18-year-old Joseph would attend the Reverend Dr. Eleazar
Wheelock's Moore's Charity School for Indians, the school eventually to
become Dartmouth College in Lebanon, Connecticut.

He [Joseph] learned to speak English and then to read and write
the language surprisingly well. The first letters of his which are
extant, while certainly not models of grammar and spelling
and penmanship, do show remarkable progress, considering
the length of his schooling—less than two years—and his very
scant knowledge of English at the start.[6]

The two years that Joseph spent in education proved to be invaluable to him.
After returning from the school, Joseph became somewhat of a jack-of-all-
trades, exercising a competence at numerous activities: entrepreneurship,
farming, guiding, as well as interpreting for missionaries and diplomats
seeking rapport with the Mohawks and the members of the Confederacy.
It wasn't until his exposure to the aristocracy of Britain, that it proved
powerful.

Joseph's appearance at court [King George III] and his endorsement by the ministry [North] quickly conferred on him a sort
of social distinction... Though Joseph's entry into fashionable
circles was no doubt at first promoted by the government, his
continued acceptance must have owed something to his own
personal qualities. Here again, his smattering of education
stood him in good stead.[7]

Joseph's education and his ability to use it advantageously, would enable
him to assume the position between the Confederacy and the British. It was
for this reason and others that Joseph could continue to bring the European

concepts of education for the member Nations of the Confederacy to experience and use in a like fashion.

With the school established at the Mohawk Village in 1785, the European style of education was quickly grasped by those at the village, and by 1792 the school had "Sixty-six students, some of whom had excellent capacities for learning, and read distinctly and fluently."[8] The school at Mohawk Village was eventually closed in 1813 due primarily to the War of 1812.

1818–1877

The period between 1818 and 1877 witnessed successive efforts to establish institutions of education for and by the Six Nations people at Grand River.

In November of 1818, Reverend Ralph Leeming of Ancaster responded to a request by the Tuscarora Chiefs to establish a school at the Tuscarora settlement. With between 30 to 35 students, Rev. Leeming attempted to have the school brought under "a proper authority" and endowed by the Society for the Propagation of the Gospel in Foreign Parts (SPG). By 1825, the school closed due to poor attendance.

At about the same time, in 1821, Chief Thomas Davis secured an agreement with the Methodist Episcopal Church Missionary Society for a school master. The school opened in 1824 under the entire responsibility of the Methodist Church.

By 1826, "twenty, sometimes twenty-five Indian children regularly attended,"[9] and by 1829, a second school was built at Salt Springs by the Methodist Church.

After Joseph Brant's passing in 1807, Joseph's son, John, had been able to maintain a degree of Joseph's influence. In 1822, while in England, John Brant had successfully negotiated for a school with the British Government. The school opened in 1824 at Grand River, following closely on the heels of the New England Company (NEC) schools; two NEC facilities both opened in 1823.

Of the two facilities under the auspices of the NEC, one was at the Tuscarora settlement on the banks of the Grand River, the other at the Mohawk settlement, near the present location of the Woodland Cultural Centre.

By 1829, the NEC had established two more schools, one for the Onondagas and the Senecas, and the other for the Delawares.

In 1830, the NEC school at the Mohawk settlement, under the direction of Rev. Robert Lugger, experienced expansion. Additional buildings were added for "teaching handicraft trades to Indian youth . . . [and] a mechanic shop and two rooms for teaching girls to spin and weave and two rooms for teaching boys tailoring and carpentering."[10]

This expanded facility was given the name "Mechanic Institution," to develop later into the Mohawk Institute and ultimately the Woodland Indian Cultural Educational Centre.[11]

Also in 1830, the Thomas School House was established by the Confederacy Council. In later years, this school would take on a much greater importance, as the control over education at Six Nations would become a contentious issue.

In 1833, under the direction from the NEC in England, Rev. Lugger "opened the Institution for ten boys and ten girls from the Six Nations, to be boarded and taught (with the day schoolers), and to be instructed in farming and gardening as well as handicrafts."[12]

By 1844, after some difficulty in getting Indian children to attend, enrollment had climbed to fifty and there were fifty more on a waiting list.

From the 1840s onward, "there were many instances of Indian youths who, on leaving the institution and being supplied with tools and materials for work, followed their respective trades with considerable success among their own people."[13]

In 1858, the Institute was destroyed by fire. A larger building was erected to accommodate more boarders, the master and mistress, and in 1859, enrollment was fixed at sixty and was not expanded until after Confederation.

Through the 1850s the Six Nations people established three schools. One near Chief William Smith's Corner, the second at the Onondaga Township and the third in Ohsweken. In the 1860s they established several more schools, one with a grant of twenty pounds from the New England Company.

In 1872, Rev. Robert J. Roberts of the NEC with the people of Six Nations established a school near Beaver's Corner and another near Chief Joseph S. Johnson's settlement.

By 1877, the NEC had established and/or controlled nine schools; the Wesleyan Church, two; and the Confederacy Council, one.

Missionary Involvement in Six Nations Education

As was stated in the introductory section of this history, the missionaries from the European religious community were a part of the first experience Iroquois people would have with European values, culture and ideals. The role they played in the development of education services at Six Nations best defines the nature of the conflicts and transitions experienced over history.

Education of Indians, except in isolated instances, was left outside government policy. The missionaries flowed into the vacuum. In part, this **was** government policy: the Protestant missionaries among the Iroquois provided a means of balancing the Catholic missionary influence among the "French Indian." The churches were willing to assume a financial burden so that the government need not carry it. For the Iroquois, though, this arrangement between the British political authorities and the Protestant churches meant that they had little choice: to get the education, they had to deal with the missionaries and their religion.[14]

The Dutch Missionaries

The initial introduction to the structured process of education practiced by the European was first introduced to the Iroquois by Dutch missionaries. Although they never established missions or schools with the Confederacy, their main trading centres served as the point of exposure.

Up until the British takeover of their colony in 1664, the Dutch missionaries Christianized and educated many of the Iroquois peoples.

French Missionaries

The Jesuit influence in Iroquois education spanned a period of some 115 years. In 1655, the Iroquois requested Jesuit presence in their communities following a peace agreement between New France and the Iroquois Confederacy.[15]

This agreement, as did numerous others that followed to around 1760, failed and the Confederacy and French were at war. These intermittent periods between wars left little time for the Jesuit priests to actually educate the Iroquois to read and write, and therefore, they restrained their activities to simply conversion of the Iroquois to Catholicism.

Between 1666 and 1687, a span of some twenty years, the Jesuits had been able to baptize some 4,000 adults and children.[16] This in effect caused the Confederacy to weaken with the creation of many "French Villages" of "Praying Indians," to which many Mohawks, Oneidas and Onondagas defected.

This arrangement became questionable in 1760, when Sir William Johnson attacked Montreal. The Iroquois in the villages around Montreal did not assist in its defence for they had agreed to remain neutral through the Confederacy.

The Society for the Propagation of the Gospel in Foreign Parts

The SPG was an organizational wing of the Church of England created by Royal Charter on June 16, 1701. One of its objectives was "to seek the conversion of the heathens."[17]

In 1709, four Iroquois Sachems visited England to confirm a peace treaty, and while there, requested Queen Anne "to take measures for the instruction of their subjects in the truths of Christianity."[18]

In 1712, Rev. William Andrews was appointed Minister and Schoolmaster, and upon his arrival in Albany, began his mission. Early in 1713, the Mohawks built a school house, 30 feet long and about 12 feet wide, with 40 children in attendance.[19]

Although the initial start was encouraging, by 1717, only five or six children were in attendance, and the conversion of the adults was not progressing. It was therefore closed.[20]

The SPG, in the guise of Rev. Henry Barclay, brought to the forefront the potential of instructing the Mohawks and, by 1743, sought approval of the SPG and the Indian Commissioners of New York to appoint two Mohawk Schoolmasters.[21]

Rev. Barclay appointed "One Cornelius a Sachem at the lower, and One Daniel at the Upper Town,"[22] and in a 1743 report informed the SPG that "both [are] very diligent, and teach the young Mohawks with surprising success."[23]

Up to 1766, there seemed to be some concern for future school development for the Iroquois, specifically the Mohawks. The issue at hand was essentially the merits of sponsoring segregated boarding schools for Indians over the provision of education services within the Mohawk communities, close to their families and homes.

The SPG requested Sir William Johnson to prepare a plan, wherein Johnson responded,

> to establish on some regular system proper Missionaries of Schools in most of their Towns which is the only effectual means of Converting and Reducing them to Order. A few struggling Missions or Schools out of their country will never answer the end proposed the more distant Indians being extremely averse to sending their Children abroad for Instruction, and if they

did, they are apt to relapse afterwards. I have seen examples amongst the best of them sufficient to justify my opinion.[24]

The SPG heeded the advice of Sir William Johnson, and until the start of the American War of Independence, the SPG opened a number of schools in what is now New York State. In this way, "by the end of the American Revolutionary War, the missionaries had laid firmly the grounds for formal European schooling among the Iroquois."[25]

With the reorientation of the SPG in Canada to become the NEC, there was renewed involvement at Six Nations with the settlement in Grand River Valley. In an 1820 treaty with the SPG,

> 20,000 acres of land in the Missaga [sic] and 40,000 in that of the Mohawk "districts" were added to the Government, and Sir Peregrine Maitland expressed his readiness to appropriate the lands themselves, or the money arising from their sale, to the Society in trust to provide the said Indians with Missionaries, Catechists, and Schoolmasters. The Society approved of the proposal, and requested the Bishop of Quebec to act in the matter. The Mohawk devoted a portion (£600) of the proceeds of the land sold by them to the building of a parsonage on the Grand River, and added a glebe of 200 acres.[26]

The relationship between the NEC and the Confederacy Council continued to develop with some success. However, financial difficulties experienced by the NEC placed a strain on the relationship, and by 1877 the two had reached a point of conflict.

Six Nations School Board—1878

With the development of so many schools came the inherent costs of maintenance and support. As so aptly summed up by a letter from Reverends James Chance, Robert J. Roberts and Robert Ashton of the NEC in September of 1877 to Colonel J. T. Gilkison, Visiting Superintendent and Commissioner of the Six Nations,

> The employment of interpreters, the building of school teacher's houses, the clothing of some of the children, etc., effectually prevented this limited [fixed at 750 pounds annually in 1821] from being strictly adhered to. It was soon increased to £1000, and again to £1300 a year nominally, and indeed for 30 years

was in fact several hundred pounds a year more than this last limit. For the last ten or twelve years, the Company's [NEC] annual expenditures at the Grand River has always exceeded £2000 and after £3000, and even £4000.[27]

The NEC had grown impatient with the refusal of the Six Nations Council to contribute towards these ever-increasing costs. The Council maintained that by an 1820 treaty with the SPG, a great contribution had already been made. The treaty, which was inherited by the NEC in 1827, in part read,

> 20,000 acres of land in the Missaga [sic] and 40,000 in that of the Mohawk "districts" were added to the Government, and Sir Peregrine Maitland expressed his readiness to appropriate the lands themselves, or the money arising from their sale, to the Society in trust to provide the said Indians with Missionaries, Catechists, and Schoolmasters. The Society approved of the proposal, and requested the Bishop of Quebec to act in the matter. The Mohawk devoted a portion (£600) of the proceeds of the land sold by them to the building of a parsonage on the Grand River, and added a glebe of 200 acres.[28]

The NEC threatened to terminate all assistance to the Six Nations, and as demonstrated in a letter to Colonel Gilkison from Walter C. Vennino,

> When the Council of Indian Chiefs comes thus to understand that it costs in the discretion of the New England Company to continue or to withdraw their assistance to them, and their children, they will probably cherish the more their present advantages, and be willing to give some proof of their gratitude, as for instance, by complying with the request of the Company that the Chiefs in Council should authorize a grant from the Indian Funds.[29]

On March 13, 1875, Colonel Gilkison appeared before the Chiefs in Council at their invitation to explain the NEC threat. In responding, the Speaker of the Council countered that "the Six Nations had contributed towards education, in revenue derived from lands held by the Company near to Brantford and elsewhere."[30]

He demanded that Col. Gilkison give an estimate of the financial value of their lands which had been acquired by the NEC for education purposes.

In November of 1875, Revs. Chance, Roberts and Ashton were appointed a Canadian Sub-Committee of the New England Company to solve this particular dilemma. After a series of proposals and counter-proposals, the Canadian Sub-Committee proposed that

> the Chiefs of the Six Nations be required to make a grant of at least fifteen hundred dollars per annum (the New England Company at present contributing a like amount) for purely educational purposes in the Company's nine day schools on the Reserve, and that management of a School Board.[31]

The School Board consisted of the visiting Superintendent of Indian Affairs, three Six Nations representatives, and three representatives of the New England Company. The Wesleyan Conference would also come under the Management of the Board, provided it had a representative on the Board commensurate with the amount of its contribution.

The proposal was submitted to the DIA in September of 1877 and approved three months later by the Superintendent General.

On July 17, 1878, the Confederacy Council named Chiefs John Hill, Richard Hill and Moses Martin to the School Board on an annual basis; the NEC appointed Canon Abraham Nelles, Reverends Robert J. Roberts and Robert Ashton for indefinite terms; with the Departmental representative the Superintendent in the Grand River Valley.

By Order-In-Council dated November 18, 1878, financial conditions of the Six Nations Council contribution were articulated as follows:

> The Six Nations Indians Council by a recent resolution unanimously voted a grant of . . . Fifteen hundred dollars per annum, to be paid from their funds, towards the support of the nine New England and two Wesleyan Methodist Schools on the Reserve, in the Township of Tuscarora—said grant to be subject to the condition that it is annually voted by the Six Nations Council and to be supplementary of the contribution of . . . Five hundred and fifty dollars per annum paid from the Indian School Fund, and of the amount contributed by each of the Corporations above-mentioned towards those schools.[32]

In December of 1878, both the NEC and the Six Nations Council approved of the contributions and the Six Nations School Board was struck.

The immediate priorities of the trustees of the School Board were the improvement of the school facilities, the acquiring of trained teachers and the improvement of student attendance. Between 1879 and 1882, the Board began "gradually making changes, improvements and repairs, alike calculated to promote efficiency, comfort of teachers and pupils and their eight schools more attractive."[33]

By 1882, "all schools are replete with all material for the instruction and comfort of pupils."[34] By 1883, "the best of order, one of them a building of brick recently erected; each is furnished with that is required for the pupils and the teachers."[35] By 1895, the School Board had spent large amounts of money to bring all the schools to a condition of relative excellence. These expenditures included the following:

> School No.-1. Repairing and screening closets, finishing fences, new sidewalks, new stove, general repair.
>
> School No.-2. Repairing and screening closets, re-shingling roof, repairing plaster, whitewashing, new stove, etc.
>
> School No.-3. Lot enlarged, re-fenced, school-house moved, interior sheeted, re-floored, closet removed and screened, new sidewalk, all buildings painted inside and outside, new stove, etc,
>
> School No.-5. Roof, fences, closet, foundation, steps and plaster repaired, exterior painted, and interior whitewashed, generally repaired.
>
> School No.-6. Closets screened, fences, sidewalk conductors and windows repaired.
>
> School No.-7. Lot graded, new fences, closet screened, sidewalk and steps, interior repainted and whitewashed.
>
> School No.-9. Lot graded and re-fenced, school-house roof and window repaired, closets screened and painted, general repair.
>
> School No.-10. Repainted and generally repaired.
>
> School No.-11. Closets screened and painted, new front steps, etc.[36]

By 1897, five new school houses had been erected and three others improved and refurnished. By 1900, four more school houses had been built and two others improved.

During the period between 1879 and 1897, in addition to the betterment of actual facilities under the control of the School Board, was the acquisition of trained and "competent" teachers. The Mohawk Institute, previously referred to as the Mechanic Institution, took on a special role.

The training of teachers was begun immediately in 1878, so that by 1881, most of the "seven competent Indian teachers" in the boards schools were graduates of the Institute.[37] By 1884, all schools under the Board's control had been placed under the "instruction of qualified and trained native teachers" from the Mohawk Institute.[38]

Records concerning teachers and other information are sketchy and rather limited, however some lists do exist, including the following:

1882

No.-2; Miss F. Maracle

No.-3; Miss L. Lewis

No.-5; Wm. Russel

No.-6; Miss E. Hill (non-Indian)

No.-7; Miss A. Jones

No.-8; Miss L. Davis

No.-9; Wm. N. Monture

No.-10; Wm. Martin[39]

1886

Board School—Council House, Ohsweken; Miss Floretta Maracle

Thomas School; Mr. John Miller

Red Line School; near Grand River Church; Miss Cross

No.-8; near Kanyenga Church; Miss Maggie Davis

No.-6; Benjamin Carpenter

No.-10; Mr. John Lickers

No.-5; Mrs. E. Tobicoe

Stone Ridge Schoolhouse; Miss Hyndman

No.-3; Miss Susan Davis

No.-7; Miss Elisabeth Johnson

No.-9; Claybren Russel[40]

1891

No.-1; Miss Hyndman

No.-2; Miss Catherine Maracle

No.-3; Miss Wetherell

No.-5; Mr. Elam Bearfoot

No.-6; Mr. Thomas Miller

No.-7; Miss Sara Russell

No.-8; Miss Maggie Davis

No.-9; Mrs. Scott

No.-10; Miss Sara Davis

No.-11; Miss Francis Davis

Thomas School; Mr. John Miller

Stone Ridge 1890; Mr. Joseph Monture

New Credit; Miss Meehan[41]

School Board Re-Organization—1901

> that as the Company's [NEC] charter, dated 1661, directs that the funds of the Company are to be "applied to the propagation of the Gospel among the heathen natives" in British North America, they consider that the work carried on in the Eastern provinces of Canada for the last seventy to eighty years is now, might be considered, some what beyond the limits of their Charter.[42]

It was for this reason that in December of 1896 the New England Company terminated its already reduced annual grant (reduced by $500 per annum in 1883) of $1,000 to the Six Nations School Board. This decision was not, however, communicated to the Six Nations Chiefs, but instead to the Department of Indian Affairs.

In January of 1897, Hayter Reed, Deputy Superintendent General, wrote to Colonel Cameron to "inform the Council that this portion of the appropriation for the school purpose will hereafter be charged to their own funds."[43]

Further to this matter, Rev. Ashton, one of the three NEC representatives, and later Colonel Cameron, advised Duncan Campbell Scott, then Acting Deputy Superintendent General, that the "present representatives of the Company be invited by the Department to continue on the Board of Management, and that the present system of management be not changed."[44]

As could be expected, the Chiefs were angered at what they clearly perceived as a violation of the School Board constitution agreed to in 1878. Adding fuel to fire, the Chiefs learned that Rev. Ashton intended to resign from the Board, June 30, 1900, while simultaneously the Wesleyan Conference was to terminate both its contribution and its representative. In effect, the Chiefs would assume full financial responsibility for the day schools as of July 1900, apart from the Department of Indian Affairs' share.[45]

In response, in February of 1900, the Chiefs presented the Superintendent General with a petition, which stated,

> That as the expense and maintenance of all the schools on their Reserve are now borne by the band out of their own funds in trust with the Government of the Dominion, they beg humbly to submit that they be allowed to assume full and complete control of the same, that is, The School Board to be composed as follows: - The local Visiting Superintendent to represent the

> Department of Indian Affairs and a committee of members of the Reserve appointed by the Chiefs in Council.[46]

In so doing, the Chiefs reminded the Superintendent General that they had total control of the Thomas School, and that

> it is the only School upon this Reserve which has prepared pupils to a standard which enabled them to pass the prescribed entrance examination into the Collegiate Institute, and not one of the board Schools has Passed a pupil into the Collegiate Institute.[47]

For the duration of one year, memorandums, reports and seemingly coincidental absences of key Departmental decision-makers, the matter of the Six Nations School Board remained contentious.

In his second of two reports, Colonel Cameron suggested the establishment of a School Board consisting of seven trustees, three to represent the Six Nations Council, and four representing the Department of Indians Affairs. He suggested that Revs. Ashton and Strong of the NEC and Rev. Wilkinson of the Wesleyan Conference be appointed as Departmental representatives, and that the new Board should have control of the schools, subject to Departmental approval.

Upon his return from Europe, the Superintendent General of Indian Affairs accepted Cameron's suggestions and upon notification, the Chiefs in Council on January 9, 1901, reluctantly approved.[48]

But this was not to be the final solution to the issue of control, for the next 25 years would witness successive efforts, both by the Department of Indian Affairs and the Confederacy Council, to bring each other into their concept of control and management.

History of Education on the Six Nations Reserve—1784-1902

The following history of education was an excerpt from a speech given by Chief Josiah Hill at the Opening Ceremonies of Number 2 school on May 24, 1902. The speech was included in the cornerstone of the school and was returned to Mr. Arthur Anderson, Secretary to the Six Nations Confederacy Council when the school was demolished.

Our sincere gratitude is extended to Mrs. Mary Longboat for making those historical documents available to our community. The documents will be catalogued and eventually placed on microfilm in the archives at the Woodland Cultural Centre.

By: Tom Hill, Museum Director

About the year 1784 the first school was established in Canada by the Government authorities in the Mohawk settlement. We are unable to find any available history relating to the progress in education made by the pupils of this first of primeval Schools beyond the fact that the teacher was chosen and appointed by the Chiefs and other members of the band interested in education.

Previous to this period, Indian Schools had been established in what is now known as the State of New York this was before the War of Independence in 1776. In these schools reading and writing in the Indian language alone were taught and our forefathers appointed their own teachers and had full control of the conduct of their schools.

Education in the Mohawk language was also conducted in the Mohawk settlement in Canada up to about 1835. During that period quite a number of our people, especially the Mohawks, could read and write in the Mohawk language, hence came the necessity to have portions of the New Testament and the book of Common Prayer, translated into the Indian tongue at various periods, by different translators, amongst whom were Capt. Brant, Wm. Hess, John Hill and others.

The latest versions of these translations were revised and corrected by the late John Wilkes, who was of English descent, but who had acquired a complete mastery of the Mohawks language. His brother Jas. Wilkes an esteemed citizen of the city of Brantford, was as his late brother well known to many of the other Chiefs and people of this Reserve, and whom we believe is still alive.

It was also found necessary to have the Church hymns translated into the Mohawk language, this had been done while yet our people lived in the Mohawk Valley revised by different translators in Canada.

These hymn books and the book of Common Prayer, revised as they have been, are still used in our missions and Chapels of worship. An edition of the book of Common Prayer was translated into the Mohawk language and prepared for the press under the direction of the late Rev. Archdeacon Nelles, Chief Missionary of the New England Company for the convenience of those who were educated to read and write in the Mohawk language so that they could take part in the services of the Church of England.

The missionaries, the Revd Archdeacon Nelles and the Revd Adam Elliott, used to read the services in the Indian language. In that year 1827 the Revd. Robert Lugger, came to the Mohawk settlement and was joined in 1831 by the Rev. Abraham Nelles.

The first schools built here were in 1823, on the River bank, Tuscarora and one where the Mohawk now stands near Brantford.

In the year 1836, three School lots known as the Oneida, Onondaga, and Delaware School lots were granted to the New England Company for the purpose of educating the youth of this Reserve. These School lots were comprised of one hundred acres each and upon each a School was established, all these lots have long since been sold by the Company.

Early in the year 1850 the School now known as the No. 1 School near Chief William Smiths' corners was opened, and another at the Tuscarora Village near the old St. John Cemetery in the Township of Onondaga.

Some years afterwards a School house was opened in a log house which was situated, where the Village of Ohsweken now stands, and within 300 yards from where this beautiful School house is now being erected. The late Augustus Johnson, was the School teacher, and latterly the School was conducted by Thomas Thomas until his death, after which the School was closed and the old log school house was sold.

Subsequently another School was opened in a log house near the McKenzie Creek on the property of Chief Abram S. Hill, and therefore the School was removed to the other corner on the north half of Lot No. 12, Concession 4 Tuscarora. This School was taught by Mr. John S. Kingston, a man of Irish extraction and from this School Mr. Kingston was transferred to the Onondaga Baptist Church, now known as the Johnsfield Baptist Church. in which the School was conducted for some years. Owing to the removal of Mr. Kingston from our midst, this section of the Reserve was entirely deprived of School advantages for years and it was for that reason that the School now known as Thomas' School, came into existence. This school had many hard struggles at its inception. For several years the teacher was paid by the parents of the pupils, from the proceedings of tea meetings and other services, including private subscriptions. The late George E. Bomberry, M.D. was its first pedagogue and eventually the New England Company assumed control of the School and engaged Mrs. R. J. Roberts. This School and that of the Kanyengeh, was given in charge of the Rev'd R. J. Roberts as teacher. This School and that of Kanyengeh, was given in charge of the Rev'd R. J. Roberts assistant missionary by the New England Company, and they were independent from those Schools which were under control and charges of the Rev. Canon Nelles. This School was closed by the opponents of the School and refused to reopen it. It was at this juncture that the residents of this section, now in the immediate vicinity of Ohsweken Village took advantage of the favourable conditions presented to them for securing a School.

The residents of this district approached Revd. R.J. Roberts with a view to securing a School for this corner and he immediately wrote to the Company *explaining the desire of the people of the Council House, that they would be pleased to have a School and would willingly help to build a School house. Ex Chief John Hill offered a School plot, and in a few weeks Mr. Roberts received an answer from the Company, agreeing to the request of the people of this section and enclosing a cheque for £20, as a grant towards building the School house and the building of this School house was commenced by the people at once, and in a few weeks the Ohsweken School house had evolved from their labour and in it the children of this village are being taught today.*

Revd. R. J. Roberts, was transferred in the year 1872 from the Kanyengeh Mission to the Cayuga Mission and consistently with his energetic manner in the cause of education he immediately set to work and inaugurated a School near Beaver's Corners and another one near Chief Joseph S. Johnson's settlement.

About the year 1878, the New England Company approached the Six Nations Council with a view to the formation of a School Board under whose charge and control the Schools upon the Reserve under the supervision of the New England Company would thereafter be conducted. It was agreed at the time that the New England Company would be represented by 3 representatives, the Six Nations Council by 3 Chiefs, the Methodist Conference by one member, and the Department of Indian Affairs was to have one representative in the person of the visiting superintendent, and the School funds were to be made up as followsA: $1500.00 from the New England Company; $1500.00 from the Six Nations Council; $500.00 from the Methodist Conference; and $50.00 was voted to each School by the Department of Indian Affairs. Thomas School was not included in these grants, as it was understood that the Council must continue to conduct this School, which was at that time as it is now, under control and management of the Chiefs in Council.

The action of the Chiefs in thus reserving this School to be solely managed and controlled by the Council was a wise stroke of policy, for in after years it proved to be an influence to other Schools which were managed by the School Board, as it became patent to the latter that their standard of education was inadequate and that efforts towards the obtaining of a higher standard were necessary to be put forth.

After many hard struggles covering a period of a quarter of a century the Council and the members of the School Board have at least gained grounds in the right direction. They have now secured to us a higher standard of education, in many particulars identical with the Ontario School system, and we, also, now have our qualified teachers, educated and trained under the Ontario School system and the Model Schools of Ontario for teachers.

In conclusion, we in behalf of the Council tender our thanks to the New England Company for the services they have rendered in the cause of education and the Christian Missions amongst the Six Nations in the past. Having withdrawn their grant to our schools in June 1897, and the Methodists in June 1899.

We are grateful for their kindness to us in supplying materials and for the maintenance of these Schools up to the time of the formation of the School Board and we now rejoice to know that their long and untiring work has been rewarded by awakening amongst the Chiefs and people of the Six Nations, a sense of the importance of education.

We sincerely trust that this School the cornerstone of which is now about to be well, truly and firmly laid by Chief Elias Lewis, speaker assisted by Chief William Wage will greatly enhance and espouse the cause of education and that the day may not be far distant when we may be able to assume the responsibilities incumbent upon a full control and charge of all our educational institutions upon this Reserve.

We are firm in the belief that should this take place it would redound in much good to the youth of our band by teaching them business principles and self reliance, which in the School of life is the first essentials to success.

We fervently hope and trust that the almighty God, who rules all things may be pleased to bless the efforts of the Six Nations Chiefs, and the Department of Indian Affairs who decided that this beautiful building should be erected for the benefit of our children and posterity for years to come and that it may prove the means of bringing them out of the dark recesses of ignorance into the sunshine of education, industry, honesty, sobriety, and a charitable Christian life.

Signed on behalf of the Six Nations Council by the Committee, this 24th day of May A.D. 1902—Chief Josiah Hill, Secretary of Six Nations Council

Control of Education—1925-1972

The period between 1901 and 1925 contained many efforts on the port of the Confederacy Council to gain control of the Six Nations School Board and the education system in place at that time. However, other events would influence the activities of the Council.

Of the many things which occurred, two of the most influential was, first, the First World War, which many of the Six Nations people participated, in both active duty and in the auxiliary services for those in active duty. The other influence was the change in the system of government occurring in 1924, wherein the Elective system replaced the Confederacy Council.

In 1925, the Elective Band Council assumed the responsibility for education, and proceeded to repair and make improvements in the schools. However, the Department of Indian Affairs began moving in the direction of greater control of residential or day schools in Canada. At Six Nations, the Indian Superintendent became responsible for the supervision of the operations of the schools.

Yet, the Department considered the formation of an all-Indian School Board, which had been a contentious issue for some thirty years past. In 1926, the Department proposed "Regulations for the Management of the Six Nations Day Schools," under which "a School Board consisting of six members—five Indians to be chosen by the Six Nations Council and the Indian Superintendent who shall Act as Chairman."[49] Their regulations were essentially the same as those submitted by the Confederacy Council in 1906.[50]

In 1928, all Indians in Canada were granted free education. Charles Stewart, Superintendent General of Indian Affairs, said,

> Free education for the Indians was definitely imposed by treaty in some provinces and by usage in others and was the only exceptions to the general rule were made in the case of Indians of the provinces of Ontario and Quebec who were fortunately in the possession of tribal funds, it seemed discrimination to refuse to extend to them the bounty of the Government in this regard. It has therefore been decided that in the future the education of these Indians shall be carried on without cost to them, thus completing a system of free education to all the Indian wards of the Crown in Canada.[51]

The Six Nations School Board was in operation until 1933, and although no record seems to exist, its termination is implied in a letter dated March 23, 1934, from Lt. Colonel Morgan to A. F. McKenzie, Departmental Secretary, which stated,

> I am in receipt this morning of a Departmental letter No. 15-32 upon this subject which is a reply to a letter I wrote to the Deputy Superintendent General regarding Truant Officers and it appears that the purpose of my letter was not fully understood

as it was far from my intention to suggest the re-appointment of a School Board or to infer that the Truant Officer should carry out the duties formerly performed by the Trustees.[52]

There are numerous other letters and directives between Departmental officials regarding financial matters, which had a limiting effect on the decision-making capacity of the School Board. Resolutions of the Six Nations Elective Council were rejected based on the financial control exercised by the Department, and it can only be assumed that this was a contributing factor to the termination of the Six Nations School Board in 1933.

By 1934, all Indian School Boards or Band Council had ceased participation in the control and management of their education. In 1946, a Special Joint Committee of the Senate and House of Commons began an inquiry into the legislative relation between the Government of Canada and the Indians of Canada. Education was a concern of this inquiry and the Six Nations Elective Council expressed concern over religious freedom in the residential schools (Mohawk Institute).

As one of its delegate, Reginald Hill told the members of the Special Joint Committee,

> We specified undenominational residential schools largely for the protection of those children whose parents still believe in the original teachings of our people. We feel it is entirely unfair to take these children and expose them to a different religious training from that which their own parents followed.[53]

In all, the Special Joint Committee held 128 meetings heard 122 witnesses, received 411 written briefs from Indian Bands, organizations, and interested individuals. In 1951, on the basis of the recommendations made by the Special Joint Committee, the Indian Act was passed. In effect, the new legislation made the Minister of Indian Affairs directly and wholly responsible for Indian Education. This act has been since in effect to 1985.

Joseph C. Hill—1951–1972

The intention of the 1951 Indian Act was to place the control of education within the Department of Indian Affairs, however, that definition was never fully implemented on Six Nations. This was due primarily to the efforts of Dr. J. C. Hill.

Dr. Hill split the education administration from the office of the Department of Indian Affairs, Brantford Agency, and established it on the Six Nations Reserve. It was the only Indian Administration office located on a Reserve in Canada.

During the 1960s, Dr. Hill initiated course development on Indian Studies, History, Crafts and Arts, and introduced the teaching of Indian language, specifically Mohawk, at the time in the schools at Six Nations.

Dr. Hill also saw the employ of Indian teaching personnel as crucial to the success of the local education system. He pursued this concept and brought the number of teachers who were Indian to be in the majority.

Indian Control of Indian Education—1972–1985

The concepts and ideals of Indian Control of Indian Education are embodied in a report prepared by the National Indian Brotherhood (now the Assembly of First Nations) of 1972. It is a report which reflects the desires and wishes of bands across Canada, and was adopted by the Government of Canada as policy in 1973.

It is a lengthy report, and should be reviewed as the state of affairs guiding present activities by Federal Government regarding Indian Education. But in keeping with the nature of this paper, a simple statement of the Six Nations perception of this concept is included here.

In his 1984 doctoral thesis, "**Iroquois Control of Iroquois Education: A Case Study of the Iroquois of the Grand River Valley in Ontario, Canada**," Abate Wori Abate drew the following summary:

> Local education control is perceived in two ways. In the first place, it is perceived as the Indianization of decision-making responsibility on the Reserve. But the Six Nations people have no desire to assume control of their education for two unrelated reasons. They would like constitutional or legislative guarantee of the funding before considering the local control of their education. On the other hand, they are aware that local education control would be a very sensitive political issue, given the existence of two Council systems on their Reserve.
>
> Education is considered a political, and it is the only institution which, employs members or supports both the Elective Band and Confederacy Council systems. Local control would mean associating it with the former Council. This would effect the jobs, and subsequently the welfare of the members of the

Confederacy Council system working in the current education climate. They might not agree to work in a system which takes its authority from the Elective Band Council. On the other hand, this Council has no desire to assume control of education.

The principals and counsellors are practically all Indians. It is generally believed that they are well placed to make effective the Indians' own ideas regarding education of the children. In addition, there is a Principal's Association and a School Committee which act as advisory bodies to the Superintendent. Moreover, parents have access to the Superintendent, principals and counsellors regarding any problems or grievances they might have.

NOTES

These notes have been lightly updated to follow contemporary citation formatting.

1. Evelyn C. Adams, *American Indian Education: Government Schools and Economic Progress* (Kings Crown Press, 1946), 12.
2. Abate Wori Abate, "Iroquois Control of Iroquois Education: A Case Study of the Iroquois of the Grand River Valley in Ontario, Canada" (PhD diss., University of Toronto, 1984), 69.
3. Charles M. Johnston, ed., *The Valley of the Six Nations: A Collection of Documents on the Indian Lands of the Grand River* (Champlain Society, 1964), 52.
4. Chief J. W. M. Elliot, *History of the Progress of Education Among the Six Nations* (Ohsweken, 1902), 5.
5. Isabel Thompson Kelsay, *Joseph Brant, 1743–1807: Man of Two Worlds* (Syracuse University Press, 1984), 57.
6. Kelsay, *Joseph Brant*, 83.
7. Kelsay, 167.
8. Johnston, *Valley of the Six Nations*, 60.
9. Johnston, 254.
10. Johnston, 256.
11. Johnston, 256.
12. Johnston, 287.
13. H. W. Busk, *A Sketch of the Origin and the Recent History of the New England Company* (Spottiswoode & Co., 1884). 38.
14. Abate, "Iroquois Control of Iroquois Education," 11.
15. Thomas Donohoe, *The Iroquois and the Jesuits* (Buffalo Catholic Publication Co., 1895), 70–71.
16. John Gilmary Shea, *History of the Catholic Missions Among the Indian Tribes of the United States* (Edward Duncan & Brother, 1855), 300.
17. Public Archives of Canada, MF78-l 4, Reel 1 (c4497).
18. Ernest Hawkins, *Historical Notices of the Mission of the Church of England in the American Colonies* (B. Fellows, 1847), 266.
19. Abate, "Iroquois Control of Iroquois Education," 56.
20. William Webb Kemp, *The Support of Schools in Colonial New York by the Society for the Propagation of the Gospel in Foreign Parts* (Teachers College, Columbia University, 1913; repr., Arno Press, 1969), 210. Citation refers to Arno Press edition.
21. Kemp, *The Support of Schools*, 210.

22 Henry Carley to Philip Bearcroft, Albany, dated November 17, 1742, in Frank J. Klingbert, *Anglican Humanitarianism in Colonial New York* (Church Historical Society, 1940), 56.
23 Hawkins, *Historical Notices*, 285.
24 SPG Letterbook in Kemp, 226.
25 Abate, "Iroquois Control of Iroquois Education," 71.
26 *Classified digest of the records of the Society for the Propagation of the Gospel in Foreign Parts, 1701-1892*, Second Edition (London, 1893), 166.
27 New England Co., *Six Years Summary of the New England Company, for the Civilization and Conversion on Indians, Blacks and Pagans in the Dominion of Canada and the West Indies, 1873-1878* (Gilbert & Rivington 1879), 163.
28 *Classified digest of the records of the Society for the Propagation of the Gospel in Foreign Parts, 1701-1892*, Second Edition (London, 1893), 166.
29 Public Archives of Canada, Indian Affairs, Reel No. C11133 (RG10, Vol. 2007, File 7825-18).
30 Public Archives of Canada, Indian Affairs, Reel No. C11133 (RG10, Vol. 2006, File 7825-1A).
31 *Six Years Summary*, 166.
32 Canada, Order-In-Council dated November 18, 1878.
33 Canada, 43 Victoria, Sessional Papers (No.4), A. 1880, Volume 3, 18.
34 Canada, 46 Victoria, Sessional Papers (No.5), A. 1883, Volume 4, 2.
35 Canada, 47 Victoria, Sessional Papers (No. 4), A. 1884, Volume 3, np.
36 Canada, 59 Victoria, Sessional Papers (No. 14), A. 1896, Volume 10, 23.
37 Canada, 46 Victoria, Sessional Papers (No. 5), A. 1883, Volume 4, 2.
38 Canada, 48 Victoria, Sessional Papers (No. 3), A. 1885, Volume 3, 19.
39 Lloyd King, unpublished manuscript.
40 Lloyd King, unpublished manuscript.
41 Lloyd King, unpublished manuscript.
42 Public Archives of Canada, Indian Affairs, Reel No. C111CC (RG10, Vol. 2007, File 7825-18).
43 Public Archives of Canada, Indian Affairs, Reel No. C111CC (RG10, Vol. 2007, File 7825-18).
44 Public Archives of Canada, Indian Affairs, Reel No. C111CC (RG10, Vol. 2007, File 7825-18).
45 Abate, "Iroquois Control of Iroquois Education," 128.
46 Public Archives of Canada, Indian Affairs, Reel No. C11133 (RG10, Vol. 2007, File 7825-18).
47 Public Archives of Canada, Indian Affairs, Reel No. C11133 (RG10, Vol. 2007, File 7825-18).
48 Public Archives of Canada, Indian Affairs, Reel No. C11133 (RG10, Vol. 2007, File 7825-18).
49 E. R. Daniels, "The Legal Context of Indian Education" ((PhD diss., University of Alberta), 1973.
50 Canada, Order-In-Council dated February 16, 1906.
51 Canada, *Annual Report of the Department of Indian Affairs, 1928* (King's Printer, 1929), 14.
52 Public Archives of Canada, Indian Affairs, Reel No. C-8218 (RG10, Vol. 6167, File 434-5, Part-3).
53 Canada, *Proceedings of the Special Joint Committee of the Senate and House of Commons on the Indian Act, 1947* (King's Printer, 1947), 1274.

Appendix 2

Mohawk Institute Students Who Became Teachers

Compiled by Alison Norman

Below is a list of Mohawk Institute graduates who became teachers (including the year they graduated from the Mohawk Institute). The list is not complete, but it includes all those whose names appeared in the records that were searched.

SOURCES:

MH = from Russell T. Ferrier's 1930 list of "successful graduates" reprinted in Elizabeth Graham, *The Mush Hole: Life at Two Indian Residential Schools* (Heffle Publishing, 1997), 86, 219–21

SH = from a list written by teacher Susan Hardie in Olive Moses, Doris Henhawk, and Lloyd King, *History of Education on the Six Nations Reserve* (Woodland Cultural Centre, 1987)

WCC = Woodland Cultural Centre collections

1850s—Elizabeth Martin Powless attended the school at the Martin Settlement on-reserve but then completed her education at the Mohawk Institute (MI) before becoming a teacher at No. 4 School.[1]

1859—Isaac Bearfoot graduated from the MI, taught at a local day school, then appointed a teacher at the MI in 1869, teaching there for nine years. He then attended Hellmuth College and was ordained a clergyman of the Church of England. (MH, SH)

1859—Albert Anthony graduated and began working at No. 5 School.

1860s—George Powless, Isaiah Joseph, and Daniel Simon, all MI graduates, were by 1871 working as teachers in reserve schools and hoping to get funding to attend Huron College, which was denied.[2]

1873—Elijah Powless graduated and taught at No. 3 School. (MH)

1876—Lucius Henry left and taught at Ojibway School in Munsey. (MH)

1876—Moses Walker left and taught at Moraviantown and at Chippeway Hill. (MH)

1876—John Schuyler left and taught at Oneida. (MH)

1876—Louis Scanado left and taught at Oneida. (MH)

1876—Amelia Checkock graduated and taught at Muncey Town, at Stone Ridge, and at Shawanaga/Parry Sound. (MH)

1878—Scobie Logan graduated and then taught at Muncey before he became chief and councillor. (MH)

1879—Adam Sickles graduated and then apprenticed as a blacksmith. He then taught at Moraviantown. (MH)

1879—Anna Jones attended the Brantford Collegiate Institute (BCI) from the MI, graduated in 1879, taught at No. 7 for several years. (SH)

1880—Lydia Lewis passed the entrance exam, graduated from BCI in 1880, taught at No. 3 for several years. Married Robert Brant and had a son, Lieutenant Cameron Brant. (SH)

1880—Catherine Maracle passed her entrance exam and graduated in 1880. Taught at St. Regis, Bay of Quinte, and at Six Nations No. 2. (SH, MH)

1880—Sarah Davis obtained the highest marks in the entrance exam. Attended Brantford Collegiate, graduated in 1880, taught at different schools on the reserve for more than twenty-five years. "She was a great reader and a well informed woman." She had a lot of influence on the reserve. (SH)

1880—Claybran Russel left in 1880, taught at No. 5 School for three years, then went to Chicago. (MH)

1881—Floretta Maracle passed her entrance exam and graduated in 1881, then taught at No. 2 for ten years. Then held a position with the Indian Department for many years. Retired on a pension. Married Allen Johnson. (SH)

1881—Jane E. M. Osborne passed her entrance examination and graduated in 1881, then became a governess at Toronto Ladies College before going to Winnipeg. (MH)

1882—Elam Bearfoot passed the entrance exam, attended Brantford Collegiate, then taught at Six Nations for twenty years. Then worked on a fruit farm for seven years. Worked at Cockshutt Plow Works, having charge of one of the Depts. (SH, MH)

1882—Isabella L. and Maggie Maracle both completed the training course. Isabella subsequently hired at No. 6, while Margaret Maracle graduated with a teaching certificate. (WCC)

1883—Jessie Osborne passed the entrance exam and attended BCI for three years, obtaining a second-class certificate and graduating in 1883. Taught in the MI before moving to Winnipeg to teach school.

1883?—Mary Monture passed her entrance and attended BCI, graduating in 1886. Taught at No. nine for years, then married Andrew Scott. (SH)

1885—Christopher Monture left in 1885. Passed the entrance exam, attended BCI for a short time, and was awarded a scholarship. Taught school on the reserve for a while then went working out. (SH)

1885—John Lickers left in 1885. Passed entrance exam, was awarded a scholarship, and attended BCI. Taught school on the reserve for many years before becoming a truant officer. (SH)

1886—Susan Hardie admitted to MI in 1878 at age eleven, attended BCI, obtained a second-class certificate. Took a model school course, graduated in 1886. Taught at the MI for one year, then attended the Toronto Normal School for one year, obtaining a professional second-class certificate. Taught at the MI until retirement in 1936. (MH, SH)

1886—Mary Monture passed the entrance exam, attended BCI, and then taught at No. 9 School for years. (MH)

1886—Robert Hill passed his entrance exam and taught at No. 11 School. (SH)

1887—Phoebe Waddilove passed the entrance exam and attended BCI before teaching at the Oneida School. (MH)

1887—Sarah Latham passed the entrance examination, attended BCI, and graduated in 1887. Taught at No. 6, then went into service in Buffalo. (SH)

1888—Josephine Good attended BCI, did the six-month training certificate at MI, and then taught in Parry Island. (MH)

1888—Sarah Russell attended BCI, did the six-month training certificate at MI, and then taught at No. 7 on-reserve. (MH)

1880s (late)—Willis Tobias, obtained third-class certificate and appointed teacher in Moraviantown. (MH)

1880s (late)—Lucy Hill passed the necessary exams, completed the six-month course at MI, and was hired at a school at Muncey. (MH)

1880s (late)—Francis Davis passed the necessary exams, completed the six-month course at MI, and was hired at No 11 School. (MH)

1893—Peter Adams passed his entrance exam and then did his training as a teacher. He taught on the reserve for many years. (SH)

1895—Naomi Latham taught at No. 7 School for three years before moving to Chicago. She had a second-class teacher's certificate. (SH)

1897—Alex Leween passed the entrance examination and then taught at the Bay of Quinte for many years. (MH)

1900—Edith Good attended BCI and then obtained a certificate to teach. She taught at the Mission School at the Mohawks of the Bay of Quinte for many years. (MH)

1901—Edith Styres was appointed a junior officer in the MI, then became the sewing teacher for two years. (MH)

1909—Susana Latham attended Brantford College and then obtained a certificate to enter normal school. She was hired as a teacher in the junior school at the MI. She later went to Chicago to attend nursing school. (MH)

1910—Jessie Van Every attended collegiate for one year, left in 1910, and taught at No. 8 School for two years. (SH)

1913—Arnold Moses left in 1913 after attending BCI for three years. Taught at No. 7 before enlisting to fight in the First World War. After the war, he became a farmer. (MH)

1914—Jesse Moses left in 1914, attended BCI for four years, taught on the reserve, and then became a successful farmer and councillor. (MH)

1918—Wilma Smith attended BCI and then Hamilton Normal School. She taught at No. 8 School from 1920 to 1929. (MH)

1921—Ruby Smith attended BCI and obtained her first-class teaching certificate. She attended Hamilton Normal School and taught at No. 3 School. (MH)

1921—Elva Miller attended continuation school and BCI, obtaining a teaching certificate. She taught at No 4 School in 1930. (MH)

1922—Carrie Crowe, from Muncey, attended business college and then taught at a school on the Muncey Reserve before returning to the MI and working as a housekeeper. (MH)

1922—Sylvia Jamieson attended continuation school in Onondaga, BCI, and then earned her certificate at Hamilton Normal School. She taught at No. 3 School in 1930 as well as other schools. (MH)

1923—Floretta Elliott completed a course in telegraphy, took a position working at the MI after she graduated, volunteered with the Girl Guides, and also worked in domestic service in Toronto. (MH)

NOTES

1 She is not included in Hardie's or Ferrier's lists. For more about her life, see Alison Norman, "'Teachers Amongst Their Own People': Kanyen'kehá:ka (Mohawk) Women Teachers in 19th Century Tyendinaga and Grand River, Ontario," *Historical Studies in Education / Revue d'histoire de l'éducation* 29, no. 1 (2017): 32–56.

2 "Report of the Hon. A. E. Botsford, Commissioner of the New England Company, on Their Missionary Stations on the Grand River, Near Brantford, Ontario," appendix VII in *History of the New England Company: From Its Incorporation, in the Seventeenth Century, to the Present Time: Including a Detailed Report of the Company's Proceedings for the Civilization and Conversion of Indians, Blacks, and Pagans in the Dominion of Canada, British Columbia, the West Indies and S. Africa, During the Two Years 1869–1870* (Taylor, 1871), 318–32.

Suggested Reading

The following is not intended as an extensive list but rather as a starting point for those who wish to learn more about the Mohawk Institute and the history of residential schools in Canada.

Archival Collections

Government records that detail the running of the school can be found at Library and Archives Canada in Record Group 10. See the helpful overview of Indian Residential School records at https://library-archives.canada.ca/eng/collection/research-help/indigenous-heritage/Pages/residential-schools.aspx.

There are multiple archival collections of interest for those wishing to conduct further study on the history of the Mohawk Institute. Many people start with Elizabeth Graham's important 1997 book, *The Mush Hole: Life at Two Indian Residential Schools*. Graham reproduces many archival sources, including documents from the New England Company, Department of Indian Affairs reports, and letters between church and departmental officials, as well as interviews with survivors of the school.

The National Centre for Truth and Reconciliation has also published an extensive narrative about the Mohawk Institute that includes over three documents such as annual reports, primary documents about the school, NEC reports, plans and maps of the school, etc. The narrative can be found at https://archives.nctr.ca/NAR-NCTR-080.

See also the following collections:

Mohawk Institute Fonds, Diocese of Huron, Verschoyle P. Cronyn Archives, Huron University College, London, Ontario.

New England Company records, including Minutes, Letters Sent, London Metropolitan Archives, London, England.

Woodland Cultural Centre, Library and Archives, various collections.

The National Centre for Truth and Reconciliation Archives also has a significant and growing collection of digitized photographs and archival records. These are available through the NCTR website, at https://archives.nctr.ca/.

Six Nations Education History and Mohawk Institute History

Acres, William. "Documents of the Mohawk Institute: The Journals and Reports of Robert Ashton, 1872–1876, and the Diary of Alice Ashton, 1877." *Journal of the Canadian Church History Society* 59 (2021–22).

Abate, Abate Wori. "Iroquois Control of Iroquois Education: A Case Study of the Iroquois of the Grand River Valley in Ontario, Canada." PhD thesis, University of Toronto, 1984.

Graham, Elizabeth. *The Mush Hole: Life at Two Indian Residential Schools.* Heffle Publishing, 1997.

Groat, Cody. "Commemoration and Reconciliation: the Mohawk Institute as a World Heritage Site." *British Journal of Canadian Studies* 31, no. 2 (2018): 195–208. https://www.liverpooluniversitypress.co.uk/doi/10.3828/bjcs.2018.14.

Jamieson, Julia L. *Echoes of the Past: A History of Education from the Time of the Six Nations Settlement on the Banks of the Grand River in 1784 to 1924.* Self-printed, n.d.)

Jamieson, Keith. *History of Six Nations Education.* Woodland Indian Cultural Educational Centre, 1987.

Moses, Olive, Doris Henhawk, and Lloyd King. *History of Education on the Six Nations Reserve.* Woodland Cultural Centre, 1987.

Norman, Alison. "The History of Education at Six Nations of the Grand River, 1828–1939." In *Ontario Since Confederation: A Reader*, 2nd ed., edited by Lori Chambers, Edgar-Andre Montigny, James Onusko, and Dimitry Anastakis, 87–108. University of Toronto Press, 2024.

Norman, Alison. "'Teachers Amongst Their Own People': Kanyen'kehá:ka (Mohawk) Women Teachers in 19th Century Tyendinaga and Grand River, Ontario." *Historical Studies in Education / Revue d'histoire de l'éducation* 29, no. 1 (2017): 32–56. https://educ.ubc.ca/special-issue-historical-studies-in-education-spring-2017/.

Norman, Alison. "'True to My Own Noble Race': Six Nations Women Teachers at Grand River in the Early Twentieth Century." *Ontario History* 107, no. 1 (2015): 5–35. https://www.erudit.org/en/journals/onhistory/2015-v107-n1-onhistory03913/1050677ar/abstract/.

Pettit, Jennifer. "From Longhouse to Schoolhouse: The Mohawk Institute, 1834–1970." Master's thesis, University of Western Ontario, 1992.

Truth and Reconciliation Commission of Canada. *Mohawk Institute Indian Residential School IAP School Narrative.*

National Centre for Truth and Reconciliation, 2013. https://t-r-c.ca/nctr/school_narratives/mohawk_institute.pdf.

General Residential School History

Battiste, Marie, and Jean Barman, ed. *First Nations Education in Canada: The Circle Unfolds*. University of British Columbia Press, 1995.

Barman, Jean. "Schooled for Inequality: The Education of British Columbia Aboriginal Children." In *Children, Teachers, and Schools in the History of British Columbia*, edited by Jean Barman, Neil Sutherland, and J. D. Wilson, 57–80. Detselig, 1995.

Barman, Jean, and Jan Hare. *Good Intentions Gone Awry: Emma Crosby and the Methodist Mission on the Northwest Coast*. University of British Columbia Press, 2007.

Chartrand, Larry N., Tricia E. Logan, and Judy D. Daniels. *Métis History and Experience and Residential Schools in Canada / Histoire et expériences des Métis et les pensionnats au Canada*. Aboriginal Healing Foundation, 2006. https://www.ahf.ca/files/metiseweb.pdf.

Chrisjohn, Roland David, Sherri Lynn Young, and Michael Maraun, *The Circle Game: Shadows and Substance in the Indian Residential School Experience in Canada*. Theytus Books, 2006.

Deiter, Constance. *From Our Mothers' Arms: The Intergenerational Impact of Residential Schools in Saskatchewan*. United Church Publishing House, 1999.

Fontaine, Phil, and Aimée Craft. *A Knock at the Door: The Essential History of Residential Schools from the Truth and Reconciliation Commission of Canada*. University of Manitoba Press, 2015.

Fraser, Crystal Gail. *By Strength, We Are Still Here: Indigenous Peoples and Indian Residential Schooling in Inuvik, Northwest Territories*. University of Manitoba Press, 2024.

Grant, Agnes. *Finding My Talk: How Fourteen Canadian Native Women Reclaimed Their Lives After Residential School*. Fifth House Books, 2004.

Grant, Agnes. *No End of Grief: Indian Residential Schools in Canada*. Pemmican Publications, 1996.

Jaine, Linda. *Residential Schools: The Stolen Years*. University of Saskatchewan, University Extension Press, 1993.

King, David. *A Brief Report of the Federal Government of Canada's Residential School System for Inuit / Bref compte-rendu du Régime du pensionnats pour les Inuit du gouvernement fédéral du Canada.* Aboriginal Healing Foundation, 2006. https://www.ahf.ca/files/kingsummaryfweb.pdf.

Lascelles, Thomas A. *Roman Catholic Indian Residential Schools in British Columbia.* Order of OMI in BC, 1990.

MacDonald, David Bruce. *The Sleeping Giant Awakens: Genocide, Indian Residential Schools, and the Challenge of Conciliation.* University of Toronto Press, 2019.

McCallum, Mary Jane Logan. "'I Would Like the Girls at Home': Domestic Labour and the Age of Discharge at Canadian Indian Residential Schools." In *Colonization and Domestic Service: Historical and Contemporary Perspectives,* edited by Victoria K. Haskins and Claire Lowrie, 191–209. Routledge, 2014.

Miller, J. R. *Residential Schools and Reconciliation: Canada Confronts Its History.* University of Toronto Press, 2022.

Miller, J. R. *Shingwauk" Vision: A History of Native Residential Schools.* University of Toronto Press, 1996.

Milloy, John Sheridan, and Mary Jane McCallum, *A National Crime: The Canadian Government and the Residential School System.* Anniversary ed. University of Manitoba Press, 2017.

National Indian Brotherhood. *Indian Control of Indian Education.* National Indian Brotherhood, 1972.

Niezen, Ronald. *Truth and Indignation: Canada's Truth and Reconciliation Commission on Indian Residential Schools.* University of Toronto Press, 2013.

Nuu-Chah-Nulth Tribal Council. *Indian Residential Schools: The Nuu-chah-nulth Experience.* Nuu-chah-nulth Tribal Council, 1996.

Truth and Reconciliation Commission of Canada. *The Final Report of the Truth and Reconciliation Commission of Canada.* Vol. 1, *Canada's Residential Schools: The History, Part 1, Origins to 1939.* McGill-Queen's University Press, 2015.

Truth and Reconciliation Commission of Canada. *The Final Report of the Truth and Reconciliation Commission of Canada.* Vol. 2, *Canada's Residential Schools: The History, Part 2, 1939 to 2000.* McGill-Queen's University Press, 2015.

Truth and Reconciliation Commission of Canada. *They Came for the Children: Canada, Aboriginal Peoples and Residential Schools.* Truth and Reconciliation Commission of Canada, 2012.

Watson, Scott, Keith Wallace, and Jana Tyner, eds., *Witnesses: Art and Canada's Indian Residential Schools.* Morris and Helen Belkin Art Gallery, 2013.

Woolford, Andrew. *This Benevolent Experiment: Indigenous Boarding Schools, Genocide, and Redress in Canada and the United States.* University of Nebraska Press, 2015.

Individual Residential School History

Barman, Jean. "Separate and Unequal: Indian and White Girls at All Hallows School, 1884–1920." In *Children, Teachers and Schools in the History of British Columbia*, edited by Jean Barman, Neil Sutherland, and J. D. Wilson, 337–58. Detsilig, 1995.

Cariboo Tribal Council. *Impact of the Residential School.* Cariboo Tribal Council, 1991.

Cross, Natalie, and Thomas Peace. "'My Own Old English Friends': Networking Anglican Settler Colonialism at the Shingwauk Home, Huron College, and Western University." *Historical Studies in Education / Revue d'histoire de l'éducation* 33, no. 1 (2021). https://doi.org/10.32316/hse-rhe.v33i1.4891.

Dyck, Noel. *Differing Visions: Administering Indian Residential Schooling in Prince Albert, 1867–1967.* Fernwood Publishing, 1997.

Fiske, Jo-Anne. "Gender and the Paradox of Residential Education in Carrier Society." In *Women of the First Nations: Power, Wisdom, Strength*, edited by Christine Miller and Patricia Chuchryk, 167–82. University of Manitoba press, 1996.

Fleming, Thomas, Lisa Smith, and Helen Raptis. "An Accidental Teacher: Anthony Walsh and the Aboriginal Day Schools at Six Mile Creek and Inkameep, British Columbia, 1929–1942." *Historical Studies in Education / Revue d'histoire de l'éducation* 19, no. 1 (2007): 1–24.

Furniss, Elizabeth. *Victims of Benevolence: The Dark Legacy of the Williams Lake Residential School.* Arsenal Pulp Press, 1995.

Glavin, Terry, and former students of St. Mary's. *Amongst God's Own: The Enduring Legacy of St. Mary's Mission.* Longhouse Publishing, 2002.

Graham, Elizabeth. *The Mush Hole: Life at Two Indian Residential Schools.* Heffle Publishing, 1997.

Haig-Brown, Cecilia, Garry Gottfriedson, Randy Fred, and the KIRS Survivors. *Tsqelmucwílc: The Kamloops Indian Residential School—Resistance and a Reckoning*. Arsenal Pulp Press, 2022. Includes the original text of Celia Haig-Brown's 1988 book *Resistance and Renewal: Surviving the Indian Residential School* as well as new material.

Haig-Brown, Celia. *Resistance and Renewal: Surviving the Indian Residential School*. Arsenal Pulp Press, 1988.

Jack, Agnes. *Behind Closed Doors: Stories from the Kamloops Indian Residential School*. Theytus Books, 2006.

Knockwood, Isabelle. *Out of the Depths: The Experiences of Mi'kmaw Children at the Indian Residential School at Shubenacadie, N.S.* Fernwood Publishing, 2015.

McCallum, Mary Jane Logan. *Nii Ndahlohke: Boys' and Girls' Work at Mount Elgin Industrial School 1890–1915*. Friesen Press, 2023. Book and audiobook. https://www.niindahlohke.ca.

Memoirs

Bear, Chief, Arthur. *My Decade at Old Sun, My Lifetime of Hell*. University of Athabasca Press, 2016.

Fontaine, Theodore. *Broken Circle: The Dark Legacy of Indian Residential Schools: A Memoir*. Heritage House Publishing, 2022.

Highway, Tomson. *Permanent Astonishment: Growing Up Cree in the Land of Snow and Sky*. Anchor Canada, 2022.

Johnston, Basil H. *Indian School Days*. University of Oklahoma Press, 1988.

Kinew, Wab. *The Reason You Walk: A Memoir*. Penguin Canada, 2017.

Merasty, Joseph Auguste, and David Carpenter. *The Education of Augie Merasty: A Residential School Memoir*. New ed. University of Regina Press, 2017.

Metatawabin, Edmund, and Alexandra Shimo. *Up Ghost River: A Chief's Journey Through the Turbulent Waters of Native History*. Vintage Canada, 2015.

Montour, Enos T., and Mary Jane Logan McCallum. *Brown Tom's Schooldays*. 2nd ed. University of Manitoba Press, 2024.

Sasakamoose, Fred. *Call Me Indian: From the Trauma of Residential School to Becoming the NHL's First Treaty Indigenous Player*. Penguin Canada, 2022.

Sellars, Bev. *They Called Me Number One: Secrets and Survival at an Indian Residential School.* Talonbooks, 2012.

Survivors of the Assiniboia Indian Residential School, *Did You See Us? Reunion, Remembrance, and Reclamation at an Urban Indian Residential School.* University of Manitoba Press, 2021.

Films

Campanelli, Stephen, ed. *Indian Horse.* 2018. https://www.indianhorse.ca/en/film.

The Chanie Wenjack Heritage Minute. 2016. https://www.historicacanada.ca/content/heritage-minutes/chanie-wenjack.

Downie, Gord, dir. *The Secret Path.* 2016. https://secretpath.ca/#Film.

Moynihan, Kevin, dir. *They Came for the Children* (a five-part film based on the TRC's final report), 2019. https://jesuits.ca/stories/they-came-for-the-children-a-film-in-5-parts-based-on-the-trc-final-report-on-residential-schools-in-canada/.

Obomsawin, Alanis. *Christmas at Moose Factory.* 1971. https://www.nfb.ca/film/christmas_at_moose_factory/.

Pittman, Bruce, dir. *Where the Spirit Lives.* 1989. https://www.youtube.com/watch?v=Os5KqErc7XY.

Sanfilippo, John, dir. *Wawahte: Stories of Residential School Survivors.* 2016. https://www.youtube.com/watch?v=oGrJNUCQ-r4.

Wolochatiuk, Tim, dir. *We Were Children.* 2012. https://www.nfb.ca/film/we_were_children/.

Acknowledgements

Several years ago, Rick Hill brought a group of about a dozen historians together to begin discussing and sharing their work about the history of the Mohawk Institute. At that time Rick observed that, although a lot of research had been done on the school, very little of it had been published in formats that were accessible to the public. This book is the product of those early meetings, and it is important that Rick be recognized for bringing us together and guiding this project to completion.

Many of these chapters would also not have been possible without the 1997 book *The Mush Hole: Life at Two Indian Residential Schools* by Elizabeth Graham. For several decades, this book was (and indeed remains) the go-to source for anyone interested in learning about the history of the Mohawk Institute. We were privileged to have her join our group during one of our early meetings, and we want to formally recognize her here.

Several students and colleagues were integral to preparing this book for publication. Specifically, we would like to recognize Natalie Cross, who provided a careful proofread and counsel during the editing phase. Erdanya Anderson also helped compile the "Suggested Readings" list and reviewed several of the chapters. Special thanks to Andrew Porteus for preparing the detailed index.

It takes significant financial resources to publish a book like this, especially in an open access format. We are grateful to the Dean's Office at Mount Royal University, the research committee at Huron University College, and Huron's Community History Centre for providing the funding to make this publication a reality. Likewise, the Social Sciences and Humanities Research Council of Canada funded the research for several of the chapters in this volume.

Finally, we need to acknowledge the survivors of the Mohawk Institute, many of whom have helped shape the chapters that appear in this volume. These are the people who carried the burden of this dark history for decades before the Canadian public began to understand what had happened at this school. Their perseverance and willingness to share their experiences have helped us to better understand the history and legacy of what happened behind the bricks.

Contributors

William Acres teaches comparative religion and history in the Faculty of Theology at Huron University College and is particularly interested in the New England Company and its Indigenous missions in Canada.

Diana Castillo obtained her bachelor of arts in sociology from the University of Calgary and a juris doctor from Osgoode Hall Law School. She is a member of the Ontario Bar and has focused her legal practice on child protection matters. She is a native of Colombia and currently resides in Toronto.

Sarah Clarke is an archaeologist and researcher at ARA Ltd. who lives in her hometown of Brantford. She considers it a privilege to have led the collaborative volunteer archaeological project at the Mohawk Institute from 2017 to 2019 while working with more than one hundred volunteers over the course of the project.

Jimmie Edgar is Anishnaabe, Scugog Island. He attended the Mohawk Institute (Mush Hole) from 1950 to 1960.

Wendy L. Fletcher is professor of religious studies and history, as well as the director of the Centre for Interreligious Spirituality and Wisdom Practices at Renison University College, affiliated with the University of Waterloo. Her research is situated at the intersection of religion and culture, most recently focusing on the history of racism and religious affiliations that fuel hatred in Canada and beyond.

Bonnie Freeman is Algonquin/Mohawk, a member of the Six Nations of the Grand River Territory, and co-appointed as an associate professor in the School of Social Work and the Indigenous Studies Department at McMaster University. Bonnie is the daughter of a residential school survivor and has an interest in historical trauma and resiliency.

Tara Froman comes from the Cayuga Nation, Wolf Clan, and works as the collections registrar at the Woodland Cultural Centre. Her paternal grandmother, Minnie Froman (née Green), attended the Mohawk Institute in the 1920s. The names left on many of the artifacts she now works to preserve are connected to faces and stories that ring with familiarity for her and many people in the community of Six Nations of the Grand River.

Alexandra Giancarlo is a settler scholar and an assistant professor in the Faculty of Kinesiology at the University of Calgary, where she applies her broad social sciences training to socio-cultural studies of sport and physical activity, broadly understood. The bulk of her work comprises community-engaged research with residential school survivors and their families.

Cody Groat is an assistant professor in the Department of History and the Indigenous Studies Program at Western University. He is a Kanyen'kehaka citizen and a band member of Six Nations of the Grand River Reserve. His grandparents, Stanley Groat and Sarah (Jean) Maracle, were survivors of the Indian residential school system.

Evan J. Habkirk is a settler historian and lecturer at University of British Columbia, Okanagan Campus, in the Indigenous Studies Program.

Rick Hill, Tuscarora Nation of the Haudenosaunee, is a community-based historian at Six Nations of the Grand River. He was formerly assistant director for public programs at the National Museum of the American Indian and assistant professor in Native American studies at University of Buffalo. He currently serves as Indigenous innovations specialist at Mohawk College, Hamilton, Ontario.

Keith Jamieson, a Mohawk of the Six Nations of the Grand River, has worked extensively as an ethno-historian, a curator of museum exhibits, and an adjunct professor and guest lecturer internationally. He has written extensively, including a book on Dr. Oronhyatekha, as well as exhibit catalogues and commentaries for news media. He lives in Ohsweken, Ontario.

Sandra Juutilainen is Haudenosaunee (Oneida Nation of the Thames, Turtle Clan) and Finnish Canadian. She is an assistant professor, Indigenous health and nutrition, in the School of Nutrition at Toronto Metropolitan University and holds an adjunct assistant professor appointment in the School of Public Health Sciences at the University of Waterloo.

Magdalena Miłosz is a Polish Canadian architectural historian and writer living in Kitchener, Ontario, a city situated within the Haldimand Tract granted to the Six Nations. She was trained as an architect at the University of Waterloo and is a PhD candidate at McGill University.

David Monture, Bear Clan Mohawk, grew up on the Six Nations Reserve. He is a retired part-time student about to commence a third degree at Western, this one in fine art. He explores poetry, flash fiction, and the novel. He is a member of the Indigenous Writers' Circle, an independent Indigenous creative voice.

Sge:no, Deyowidron't ni'gya:sǫh, otahyoni niwagesyao'dę:, gayagǫho:no^ niwagehwęjodę. My name is **Teri Morrow**, Wolf Clan from the Haudenosaunee Cayuga Nation. I am a registered dietitian at Ogwaya'dadogehsdoh; Alignrbody in Six Nations of the Grand River, One Dish wampum territory.

A former director (retired) of Repatriation and Indigenous Relations at the Canadian Museum of History, **John Moses** (Delaware and Upper Mohawk bands, Six Nations of the Grand River Territory), is an independent consultant providing Indigenous advisory services for museums and heritage institutions.

Alison Norman is a settler historian who works for the federal government at Crown-Indigenous Relations and Northern Affairs Canada. She is also a graduate faculty member in the Frost Centre for Canadian Studies and Indigenous Studies at Trent University.

Thomas Peace is a historian at Huron University College. He is the author of *The Slow Rush of Colonization: Spaces of Power in the Maritime Peninsula, 1680–1790*, and an editor at ActiveHistory.ca.

Jennifer Pettit is the dean of the Faculty of Arts and a professor of history and Indigenous studies at Mount Royal University. Jennifer is a settler scholar living in Treaty 7 territory committed to education-based reconciliation. Her research focuses on government policy for Indigenous peoples, with a focus on the residential school system.

Paul Racher is the managing principal at Archaeological Research Associates Ltd. Much of his professional career has been focused on his discomfort with the fact that key decisions about Indigenous heritage are made without input from Indigenous peoples. He is a former lecturer in anthropology at Wilfrid Laurier University and a past president of the Ontario Archaeological Society.

Bud Whiteye is Delaware-Turtle Clan, Moraviantown. He attended the Mohawk Institute (Mush Hole) from 1955 to 1961.

Index

Page numbers in italics refer to tables, figures, and illustrations

Abate, Abate Wori, 475
Aberdeen, Earl & Lady, 137
Aboriginal Affairs and Northern Development, 226. *See also* Indian Affairs (government department)
Aboriginal Healing Foundation, 92
Acres, William, 4-5, 495
Adams, Peter, 482
Adams Wagon Company, 325, 329
adoption, 47, 85
Ahyonwaeghs John Brant, 32, 174–176, 277, 283–284, 371, 457
Albert, Martha, 433-434
Albrecht, Beverly, 257, 259–260, 261-262, 265, 266, 267-269, 419, 422, 428
alcohol, 37, 67–68, 90, *306*, 319, 338, 345n29, 345n33, 423
Alderville Industrial School, 41, 56n100, 283
Alexander, Mr., 244, 251n14
All Hallows School for Girls, 331
Alnwick Industrial School, 41
American Revolution, 26-27, 33, 174, 216n13, 276, 278, 279, 377, 469
Anderson, Arthur, 468
Andrews' report, 74
Andrews, William, 460
Anglican church, 13, 32, 45, 60, 89, 91, 112, 143, 227, 298-299, 393, 398, 399–402, 409–410, 412n5
Anthony, Albert, 111, 112, *113*, 114, 123, 370, 479
Antoine, Isaiah, 244-247
apologies, 2, 60, 89
Appleyard, Bishop, *125*
Archaeological Research Associates, 376, 377, 379
archaeology, 1, 5–6, 7, 89, 389. *See also* Mohawk Institute Archaeological Site
architecture, 3, 171, 180-181, 189, 196–197, 231–237. *See also* Mohawk Institute—architecture; residential schools—architecture
Arnold, Oliver, 33, 278, 279, 281, 282
arson, 2, 4, 5, 25, 42, 51–52, 60, 61, 63, 193, 243, 244–247, 295, 298, 317, 318
Ashton, Alfred Nelles, 4, 66–68, 136, *138*, 139, *140*, *141*, 142, 148n14, 220n131, 248–250, 297, 319, 333, 337, 338, 342, 379, 409, 416
Ashton, Alice Turner, *See* Boyce, Alice Ashton
Ashton, Ernest Charles., 136, 137, 138, 140, 142, 143, 148n14, 148n22, 196–197, 220n131, 298
Ashton, Minnie, 317–318, 326, 329
Ashton, Nelles. *See* Ashton, Alfred Nelles
Ashton, Robert, 2, 4–5, 44, 47, 49–50, 61, 63, 65, 66, 67, 69, 107, 117–119, 121, 123, 124–128, 131n57, 134, 137, 139, 142, 147, 148n14, 149n38, 184, 196–197, 295–300, 302–307, *306*, 307–319, 323–343, 343n1, 343n4, 343n5, 379, 461, 463, 467, 468
Assembly of First Nations, 89, 226
Assembly of Manitoba Chiefs, 228
assimilation. *See* Indigenous peoples—assimilation of; Mohawk Institute—assimilation
Association of Iroquois and Allied Indians, 214, 228
Audette, Louis Arthur, 340

Babcock Lot, 43, 70, 317, 318, 324–325, 326, 327–329, 330, 343n4, 343n7
Bagot Commission, 39

Bagot, Sir Charles, 39
Bailey, Pearce, 154
Barclay, Henry, 460
Barker, Adam J., 30, 53n24
Battleford Industrial School, 46
Bay of Quinte, 283
Bearfoot, Elam, 481
Bearfoot, Isaac, 3, 43, 110, 111, 114, *115*, 126, 130n33, 130n39, 135, 305, *306*, 309, 310, 316, 320n20, 351, 370, 479
Beaver, John, 318
Beaver, Marguerite, 428
Beaver, Yagoweia Loft, 111
Bedard, Joanna, 230, 236
begging, 14, 21
Behind the Bricks (book), xix, 1–9, 97, 290
Bennett, Tony, 185
Benson, Martin, 50–51, 56n100, 127, 191, 192, 246–247, 310, 312, 314, 343n7
Berger, John, 7
Bethany Baptist Mission, 250
Bible, The, 30, 288, 289, 396, 403, 405
biopolitics, 406–409, 411
biopower, 397, 406–409, 411
Black Americans, 154, 157
Blackbird, Jennie, 198, 201, 202, 428
Blake, Samuel H., 65, 332–333, 341
boarding schools, 25, 35, 50, 52n4, 58n155, 60–61, 63, 64, 72, 75, 78, 147n9, 197, 290
Bomberry, Beverly. *See* Albrecht, Beverly
Bomberry, George, 470
Bomberry, Tony, 421, 436
Bond Head, Francis. *See* Head, Francis Bond
Botsford, Amos Edwin, 111, 302, 324, 361
Bouslaugh, Mr. & Mrs., 309
Boyce, Alice Ashton, 67–68, 69, 70, 72, 74, 116, 142, 143, 297, *306*, *310*, 311, 313, 316, 324, 338, 340, 341, 345n42
Boyce, George, 412n11, 412n14
Brandon Industrial Institute, 156, 192
Brant, Cameron, 480
Brant, Henry, 286
Brant, Jacob, 277
Brant, John (Ahyonwaeghs). *See* Ahyonwaeghs John Brant
Brant, Joseph (son of Thayendanegea), 277
Brant, Joseph (Thayendanegea). *See* Thayendanegea Joseph Brant
Brant, Margaret, 455
Brant, Molly, (Konwatsi'tsiaiénni). *See* Konwatsi'tsiaiénni Molly Brant
Brant, Robert, 480
Brant County, ON, 37, 142
Brantford Collegiate Institute, 119, 120, 121, 123, 126, 127, 308
Brantford Collegiate Institute Cadet Corps, 134, 137, 143
Brantford Grammar School, 356, 369
Brantford, ON, 1, 37–38, 43, 77, 85, 137, 142, *178*, 197, 253, 324, 328, 330; employment, 325; housing, 325
Brantford Women's Council, 82, 207
Brant Historical Society, 227–228
Brewster, Willoughby Staples, 335
bricks, xviii, 1, 86, 97, 147, 171, 215, 218n52, 382; *387*, 388–389, 435–436, *436*. *See also* Mohawk Institute—architecture
British Empire, 137, 138. 144, 189, 194
Bromley, Walter, 281–282, 283

499

Browell, Edward Mash, 296-297
Bowell, Herbert Henry, 330, 344n14
Bryce, Peter H., 64
Burnham, Elwood, *350*
Burning, Harrison, 198, 221n145, 419, 420, 422
Burrows, Major-General, 366
Busk, Charlotte, 320n13
Busk, Edward, 320n13

cadets, 137-138, 139, 140, 143, 145-147. *See also* Brantford Collegiate Institute Cadet Corps; military; Mohawk Institute Cadet Corps; Mohawk Institute—military training
Caldwell Report, 84
Calls to Action. See Truth and Reconciliation Commission—Calls to Action
Cameron, Colonel, 467, 468
Canada, 2, 42, 46; apology 60, 90, 92; lawsuits against, 91-92; oversight of residential schools, 4, 26, 43, 45, 48, 49, 62-63, 66, 90, 213; population, 60; relationship with Indigenous peoples, 27, 42, 43, 89-90, 298, 390-391, 474.*See also* Indian Affairs (government department)
Canada Starch Company, 329, 343n3
Canadgaranuncka, Brant, 455-456
Canadian Armed Forces, 141, 146-147
Canadian Expeditionary Force, 142
Canadian Mounted Rifles, 142
Canajoharie, 284
Carleton, Sean, 64
Carleton, Thomas, 278
Carlisle Indian Industrial School, 172, 185
Carpenter, Mary, 296
Carpenter, Susannah, 112-114, 370
Carpenter, William, 120
Carr, Geoffrey, 171-172
Carter, James, 302
Castillo, Diana, 4, 67, 495
Castledon, Hugh, 79
Caswell, Rev. & Mrs., *119*
Catholic Church, 37, 218n62, 275, 278, 307, 361, 459
Cayuga Nation, 26, 109, 317, 321n49
celebrations, 12, 29, 134, 137, 143, 144, 225, 236, 404
Central Canada Exhibition, 134, 137
Chance, James, 113, 116, 302, 461, 463
Chapleau Residential School, 197
Charity Commission, 310, 232, 335
Charter of Rights and Freedoms, 89
Checkock, Amelia (Jones), 116, 130n44, 480
Chene, Jean Dosithe, 197
child abuse, 6, 15, 89, 339, 409-410. *See also* Mohawk Institute—corporal punishment; Mohawk Institute students—abuse of
children, xix, 3, 5, 13, 15, 25, 26, 29, 32, 33, 34-35, 253-254, 389-390, 453; removal from parents, 1, 4, 34, 49, 62-63, 93, 176, 182, 184-185, 258, 261-262, 265, 278, 280-281, 286, 288, 351, 389-390, 411, 443. *See also* Indigenous peoples—removal of children
Children's Aid Society, 90
child welfare, 158
Chipman, Ward, 278
Chisholm, Andrew Gordon, 334, 336, 339-340, 341, 342, 343, 347n63
Christian Island, *80, 81*
Christianity, 32; conversion to, 26, 27, 29-30, 36-37, 63, 109, 174, 278
"Christianizing and civilizing," 26, 27-30, 32-33, 35, 40, 43, 50-51, 61, 79, 97, 98n7, 107, 108, 134, 143-144, 174, 230-231, 265, 291n8, 296, 327, 403-404
Christmas, Benjamin (Basamai Nachecallassootmamk), 368-369

Church of England. *See* Anglican church
churches, 2, 29-30, 95, 189, 213, 216n13, 291n91, 331; oversight of residential schools, 62-63, 213; partnership with state, 397-402; relations with Indigenous peoples, 36
civilization program 6, 22, 28-30, 31, 32-33. *See also* "Christianizing and civilizing"
Clark, C. A. F., *159*, 208-209
Clark, William, 305
Clarke, A. L. G., 82
Clarke, Sarah, 5, 495
Claus, Daniel, 174
Cockenoe, 276
Cockshutt family, 317-318, 325, 326, 329, 338, 344n9
Cockshutt, Ignatius, 326
Cockshutt Plow Company, 326, 343n4
Cockshutt, William Foster, 317-318, 326, 327, 329, 333, 338
Coffin, John, 278
Colborne, John, 176
collective trauma, 6, 394, 395-396, 410, 411
colleges, 31
colonialism, *See* settler colonialism
Commanda, Jacqueline, 434
Commanda, Joey, 434
Commanda, Loretta, 434
Commanda, Rocky, 434
commemoration, 86, 92, 94, 96, 215, 225-237
community, 2
competitions, 66
Connaught, Duke of, 137
Cooke, Donald, *81*
Cooper, Mary Ann (Marguerite) Cooper (Number 33), 434-436
Creation Story, 260, *260*
Cree School Board of Quebec, 227
criminal behaviour, 4, 47, 51-52, 71, 75, 77, 82, 339, 342, 389, 409-410, 416
Cromarty, Sara Jane, 417-418
Cromb, G. D., 214
Cronyn, Benjamin, 112, 117, 305
Crowe, Carrie, 482
cultural genocide, 31, 61, 90, 94, 191, 214, 215, 226, 230, 236-237
cultural heritage, 226, 228
cultural resurgence, 214, 230, 236-237
Curley, Jo-Bear, 425-426
Curley, Kelly, 212, 436
Cusick, C., *138*, 148n22

Darling, H. C., 27, 29
Davids, Lawrence, 109-110, 129n13
Davin, Nicholas Flood, 46
Davis, Francis, 482
Davis, Laura, 432-433
Davis, Sarah, *118*, 119-120, 480
Davis, Thelma. *See* Moses, Thelma (Davis)
Davis, Thomas, 34, 457
day schools, 29, 31, 32-35, 42, 51, 58n155, 60, 63, 78, 85, 107, 109, *118*, *119*, 119, 127, 232-233, 283-285, 291n18, 307, 320n9. *See also* Mohawk Village Day School; Red Bank Day School
Debo, Jesse, 244-247
Debo, Mathew, 246
Dee, Robert, 364
Delaporte, Helen L., 162
Delaware Settlement, 109, 457, 470
de Leeuw, Sarah, 172
Department of Indian Affairs. *See* Indian Affairs (government department)
destitution, 46-47, 48, 51, 65, 69
Dibblee, Frederick, 279-280

500   Index

Dingman, Absalom, 316
Dixon, Paul, 434, 437
Doctrine of Discovery, 30
"Documenting the Early Residential Schools" project, 5, 352
Doherty, R, 367
Dominion Natural Gas Company, 329
Doxtator, Frederick, 149n45
Dufferin Rifles, 38th, 136, *138*, 138–139, 140, 148n14, 149n38, 220n131
Dunbow Industrial School, 46

Earth to Table legacy project, 267
Edgar, Jimmie, 449–450, 495
education, 26, 29, 32, 34–37, 403–404; academics, 35; apprenticeships 33; compulsory, 49, 64; farming, 4, 35; higher education, 68, 107, 116–120, 121–128; household duties, 35; policy 60, 67, 68; trades, 35. *See also* subtopic "education" under numerous topics
Edward, Prince of Wales (Edward VII), 42, 185
Edward, Price of Wales (Edward VIII), 69, 137, 143
Elbourne, Elizabeth, 284
Eliot, John, 276
Elliott, Adam, 110, 300, 302, 320n13, 469
Elliott, Floretta, 483
Elliott, John R., 430–431, *431*
employment, 11–12, 61
Enfranchisement Act, 43
English, Sally, 228–229
Enmegahbowh, 368
Erasmus, Georges, 90
eugenics, 155

farming, 4, 13–14, 19, 20, 35, 37–38, 43, 46–47, 64, 98n20. *See also* Mohawk Institute—farming
Fear-Segal, Jacqueline, 172, 185
Felton Industrial School. *See* Middlesex Industrial School
Ferrier, Chester, 246
Ferrier, Russell, 72, 100n76, 124, 159
File Hills Boarding School, 64
Fingard, Judith, 280
First Nations Peoples. *See* Indigenous Peoples
Fisher, Jennie, *306*, 309, 320n21
Fiske, Jo-Anne, 172
Fletcher, Wendy, 6, 90, 393, 495
Fontaine, Phil, 89, 228–229, 236
food, 4, 13–14, 18–19, 254–264, 265, 266–270. *See also* Mohawk Institute—food
Ford, John Walker, 297, 319, 332
Forsyth, Janice, 139
Fort Alexander Indian Residential School, 228–229, 236
foster care, 263–264, *438*, 439
Foucault, Michel, 397, 406–409, 411
Freeman, Bonnie, 4, 495
Friendship Centres, 267
Froman, Tara, 5, 495
From Longhouse to Schoolhouse: The Mohawk Institute 1934-1970 (thesis), 8
fur trade, 27, 378–379

Gamble, F. C., 366
Gathering Strength: Canada's Aboriginal Action Plan, 91
Gell, Molly Ann, 282, 290
General, Emmert, 420, *421*, 425
General, Salli, 422
General, William, 131n64
genocide, 94. *See also* cultural genocide; Indigenous peoples—eradication efforts
George, Baptist, *81*
George, Deane, 440–442

George, Doug (Number 73) (Kanentiio), v, xviii, 87, 417, *418*, 439, 440–442
George, Kenneth, 428
Giancarlo, Alexandra, 3, 192, 495
Gibson, Robert, 339
Gilkison, Jasper T., 47, 121, 123–124, 461–462
Glebe Lot. *See* Mohawk Glebe
Glenelg, Lord
Goderich, Viscount, 36
Goffman, Erving, 185
Good, Edith, 482
Good, Josephine, 126–127, 481
Gordon's Indian Residential School, 146
Gould, Lewis, 341
Graham, Elizabeth, 6, 8, 88, 155, 164, 367, 408, 416
Gramsci, Antonio, 397
Grand Council of Indians of Ontario, 116
Grand River, 4, 33, 377
Grand River Navigation Company, 324, 339
Grand River Reserve. *See* Six Nations Reserve
Grand River Station, 4–5, 33–34, 297, 300, 302, 304, 323, 326–327, 331, 340
Grand River Tract. *See* Haldimand Tract
graves, xix, 1, 95, 390, 432
Great Britain, 26–27, 30, 39, 40, 42, 136, 180, 188, 189, 455, 456
Great Law of Peace (*Kayanerenko:wa*), 26, 256, 268, 269, 453
Great Northern Railway Company, 329
Green, Tom, 310, 316
Griffin, Egerton, 363
Griffith, Thomas, 309, 352, 357, 358, 367
Griffith, Mrs., 309
Groat, Cody, 3, 495
Groat, Edward (Russell) S., 204, 429
Groat, Marjorie J., 204

Habkirk, Evan, 3, 66, 495
Haldimand, Frederick, 27, 32, 174, 284
Haldimand Rifles, 37th, 138, 148n25
Haldimand Tract, 27, 287, 377, 455, 496
Haldimand Treaty, 27
Hankins, Jean Fitz, 276
Hardie, Susan, 74–75, 124–125, *125*, 126, 338, 432–433, 481
Hardy, A. D., 245, 330
Harper, Elijah, 94
Harper, Stephen, 92–93
Harvard Indian College, 276, 277
Haudenosaunee Confederacy: archaeology (*see* Mohawk Institute Archaeological Site); ceremonies, 257–259, 266, 267, 268, 454; chiefs, xviii, 37, 39, 45, 73, 123, 181, 286, 300; crops, 254, 260; education system, 26, 32, 51, 108, 284, 317, 453–476; elective band council, 473, 475, 476; families, 265; food, 254–255, 257–269; history, 8–9, 26, 174, 453; health, 254–255; Knowledge Keepers, 261, 269; land, 257–258; nutrition, 254–255, 260–261; population, 37; relationship with Great Britain, 26, 181, 284; relationship with the Anglican church, 45; relationship with The New England Company, 26, 32–34, 45–46, 277, 283–284, 403–404, 461; teachers, 43, 108, 123, 475; traditional way of life, 254–255, 257–261, 299. 453; trauma, 265, 393; women, 26, 257, 268–269. *See also* Cayuga Nation; Mohawk Nation; Oneida Nation; Onondaga Nation; Seneca Nation; Six Nations of the Grand River; Tuscarora Nation
Haudenosaunee Confederacy Council of Chiefs, xviii, 45, 73, 298, 316, 317, 318, 333–334, 336–337, 341, 461–463, 467–468, 471, 472, 475–476. *See also* Haudenosaunee Confederacy—chiefs

Index *501*

Hawthorn Report, 84
Hazen, William, 278
Head, Francis Bond, 28–29
healing, 92, 95, 96, 236, 260, 394–395
healing fund, 91, 92, 96
Hellmuth College, 112, 113, 114, 367–368, 370
Hellmuth, Isaac, 112
Hellmuth Ladies' College, 112, 113
Henry, Edward Lamson, *181*
Henry, Geronimo, 422, *423*
Henry, Lucius, 116, 480
heritage designation, 3, 88, 235, 236
Heron, Alex H., 366
Hess, Marie, 196
Hesse, William, 285
High River Industrial School, 46
high schools, 65
Hill, Abram S., 470
Hill, Asa, 336, 340
Hill, David, 455
Hill, Dawn, *438*
Hill, Frank, 424
Hill, George, 369
Hill, James, 111
Hill, John, 463, 470
Hill, Joseph C., 78, 401, 402, 474–475
Hill, Josiah, 338, 468, 472
Hill, Lucy, 482
Hill, Lydia, 115
Hill, Mark, 390
Hill, Martha, 201–202, 221n147, 424
Hill, Pat, 426, *427*
Hill, Peggy, 420, 425
Hill, Raymond (Ross), 429, *430*
Hill, Reginald, 474
Hill, Richard (Rick) W., Sr., 1, 6, 223n183, *421*, 463, 495
Hill, Robert, 481
Hill, Roberta (Number 34), *80*, 434, 437, *438*, 439, *440*
Hill, Susan M., 175
Hill, Tom, 9
Hill-Easton, Blanche, 426
historic plaques, 86, 226, 227–228, *229*, 229–230, *230*, 231, 236
Historic Schools of Canada (study), 231–232, 233
Historic Sites and Monuments Act, 231, 236
Historic Sites and Monuments Board of Canada, 225–226, 231–237
History of Six Nations Education (essay), 8
Hoey, Robert A., 78, 156, 401
Hoffman, David, 62
Hough, W., 34
Howells, Thomas, 128n4
hunting, 28
Huron College, 112, 114, 117, 297, 370
Hyde, L.F., 244–247

immigrants, 50, 61, 154–155. *See also* settlers
indentured servitude, 4, 280–283, 286
Indian Act, 46, 64, 67, 79, 84, 191, 222n169, 227, 244, 249, 257, 474
Indian Affairs (government department), 12, 14, 17, 26, 41, 42, 46, 47, 48, 51–52, 64, 68, 72, 78, 81–82, 90, 120, 121, 145, 155–157, 197, 207–208, 211, 214, 223n183, 226, 227–228, 231, 234, 251n14, 298, 307, 318, 329, 330, 333, 336, 340, 341–343, 399–401, 463, 467–468, 472, 475
Indian agents, 29, 42, 49, 77, 191, 358, 406, 425, 442
Indian and Northern Affairs Canada. *See* Indian Affairs (government department)
"Indian Education" event, 233

"Indian Lands" 324, 326, 329
Indian Normal School, The. *See* Mohawk Institute Certificate
"Indian Problem, The," 27, 75, 84, 96
Indian Residential Schools Settlement Agreement, 91–92, 225
Indian Rights Association, 66
Indian Teachers' Certificates, 121, *122*. *See also* Mohawk Institute Certificate
Indians of Canada Pavilion (Expo 67), 15
Indigenous architecture, 214
Indigenous Heritage Circle, 236
Indigenous peoples: archaeology, 377 (*see also* Mohawk Institute Archaeological Site); as farmers, 28, 44, 72; as federal government employees 12–13; as manual labourers, 44; assimilation of, 2, 26, 29–30, 31, 36, 37, 51, 60, 61–62, 90, 92–93, 94, 96–97, 128, 145–147, 171–173, 177, 184–185, 191, 194, 207, 227, 230–231, 285, 389–390, 395–396, 404; "civilization" of, 3, 27–30, 50, 61–62, 79, 92–93, 97, 109, 111, 136–137, 162,171–172, 177, 185, 230, 397–398; commemoration, 225–237; definition of, 67, 79, 84; dignity of, 90, 208; education, 2–3, 13, 28, 29, 36, 39, 40–41, 43, 49, 58n155, 60–62, 64, 67, 69, 72, 73, 75, 78, 79, 84, 90, 108–114, 121, *122*, 123–128, 153, 176, 227, 232, 371, 453–454, 473–475; employment, 2–3, 12–13, 28, 43. 44, 50–51, 60–61, 78; eradication efforts, 28, 30–31, 94, 232; family relations 15, 31, 90, 91, 236; governance, 43–44, 79, 89, 91, 92–93, 96; health, 298; "inferiority of," 31, 46, 153, 155–157, 184–185, 279, 398; integration, 28, 79, 227; intelligence of, 3, 31, 153–154, 155–164; isolation of, 61–62; language, 16, 29, 31, 39, 69, 93, 108, 110, 111, 113, 155, 176, 253; legal affairs, 249; living conditions, 29; military, 150n68; population, 50; religion, 29, 31, 37, 397–402; removal of children, 4, 49, 62–63, 93, 176, 182, 184–185, 253–254, 286, 406; self government, 89; social conditions, 37, 69, 90, 156; sovereignty, 89, 287; teacher training, 2–3, 43, 78, 107–110 (*see also* Mohawk Institute Certificate); trade, 378–379; wage equity, 65, 110, 115; way of life, 27–28, 29, 253–262; women, 26, 257
Industrial School for Boys, 135
industrial schools, 29, 35, 39, 40, 41–42, 46, 47, 50–51, 52n4, 58n155, 60–61, 63, 64, 65, 71, 72, 75, 135, 197, 300; investigations, 64, 65
industrialization, 326–328
Inglis, Charles, 279
intelligence testing, 154–164. *See also* Indigenous Peoples—intelligence testing; Mohawk Institute—intelligence testing; residential schools—intelligence testing; racism
Inuit Peoples. *See* Indigenous Peoples
I.O.D.E., 20, *85*, 143–144, 150n60
IQ. *See* intelligence testing
Iroquois Confederacy. *See* Haudenosaunee Confederacy
Iroquois Control of Iroquois Education: A Case Study, 475
Isaac, Edith, 247–250
Isaac, Emma, 247–250
Isaac, Jefferson D., 248
isolation, 28, 61, 92, 202, 279, 281, 390, 459

Jacobs, John, 370
Jagz, Ken, 409
Jamieson, Andrew, 158
Jamieson, Elmer, 153, 155, 158–161, 162
Jamieson, Keith, 8, 453, 495
Jamieson, Sylvia, 483
Jesuits, 35, 275, 283, 358, 454, 459
Johnny, 439
Johnson, Allen Wawanosh, 121, 480
Johnson, Augustus, 470

Johnson, Dana, 231–232, 235
Johnson, Evelyn, 73, 123, 131n64
Johnson, Joseph S., 458, 471
Johnson, Lonnie, 420, 429
Johnson, Molly, 433
Johnson, Pauline, 73, 121, 123, 131n64
Johnson, William, 123, 180, *181*, 218n59, 284, 456, 459–461
Johnson Hall, 180–181, *181*
Jones, Anna, 480
Jones, Charles Kejedonce, 130n44
Jones, H. M., 83
Jones, Melvin, 331, 344n16
Jones, Peter (Kahkewaquonaby). *See* Kahkewaquonaby Peter Jones
Jones, Spencer A., 369
Joseph, Isaiah, 111, 369, 480
Juutilainen, Sandra, 4, 495
Juvenile Delinquents Act, 245

Kahkewaquonaby Peter Jones, 36
Kalman, Harold, 180
Kamloops Indian Residential School, xix, 95
Kanentiio, Douglas George. *See* George, Doug (Number 73) (Kanentiio)
Kayanerenko:wa. *See* Great Law of Peace
Kelly, Hugh Thomas, 248–249
Kelly, J., 47
Kempt, James, 29
Kenyengeh Mission Church, 302, 328
Kidd, Kenneth E., 161–162
Kingston, John S., 470
Kingston Penitentiary, 193, 243
Kirkland, Samuel, 279
Kitigan Zibi Reserve, 11
Kiyoshk, Ramona, *441*
Konwatsi'tsiaiénni Molly Brant, 123, 180, 218n59, 284
Korean War, 11, 15, 150n68
Ktunaxa/Kinbasket Tribal Council, 234

Lager, C. H., 433
Laird, David, 61, 314
land, 28, 29, 31, 43, 44, 60, 62, 79, 89, 116, 129n13, 174–175, 180, 183, 253, 285–286, 298, 310, 317, 318, 321n50, 323–343; expropriation, 326, 329, 330–331, 335; land registry, 330. *See also* Babcock Lot; "Indian Lot;" Manual Labour Lot; Mohawk Glebe; Mohawk Institute grounds; Mohawk Institute Manual Labour Farm; Six Nations Reserve—land
language, 30, 32, 110, 111, 113, 124, 469. *See also* Mohawk Institute students—language
Latham, Naomi, 482
Latham, Sarah, 481
Latham, Susana, 482
Lawrence, David, 285
lawsuits, 91–92, 231, 247–250, 297, 326, 327, 330, 334–335, 340, 341–342, 439
Leeming, Ralph, 457
legal system, 245–250
Leighton, Douglas, 36
Leonard, George, 278, 279
Leslie, John, 89
Leween, Alex, 138, 148n22, 482
Lewis, Elias, 472
Lewis, Lydia, 480
Lickers, John, 481
Lickers, Norman, 93, 228
Lister, H. J., 42–43
Litt, Paul, 230
Logan, Scobie, 116, 130n49, 480
London Metropolitan Archives, 297, 343n2

Longboat, Jan, 268
Longboat, Mary, 468
Longboat, Tom, 432
Long Plain First Nation, 221n139
Lorna, 419, 420, 424, 439
Lorne, Marquis of, 136–137
Lougheed, James, 342
Louise, Princess, 136–137
Lowman, Emma Batell, 30, 53n24
Lugger, Robert, 34, 37, 176, 285, 288–289, 316, 457–458, 469
Luxton, George, 398
Lytton Residential School. *See* St. George's Residential School

MacDonald, John A., 124, 389–390
MacInnes, T. R. L., 156
Maitland, Peregrine, 285, 461, 462
Manitoulin Island, 28
Manual Labour Lot. *See* Mohawk Institute Manual Labour Farm
Maracle, Alexander, 244–247
Maracle, Catherine, 480
Maracle, Chandra, 266–267
Maracle, Elizabeth, 257, 264, 265, 267–268
Maracle, Floretta K., *120*, 120–121, 131n64, 480
Maracle, Isabella L., 481
Maracle, Margaret, *122*, 481
Martin, Charlotte, 131n64
Martin, George, 369
Martin, John, 422, 429
Martin, Moses, 463
Martin, Tammy, 142
Martland, John, 184, 358, 362, 364, 369
Massey-Harris Company, 325, 329
Mathews, Ernest, 319, 339
Matunga, Hirini, 214
Mayhew, Thomas, 276
McCallum, Mary Jane Logan, 41, 128, 192
McDowall, James
McKenzie, A. F., 473
McKenzie, Brad, 265
McKenzie, Kathleen, 64
McMaster University, 86
Mechanics' Institute, 34, 52n4, 217n26, 287–288
Meighen, Arthur, 340
memorials. *See* commemoration; historic plaques; Mohawk Institute—as memorial; Mohawk Village Memorial Park; National Historic Sites; Residential schools—memorials; Woodland Cultural Centre
Methodist Church, 41, 156, 165n23, 283, 307, 457, 463, 471, 472
Métis Peoples. *See* Indigenous Peoples
Middlesex Industrial School, 197, 220n131, 295, 296, 298–299, 309, 312
Mi'kmaq Nation, 279–280, 290
military, 3, 11, 12, 15, 26, 66, 69, 70, 79, 137–138, 141–143, 150n68. *See also* Brantford Collegiate Institute Cadet Corps; Canadian Expeditionary Force; Canadian Mounted Rifles; Mohawk Institute Cadet Corps
militia, 136, 137. *See also* Dufferin Rifles, 38th; Haldimand Rifles, 37th
Miller, Calum, *152*
Miller, Elva, 482
Miller, George, 247, 248
Miller, Hazel, 4, 67, 243–244, 247–250
Miller, J. R., 156, 188, 229
Miller, Robert Gary, *394*, 410, 419, 421, 428, 432, 434, 440
Miller, Ruth, 4, 67, 243–244, 247–250
Milloy, John, 90, 156

Miłosz, Magdalena, 3, 496
Mimico Industrial School, 193, 243, 245, 246
missing children, 95
Missing Children Project, 95
missionaries, 30, 32–33, 112, 250, 276, 277, 283, 300, 327, 403–404, 458–461; Dutch, 458; French, 458–459
Missionary Society of the Church of England in Canada, 65, 341, 399
mission stations, 33–34
Mississauga Nation 376
Model Indian School, 185
Mohawk Chapel, 24, 32, 34, 78, 125, 126, 142, 174,178, 198, 216n13, 221n147, 242, 314, 342, 357, 400, 402, 402, 404
Mohawk Glebe, 324, 325, 325, 326, 328, 329, 330, 331–333, 335, 336, 337, 340, 343n3, 343n4, 344n16, 461
Mohawk Institute, xvii; 24, 96–97, 170, 180, 182, 188, 190, 194, 209, 283; academics, 35, 39, 47, 50, 73, 76, 307–308, 317, 320n13, 360, 384, 388; adaptive reuse, 235; apprenticeships 33, 109, 177, 386; archaeology (see Mohawk Institute Archaeological Site); architecture, 3, 172–173, 179–181, 185–186, 186, 187–192, 193–194, 195, 196–197, 199, 200, 201, 204, 209, 214–215; as crime scene, 389; as memorial, 86–87, 226; assimilation, 137–138, 143, 181–182, 191, 207, 208, 236, 296, 379–382, 384–386, 397, 404–405, 406–407; attendance, 5, 15, 34, 35, 45, 47, 71, 161, 227, 353, 355–356; attendance register, 5, 352–353, 354, 355–371; books, 41, 47, 126, 150n60, 262, 289, 360; Boy Scouts, 143, 146, 149n53; boys' activities and resources (see gender based activities and resources); Brownies, 143, 146; bugle band, 143; buildings, 42, 44, 45, 48, 51–52, 63, 66, 72, 82, 86–87, 172–173, 176–177, 183, 184, 185, 188–189, 196, 203–204, 208–210, 210, 217n21, 223n183, 233, 287, 310, 311, 375, 376; clergy training, 13, 112; closure, 2, 47, 84–87, 96, 116, 214, 227; commemoration, 225–229, 229, 230, 230, 231–237; community education, 68; corporal punishment, 48, 65–66, 74–75, 78, 83, 202, 243, 247–250, 266, 345n42, 405–409, 412n21, 417, 424–431, 439, 442; Cubs, 146; curriculum, 3, 5, 19, 38, 39, 47, 66, 72–73, 75, 76, 108, 153, 162, 207, 287, 289, 314, 317, 358, 359; discipline, 44, 46, 48–49, 67, 71, 73, 74, 83, 134, 136, 191, 201–202, 215, 247–250, 263–264, 300, 313, 317, 338–339, 385–386, 405–409, 412n21, 417; dormitories, 48, 49, 51, 63, 176, 183–184, 187, 189, 209–210, 312–313, 316, 363, 367, 417; economic aspects, 38, 40, 45–46, 48, 50, 51, 61, 66, 70, 71–72, 73, 75, 76, 82, 85–86, 90, 116–117, 123, 298, 305, 308, 310–311, 316, 321n27, 327–331, 334–335, 338, 339, 341, 399–400; electricity, 189, 190, 208, 226, 313, 327, 329; enrollment, 38–39, 42, 47, 48, 63, 65, 66, 68, 73, 79, 82, 84, 85–86, 89, 176–177, 179, 190, 193, 207, 213, 286, 288, 289, 307, 308, 351, 353, 355–356, 458; examinations, 65, 117, 121, 123, 124, 125, 126, 129n30, 131n57, 132n93, 303, 307, 352, 353, 358, 371; family visits, 15, 67, 186, 201, 202, 211, 301; farming, 38, 43, 45, 50, 64, 66, 71, 73, 75, 76, 134–135, 183, 191–192, 204–206, 274, 289, 300, 309–311, 321n27, 326, 338, 339, 360, 361, 379, 386, 424; fires, 2, 4, 5, 25, 42, 51–52, 60, 61, 63, 179, 193, 218n51, 243, 244–247, 295, 298, 317, 318, 382, 458; food, 4, 18–20, 68, 73, 192, 202, 247–249, 254, 259, 262, 266, 268–269, 309–311, 312, 338, 386–388, 387, 425; gender based activities and resources, 34, 38, 41, 42, 45, 48, 49, 50, 63–64, 65, 66, 67, 70, 108–109, 117, 134–135, 136, 142, 143, 148n12, 158, 176, 177, 183–184, 186–187, 189, 190, 191–192, 193, 196, 198, 201, 202–204, 206, 207, 212, 287, 307–308, 310–314, 315, 336, 338, 352, 355, 358, 359, 359–361, 363, 364, 370, 386, 421, 424, 457–458;
Girl Guides, 143, 144; girls' activities and resources (see gender based activities and resources); goals, 37, 90, 117, 137, 327–328; grounds, 37, 42, 43, 45, 47, 86, 95, 170, 182, 183, 184, 192, 204–205, 205, 206, 320n12, 326, 343n4; half-day system, 39, 160, 164, 203, 205, 299, 309, 357; history, xvii–xix, 1–2, 4–7, 12, 13, 25–26, 34–46, 96, 173–177, 283–284, 285–287, 351, 457–458; household duties, 38, 66, 109, 176, 204; human remains, 375, 390; impact on students, 2, 4, 22, 254, 256–257, 263, 337, 389; impact on survivors, 2, 96, 256–257, 289, 389; Indian reception room, 186, 201, 202, 211; intelligence testing, 3, 153, 157–164; integration, 211–212, 314; investigations, xviii, 67, 68, 71, 73–75, 81–82, 90, 158, 159, 183–184, 208, 218n73, 248, 338; labour, 39, 47, 50, 65, 66, 158, 166n36, 177, 183, 189, 192, 203–205, 215, 289, 308–313, 326, 336, 360–361, 384, 386; legacy, xix, 2, 22, 60, 386; legal affairs, 67, 75, 95, 243–244, 248–250, 326, 327, 340–342; ledgers, 308, 382, 386; living conditions, 90, 158, 208, 288, 296; management of, 44, 47, 65, 68–69, 71, 73, 75, 76, 77, 135–136, 162–163, 299–300, 302–310, 336–337, 399–400, 406–409; maps, 14, 178, 325; militarization, 132–147, 148n14; military training, 13, 49, 134, 136–138 (see also Mohawk Institute Cadet Corps); model for residential schools, 26, 40–41, 46, 52, 72, 177, 197, 296; modernization, 211–212, 213, 295–296, 329; natural gas, 329; nutrition, 68, 88, 247–249, 254, 262, 312, 338; outbuildings, 67, 81, 173, 185, 191–192, 208; oversight of, 4, 25–26, 31, 47, 50, 65, 69, 70, 82, 213, 286–287, 304, 305, 323, 335, 341, 342, 395, 400, 401; physical education, 139, 358; policy, 96, 116, 117, 208; public memory, 237; public relations, 136–137, 211–212, 368; punishment room, 48–49, 67, 191, 201–202, 215, 243, 247–248; quality of education, 153; relations with local community, 2, 4, 70, 96, 134–135; religion and, 6, 20, 22, 75, 393–396, 404–405; renovation and restoration of, 3, 5, 42, 44, 46–47, 82, 173, 176, 183–185, 188, 188–191, 190, 193–194, 196–198, 199, 200, 208–212, 213, 310, 317, 319n3, 375, 379; rifle range, 67, 140, 149n38; safety, 76–77, 191, 198, 212, 367; sanitary conditions, 80–81, 82, 184; schedule, 19–20, 299, 313, 315, 357, 404–405; school trips, 77, 80, 81, 81, 133, 134, 138, 361; solitary confinement, 49, 136, 191, 201–202, 247–250, 338, 345n42, 424, 426, 428, 431; swimming pool, 211–212, 435; teacher training, 2–3, 43, 65, 108, 112, 116–119, 121, 122, 123–128, 131n57, 217n39; teams, 309–310; television, 425; trades, 35, 38, 39, 42, 43, 48, 50, 51, 60, 64, 204, 287, 288, 289, 384, 457, 458; vacations and holidays, 47, 70, 74, 80, 85, 318, 362; visitors, 5, 8, 72, 134, 177, 182, 184, 185, 186, 215, 352, 353, 364, 365–369; war surplus, 142, 145, 208–209, 210; World War I, 141–144, 149n45, 150n61. See also Woodland Cultural Centre
Mohawk Institute Archaeological Site, 5, 7, 89, 375–376, 385; artifacts, 5–6, 7, 89, 376, 377–378, 379, 380, 381, 379–388, 385, 387; assimilation, 379–382, 384–386, 385; fires, 382; food, 386–388, 387; identity, 383–384; names, 381–383, 388–389; resistance, 382–383, 386–389; settlements, 377; tools, 377
Mohawk Institute Cadet Corps, 3, 66, 70,133, 134, 135, 136–137, 138, 140, 141, 146, 379; assimilation, 134, 136–138, 146; awards, 133, 134, 137–138, 138, 139, 140, 143, 149n50; funding, 139, 145; public relations, 134, 136–137, 145–146; Sea Cadets, 146; uniforms, 133, 135, 136, 137, 138, 138, 139, 140, 141, 378; World War I, 141–145, 149n45; World War II, 145
Mohawk Institute Certificate, 117, 118, 121, 122, 123–128, 131n58

504   Index

Mohawk Institute graduates, 39, 42, 43, 44, 50, 51, 65, 68, 69–70, 74, 109, *118*, *120*, 127, 132n100, 153, 164, 289, 308, 367, 369–370; as clergy, 112, 114, 351, 369–370; as teachers, 2–3, 43, 65, 74–75, 107, 108, 109–111, 112–114, 115–120, 121, 123–128, 131n72, 351, 356, 369–370, 465; higher education, 68, 74, 107, 110–111, 112–114; 116–118, 126, 164, 308, 367, 369; wage equity, 65, 115. *See also* Mohawk Institute survivors

Mohawk Institute Manual Labour Farm, 37, 47, 70, 71, 204–205, *205*, 221, 296, 323, 324, 326, 328, 329, 330, 331–333, 340–343

Mohawk Institute Research Group, 6–7

Mohawk Institute staff, *xvii*, 21–22, 43, 66, 71–72, 73, 74–75, 78, 188, 194, *195*, *213*, *306*, 309; criminal behaviour, 4, 75, 89, 223n183, 319, 338, 339, 342, 395, 409–410; gender, 108; Indigenous, 108, 114, 124, 370, 426, 479–483; principals, 2, 4–5, 12–13, 44, 66–69, 71–75, 77–79, 189, 202, 209–210, 212, 227–228, 295–300, *306*, 295–319, 323–343, 399–402, 407–409, 412n5, 412n7; superintendent, 4, 41, 63, 134, 139, 186, 297, 302–307, 323; teachers, 66, 108, 110, 111, 114, 124, 126, 128n4, 131n72, 161–162, 165n20, 229–230, 338, 339, 415, 425, 479–483

Mohawk Institute students, *xvii*, xvii–xix, 2, 5, *10*, 59, 77, *106*, 134–135, 194, *195203*, *213*, *242*, *274*, *301*, *350*, 351–371, *441*; abuse of, 6, 21, 90, 172, 201–202, 223n183, 290, 319, 337, 338, 339, 356, 389, 395, 405, 406–410, 416–445; arrival, 49, 182, 195, 196, 202, 205, 280, 317, 353, 355, 356, 384, 417–419, 434, 441; art, 384, *394*, 394–395, 440; attendance, 5; awards, 48, 70, 126, 132n93, 136, 313, 316; begging, 14, 21; bullying, 21; cadets, (*see* Mohawk Institute Cadet Corps; military training); civilization of, 6, 134, 136–137, 143–146; 403–409; clothing, 20, 70, 128n4, 136, 203, 207, 312–313, 361, 382, 384, 424, 425, 440; crime, 47, 51–52, 71, 77, 193, 243, 244–247, 298, 407; deaths of, 5, 76–77, 307, 339, 357, 363, 364, 365, 371, 432–434; diet of, 1, 4, 67, 68, 312, 338; dignity of, 208, 405; disease of, 5, 71, 363; education, 19, 128, 371; expulsion, 248, 355, 357; family, 383; fighting, 74, 416, 421–422, 425, 427, 443; gender segregation, 45, 67, 73, 74, 186–187, 188–189, 196, 201, 203, 211, 212, 214, 262–263, 425; hair, xviii, 49, 67, 194, 248, 249, 265, 362, 384–385, 418, 419–420, 425, 428, 440; hate, 422–423, 427, 429–443; health, 5, 19, 70, 74, 362, 365, 371, 424, 425; humiliation, 248–249, 431; hunger, 6, 73, 77, 88, 205, 247, 259, 387, 416, 420; hygiene, 49, 70, 76, 80, 208, 296, 364, 365, 371; identity, 88, 265, 383–384, 406–411, 439; isolation of, 67, 136, 196, 416, 424; language, 39, 45, 69, 84, 108, 111, 176, 202, 253, 357–358, 366–367, 428–429; living conditions, 90, 208, 371, 407–411; loneliness, 6, 88, 416, 418–419, 423, 434–435, 439; love, 265, 383, 386, 409, 416, 418, 422–423; manual labour, 13–14, 19–20, 35, 39, 40, 47, 52n4, 70, 71, 73, 77, 97n3, 139, 158, 204, 296, 310–311, 361; memoirs, 11–22, 415–445; menstruation, 80, 424; missing, 433; monitors, 45, 48, 316; names, *14*, 49, 88, *381*, 381–383, 384, 388–389; numbering, *14*, 49, 57n151, 88, 203, 264, 384, 389; privacy, 187, 313, 367, 383–384; punishment 19, 48–49, 67, 83, 201–202, 215, 243, 245–248, 266, 405, 407, 408–410, 424–432, 433; recreation, 5, *59*, 66, 70, 80, 139, 146, 148n12, 192–193, 202–203, 206, 211, 212, 314; religion and, 6, 361, 398, 399, 404–409; resistance, 2, 4, 5, 25, 61, 74, 173, 177, 243–250, 298, 317, 356–357, 382–383, 386–389, 417; runaways, 4, 5, 21, 67, 71, 73, 74, 82, 156, 193, 201–202, 247–250, 288–289, 317, 353, 356–357, 366, 368, 407, 408, 424, 425, 427, 429–432; sexual abuse, 290, 395, 407, 409–410, 416, 424, 427, 434–437, 439; sexuality, 21, 71, 83, 425; social hierarchy, 18;

socialization of, 6, 134, 143, 156; suicide, 433–434, 440; survival techniques, 4, 139, 207, 356–357, 411, 417, 439; teacher training, 2–3, 43, 65, 108–110, 117–120; trauma, *394*, 395–396, 406–410, 411, 439, 441–442; underachievement, 155; vaccinations, 364. *See also* Mohawk Institute graduates; Mohawk Institute survivors

Mohawk Institute survivors, xviii, 39, 43, 95, 128, 215, 247, 389, 393–394; apologies to, 2, 60, 89; commemoration, 226; employment, 44, 46, 50–51, 61, 65, 117, 119–120, 128; lawsuits, 91–92, 297; recollections, 6, 11–22, 70–71, 87, 88–89, 116, 158, 195, 198, 201–204, 205, 212, 229–230, 259–261, 261–266, 290, 367, 408–409, 415–445; recovery, 439–442; research, 256–257, 389; religion and, 396–397, 410; trauma, 265, 393–396, 405, 409–410, 411, 415–416, 427, 439, 441–445. *See also* Mohawk Institute graduates; Residential School Syndrome; survivors

Mohawk Nation, 26, 457

Mohawk Parsonage, 311

Mohawk Village, 32, 34,172, 216n13

Mohawk Village Day School, 32, 173–175, *175*, 284–285, 455

Mohawk Village Memorial Park, 87, 225, 226, 236, 376, 379

Mohawks of the Bay of Quinte, 226, 228

Mohr, Jean, 7

Montequassum, 276

Montour, O., *138*, 148n22

Monture, Bill, 419

Monture, Christopher, 481

Monture, David, vii, 497

Monture, Edith Anderson, 11

Monture, Mary, 481, 481

Monture, Nelles A., 112–113, 114, 370

Monture, Rick, 173–174, 287

Moore, Flora, 83

Moor's Indian Charity School, 33, 173, 277, 284, 456

Moran, Ry, 235

Morgan, Laverne, 412n11

Morgan, Lt. Colonel, 473

Morrison, Dr., 432–433

Morrissette, Vern, 265

Morrow, Teri Lyn, 4, 497

Mosby, Ian, 269

Moses, Arnold, 482

Moses, Helen Monture, 11

Moses, J., *138*, 148n22

Moses, Jesse, 482

Moses, Jim, 11

Moses, John, 2, 11, 497

Moses, Nelson, 12, 13

Moses, Russ, 2, *10*, 11–22, *13*, 83, 205–206

Moses, Ted, 12, 13

Moses, Thelma (Davis), *10*, 15

Mount Elgin Industrial School, 8, 41, 56n100, 70, 71, 192, 197, 207, 233, 442, *444*

Mugerauer, Robert, 182

Mush Hole vii, 18, *80*, 88, 247, 253, 257, 262, 371, 375. *See also* Mohawk Institute

Mush Hole, The (art exhibit), 394–395, 410

Mush Hole, The: Life at Two Residential Schools (book), 6, 8, 195, 416

Nachecallassootmamk, Basamai (Benjamin Christmas), 368–369

National Centre for Truth and Reconciliation, 95, 235; Memorial Register, 364

National Cost Sharing Program, 234

Index   *505*

National Day for Truth and Reconciliation, 94
National Health and Welfare Service, 90
National Historic Events, 232, 235
National Historic Sites, 87, 216n13, 221n139, 231–237
National Indian Brotherhood for First Nations, 84, 89, 475
National Indigenous Residential School Museum of Canada, 221n139
National Native Nurses Association of Canada, 11
National Negro School, 34
Navy and Army Illustrated (magazine), 134, 137
Neary, Bernard F., 80, 163, 164
Nelles, Abraham, 2, 34, 38–39, 44–45, 107, 109–110, 112, 116–117, 128, 134, 176, 179, 183, 289–290, 295, 297, 299, 302, 304–306, 308, 309, 314, 343n1, 351–352, 367, 371, 463, 469, 470
Nelles, Hannah, 108
Nelles Medal, 126, 132n93
Nesuton, Job, 276
New Brunswick, 278
New England Company, xviii, 4–5, *23*, 26, 32–34, 37, 40, 42–43, 44–46, 60, 70, 71, 72, 108, 112, 118–119, 124–125, 174, 207, 297, 461–468; Board of Missionaries, 302–305, 306, 307; divestment of Mohawk Institute, 331–336, 340–342; history, 275–277, 285–287, 291n2, 323, 399, 457; land, 323–343; missionaries, 276, 403–404; oversight of Mohawk Institute, 47, 50, 65, 69, 75, 78, 82, 90, 108, 110–111, 116–117, 177, 179, 207, 248, 284, 285–287, 290–291, 295–300, 302–307, 310, 318–319, 323–343, 399–401; oversight of Sussex Vale Indian School, 278, 280–281, 290–291; relationship with the Haudenosaunee, 26, 43, 277, 286, 461. *See also* Grand River Station
Newman, Henry, 369
newspaper reports, xviii, 51, 73, 85, 86, 124, 139, 140, 149n45, 192, 193, 207, 212, 245, 433, 443–445
Niblock, Mr., 339
Nightingale, Florence, 295–296, 355, 357, 358, 362, 365
Normal Schools, 2, 43, 110, 111, 114, 116–117, 124, 126, 127–128, 369–370. *See also* Mohawk Institute Certificate
Norman, Alison, 2–3, 142, 358, 367, 369, 497
Norton, John, 28
Norway House Boarding School, 156
Number 33 (Mary Ann [Marguerite] Cooper), 434–436
Number 34 (Roberta Hill), *80*, 434, 437, *438*, 439, *440*
Number 73 (Doug George) (Kanentiio), v, xviii, 87, 417, *418*, 439, 440–442
nutrition, 254–255

Obey, John, 289
Ogilvie, Robert M., 232
Oliver, Frank, 51, 60, 62
O'Meara, Frederick Augustus, 110, 183
Oneida Nation, 26, 470
Onondaga Nation, 26, 286–287, 457, 470
Ontario Archaeological Society, 376
Ontario Department of Education, 123–125, 160
Ontario Heritage Trust, 225–231
Oral histories. *See* Mohawk Institute survivors—oral histories; survivors—oral histories
Orange Shirt Day, 94
Order of Ontario, 445
orphans, 35, 46–47, 48, 51, 65, 69, 73, 74, 76, 79, 96
Orr, Roland Guerney, 197–198, *199*, *200*, 221n145
Osborne, Jessie, 123–124, 481
Osborne, Jane, 123, 124, 480
Ottawa, ON, 11–12

Palmer, Dr., 432–433
parents, 22, 46–47, 49, 67, 69, 70, 74, 246, 337, 422. *See also* children—removal from parents

Park, Robert, 309, 324
Parks Canada, 234, 235
Pawling, Micah, 279
Peace, Thomas, 4, 5, 31, 89, 497
Peachey, James, 174, *175*
Peatman, Henry, 128n4
Pedley, Frank, 61, 62, 98n7
Pengelley, O. R. (Roy), 415
Pennefather, Richard T. 42
Perkins, Mary Ellen, 230
Peters, A., *138*, 148n22
Petrus, Paulus, 284
Pettit, Jennifer, 2, 7, 497
Pheasant, Emily, 71
Phelan, Philip, 157
photography, 7, 194, 203–204, 208–209, 212
Pikwakanagan Reserve, 11
Places of Memory and Indian Residential Schools (report), 235
Planter, O., *138*, 148n22
plaques. *See* historic plaques
poetry v, vii, *441*, 449–451
Portage La Prairie Residential School, 197, 221n139, 235
Powless, Elijah, 480
Powless, Elizabeth Martin, 111, 479
Powless, George, 480
Powless, Isaac, 351
Powless, Velma, 432–433
"praying towns," 276, 277, 291n8
Presbyterian Committee to Investigate Schools, 64
Primer for the Use of the Mohawk Children, 174
Printer, James (Wowaus), 276
proof of life, 15
Proulx, Geoge, 278

Qu'Appelle Industrial School, 46

Racette, Sherry Farrell, 194, 204
Racey, Henry, 128n4
Racher, Paul, 5, 497
racism, 44, 50, 61, 96, 145, 154–157, 160, 161, 164, 172, 188–189, 211, 215, 243, 339, 398, 401–402, 405
Ragged Schools for Indigent Children, 296
Railway Act, 329
railways, 325, 326, 327, 328, 329, 330, 331
Rand, Silas, 368–369
Raymer, Ken, 229–230
reconciliation, xix, 4, 7, 25, 60, 89, 97, 254, 391
recovery. *See* Mohawk Institute survivors—recovery
Red Bank Day School, 232
Red Crow, 124
Red Jacket, 123
Reed, Hayter, 47, 49
reformatory schools, 5, 36, 44, 135
Regan, Paulette, 7
religion, 6, 397
Renison University College, 394–395
Report on the Indian Schools of Manitoba and the North West Territories, 64
reserves, 28, 29, 61, 96
Residential School Syndrome, 90
residential school survivors, vii, vii, 1–2, 93, 257; apologies to, 92–93; art, 7, 61, 243, 260, 261, 394–395; commemoration, 226–231, 235; employment, 39, 50–51; intergenerational survivors, 15, 91, 226, 235, 257, 265–266, 268, 405; lawsuits, 91–92; recollections, 6, 7, 11–22, 93, 94, 261–270; trauma and, 6, 228–231, 263–264, 265, 393–396; traditional way of life, 261, 268
residential schools 1, 4, 7, 11–12, 25, 29, 34–35, 52n4, 72, 75–76, 97n3, 341, 375, 389; abuse, 89, 90, 92–93,

147, 228–229, 406–409; academics 40–41, 83, 155; adaptive reuse, 235–236; apologies, 2, 60, 89, 92; architecture, 171–172, 177, 181, 196–198, 207, 211, 214–215; attendance, 49, 65, 84; "civilizing," 61, 90, 145–147, 171, 185; closures, 2, 84–85, 87, 89, 96, 146, 227; commemoration, 226–237; curriculum, 3, 161; deaths, 64, 93, 95, 97, 390; diet, 35, 41, 42, 262; economics 40, 66, 68, 90, 197, 399; enrollment, 83, 85; farming 40–41; governance, 213, 227, 295–296, 337, 399; graves (*see* graves); history, 275, 295; impact on Indigenous Peoples, 90–94, 96, 97, 228–229, 257; intangible significance, 227, 232, 233, 234, 236, 237; integration, 212; intelligence testing, 155–156; investigations, 8, 65, 83, 89–90, 211, 230, 234, 281; labour, 40–41, 83, 192; legacy, 265; living conditions, 90; memorials, 87–88, 92, 96, 226–231; militarization, 147n9; models, 26, 35, 40–41, 72, 177, 197, 283, 295–296, 298–300; modernization, 211–212; National Historic Sites, 231–237; objectives, 92–93, 177; oversight, 39, 40–41, 72, 393; perception of, 172, 185; physical education, 145; principals, 11–12, 17; religion, 275, 474; school committees, 83; sexual abuse, 89, 93, 229; socialization, 147n9, 232; staff, 83, 163, 165n20; student underachievement, 155, 163; war surplus, 145, 208–209. *See also* boarding schools; day schools; industrial schools; mechanics institutes; Mohawk Institute

Richardson, William, 108–109, 305, 317, 343n1
Riley, Delbert, 437
Riley, Violet, *444*
Rite of Passage, 268
Roberts, Mrs. R. J., 470
Roberts, Robert J., 110, 302, 305, 331, 458, 461, 463, 470, 470
Robertson, Geraldine Maness, 419, 442–445, *443*, *445*
Rogers, Sydney, 72–74, 143, 160, 311, 400
Royal Canadian Air Force, 15
Royal Canadian Mounted Police, 95, 146–147, 406
Royal Commission on Aboriginal Peoples, 89–91, 230, 231
Russell, Claybran, 480
Russell, Sarah, 126–127, 481
Ryerson, Egerton, 39, 40
Ryerson, George, 284–285

Sahonwadi, Paulus, 174, *175*
Sahonwagy, 284
Salli, 423
Sandiford, Peter, 153, 155, 160–161
Sandy, Hilton, *81*
Sault, Albert, 408
Sault, Calvin, 408
"Save the Evidence" campaign. *See* Woodland Cultural Centre—"Save the Evidence" campaign
Scanada, Louis, 116, 480
school boards, 45, 114, 117, 118, 127
schools, 32, 34, 69–70, 73, 76, 100n76, 112, 115, *118*; adaptive reuse, 235; architecture, 171, 232; arson, 246–247; assimilation, 285; attendance, 65; economic aspects, 39, 61, 63, 66, 68, 78, 90; higher education, 48, 61, 68, 74, 155; historic, 231–232, 457–458; inspectors, 50, 64, 73, 82, 90, 114, 118–119, 130n39, 132n89, 153, 156, 157, 160, 163; integration, 207; intelligence testing, 155–164; investigations, 41, 50, 64, 90, 281–282; policy, xviii, 2, 3, 27, 39, 44, 60–63, 67, 68, 76, 90; provincial schools, 83, 84–85; resistance, 246–247; scandals, 61, 66. *See also* Boarding schools; Day schools; Industrial schools; Mechanics Institute; Mohawk Institute; Normal schools; reformatory schools; Sussex Vale Indian School

Schultz Brothers Company, 72
Schuyler, John, 116, 480
Scott, Andrew, 481
Scott, Duncan Campbell, 62, 67, 69, 71, 79, 120–121, 174, 184, 198, 248, 319, 333–334, 335, 336, 337, 339, 340, 341–342, 467–468
Seager, C. A., 163, 401–402
seeds, 255, 261, 267-268
segregation, 2, 3, 79, 154, 172, 173, 179, 186, 196, 201, 215; *See also* gender segregation
Seneca Nation, 26, 123, 457
Sergeant, John, 35
settler colonialism 7, 9, 27, 30–32, 177, 179, 181–182, 184, 190, 194, 230, 269, 276, 282, 289, 390–391, 397–39, 454
settlers, 27, 28, 30, 60–61; "superiority" of, 30, 185, 190
sexual abuse, 4, 33, 229, 282, 290, 409–410
Shanahan Research Associates, 229–230
Shawahnahness, Chief, 36
Shawanda, June, 423
Shingwauk Industrial School, 71, 100n67, 283, 327
Shingwauk Residential Schools Centre, 352
Shogesjowaueh, 366, 368
Shubenacadie Indian Residential School, 235–236, 237n14
Sickles, Adam, 116, 480
Sickles, Obadiah, 316
Sifton, Clifford, 50
Simon, Daniel, 111, 480
Sinclair, Murray, 25
Sinclair, Robert, 316
site of conscience, 215, 223n199, 390
site of remembrance. *See* Woodland Cultural Centre
Six Nations Inspectorate of Schools, 90
Six Nations of the Grand River, 4–5, 12, 26, 33, 86, 95, 114, 174, *181*, 214, 248, 265, 376; ceremonies, 255; commemoration, 226, 227–228; education, 26, 32, 39, 45, 46–47, 56n86, 60, 65, 117–119, 175, 213, 286, 308, 334, 343, 453–476; farming, 135, 183; governance, 43–44; intelligence testing, 155, 158; land, 37, 114, 118–119, 158, 174–175, 177, 285–286, 298, 317, 323, 326, 333–335, 340, 342, 343; military, 69, 142, 143–144, 148n25, 149n41; population, 37; relationship with Canada 43–44, 96, 334; relationship with Great Britain, 181; religion, 37, 255; research, 256–257; schools, 90, 114, 118–119, 158, 233, 284–285, 286, 299, 304, 333–335, 464–466, 469–471, 474–476; social conditions, 28, 35, 299. *See also* Haudenosaunee
Six Nations Reserve, 27, 32, 37, 42, 71, 285–286, 319, 326, 375–376; land, 324, 326, 331, 335, 342–343
Six Nations School Board, 114, 118–119, 158, 317, 323, 461–468, 471–474
"sixties scoop," 85, 280
Skye, Christine, *261*, 261
Slow Rush of Colonization, The (book), 31
Smith, Edward, 339
Smith, Effie, 432–433
Smith, Gordon, 142
Smith, Peter, 158, 205, 206, 207, 420, 429
Smith, Ruby, 482
Smith, William, 127
Smith, Wilma, 482
Snake, Leander (Lee), 433, 436
Snake, Phoebe, 117
Snell, Horace W., 75, 76, 164, 166n36, 399, 400–401, 424, 432–433
Society for the Propagation of the Gospel in Foreign Parts, 277, 285, 457, 460–461
Soney, Sylvia, 202, 203, 204, 206, 207
Staats, Greg, *426*, *435*, *445*
Standing, T. W., 130n39, 132n89

Stanton, F. C., 366
Stephen, Anne, 163
St. Eugene's Indian Residential School, 231, 234
Stewart, Stewart & Taylor Architects, 197, 221n134, 221n135
St. George's Residential School, 330, 331, 336, 342
Stothers, C. E., 162
Strachan, John, 342
Strathcona Trust, 139
Strong, James Leonard, 298, 328, 468
students, 1-2 ; graves, xix, 1, *118*. See also Mohawk Institute—students; Sussex Vale Indian School—students
Styres, Edith, 482
Styres, James, 110
Styres, Vera, 201, 424
suicide, 90, 433-434
Sunseri, Leni, 269
Superintendent of Schools, 90
survivors. *See* Mohawk Institute survivors; residential school survivors
Survivors' Secretariat, 95, 390, 432
Sussex Corner, NB, 278
Sussex Vale Indian School, 4, 33, 275; abuse, 281, 290; Board of Commissioners, 278, 280, 281; closure, 280, 283; curriculum, 280, 281-282; economic considerations, 279, 280; enrollment, 279, 280, 281; gender segregation, 280, 281; history, 275, 278-280; indentured servitude, 4, 280-281; investigations, 281; manual labour, 281, 290; social impact, 282-283, 289; students, 280-281; teachers, 279-280
Symbols, 393-394, 396

Teachers: Indigenous, 108-109, 124-126; teacher training, 2-3, 65, 110-111, 112-114, 131n72. *See also* Mohawk Institute graduates—as teachers; Mohawk Institute staff—teachers; Suusex Vale Indian School—teachers
Tekarihogen John Brant. *See* Ahyonwaeghs John Brant
terror, 45, 389, 397, 409, 411, 437
Thanksgiving address, 253
Thayendanegea Joseph Brant, 26, 28, 32, 123, 173-174, 216n14, 277, 284, 287, 455-457
Thomas, Jake, *260*, 260-261
Thomas, Thomas, 110, *306*, 470
Thomas School House, 458, 468
Thompson, Andrew, 73, 74
Titley, E. Brian, 30
Tk'emlúps te Secwépemc community, 95, 390
Tobias, John L., 76
Tobias, Willis, 481
Toronto (Normal) Training School. *See* Normal Schools
trauma, 6, 228-231, 263-264, 265, 393-396, 405, 406-410, 411, 415-416, 427, 439, 441-445
Trauma (painting), *394*
Trent University, 162
Trinity College, 276
Truth & Reconciliation Commission of Canada, 1, 7, 25, 31, 91, 92-94, 225, 234, 237; Calls to Action, 94, 231, 254; findings, 157, 158; hearings, 93-94, 150n68
Truth Telling: Gardens, Faming and Food Experiences at the Mohawk Institute (research project), 254, 256
Turnell, Cyril Mae., 68, 202, 307, 311, 335, 336, 337-339, 340, 345n33, 433
Tuscarora Nation, 26, 298, 320n13, 327-328, 457, 469
Two Row Wampum, 216n15
Tyendinaga Mohawk Territory, 12, 214

United Church of Canada, 156
United Empire Loyalists, 26-27, 33, 277, 278, 279
United Nations Declaration on the Rights of Indigenous Peoples, 236

Upham, Joshua, 278
Urion, Carl, 25

Van Every, Hazel, 432-433
Van Every, Jessie, 482
Vankoughnet, Lawrence, 121
Venning, W. J., 343n6, 344n13
Vennino, Walter C., 462
Verity Plow Company, 325, 329, 331, 338, 344n16
Verschoyle Phillip Cronyn Memorial Archives, 352
Victoria, Queen, 116
Vidal, James H., 366

Waddilove, Phoebe, 481
Wage, William, 472
Wahta Mohawks, 214, 226, 228
Walker, Moses, 116, 480
Wallace, Sgt., 245
War of 1812, 27, 174, 457
Warrick, Gary, 389
Warriors, Veterans, and Peacekeepers (exhibition), 142
Watts, Mr., 317-318
Wawanosh Homes, 283
Webb, C. Augustus, 330, 332, 335, 338, 344n13
Webstad, Phyllis, 94
Webster, J. O., 163
Webster, W. F., 64, 298, 318, 321n50, 331-332
Weld, Henry, 341
We Share Our Matters (book), 287
Wesley, Charles, 149n45
Wesleyan Conference, 458, 463, 467
West. John, 33, 34, 281, 282-284, 285
Western University, 112
Wheelock, Eleazar, 277, 279, 284
Whiteye, Bud, 290, 434, *435*, 436, 451, 497
Whiteye, Robert, *81*, 408
Whitlow, Paula, 142, 235
Wikwemikong Industrial School, 71, 100n67, 358
Wilkes, James, 469
Wilkes, John, 469
Wilkinson, Rev., 468
Williams, David, 144, 333, 337-338, 341, 342, 400, 401
Williams Lake Residential School, 8
Wilson, David, *125*, 408
Wilson, Roy, 244-247
Winney, Frank, 244-247
Winslow, Edward, 278, 279
Wolastoqiyik Nation, 279-280, 290
Woodland Cultural Centre, 1, 3, 8-9, 86-87, 88, 97, 142, 214-215, 223n198, 225, 226, 227-231, 235, 236, 327, 352, 377, 416, 468; "Save the Evidence" campaign, 3, 87, 214, 235. *See also* Mohawk Institute
Woolford, Andrew, 92
Workers Among the Methodist Workers of Manitoba, 156
Workman and Watts, 317, 343n3
World War I, 13, 68, 69, 72, 141-145, 198, 325, 472
World War II, 13-14, 79, 82, 87, 145, 150n68, 208, 402
Wowaus James Printer, 276
Wright, Janet, 171

"Year of Reconciliation with Aboriginal Peoples, A," 89
Yeoward, R., 128n4
York and Cornwall, Duke and Duchess of, 137
Young, John, 124

Zimmerman, Gladys, 297
Zimmerman, William John, 79, 82-83, *125*, 146, 164, 212, *213*, 223n183, 227-228, 236, 237n12, 297, 402, 407-408, 424-425, 426-427, 429, *440*, 442-444

www.ingramcontent.com/pod-product-compliance
Lightning Source LLC
Chambersburg PA
CBHW041731300426
44115CB00022B/2969